Library of Congress Cataloging-in-Publication Data

Miller, Robert D. (Robert Desle), 1947–
Problems in health care law / Robert D. Miller. — 7th ed.
p.   cm.
Rev. ed. of: Problems in hospital law / Robert D. Miller. 6th ed. © 1990.
Includes bibliographical references and index.
ISBN 0-8342-0767-2
1. Hospitals—Law and legislation—United States.   2. Medical care—Law and legislation—United States.   I. Miller, Robert D. (Robert Desle), 1947–   Problems in hospital law.
II. Title.
KF3825.M53   1996
344.73′03211—dc20
[347.3043211]
95–23511
CIP

Editorial Resources: Sandra L. Lunsford

Library of Congress Catalog Card Number: 95-25311
ISBN: 0-8342-0767-2

Printed in the United States of America

1   2   3   4   5

Proble[m]
Health Care[...]

Seventh[...]

Robert D. Miller, J[...]

AN ASPEN [...]
Aspen [...]
Gaithersb[...]

Table of Contents

Preface

New material has been added throughout this edition to address many of the problems arising from the revolutionary changes in the health care system since the last edition. This expanded perspective has led to the change in the title of the book to **Problems in Health Care Law**. Prior editions were titled *Problems in Hospital Law*. Although hospitals remain an important component of the health care system, there have been so many changes in the health care field that its legal problems can no longer be defined or addressed solely from the perspective of the hospital.

Acknowledgments

Many individuals and organizations assisted in the preparation of this book. My students at the University of Iowa and the University of Miami helped to establish the structure. My hospital, physician, and other health care clients have taught me the practical aspects of applying law to the day-to-day provision of health care services. They have also presented the questions that have led me to confront many of the problems of health care law that are addressed in this book.

LEXIS-NEXIS®, a member of the Reed Elsevier plc group, provided its LEXIS CheckCite™ Report service to review the entire manuscript, checking court cases cited in the endnotes to determine if they were properly cited and if they had been overruled or superseded. This service enabled me to provide more accurate and complete endnotes than in previous editions. I thank LEXIS for this helpful assistance.

My colleagues in the health law section of Shutts & Bowen, especially James Farrell and Marvin Kirsner, reviewed drafts and made many helpful suggestions.

My law firm's library made the research on this book possible. Richard Korman, the librarian, and his assistant, John Moder, provided important assistance in locating some of the information in this book. Michelle Comerford of the Shutts & Bowen information systems staff provided assistance in performing the LEXIS™ CheckCite of the manuscript.

The strong support and cooperation of Sandy Lunsford and the rest of the Aspen staff once again made the preparation of this book an enjoyable experience.

Special thanks are due to my wife, Jill, and my daughter, Katie. They have patiently continued their support as I spent long hours preparing this book. I thank them for their continued understanding and encouragement.

1

Introduction to the American Legal System

Many decisions that health care administrators, professionals, and technical staff must make each day are affected by legal principles and have potential legal consequences. Legal advice cannot be obtained before each decision, so health care providers should develop an understanding of the law to help identify problems requiring legal counsel and to help make other decisions consistent with applicable legal principles.

This chapter includes general information about law, including the workings of the legal system and the roles of the branches of government in creating, administering, and enforcing the law.

THE NATURE OF THE LAW

Law can be defined as a system of principles and processes by which people who live in a society attempt to control human conduct to minimize the use of force in resolving conflicting interests. Through law, society specifies standards of behavior and means to enforce those standards. The purpose of law is to avoid conflict between individuals and between government and individuals. Since conflicting interests are inevitable, law also provides a way to resolve disputes.

Like medicine, law is not an exact science. Lawyers are frequently unable to provide a precise answer to a legal question or to predict with certainty the outcome of a legal conflict because much of the law is uncertain. Some questions have never been precisely addressed by the legal system. Even when questions have been addressed and answered through the law, the legal system may change those answers in response to changing conditions. The ability of the law to adjust is one of its strengths. Legal uncertainty is similar to the uncertainty encountered in making medical and nursing diagnostic and treatment decisions. When dealing with systems as complicated as the human body or human society, uncertainty is inevitable. A lawyer's advice is still valuable, just as a physician's advice is valuable, because the lawyer can use knowledge of how the law has addressed similar questions to predict the most probable answer. After a dispute has arisen, a lawyer can play a valuable role as an advocate to assure that legal dispute resolution mechanisms are used to the client's advantage.

In daily life, law is a guide to conduct. Most disputes or controversies between persons or organizations are resolved without lawyers or courts. The existence of the legal system is a stimulus to orderly private dispute resolution. Legal principles reinforce those settlements. The likelihood of success in court affects the willingness of parties to negotiate private settlements. Knowledge of the law is important in resolving disputes.

Laws govern relationships of private individuals and entities with each other and with government. Law can be divided into civil law and criminal law.

Civil law can be divided into contract law, tort law, and other governmental statutes and regulations. Contract law concerns enforcement of agreements and payment of compensation for failure to fulfill those agreements. Tort law defines duties that are not based on contractual agreement and imposes liability for injuries that are caused by breaches of those duties.

A third area of civil law includes the governmental statutes and regulations that require individuals and organizations to act in specified ways. Many of the areas addressed affect hospitals, including cost containment, health care quality, medical device safety, hazardous waste disposal, labor relations, employment policies, facility safety, and other important topics. The primary goal of many of these regulations is to attain compliance, not to punish offenders.

Criminal law forbids conduct deemed injurious to public order and provides for punishment of those who engage in the forbidden conduct. Criminal law has become a more significant concern for hospitals as the government has expanded its use of criminal law to restructure the health care system. Some traditional conduct in the health care system has been redefined as criminal, and criminal penalties have been added for violations of some regulations.

GOVERNMENTAL ORGANIZATION AND FUNCTIONS

Government is divided into three branches—the legislative, executive, and judicial branches. Their primary functions are as follows: the legislature makes laws, the executive branch enforces laws, and the judiciary interprets laws. Actual functions of the branches overlap in practice. This separation of powers means that none of the branches is clearly dominant over the other two; each branch may affect and limit the functions of the others.

Separation of powers—sometimes called a system of checks and balances—is illustrated by the process for enacting legislation. On the federal level, statutes are enacted by Congress; however, until a bill enacted by Congress is signed by the president (or passed over his veto by a two-thirds vote of each house of Congress), the bill does not become law except when the president allows it to become law by failing to veto or approve it within the time allowed. By a veto the president can temporarily prevent a bill from becoming law and possibly prevent it from becoming law at all. A bill that has become law may ultimately be declared invalid by the United States Supreme Court or another court in the judicial branch if the court decides that the law violates the Constitution.

The executive and legislative branches affect the composition of the judicial branch. The president's nominees to be federal judges, including Supreme Court justices, must be approved by the Senate. While a Supreme Court decision is final concerning the specific controversy before the Court, Congress and the president may enact revised legislation to change the law. Another method of overriding a Supreme Court decision, while complex and often time consuming, is to amend the Constitution.

Each branch has a different primary function. The function of the legislative branch is to enact new laws and amend existing laws. The legislature determines the need for new laws and for changes in existing laws. Legislatures generally assign legislative proposals to committees charged with oversight of the areas addressed by the proposals. The committees investigate, holding hearings at which interested persons may present their views. These hearings provide information to assist the committees in considering the bills. Hearings are often used to publicize issues to develop public support for action. Some bills eventually are released from the committees and reach the full legislative body, where, after consideration and debate, the bills may be either approved or rejected. The Congress and every state legislature except Nebraska consist of two houses. (Nebraska has only one house.) Both houses must pass identical versions of a bill before it can be presented to the chief executive. Differences in the versions passed by the two houses are sometimes resolved by a joint conference committee composed of leaders from both houses, and their compromise is then voted on in both houses.

The primary function of the executive branch is to enforce and administer laws. The chief executive, whether a state governor or the United States president, also has a role in law creation through the power to approve or veto bills passed by the legislature, except in North Carolina where the governor has no veto power.[1] If the chief executive approves a passed bill, it becomes law. If the chief executive vetoes the bill, it can become law if the legislature overrides the veto.

The executive branch is organized into departments. The departments are assigned responsibility for specific areas of public affairs and enforce the law within their assigned areas. Much of the federal law affecting hospitals is administered by the Department of Health and Human Services. In most states there is a department assigned responsibility for health and welfare matters, including the administration and enforcement of most laws affecting hospitals. Other departments and governmental agencies may also affect hospital affairs. On the federal level, for example, laws concerning wages and hours of employment are enforced by the Department of Labor.

The function of the judicial branch is adjudication—deciding disputes in accordance with law. For example, courts decide suits brought against hospitals by patients seeking compensation for harm they feel was caused by the wrongful conduct of hospital personnel. While news of malpractice suits and suits by the government against hospitals frequently receives the greatest attention, hospitals also sue to enforce rights or to protect legally protected interests. For example, hospitals initiate suits to challenge acts by governmental agencies, to have legislation concerning hospitals declared invalid, to collect unpaid hospital bills, and to enforce contracts.

Many disputes are resolved by negotiation or arbitration without resort to courts. However, sometimes a controversy cannot be ended without submitting it to the adjudicative process of courts. When a dispute is brought before a court, the judicial process decides the meaning of agreements and laws, decides what the facts are, and applies the law; this application of law to determined facts is the essence of the judicial process.

SOURCES OF LAW

Four primary sources of law are constitutions, statutes, decisions and rules of administrative agencies, and decisions of courts. Private agreements can be viewed as a fifth source of law. In many contexts, the legal constraints that are self-imposed through the private ordering of contracts have more direct impact on day-to-day decision making than the other governmental sources of law.

Constitutions

The Constitution of the United States is the supreme law of the land. It establishes the general organization of the federal government, grants powers to the federal government, and places limits on what the federal and state governments may do. The Constitution establishes the three branches of the federal government and grants them powers.

The Constitution is a grant of power from the states to the federal government. The federal government has only the powers that the Constitution grants expressly or by implication. Express powers include, for example, the power to collect taxes, declare war, and regulate interstate commerce. The federal government is also granted broad implied powers to enact laws "necessary and proper" for exercising its other powers. When the federal government establishes law within the scope of its powers, that law is supreme. All conflicting state and local laws are invalid. The Constitution also limits what the federal and state governments may do. Many limits on federal power appear in the first ten amendments to the Constitution, the Bill of Rights. The rights protected by the Bill of Rights include free speech; free exercise of religion; freedom from unreasonable searches and seizures; trial by jury; and no deprivation of life, liberty, or property without due process of law. Some of the most frequently applied limits on state power are stated in the Fourteenth Amendment: ". . . nor shall any State deprive any person of life, liberty, or property, without due process of law; nor deny to any person within its jurisdiction the equal protection of the laws." These clauses are frequently referred to as the due process clause and the equal protection clause. Another constitutional limit on state and federal governmental power that may affect hospitals and health care professionals is the right of privacy.

Due Process of Law

The due process clause restricts state action, not private action. Actions by state and local governmental agencies, including public hospitals, are state actions and must comply with due process requirements. Actions by private individuals at the behest of the state can also be subject to these requirements. In the past, private hospitals were sometimes considered to be engaged in state action when they were regulated or partially funded by governmental agencies. As discussed in Chapter 7, it is now rare for private hospitals to be found to be engaged in state action.

The due process clause applies to state actions that deprive a person of "life, liberty, or property." Liberty and property interests can include a physician's appointment to the medical staff of a public hospital and a hospital's institutional license. Thus, in some situations public hospitals must provide due process, and in other situations hospitals are entitled to due process. The process that is due varies depending on the situation. The two primary elements of due process are that (1) rules must be reasonable and not vague, and (2) fair procedures must be followed in enforcing rules. Rules that are too arbitrary or vague violate the due process clause and are not enforceable. The primary elements of a fair procedure are notice of the proposed action and an opportunity to present information as to why the action should not be taken. The phrase "due process" in the Fourteenth Amendment also has been interpreted by the Supreme Court to include nearly all of the rights in the Bill of Rights. Thus, state governments may not infringe on those rights.

Equal Protection of the Laws

The equal protection clause also restricts state action, not private action. Equal protection means that like persons must be dealt with in a like fashion. The equal protection clause addresses the classifications used to distinguish persons for various legal purposes. When a classification is challenged, the court must determine whether a difference between persons justifies the particular difference in rules or procedures. Courts generally require governmental agencies to justify differences with a "rational reason." The major exceptions to this standard are the strict scrutiny courts apply to distinctions based on "suspect classifications," such as race, and the intermediate level of scrutiny applied to sex-based classifications.

Right of Privacy

In 1965 in the case of *Griswold v. Connecticut* the Supreme Court recognized a constitutional right of privacy.[2] The Court has ruled that the right of privacy limits governmental authority to regulate contraception, abortion, and other decisions affecting reproduction. These reproductive issues are discussed in Chapter 15. Several state courts have ruled that the right of privacy permits terminally ill patients and those acting on their behalf to choose to withhold or withdraw medical treatment. Due to the changed composition of the Supreme Court, it is not clear to what extent the federal courts still recognize a right of privacy in the U.S. Constitution. In 1990 the Supreme Court found a constitutional right to refuse medical treatment in the due process clause instead of the right of privacy.[3] These issues are discussed in Chapter 13. Some state constitutions have an express right of privacy.[4]

State Constitutions

Each state has a constitution. The state constitution establishes the organization of state government, grants powers to state government, and places limits on what state government may do. Many state constitutions contain rights similar to the rights in the U.S. Constitution, plus some provide additional rights.

Statutes

Another major source of law is statutory law, which is law enacted by a legislature. Legislative bodies include the United States Congress, state legislatures, and local legislative bodies, such as city councils and county boards of supervisors. Congress has only the powers delegated by the Constitution, but those powers have been broadly interpreted. A state legislature has all powers not denied by the United States Constitution, by valid federal laws, or by the state constitution. A local legislative body has only those powers granted by the state. Some states have granted local governments broad powers through either statutes or constitutional amendments authorizing "home rule."

When state or local law conflicts with federal law, valid federal law supersedes. Federal law preempts some areas of law, and in those areas state law is superseded even when it is not in direct conflict. Some laws, such as bankruptcy laws and the Employee Retirement and Income Security Act (ERISA),[5] explicitly forbid dual state regulation. In other laws, courts find that preemption is implied from the aim and pervasiveness of the federal scheme, the need for uniformity, and the likelihood that state regulation would obstruct the full goals of the federal law. Courts tend not to find implied preemption when the state is exercising its police power to protect public health. For example, in 1960 the Supreme Court ruled that the extensive federal regulation of shipping did not preempt a city ordinance concerning smoke emissions, so a federally licensed vessel could be prosecuted for violating the pollution ordinance.[6] In 1985 the Supreme Court ruled that county ordinances regulating blood plasma collection were not preempted by federal regulation of drugs.[7] Some federal laws preempt only some aspects of an area, leaving others to state regulation. For example, the Minnesota Supreme Court ruled in 1986 that federal law preempted state licensure of air ambulances, but that the state could enforce staffing, equipment, and sanitation requirements.[8]

When local laws conflict with state laws, valid state laws supersede. State law can preempt an entire area of law, so that local law is superseded even when it is not in direct conflict.[9]

When a statute does not specifically authorize private individuals to bring a lawsuit to enforce the statute, the courts have to determine whether there is a private right of action implied.[10] If there is no private right of action, then only the government can enforce the statute.

Decisions and Rules of Administrative Agencies

The decisions and rules of administrative agencies are another source of law. Legislatures have delegated to administrative agencies the responsibility and power to implement various laws. These delegated powers include the quasi-legislative power to adopt regulations and the quasi-judicial power to decide how the statutes and regulations apply to individual situations. These powers are delegated because a legislature does not have the time or expertise to address the complex issues concerning many regulated areas. Examples of federal administrative agencies include the Health Care Financing Administration (HCFA), Food and Drug Administration (FDA), the National Labor Relations Board (NLRB), and the Internal Revenue Service (IRS). HCFA administers the Medicare program and the federal aspects of the Medicaid program. The FDA promulgates regulations and applies them to individual determinations concerning the manufacturing, marketing, and advertising of foods, drugs, cosmetics, and medical devices.

The NLRB decides how national labor laws apply to individual disputes. The IRS promulgates regulations and applies them to individual disputes concerning federal taxation. Many administrative agencies seek to achieve some consistency in their decisions by following the position they adopted in previous cases involving similar matters.[11] This is similar to the way courts develop the common law discussed later in this chapter. When dealing with these agencies, previous decisions, as well as rules, should be reviewed.

Administrative regulations are valid only to the extent they are within the authority validly granted by legislation to the agency. Delegation can be invalid when it violates the constitutional requirement of separation of powers by not sufficiently specifying what regulations the administrative body may make. Delegations by Congress have seldom been found to be invalid. Broad delegation, specifying the general area of law, has been permitted.[12] In the past, state courts often declared delegations to be unconstitutional unless there was considerable specificity. Today state courts also permit much broader delegation.

The Congress and many state legislatures have passed administrative procedure acts. These laws specify the procedure for administrative agencies to adopt rules and to reach decisions in individual cases when no other law specifies different procedures for the agency. Generally these laws require proposed rules to be published so that individuals have an opportunity to comment before finalization. Many federal agencies must publish both proposed and final rules in the *Federal Register*. Some changes do not have to be published.[13] Many states have similar publications that include proposed and final rules of state agencies. Hospitals should monitor proposed and final rules through these publications, publications of professional or hospital associations, or other sources. Despite their expertise, administrative agencies do not know all the implications of their proposals. They rely on the public and those regulated to alert them to potential problems through the comment process.

Agency enforcement of statutes and regulations is constrained by the resources of the agency. Sometimes when legislators are opposed to a law or regulation that they cannot repeal directly through political or procedural means, they curtail or eliminate the funding for enforcement.[14] Even when an agency is not targeted in this fashion, its funding generally is limited for budgetary reasons. Enforcement funds and practices often define what the meaning of the regulations are in practice. When approvals from the government are required, this can lead to delays in approvals.[15]

Court Decisions

Judicial decisions are a fourth source of law. The role of courts is to resolve disputes. In deciding individual cases, courts interpret statutes and regulations;

determine whether specific statutes and regulations are permitted by the state or federal constitution; and create the common law when deciding cases not controlled by statutes, regulations, or a constitution.

There is frequently disagreement over the application of statutes or regulations to specific situations. Often an administrative agency has the initial authority to decide how they will be applied. Under the doctrine of primary jurisdiction, courts generally will refuse to accept a suit until the administrative remedies have been pursued.[16] This is sometimes referred to as the requirement of exhaustion of remedies. The final administrative decision can usually be appealed to courts. Courts generally defer to decisions of administrative agencies in discretionary matters. While there is some deference to an agency interpretation of the law concerning the agency, there is no presumption that the agency conclusions of law are correct.[17] Courts review whether the delegation to the agency was constitutional and whether the agency acted within its authority, followed proper procedures, had a substantial basis for its decision, and acted without arbitrariness or discrimination. The court may have to interpret a statute or regulation or decide which of several conflicting statutes or regulations applies. Courts have developed rules for interpreting statutes. Some states also have a statute specifying interpretation rules. These rules or statutes are designed to help determine the intent of the legislature.

Courts also determine whether statutes or regulations violate the Constitution. All legislation and regulations must be consistent with the Constitution. Courts may declare legislation invalid when it is unconstitutional.[18] Laws can be unconstitutional because of their content or because of how they are enacted. For example, in Florida, like in some other states, an appropriation bill cannot change the law that says how the money will be spent, so in 1995 the Florida Supreme Court ruled that a provision of the Medicaid appropriation bill which purported to reinstate pharmacy copayments was unconstitutional.[19] The legislature would have to make the change in the nonappropriation bill.

Many legal principles and rules applied by courts are the product of the common law developed in England and the United States. The term *common law* refers to principles that evolve from court decisions. Common law is continually being adapted and expanded. During the colonial period English common law applied. After the Revolution, each state adopted part or all of the existing common law. Subsequent common law has been developed by each state, so common law differs from state to state. The federal courts have also developed a federal common law. Statutory laws have been enacted to restate many legal principles that initially were established by courts as part of the common law. Many cases, especially disputes among private entities, are decided according to the common law. The common law may be changed by statutes that modify the principles or by court decisions that establish different common law principles.

ORGANIZATION OF THE COURT SYSTEM

The structure of the court system determines which court decisions serve as precedents in a geographic area. There are over 50 court systems in the United States, including the federal system, each state's system, the District of Columbia's system, and the systems of Puerto Rico and the territories. These courts do not all reach the same decisions concerning specific issues. Frequently a majority approach and several minority approaches exist on an issue. Careful review is necessary to find the court decisions applicable to an individual hospital and, if there are no such court decisions, to predict which approach courts are likely to adopt.

The federal court system and many state court systems have three levels of courts—trial courts, intermediate courts of appeal, and a supreme court. Some states do not have intermediate courts of appeal.

Trial Court

In both the state and federal trial courts the applicable law is determined, and the evidence is assessed to determine what the "facts" are. The applicable law is then applied to those facts. The judge determines what the law is. If there is a jury, the judge instructs the jury as to what the law is, and the jury determines the facts and applies the law. If there is no jury, the judge determines the facts also. In some cases everyone agrees on the facts, and the court is asked only to determine what the law is. In other cases everyone agrees what the law is, but there is disagreement over the facts. Many cases involve both questions of law and questions of fact.

The determination of facts must be based on evidence properly admitted during trial, so "facts" are not necessarily what actually happened. To determine facts for purposes of deciding a case, the credibility of witnesses and the weight to be given to other evidence must be determined.

When analyzing any statute or legal principle, it is helpful to identify the default outcome, that is, what happens if no one can prove that something else should happen. If the default outcome is not desirable, then it is helpful to identify what must be proven with admissible facts to meet the *burden of proof* to convince the judge or jury to determine that the default outcome should not occur. Generally, in a trial the plaintiff who brings the suit has the initial burden of proof, but when that initial burden is met, frequently the burden shifts to the defendant to prove that an exception applies. Much of legal planning is to make the default outcome favorable or at least to design documentation to meet the *burden of proof* for the desired outcome.

An example of this analysis is a Florida case in which a hospital sought to collect from a guarantor the balance of the bill that had not been paid by insurance. The trial court placed the burden of proof on the hospital to demonstrate that the

court not to apply the previous rule to the current case. Even when such differences are absent, a court may conclude that a common law principle no longer is appropriate and may depart from precedent. An example of this overruling of precedent is the reconsideration and elimination of the common law principle of charitable immunity, which for many decades provided nonprofit hospitals with virtual freedom from liability for harm to patients.[22] Courts in nearly every state overruled precedents that had provided immunity, so now nonprofit hospitals can generally be sued[23] except in the few states that have re-established charitable immunity by statute.[24]

When a court is presented with an issue, it is bound by the doctrine of *stare decisis* to follow the precedents of higher courts in the same court system that have jurisdiction over the geographic area where the court is located. Each appellate court, including the highest court, is generally also bound to follow the precedents of its own decisions unless it decides to overrule such precedent due to changing conditions. However, many courts issue some opinions that are not published and cannot be used as precedent.[25] Another reason that a court may change its prior position is that controlling statutes or regulations have changed. Most decisions by a federal circuit court of appeals are made by a panel of three judges. There is a special procedure, called *en banc* review, by which all the active judges in the circuit can review the decision of a panel and overrule the decision.[26]

Decisions from equal or lower courts do not have to be followed. Federal circuit courts consider, but do not defer, decisions of other circuits.[27] Usually decisions from courts in other court systems do not have to be followed. One exception is when a federal court is deciding a controversy between citizens of different states and must follow state law as determined by the highest court of the state whose law governs under applicable choice of law principles. Another exception is when a state court is deciding a controversy involving a federal law or constitutional question and must follow the decisions of the United States Supreme Court. State courts do not have to follow decisions of other federal courts, however, even when deciding federal law questions.

A third exception occurs when a court determines that the law of another jurisdiction governs some aspect of the case. The court must then follow the decisions of the highest court in the state or country whose law governs. With the growth of interstate and international transactions and travel, courts are frequently confronted with issues of *choice of law*, having to decide what law governs. It is not unusual for the law of another state or country to govern some or all aspects of a case, especially in contract disputes, where the contract often specifies that the law of another jurisdiction governs. Many courts will not research foreign law. They place the burden of proof on the person who is relying on the foreign law to prove what that law is and adopt the default outcome of assuming that the other law is no different than the forum state's laws.

When a court is presented with a question that is not answered by statutes or regulations and that has not been addressed by the applicable court system, the court will usually examine judicial solutions in other systems to help decide the new issue. Judicial decisions from other systems are also examined when a court reexamines an issue to decide whether to overrule precedent. Court systems tend toward consistency. A trend across the country provides a basis for a reasonable legal assessment of how to act even when courts in a hospital's area have not decided the issue. However, a court is not bound by decisions from other systems, and it may reach a different conclusion.

There can be a majority approach to an issue that many state court systems follow and one or more minority approaches that other state courts follow. State courts show more consistency on some issues than others. For example, nearly all state courts have completely eliminated charitable immunity. However, while nearly all states require informed consent to medical procedures, some states determine the information that must be provided to patients by reference to what a patient needs to know, and other states make the determination by reference to what other physicians would disclose.

Courts may reach different conclusions because state statutes and regulations differ. For example, Georgia had a statute that specified that a physician need only disclose "in general terms the treatment or course of treatment" to obtain informed consent.[28] In 1975, a Georgia court interpreted that statute to eliminate the requirement that risks be disclosed to obtain informed consent.[29] As a result, Georgia courts stopped basing liability on failure to disclose risks[30] until 1989, when a state statute again required risk disclosure for most surgery and some other procedures.[31] Courts in other states are unlikely to consider Georgia court decisions concerning this issue because these decisions are based on Georgia statutes, not on a change in Georgia common law.

In summary, while it is important to be aware of trends in court decisions across the country, legal advice should be sought before taking actions based on decisions from court systems that do not have jurisdiction over the geographic area in which the hospital is located.

Res Judicata

Another doctrine that courts follow to avoid duplicative litigation and conflicting decisions is *res judicata*, which means "a thing or matter settled by judgment." When a legal controversy has been decided by a court and no more appeals are available, those involved in the suit may not take the same matters to court again.[32] This is different from stare decisis in that *res judicata* applies only to the parties involved in the prior suit and to issues decided in that suit. The application of *res judicata* can be complicated by disagreements over whether specific matters were actually decided in the prior case.

Standing

Another important requirement is that the person bringing the suit must have *standing*. Courts can only decide actual controversies, and the person bringing the suit must have an actual stake in the controversy. Persons with such a stake are said to have standing. Sometimes parties with a stake do not have standing for other reasons. For example, in some states governmental entities do not have standing to challenge the constitutionality of state statutes.[33]

NOTES

1. *Last governor without veto: Era is ending*, N.Y. TIMES, Feb. 12, 1995, at 13 [amendment to N.C. state constitution likely to be voted on in 1996].

2. Griswold v. Connecticut, 381 U.S. 479 (1965).

3. Cruzan v. Director, Missouri Dep't of Health, 497 U.S. 261 (1990).

4. *E.g.*, FL. CONST. Art. I, § 23.

5. 29 U.S.C.A. § 1144 [ERISA preemption]. There is still disagreement among the courts on the scope of ERISA preemption, *see* discussion in Chapter 4.

6. Huron Portland Cement Co. v. Detroit, 362 U.S. 440 (1960).

7. Hillsborough County v. Automated Medical Labs., 471 U.S. 707 (1985).

8. Hiawatha Aviation of Rochester, Inc. v. Minnesota Dep't of Health, 389 N.W.2d 507 (Minn. 1986).

9. *E.g.*, Robin v. Incorporated Village of Hempstead, 30 N.Y.2d 347, 285 N.E.2d 285 (1972).

10. *E.g.*, Suter v. Artist M., 112 S.Ct. 1360 (U.S. 1992) [child beneficiaries of Adoption Act cannot enforce requirement of reasonable state efforts to keep children in their homes]; Gentry v. Department of Pub. Health, 190 Mich. App. 102, 475 N.W.2d 849, *app. denied*, 439 Mich. 871, 478 N.W.2d 99 (1991) [no private right of action to enforce nursing home patient bill of rights]; Evelyn V. v. Kings County Hosp. Ctr., 819 F. Supp. 183 (E.D.N.Y. 1993) [Medicaid recipients have no statutory right to enforce Medicaid regulations against provider]; *but see* Wilder v. Virginia Hosp. Ass'n, 496 U.S. 498 (1990) [providers can enforce Medicaid "reasonable rates" requirement]; Arkansas Med. Soc'y, Inc. v. Reynolds, 6 F.3d 519 (8th Cir. 1993) [Medicaid recipients can challenge reimbursement rate as violation of equal access to care provision]; Sobky v. Smoley, 855 F. Supp. 1123 (E.D.Cal. 1994) [in challenge to county option on Medicaid coverage of methadone maintenance treatment, recipients can enforce requirement of state-wide Medicaid applicability]; Fulkerson v. Comm'r, Maine Dep't. of Human Servs., 802 F. Supp. 529 (D. Me. 1992) [Medicaid recipients may enforce equal access to care provision].

11. *E.g.*, Citrosuco Paulista, S.A. v. United States, 704 F.Supp. 1075, 1088 (Ct. Int'l Trade 1988).

12. Yakus v. United States, 321 U.S. 414 (1944) [broad price control delegation during World War II upheld].

13. *E.g.*, National Med. Enterprises v. Shalala, 43 F.3d 691 (D.C. Cir. 1995) [reclassification of labor costs to different cost center for Medicare payment purposes was not substantive rule requiring notice and comment]; Association of Am. R.R. v. Dept. of Transp., 309 U.S. App. D.C. 7, 38 F.3d 582 (1994) [when final rule differs from proposed rule, agency is not required to give separate notice if final rule is "logical outgrowth" of rule-making proceeding].

14. *See House GOP hopes to cut funding used to enforce dozens of U.S. regulations*, WALL ST. J., June 1, 1995, at A16.

15. *E.g.*, *Lack of funds forces HCFA to revise survey priorities*, 4 HEALTH L. REP. [BNA] 407 (1995) [HCFA cannot complete survey and certification of home health agencies (HHAs), which may lead to moratorium on new HHAs].

16. *E.g.*, Johnson v. Nyack Hosp., 964 F.2d 116 (2d Cir. 1992), [physician must first pursue N.Y. state administrative remedies before suit challenging privilege termination].

17. *E.g.*, Keeton v. D.H.H.S., 21 F.3d 1064 (11th Cir. 1994).

18. Marbury v. Madison, 5 U.S. (1 Cranch) 137 (1803).

19. Moreau v. Lewis, 648 So.2d 124 (Fla. 1995).

20. Public Health Trust v. Holmes, 646 So.2d 266 (Fla. 3dDCA 1994).

21. *E.g.*, Trent v. Dial Med. of Fla., Inc., 33 F.3d 217 (3d Cir. 1994).

22. *E.g.*, Mikota v. Sisters of Mercy, 183 Iowa 1378, 168 N.W. 219 (1918) [established charitable immunity].

23. *E.g.*, Haynes v. Presbyterian Hosp. Ass'n, 241 Iowa 1269, 45 N.W.2d 151 (1950) [overruled charitable immunity].

24. *E.g.,* Marsella v. Monmouth Med. Ctr, 224 N.J. Super. 336, 540 A.2d 865 (1988).

25. Hamilton v. Brown, 39 F.3d 1574 (Fed. Cir. 1994).

26. *E.g.*, Atchison, Topeka & Santa Fe Ry. Co. v. Pena, 44 F.3d 437 (7th Cir. 1994) *(en banc) cert. granted*, 132 L.Ed.2d 826 (U.S. 1995).

27. *Id.*

28. GA. CODE ANN. § 31-9-6(d) (1985).

29. Young v. Yarn, 136 Ga. App. 737, 222 S.E.2d 113 (1975).

30. *E.g.*, Padgett v. Ferrier, 172 Ga. App. 335, 323 S.E.2d 166 (1984). The Georgia Supreme Court has interpreted a similar statute concerning consent to sterilization as limiting the applicability of the informed consent doctrine, Robinson v. Parrish, 251 Ga. 496, 306 S.E.2d 922 (1983).

31. GA. CODE ANN. § 31-9-6.1 (1988 Supp.).

32. *E.g.*, Lim v. Central DuPage Hosp., 972 F.2d 758 (7th Cir. 1992) *cert. denied*, 113 S.Ct. 1586 (U.S. 1993) [physician's second antitrust suit barred by res judicata].

33. *E.g.*, Trustees of Worcester State Hosp. v. Governor, 395 Mass. 377, 480 N.E.2d 291 (1985).

The case citations following the case names are explained at the beginning of the Index of Cases at the end of this book.

2

The Legal Basis and Governance of Health Care Organizations

A hospital or health care organization is a legal entity that derives its powers and many limitations on its powers from its legal basis. Familiarity with the entity's legal basis is essential to an understanding of its organization and powers. A hospital or other health care entity can be one of five types of organizations—a governmental agency, a nonprofit corporation, a for-profit corporation, a partnership (limited or general), or a sole proprietorship. In some cases the hospital or health care organization is not a distinct entity but is an owned component or division of an entity that is one of these types.

The organization of most health care organizations, regardless of their type, includes a governing body and a chief executive officer. The organization of most hospitals also includes an organized medical staff. The governing body has the ultimate responsibility and authority to establish goals and policies, select the chief executive officer, and appoint medical staff members. The governing body will be called the "board" hereinafter, but it can have other names. The chief executive officer is delegated responsibility and authority to manage day-to-day business within policies established by the board. The organized medical staff is delegated responsibility and authority to maintain the quality of medical services in the hospital, subject to ultimate board responsibility. The duties, authority, liability, selection, and rights of the board, chief executive officer, and medical staff are discussed in more detail in this chapter and in Chapter 7.

The hospital is a unique organization because many decisions concerning use of its staff, equipment, and supplies are made by physicians who are not employees or agents of the hospital. Physicians are usually legally independent of the hospital and accountable primarily through the organized medical staff. In the mid-1990s this is changing; increasingly physicians are becoming employees of hospitals, medical groups, or other entities. As discussed further in Chapter 7, changes in the relationship between physicians and hospitals are therefore likely.

This chapter focuses predominantly on hospitals, but the same principles apply to other health care entities.

LEGAL BASIS

The hospital's powers and governance structure are derived from its legal basis, which also imposes limitations on those powers. Some states may not permit certain forms of ownership. In 1987 the Rhode Island Supreme Court ruled that the state could ban ownership of health care facilities by corporations with publicly traded stock.[1] In 1989 the Arkansas Supreme Court ruled that ownership of retail pharmacies by nonprofit hospitals could be banned.[2]

While hospital powers usually cannot be expanded without changing the underlying legal basis, many additional limitations are imposed by government regulations or by private actions, such as through the restrictions in gifts and bequests that the hospital accepts and through the contracts the hospital enters.

Governmental Hospitals

The legal basis of governmental hospitals is found in state and federal statutes and in local ordinances. Governmental hospitals are not corporations in most states. They are created by a special statute for the specific hospital or by a governmental unit, pursuant to a statute explicitly or implicitly authorizing such units to create hospitals. For example, counties and cities create hospitals under laws authorizing counties to establish hospitals.

These statutes often include specific duties or limitations. In some states, county hospitals are required to care for indigent residents. Some county hospital statutes prohibit purchases from board members and restrict how and to whom hospital property may be sold or leased. Illinois law gives county commissioners the power to establish a limit on expenditures by county hospitals regardless of the source of funds.[3]

Asset transfers or facility leases from public hospitals to corporations have frequently been challenged. A North Carolina court ruled that a county hospital could not be leased to a for-profit management company because (1) there was no statutory authority for the lease and (2) the lease violated a restriction in the deed to the property that would have caused the loss of the property.[4] A Michigan appellate court upheld the leasing of a county hospital because the patient care management system in the contract fulfilled the county's duties.[5] In 1985 the Georgia Supreme Court upheld the restructuring of a county hospital in which the hospital was leased to a nonprofit corporation governed by a board controlled by members of the county hospital authority.[6] The court found that public hospitals needed to be more competitive and that the lease would enable the hospital to better serve the public health needs of the community. The Kansas Supreme Court upheld the transfer of assets of a county hospital to a nonprofit corporation because the transfer was authorized by statute.[7]

When a governmental entity acts outside its authority, its actions are usually void. For example, in 1988 a Tennessee court ruled that a hospital district created for certain counties could not operate a home health agency outside those counties.[8] In 1986 the North Carolina Supreme Court ruled that a three-year contract with a public hospital administrator was unenforceable. The board's authority to enter long-term contracts had been revoked by implication when it adopted a resolution of intent to transfer control to a nonprofit corporation.[9] In 1971 the Missouri Supreme Court ruled that a bank could not collect on certain debts that a public hospital had endorsed because the hospital did not have authority to endorse them.[10]

In some states, governmental hospitals are subject to open meetings and open records laws. For example, in 1985 a Minnesota appellate court ruled that a county hospital board could not give the chief executive officer a private performance evaluation because of the state open meetings law.[11] States vary as to whether open meetings and records laws apply to governmental hospitals that are leased to private entities.[12] Some public hospitals have sought exemption from open meetings laws.[13]

Many governmental hospitals are converting to nonprofit hospitals because they believe that will make them more attractive to other nonprofit hospitals as potential partners.[14]

Corporations

A corporation is a separate legal entity distinct from the individuals who own and control it. In the past, each corporation was created by an individual act of the state legislature, granting articles of incorporation. In some states, nonprofit corporations were created under judicial petitions filed by citizens. Today states have general corporation laws that authorize a state official to create a corporation by issuing articles of incorporation.

One legal benefit of incorporation is that each owner's liability is generally limited to that owner's investment in the corporation. An owner is generally not individually liable beyond this investment except when the owner causes the injury by personal acts or omissions, fails to observe the corporate formalities, or personally guaranties the corporation's debts or when special statutory liabilities apply, such as environmental and pension laws. The corporation itself is liable to the extent of its resources, which include the owners' investments.

Another benefit is corporate perpetual life. Death of an owner does not terminate the corporation; only ownership is changed.

Unless the corporation is tax exempt or elects another special tax status, the corporation must pay taxes on its earnings, but in most situations the owners do not have to pay personal income tax on corporate earnings until the earnings are distributed to them.

Corporations may be for-profit or nonprofit. A for-profit corporation is operated with the intention of earning a profit that may be distributed to its owners. The earnings of a nonprofit corporation may not be distributed for the benefit of individuals. A nonprofit hospital is sometimes called a charitable hospital, while a for-profit hospital is sometimes called an investor-owned or a proprietary hospital.

For-profit hospitals can be owned in various ways. Some are closely held by a small number of investors. Some are wholly owned by a multihospital system or other parent corporation. The parent may then have publicly traded stock that may be purchased through the stock market. The stock of some hospitals has been owned by their employee's pension plans through an Employee Stock Ownership Plan (ESOP). In some cases the parent owns only part of the stock in the hospital and other local investors, frequently physicians, own the rest. Sometimes the ownership of a hospital is structured as a partnership, which is discussed later in this chapter. There is extensive federal and state regulation of the offering and sale of stock and partnership interests.

Many hospitals, both for-profit and nonprofit, are part of multihospital systems. For financial and liability reasons, each hospital is usually owned by a distinct entity, and those entities are owned or controlled by a parent corporation. The parent corporation generally retains control over many aspects of the hospital to take advantage of size efficiencies and to achieve other parental goals, but usually leaves some aspects to local control of the individual hospital. Various structures are used to achieve the parental control. They limit the latitude of the local corporation.

The powers of a corporation include only those powers expressed or implied in the articles of incorporation. Some corporations have articles that limit the type of business the corporation may conduct. When a hospital corporation plans to start a new line of business or abandon a present activity, the articles must be examined. Many modern corporations have articles that do not limit the scope of their activities; the articles authorize any business that a corporation may lawfully conduct. Other corporations may find it necessary to amend their articles before substantially changing their scope of business.

Express Corporate Authority

Any corporation derives authority to act from the state that creates it. The articles of incorporation state the corporation's purposes and its express powers to carry out those purposes. State corporation laws also grant some express authority. Acts performed within the scope of this express authority are proper, while expressly prohibited acts are improper.

Implied Corporate Authority

In addition to express authority, implied powers are inferred from corporate existence. Examples of implied authority include the power to have a corporate seal and perpetual existence, to enact corporate bylaws, and to purchase and hold property. These powers are often enumerated in express authority.

Corporations have implied authority to do any acts necessary to exercise express authority and to accomplish corporate purposes. While an act need not be indispensably necessary, the act must tend to accomplish the corporate purpose in a manner not otherwise prohibited by law. Benefit or profit alone to the corporation is usually not sufficient.

Some hospital corporations have articles of incorporation that limit them to hospital-related activities. Activities that provide services for patients, their families, and other visitors are usually considered hospital related. Examples include a clinical laboratory, cafeteria, gift shop, and parking lot. The scope of hospital-related activities has tended to expand.

The authority of nonprofit hospitals to maintain nursing residences or physician offices is sometimes challenged because there is also a direct benefit to users. Courts weigh hospital benefit against user benefit to determine if the facilities are intended primarily to accomplish hospital purposes. Implied authority for nursing residences is generally recognized because residences place nurses within easy call and help attract nurses to staff the hospital. The same reasoning generally applies to physician offices. A Connecticut court allowed a hospital to construct a medical office building on land that had been donated for a general hospital because such offices aid the work of general hospitals.[15]

When a hospital engages in new activities, such as ownership of an oil well, manufacturing company, shopping center, or fast food outlet, courts are less likely to find implied authority if the articles of incorporation narrowly define the corporation's purpose. When considering these activities, hospitals with narrow corporate powers must consider changing their articles of incorporation or creating subsidiary corporations to avoid acting outside their powers.

Consequences of Ultra Vires *Acts*

When a corporation acts outside its authority, the act is said to be *ultra vires*. In some states an *ultra vires* contract cannot be enforced. Courts in these states will not require parties to complete what they have agreed to do and will not order one party to pay the other for its injuries when the contract is not fulfilled. In other states the defense of *ultra vires* actions has been abolished, so these contracts are enforced. A corporate member or the state generally has the right to obtain an injunction to prevent performance of *ultra vires* acts. For example, a California appellate court ruled that the articles of incorporation required a nonprofit corporation to continue operating a hospital, so the board could not lease the hospital and use the rent to operate clinics.[16] *Ultra vires* acts can also justify revocation of the articles of incorporation by the state, thus dissolving the corporation.

If an *ultra vires* act is already completed, courts will normally permit it to stand unless the state intervenes. The state may obtain an order for the corporation to erase the *ultra vires* act by disposing of property, discontinuing services, or taking other steps.

Some courts have imposed a stricter standard on nonprofit corporations because of the public interest in their charitable activities.

Changing Corporate Documents

Articles of incorporation and bylaws are changed for many reasons, including (1) to permit expansion into new activities, (2) to reorganize the corporation, and (3) to adapt to other environmental changes. Corporate document changes can be made if proper legal procedures are followed and if other corporate members are treated fairly.

Articles can be changed for reasons other than altering corporate business. A Vermont hospital amended its articles to require a one-dollar contribution from members. Previously, any adult resident of certain regions of Vermont could be a member without making any contribution. The hospital made the change to determine its membership more easily.[17]

When basic corporate documents are changed, the hospital has a duty to deal fairly with other members of the corporation. If this duty is violated, changes may be declared void. An Arizona court ruled that an amendment to the articles of incorporation was void because of the unfair way it was adopted.[18] A few hours before the vote on the amendment, the board designated 159 new corporate members from among their associates so that, together, they would have more votes than the 60 physicians who were the other corporate members. Though the board had authority to appoint new members, the court found the appointment of the new members, plus the way their proxy votes were used, to be unfair.

Members can lose their power to block change. A California appellate court upheld an amendment to the bylaws of a health maintenance organization (HMO) deleting the right of the founding health insurer to appoint corporate members. The court noted that the HMO was legally required to be independent from the health insurer and that the health insurer had told the state that the HMO was independent. Thus, the health insurer was not permitted to challenge the bylaw change implementing this independence.[19]

The legislature that creates the corporation reserves the power to amend corporation laws and the articles even if the corporation or its members do not want change. The highest court of New York upheld a legislative amendment to the articles of a hospital requiring outgoing board members to be replaced by persons selected by the remaining board members, rather than by a vote of the corporation's membership.[20]

Corporations have broad powers to change their bylaws if they comply with the procedures and restrictions in their articles and in state corporation law. The Illinois Supreme Court ruled that, since the corporate articles did not forbid the change, a board could amend the bylaws to end elections of board members and to provide for the selection of replacement board members by present board members.[21]

Bylaws and bylaw amendments can be adopted orally, in writing, or by acts as well as words except where a statute or the corporate articles require a certain mode of adoption. Courts may find implied adoption of bylaws from a uniform course of conduct.[22] There is less room for dispute when bylaws are formally adopted in writing.

Partnership

A business can be organized as a partnership of several individuals or organizations. One benefit of a partnership is that income tax is paid only by the partners; no separate income tax is paid by the partnership. However, it is more difficult to arrange partnership affairs to survive the death or withdrawal of a partner.

There is no limit on the potential liability of general partners. The potential liability of some partners can be limited through a limited partnership. Limited partners are only liable to the extent of their investment, provided they do not participate in the management or operation of the business or interfere with control of the business.[23] Physicians and others who invest as limited partners in hospitals need to limit their involvement in control of the business, unless they are willing to accept the risk of unlimited liability beyond any insurance coverage that is provided. There must be at least one general partner whose liability is not limited. Usually the general partner will be a corporation. In multihospital systems, the general partner is generally controlled by the parent corporation.

Liability of general partners can include criminal liability. A New York court ruled that, without any showing of individual culpability, the 42 partners in a hospital could be charged in an indictment that alleged the hospital permitted an unauthorized person to participate in a surgical procedure and falsified records to conceal the crime.[24]

Some states permit limited liability partnerships (LLPs) that permit partners to fully participate in management and operations while limiting their individual liability for their partners' acts to their investment in the partnership.

Sole Proprietorship

A business can also be organized as a sole proprietorship, which means it is owned by one individual who has not incorporated the business. All income of the business is taxed as personal income of the owner, and there is no limitation on the owner's potential liability. Hospitals are seldom operated as sole proprietorships.

GOVERNING BOARD

Most hospitals have a governing board, which has the ultimate governance responsibility for the hospital. The chief executive officer and the organized medical staff also have roles in hospital governance that are discussed later in this chapter and in Chapter 7.

The governing board has ultimate legal responsibility for hospital operations. Active involvement of members is essential as communities, governmental agencies, and courts hold the board accountable for hospital activities.

The same general duties of supervision and management are applicable to the boards of for-profit and nonprofit hospitals. Most governmental hospital boards have similar duties. Each member has a duty to act as a reasonably prudent person would act under similar circumstances when faced with a similar problem.

In some multihospital systems, the local board may have only some of the powers and duties of the board of an independent hospital. Some powers and duties may be centralized in the board of the parent.

Duty To Act with Due Care

Board members have a duty to exercise reasonable care and skill in the management of the entity's affairs and to act at all times in good faith and with complete loyalty to the entity. This general duty applies to boards of governmental, nonprofit, and for-profit hospitals.

This duty of due care requires each board member to fulfill membership functions personally. The board member must attend meetings and participate in the consideration of matters before the board. All board members assume responsibility for board decisions that they do not oppose.

Board members cannot bargain away their duties. A Minnesota case declared void an agreement by two individuals not to take part in hospital management if elected to the board.[25] A District of Columbia court found that delegation of investment decisions to a committee of board members without any supervision by the board was a failure to use due diligence.[26]

Preservation of Assets

The general duty to act with due care and loyalty requires reasonable steps to preserve hospital assets from injury, destruction, and loss. Prudent judgment must be exercised to decide which property should be protected and how. The duty applies beyond land, buildings, equipment, and investments to include rights under contracts, wills, and other legal claims and protection against liability losses.

Buildings and equipment should be maintained in good repair. Adequate insurance against fire and other risks should also be maintained. Most boards have a duty to protect the hospital from liability losses. This duty can be satisfied by purchasing insurance. Many hospitals have elected to self-insure a large part of their risk exposure by setting aside funds for this purpose, but they usually purchase excess or stop-loss insurance against larger losses when available.

Hospitals in some states have complete or partial immunity from liability based on their governmental or charitable nature. In some states, liability insurance may not be necessary, but purchasing liability insurance is seldom considered beyond the board's authority. However, sometimes purchasing insurance waives immunity to the extent of the insurance.

The board has a duty to pay all taxes; they should be paid when due to avoid penalties. The board should treat tax exemptions as corporate assets to be preserved and protected like other assets. There are circumstances where it may be prudent deliberately to relinquish this asset, like others.

The board must enforce the hospital's rights. This includes supervising the collection of bills for hospital services and authorizing appropriate legal suits when justified. When the hospital is entitled to property under a will, the hospital's interest should be protected. The board has a corollary duty to defend the hospital from claims. The board must act reasonably under the circumstances. Some claims are not worth pursuing or should be settled out of court. The board's duty will generally be satisfied if the board conforms to sound business practices.

Basic Management Duties

The board has general authority to manage hospital business. This authority is absolute when the board acts within the law. Questions of policy and internal management are usually left by courts wholly to board discretion. When departure from board duties is clear, courts will intervene.

Basic management functions of the board include:

1. selection of corporate officers and other agents,
2. general control of compensation of such agents,
3. delegation of authority to the chief executive officer and subordinates,
4. establishment of policies,
5. exercise of businesslike control of expenditures,
6. provision for planning, and
7. supervision of and vigilance over the welfare of the whole corporation.

Specific management duties peculiar to hospitals include (1) determining hospital policies in connection with community health needs, (2) maintaining proper professional standards in the hospital, (3) assuming general responsibility for adequate patient care throughout the hospital, and (4) providing adequate financing of patient care.

Authority to manage hospital business may be delegated to the chief executive officer or to committees. In practice, much authority is expressly or implicitly delegated. If authority is not delegated or is not conferred on officers by statute or by the articles or bylaws, the board is the only body authorized to exercise that authority and to represent the corporation. The board has no obligation to delegate any management functions. Any delegation of policy-making functions is subject to revocation by the board at any time. If revocation breaches a contract, the hospital may have to pay for injuries the revocation causes.

The board cannot delegate its responsibility. The power to delegate authority is implied from the business necessities of managing corporations. To avoid abdicating its responsibility, the board should have some procedure to oversee the use of delegated authority.

The board has inherent authority to establish hospital policies. The board may directly exercise this authority by adopting rules, or it may delegate the authority. An example of this policy-making power is a Georgia Supreme Court decision upholding a hospital rule requiring all computerized tomography (CT) scans of hospital patients to be performed with the hospital machine, not with an external machine.[27] Similarly, the Arkansas Supreme Court upheld a hospital rule prohibiting megadose vitamin therapy for allergies.[28] A Florida appellate court upheld a board rule that the surgeon, not the anesthesiologist, shall make the final decision on whether to attempt emergency surgery.[29] Hospital chief executive officers, their subordinates, or hospital committees are often permitted to make policies or formulate rules and regulations.

Courts have reviewed several board actions concerning affiliation, relocation, sale, or dissolution of hospitals. These are discussed in Chapter 7.

Duty To Provide Satisfactory Patient Care

The duty to provide satisfactory patient care is an essential element of the board's duty to operate the hospital with due care and diligence, applying equally to for-profit and nonprofit hospitals. Through fulfillment of this duty, the basic purpose of the hospital is accomplished. Actions required by this duty extend from the purchase of suitable equipment for patient treatment (subject to the hospital's financial ability) to the hiring of competent employees. Two important required actions are (1) selection and review of the performance of medical staff and (2) selection and supervision of a competent hospital chief executive officer.

The board has the duty to select medical staff members as part of its duty to manage the hospital and maintain a satisfactory standard of patient care. The board, while cognizant of the importance of medical staff membership to physicians, must meet its obligation to maintain standards of good medical practice in dealing with matters of staff appointment and discipline.

In 1965, the Illinois Supreme Court ruled in the famous *Darling* case, that the board has a duty to establish procedures for the medical staff to evaluate, advise, and, where necessary, take action when an unreasonable risk of harm to a patient arises from the treatment being provided.[30]

In 1981, in the *Misericordia Community Hospital* case, the hospital was found liable for failing to exercise due care in evaluating and checking the claimed credentials of an applicant for medical staff membership.[31] This has evolved into the corporate liability doctrine discussed in Chapter 10. Hospitals should have appropriate procedures for evaluating the competency of candidates for staff appointments and for determining privileges to be given to physicians. Hospital responsibilities and physician rights concerning medical staff matters are discussed further in Chapter 7.

Duty of Loyalty

The board's duty of loyalty to the hospital can be violated by seizing corporate opportunities, self-dealing, and not disclosing conflicts of interest.

Corporate Opportunities

A board member who becomes aware of an opportunity for the corporation has a duty not to seize that opportunity for private gain unless the corporation elects not to pursue the opportunity. One example of such a seizure concerns a professional service corporation that contracted to provide services to a hospital in Illinois.[32] While the corporation was negotiating with the hospital to continue the contract, one of the two board members of the corporation created a competing corporation that contracted with the hospital to provide the services. The court found the new contract was an improper seizure of a corporate opportunity, violating the duty of loyalty to the first corporation.

As hospitals become involved in corporate ventures with competitors and place hospital officers on the boards of those corporations, they should structure the relationship so those corporations cannot claim a right to corporate opportunities that the hospitals identify.

Self-Dealing

Self-dealing is a contract between the corporation and an entity in which a board member has a financial interest. Statutes in some states specifically forbid some types of self-dealing transactions. One state makes it a crime for trustees or officers of a public hospital to own stock in any company that does business with the hospital.[33] Forbidding all self-dealing may be disadvantageous to a hospital because sometimes the most advantageous contract is with a board member or with a company in which a board member has an interest. Unless there is a statutory prohibition, most hospitals permit contracts between the corporation and a board member if (1) the contract is fair; (2) the interested board member does not speak or vote in favor of the contract; and (3) the board member makes full disclosure of all important facts concerning the interest, including both favorable and unfavorable facts. Courts generally believe the disinterested remainder of the board is able to protect corporate interests.

Courts have the power to declare any self-dealing contract void. In a South Carolina case, two board members challenged the sale of hospital land to another board member.[34] Although the purchaser did not participate in the final vote on the sale, a board member who was his business associate actively participated. The court declared the sale void because the board members did not meet the high standard of loyalty. If the fairness of the contract is questioned, the burden of proving fairness falls upon the board member with the financial interest. For example, the North Carolina Supreme Court required those involved to prove the fairness of a lease of an entire hospital to one board member.[35]

Courts often adopt a strict view of the responsibility of board members of governmental hospitals. In a 1960 Arkansas case, the court held that a contract between a board member and a governmental hospital for laundry service was improper although the board member's bid was the lowest bid.[36] The court allowed the hospital to pay the fair value of services already performed. Membership on the board of a governmental hospital is a public office. Many courts consider the danger of conflicts of interest of public officers to justify holding all contracts between board members and governmental hospitals improper and invalid even when otherwise advantageous to the hospital. However, the Mississippi Supreme Court ruled that it was not a violation of ethics or the prohibition of contracts with state officers for a public hospital to grant a physician board member medical staff membership and clinical privileges.[37]

Conflict of Interest

Conflict of interest is closely akin to self-dealing. While no actual self-dealing may be involved, nondisclosure of conflicting interests may result in statutory penalties or breach of common law fiduciary duties. All boards should require periodic disclosure of all potentially conflicting interests.

One of the most extensive judicial discussions of duties of board members concerning self-dealing and conflicts of interest arose out of Sibley Hospital, a nonprofit hospital in the District of Columbia.[38] The board had routinely approved financial arrangements made by two members, the treasurer and the chief executive officer. When the chief executive officer died, the other trustees discovered that substantial hospital assets were in bank accounts drawing inadequate or no interest and that the banks were associated with several board members.

The court ruled that board members have a general financial responsibility and breach their duty to the hospital if they (1) fail to supervise actions of persons to whom responsibility for making those decisions has been delegated; (2) allow the hospital to conduct a transaction with a business in which they have a substantial interest or hold a significant position without disclosing their interest and any facts that would indicate such a transaction would not be in the hospital's best interest; (3) vote in favor of or actively participate in decisions concerning transactions with any business in which they have a substantial interest or hold a significant position; or (4) fail to perform their duties honestly, in good faith, and with a reasonable amount of care and diligence. Although the court found that the board members had breached their duty, it did not remove the members from their positions. Written financial procedures and policies were required, and board members were required to disclose their interests in financial institutions with which the hospital dealt. Written financial statements were to be issued to the board before each meeting. In addition, the court required newly elected board members to read the court's directions.

Liability of Board Members

Criminal Liability

Board members can be criminally liable. A federal court affirmed criminal convictions of several members of a county council, which served as the county hospital board, for soliciting and receiving kickbacks from architects in return for awarding contracts for a hospital project financed with federal funds. They were each sentenced to one year in prison.[39]

Civil Liability

Although board members are sometimes called trustees, they are usually not held to the strict standard of a trustee of a trust, but instead are judged by the standard applicable to directors of other business corporations. Trustees of trusts are generally liable for simple negligence. Directors of business corporations are generally not liable for mere negligence in exercising their judgment concerning corporate business; they are liable for only gross or willful negligence. This "business judgment" rule offers board members wide latitude for actions taken in good faith. The business corporation standard was applied to hospital board members in the Sibley Hospital case.[40] Board members were not personally liable for the money lost while hospital funds were earning inadequate interest.

Board members are sometimes named as individual defendants in malpractice suits involving hospitals. A board member is generally not personally liable for medical malpractice unless the member participated in or directed the wrongful act that caused the injury. A South Carolina court ruled that board members could not be sued for a patient's death during an operation due to erroneous installation of a medical gas system in which the oxygen and nitrous oxide lines were crossed.[41] The court said that board members would not be personally liable even if the plaintiff's claims—that the board members failed to hold meetings, oversee hospital management, and confirm inspection of the medical gas unit—were correct. While the hospital could be liable for the consequences of the crossed lines, board members could not. However, when a corporate officer or director knows that the corporation is violating a standard of care and fails to take any action, the officer or director may be personally liable. A District of Columbia court ruled that a corporate officer of a clinic could be personally liable to a patient harmed by overnight treatment prohibited by local law when the officer knew of the practice and did nothing to stop it.[42]

Some federal laws impose personal liability on directors. Directors can be personally responsible for the costs of some environmental cleanup of lands owned by the corporation.[43]

Liability Limits and Insurance

Some state laws limit the liability exposure of directors of nonprofit corporations for their actions as directors. For example, Illinois forbids suits against uncompensated directors unless their actions are willful or wanton.[44] Even though the liability exposure of board members is limited, defense of these suits can be costly. It is not reasonable to expect board members to serve unless the corporation protects them from defense costs and from liability for good faith actions. Corporations generally may indemnify directors for defense costs, judgments, fines, and other expenses resulting from civil or criminal actions if the directors acted in good faith and reasonably believed their actions to be lawful and in the corporation's best interests. Many hospitals purchase insurance to protect board members from these costs. This insurance is generally called directors and officers (D & O) liability insurance. However, some D & O insurance policies may not provide the protection they appear to provide. A federal district court ruled that one officer's misrepresentations in the insurance application invalidated the coverage for all directors and officers.[45]

Selection and Dismissal of Board Members

Selection

Board members are selected in several ways. Many boards are self-perpetuating. Vacancies are filled by replacement members selected by the remaining board members. Some boards are elected by stockholders or corporate members.

Board members for governmental hospitals are frequently elected by a vote of the people in a governmental subdivision or appointed by elected officials.[46]

Usually terms of office are staggered so that all members are not replaced at the same time. Experienced members can provide continuity of governance.

If board members are not selected in accord with applicable laws, articles of incorporation, and bylaws, courts may declare board actions void. In a Tennessee case, board members were not selected as specified in the articles, and several members did not satisfy membership qualifications.[47] As a result, the court declared a board vote to transfer ownership of the hospital to the county to be void.

As discussed earlier in this chapter, it is usually possible to change the board member selection procedure by changing corporate documents.

When persons are selected by proper procedures, they must still satisfy membership qualifications before they can become board members. A 1980 California case presented a challenge to one person's membership on a public hospital board.[48] He had been elected by the proper procedure, but he was also president of a nonprofit private hospital serving the same area. Under California law, anyone who is an officer of a private hospital serving the same area is not qualified to be a member of a public hospital district board. The court set aside the election.

Other membership qualifications have been challenged. A Kentucky court ruled that a private hospital could require that all board members be women.[49] A California court ruled that a prohibition of employees from serving on a public hospital board violated a state law that prohibited local entities from restricting employee political activities.[50]

The composition of the board is one of the factors that the Internal Revenue Service (IRS) uses in determining whether a nonprofit corporation is eligible for tax exemption, so nonprofit hospitals need to consider IRS guidelines in selecting board members. IRS guidelines are discussed in Chapter 4.

At least one legislature has controlled the composition of boards. West Virginia requires 40 percent of the board of each nonprofit or local governmental hospital to be consumer representatives selected in equal proportions from small businesses, organized labor, older persons, and lower-income persons. Special consideration must also be given to women, racial minorities, and the disabled. Failure to comply can result in loss of the hospital's license, a fine, or imprisonment.[51] Federal courts have ruled that the statute is constitutional.[52]

Dismissal

Sometimes a board tries to remove a member. The procedure specified in the articles and bylaws must be followed. In New Jersey, a private hospital board member must be provided with notice of the reason for the action and an opportunity to be heard even if the articles and bylaws do not require these steps—a rule established in an 1897 case in which the court ordered the person restored to the board because this procedure had not been followed.[53] In an Oregon case, the court affirmed the removal of a public hospital board member by the board of county commissioners after he was provided with notice and opportunity to be heard pursuant to a lower court order.[54] The court ruled that substantial evidence supported the commissioners' decision that the member's lack of candor caused a lack of trust, which diminished his effectiveness as a board member, and that this was sufficient reason to remove him from the board.

CHIEF EXECUTIVE OFFICER

The chief executive officer (CEO) of the hospital is concerned with all the topics covered in this book. The CEO's personal intervention will probably be required when many legal problems arise. In this section the CEO's duties, authority, qualifications, and personal liability will be covered.

Duties of the CEO

The hospital CEO is directly in charge of the hospital and is generally responsible to only the governing board, but may be responsible to systems officers when the hospital is part of a multiple hospital system. The CEO is the general supervisor of all hospital operations and is delegated powers by the board to fulfill this responsibility. Although areas of responsibility are usually delegated to subordinates, the CEO is primarily responsible for hospital management. The CEO is the agent and usually the employee of the governing board and is subject to its superior authority. Even when the CEO is also a board member or a part-owner of the hospital, the CEO is a board agent and has a duty to carry out board policies.

Many hospitals are part of a larger organization. Both for-profit and nonprofit organizations apply systemwide policies concerning many aspects of management. To promote efficiency, the organization often uses shared services, uniform accounting procedures, centralized support services, and other management methods made possible by the umbrella structure. A CEO in a multiple hospital system may or may not be an employee of the larger organization, but will be subject to its policies.

Governmental hospital CEOs are usually appointed public officials. Whether public officials or hired supervisors, they are directly responsible to the governmental body that controls the hospital. Their conditions of employment may fall within civil service laws.

The CEO has only the duties either imposed by law or delegated expressly or by implication by the board. The CEO is usually charged with certain general hospital management duties. By resolution, bylaw, order, or contract, the board may assign the CEO additional duties. Following are examples of duties often delegated.

The CEO has the general duty to oversee every activity in the hospital for the board. The CEO's responsibility is to the board, which has ultimate legal responsibility for the hospital. The CEO is responsible for implementing board policies, including obtaining required governmental approvals. The CEO transmits and interprets board policy to the medical staff and other personnel and is responsible for informing patients, visitors, hospital personnel, medical staff members, and others of hospital rules. The CEO is responsible for taking appropriate corrective action concerning noncompliance with hospital rules except when disciplinary authority has been retained by the board or delegated by the board to others. The CEO also has the general duty to make periodic reports to the board concerning hospital operations.

The CEO is usually authorized to select or recommend selection of administrative department heads. The CEO is normally responsible for employment in the hospital and, within budgetary limits and salary guidelines, is generally given authority to fix individual salaries and wages. Some CEOs delegate to department heads the authority to select their assistants. The CEO remains responsible for the performance of any duties delegated to subordinates.

CEOs are generally responsible to have systems in place to provide satisfactory care of patients. They should have proper admission and discharge procedures implemented. They should cooperate with the medical and professional staff in maintaining satisfactory standards of patient care. They should arrange for hospital departments to work in coordination with each other and with the medical staff to provide satisfactory patient care. CEOs also assist the medical staff with its organizational and administrative problems and responsibilities.

The CEO is usually responsible for corporate operating funds and for planning and analysis for the board. The CEO generally advises the board on policy formation; proposes organizational plans; prepares plans for achieving hospital objectives; submits a proposed annual budget; recommends charges for hospital services; submits periodic and special reports to the board, showing the service and financial experience of the hospital; and deals with other matters as requested by the board.

Unless otherwise directed by the board, the CEO or a delegate is expected to attend all meetings of the board and its committees and to advise the board of significant trends that may affect its policy-making function. These trends can include societal, economic, legal, medical, and technical trends as well as changing conditions in the hospital and in the health care field.

CEOs sometimes have dual roles in which they also serve as board members. When CEOs are nonvoting members, their positions do not present legal difficulties. When CEOs serve as voting members of a nonprofit hospital board, caution is required; CEOs cannot vote on any question concerning their personal status or compensation.

When a new CEO is appointed, there is often a duty to abide by many of the contractual and other commitments of the predecessor until the commitments are legally terminated. For example, at one hospital, a new president committed an unfair labor practice by refusing to bargain with a union the predecessor had voluntarily recognized.[55]

In addition to delegated duties, duties are imposed on CEOs by statutes and regulations. These duties may include reporting vital statistical information (births and deaths) to health authorities and furnishing communicable disease and gunshot wound treatment reports, unless state law imposes those duties on an entity other than the hospital. Sometimes it is not possible to obey all legal requirements because they conflict with each other or because of other reasons. Legal advice should be sought in these situations to determine the proper procedure for resolving the conflict or to seek appropriate temporary or permanent waivers of the requirements.

The most important skill needed to accomplish these varied responsibilities is the art of negotiation. Hospital administration is a series of negotiations. Arrangements must be made that appropriately accommodate the interests of the hospital, community, and other interested groups. The following list of some of these groups suggests the complexity of negotiations required: patients, their families, physicians, nurses, other hospital staff, board members, community groups, insurers, other third party payers, bankers, other lenders, politicians, government officials, and reporters. An adversary or any other interested party can always find fault with the CEO's assessment of a situation, choice of strategy to solve a problem, or decisions and actions. The CEO's performance should be judged as a whole. Not every negotiation will be successful. When evaluating administrative actions, the board should take into account the complexity of tasks and inherent difficulties in successful negotiation.

Authority of the CEO

The CEO's primary source of authority is the governing board, which normally delegates to the CEO the duty and responsibility of managing the hospital, together with the authority to accomplish this duty. Board resolutions or policies may specify the CEO's authority or grant special authority to deal with certain problems. Some authority may be granted in legal documents organizing the hospital, such as hospital articles or bylaws, while other aspects of the CEO's authority may be covered in an employment contract. State statutes or regulations may provide for certain administrative powers.

Authority may be either express or implied. Express authority is a written or oral grant giving the CEO power to accomplish certain ends. The scope of the CEO's express authority may be as broad or as limited as the board desires. Implied authority consists of those powers that are deemed to be conveyed along with express authority so that desired ends may be accomplished. For example, when the CEO is given responsibility to maintain hospital safety, authority to create rules is implied—one such rule might require that specific clothing be worn in certain hospital areas. The CEO may possess only those powers and duties that can be properly delegated. The board cannot delegate authority that it does not possess, and it cannot delegate certain responsibilities that are nondelegable. For example, in some states, the board probably cannot delegate the power to grant appointments to the medical staff, except on a temporary basis.

The CEO may be able to do many things that are not challenged, either because people are unaware of the actions or because people with the right to challenge or forbid them do not care to do so. Acts that could be successfully challenged are said to be beyond the scope of the CEO's authority. A CEO acting beyond authority is subject to several possible legal consequences, including being dismissed by the board in accordance with its established rules, being sued by the hospital for breach of the employment contract and for any resultant financial damage to the hospital, being held liable by employees or other persons for damages resulting from negligence or intentional wrongdoing, and being subjected to prosecution for any specific criminal laws violated.

Selecting, Evaluating, and Discharging the CEO

Governing boards are responsible for selecting CEOs to act as their agents in hospital management. Boards that try to run hospitals without CEOs are subject to extensive criticism and risk legal liability.[56] Some boards use temporary CEOs while searching for permanent CEOs.[57] The board must select a competent CEO who will set and maintain satisfactory patient care standards. Minimum standards for CEOs are contained in some hospital licensing statutes and regulations and in some statutes creating governmental hospitals. Where legal requirements exist, the CEO must satisfy at least those requirements. Boards, especially those of hospitals with more complex operations, often find it necessary to appoint CEOs with qualifications that exceed the minimum.

Even when no statutory or regulatory standards exist, the board has a duty to select a competent CEO. This board responsibility was discussed in a federal court case concerning a county hospital board that had selected a CEO with no prior hospital management experience. The CEO padded bills of patients covered by hospitalization insurance, and the insurance company sued to recover the overcharges. The court criticized the hospital board for selection of the CEO.

> To select a governing board for an institution as complex as a hospital in the manner used here, chosen as political patronage by County Supervisors from their respective districts without any requirement of training, experience or knowledge of what was expected of them was calculated to bring about the very result which developed here. Failing to appreciate their duties and responsibilities led these Trustees to feel, according to their testimony, that they had discharged their duties by picking as Administrator, Salter, a former school teacher, apparently as ignorant of operating a hospital as they themselves were. Their attachment to him was such that, despite the refusal of other agencies to deal with Salter in certain respects, and his dismissal, these Trustees again rehired and restored him to the position of Administrator of the hospital. They seemed to think because Salter had changed the hospital's financial position from a deficit of several thousand dollars to one of approximately the same amount on the black side of the ledger, this justified his restoration.[58]

After appointing a CEO, the board must periodically evaluate the CEO's performance. To provide accountability, it is helpful to set performance standards and procedures for measuring administrative performance. The board is liable if patient care becomes inadequate because the board has failed to properly supervise the CEO's management. When not satisfied with performance, the board should take appropriate corrective action, including replacement, if necessary. Failure to remove an incompetent CEO or agent is as much a breach of duty of due care and diligence as is failure to appoint a competent one.

When the board is considering replacement of the CEO, it should follow the procedures in applicable law, the articles of incorporation, and the bylaws. Some courts have declined to intervene even when bylaws are not followed. For example, the Louisiana Supreme Court declined to order reinstatement of a public hospital CEO even though the bylaws had not been followed.[59] The bylaws required a warning and an opportunity to correct any deficiencies before dismissal. The court ruled that it would order reinstatement only if the CEO could prove that he had relied on the bylaws to his detriment. Similarly, the Minnesota Supreme Court refused to intervene when a CEO was discharged.[60] The applicable law provided that the CEO served "at the pleasure of the county board," so he was not entitled to a hearing.

Generally courts will not order reinstatement of removed CEOs, but the hospital will generally be liable to pay damages when the removal breaches a contract[61] or is done in an improper manner.[62]

Under some state laws it may be possible for someone other than the board or a court to order removal of a CEO. A New York court ruled that the state's Department of Health had authority to order removal of a CEO for not being sufficiently qualified by education or experience.[63]

Liability of the CEO

Criminal Liability

CEOs who become involved in fraudulent schemes can be held criminally liable, as can those in other industries. For example, a Florida CEO who caused a hospital to issue 21 checks, fraudulently endorsed them, and appropriated the proceeds, which exceeded $850,000, was sentenced to 25 years in prison.[64] Embezzlement and bribery are also federal crimes when committed by an agent of an organization that received over $10,000 under a federal program in a one-year period that includes the offense.[65] A hospital CEO has been convicted under this law.[66]

Fraudulent schemes can also result in forfeiture of benefits. An Ohio court ruled that a CEO who had embezzled funds forfeited all compensation, including deferred compensation, during the period of faithlessness.[67]

Some prosecutors have pursued criminal charges against CEOs for treatment of patients. The Wisconsin Supreme Court upheld the conviction of a nursing home CEO for abuse of residents, but reversed a conviction for reckless conduct causing death.[68] One resident had died of exposure after walking away from the facility. Other residents had lost weight and had developed bed sores. The state claimed this was due to understaffing by the CEO.

Several other nursing home administrators have been convicted of patient abuse or neglect.[69]

Civil Liability

CEOs, like other members of society, may be individually liable for their own wrongful actions that injure others.

A CEO can be liable for injuries caused by a subordinate only when the CEO is at fault due to negligent supervision or careless hiring of the subordinate. A CEO who is not personally at fault is not liable for injuries caused by subordinates.[70] Employers are liable for the injuries wrongfully caused by their employees, but CEOs are not the employers of their subordinates, the hospital is. Since CEOs are hospital employees, the hospital may be liable for wrongful acts of CEOs. If the hospital pays money to an injured person as the result of a lawsuit, it usually has the right to repayment from the employee who caused the injury. Hospitals rarely exercise this right of indemnification beyond the employee's individual insurance coverage. Liability issues are discussed in more detail in Chapters 10 and 11.

CEOs are not personally liable for contracts they make on behalf of the hospital when acting within their authority to contract. When CEOs enter contracts that exceed their authority, the hospital may not be bound by the contract. CEOs may be personally liable to the other party to the contract for the loss resulting from the failure to bind the hospital. CEOs are not liable if the hospital ratifies the contract and adopts it as its own. CEOs are generally not liable for unauthorized acts if they innocently believe they have the power to make the contract and the hospital clothed the CEOs' position with such apparent authority that the other contracting parties reasonably believed the CEOs had authority. If the hospital creates this apparent authority, so that innocent third parties are misled, then the law imposes liability on the hospital. If the other contracting parties should have suspected the CEO lacked authority, they are required to make appropriate inquiries. If the inquiries would have disclosed the lack of authority, no recovery is allowed against the hospital. The CEO is liable to the other contracting parties even when the CEO has apparent authority, if the CEO made the contract with intent to defraud.

In a case in Mississippi, an insurance company sought to recover excessive amounts it had paid to a hospital because the CEO had padded bills.[71] The court found both the CEO and the hospital liable to repay overcharges.

CEOs may be liable civilly or criminally for breach of duties imposed on them by statute. For example, when a license or permit is required before the hospital may perform certain acts, often the CEO is required to obtain the license or permit; failure to obtain it may lead to fine or imprisonment. CEOs may also be required to submit certain reports to the state. While hospital CEOs are seldom fined personally for failure to discharge such a statutory duty, the possibility exists. In a Mississippi Supreme Court case involving the same CEO and hospital as the case discussed above, a state auditor sought to force the CEO and the hospital board to repay county hospital funds that had been spent without authority.[72] The court analyzed each type of expenditure the state auditor claimed to be unauthorized and found several to be unauthorized, requiring personal repayment by the CEO and the board members.

Some federal laws impose personal liability on CEOs. For example, the CEO can be personally liable for unpaid wages under the Fair Labor Standards Act.[73] A federal court in New York ruled that a new CEO could be personally sued for sex discrimination for excluding the vice-president/chief nursing officer from vice-presidential meetings, refusing to meet with her, and firing her.[74]

A CEO may also be civilly liable to a person harmed by violations of statutes. Thus, if a statute imposed a duty on officials to keep medical records confidential, an official who improperly made such records public could be liable to those injured by the violation.

The federal government and some states have provided some official immunity from personal civil liability for some public officials when following a legal mandate (i.e., performing a "ministerial duty") or when exercising administrative judgment (i.e., performing a "discretionary duty"). Rules vary considerably, and courts tend to restrict the application of immunity doctrines.

Management Contracts

Many hospital boards have entered contracts with other corporations to manage their hospitals. The CEO is generally supplied by the management corporation.

The board retains ultimate authority, so no change is required in the hospital's license in most states. The authority of the board and the contractor should be carefully defined. The board should preserve its authority to terminate the contract without prohibitively onerous penalties.

These contracts are sometimes difficult to terminate. A Mississippi board tried to terminate a management contract after the management company increased hospital rates and revised the hospital budget without the board approval required in the contract. The court ruled that termination was not justified because the board had authority to nullify the breach without termination.[75]

Hospitals that have or plan to issue tax-exempt bonds need to consider the IRS requirements limiting the length and other features of such contracts.[76]

Often hospitals enter management contracts because of confidence in individuals who own or manage the management corporation. They do not want to be managed by others, so they restrict assignment of the contract. Restrictions on assignment of contracts with corporations can easily be avoided by sale of the management corporation's stock. Unless provided in the contract, the hospital will not be able to terminate the contract when these stock sales occur. An Alabama hospital sued when all the stock of a management company was sold to another company despite a prohibition of assignment of the management contract. The court upheld a temporary injunction of transfer of hospital funds, conversion of the hospital into an abuse facility, and movement of property out of the hospital.[77] Hospitals should not rely on courts to provide these protections. It is prudent to require the management corporation to inform the hospital of all substantial changes in stock ownership and to give the hospital the option to terminate the contract after such a change.

NOTES

1. In re Advisory Opinion to House of Representatives Bill, 519 A.2d 578 (R.I. 1987).

2. Arkansas Hosp. Ass'n v. Arkansas State Bd. of Pharmacy, 297 Ark. 454, 763 S.W.2d 73 (1989).

3. County of Cook v. Ayala, 76 Ill. 2d 219, 390 N.E.2d 877 (1979).

4. National Med. Enters., Inc. v. Sandrock, 72 N.C. App. 245, 324 S.E.2d 268 (1985).

5. University Med. Affiliates, P.C. v. Wayne County Executive, 142 Mich. App. 135, 369 N.W.2d 277 (1985). Leases have also been upheld in Kromko v. Arizona Bd. of Regents, 149 Ariz. 319, 718 P.2d 478 (1986) and Local Union No. 2490 v. Waukesha County, 143 Wis. 2d 438, 422 N.W.2d 117 (Ct. App. 1988).

6. Richmond County Hosp. Auth. v. Richmond County, 255 Ga. 183, 336 S.E.2d 562 (1985).

7. Ullrich v. Board of County Comm'rs, 234 Kan. 782, 676 P.2d 127 (1984).

8. Professional Home Health & Hospice, Inc. v. Jackson-Madison County Gen. Hosp. Dist., 759 S.W.2d 416 (Tenn. Ct. App. 1988).

9. Rowe v. Franklin County, 318 N.C. 344, 349 S.E.2d 65 (1986).

10. Fulton Nat'l Bank v. Callaway Mem. Hosp., 465 S.W.2d 549 (Mo. 1971); *accord* Board of Trustees v. Peoples Bank, 538 So.2d 361 (Miss. 1989) [copier lease void because not approved by purchasing department].

11. Itasca County Bd. of Comm'rs v. Olson, 372 N.W.2d 804 (Minn. Ct. App. 1985).

12. *E.g.,* Memorial Hosp. Ass'n, Inc. v. Knutson, 239 Kan. 663, 722 P.2d 1093 (1986) [private lessee not subject to Kansas open meetings law]; State ex rel. Fostoria Daily Review Co. v. Fostoria Hosp. Ass'n, 40 Ohio St. 3d 10, 531 N.E.2d 313 (1988) [private lessee subject to Ohio open records law].

13. S. Lutz, *Texas hospital bids for closed meetings,* MOD. HEALTHCARE, Feb. 20, 1995, at 20.

14. K. Shriver, *Municipal hospitals becoming converts,* MOD. HEALTHCARE, Feb. 27, 1995, at 46.

15. Charlotte Hungerford Hosp. v. Mulvey, 26 Conn. Supp. 394, 225 A.2d 495 (1966); *contra,* Prichard v. Cleveland, 314 So.2d 729 (Miss. 1975) [governmental hospital did not have authority under statute to convert nurse's quarters into private doctor's offices].

16. Queen of Angels Hosp. v. Younger, 66 Cal. App. 3d 359, 136 Cal. Rptr. 36 (2d Dist., 1977).

17. Langrock v. Porter Hosp., Inc., 126 Vt. 233, 227 A.2d 291 (1967).

18. Hatch v. Emery, 1 Ariz. App. 142, 400 P.2d 349 (1965); *contra,* Harris v. Board of Directors, 55 Ill. App. 3d 392, 370 N.E.2d 1121, 13 Ill. Dec. 94 (1st Dist. 1977) [board could unilaterally amend bylaws to become self-perpetuating despite desire of members to remove board].

19. Health Maintenance Network v. Blue Cross, 202 Cal. App. 3d 1043, 249 Cal. Rptr. 220 (2d Dist. 1988).

20. In re Mt. Sinai Hosp., 250 N.Y. 103, 164 N.E. 871 (1928).

21. Westlake Hosp. Ass'n v. Blix, 13 Ill. 2d 183, 148 N.E.2d 471, *appeal dismissed,* 358 U.S. 43 (1958).

22. *E.g.,* In re Rye Psychiatric Hosp. Ctr., Inc., 101 A.D.2d 309, 476 N.Y.S.2d 339 (1984) [implied amendment recognized], *rev'd,* 66 N.Y.2d 333, 488 N.E.2d 63 (1985) [number of directors may not be determined by custom].

23. *See* Annotation, *Liability of limited partner arising from taking part in control of business under Uniform Limited Partnership Act,* 79 A.L.R. 4TH 427.

24. People v. Smithtown Gen. Hosp., 92 Misc. 2d 144, 399 N.Y.S.2d 993 (Sup. Ct. 1977).

25. Ray v. Homewood Hosp., 223 Minn. 440, 27 N.W.2d 409 (1947).

26. Stern v. Lucy Webb Hayes Nat'l Training School, 381 F. Supp. 1003 (D. D.C. 1974).

27. Cobb County-Kennestone Hosp. v. Prince, 242 Ga. 139, 249 S.E.2d 581 (1978).

28. Brandt v. St. Vincent Infirmary, 287 Ark. 431, 701 S.W.2d 103 (1985).

29. Martin Mem. Hosp. Ass'n, Inc. v. Noble, 496 So.2d 222 (Fla. 4th DCA 1986).

30. Darling v. Charleston Community Mem. Hosp., 33 Ill. 2d 326, 211 N.E.2d 253 (1965), *cert. denied,* 383 U.S. 946 (1966).

31. Johnson v. Misericordia Commun. Hosp., 99 Wis. 2d 708, 301 N.W.2d 156 (1981).

32. Patient Care Servs., S.C. v. Segal, 32 Ill. App. 3d 1021, 337 N.E.2d 471 (1975).

33. N.C. GEN. STAT. § 14-234 (1986 Supp.); N.C. Att'y Gen. Op. Dec. 6, 1982.

34. Gilbert v. McLeod Infirmary, 219 S.C. 174, 64 S.E.2d 524 (1951).

35. Fowle Mem. Hosp. v. Nicholson, 189 N.C. 44, 126 S.E. 94 (1925).

36. Warren v. Reed, 231 Ark. 714, 331 S.W.2d 847 (1960).

37. State by Mississippi Ethics Comm'n v. Aseme, 583 So.2d 955 (Miss. 1991).

38. Stern v. Lucy Webb Hayes Nat'l Training School, 381 F. Supp. 1003 (D. D.C. 1974).

39. United States v. Thompson, 366 F.2d 167 (6th Cir), *cert. denied*, 385 U.S. 973 (1966).

40. *Id.*; *accord*, Beard v. Achenbach Mem. Hosp. Ass'n, 170 F.2d 859 (10th Cir. 1948).

41. Hunt v. Rabon, 275 S.C. 475, 272 S.E.2d 643 (1980).

42. Vuitch v. Furr, 482 A.2d 811 (D.C. 1984).

43. 42 U.S.C.A. §§ 9601(20)(a), 9607(a); Sidney S. Arst Co. v. Pipefitters Welfare Educ. Fund, 25 F.3d 417 (7th Cir. 1994).

44. ILL. REV. STAT. ch. 32, § 108.70(a).

45. Shapiro v. American Home Assurance Co., 584 F. Supp. 1245 (D. Mass. 1984); *but see* Shapiro v. American Home Assur. Co., 616 F. Supp. 900 (D. Mass. 1984) [due to severability provision in policy, Securities Act policy must provide coverage despite fraud of other insureds].

46. *E.g.*, State ex rel. Board of Trustees of City of North Kansas City Mem. Hosp. v. Russell, 843 S.W.2d 353 (Mo. 1992) [board members selected by mayor with approval of city council, could be removed by city government].

47. Bedford County Hosp. v. County of Bedford, 42 Tenn. App. 569, 304 S.W.2d 697 (1957).

48. Franzblau v. Monardo, 108 Cal. App. 3d 522, 166 Cal. Rptr. 610 (1st Dist. 1980).

49. Pattie A. Clay Infirmary Ass'n v. First Presbyterian Church of Richmond, 605 S.W.2d 52 (Ky. Ct. App. 1980); *see also Ex-Chronicle chairwoman loses lawsuit*, N.Y. TIMES, May 27, 1995, at 27 [upholding bylaw barring directors over age 73; state age discrimination law did not apply because directors are not employees].

50. Eldridge v. Sierra View Local Hosp. Dist., 224 Cal. App. 3d 311, 273 Cal. Rptr. 654 (5th Dist. 1990), *rev. denied*, 1990 Cal. LEXIS 5673 (Dec. 20, 1990).

51. W. VA. CODE § 16-5B-6a; Christie v. Elkins Area Med. Ctr, Inc., 179 W.Va. 247, 366 S.E.2d 755 (1988).

52. American Hosp. Ass'n v. Hansbarger, 594 F. Supp. 483 (N.D. W. Va. 1984), *aff'd*, 783 F.2d 1184 (4th Cir. 1986), *cert. denied*, 479 U.S. 820 (1986); *see also* Blue Cross v. Foudree, 606 F. Supp. 1574 (S.D. Iowa 1985) [upholding required subscriber majority on board].

53. State ex rel. Welch v. Passaic Hosp. Ass'n, 59 N.J.L. 142, 36 A. 702 (1897).

54. Coldiron v. Board of Comm'rs, 39 Or. App. 495, 592 P.2d 1053 (1979).

55. Exxel/Atmos, Inc. v. N.L.R.B., 307 U.S. App. D.C. 376, 28 F.3d 1243 (1994), *reh'g denied*, 308 U.S. App. D.C. 411, 37 F.3d 1538 (1994).

56. *Community hospital's questionable ethics*, and Barkholz, *Maryland system's board refutes allegations, promises improvements*, 15 MOD. HEALTHCARE, June 7, 1985, 5, 44 [hospital operated 18 months without CEO].

57. Droste, *Temporary CEOs take up the slack in hospitals*, 63 HOSPS., Sept. 20, 1989, at 104.

58. Reserve Life Ins. Co. v. Salter, 152 F. Supp. 868, 870 (D. Miss. 1957).

59. Lamm v. Board of Comm'rs, 378 So.2d 919 (La. 1979).

60. State ex rel. Stubben v. Board of County Comm'rs, 273 Minn. 361, 141 N.W.2d 499 (1966); *accord* Heath v. Redbud Hosp. Dist., 620 F.2d 207 (9th Cir. 1980) [CEO not entitled to hearing before termination].

61. *E.g.*, Browning v. Salem Mem. Dist. Hosp., 808 S.W.2d 943 (Mo. Ct. App. 1991).

62. *E.g.*, American Med. International, Inc. v. Giurintano, 821 S.W.2d 331 (Tex. Ct. App. 1991) [Hospital, assistant administrator, and individual physicians liable to prospective hospital administrator for intentional infliction of emotional distress for spreading rumors, other actions to prevent his appointment. After he resigned former position, told not to report for work due to opposition by employee physicians].

63. Harlem Hosp. Center Med. Bd. v. Hoffman, 84 A.D.2d 272, 445 N.Y.S.2d 981 (1st Dep't 1982).

64. Bronstein v. State, 355 So.2d 817 (Fla. 3d DCA 1978); *see* Touche Ross & Co. v. Sun Bank, 366 So.2d 465 (Fla. 3d DCA), *cert denied*, 378 So.2d 350 (Fla. 1979) [effort by hospital to recover losses due to CEO's crimes]; *see also Former Hermann Hospital exec released from prison*, 17 MOD. HEALTHCARE, Dec. 18, 1987, 21.

65. 18 U.S.C.A. § 666.

66. United States v. Stout, Crim. No. 89-317-1-2-3. 1990 U.S. Dist. LEXIS 12343 (E.D. Pa. Sept. 18, 1990), *post-conviction proceeding*, 1994 U.S. Dist. LEXIS 3182 (E.D. Pa. Mar. 21, 1994). *aff'd without op.*, 39 F.3d 1173, 1994 U.S. App. LEXIS 31128 (3d Cir. 1994); *see also* United States v. Sadlier, 649 F. Supp. 1560 (D. Mass. 1986) [denying dismissal of charges against respiratory therapist].

67. Roberto v. Brown County Gen. Hosp., 59 Ohio App. 3d 84, 571 N.E.2d 467 (1989).

68. State v. Serebin, 119 Wis. 2d 837, 350 N.W.2d 65 (1984).

69. *E.g.*, State v. Cunningham, 493 N.W.2d 884 (Iowa Ct. App. 1992); State v. Springer, 585 N.E.2d 27 (Ind. Ct. App. 1992); Annotation, *Criminal liability under statutes penalizing abuse or neglect of the institutionalized infirm*, 60 A.L.R. 4th 1153.

70. *E.g.*, Portlock v. Perry, 852 S.W.2d 578 (Tex. Ct. App. 1993) [investor/president of diagnostic radiology center not liable for death of child after technicians gave too much chloral hydrate for sedation; claimed failure to have adequate policies and procedures not sufficient to impose personal liability].

71. Reserve Life Ins. Co. v. Salter, 152 F. Supp. 868, 870 (D. Miss. 1957).

72. Golding v. Salter, 234 Miss. 567, 107 So.2d 348 (1958).

73. Fegley v. Higgins, 19 F.3d 1126 (6th Cir. 1994), *cert. denied*, 115 S.Ct. 203 (U.S. 1994).

74. Dirschel v. Speck, No. 94 Civ. 0502 (LLM) (S.D. N.Y. July 6, 1994), *as discussed in* 3 HEALTH L. REP. [BNA] 954 (1994).

75. UHS-Qualicare, Inc. v. Gulf Coast Commun. Hosp., 525 So.2d 746 (Miss. 1987), *pet. reh'g withdrawn*, 525 So.2d 758 (Miss. 1988) [settlement].

76. Rev. Proc. 93-17, 93-19; *IRS issues proposed regulations on private activity bond restrictions*, 59 FED. REG. 67658 (Dec. 30, 1994) [to replace Rev. Proc. 93-17, 93-19].

77. Ex parte Health Care Management Group, 522 So.2d 280 (Ala. 1988).

3

Regulation and Accreditation

Hospitals and other health care entities are among the most extensively regulated institutions. They are regulated by all levels of government and by numerous agencies within each level. They occasionally are confronted with conflicting mandates. Since this problem has received more attention, relief has been provided in some areas. Conflicts still remain because of underlying conflicts in societal goals. There are also numerous private entities that develop standards and accredit institutions that satisfy their standards.

Licensure is different from accreditation. Licensure is governmental regulation. For example, the state legislature grants an administrative agency authority to adopt standards hospitals must meet, to grant licenses to complying institutions, and to enforce continuing compliance. Hospitals are barred from operating without a license. Persons who operate hospitals that violate the standards can lose their licenses, be fined, or penalized. Numerous other health care entities must obtain state and local licenses and comply with licensing standards. Each state has a different list of required licenses. Some of the entities that are licensed include health maintenance organizations, nursing homes, ambulatory surgery centers, hospices, home health agencies, clinical laboratories, and employee leasing organizations.

In contrast, accreditation is granted by private authorities and is not legally mandated. Many hospitals are accredited by the Joint Commission on Accreditation of Healthcare Organizations (Joint Commission), formerly called the Joint Commission on Accreditation of Hospitals, an organization that includes representatives from the American College of Physicians, the American College of Surgeons, the American Dental Association, the American Hospital Association, the American Medical Association, and the American Nurses Association, plus representatives of the public. Hospitals seeking accreditation apply to the Joint Commission, pay a fee, and submit to a survey to determine whether they satisfy the standards established by the Joint Commission and published in its *Comprehensive Accreditation Manual for Hospitals*.[1] When hospitals cease to meet the standards, they can lose their accreditation. The American Osteopathic Association (AOA) accredits osteopathic hospitals and functions in a manner similar to that of the Joint Commission. Several states accept Joint Commission or AOA accreditation as a basis for full or partial licensure either without further state inspection or with state inspection of only areas not covered by the accrediting entity. This acceptance is part of an effort to reduce duplicative hospital inspections.

There are accrediting bodies for other health care entities. For example, the Joint Commission also accredits long-term care facilities; mental health, chemical dependency, and mental retardation/developmental disabilities services; home care; and pathology and clinical laboratory services. The National Committee for Quality Assurance (NCQA) and the Joint Commission accredit managed care entities.

Medicare has standards, called "conditions of participation"[2] for the operations of health care organizations, including hospitals, intermediate care facilities for the mentally retarded, home health agencies, comprehensive outpatient rehabilitation facilities, organ procurement organizations, rural primary care hospitals, and providers of outpatient physical therapy and speech-language pathology services. They are not licensing standards, but health care organizations must comply to qualify for Medicare payment for most services to Medicare beneficiaries. The Medicare law provides that hospitals accredited by the Joint Commission or AOA are deemed to meet most conditions of participation unless a special Medicare inspection finds noncompliance.[3]

Some regulatory or accrediting agencies focus on entire institutions. Other agencies focus on individual services or activities such as pharmacies, laboratories, radiology, or elevators. Some agencies can focus on the institution or on individual activities depending on the circumstances. For example, a certificate-of-need agency must give its permission before a new hospital or many new services can be started. Numerous other regulations apply to other aspects of hospitals such as financing, taxation, waste disposal, communications, transportation, and labor relations.

Licensing of individuals is the focus of other regulatory agencies discussed in Chapter 8.

Many institutions are subject to other private standards that they have voluntarily accepted. For example, hospitals operated by the Roman Catholic church are subject to the rules of the church, including canon law. Canon law has an important role in many decisions of these hospitals.[4]

LICENSURE OF INSTITUTIONS

States regulate each hospital as an institution through licensure. The major legal issues concerning licensure are the authority for licensure, scope of regulations, inspections, and penalties for violations.

Authority

The police power provides state governments with authority to regulate hospitals. All states have enacted hospital licensing statutes. These statutes usually grant an agency authority to adopt standards, to grant licenses, and to revoke licenses or impose other penalties when standards are violated. Licensing statutes and regulations must be a reasonable exercise of the police power and must not deny due process or equal protection of the laws. To be enforceable, agency rules must be within authority properly delegated to the agency by statute. Rules must be adopted using the state procedure for administrative rule making. This procedure usually includes public notice of proposed rules and an opportunity for public comment before the rules become final. Some states require additional steps, such as an economic impact statement, before a rule becomes enforceable.[5]

Rules are difficult to challenge if they are within the statutory authority of the agency, do not violate due process by being vague or arbitrary, and are adopted through proper procedures. For example, detailed hospital licensing rules were contested in Pennsylvania on the ground that they were an attempt by the Department of Health to take away "management prerogatives" of hospital boards and administrators. The Pennsylvania Supreme Court decided that the department had statutory authority and upheld the rules even though they might supplant part of traditional management authority.[6]

Most actions that states take under licensing laws have been interpreted not to constitute a taking of private property, so the constitutional requirement of just compensation for takings generally does not apply.[7]

Scope of Regulations

Hospital licensing regulations usually address hospital organization and require an organized governing body or some equivalent, an organized medical staff, and an administrator. The relationship among these elements usually is also addressed. Regulations may require general hospitals to provide certain basic services, including laboratory, radiology, pharmacy, and some emergency services. Regulations generally require use of adequate nursing personnel. They also may establish standards for facilities, equipment, and personnel for specific services, such as obstetrics, pediatrics, and surgery. Regulations may also address safety, sanitation, infection control, record preparation and retention, and other matters.

All standards do not have to be in objective numerical terms to satisfy due process requirements, but some courts are reluctant to uphold overly subjective rules. A New York court found that several nursing home rules violated due process requirements because they were so subjective that they did not provide adequate notice of the conduct required.[8] The invalidated rules required nursing staff, linen laundering, and sewage facilities to meet the "approval" and "satisfaction" of the Commissioner of the Department of Health. No objective standard was included in the rules. The court upheld another rule that required nursing staffing based on "needs of the patients." The court considered this to be an objective standard because it believed the needs would be "reasonably well identifiable by all competent observers." Courts recognize that in some areas objective standards either are impossible to develop or, if developed, would be too arbitrary. Thus, courts have upheld enforcement of subjective standards if fairly applied. This is illustrated by another New York nursing home case in which somewhat vague standards were upheld because the actual violations clearly deviated from the rules' objective and the agency had provided written explanations of violations to the owners.[9]

One focus of hospital licensure is the integrity of hospital buildings. Numerous special building code and fire safety code regulations apply to hospitals and are frequently enforced through the licensing mechanism. These codes can provide for inspections of the hospital by building inspectors and fire marshals who may either have authority to initiate action through their own agencies or refer the matter to the licensing agency to initiate action. Generally, local government authorities must issue a permit, often called a certificate of occupancy (CO), before a new building can be used. Usually the local authorities require a hospital building also to pass an inspection by the hospital licensing agency before granting a CO.[10]

Often administrative agencies have authority to permit exceptions to their rules by granting a waiver or variance. Undue hardship may result from an unbending application of the rules, and the public's best interest may not be served by inflexibility. For example, one state required all hospital rooms to have showers for patients. When the rules were written, apparently no one thought of intensive care units where patients could not use showers, so it was necessary for hospitals to obtain waivers until the rule could be changed. Waivers are sometimes needed because some rules, especially building and fire codes, are so complex that individual rules contradict each other when applied to unusual situations. It may be necessary to obtain an official determination of which rule to follow and a  waiver of conflicting rules. Waivers may also be necessary to implement innovative practices. Waivers are generally granted only when (1) a substantial need exists for relief from the rule, (2) the public purpose will be better served by the exception, and (3) the exception will not create a hazard to the health and well-being of patients or others that is excessive in light of the public purpose being served.

Hospital licenses usually specify the number of beds the institution is permitted to operate. The license may stipulate that certain numbers of beds are approved for a specified use. In 1992, a Washington court ruled that a lessee/operator of a nursing home facility did not breach its lease or other agreements by entering into an agreement with the state agency to reduce its number of licensed beds.[11] States usually look to the licensed operator for issues related to licenses. Thus, owners and lenders need to clearly specify in their contracts with operators any limits on their authority to modify the license.

Inspections

Generally, licensing agencies have a right to make unannounced inspections of complex licensed entities, like hospitals. Applying for the license is viewed as consent to reasonable inspections within the scope of the agency's authority. However, some inspections, even with search warrants, can be conducted in such a manner as to violate the rights of those searched. Pursuant to a search warrant, an agency searched a birthing clinic at 2 A.M., rousting and photographing newborns and parents. The basis for the search was suspected practice of medicine without a license. A federal appellate court ruled that those involved in the search could be sued for violating the civil rights of the newborns and parents.[12]

Violations and Sanctions

Two fundamental elements of due process are notice and an opportunity to be heard. Unless hospital deficiencies immediately threaten life or health, the state can close a hospital or impose other penalties for licensing law violations only after giving the hospital adequate notice of violations and an opportunity to be heard. For example, a New York court ordered the hospital licensing agency to provide a hearing before deciding not to renew a hospital's license even though the hospital lacked many basic services.[13]

Some state statutes and regulations require licensing agencies to give a hospital an opportunity to correct deficiencies before imposing sanctions. Although this opportunity is not constitutionally required, it must be provided when guaranteed by state law, or any sanctions will be invalid unless immediate action is justified by deficiencies that threaten life or health.

Some hospital licensing statutes recognize that it may not be in the public interest to revoke a hospital's license for minor violations. These statutes provide a range of lesser penalties, such as money penalties, and reserve license suspension or revocation for "substantial" violations. States' definitions of substantial violation vary. In every state, sufficiently serious violations lead to license revocation.[14] When a licensing agency makes an adverse decision, the hospital can generally seek judicial review. In most states, courts will review only the administrative hearing record and will not accept additional evidence. Courts will overrule the agency only if the decision was beyond the agency's authority, the agency did not follow proper procedures, or the evidence was insufficient to justify the decision.

In addition to fines and license suspension or revocation, some hospital licensing statutes provide criminal penalties for violations. For example, the operation of a hospital without a license may lead to criminal prosecution. The law protects persons who report violations to appropriate government agencies. For example, after visiting a nursing home in which they were planning to place a relative, family members reported to federal and state officials what they believed to be violations. The home lost its Medicare and Medicaid eligibility and was not allowed to admit new patients during a state investigation. The nursing home sued the family members, claiming that they had conspired and tortiously interfered with its business relationships. A federal appellate court upheld a summary judgment in the family members' favor because any interference was justified by the greater public interest in the proper operation of such facilities.[15]

Private individuals sometimes use licensing requirements in disputes with hospitals and other health care entities. A hospital avoided honoring a contract with a nurse staffing agency because the agency did not have the license that was required by state law.[16] Employee groups and others sometimes use regulatory violations to try to apply pressure.[17] Violations of regulations can sometimes be used to help establish liability in malpractice suits.

Generally, agencies have discretion whether to invoke the penalties authorized by law. Private individuals cannot compel licensing agencies to take action.[18] However, they cannot exercise this discretion on discriminatory grounds, such as religion. A federal appellate court permitted the orthodox Jewish operators of a nursing home to sue state officials for allegedly citing their facility because of discrimination against their religion.[19]

CERTIFICATE-OF-NEED LAWS

Some states require hospitals and other health care providers to obtain a certificate of need (CON) from a state agency before expenditures can be made on certain new buildings, equipment, or services.

In the 1970s, all states had CON laws. The National Health Planning and Resources Development Act of 1974[20] required states to have a CON law to qualify for certain federal health funds. The state CON programs were tied into a national health planning system. When the federal requirement was repealed,[21] many states repealed their CON laws.

In states that still have CON laws, hospitals that plan capital expenditures or program changes must comply with applicable state CON requirements. These requirements define (1) the expenditures that are subject to review, (2) the criteria for evaluating need, and (3) the review procedures. Hospitals, other than the applicant, will often participate in the review process to challenge the need for additional competitors.

Review is generally required for all capital expenditures that (1) exceed a specified threshold, (2) are for starting a new institution, (3) change bed capacity more than a specified amount, or (4) are for starting new services that will involve ongoing annual operational costs that exceed a defined threshold. Some states also require a CON to close certain services.[22]

The review criteria now vary among the states, but they generally focus on the health care provider's relationship to the existing health care system and to applicable health plans. Some criteria are numerical, such as bed need formulas based on population, while others are more subjective.

Some states favor institutions that treat Medicaid and indigent patients, but at least one state favored a private nursing home over a facility that projected 65 percent Medicaid utilization, because the state had insufficient Medicaid funds.[23]

Procedures also vary, but they generally involve an application, public notice, a hearing with the right to present evidence, a timely decision, and an opportunity to appeal. Most states require technical compliance with the application requirements before an application may be processed.[24] In some states, if the agency does not act on the application within a specified time, the CON is automatically approved.[25]

CONs generally specify the timetable for completing the approved project and the maximum amount of authorized capital expenditures. If a good-faith effort is not made to meet the timetable, the CON can be withdrawn. If the actual expenditures are expected to exceed the maximum, the project can be subject to further review. The withdrawal of a CON after a project is commenced could have a serious adverse effect on a hospital, so a realistic timetable and budget are essential elements of a prudent CON application.

Financial institutions, bond underwriters, and other lenders require providers seeking funds for construction, expansion, or modernization to obtain all necessary approvals from the state planning agency. Thus, in states with CON laws, lenders will expect a timely CON application, plus appropriate actions to preclude withdrawal of the CON. Planning agency approval does not guarantee financing. Lenders may require a feasibility study in addition to the planning process. In some instances, projects that have received planning approval have not been constructed because of unfavorable findings in feasibility reports.

Some states have enacted limits on the total capital expenditures in the state for health care. Other states have imposed moratoria on approvals of all capital expenditures of certain types, such as expenditures for new hospital beds.[26] These moratoria and limits have been successfully challenged only when they were not authorized by state statute.[27]

Hospitals that are granted CONs generally can be ordered to comply with them. After an Alabama hospital obtained a CON to operate a long-term facility, but operated it with an average length of stay of 6.6 days, a court ordered that the hospital be limited to an average length of stay of 30 days or more.[28] Hospitals that make promises in the course of obtaining a CON are generally required to honor their commitments. To settle a CON challenge, a Florida hospital agreed to provide a certain amount of indigent care or to pay a local governmental hospital any shortfall. When the care was not provided, the hospital was ordered to make the payment.[29]

Failure to have a CON for a service has been ruled not to be a defense to a collection action for that service. A federal appellate court ruled in favor of the hospital in its suit to collect for a transplant procedure, even though the hospital did not have a CON for the service.[30]

ZONING LAWS

Zoning is another potential barrier to opening a new hospital or making substantial changes in an existing hospital's services. Zoning ordinances are laws adopted by local governments that specify where certain types of land use are permitted. Local ordinances usually are not permitted to exclude hospitals. However, when an ordinance permits hospitals in one area, the ordinance would be difficult to attack if a hospital wanted to locate in a forbidden area. Zoning ordinances also limit the height, size, and design of buildings. These limitations can restrict expansion or require time-consuming efforts to obtain waivers, variances, or amendments to zoning ordinances.

Zoning rulings can also create problems after projects are commenced. In 1988, a Florida hospital obtained a city building permit to build a staff tower and diagnostic clinic on land adjacent to the existing hospital. The tower was designed and planned to provide offices for the medical staff. After construction was commenced, the city attorney issued an opinion that the term "staff offices" in the zoning ordinance permitted offices only for physicians employed full time by the hospital. Because most of the medical staff were not full-time employees, this ruling made it impossible to obtain permanent construction funding or to lease the office space. In 1989, a federal court issued a preliminary injunction preventing enforcement of the interpretation because it was likely the hospital could show due process violations.[31] The hospital and city settled several weeks later, with the city dropping its interpretation, the hospital agreeing to pay property taxes on the building, and the physicians with offices in the building being subject to an annual city occupational license fee.[32]

When zoning laws are changed, usually existing uses are permitted to continue as nonconforming uses either indefinitely or for a specified period of time. Generally there are limits on the improvements that can be made to nonconforming uses. In 1980, a Pennsylvania court found that a hospital had sufficiently used its helipad to establish it as a nonconforming use, so the hospital did not have to obtain the special exception required for new helipads. The court also ruled that the adding of paving and lighting to the pad did not exceed permitted improvements.[33]

LICENSURE AND PERMITS FOR SERVICES

Hospitals that have institutional licenses may also be required to obtain licenses or permits for individual departments or services. Many state and local governments require separate licenses or permits for hospital pharmacies, clinical laboratories, radiological equipment, renal dialysis facilities, substance abuse centers, food services, vending machines, elevators, hospital vehicles, waste disposal, and other services. Some states exempt hospitals from having to obtain licenses or permits for some of these services. If the hospital offers the service to other hospitals or to persons other than hospital patients and staff, the exemption may be lost in some states, so applicable laws should be carefully examined before offering services to others.

The federal Clinical Laboratory Improvement Amendments of 1988 (CLIA) strictly regulate clinical laboratories in hospitals, physician's offices, and other locations.[34]

Hospitals and other providers must obtain a federal certificate before providing mammography services.[35]

Other Regulations

Many types of laws and regulations do not require licenses and permits. They mandate certain conduct and specify the sanctions for failure to comply. Many regulations are associated with the governmental financing and taxation laws discussed in Chapter 4 and the labor laws discussed in Chapter 9.

Local governmental regulations can affect hospitals.[36] For example, local ordinances banning smoking in public places may apply to hospitals. In 1986, an Illinois appellate court ruled that a hospital could be liable for brain damage to an infant, which it found to be due to the violation of a city ordinance requiring a specially trained nurse to supervise each nursery.[37]

REGULATION OF DRUGS AND MEDICAL DEVICES

The use of drugs and medical devices is heavily regulated. State laws regulate pharmacies. Federal laws regulate the production, distribution, and use of drugs and medical devices, especially drugs and medical devices involved in interstate commerce. State laws usually regulate intrastate commerce involving drugs that is not regulated by federal laws.[38] Joint Commission standards and the Medicare conditions of participation also address hospital pharmacies.[39]

Medical care requires the availability of drugs, so hospitals must provide pharmaceutical services. The Medicare conditions of participation and hospital licensing laws require that pharmaceutical services be under the direction of a qualified pharmacist.[40]

State Regulation

Some states require hospitals to obtain a separate license for the hospital pharmacy. Other states regulate hospital pharmacies through the hospital licensing system, exempting hospital pharmacies from the pharmacy licensing system.[41] Some exemptions apply only to dispensing inpatient drugs and take-home drugs in conjunction with a hospital visit, but not to other refills, so that pharmacy licensure is required for nonexempt dispensing. Some states that license hospital pharmacies require a separate community pharmacy license before the pharmacy may fill prescriptions for staff or others for use outside the hospital. Pharmacies in nonprofit hospitals that fill such prescriptions also need to comply with the limitations on the use of drugs that are acquired at special prices for the hospitals' own use. These limitations are discussed in Chapter 5.

Regulations usually include staffing requirements. The scope of permitted uses of unlicensed technical staff varies.

Hospital Formularies

Hospitals generally promote rational and cost-effective drug use through a hospital formulary system that selects the drugs to be available for use. When a medical staff committee determines that two or more drugs are equivalent, only one is primarily stocked. It is selected by negotiation with or bidding from competing suppliers. When a physician prescribes a drug for which an equivalent is stocked, the equivalent drug is dispensed unless the physician specifies on the prescription form or order that no substitutions are permitted. Hospital or medical staff rules determine when such a specification will result in obtaining the specified drug and when it will result in an educational effort or other response. Formulary systems are required by Medicare conditions of participation.[42] The Joint Commission requires a procedure for selecting medications available in the hospital.[43]

Formulary systems have been legally challenged on the basis of state antisubstitution or generic substitution laws, federal or state drug laws, and trademark laws. These challenges have not been successful when there is an agreement between the prescriber and dispenser that an equivalent drug may be dispensed. The equivalent drug is what is actually being prescribed by the symbols on the prescription. Usually the agreement is in the medical staff bylaws or rules, which each medical staff member accepts to obtain and retain medical staff membership.

Price Advertising

Many states used to have laws limiting prescription price advertising. In 1976, the Supreme Court declared unconstitutional all laws that prohibit or unnecessarily restrict advertising of prescription price information. The Court left room for states to control some aspects of advertising, including restrictions on time, place, manner, and false or deceptive practices.[44] Some states now require the posting of prices in pharmacies.

Controlled Substances Act

The Comprehensive Drug Abuse Prevention and Control Act of 1970,[45] commonly known as the Controlled Substances Act (the Act), regulates hospital distribution systems and also deals with rehabilitation programs, research in and treatment of drug abuse, and importation and exportation of controlled substances. The Act should be reviewed when hospitals create or revise procedures for handling and administering controlled substances.

Hospitals are defined as "institutional practitioners"[46] and must register under the Act.[47] Each registrant must take a physical inventory every two years.[48] A separate inventory is required for each registered location and for each independent activity registered. Each registrant must also maintain records of all controlled substances received and disposed of.[49]

Controlled substances are classified into lists, called schedules, by the degree to which they are controlled.[50] The Drug Enforcement Administration (DEA) of the Department of Justice has discretion in determining in which schedule to classify a substance.[51] Schedule I has the tightest controls. Controlled substances in Schedules I through IV may be dispensed only upon the lawful order of a practitioner. For outpatients, the order must be a prescription that complies with legal requirements.[52] For inpatients, a chart order satisfies the requirement.[53] The practitioner who signs the order must be registered with the DEA or exempt from registration.[54] State law determines which professionals may be practitioners.[55]

All institutions and individual registrants must provide controls and procedures to guard against theft and diversion of controlled substances. Only authorized personnel should have access to the central storage area and to other areas where drugs are kept in the hospital. Controlled substances stored at nursing units should be securely locked up.

Substantial federal criminal penalties, including fines and imprisonment, are imposed for violating the Act. In addition, violators can lose the authority to possess, prescribe, and dispense controlled substances. Most states have controlled substances acts that parallel the federal law, so state sanctions are also possible.[56]

Food and Drug Administration

The Food and Drug Administration (FDA) enforces a complex system of federal controls over the testing, manufacturing, labeling, and distributing of drugs, cosmetics, and devices.[57] These controls appear in the Federal Food, Drug, and Cosmetic Act, which includes the Medical Device Amendments of 1976, and in FDA regulations.[58]

The definitions of drug and device are broad. For example, human blood is considered a drug. Virtually all equipment and supplies used in patient care are regulated as devices. In addition to such obvious devices as hip prostheses, pacemakers, and artificial hearts, the term includes common equipment and supplies such as catheters, hospital beds, specimen containers,[59] support stockings, scissors, adhesive tape, elastic bandages, tongue depressors, and sutures. In 1992, a federal appellate court upheld an FDA rule defining replacement heart valve allographs as medical devices.[60] A heart valve allograph is a human heart valve that has been processed and preserved so that it can be stored until needed for implantation.

The FDA has broad discretion to decide whether to use its powers to investigate or penalize specific activities. When the FDA declined to investigate drugs used to execute condemned criminals, the Supreme Court was asked to order an FDA investigation. The Court ruled that the FDA and other federal agencies have prosecutorial discretion to decide whether to exercise their discretionary powers in individual cases, so courts cannot review such decisions in most situations.[61]

The FDA has been attacked for the time it takes to approve new drugs and devices and for the cost of compliance with its requirements, among other factors.[62] It has been defended for its contribution to protecting public safety. In 1995, Congress began considering reforms. The FDA then announced some reforms to speed review, including exempting many low-risk devices from review.[63] The balance among cost, safety, access, and other factors will undoubtedly periodically shift.

Investigational Drugs and Devices

Before new drugs and devices may enter general use, an elaborate procedure must be followed to establish their safety and effectiveness. The investigational new drug (IND) and investigational device exemption (IDE) requirements must be met to use investigational drugs and devices lawfully. With few exceptions, these drugs and devices can be used only in research projects approved by an institutional review board, conducted by a qualified investigator, and sponsored by an appropriate company or institution.[64]

Investigators need to maintain complete and accurate records. The FDA can use criminal sanctions to enforce its record-keeping requirements. A Minnesota investigator was convicted of mail fraud and making false statements to the government for submitting false information concerning a study.[65]

New drugs generally have three testing phases.[66] Phase I focuses on determining the pharmacological action of the drug, the side effects, and the maximum tolerated dose. Phase I studies may involve normal volunteers. Phase II consists of small controlled clinical studies on patients to evaluate effectiveness for particular indications and side effects. Phase III consists of expanded controlled and uncontrolled studies to gather additional information on effectiveness and safety, evaluate the risk-benefit relationship, and provide an adequate basis for labeling. Some drugs that appeared promising in earlier phases have failed in Phase III.[67] In some circumstances there are Phase IV postmarketing studies.[68]

The FDA can approve a treatment IND that permits use outside of clinical trials for a drug for a serious or immediately life-threatening disease when no satisfactory alternative therapy is available.[69] There is also a procedure for approval of emergency shipments prior to IND approval.[70]

Subjects in clinical studies generally do not have a legal right to continued access to investigational drugs after they cease to be subjects.[71] However, consent documents can create a contract to continue to supply the drug.[72]

One controversial aspect of use of investigational drugs and devices is that some third party payers refuse to pay for their use. This has led to malpractice suits as discussed in Chapter 10.

In 1994, the Office of Inspector General of the Department of Health and Human Services (HHS) issued a subpoena seeking the records of all uses of investigational devices at many hospitals.[73] The scope of the subpoena was eventually focused on certain cardiac devices. There was a concern that HHS was taking the position that when an investigational device was used during a hospitalization the entire hospitalization was not eligible for Medicare or Medicaid payment, even making the submission of a bill for that hospital stay a false claim. This led some hospitals to either stop enrolling Medicare and Medicaid patients in clinical device trials or halting all uses of investigational devices until the implications of the use of the devices were clarified.[74]

Approved Drugs or Devices

When the FDA is convinced that a new drug or device is safe and effective for certain uses, it approves the drug for general sale. The approval may permit either over-the-counter sales or sales by order of a practitioner. Approval of devices may include additional restrictions on the use of the device.

The approval specifies which uses of the drug or device may be included in labeling. In the past, only uses that had been fully proven in controlled studies could be on labels. Special studies on children were required before any uses for children could be on the label, so there was limited label information about uses for children. In 1995, the FDA began permitting more label information about uses for children.[75] In 1995, a lawsuit was pending in federal court, generally challenging the ban on marketing of off-label uses of drugs and devices and claiming that the ban is a violation of First Amendment free speech rights.[76]

Frequently, medical practice changes more rapidly than do FDA approvals, so drug or device use is often different from the approved uses listed on labels.[77] Drugs are often given for other conditions or in different dosages. Such use is often referred to as "off label" use. It is not a violation of federal law for physicians to order such unapproved uses or for pharmacists to dispense drugs pursuant to such orders. However, unapproved uses that result in injuries to patients may result in liability. Some courts consider FDA-approved labeling to be sufficient evidence of proper use, so that no further expert testimony is required.[78] However, when defendants introduce evidence that FDA-approved uses lag behind current medical practice, deviations from FDA-approved uses alone do not conclusively prove negligence. Juries are permitted to consider the FDA position along with other testimony concerning accepted practice in deciding whether the use was negligent.[79] The most prudent practice is for the physician to explain the unapproved use and the reasons for the use to the patient and to obtain the patient's informed consent.

Prescriptions

Prescriptions must be properly documented. Written prescriptions or orders in the medical record satisfy the documentation requirement. The Act requires oral prescriptions to dispense drugs to be "reduced promptly to writing and filed by the pharmacist. . . ."[80] This is generally interpreted not to preclude registered nurses and other appropriate personnel to transcribe oral orders to administer drugs in institutional settings. Hospitals should review these requirements and other state requirements, such as hospital licensing regulations, to assure that telephone orders are accepted by proper personnel.

Device Tracking

Manufacturers have a duty to have a method for tracking certain devices, including permanently implantable devices, life-supporting devices for use outside of a hospital, and other devices designated by rule.[81] Hospitals and other distributors are required to provide the necessary information to the manufacturer, unless an exemption is obtained.[82]

Manufacturing

Every person who owns or operates any establishment engaged in interstate or intrastate "manufacture, preparation, propagation, compounding or processing" of drugs must register each such establishment.[83] The terms *manufacture, preparation, propagation, compounding*, and *processing* include prepackaging or otherwise changing the container, wrapper, or labeling of drugs for distribution to others who will make the final sale or distribution to the ultimate consumer. The Act also requires manufacturers to maintain certain records, file specified reports, be periodically inspected, and satisfy other requirements. Manufacturers must file a list of all drugs they manufacture. The FDA exempts most hospitals from these requirements if the hospitals are "in conformance with any applicable local laws."[84] However, if a hospital pharmacy supplies compounded or repackaged drugs to other institutions or pharmacies under circumstances other than emergencies, it may be considered a manufacturer.

The Prescription Drug Marketing Act of 1988[85] places additional restrictions on transfers of drugs to persons other than patients. Drugs can be resold or even returned to manufacturers and distributors only if the proper procedures are followed.[86]

Hospital blood banks must register and comply with regulations concerning good manufacturing practices for blood and blood components.[87]

Poison Prevention Packaging Act

The Poison Prevention Packaging Act[88] requires most drugs to be dispensed in containers designed to be difficult for children to open. Exceptions are permitted when authorized by the prescribing physician.

Tissues for Transplantation

The FDA also regulates the use of many human tissues intended for transplantation, requiring certain inquiries and tests, including HIV and hepatitis tests.[89]

NOTES

1. Joint Commission on Accreditation of Healthcare Organizations, COMPREHENSIVE ACCREDITATION MANUAL FOR HOSPITALS (1995) [hereinafter 1995 Joint Commission CAMH].
2. 42 U.S.C.A. § 1395x(e) [hospitals]; 42 C.F.R. pt. 482 [hospitals]; 42 C.F.R. §§ 483.400–483.480 [ICF/MR]; 42 C.F.R. pt. 483 [HHA]; 42 C.F.R. §§ 485.50–485.74 [CORF]; 42 C.F.R. §§

485.301–485.308 [organ procurement]; 42 C.F.R. §§ 485.601–485.645 [rural primary care hospitals]; 42 C.F.R. §§ 485.701–485.729 [physical therapy and speech pathology]. Medicare also has requirements for long-term care facilities. 42 C.F.R. §§ 483.1–483.75.

3. 42 U.S.C.A. §§ 1395aa(c), 1395bb; *see also* Holthaus, *HCFA's surprise surveys can be costly*, 63 HOSPS., July 20, 1989, at 50; Cospito v. Heckler, 742 F.2d 72 (3d Cir. 1984), *cert. denied*, 471 U.S. 1131 (1985) [not constitutional violation for patients at psychiatric hospital to lose Medicare and Medicaid benefits when hospital lost JCAH accreditation].

4. *E.g.*, Burda, *Abortion a business hurdle for nation's Catholic hospitals*, 19 MOD. HEALTHCARE, Aug. 25, 1989, at 40.

5. Department of Health & Rehabilitative Servs. v. Delray Hosp. Corp., 373 So.2d 75 (Fla. 1st DCA 1979).

6. Hospital Ass'n of Pa. v. MacLeod, 487 Pa. 516, 410 A.2d 731 (1980).

7. *E.g.*, Hospital Ass'n of N.Y.S. v. Axelrod, 164 A.D.2d 518, 565 N.Y.S.2d 243 (3d Dep't 1990); Village of Herkimer v. Axelrod, 88 A.D.2d 704, 451 N.Y.S.2d 303 (3d Dep't 1982), *aff'd*, 58 N.Y.2d 1069, 462 N.Y.S.2d 633, 449 N.E.2d 413 (1983).

8. Koelbl v. Whalen, 63 A.D.2d 408, 406 N.Y.S.2d 621 (3d Dep't 1978).

9. Eden Park Health Servs., Inc. v. Whalen, 73 A.D.2d 993, 424 N.Y.S.2d 33 (3d Dep't 1980).

10. *E.g.*, Miami Heart Inst. v. Heery Architects & Eng's, Inc., 765 F. Supp. 1083 (S.D. Fla. 1991), *aff'd without opinion*, 44 F.3d 1007 (11th Cir. 1994). [Alleged breach of contract from failure to draw plans and specifications for hospital in accordance with relevant codes. Hospital failed inspections by state hospital licensing agency and City of Miami Beach delaying certificate of occupancy for nearly a year.]

11. Watkins v. Restorative Care Ctr., Inc., 66 Wash. App. 178, 831 P.2d 1085, *rev. denied*, 120 Wash. 2d 1007, 841 P.2d 47 (1992).

12. Hummel-Jones v. Strope, 25 F.3d 647 (8th Cir. 1994).

13. Woodiwiss v. Jacobs, 27 Misc. 2d 602, 211 N.Y.S.2d 217 (Sup. Ct. 1961). For a similar result concerning a nursing home, *see* Bethune Plaza, Inc. v. Lumpkin, 863 F.2d 525 (7th Cir. 1988) [issuing conditional license without prior hearing violates due process when no emergency].

14. Harrison Clinic Hosp. v. Texas State Bd. of Health, 400 S.W.2d 840 (Tex. Civ. App.), *aff'd*, 410 S.W.2d 181 (Tex. 1966) [multiple violations of fire, safety rules, multiple citations for poor sanitation justified license revocation].

15. Brownsville Golden Age Nursing Home, Inc. v. Wells, 839 F.2d 155 (3d Cir. 1988).

16. U.S. Nursing Corp. v. Saint Joseph Med. Ctr., 39 F.3d 790 (7th Cir. 1994).

17. *E.g.*, *Unions search for regulatory violations to pressure firms and win new members*, WALL ST. J., Feb. 28, 1992, at B1.

18. *E.g.*, Mullen v. Axelrod, 74 N.Y.2d 580, 549 N.Y.S.2d 953, 549 N.E.2d 144 (1989).

19. Sherwin Manor Nursing Ctr, Inc. v. McAuliffe, 37 F.3d 1216 (7th Cir. 1994), *reh'g denied (en banc)*, 1995 U.S. App. LEXIS 7501 (7th Cir. Mar. 31, 1995).

20. Pub. L. No. 93-641, 88 Stat. 2225, § 1523(a)(1)(4) (1975) (codified at 42 U.S.C.A. § 300m-2(a)(1)(4)). For a short history of the law of health planning, *see* R. Miller, PROBLEMS IN HOSPITAL LAW, 95–108 (5th ed.).

21. Pub. L. No. 99-660, 100 Stat. 3799 (1986).

22. FLA. STAT. § 395.0146 [CON required to close emergency room].

23. National Health Corp. v. South Carolina Dep't of Health & Environ. Control, 298 S.C. 373, 380 S.E.2d 841 (Ct. App. 1989).

24. *E.g.*, In re Nashua Brookside Hosp., 636 A.2d 57 (N.H. 1993) [error of law to review application to convert substance abuse beds to psychiatric beds without required letters from state mental health agency].

25. *E.g.*, In re VHA Diagnostic Servs., Inc., 65 Ohio St.3d 210, 602 N.E.2d 647 (1992).

26. *E.g.*, Ex parte Shelby Med. Ctr., Inc., 564 So.2d 63 (Ala. 1990).

27. *E.g.*, Balsam v. Department of Health & Rehabilitative Servs., 452 So. 2d 976 (Fla. 1st DCA 1984); Arkansas Dept. of Human Servs. v. Greene Acres Nursing Homes, Inc., 296 Ark. 475, 757 S.W.2d 563 (1988).

28. Hospital Corp. of Am. v. Springhill Hosps., Inc., 472 So.2d 1059 (Ala. Civ. App. 1985).

29. South Broward Hosp. Dist. v. Nu-Med Penbroke, 603 So.2d 11 (Fla. 1st DCA 1992).

30. Rush-Presbyterian-St. Luke's Med. Ctr. v. Hellenic Republic, 980 F.2d 449 (7th Cir. 1992), *reh'g denied* (*en banc*), 1993 U.S. App. LEXIS 2544 (7th Cir. Feb. 16, 1993).

31. Mount Sinai Med. Ctr. v. City of Miami Beach, 706 F. Supp. 1525 (S.D. Fla. 1989).

32. *Miami Beach settles with Mount Sinai*, 2 FLA. MED. BUS. (S. Fla. ed.), Feb. 28, 1989, at 16.

33. Appeal of Suburban Gen. Hosp., 48 Pa. Commw. 273, 410 A.2d 85 (1980).

34. Pub. L. No. 100-578, 102 Stat. 2903 (1988) (codified at 42 U.S.C.A. § 263a); 42 C.F.R. pt. 493.

35. 42 U.S.C.A. § 263b; 21 C.F.R. pt. 900.

36. *E.g.*, Northern Trust Co. v. Louis A. Weiss Mem. Hosp., 143 Ill. App. 3d 479, 493 N.E.2d 6 (1st Dist. 1986) [county ordinance regulating qualifications of nurses in special units].

37. *Id.*

38. *E.g.*, *Florida allows 2 firms to market interferon under law on cancer*, WALL ST. J., Nov. 4, 1983, at 46.

39. 1995 Joint Commission CAMH, *supra* note 1 at 139–50; 42 C.F.R. § 482.25.

40. 42 C.F.R. § 482.25.

41. *E.g.*, Missouri Hosp. Ass'n v. Missouri Dep't of Consumer Affairs, 731 S.W.2d 262 (Mo. Ct. App. 1987).

42. 42 C.F.R. § 482.25(b)(9).

43. 1995 Joint Commission CAMH, *supra* note 1 at 139.

44. Virginia State Bd. of Pharmacy v. Virginia Citizens Consumer Council, 425 U.S. 748 (1976).

45. Pub. L. No. 90-513, 84 Stat. 1236 (codified as amended in scattered sections of 18, 21, 26, 31, 42, 46, 49 U.S.C.).

46. 21 C.F.R. § 1306.02(c).

47. 21 U.S.C.A. § 822.

48. 21 U.S.C.A. § 827.

49. *Id.*

50. 21 U.S.C.A. § 812.

51. *E.g.*, Alliance for Cannabis Therapeutics v. D.E.A., 304 U.S. App. D.C. 400, 15 F.3d 1131 (1994) [upholding DEA order refusing to change classification of marijuana to Schedule II].

52. 21 C.F.R. pt. 1306.

53. 21 C.F.R. §§ 1306.02(f), 1306.11(c), 1306.21(c), 1306.31(c).

54. 21 C.F.R. § 1301.24 [exempting residents, some agents].

55. 21 C.F.R. § 1306.2(b).

56. *E.g.*, Schmidt v. Iowa State Bd. of Dental Examiners, 423 N.W.2d 19 (Iowa 1988) [dental license suspended for 30 days for diversions of drugs due to ineffective office controls]; Schmidt v. Iowa

State Bd. of Dental Examiners, 872 F.2d 243 (8th Cir. 1989) [suspension not a denial of due process].

57. *See, e.g.*, Kessler, Pape & Sudwall, *The federal regulation of medical devices*, 317 N. ENGL. J. MED. 357 (1987).

58. Title 21 of the United States Code; Title 21 of the Code of Federal Regulations.

59. *E.g.*, United States v. Undetermined Number of Unlabeled Cases, 21 F.3d 1026 (10th Cir. 1994) [specimen containers for testing for HIV are devices].

60. Alabama Tissue Ctr. v. Sullivan, 975 F.2d 373 (7th Cir. 1992); Annotation, *What is a "drug," a "device," and a "new drug" within the definitions of these terms in sec. 201 (g)(1), (h), and (p) of the Federal Food, Drug, and Cosmetic Act as amended*, 3 A.L.R. FED. 843; *but see* Northwest Tissue Ctr. v. Shalala, 1 F.3d 522 (7th Cir. 1993) [permitting challenge to applying of regulations].

61. Heckler v. Chaney, 470 U.S. 821 (1985).

62. *E.g.*, *F.D.A. becomes target of empowered groups*, N.Y. TIMES, Feb. 12, 1995, at 12; *FDA moves too slowly in approving medical devices, industry critics say*, 3 HEALTH L. RPTR. [BNA] 884 (1994) [hereinafter HEALTH L. RPTR. cited as H.L.R.].

63. *Administration announces more reforms to speed drug, medical device reviews*, 4 H.L.R. 562 (1995).

64. 21 C.F.R. pt. 50, 56, 312, 812, 813. For a summary of FDA actions for scientific misconduct from 1975 through 1983, see Shapiro & Charrow, *Scientific misconduct in investigational drug trials*, 312 N. ENGL. J. MED. 731 (1985).

65. United States v. Garfinkel, 29 F.3d 1253 (8th Cir. 1994).

66. 21 C.F.R. § 312.21.

67. *E.g.*, *The tale of a dream, a drug and data dredging*, WALL ST. J., Feb. 7, 1995, at B1 [drug designed to heal wounds did well in all tests until it failed to out perform a placebo in its Phase III clinical trial].

68. 21 C.F.R. § 312.85.

69. 21 C.F.R. § 312.34.

70. 21 C.F.R. § 312.36.

71. *E.g.*, Kraemer-Katz v. United States Pub. Health Serv., 872 F. Supp. 1235 (S.D. N.Y. 1994).

72. *E.g.*, Dahl v. HEM Pharmaceuticals Corp., 7 F.3d 1399 (9th Cir. 1993).

73. *IG nationwide hospital investigation seeks data on non-FDA approved devices*, 3 H.L.R. 836 (1994).

74. *E.g.*, L. Scott, *Hospitals try to devise solutions in device debate*, 25 MOD. HEALTHCARE, Feb. 20, 1995, at 34.

75. 21 C.F.R. § 201.57(9).

76. Washington Legal Found. v. Kessler, 880 F. Supp. 26 (D. D.C. 1995). [dismissal denied].

77. *E.g.*, T.A. Ratko, *Recommendations for off-label use of intravenously administered immunoglobulin preparations*, 273 J.A.M.A. 1865 (1995).

78. *E.g.*, De Paolo v. State, 99 A.D.2d 762, 472 N.Y.S.2d 10 (2d Dep't 1984).

79. *E.g.*, Young v. Cerniak, 126 Ill. App. 3d 952, 467 N.E.2d 1045 (1st Dist. 1984).

80. 21 U.S.C.A. § 353(b).

81. 21 U.S.C.A. § 360i(e); 21 C.F.R. pt. 821.

82. 21 C.F.R. § 821.30.

83. 21 U.S.C.A. § 360.

84. 21 C.F.R. § 207.10(b).

85. Pub. L. No. 100-293, 102 Stat. 95 (codified at 21 U.S.C.A. §§ 331(t), 333(b), 353(c)(3), 353(d), 353(e)).

86. Holthaus, *Network of laws governs resale of products*, 62 HOSPS., Sept. 20, 1988, at 54.

87. 21 C.F.R. pt. 607 [registration]; 21 C.F.R. pt. 606 [manufacturing practices].

88. Pub. L. No. 91-601, 84 Stat. 1670 (codified as amended in scattered sections of 7, 15, 21 U.S.C.).

89. 21 C.F.R. pt. 1270.

4

Payment, Managed Care, and Taxation

One duty of the governing body is to maintain the financial integrity of the hospital. Most actions necessary to accomplish this goal are the responsibility of the CEO, who must conceptualize and recommend actions to the governing body and then implement its decisions.

The hospital's mission, and resulting scope of activities, must be within the attainable financial means of the institution. The resulting financial requirements must be met, or the hospital cannot continue to operate. This is accomplished through realistically establishing the scope of the hospital's activities within available resources; entering appropriate contracts and other arrangements with insurers, providers, and others to assure the planned role in health care delivery with appropriate payment; developing a realistic budget to allocate resources to carry out those activities; setting appropriate charges and pricing practices; obtaining payment from third parties and individuals; initiating appropriate cost-containment and restructuring measures; arranging for appropriate capital financing; protecting the hospital's assets; and minimizing the impact of taxes, including preserving appropriate tax exemptions.

It is becoming more challenging to identify and pursue a viable path. The available options for mission, activities, and arrangements are changing as society reexamines and changes the organization of the delivery and financing of health care. Each institution needs to strike the appropriate balance between the long-term commitments and short-term flexibility to respond to these changes.

Health care reform will continue to accelerate. In 1993–94, major proposals for national system reform were debated, but not enacted. Attention was focused on the need for change. While the federal debate continued, rapid and significant change continued in the private sector and at the state level. Managed care enrollments continued to increase dramatically, and in 1994 employer costs for health care declined. There was an increase in mergers and other substantial linkages among providers and among insurers. However, many of the underlying forces driving reform remained, so providers should expect further governmental and private action to significantly change the system.

FINANCIAL REQUIREMENTS

A hospital's financial requirements include its current operating needs plus an operating margin. In addition to caring for paying patients, many hospitals also provide charity care, education, and research, and these activities also contribute to current operating needs. An operating margin is necessary to provide working capital and meet other capital requirements. For-profit hospitals also seek profit so that they can pay dividends to their investors. Working capital is needed to assure immediate stability and the ability to make timely payment of current obligations without costly short-term borrowing. Other capital requirements include renovations and major repairs, replacement of buildings and equipment, expansion, and acquisition of new technology.

One aspect of meeting financial requirements is minimizing the cost of the services provided, while maintaining acceptable quality. This restructuring of costs is rapidly moving from incremental and traditional methods to major cuts[1] and actual changes in the way health care is delivered.

MAKING ARRANGEMENTS FOR PATIENTS

In order to have financial requirements, a hospital or other health care provider must have patients. Since the development of modern medicine, much health care has always been too expensive for the average individual, so individuals have had to rely on third party payment or charity and have had to seek care where the applicable third party payer would pay. In the past, Medicare, Medicaid, and most private third party payers permitted a fairly wide range of choices of provider. Thus, providers could market their services directly to patients and, more significantly, to physicians who for the most part decided where the patients were admitted. Today a rapidly increasing proportion of persons who have third party coverage are in plans that either (1) require the use of a specific provider or a member of a panel of providers or (2) pay a significantly smaller portion of the costs when a non-panel provider is selected, creating a strong incentive to use the panel, especially for more expensive treatments, such as hospitalization. In 1994, enrollment in the most restrictive plans, health maintenance organizations (HMOs), topped 50 million, approximately 20 percent of the population.[2] Thus, it is essential that a hospital have arrangements with managed care entities and other third party payers to be on the approved panel.

Contracts Among Providers To Position Themselves To Compete

Providers are forming an increasingly wide variety of arrangements to be part of a large enough group to be able to effectively and efficiently compete in the market for arrangements with third party payers. These arrangements include such examples as the mergers and reorganizations discussed in Chapter 6, physician–hospital organizations (PHOs) and practice purchases discussed in Chapter 7, and integrated delivery systems (IDSs). New forms of these arrangements will continue to develop.

There is no one best approach. Local market conditions, local politics, institutional culture, available resources, leadership personalities, and many other factors will determine which approaches are viable at each institution.

There are legal constraints on the structuring of these arrangements that are discussed later in this chapter. In most cases it is possible to structure an arrangement that meets the business goals within these constraints, provided that from the start the entire development of the arrangement is made with these constraints in mind. In some situations, the stated reasons for an arrangement can be more damaging to the legality of the arrangement than its actual structure.

Contracts with Managed Care Entities and Other Third Party Payers

Hospitals, and the larger groups of which they are often a part, seek contracts with managed care entities and other third party payers to assure that they are at least included in the panel of permitted providers for the persons covered by that payer. When possible, hospitals seek exclusive agreements that restrict the extent that competing providers can be on the panel. Some of these restrictions can raise antitrust problems in some circumstances which are discussed in Chapter 5.

Some states have responded to the concerns about provider access to patients and patient access to providers by passing "any willing provider" laws, which require managed care entities to offer contracts to any provider willing to meet their criteria.[3] Managed care entities and purchasers of their services have expressed concern that these laws destroy the ability to offer less expensive coverage by selecting a small panel of efficient providers that can be efficiently monitored. Providers excluded from the panels and some consumer groups have expressed concern about the loss of continuity of care when patient–provider relationships are disrupted when patients are limited to a small panel. There is a split in the courts over whether any willing provider laws apply to managed care plans that are covered by the Employee Retirement Income Security Act (ERISA),[4] which is discussed in more detail later in this chapter. Even when any willing provider laws apply, providers who refuse to accept the economic terms offered by the plan are not "willing" and have no right to demand participation on their own terms.[5]

The payment arrangements with managed care plans and other third party payers can include charges (usually discounted), per diem rates (a fixed payment per day the patient is in the hospital, which may vary depending on whether intensive care or other special services are provided), and per admission rates (which may vary by diagnosis or other factors). These rates may be adjusted so that the provider shares some of the risk and benefit of overall cost savings from efficient practice.

In some cases, the payment is by capitation, under which the provider agrees to provide to a defined population all the services within the service capacity of the institution for a fixed rate per person per month. Under capitation, the provider receives the same payment whether no services or a large number of services are provided, so the incentive is to promote health, efficient practice, and empty beds rather than to fill the hospital.

State law must be reviewed in structuring capitation arrangements because some arrangements may require the hospital to qualify as an insurance company. However, under some state laws, as long as the hospital is only accepting capitation to provide its own services and not agreeing to pay other providers that are not part of the hospital, the arrangement will not require the hospital to qualify as an insurer. Under some state laws, the arrangement may have to be with a managed care entity, and not directly with an employer, to avoid having to qualify as an insurer.

There are legal restraints on arrangements with third party payers that are discussed later in this chapter.

The organization of managed care entities varies widely. Three types of organizations are HMOs, preferred provider organizations (PPOs), and IDSs.

A staff–model HMO generally provides services directly to patients through HMO employees, while an independent practice association (IPA) model HMO provides services through other providers with which the HMO contracts. In exchange, the HMO receives a fixed premium payment from or on behalf of the patient. Except for some emergency services and some services provided while the patient is out of the HMO's service area, the HMO pays for services only if they are provided by HMO employees or contractors. While some HMOs own hospitals, most HMOs make arrangements with other hospitals. These arrangements vary widely. In many HMO contracts the provider agrees not to bill the patient even if the HMO fails to pay. Many hospitals have lost large amounts when HMOs have become bankrupt.[6] Even when the HMO contract does not contain this restriction, federal law prohibits hospitals from billing Medicare patients directly when their HMOs fail to pay the provider.[7] Some states forbid direct provider billing to any HMO patients. One bankruptcy court took the unusual further step of enjoining providers from all direct billing of any patients of a bankrupt HMO.[8]

A PPO generally does not provide services directly. It contracts with other providers to provide care at an agreed rate. Patients are given a financial incentive to use these preferred providers, such as lower deductibles and copayments. The PPO pays for services provided by other providers, but usually at a lower rate, so the patient pays higher out-of-pocket expenses. PPOs are often marketed to self-insured employers on a cost-plus-processing-fee basis. Thus, the PPO often does not assume the risk of higher health care costs; the PPO is usually an administrative service, not an insurer. In some cases there is no PPO entity; the PPO is the result of the direct contracts an insurer enters with providers. Some providers have attempted to convince courts and regulators that PPOs are violations of federal antitrust laws, but these attacks have generally been unsuccessful.[9]

Although the term *IDS* is used for a wide variety of arrangements, an IDS generally refers to entities that bring a broad range of services under one organization so that they can offer comprehensive services to a population. HMOs can be IDSs, but an IDS need not be an HMO. Some IDSs are groups of health care providers.

Contracts with Employers and Other Ultimate Payers

Managed care entities and other third party payers contract directly with employers and other ultimate payers to provide care through the networks that are created by the agreements discussed in the previous section. In an effort to reduce the number of intermediate layers of administration and control, some hospitals and groups of providers seek to contract directly with employers and other ultimate payers to provide services. These contracts have to be carefully structured to comply with state insurance and other laws.

Federal law requires employers who provide certain health care benefits to offer their employees the option of coverage by an HMO.[10] However, only the federal government can enforce this law. An HMO cannot sue an employer to compel the employer to provide the option.[11]

Control of "Lives"

Insurers and managed care plans refer to the persons they cover as "lives." They use the control of the revenue stream for the coverage of those lives (1) as a source of bargaining power in negotiating with providers and (2) as a marketable asset that may permit them to sell the plan. When entering any service contracts in the health care field, it is important to identify and be comfortable with who ultimately controls the lives involved. Providers need to be careful so that they do not unintentionally turn over lives that they already control. There have been major custody battles over lives when service contracts have ended.[12]

Generally an individual, covered person cannot challenge the sale of the plan.[13]

Legal Constraints on Arrangements

There are several legal constraints on arrangements among providers and between providers and third party payers, including federal and state laws that forbid kickbacks and fee-splitting; restrictions on self-referral arrangements;

restrictions on disincentives for treatment; antitrust laws; and state insurance laws. Federal income tax concerns and qualification for Medicare payment may also affect the structure as discussed later in this chapter.

Kickbacks: Medicare and Medicaid Fraud and Abuse. Those who are involved in providing services and supplies for Medicare and Medicaid patients are subject to strict anti-fraud and abuse requirements.[14] Kickbacks, bribes, rebates, and other inducements for referrals of Medicare and Medicaid patients are all felonies. Both paying and receiving inducements are offenses. Payment need not be completed. Solicitations and offers of inducements are also offenses. In addition, the Secretary of the Department of Health and Human Services (HHS) can impose civil penalties, including exclusion from participation in the Medicare and Medicaid programs.

In 1989, a federal appellate court ruled that any payment to induce future referrals can be a violation even if the payment is for actual services.[15] The court decided that a payment for professional services is permitted only if it is wholly and not incidentally attributable to the delivery of goods and services. Also in 1989, another federal appellate court upheld the convictions of an ambulance company and a hospital training director who was paid by the ambulance service for serving as its part-time training consultant.[16] The director served on the hospital committee that wrote specifications, reviewed bids, and recommended contracting with the ambulance company. The court ruled that he did not have to be in a position to make a referral, but could violate the statute by being in a position to recommend or arrange a referral.

In 1995, in the first major setback for HHS, the Federal Court of Appeals for the Ninth Circuit ruled that the Hanlester Network had not violated the kickback prohibition through its joint venture laboratory arrangements with physicians.[17] HHS claimed that the payments to the limited partner physicians were to induce referrals. The law requires that the acts be "knowing and willful" to be illegal. The court interpreted the knowing and willful requirement to mean that it must be proved that the defendants knew the conduct was unlawful and acted with specific intent to disobey the law. Thus, unlike most areas of the law, ignorance of the law is an excuse. This interpretation of "willful" is unusual. The court relied on a 1994 U.S. Supreme Court decision that applied this interpretation to the law against structuring currency transactions.[18] Previously this interpretation had been applied by the U.S. Supreme Court only to federal income tax cases.[19] Federal courts have been reluctant to expand the scope of those rulings.[20] Thus, it is not clear whether federal courts outside the Ninth Circuit will follow *Hanlester* on this point. *Hanlester* is binding law only in the Ninth Circuit.

The court concluded that acts by the Hanlester officials, with the exception of those of one agent, had not been knowing and willful. The court found that Hanlester was responsible for the one agent who had specific intent to disobey the law, but that this was not sufficient to justify its exclusion from Medicare and Medicaid. This was a case where program exclusion was not mandatory. The court ruled that such permissive exclusion was permitted only when there was evidence of risk of future conduct harmful to the Medicare program. Conduct by a non-control agent who was no longer involved with the organization would seldom be sufficient to show such a risk.

Hanlester noted that the payments alone were not enough to violate the law. One can make profit from referrals if it is not the result of a payment "to induce" referrals.

Hospitals must still be careful, when structuring business relationships with physicians and other providers, to avoid making payments that are forbidden kickbacks.

The statute expressly states that payments to physicians are not considered kickbacks if the physician is a bona fide employee of the entity making the payment. Regulations have been issued that define other "safe harbors," conduct that will not be considered a violation.[21] There are safe harbors for space rentals, equipment rentals, investment interests, personal service and management contracts, referral services, warranties, discounts, group purchasing organizations, waiver of hospital copayments and deductibles, and sale of medical practices to other physicians. Additional safe harbors were added in 1992 that address health care plans, such as HMOs and PPOs.[22] Proposals have been published to change the safe harbors, but have not been finalized.[23] Each of these safe harbors is subject to detailed limitations. When possible it is safest to stay within them, but few real transactions in the actual marketplace fit within the safe harbors. Venturing outside the safe harbors does not mean that the law is necessarily being violated.

Several "fraud alerts" have been issued by the Office of Inspector General (OIG) of HHS that state that certain conduct is prohibited or suspicious. The fraud alerts address

1. joint venture arrangements,
2. waiver of copayments and deductibles,
3. hospital incentives to physicians,
4. prescription drug marketing,
5. clinical laboratory arrangements,
6. home health care, and other areas.[24]

Otherwise, the federal government has been hesitant to provide authoritative guidance as to what conduct is permitted. A federal court refused to decide whether it would be a violation for a physician who admitted patients to a hospital to also own part of the hospital.[25] When the federal government approves certain conduct, it is not permitted to prosecute that conduct as fraud and abuse.[26]

One area of concern is the recruitment of physicians and the purchase of their practices. This is an important step in putting together a network or IDS. The legal constraints on recruitment and practice acquisition are discussed in Chapter 7.

Another reason to be careful about fraud and abuse issues is that even when the government chooses not to challenge the arrangement, one of the parties can try to use a violation as a basis for avoiding its responsibilities in the arrangement. Illegality of a contract can be a reason to declare a contract void and unenforceable. One Texas court declared a physician recruitment contract void as an illegal inducement of referrals, so when the physician violated the contract by refusing to make required repayments, the hospital could not recover the money it had advanced.[27] A California court ruled that a hospital's free rent office arrangement with a physician was an illegal inducement for referrals, so the hospital could get out of the lease.[28] A federal court in Illinois found that a laboratory management agreement was unenforceable because it was illegal inducement for referrals. Although the court questioned whether there was sufficient proof of wilfulness for any crime to have occurred yet, the court ruled that future performance would be willful after the decision in the case was issued.[29] These attacks do not always succeed. A California jury rejected a radiologist's challenge to a marketing agreement with a hospital and required him to pay the fee under the contract.[30]

Kickbacks and Fee-Splitting: State Law. Some states have laws that forbid kickbacks for referrals[31] or splitting of fees.[32]

Self-Referral: Stark II. Congress has directly prohibited many referrals by a physician to an entity in which the physician or a family member has an ownership interest or other financial relationship.[33] Initially these restrictions applied only to referrals for laboratory services,[34] but a 1993 amendment expanded the restrictions effective January 1, 1995, to apply to a wide range of services.[35] Representative Stark of California was the sponsor of the original legislation and the 1993 amendment, so the original legislation is often called the Stark Amendment and the amended law is called Stark II. A 1994 technical amendment clarified that not all diagnostic services are covered.[36] There are several safe harbors stated in the statute. For example, most payments to employees are permitted. Unlike the Medicare fraud and abuse law, venturing outside those safe harbors violates the law and there is no requirement to prove the act is knowing or willful.

Self-Referral: Federal Income Tax Exemption. Tax-exempt hospitals cannot enter most self-referral arrangements without endangering their federal income tax exemption.[37]

Self-Referral: State Law. Some state laws also regulate such self-referrals.[38]

Treatment Disincentives. Under many payment systems, especially capitation and per admission payment, hospitals make more money when fewer services are given. Some hospitals structured financial rewards for physicians who arranged for more efficient treatment of patients. Due to concerns that this could promote insufficient treatment, the Medicare law was amended in 1986 to make it illegal to offer financial incentives to physicians not to provide services.[39] In 1990, special rules for Medicare HMOs were adopted that placed restrictions on their physician incentive plans.[40]

Antitrust. Antitrust law, which is discussed in Chapter 5, restricts many activities between competitors, so arrangements should be designed with antitrust compliance in mind.

One special antitrust concern in contracts with third party payers is the "most favored nation" clause (MFN). The MFN clause states that when the provider gives anyone else a lower price, that price becomes the price the third party payer must pay. In effect, it precludes any other entity from getting a better price. The MFN clause has been challenged by antitrust authorities and has had to be dropped from several agreements as part of settlements of the cases.[41] One state court has ruled that MFN clauses do not violate state antitrust laws.[42]

State Insurance Laws. As discussed earlier in the chapter, some payment arrangements may require the hospital to qualify as an insurer or HMO under state law. Usually it is better to structure the arrangement to avoid this outcome. In some situations, it is feasible and advantageous to either directly qualify as an insurer or HMO or to qualify by sufficiently involving an insurer in the arrangement.

SETTING CHARGES

Even though an increasing portion of hospital payments is determined by contracts with managed care entities and insurers, hospitals still must set charges for those not covered by contracts. These charges are often limited by law either for specific groups of patients, such as those covered by workers' compensation or Medicare, or for all patients, such as through rate regulation. This section focuses on some legal considerations in setting charges.

Some uninsured patients have challenged having to pay full charges. The challenges have been based on the fact that the implied contract for hospital services is to pay "reasonable" charges. Some cases focus on the fact that higher charges are designed to help cover the cost of those who cannot pay, so-called "cost-shifting." Courts have generally recognized that this is necessary and reasonable. The law cannot mandate care to those who cannot pay for that care and then block the other avenues to cover the associated costs. The other focus of the challenges is on the markup on individual items, e.g., the $10 aspirin. These cases seldom reach the appellate courts because of settlements or acceptance of lower court decisions. A class action in Florida is exploring this issue.[43]

Rate Regulation

Some states have an agency that monitors, reviews, or establishes charges or revenue limits for hospitals. The role of this agency varies greatly among the states. The programs use different data as a basis for their evaluations. Some programs establish peer groups of hospitals and compare the hospitals in each group. Courts have generally upheld peer comparisons and administrative latitude in grouping hospitals.[44] Other programs focus on historical data from the individual hospital, evaluating the current year by comparison to a base year. The data are evaluated based on (1) formulas, (2) budget analysis, (3) negotiation, and (4) a combination of these approaches. Formula review compares submitted data to a standard calculated from a formula. Budget review analyzes the appropriateness of particular expenditures in the hospital's proposed budget. Some programs involve negotiation between the hospital and the regulatory agency concerning the appropriate rates or budget. Mandatory rate regulation has led to many controversies.[45]

Rate limits can be placed on some types of providers and not on others. A federal appellate court ruled that it was not a violation of equal protection for Florida to exempt hospitals and group practices from its fee cap on diagnostic imaging services.[46]

The Massachusetts Nurses Association challenged the state rate regulation system, claiming payment restrictions illegally interfered with collective bargaining efforts with hospitals. A federal appellate court ruled in 1984 that the law did not violate the nurses' collective bargaining rights because it affected labor–management relations only indirectly.[47]

Some third party payers have challenged rate regulation systems. For example, a pension plan challenged a New York system that prevented self-insured employee benefit plans from negotiating rates lower than those set by the system. A federal appellate court upheld the law in 1984,[48] finding it not to be preempted by ERISA[49] because the impact on pension plans was only tangential. States probably have authority to freeze hospital rates. In 1985, a federal appellate court upheld a West Virginia law that froze all hospital rate schedules.[50]

Where market forces are more developed, it is likely that state rate regulation will increasingly be recognized as obsolete. As early as 1989, Washington repealed its rate-setting law.[51]

However, where market forces do not keep hospital rates within politically acceptable limits, government is likely to act. Government has broad powers to regulate rates without the regulations being considered a "taking" of private property, which requires compensation under the Fifth Amendment.[52]

Bonding Covenants

When hospitals borrow money through bonds or other mechanisms, they usually pledge certain property or revenues to guarantee repayment. One pledge is usually a promise to set rates sufficiently high to repay the loan and maintain hospital operations until the loan is repaid. These pledges must be respected to the extent permitted by law in setting rates.

LEGAL BASIS FOR OBTAINING PAYMENT

There are fundamentally four legal bases for obtaining payment for health care services: (1) statute or regulation under a governmental program, such as Medicare or Medicaid; (2) direct contract with payers; (3) assignment of or liens against patient claims against a payer; or (4) express or implied contract with the patient, family, or individual guarantors.

GOVERNMENT PROGRAMS

There are several federal government programs that provide payment for health care, including Medicare, Civilian Health and Medical Program for the Uniformed Services (CHAMPUS),[53] Federal Employee Health Benefits Program (FEHBP),[54] and the Veterans Administration. There are federal–state programs, especially Medicaid. There are also various state programs. Participation in some government programs is limited to those who have a contract with the appropriate government agency. However, because of the latitude of government to unilaterally change most of the programs, the right to payment is often determined more by the current statute and regulations than by the contract. This section focuses on Medicare and Medicaid and then discusses state programs.

Medicare

The 1965 Amendments to the Social Security Act[55] added Title XVIII to the Act. Title XVIII established a two-part program of health insurance for the aged known as Medicare. Persons are eligible to participate in Part A, the hospital insurance program, if they (1) are 65 years of age or older and are receiving retirement benefits under Title II of the Social Security Act or the Railroad Retirement Act, (2) qualify under a special program for persons with end-stage renal (kidney) disease, or (3) qualify under the special transitional program. Persons not qualifying otherwise who are 65 years of age or older may still participate in Part A by paying premiums. Anyone age 65 or older who is a United States citizen or has been a permanent resident alien for five years may elect to enroll in Part B, a program of supplementary medical insurance. Medicare applies to all qualified people without regard to financial need. It is administered federally, so it is intended to have nationally uniform benefits. Provider relations and payments are federally administered on a regional basis, so some regional variations exist.[56]

Part A is a program of hospital insurance benefits for the aged and selected others that is financed by a special tax on employers, employees, and the self-employed. The coverage includes a specified number of days of care in hospitals and extended care facilities for each benefit period plus home care after hospitalization. The Medicare Catastrophic Coverage Act of 1988[57] removed the limits on the number of hospital days and increased the limits for other coverages. There was strong opposition by the elderly to the surtax that funded the 1988 benefit expansion, so Congress repealed the Act in 1989, restoring the coverage limits and eliminating the surtax.[58]

Claims must be presented to trigger reimbursement. Until 1983, reimbursement under Part A was based on the allowable costs of the facility providing the care, but was subject to several reimbursement limits. This was changed by the Social Security Amendments of 1983,[59] so that payment to hospitals for inpatient care is based on a prospectively determined amount per discharge according to the patient's diagnosis and the facility's location. Beneficiaries have to pay certain deductible and coinsurance payments. A deductible is the amount of health care charges that the patient must incur and owe before Medicare pays for any of the remainder. Medicare will pay only a percentage of some of the remaining allowable payments for some services; the percentage not paid by Medicare is called a coinsurance payment and is owed by the patient. Some hospitals and physicians routinely waive deductibles and copayments. However, at least one state has forbidden this practice.[60] There is concern that some waivers may be viewed as violations of Medicare anti-fraud and abuse laws. Some waivers by hospitals are within the safe harbors permitted by regulation.[61]

Part B is a program of supplementary medical insurance covering a substantial part of physician and other practitioner services, medical supplies, and X-rays and laboratory tests incident to physician services, as well as other services not covered under Part A, such as ambulance services and prosthetic devices. Enrollment is voluntary. The program is funded from contributions by beneficiaries and the federal government. Beneficiaries must pay a deductible and a 20-percent coinsurance amount.

Provider payment under Part B was based on "reasonable charges," which are subject to numerous arbitrary limits.[62] Since 1992, physicians have been paid based on a resource-based relative value scale (RBRVS).[63] Some procedures, such as cataract surgery, have been paid for through a bundled single global fee for the surgical facility and surgeon.[64] Medicare payments can be made to only the provider who provides the services and certain entities permitted to bill for that provider; other reassignments of payments are prohibited.[65] Thus, some billing arrangements are not permitted. Each physician has a unique physician identification number (UPIN) that must be put on each bill.[66] Another billing problem is that physicians may bill for services, such as X-rays, provided by others, such as technicians, only when the services are provided in a way that meets the technical requirements to be "incident to" the physicians' services.[67]

One important issue for all providers is proper coding of the services provided. The diagnoses and certain other features of the patient's condition or treatment must be coded on the claim. Hospital claims are coded according to the International Classification of Diseases, Ninth Edition, Clinical Modification (ICD-9-CM). Physician claims are coded according to the Health Care Financing Administration (HCFA) Common Procedure Coding System (HCPCS), which includes the Physician's Current Procedural Terminology (CPT).[68]

The secretary of HHS has the overall responsibility for Medicare. The operation of the program has been assigned to the HCFA. Congress authorized the delegation of much of the day-to-day administration to state agencies and public and private organizations operating under agreements with the secretary of HHS. Most payment claims are processed by private agencies that have entered agreements to serve as "intermediaries" for Part A or "carriers" for Part B. They make initial determinations whether services provided to beneficiaries are payable by the program and how much payment is due. Hospitals must be cautious in acting on information provided by intermediaries and carriers. The U.S. Supreme Court ruled in 1984 that HCFA could recover Medicare overpayments from a provider despite the fact that the overpayments were due to erroneous information from the intermediary.[69] The Court stated that providers are expected to know the law and cannot rely on information provided by governmental agents. Some intermediaries have been charged with defrauding the government while acting in that capacity.[70]

Participating Providers

To be a participating provider of services and receive payments from Medicare, a hospital must sign an agreement with HHS and meet the conditions of participation.[71] The only exception is that Medicare will pay for some emergency services in nonparticipating hospitals. The participating provider agreement specifies that the hospital will not bill Medicare patients for services except for (1) deductible and coinsurance payments required by law and (2) charges for services that Medicare does not cover. Charges can be made for noncovered services only if the patient has been given adequate notice that they are not covered. A hospital is deemed to meet the conditions of participation if it is accredited by the Joint Commission or the American Osteopathic Association unless a Medicare inspection indicates noncompliance.[72]

Physicians who become participating providers are paid directly by Medicare and may charge patients only allowed copayments and deductibles. When patients are treated by nonparticipating physicians, Medicare pays the patient directly. The physician then bills the patient. The amount the nonparticipating physician may bill the patient is limited to a maximum allowable actual charge (MAAC).[73] Physicians who bill more than the MAAC can be assessed substantial civil money penalties and barred from Medicare payments for up to five years.[74] Some states have required physicians to accept the Medicare payment amount as payment in full.[75]

HHS frequently threatens to revoke participating provider status, but most hospitals are able to make changes and reach settlements that avoid revocation.[76] Rarely have hospitals had their status revoked.[77]

Prospective Payment

The Social Security Amendments of 1983[78] established a Medicare prospective payment system (PPS) based on diagnosis-related groups (DRGs) to pay hospitals for inpatient care. The system has been modified by numerous amendments. The following is a summary of the system, based on the statute and implementing regulations[79] as amended after the 1994 amendments. All Medicare acute care inpatients are divided into 492 DRGs based on their principal diagnoses, complications, comorbidities, and whether certain procedures are performed.[80] The principal diagnosis is the one chiefly responsible for the admission. The DRGs are numbered 1 through 495, omitting numbers 109, 438, and 474, which were deleted as the classification system was changed. Medicare will pay for 490 of the groups. Groups 469 and 470 involve unacceptable diagnoses and invalid data. By statute, no administrative or judicial review is permitted for either the DRG groups, assignment to a group, or the weight given to the group.[81] One criticism of the DRG system is that it does not equitably adjust for the cost of treating more severely ill patients in each group. Various severity of illness adjustments have been proposed and are under review by HCFA.[82]

With a few exceptions, the hospital receives one payment for the entire admission, based on the DRG and facility location. The payment also covers some preadmission services.[83] In early 1995, 4,600 hospitals were sent letters by HCFA, which threatened civil prosecution for billing for nonphysician outpatient services prior to admission.[84]

There is no extra payment for longer stays or more procedures unless the patient becomes an outlier. An outlier is a patient with an extraordinarily long length of stay or high total cost of care. Medicare makes an extra payment for outliers,[85] some bad debts,[86] and some costs of copying and mailing medical records for review by Professional Review Organizations.[87] Another exception is that direct educational costs and kidney acquisition costs are not included in the prospective payment; they are paid on a cost basis.[88] Initially capital costs were paid separately on a cost basis, but starting in 1991 new capital costs are paid prospectively and prior capital expenditures are handled through a transitional formula.[89]

An adjustment for indirect medical education costs increases payments to hospitals with medical residency programs.[90] Children's hospitals, long-term care hospitals, psychiatric hospitals, and rehabilitation hospitals are exempt from the PPS so they can continue to receive cost-based payment from Medicare.[91] Psychiatric and rehabilitation units of general hospitals can be exempt if they apply for an exemption.

There is an adjustment for some hospitals that serve a disproportionate share of low-income or Medicaid patients,[92] are sole community providers,[93] are referral centers,[94] are essential access community hospitals,[95] or experience other extraordinary circumstances.

PPS is prospective only in the sense that the amount paid is calculated based on circumstances at the time of admission. Payment is made only after services are provided. PPS has completely changed provider incentives. Under the previous cost-based system, additional hospital days and services meant additional payment, so there was an incentive to give patients all the services that could possibly benefit them. In some situations, unnecessary services were provided, but Medicare refused to pay for them, when discovered.

Under PPS the incentive is to minimize services and shorten stays. Hospitals lose money if services exceed the prospective payment, and they can keep savings when services cost less than the payment.

Interhospital transfers may be affected by the change to prospective payment. Those fashioning PPS wanted to make one payment to be shared by all hospitals that provided care to the patient, but the Act did not authorize shared payment. The hospital from which the patient is finally discharged receives a full prospective payment based on the patient's DRG. The hospital that cares for the patient before transfer is paid a per diem rate equal to the prospective payment for the DRG divided by the average length of stay for that DRG, but the total cannot exceed the full DRG payment. The transferring hospital can qualify for additional payment if the patient becomes an outlier due to high costs.[96]

It is likely that Medicare will be significantly changed. There may be expansion of use of the DRG approach. In 1995, HHS recommended to Congress the adoption of a PPS for hospital outpatient care, involving Ambulatory Patient Groups (APGs).[97] There are likely to be more drastic changes. The Hospital Insurance Trust Fund Board of Trustees reported in 1995 that the fund is expected to be exhausted in 2002.[98] Medicare at present offers an option to enroll in a prepaid health plan,[99] but payment is based on adjusted average per capita costs (AAPCC). It is likely that other capitation approaches will be developed and the prepaid option will be made more attractive to individuals covered by Medicare.[100]

Appeals

Depending on the amount of money in controversy, hospitals may appeal payment decisions under the old cost reimbursement systems to the Provider Reimbursement Review Board (PRRB) (larger amounts) or to their Medicare intermediary (smaller amounts). When the issues being appealed apply to several hospitals, group appeals are frequently pursued to reduce the cost to individual hospitals. The secretary of HHS has the authority to modify the decisions of the

PRRB or the intermediary. The final decision of HHS concerning a payment issue can sometimes be appealed to the federal courts. Administrative remedies must be exhausted before resort to the courts.[101]

The number of issues that can be appealed is limited.[102] In 1993, the U.S. Supreme Court decided that HHS is not required to give providers an opportunity to establish entitlement to payment in excess of limits stated in the regulations.[103]

In 1995, the U.S. Supreme Court upheld the HHS guidelines for treatment of bond defeasance losses, finding that HHS did not have to adhere to generally accepted accounting principles (GAPP) in developing its cost determination principles.[104]

Medicaid

Medicaid is a joint federal–state program designed to provide medical assistance to individuals unable to afford health care. Although the Medicaid program is authorized by federal law (Title XIX of the Social Security Act),[105] states are not required to have Medicaid programs. Each state must pass its own law to participate. All states now participate. Under Medicaid the federal government makes grants to states to enable them to furnish (1) medical assistance to families with dependent children and to aged, blind, or disabled individuals whose income and resources are insufficient to pay for necessary health services; and (2) rehabilitation and other services to help such families and individuals obtain or retain the capability for independence or self-care. The secretary of HHS is responsible for administration of federal grants-in-aid to states under Medicaid.

Medicaid is different from Medicare in that it provides medical assistance for categories of persons in financial need, while Medicare provides medical assistance primarily to people 65 years of age or older without regard to financial need. Medicaid varies widely among the states, while Medicare is uniform. Medicaid is financed by general federal and state revenues, while Medicare is financed by a special tax on employers and employees for hospital insurance and by contributions by beneficiaries and the federal government for supplementary medical services. Medicaid is basically a welfare program, while Medicare is considered a form of social insurance.

Some states tried to generate some of the state share of the cost of Medicaid through special taxes on providers. Most providers accepted this tax because they got the money back with the addition of federal matching funds. In 1991, Congress outlawed this practice.[106] The tax itself is not illegal[107]; it is the use of the funds to pay for Medicaid that is prohibited. In 1995, the federal government sought repayment of the additional federal matching monies due to continued use of such provider taxes after 1991.[108]

Beneficiaries and Scope of Benefits

Any state adopting a Medicaid plan must provide certain minimum health benefits to the categorically needy. The categorically needy includes individuals receiving financial assistance under the state's approved plan for Supplemental Security Income (Title XVI of the Social Security Act)[109] or for Aid to Families with Dependent Children (Title IV-A of the Social Security Act).[110] Several other groups are included in the categorically needy if they qualify for financial assistance under the state plans except for certain characteristics that Medicaid requires to be ignored. States have the option of including other persons within their plan as medically needy if (1) they would qualify for assistance under one of the above programs if their incomes were lower and (2) their incomes would be low enough to qualify for assistance under that program if they were permitted to subtract the health care expenses they have already incurred. This is sometimes called the "spend-down" option because the persons must in effect spend their income down to the threshold level for the other programs to be eligible for Medicaid.

Undocumented aliens are ineligible for nonemergency Medicaid.[111]

There have been challenges to the age requirements for certain Medicaid benefits. The U.S. Supreme Court ruled that Congress may limit coverage in public health institutions to persons under 21 and over 65 years of age.[112] The Arizona Supreme Court ruled that the Medicaid law does not permit states to limit liver transplants to minors.[113]

Eligible recipients must apply to the designated state agency before Medicaid will pay for the services they receive. State Medicaid plans must meet many conditions before they can be approved, but states are permitted substantial flexibility in the administration of their own programs. States may decide, within federal guidelines, who in addition to the categorically needy will be eligible for medical assistance. In determining scope of benefits, states are required to provide only five basic services to the categorically needy, but are free to provide additional optional services. Although the states are given wide latitude in the administration of their programs, they are sensitive to federal direction because 50 percent or more of the financial support for Medicaid comes from the federal government.

Courts have disagreed on whether recipients have a right to sue providers to force compliance with Medicaid regulations.[114]

Providers and Payment

Institutional providers of services generally become participants in the Medicaid program by contracting with the state to provide services to Medicaid recipients in exchange for the payment permitted by the state. Payment cannot be collected from the patient except to the extent permitted by federal law. Noninstitutional providers generally are not required to enter into any contract with the state, but participate merely by treating Medicaid recipients and then billing the state. States may directly reimburse physicians who provide covered services to the medically needy, or they may pay the individual beneficiaries, leaving them with the obligation to pay the physician. Payment for physician services can be made only if the physician agrees to accept charges determined by the state as the full charges.

States have considerable latitude to determine the services to be covered and the amount of payments. States are generally free to establish their own methods of payment for inpatient hospital services as long as the costs do not exceed the Medicare payment for the same services. The Boren Amendment requires the state to find that the rates are "reasonable and adequate to meet the costs which must be incurred by efficiently and economically operated facilities."[115] In 1990, the U.S. Supreme Court ruled that the Boren Amendment created a substantive federal right to adequate reimbursement that could be enforced by health care providers.[116] There have been many lawsuits challenging the adequacy of Medicaid payment rates.[117] Some cases have required states to reinstate prior payment approaches until proper procedures are followed,[118] while others have upheld the state payment rates.[119] States still have considerable latitude if they follow the proper procedures in adopting their payment mechanisms.

Many states have reduced services. When Tennessee reduced the covered days of inpatient care from 20 to 14, the reduction was challenged as a violation of the federal laws prohibiting discrimination against the disabled because they generally need longer stays. The U.S. Supreme Court rejected this challenge, ruling that the handicapped nondiscrimination law does not guarantee equal results from Medicaid services.[120] The Court did not rule on whether the limit was consistent with the Medicaid law. Lower courts have ruled that limits on the number of inpatient days, such as South Carolina's 12-day limit, are consistent with the Medicaid law.[121]

Other states have placed other limits on payment to providers. Several states have adopted PPSs for Medicaid similar to the Medicare payment system.[122] Minnesota went one step further in its nursing home payment system. Minnesota will pay nursing homes through its Medicaid system only when the nursing home agrees not to charge non-Medicaid patients more than Medicaid pays for comparable care. This system has been upheld by both the federal and the state courts.[123] In 1985, a Minnesota court ruled that neither the state nor Medicaid patients could stop a nursing home from phasing out participation in Medicaid.[124]

Some states still use cost-based payment systems.[125] Some states have calculated allowable costs, assuming facility occupancy is at least a certain percentage, such as 85 or 90 percent. These formulas have generally been upheld by the courts.[126]

Medicaid plans are undergoing rapid transformation. In 1994, Medicaid consumed approximately 20 percent of state budgets. Medicaid is one of the fastest growing parts of the budgets of many states. Faced with the unacceptability of tax increases and with other important budgetary needs, especially education and law enforcement, most states are seeking ways to control that Medicaid growth. Medicaid is also a major budget element at the federal level. Congress is exploring various ways to change Medicaid. Thus, further change is likely.

Many states have significantly modified their Medicaid programs, usually by adopting managed care approaches, including contracting with private HMOs. Medicaid includes a freedom-of-choice of providers requirement under which eligible persons may select any participating provider.[127] Initially the managed care approaches were voluntary.[128] However, the Medicaid law authorizes federal waivers of various requirements, including freedom of choice.[129] Several states have obtained waivers[130] or are requesting waivers. Congress has mandated that some individual waivers be granted.[131] Starting in 1995, waiver requests and decisions are being published in the *Federal Register*.[132]

Significant change at the federal level is also likely. A 1995 General Accounting Office (GAO) report examined the following three options: (1) replacing Medicaid with federal block grants to states, (2) making Medicaid a federal program relying entirely on federal financing, and (3) splitting Medicaid into two programs for acute/primary services and long-term services.[133]

Government is confronted with difficult allocation decisions. In ruling that the Medicaid law does not grant an enforceable right to compel expenditure of funds to provide a particular treatment, a federal court in Minnesota stated,

> Unfortunately, funds available for these programs are finite. Ordering the development of the requested facility, at cost far above the currently available funding limits, would rob Peter to pay Paul. Society, through its elected representatives and appointed agency administrators, has made the difficult decisions regarding the amount and allocation of these funds.[134]

Actual and proposed changes in Medicaid and other funding can also affect hospital financing in other indirect ways. For example, soon after New Jersey announced plans in early 1994 to reduce Medicaid payments to hospitals, Standard & Poor's Rating Group scheduled meetings with New Jersey hospitals to discuss the impact.[135]

Medicare and Medicaid Fraud and Abuse

In addition to the anti-kickback restrictions discussed previously in this chapter, those who are involved in providing services and supplies for Medicare and

Medicaid patients are subject to other anti-fraud and abuse requirements.[136] Misrepresentations in claims and reports are felonies, subject to a maximum penalty of $25,000 and/or five years in prison. For example, in 1987 a federal appellate court upheld a Medicaid fraud conviction of a physician for using improper billing codes on claims.[137]

Abuse is a broader term than fraud. While fraud requires deliberate deceit, the government considers it abuse to operate a hospital in a manner that is inconsistent with accepted principles of medical practice and business and that results in excessive and unreasonable expenditures by Medicare and Medicaid. In general, abuse is subject to civil sanctions, such as suspension of payments, suspension from the program, and repayment of overpayments, rather than to criminal sanctions.

In 1981, the Social Security Act was amended to permit HHS to impose civil money penalties and assessments for filing false claims. Penalties of $2,000 per item or service and assessments of twice the amount claimed may be imposed.[138] A penalty of $1,791,000 has been assessed against one provider.[139] In 1989, the U.S. Supreme Court ruled that the constitutional prohibition against double jeopardy limits the amount that can be claimed in a governmental civil penalties suit after a criminal prosecution for the same conduct.[140] This may have little practical significance because (1) the government can avoid this limit by pursuing the civil suit simultaneously with the criminal prosecution and (2) the limit does not apply to civil penalty suits by private persons. Other federal criminal and civil penalty statutes can be applied to wrongful acts related to Medicare and Medicaid.[141] In 1988, a federal appellate court upheld a finding that an ophthalmologist had violated the false claims statute by billing for procedures that were not performed or were medically unnecessary.[142] One of the grounds for the lack of medical necessity was the improper way in which the procedures were performed.

State Programs

Several states have state and local programs that pay for some health care for indigent persons who cannot qualify for Medicaid. These programs vary greatly. Under the statutes of some states, counties or other units of local government are responsible for paying for some health care on behalf of their residents who are unable to pay. Some of these statutes provide that prior notice must be given[143] or authorization must be obtained from appropriate government officials. Other statutes do not require prior approval to create an obligation, especially in emergencies.[144] Some states require that claims for payment be made in a certain way, and courts affirm nonpayment when the proper procedures are not followed.[145] In many states, local governmental units or their police departments are obligated to pay for the care of persons in their custody who are charged with crimes.[146] However, police generally do not assume financial responsibility by bringing someone who is not in custody to a hospital.[147] Some jurisdictions have sought to avoid the cost of caring for prisoners by not charging sick suspects or by releasing sick prisoners.[148]

DIRECT CONTRACTS WITH PAYERS

Increasingly, providers are entering direct contracts with managed care plans and other payers to provide care for persons covered by the plan for the payment specified in the contract. The payer duty to pay is based on the direct contractual relationship. Generally the specified payment provided by the contract must be accepted as payment in full. Sometimes part of that payment must be collected directly from the patient as a deductible or a coinsurance payment. The remainder is paid directly to the provider by the third party payer. A discussion of the wide range of contractual arrangements is beyond the scope of this book. See Chapter 10 for some of the legal issues concerning contracts.

Providers need to carefully evaluate what care they are promising to give. One serious problem has been the "silent PPO," where the payer tries to take advantage of the special prices in the contract for patients who are not intended to be covered by the contract.[149] Some contracts are worded so broadly that this practice may be authorized by the contract. In other cases, the payer is acting outside the contract.

Another potential problem is that in some cases the patient may become a third party beneficiary to the contract, so that the patient can sue for breach of contract when the obligation to provide services is not fulfilled.[150] Unless this is required or intended, it can usually be avoided by the wording of the contract.

Insolvency

With limited exceptions, direct contracts are only as good as the solvency of the payer. Hospitals have lost significant amounts when payers have become unable to pay.[151] Insolvency of payers can be a problem whether or not there is a direct contract, but it is particularly significant in the direct contracting situation because the direct contract will usually eliminate or limit the opportunity to pursue collection from the patient and may require acceptance of additional patients for a period of time after the insolvency occurs.

Many contracts specify that the provider cannot bill the patient even if the payer fails to pay. The provider is left with a claim in the bankruptcy or receivership of the payer. Generally providers are not given a priority in the distribution of assets.[152] Thus, to the extent possible, providers need to structure their arrangements to keep their exposure to loss within sustainable bounds. Attention should be paid to the steps the provider can take to protect itself, including when the contract can be terminated. Generally a hospital can bill HMO patients for care given after the date the hospital terminates its contract with the HMO.[153]

Insurance companies are not eligible for federal bankruptcy and instead must go through a receivership under state law.[154] When HMOs are treated as insurance companies under state law, they are not eligible for federal bankruptcy.[155]

Due to the adverse effect of payer failures, some states have strengthened the financial qualifications to be an HMO, insurer, or other payer. Many plans have private reinsurance that will sometimes, but not always, cover some payments.[156] Some plans are required to contribute to state guaranty funds that pay some of the losses when plans become insolvent. However, not all plans are covered.[157]

ASSIGNMENT OF PATIENT CLAIMS

Other third party payers do not contract with providers. These payers contract with individuals or their employers to reimburse for some or all of the cost of covered services to the individuals. The individuals must make their own arrangements with providers for the services. Some of these payers pay the individual directly, and the provider must collect from the individual. Providers usually seek assignment of these payments so that they can be paid directly.

Generally a hospital must have an assignment of the beneficiary's claim before the hospital can sue an ERISA plan directly.[158] However, some courts have ruled that a suit against a health plan by a provider with a direct contract with the plan is not affected by ERISA.[159]

Some payers have sought to forbid such assignments[160] or have permitted assignment only when the provider accepts the payment as payment in full. For example, one Michigan insurer required a physician requesting direct payment to sign a form stating the physician would accept the amount as payment in full. One Michigan physician crossed out this statement before signing the form, but a Michigan court ruled that the physician was still bound by the statement.[161] Physicians have challenged requirements that patients not be billed more than allowed by the insurance company, but these limits have generally been upheld.[162] However, without such a contractual agreement or a statutory limit, there is no limit on what the provider may charge, and the patient remains liable for any amount not paid by the payer.

After the provider gives notice to the payer of a valid assignment, the payer is generally obligated to pay amounts due directly to the provider.[163] After assignment, generally only the provider who has received the assignment has the right to sue for unpaid claims.[164]

RESPONSIBILITY OF PATIENT, FAMILY, AND INDIVIDUAL GUARANTORS

An adult patient is responsible for paying his or her hospital bill, unless the provider is barred by another contract or by law from billing the patient. This responsibility is based on either an express or an implied contract to pay for accepted services. The adult patient is responsible for the reasonable value of services furnished in good faith even if the patient is unconscious, mentally incompetent, or incapacitated at the time the services are provided.[165] The major exceptions occur when the competent, oriented adult has explicitly refused to accept the services and when the law entitles the patient to free care.

In most states a husband is responsible for paying for necessary care for his wife. In most states the wife has a reciprocal duty to pay for necessary care for her husband.[166] Most states make the father responsible for paying for necessary care for minor children. In many states the mother is also responsible.[167] In some states minors are not legally responsible for paying for care they receive unless they are emancipated. However, in other states minors are also responsible for paying for their necessary care. When there is doubt under state law concerning parental responsibility, the parents' express promise to pay is frequently obtained. When parents are divorced or separated, special rules concerning parental responsibility apply in some states,[168] so that an express promise is frequently required to make the noncustodial parent responsible.[169]

Absent a statute or an express promise, other relatives or friends are not responsible for paying for care. Some state statutes make adult children responsible for their parents' care when their parents are unable to pay.[170] By expressly promising to pay, a relative or friend or other guarantor may become responsible for paying for care, especially if the promise is written. The promise must be carefully written because some forms have been successfully challenged.[171] In most states merely arranging for care or bringing a person to the hospital does not make a relative, friend, or other person responsible for payment.

OTHER BASES FOR OBTAINING PAYMENT

In response to the perceived problem of "dumping" of patients, the Emergency Medical Treatment and Active Labor Act (EMTALA) makes the transferring hospital responsible for the financial loss to the receiving hospital as a result of an impermissible transfer.[172] EMTALA is discussed in Chapter 12.

One Florida hospital sued a nursing home that would not accept the return of a patient, in an effort to collect the cost for care of the patient during the period from when hospitalization was no longer necessary until arrangements could be made for discharge to another nursing home. The court denied the claim because neither statutes nor the transfer agreement with the nursing home required such payment.[173]

DENIAL OF PAYMENT

Payers deny payment for many reasons. Familiarity with the legal principles that are applied to these denials is helpful to providers seeking payment and to payers designing ways to control the scope of their payment liability.

ERISA

The legal principles concerning denial of payment vary significantly depending on whether the payment plan is covered by the federal Employee Retirement and Income Security Act (ERISA). ERISA applies to self-funded employer benefit plans. ERISA is designed to permit employers to offer uniform benefits nationwide. It preempts nearly all state regulation of such plans, so that ERISA-qualified plans are protected from most state law challenges to denial of payment. The preemption analysis has three levels. First, all state laws that "relate to" any covered employee benefit plan are preempted.[174] Second, there is an exception so that state laws that "regulate insurance, banking, or securities" are not preempted.[175] Third, most employee benefit plans cannot be deemed to be insurers or banks, so they cannot be subjected to state insurance or banking laws.[176] There has been extensive litigation concerning the scope of this preemption. In addition to coverage denial issues, ERISA preemption litigation has addressed attempts to avoid state taxes and other state requirements.

Basic State Legal Principles

Payers must generally act in good faith and with fair dealing. In most states, they can be assessed substantial monetary damages when they act in bad faith. However, some courts have ruled that only the covered person can sue for bad faith, so there must be an express assignment of the bad faith claim in order for a provider to be permitted to sue for bad faith.[177] Generally bad-faith claims cannot be made against ERISA plans due to preemption.[178]

Ambiguities in insurance policies are interpreted in favor of providing coverage for the insured. Frequently, when terms are not defined in the plan or policy, courts will find the terms to be ambiguous.[179] One court has held that this rule concerning interpretation of ambiguities does not apply to some ERISA plans.[180]

Exclusions in policies are generally interpreted more strictly against the insurer than are statements of coverage. This is sometimes called the *doctrine of reason-*

able expectations. Although this state common law doctrine does not apply to ERISA plans, one federal court has ruled that the doctrine of reasonable expectations is applicable to ERISA plans as part of federal common law.[181] Courts can refuse to enforce exclusions based on public policy.[182]

Disqualification of Individual

Some payment denials are based on a determination that the individual is not covered by the plan, without ever reaching the issue of whether the individual's condition or the proposed services are covered. Some misrepresentations by the insured on the application form can void all coverage.[183] Under family coverage, there are frequently disputes in which it is determined that adult children no longer qualify for coverage.[184] Under single-person policies, it is sometimes determined that babies are not automatically covered.[185] State law often requires automatic coverage of newborns, but such requirements do not apply to ERISA plans due to preemption.

Loss of employment generally results in loss of coverage by the employer's health plan, subject only to COBRA continuation rights.[186] When the employer changes insurance carriers, all employees are no longer covered by the old plan.[187]

Denial of Coverage for Individual Services

Insurance coverage for individual services is denied on a wide variety of grounds. This section surveys some of those grounds and related issues.

Pre-existing Condition. Under many health plans, payment is not made for treatment of conditions that exist at the time the person begins coverage.[188] In some plans, the pre-existing condition exclusion ceases to apply if no treatment is required for the pre-existing condition during the first year under the plan. State law can forbid pre-existing condition exclusions in plans,[189] but such laws generally do not apply to ERISA plans.

Criminal Activities. Some policies exclude coverage for injuries that occur during criminal activities. One federal court ruled that this could be applied to deny coverage for injuries that occurred while driving under the influence of alcohol.[190]

Cosmetic Procedures. Plans generally exclude coverage for most cosmetic procedures.

Dental Procedures. Medical plans generally exclude coverage for most dental procedures. There are disputes over the scope of the exclusion.[191] There are dental plans that are offered either with medical plans or as a free-standing option.

Nonemergency. Plans that have closed panels generally pay for emergency services by providers outside the panel. There are frequently disputes over what constitutes an emergency.[192]

Medical Necessity. Medicare, Medicaid, and most private plans cover only medically necessary care. A frequent basis for denial of coverage is that the care lacks medical necessity.[193] There is judgment involved in these determinations and in most plans the administrator is given discretion to make the determinations.[194] Courts will usually overturn such decisions only if they are arbitrary and capricious. When the administrator is also the insurer who is at risk for the cost, some courts find that there is a conflict of interest, so that a less deferential standard is used to review the medical necessity decisions.[195]

Those involved in making medical necessity determinations have been sued for malpractice and on other grounds with mixed results. This is discussed in Chapter 10. In an effort to avoid being sued for judgment calls, some plans adopt rules expressly excluding specific treatments.

There are substantial variations in medical necessity determinations for Medicare. Regional carriers do not agree, which is one of the ways that Medicare fails to be nationally uniform.[196]

Medical Appropriateness. Sometimes care that is otherwise medically necessary is denied on the grounds that it is not medically appropriate. For example, a federal appellate court upheld the denial of a liver transplant on the grounds that it was not medically appropriate in light of the patient's history, including contraction of hepatitis B.[197]

Likelihood of Successful Clinical Outcome. HCFA has limited lung transplant coverage to approved programs that have patient selection criteria for determining suitable candidates based on critical medical need and a "strong likelihood of a successful clinical outcome."[198]

Experimental Exclusion. Most plans have some exclusion for research or experimental procedures.[199] These exclusions have frequently been used to deny payment for new expensive procedures. Sometimes all associated care is also denied coverage.[200] This has especially been a problem with the use of new drugs and devices and with the new uses of old drugs and devices, as discussed in Chapter 3.

There appears to be an inconsistency between the strict standard of scientific, controlled, statistical proof of safety and efficacy applied to drugs and devices and the absence of any such apparent standard applied to the broad range of alternative treatments that some plans are beginning to cover.[201]

Denials of coverage have led to malpractice suits as discussed in Chapter 10. In addition, in 1993, the Texas Attorney General sued a plan after it denied certain cancer coverage on the grounds it was research. The suit claimed that the plan had violated state law by misrepresenting its policies. The suit was settled, the plan agreeing to pay for such treatment.[202]

Transplant Exclusion. There has been extensive litigation concerning exclusion of coverage of transplant procedures; usually the issue is either medical necessity or the experimental exclusion, which have already been discussed. Some plans expressly exclude or restrict transplant procedure coverage.[203] However, one court ruled that a bone marrow transplant was not an organ transplant, so an exclusion for organ transplants did not exclude bone marrow transplants.[204]

Eligibility Requirements. Some plans deny coverage for certain services when specified eligibility requirements are not met. For example, when a state plan provided attendant care to persons who were mentally alert, a federal appellate court upheld denying such care to a person who was not mentally alert.[205]

Managed Care Review. In order to make the above and other determinations required to manage care, plans use reviewers.

Some states have required that managed care plans disclose the criteria that they use to make decisions.[206] A few plans have voluntarily disclosed their criteria.[207] Some plans require compliance with practice guidelines.[208]

Managed care review decisions have been attacked through malpractice suits (see Chapter 10), state administrative procedures,[209] racketeering suits,[210] and other ways.[211] Successful attacks remain rare.

A few states have enacted laws that give patients the right to an external independent review of coverage denial decisions.[212]

Communicating Denial to Patient. One provider sued a plan administrator for defamation for the wording of the notice to the patient of denial. The suit was unsuccessful because the provider did not overcome the qualified privilege for such communications.[213] However, care should be taken in such communications to avoid acting outside the privilege.

Limits on Scope of Coverage

Cap on Benefits

In structuring or changing the structure of plans, nondiscrimination laws need to be considered. Several plans tried to limit their coverage of care for HIV-positive patients by capping benefits. It was first determined that this did not violate ERISA, which gives employers great latitude in changing benefit plans.[214] However, it was then found to violate the federal Americans with Disabilities Act.[215]

To the extent not preempted by ERISA, state nondiscrimination laws also need to be observed in structuring plans.[216]

Copayment/Deductible

Most non-HMO plans involve copayments or deductibles, which the provider is almost always given the responsibility to collect. A copayment is a portion of each bill that the patient must pay. For example, the patient might have to pay $10 for each office visit to a doctor or 20 percent of every hospital bill, with the plan paying the balance. A deductible is the amount that the patient must pay before the plan pays anything. For example, the patient might have to pay $200 in covered medical bills before the plan starts paying any of the bills. Sometimes the deductible does not have to be met before the plan starts paying for some services, typically doctor's visits. Usually the copayments do not count toward the deductible.

The biggest problem with copayments has been that some payers have said that the copayment was a certain percentage and then have calculated the amount based on full charges of the provider, not based on the discounted payments the provider contracted with the payer to accept. Thus, the payer pays a smaller percentage of the total actual payment. These practices have been challenged as overcharges by the payers. The cases have generally been settled by the payers paying a substantial settlement and changing the practice,[217] although some cases are still pending. Hospitals should avoid agreeing to collect copayments based on full charges.

Some states prohibit providers from waiving copayments and deductibles.[218] Medicare policy was discussed earlier in this chapter.

Coordination of Benefits

Most plans have a coordination of benefits provision that specifies the priorities when more than one plan or policy potentially applies. These often result in disputes between plans.[219]

CONFIRMATION OF COVERAGE

Confirmation of coverage and necessary approvals should be sought before nonemergency care is provided. Many employers have adopted health care plans that pay for hospitalization and certain procedures only if prior approval is obtained from the plan. Prior approval may require a second opinion from another physician.

In emergencies, federal law forbids delays in the medical screening or emergency treatment to make inquiries concerning insurance coverage.[220]

Courts have disagreed on whether a third party payer is bound by a confirmation of coverage. Some courts hold that oral representations cannot vary the terms of the plan. One federal appellate court upheld an HMO's denial of heart transplant coverage even though (1) the patient had joined the HMO only after obtaining oral confirmation of coverage and (2) the denial was not made until after the procedure had been performed.[221] Other courts hold that insurers cannot refuse to pay for services after verifying coverage.[222] The Florida Supreme Court ruled that an insurer can be estopped from denying coverage after confirming coverage if (1) there is detrimental reliance on the confirmation and (2) refusal to enforce coverage would sanction fraud or other injustice.[223] The detrimental reliance requirement may mean that the hospital would have to show it would not have admitted the patient or given the service if there had been no confirmation. In states that enforce coverage confirmations, careful documentation of what was confirmed is necessary.[224] If the insurer merely confirmed that the group existed or that the patient was a member of the group, the insurer did not necessarily confirm that a particular procedure was covered.

State law requirements that plans abide by coverage confirmations are generally preempted by ERISA.[225] However, the federal circuit courts have adopted somewhat different positions. Some federal courts have said that there is no remedy under ERISA for misrepresentation of coverage.[226] One federal court ruled that negligent misrepresentation claims under state law were not preempted, but that the plan could not be modified orally. Thus, confirmations based on "interpretations" could be enforced, but not confirmations that required modification of the plan.[227] Another federal court ruled that, when the plan gave a written confirmation of coverage, misrepresentation claims by the provider were not preempted.[228] Other federal courts have reached the same conclusion, viewing the coverage confirmation as a separate contract between the plan and the provider.[229]

One federal court went a step further. The plan gave pre-admission certification subject to review for pre-existing conditions. The court ruled that the plan could not later deny coverage on the basis of a pre-existing condition that it could have determined from medical records available when the initial certification was given.[230]

Plans may also be liable for refusing to provide confirmation of coverage.[231]

Providers should avoid assuring patients that procedures are covered by insurance unless they are willing to forgo payment if the insurer does not pay. A Georgia appellate court case arose when a physician tried to collect a bill after an insurer refused to pay.[232] The patient claimed the physician had stated the procedure would be covered by insurance, and the patient refused to pay. The patient had signed a document promising to pay if the insurer did not. The court decided that the patient had to pay, not because of the document, but because the patient had conducted an investigation of the insurance coverage so there was no reliance on the physician's statements.

BILLING AND COLLECTIONS

ERISA has such a pervasive effect on the relationship between providers and covered plans that, before attempting to collect from an employer-sponsored health plan, a hospital should determine whether it is an ERISA plan and, if so, follow ERISA procedures to collect.

One Ohio court did not let a hospital collect the bill from the patient after the hospital failed to timely submit the claim to the insurance company.[233] While this may not be the rule that other courts will apply, the hospital should try to promptly submit claims to known third party payers.

Content of Bill

To ensure that collections can be pursued to the full extent permitted by law, the billings must be accurately prepared and maintained. The correct name and address of the patient and the person responsible for payment must be obtained, services provided and dates clearly described, and any payments or other credits promptly reflected on the account. Some states impose additional requirements on the contents of hospital bills.[234]

Laws concerning the content, including the amount, of the bill need to be observed. Proper coding is important. Improper billing can result in proceedings under the False Claims Act or the mail fraud law.

False Claims Act

This act[235] imposes criminal penalties on anyone who knowingly presents, or causes to be presented, to the U.S. government a false or fictitious claim for payment. This includes using a false record or statement to get a false or fictitious claim paid. It is not limited to health care; it applies equally to all others who make claims for payment to the government for anything. There does not have to be specific intent to defraud the government; recklessness is enough. If the government suffered damages as a result of the false claim, the defendant can be assessed three times those damages. In addition, a penalty of $5,000 to $10,000 per false claim can be assessed. Providers have been found liable under this act.[236]

The Act permits individuals to bring suits, called "qui tam" actions, in the name of the United States as "private attorneys general."[237] The individual must be the "original source" of the information, and the government has to be given an opportunity to pursue the litigation. Regardless, the individual is entitled to keep part of any recovery in the suit. Retaliation against whistleblowers is prohibited. Qui tam actions have been brought against providers and those administering federal health programs.[238]

Mail Fraud

False claims that are sent through the mails can be punished under the mail fraud law.[239] It is not limited to claims to the government. Physicians have been convicted of mail fraud for bills submitted to private insurers.[240]

Fraud by Patients and Others

Patients who submit fraudulent claims can also be prosecuted. A 1993 case addressed friends who had lied about an injured person's identity, so that he could use one of the friend's employer-provided health insurance to obtain medical services. They were convicted of wire fraud and conspiracy.[241]

Collection Methods

When a hospital's internal collection procedures fail to produce payment, hospitals frequently use collection agencies. Usually the hospital enters a written agreement with the collection agency, specifying the permitted collection activities to assure compliance with applicable laws and hospital policies. Public hospitals usually have authority to use collection agencies, absent a specific statutory prohibition. This is illustrated by a California court ruling that a county could assign its delinquent accounts to a private collection agency, provided it first evaluated the patient's ability to pay and reserved the right to adjust or cancel any bill that would work undue hardship on the debtor.[242]

A bill is evidence of a contract to pay for services provided and is enforceable by legal action. Although small bills are usually not worth the cost of judicial proceedings, legal action may sometimes help educate patients about their obligation to pay medical bills just as they pay other bills. In some states small claims courts can be used to enforce smaller obligations at lower cost.

After the time period for filing a malpractice suit has passed, providers usually will not want to file a suit to collect the bill because in some states filing a collection suit reopens the opportunity to file the malpractice suit as a counter-claim.[243]

Some health plans impose a much shorter time limit for filing suit to recover benefits. These limits are valid under some state laws[244] and violate the laws of other states.[245] However, the shorter time limit may be valid for ERISA plans in all states due to preemption of contrary state laws.

When a court judgment is obtained, it can be enforced in several ways, including having a sheriff seize the debtor's property and imposing garnishment of the debtor's wages. Garnishment of a debtor's wages requires a court order to an employer to pay a portion of the debtor's paycheck to the creditor until the debt is paid. The federal Consumer Credit Protection Act[246] and various state laws limit the portion of a paycheck that may be garnished.

Occasionally families have alleged that patient suicides were due to collection efforts. In 1987, a New York appellate court ruled that suicide was not a foreseeable risk of aggressive collection efforts, so the hospital was not liable for the death.[247] However, also in 1987, a federal appellate court ruled that a jury properly required a physician to pay $200,000 to the surviving husband whose wife committed suicide after she received a copy of a Medicare claim that falsely indicated a diagnosis of a brain tumor.[248] The physician had instructed his staff to enter the false diagnosis because payment would have been denied for the test if a negative result had been reported.

Fair Debt Collection Practices Act

The Fair Debt Collection Practices Act (FDCPA)[249] and various state laws[250] regulate techniques that may be used to seek payment of delinquent accounts. Some of these laws apply to only collection agencies' collection activities, while others also apply to internal hospital collection activities. All persons involved in hospital collection activities should be familiar with these laws to assure compliance. In some situations failure to comply can make the debt unenforceable and even subject the hospital and individuals involved to civil liability and criminal penalties. In 1984, a collection agency attempting to collect a $552.40 bill for the Mayo Clinic was required to pay the debtor $14,400 for his emotional distress, out-of-pocket expenses, and attorney's fees because the agency violated the FDCPA.[251]

Although originally there was an exception for attorneys, it was removed, so letters and communications from attorneys are also covered by FDCPA.[252]

Fair Credit Reporting Act

The Fair Credit Reporting Act[253] regulates the collection and use of consumer credit information. Obtaining consumer reports for unauthorized uses violates this Act.[254]

Liens

Hospital liens are a special legal collection mechanism. Many states have hospital lien laws to assist hospitals in collecting for services rendered to victims of compensable accidents. If a patient is treated for injuries caused by a person who is insured or otherwise capable of paying damages, the hospital may place a lien on the proceeds of any court judgment or settlement of the patient's personal injury action against the responsible individual.[255] This lien gives the hospital some priority to payment from the proceeds. Appropriate documents must be filed with the court, the negligent party, the insurer, and the patient's attorney.

Estate Claims

When the patient dies, the patient's estate is responsible for debts of the deceased if the estate is given timely notice of the debt. Many states assign a high priority to payment of expenses for care during the last illness of the deceased. Thus, many of the other debts of the deceased cannot be paid until the hospital bill has been paid.

Bankruptcy

When a hospital receives a notice that a patient has filed for bankruptcy or has obtained discharge of debts in bankruptcy, collection efforts must cease. Federal law forbids efforts to collect debts during bankruptcy proceedings[256] or after discharge of the debts in bankruptcy.[257] A hospital can be liable for any damage it causes by violating this law. Bankruptcy issues are discussed in Chapter 6.

Ascertaining Indigency and Applying for Benefits

Although hospitals generally help patients identify and qualify for benefits, in most jurisdictions there is no legal duty to do so. However, one California trial court found such a duty and barred a hospital that had not provided such assistance from collecting half of its bill.[258]

Interest

Hospitals also need to be aware of the Truth-in-Lending Act and its implementing regulation,[259] called "Regulation Z," which specify the disclosures that must be made by entities that lend consumers money. These rules are applicable to the credit practices of many hospitals. Oral agreements involving no finance charges are generally exempt. Some other credit practices may not be affected by the rules.[260]

UNCOMPENSATED CARE

Many hospitals are required by law to provide uncompensated care to certain patients. State law requires many governmental hospitals to provide uncompensated care, especially to patients who are residents of the area providing tax support to the hospital and who are unable to pay. Federal law imposes this obligation on hospitals that have received Hill-Burton grants or loans.

The federal Hill-Burton Act[261] provided public and nonprofit community hospitals with funding for construction and modernization. Hospitals that accepted this funding are required to provide, for 20 years after completion of construction, a reasonable volume of services to persons unable to pay.[262] Virtually all hospitals have fulfilled their Hill-Burton uncompensated obligation. The Hill-Burton program retains significance because of the ongoing community service obligation[263] and because, in certain sales of hospitals, any Hill-Burton funding must be repaid to the U.S. government.[264]

Some patients have attempted to use a hospital's failure to comply with the Hill-Burton uncompensated care regulations as a defense to collection suits. Courts have disagreed on whether this may be used as a defense.[265]

CAPITAL FINANCING

Hospitals have substantial and growing needs for capital to modernize and expand.

Internal financing from current net operating revenues or funded depreciation is one source of capital, but it has become increasingly difficult to accumulate.

Private philanthropy is another source of capital and operating funds for nonprofit hospitals. Although funds from philanthropic sources have remained substantial,[266] the percentage of total hospital funds for capital expenditures from these sources has been continually decreasing. Starting in 1995, before a donor of a charitable gift of $250 or more may deduct the gift in calculating income taxes, the donor must obtain from the recipient a written acknowledgement confirming the gift and stating whether anything of value was given in return and, if so, what its value was.[267]

Another major source of capital was governmental grants, until the federal government discontinued its programs. Some states still have grant and loan programs to help fund construction and improvement of medical facilities.

Thus, bonds, equity, and conventional borrowing remain as the sources of capital.

Bonds

Tax-Exempt Bonds

Sale of tax-exempt bonds is the predominant method by which many nonprofit providers of health care obtain funds for major capital expenditures.[268] A principal advantage of tax-exempt bonds has been an interest rate lower than that on loans that pay taxable interest. Tax-exempt bonds are issued by state or local govern-mental entities. The bonds are usually revenue bonds repayable from only hospital revenues, but bonds for governmental hospitals are sometimes payable from general tax revenues. The exemption of bond interest from federal income taxation is based on section 103 of the Internal Revenue Code.[269] Bonds for private tax-exempt hospital purposes qualify if certain conditions are met.[270] This law and its implementing regulations must be complied with to assure tax exemption. For example, federal directives place limits on the contracts that may be signed with management companies or with nonemployee physicians.[271] Some incidental uses outside the scope of otherwise permitted uses are allowed, if they involve a small enough percentage of the proceeds and the space.[272]

Some states place additional limits on hospital use of tax-exempt bonds. One controversial area has been whether these bonds can be used to finance the capital needs of church-owned hospitals, but most courts have upheld such uses.[273]

Most tax-exempt bonds must be in registered form.[274] However, tax-exempt bonds generally do not have to be registered under federal securities laws,[275] but are subject to the penalties under those laws if fraudulent or deceptive practices are used. Tax-exempt bonds are not exempt from some state securities laws, so they must be registered in some states before they can be sold to residents of the state.

In 1995, the Securities Exchange Commission began requiring entities that receive monies from tax-exempt bonds, including hospitals, to make annual and special disclosures.[276]

When a for-profit corporation buys a nonprofit hospital that was financed with tax-exempt bonds, the bonds generally must be redeemed.[277]

Times when bonds are being processed can be delicate. A radiologist who lost his contract with a hospital sent to the finance commission allegedly false information that delayed approval of the bonds. A Michigan court ruled that the radiologist could be liable for tortious interference with the bonding.[278]

Taxable Bonds

For-profit hospitals borrow money using taxable bonds and other taxable debt arrangements. Some nonprofit hospitals have also used taxable bonds.

Equity

Investor-owned hospitals and other health care enterprises acquire equity capital by selling stock, partnership interests, or other equity interests to investors. Such sales have been a major source of capital. Enterprises that acquire capital through these means must comply with securities laws. These laws require disclosure of certain information as well as place some restrictions on the conduct of those involved with the enterprise.

Conventional Borrowing

Both for-profit and nonprofit hospitals borrow money through conventional borrowing, often secured by mortgages on the real and personal property of the borrower. This can lead to mortgage foreclosures on buildings that are mortgaged to secure the borrowings.[279]

Mortgage Guaranties

The Federal Housing Administration (FHA) insures conventional mortgages for constructing, modernizing, and equipping hospitals.[280] Rather than lending funds directly to hospitals, the FHA provides loan insurance. This minimizes lenders' risk, making it easier to borrow money. The FHA also guarantees and insures loans for some capital expenditures of hospitals in rural communities.[281]

Leasing

While purchasing has been the more traditional method within the health care industry for obtaining capital assets, leasing is also used. Although any type of capital asset may be leased, leases are most frequently used to obtain equipment.

Leasing is used as part of capital financing arrangements. Hospitals are sometimes sold to real estate investment trusts or other entities and then leased back on a long-term basis. Leases are also used for off–balance sheet financing of other real estate, such as medical office buildings.

ASSET PROTECTION

Hospital administrators must be concerned with protection against losses arising from injuries to patients or visitors and losses arising from damage to physical facilities, equipment, and vehicles. Patients may sue the hospital if they are injured by malpractice. Fire, theft, and other hazards may damage the hospital's physical property. A program to manage risks includes attempts to minimize the risks and maintain proper insurance coverage against the risks that remain.

Hospitals need professional and general liability insurance. Professional liability contracts generally are a combination of malpractice and product liability coverage. General liability insurance usually covers losses from injury to patients or visitors arising out of negligence of personnel other than professionals. Disputes concerning which company is obligated to provide coverage for particular incidents sometimes arise between the insurance companies that provide professional and general liability protection. Hospitals should design their coverage to avoid gaps between the policies. Hospitals are involved in many activities that are not covered by professional and general liability insurance, so separate coverage needs to be considered for these activities, such as operation of motor vehicles and workers' compensation coverage.

Property insurance includes fire, flood, windstorm, or earthquake coverage, depending on local risks. Theft losses are frequently self-insured because of the high premium cost for such insurance. However, employee fidelity insurance or a bond is frequently purchased to cover losses arising out of embezzlement, fraud, and other acts of employee dishonesty.

Hospitals frequently purchase insurance for directors and officers to protect them against personal loss from lawsuits for acts in their official capacities. However, some insurance policies may not provide the protection they appear to provide. A federal district court ruled in 1984 that one officer's misrepresentations in the application for the insurance invalidated the coverage for all directors and officers.[282]

To reduce insurance premium costs, many hospitals have adopted alternatives to commercial insurance policies, including captive insurance companies that are chartered to do business for only a particular group of patrons. Regardless of coverage, the premium is usually determined in part by the hospital's liability history. To control premium cost, hospitals have implemented loss control programs, including a thorough incident reporting system and a system of addressing identified incident patterns and handling claims. Some states require such risk management systems.[283] The Joint Commission requires the collection of data about risk management activities.[284]

Some hospitals may be able to reduce insurance costs through self-insurance of some risks. One approach to limited self-insurance has been to obtain policies with larger than standard deductibles, the amounts the insured hospital must pay before the insurance company becomes responsible for paying the remainder up to the policy limits.

STATE TAXES

There are a wide variety of state and local taxes. Some examples include income taxes; corporate franchise taxes; revenue taxes; tangible and intangible property taxes; professional and business registration and licensure fees; unemployment taxes; and transactional taxes, such as sales taxes, transfer taxes, and document stamps. In some states, the way a transaction is structured can have a large impact on the amount of taxes that are due.

Taxes on Health Services

States are increasingly placing taxes on health services.[285] Sometimes these are simply revenue-generating measures. In the past, taxes have been mechanisms for increasing a state's Medicaid expenditures to increase the flow of federal money into the state. As discussed in the Medicaid section of this chapter, that is no longer permitted. Now these taxes usually are designed to spread the responsibility for financing uncompensated care.

In 1995, the U.S. Supreme Court addressed a New York tax that was assessed on third party payments to hospitals. Different categories of payers had different tax rates, with Blue Cross exempt from the tax. Blue Cross was exempt because it was the only payer who sold individual health policies on an open enrollment basis. Plans covered by ERISA challenged the tax, claiming that it was preempted by ERISA. The Court ruled that the tax was not preempted by ERISA. The Court concluded that ERISA preemption was focused on permitting plans to offer uniform national benefits and claims processing. It was not designed to regulate the price of health care.[286]

EXEMPTION FROM STATE AND LOCAL TAXES

Governmental and charitable institutions are granted exemption from many taxes at both state and local levels for property, sales, and income taxes and at the federal level for income taxes. Classification of a hospital as exempt depends on several factors that vary depending on the type of tax. The qualifications for state tax exemptions are often different from the qualifications for federal tax exemption.

Property Taxes

Each state has the power to tax properties within its boundaries. A hospital must prove eligibility for a specific tax exemption, or its property is taxable. In some states, ownership by a nonprofit or governmental hospital is not sufficient to establish eligibility. In those states, hospitals must also show that the property is used exclusively for hospital or other exempt purposes to qualify.

Federal Hospitals

Federal hospitals are exempt from state and local taxation because the United States has the sovereign right to hold property free of taxation. This right is based in the Supremacy Clause of the U.S. Constitution and in the necessity for federal freedom from state interference when dealing with its property. Federal ownership is sufficient to qualify for this exemption.

Other Governmental Hospitals

State, county, district, and municipal hospitals are usually also exempt from property taxation because they fall within state constitutional or statutory exemptions. These exemptions are sometimes based solely on ownership regardless of property use. In some states, exemption from taxation is granted only when governmental property is devoted to a "public use," but hospital purposes are generally considered to be a public use. Questions may arise about whether other uses are valid public uses.

For-Profit Hospitals

For-profit hospitals do not qualify for tax exemption even if a profit is not earned. When for-profit hospitals are reorganized as nonprofit hospitals, some states consider the property to be tax exempt even when hospital net revenue is used to pay off bondholders who are former stockholders in the predecessor for-profit hospital; however, some courts disagree.[287]

Nonprofit Hospitals

Nonprofit hospitals are frequently exempted from state and local property taxation by state constitutions and statutes. Most exemptions require that the institution serve a charitable purpose, but specific wording determines the qualifications and extent of exemptions. Tax exemption for nonprofit hospitals is receiving renewed scrutiny and challenge. For example, the Utah Supreme Court established tighter criteria for what demonstrates charitable purpose. Those criteria limited the number of Utah hospitals that could qualify.[288] In 1992, a Pennsylvania hospital lost its tax exemption because it did not donate a substantial portion of its service. The court found that it provided free care only to the extent required by other laws and that it had participated in a lawsuit seeking higher Medicaid reimbursement.[289]

In some states a nonprofit organization's property must satisfy four tests to qualify for tax exemption: organizational test, property type test, interest test, and use test.

The organizational test usually requires that the organizational documents must state the charitable purpose and forbids financial gain to private individuals from hospital operations or distribution of assets. Actual hospital operations may be scrutinized to confirm that the hospital operates as a charitable enterprise. The prohibition of private gain does not prevent salaries to staff, contracts with vendors, and payments for services, if the payments bear a reasonable relationship to the services provided.

The beneficiaries of a charitable hospital may be restricted to some extent without loss of tax exemption. For example, children's hospitals limit their care to children, and some hospitals limit their services to persons with specific diseases or to members of an order, society, or association. However, a Missouri court ruled that a hospital owned by a railroad and open to only railroad employees and their families was not exempt from taxation because the hospital was not open to the public.[290]

For the charitable use part of the organizational test, some states accept health care services as sufficient evidence.[291] Other states require hospitals to provide free care to those unable to pay.[292] Generally, exempt hospitals may charge for services and collect bills. However, a Georgia court denied exemption to a hospital that collected payments from patients because the statutory exemption required the institution to be a "purely public charity."[293]

Some states tax real property (land and buildings), tangible personal property (e.g., movable equipment and automobiles), and intangible personal property (e.g., accounts receivable, stocks and bonds). The charitable exemption may apply to only certain types of property. Real estate owned by a charitable hospital and used for hospital purposes is usually exempt; however, personal property belonging to the hospital may not be exempt.[294]

To satisfy the interest test, usually the hospital must demonstrate that it owns or has another qualifying interest in the specific property. In some states, the hospital must have title; in other states, a lease is sufficient, although some states require the lease to be of a certain type or duration.[295]

The use test generally requires use for an exempt purpose. Many states require exclusive use for charitable purposes, but the interpretation of exclusive use varies. Generally uses that are reasonably necessary for the charitable or educational work of the institution qualify, even if they are not directly related to patient care. However, some property owned by charitable hospitals has been taxed. For example, property rented for commercial use is generally taxable even when the income is used for charitable purposes. Noncommercial rental, such as occasional rental to another charitable organization, does not destroy the property's exemption in most states.

A few states do not require exclusive use for charitable purposes. For example, Kentucky's constitutional exemption of institutions of public charity has been interpreted to extend to property rented or leased by the charity to obtain income for charitable purposes.[296]

Some states permit split listing of property so that the portion used for tax-exempt purposes can retain its tax exemption, while other portions are taxed.[297] In other states, the tax exemption of the entire property is lost if a portion is being used for other than tax-exempt purposes.

In most states, hospital property that is used for private physician offices is not exempt.[298] Hospital property used to house hospital employees, trainees, and key administrative personnel is exempt in some states. States vary on whether a cafeteria, pharmacy, or other patient and visitor amenities can be an exempt use. States also vary on whether vacant land or unoccupied buildings are exempt.[299] States vary on whether hospital property used for tennis courts, playgrounds, parks, and the like for employees or patients is exempt.[300] Most states view a hospital parking building as necessary to efficient hospital operations and thus exempt if it is used primarily by hospital personnel, patients, and visitors.[301] As nonprofit hospitals have formed chains, the tax status of corporate headquarters has been questioned. One court found the headquarters to be tax exempt in Illinois.[302]

The status of property owned by cooperatives or shared services corporations is not clear. In a 1976 Minnesota decision, the court found cooperative property to be exempt because the exempt member hospitals completely owned, managed, and financed the cooperative and received all the benefits from it.[303]

Payments in Lieu of Taxes

In some states, municipal taxing authorities have placed pressure on hospitals and other tax-exempt organizations to make payments in lieu of taxes.[304] Although there is usually no legal basis for these requests, they have sometimes succeeded in obtaining "voluntary" payments. In fact, some payments have been made voluntarily. Others have resulted from threats to challenge the hospital's tax-exempt status or to withhold approval of building permits; zoning changes; and other variances, licenses, and approvals. Hospitals may be confronted with the choice of negotiating payments, accepting delays or denials of important approvals, or resisting through the political or legal process.

Sales and Use Taxes

State and local sales and use taxes vary considerably in their coverage and exemptions. Hospitals sometimes pay taxes on purchases and sometimes collect taxes on sales. Some states exempt qualified charitable organizations from paying sales taxes, while others grant exemptions for specific products or services, rather than for entire institutions.[305] There is usually an exemption for medicines and some medicinal products.[306] There is sometimes an exemption for items purchased for resale.[307] As state and local governments search for more revenue, exemptions are being more narrowly interpreted and there is more enforcement activity in some states.

FEDERAL INCOME TAX

Federal income tax laws are an important issue for most hospitals. Hospitals either must take the steps to qualify for exemption, as discussed later in this chapter, or structure their activities to minimize taxes and pay applicable taxes.

A tax-exempt hospital still must pay taxes on unrelated business income. For example, the profit from drug sales to outpatients who are private patients of the medical staff is usually unrelated business income.[308] Care needs to be taken in structuring the provision of services to outside entities.[309] If the unrelated business income is too large a portion of total revenues, the entire tax exemption can be lost.

A for-profit hospital must pay taxes on its profits. It can deduct most of its legitimate business expenses in determining its profits. Sometimes corporations try to avoid corporate taxes by paying excessive salaries because salaries are deductible as business expenses while dividends and other distributions of profits are not deductible. The IRS will treat excessive salaries as non-deductible dividends and assess taxes, interest, and penalties.[310]

Insurance companies are taxed differently than other companies. Some for-profit IPA–model HMOs have qualified to be taxed as insurance companies.[311] Staff–model HMOs are generally not taxed as insurance companies.[312]

When reviewing IRS pronouncements, it is important to keep in mind that they have different effects, ranging from rules that are binding on the IRS through Private Letter Rulings (PLRs) that apply to only the entity that obtained the ruling and cannot be cited by others in any court.[313] Thus, while PLRs are helpful to know what the IRS was thinking at the time and, in conjunction with other materials, may suggest ways to structure the hospital's affairs, they cannot be relied on.

Federal Employment Taxes

All hospitals must pay federal employment taxes on employees. Independent contractors pay their own employment taxes. The IRS is increasingly scrutinizing relationships that are labeled as independent contractor relationships to determine if they should be considered employment relationships under tax law.[314] What the parties call the relationship is not determinative. Retroactive finding of an employer relationship can result in substantial back taxes, interest, and penalties (including the portion of the employee's income that should have been withheld by the employer).[315] Thus, independent contractor relationships need to be structured so that they will not be considered employment relationships under tax law.

Hospitals need to comply with the technical requirements concerning pensions, deferred compensation, and benefits. They have been a focus of some IRS audits.

FEDERAL INCOME TAX EXEMPTION

Section 501(c)(3)

Many nonprofit hospitals are eligible for exemption from federal income tax under section 501(c)(3) of the Internal Revenue Code.[316] It exempts organizations created and operated exclusively for certain purposes, including "charitable purposes." The scope of charitable purposes entitled to this exemption is different from the scope used to determine exemption from state and local taxes. Property may be exempt from one and not the other.

All organizations seeking section 501(c)(3) tax exemption must meet six requirements.

1. The organization must be organized and operated exclusively for one or more special purposes (religious, charitable, scientific, literary, or educational purposes; prevention of cruelty to children or animals; testing for public safety; or amateur sports).
2. No part of the net earnings can inure to any private shareholder or individual.
3. No substantial part of its activities can involve passing propaganda or otherwise attempting to influence legislation.
4. The organization cannot participate in or intervene in any political campaign on behalf of any candidate for public office.
5. The assets of the organization must be dedicated to charity, so that they go to another qualified charity if the organization is dissolved.
6. The organization must apply for classification as a tax-exempt organization on Form 1023 furnished by the IRS.

The second requirement is of particular concern to hospitals. Many of the financial arrangements that hospitals consider entering into with physicians and others can violate the second requirement by involving prohibited private inurement.[317] For example, free or subsidized services or payments to physicians or others in excess of the fair market value of the services they provide to the hospital can constitute private inurement. Such payments and services can also constitute illegal kickbacks as discussed earlier in this chapter. Excessive executive compensation can also constitute private inurement and has received increasing IRS and congressional attention.[318] In 1991, the IRS revoked the tax exemption of a Florida hospital because its sale had allegedly benefited in excess its officers and directors, who bought the hospital from the non-profit entity for $6.3 million and two years later sold it for almost $30 million. The appeal to the tax court is still pending.[319]

The fifth requirement, a charitable purpose, has received considerable attention concerning hospitals. Health care is accepted as a "charitable purpose" by the IRS. Before 1969, the IRS considered free care to the poor to be one of the essential characteristics a hospital must have to be "charitable." Then in 1969, the IRS issued a ruling that recognized promotion of health as a purpose of the law of charity, so free or reduced rate services are not required.[320] A federal appellate court upheld this ruling.[321] The U.S. Supreme Court later vacated the decision on the ground that the organization could not file the suit because it did not have sufficient interest in the outcome.[322] Thus, the 1969 IRS ruling was left in effect. The 1969 ruling found six characteristics to be important in determining whether the hospital was operated for a charitable purpose.

1. The hospital provided care on a nonprofit basis to all persons in the community who were able to pay directly or through third party reimbursement.
2. The hospital operated an emergency room that was open to all persons.
3. Any surplus of receipts over disbursements was used to improve the quality of patient care, expand facilities, and advance training, education, and research.
4. Control of the hospitals rested with a board of trustees composed of independent civic leaders.
5. The hospital maintained an open medical staff, with privileges available to all qualified medical staff.
6. The hospital permitted all members of the active medical staff to lease space in its medical office building.

This ruling was clarified by a 1983 IRS ruling that addressed a hospital that did not have all of the characteristics listed in the 1969 ruling.[323] The hospital did not have an emergency room because the state health planning agency had found it unnecessary. The IRS looked at other factors and concluded that the hospital was operated for the exclusive benefit of the community and, thus, was charitable and entitled to tax exemption. Additional flexibility is indicated in other areas, such as the approval of some profit-sharing[324] and incentive compensation[325] plans for nonprofit hospitals. It is likely that other flexibility will be recognized. The minimum characteristics necessary to assure tax exemption are not yet clear, so hospitals that desire federal income tax exemption under section 501(c)(3) should seek advice from a tax lawyer before varying from the characteristics listed in the rulings.

In 1983, the U.S. Supreme Court recognized a new requirement for exemption under section 501(c)(3) by ruling that organizations violating an "established national public policy" are not entitled to exemption.[326] The Court upheld denial of exemptions to a school with a racially discriminatory admission policy and a school with a racially discriminatory code of conduct for students. The IRS has taken the position that the Medicare fraud and abuse and self-referral laws are also such established national policies, so violations can endanger tax exemption.[327]

A tax-exempt hospital may have a for-profit subsidiary if certain conditions are met that assure separation of the entities.[328] A 1985 IRS General Counsel Memorandum outlines the four factors that are examined to determine if the parent corporation's tax-exempt status is compromised.

1. The parent and the subsidiary should have separate boards of directors with minimal overlap.
2. The parent should have no more than minimal involvement with the subsidiary's day-to-day management.
3. The subsidiary should have a separate existence and a bona fide business purpose.
4. Any services provided between the parent and subsidiary should be on an arm's length basis.[329]

However, an IRS private letter ruling has indicated that the absence of one factor may not be fatal.[330] If the IRS finds that the factors have not been sufficiently met, the actions of the subsidiary will be attributed to the parent; so, for example, any dividends paid by the subsidiary entities to other than the exempt parent could be fatal for the parent's tax-exempt status.

Hospitals need to carefully structure joint ventures to avoid prohibited arrangements.[331] Hospitals can enter certain Physician–Hospital Organizations (PHOs) without jeopardizing their tax exemption, if the PHOs are not physician controlled and fairly allocate monies.[332]

In 1992, the IRS issued Audit Guidelines for hospitals. The subsequent comprehensive audits of selected hospitals have led to a new level of scrutiny of hospital practices.[333]

When structuring arrangements to satisfy IRS requirements, the arrangements should also be designed to satisfy other legal requirements, such as those to prevent Medicare fraud and abuse. In 1989, the IRS and HHS agreed to share information on potential violations.[334]

Other Organizations

Integrated delivery systems and other new types of entities have sought tax exemption with mixed success. One approach has been to seek to qualify as a stand-alone entity. Another way to qualify has been as an "integral part" of an exempt entity.

Geisinger Health Plan, an IPA-model HMO, sought to be recognized standing alone and was denied the exemption based on the finding that it benefited its members and not the community.[335] Geisinger then tried to be recognized as an integral part of the Geisinger system and was denied the exemption again.[336]

There have been other favorable rulings on tax exemption of networks. Friendly Hills Healthcare Network,[337] Facey Medical Foundation,[338] Billings Clinic,[339] and Rockford Memorial Health Services Corporation[340] were granted stand-alone exemptions. Northwestern Healthcare Network was granted tax exemption of the parent and superparent (the parent's parent) in its regional health network as integral parts of an exempt entity.[341]

Some tax exemptions are of short-lived utility. In 1994, after obtaining tax exemption, Friendly Hills was unable to work out various issues with its affiliated medical center, so the foundation was sold to a for-profit corporation.[342]

In 1994, the IRS unofficially outlined several factors that it considered important for exemption of systems, including nondiscriminatory treatment of Medicare and Medicaid patients, open medical staff at the hospital component, community control, no more than twenty-percent control of the governing board by physicians, and purchase of assets at fair market value.[343] The twenty-percent rule remains controversial with physicians seeking greater representation. One option has been to make the system for profit.[344] Other nonprofit arrangements may be possible. In 1995, one PHO in a university context with a board that was over 80 percent physician controlled received approval where the quorum and voting requirements gave the hospital an effective veto.[345]

Some medical groups have obtained tax exemption as integral parts of hospitals, especially in academic settings.[346]

Some hospitals share services, such as data processing, warehousing, billing and collections, and laboratory and clinical services. The sharing of some services has been facilitated by section 501(e) of the Internal Revenue Code,[347] which permits the formation of tax-exempt organizations to provide some services to several hospitals. Only the services listed in section 501(e) are entitled to exemption under the section, so it is not helpful for unlisted services, such as shared laundry services.[348]

Governmental Entities

Some governmental hospitals are tax exempt under section 115 of the Internal Revenue Code[349] on the basis of being an instrumentality of the state, rather than under section 501(c)(3).

NOTES

1. *E.g., U. of Cincinnati Hospital cuts $22 million,* AM. MED. NEWS, Nov. 7, 1994, at 31.

2. M. Mitka, *HMO enrollment tops 50 million,* AM. MED. NEWS, Dec. 26, 1994, at 3.

3. See A.L. Jiranek & S.D. Baker, *Any willing provider laws: Regulating the health care provider's contractual relationship with the insurance company,* 7 HEALTH LAW., Wint. 1994–95, at 1.

4. *E.g.,* Stuart Circle Hosp. Corp. v. Aetna Health Management, 995 F.2d 500 (4th Cir.), *cert. denied,* 114 S. Ct. 579 (U.S. 1993) [no preemption of Virginia statute by ERISA, statute regulates business of insurance, so within savings clause]; Blue Cross & Blue Shield v. St. Mary's Hosp., 245 Va. 24, 426 S.E.2d 117 (1993) [no preemption by ERISA]; *contra,* BPS Clinical Labs. v. Blue Cross & Blue Shield of Michigan, 206 Mich. App. 570, 522 N.W.2d 902 (1994), *mot. granted, remanded,* 449 Mich. 860, 1995 Mich. LEXIS 1079 (1995) [Michigan any willing provider law preempted by ERISA].

5. *E.g.,* Blue Cross & Blue Shield v. St. Mary's Hosp., 245 Va. 24, 426 S.E.2d 117 (1993); HCA Health Servs. of Va., Inc. v. Aetna Life Ins. Co., No. 92-574-A (E.D.Va. June 16, 1994), *as discussed in* 3 HEALTH L. REP. [BNA] 143 (1994) [hospital exclusion from PPO resulted from unsuccessful good-faith negotiations, did not violate any willing provider law] [hereinafter HEALTH L. REP. will be cited as H.L.R.].

6. *E.g.,* Larkin, *Hospitals foot bill for Maxicare Utah's failure,* 62 HOSPS., Oct. 5, 1988, at 44 [hospitals left with $6 million in unpaid bills]; Kenkel, *Pa. hospitals denied payment from Maxicare,* 19 MOD. HEALTHCARE, July 7, 1989, at 4.

7. 42 U.S.C.A. § 1395cc; 42 C.F.R. §§ 489.20, 489.30; Klas, *Hospital may lose Medicare over lawsuits,* PALM BEACH POST, Nov. 20, 1987, at 7B.

8. *Providers not permitted to bill Maxicare enrollees,* 19 MOD. HEALTHCARE, Sept. 22, 1989, at 12.

9. *E.g.,* Barry v. Blue Cross, 805 F.2d 866 (9th Cir. 1986) [PPO did not violate antitrust laws]; Ball Mem. Hosp., Inc. v. Mutual Hosp. Ins., Inc., 603 F. Supp. 1077 (S.D. Ind. 1985) [preliminary injunction of PPO denied], *aff'd,* 784 F.2d 1325 (7th Cir.), *reh'g denied (en banc),* 788 F.2d 1223 (7th Cir. 1986); Associated Foot Surgeons v. National Foot Care Program, Inc., No. 84-271367CZ (Mich. Cir. Ct. Oakland County Feb. 1, 1984) [injunction of PPO denied], *as discussed in* 12 HEALTH L. DIG., June 1984, at 4.

10. 42 U.S.C.A. § 300e-9.

11. *E.g.,* Health Care Plan v. Aetna Life Ins. Co., 966 F.2d 738 (2d Cir. 1992).

12. *E.g.,* J. Johnsson, *Patients caught in bitter split of group, Pru Care,* AM. MED. NEWS, Apr. 25, 1994, at 1 [custody battle over 75,000 capitated patients enrolled in PruCare, treated exclusively by Austin Regional Clinic].

13. *E.g.,* Silard v. Group Health Ass'n, No. 93-CA-8678 (D.C. Super. Ct. Feb. 22, 1994), *as discussed in* 3 H.L.R. 280 (1994) [HMO member's challenge to sale of HMO to Humana dismissed as without merit. Election conducted in accordance with District of Columbia nonprofit corporation law].

14. 42 U.S.C.A. § 1320a–7b.

15. United States v. Kats, 871 F.2d 105 (9th Cir. 1989); *accord* United States v. Greber, 760 F.2d 68 (3d Cir.), *cert. denied,* 474 U.S. 988 (1985); *see also* United States v. Lipkis, 770 F.2d 1447 (9th Cir. 1985); *but see* United States v. Porter, 591 F.2d 1048 (5th Cir. 1979).

16. United States v. Bay State Ambulance & Hosp. Rental Serv., 874 F.2d 20 (1st Cir. 1989).

17. Hanlester Network v. Shalala, 51 F.3d 1390 (9th Cir. 1995).

18. Ratzlaf v. United States, 114 S. Ct. 655 (U.S. 1994).

19. *E.g.*, Cheek v. United States, 498 U.S. 192 (1991).

20. *E.g.*, United States v. Hilliard, 31 F.3d 1509 (10th Cir. 1994).

21. 42 C.F.R. § 1001.952, *published first in* 56 FED. REG. 35952 (July 29, 1991).

22. 42 C.F.R. § 1001.952, *published first in* 57 FED. REG. 52723 (Nov. 5, 1992).

23. 59 FED. REG. 37202 (July 21, 1994).

24. *Joint venture arrangements*, OIG-89-4 (Aug. 1989);*Routine waiver of copayments and deductibles under Medicare Part B*, OIG-91-23 (May 1991); *Hospital incentives to physicians* (May 1992); *Prescription drug marketing schemes*, OIG 94-18 (Aug. 1994); *Arrangements for the provision of clinical lab services*, OIG 95-03 (Oct. 1994); these five alerts were reissued together in 59 FED. REG. 65372 (Dec. 19, 1994); *Home health fraud* (June 1995); the six alerts are reprinted in MEDICARE & MEDICAID GUIDE [CCH] ¶¶ 38448, 39225, 40200, 42609, 42712, 43422 [hereinafter MEDICARE & MEDICAID GUIDE [CCH] will be cited as M.M.G.].

25. Bakersfield Community Hosp. v. Sullivan, No. 89-1056-TPJ (D. D.C. Aug. 8, 1989), *as discussed in* 17 HEALTH L. DIG., Sept. 1989, at 15; Burda, *Judge refuses to rule on hospital sale*, 19 MOD. HEALTHCARE, Sept. 1, 1989, at 7.

26. *E.g.*, United States v. Levin, 973 F.2d 463 (6th Cir. 1992) [dismissal of fraud, abuse charges against manufacturer for giving gifts to surgeons pursuant to marketing plan approved by HHS, HCFA].

27. Polk County v. Peters, 800 F. Supp. 1451 (E.D. Tex. 1992).

28. Vana v. Vista Hosp. Sys., Inc., No. 233623, 1993 WL 597402 (Cal. Super. Ct. Riverside County Oct. 25, 1993). The case settled in 1994, 3 H.L.R. 180 (1994).

29. Modern Med. Labs., Inc. v. Smith-Kline Beecham Clinical Labs., Inc., No. 92 C 5302 (N.D. Ill. Aug. 16, 1994), *reprinted in* M.M.G. ¶42754.

30. Anaheim General Hosp. v. Pacific Coast Radiology Med. Group, No. 660926 (Cal. Super. Ct. Oct. 11, 1994); B. McCormick, *Anti-kickback law no defense for not paying fee*, AM. MED. NEWS, Nov. 14, 1994, at 8.

31. *E.g.*, FLA. STAT. §§ 395.0185, 455.237; *see also* Schmidt v. Foundation Health, No. C015978 (Cal. Ct. App. 3d Dist. June 26, 1995), *as discussed in* 23 HEALTH L. DIG., July 1995, at 41 [illegal kickback for health insurance broker to rebate commission to subscribers].

32. *E.g.*, FLA. STAT. § 458.331(1)(i).

33. 42 U.S.C.A. § 1395nn; 42 C.F.R. pt. 1003 [civil money penalties], first published in 60 FED. REG. 16850 (Mar. 31, 1995).

34. Pub. L. No. 101-239, § 6204 (1989); Pub. L. No. 101-508, § 4207 (1990); 42 C.F.R. §§ 411.350-411.361, *as published in* 60 FED. REG. 41,914 (Aug. 14, 1995).

35. Pub. L. No. 103-66, § 13562(a) (1993).

36. Pub. L. No. 103-432, § 152 (1994).

37. Gen. Couns. Mem. 39,862 (Nov. 21, 1991).

38. *E.g.*, FLA. STAT. §§ 455.236 [prohibition of most self-referrals], 455.25 [required disclosure to patient].

39. 42 U.S.C.A. § 1320a-7a(b), *added by* Pub. L. No. 99-509, § 9313; *see Physician incentive payments by hospitals could lead to abuse*, Report No. GAO/HRD-86-103 (July 1986), *reprinted in* M.M.G. ¶35,538 [discussion of Paracelsus plan, other incentive plans that were tried before the law].

40. 42 U.S.C.A. § 1395mm(1)(8).

41. *E.g.*, United States v. Delta Dental Plan of Ariz., Inc., No. CIV 94-1793 PHXPGR (D. Ariz. Aug. 30, 1994), *as discussed in* 3 H.L.R. 1261 (1994) [Settlement of DOJ challenge to MFN clause by

agreeing to drop it]; United States v. Vision Service Plan, No number (D. D.C. Dec. 15, 1994), *as discussed in* 3 H.L.R. 1822 (1994) [proposed consent agreement with DOJ eliminating MFN clause]; B. McCormick, *Antitrust peril in contract clause*, AM. MED. NEWS, Sept. 19, 1994, at 1 [most favored nation clause. Delta Dental settlement].

42. Willamette Dental Group, P.C. v. Oregon Dental Service Corp., 130 Or. App. 487, 882 P.2d 637 (Ore. Ct. App. 1994), *rev. denied*, 320 Or. 508, 888 P.2d 569 (1995) [enforcement of MFN clause in prepaid dental benefit plan not violation of Oregon antitrust law], but plan agreed not to enforce MFN clause for five years in proposed final judgement after Department of Justice challenged MFN clause under federal law, United States v. Oregon Dental Serv., No. C95 1211 FMS (N.D. Cal. filed Apr. 10, 1995), *as discussed in* 4 H.L.R. 646 (1995).

43. Johnson v. Plantation Gen. Hosp. Ltd., Partnership, 641 So.2d 58 (Fla. 1994) [claims of patients in class action challenge for overcharging could be aggregated to meet amount in controversy].

44. *E.g.*, In re William B. Kessler Mem. Hosp., 78 N.J. 564, 397 A.2d 656 (1979).

45. *E.g.*, Bath Mem. Hosp. v. Maine Health Care Fin. Comm'n, 853 F.2d 1007 (1st Cir. 1988); In re 1983 Final Reconciliation Adjustments of Greenville Hosp., 214 N.J. Super. 607, 520 A.2d 809 (App. Div. 1987); Griffin Hosp. v. Commission on Hosps. & Health Care, 200 Conn. 489, 512 A.2d 199, *app. dismissed*, 479 U.S. 1023 (1986); Prince George's Doctor's Hosp., Inc. v. Health Servs. Cost Review Comm'n, 302 Md. 193, 486 A.2d 744 (1985).

46. Panama City Med. Diagnostic Ltd. v. Williams, 13 F.3d 1541 (11th Cir. 1994), *en banc reh'g denied*, 21 F.3d 1127 (11th Cir. 1994), *cert. denied*, 115 S. Ct. 93 (U.S. 1994); but a state trial court enjoined enforcement of the law as a violation of the state constitution, Physical Therapy Rehab. Ctr. v. Florida, No. 92-2736 (Fla. Cir. Ct. Leon County July 7, 1994), *as discussed in* 3 H.L.R. 1014 (1994).

47. Massachusetts Nurses Ass'n v. Dukakis, 726 F.2d 41 (1st Cir. 1984); *accord* Washington State Nurses Ass'n v. Washington State Hosp. Comm'n, 773 F.2d 1044 (9th Cir. 1985), *cert. denied*, 475 U.S. 1120 (1986).

48. Rebaldo v. Cuomo, 749 F.2d 133 (2d Cir. 1984), *cert. denied*, 472 U.S. 1008 (1985).

49. Pub. L. No. 93-406, 88 Stat. 829 (1974) (codified in scattered sections of 5, 18, 26, 29, 31, 42 U.S.C.).

50. United Hosp. Ctr., Inc. v. Richardson, 757 F.2d 1445 (4th Cir. 1985).

51. *Wash. forms health agency, will end rate-setting policy*, 19 MOD. HEALTHCARE, June 16, 1989, at 12.

52. Baltimore & Ohio RR. v. United States, 345 U.S. 146 (1953); F.C. Dreyer, Jr., *Health care rate regulations: The need for a reinvigorated "takings" analysis*, 26 J. HEALTH & HOSP. L. 161 (1993) [hereinafter J. HEALTH & HOSP. L. will be cited as J.H.H.L.].

53. 10 U.S.C.A. §§ 1079–1086, 1095; 32 C.F.R. pt. 199.

54. 5 U.S.C.A. §§ 8901–8914; 5 C.F.R. pt. 890; 48 C.F.R. chaps. 1, 16.

55. Pub. L. No. 89-97, 79 Stat. 290 (1965).

56. C. Culhane, *Medicare denial rates vary widely: Carriers inconsistent in judging medical necessity*, AM. MED. NEWS, Apr. 18, 1994, at 3.

57. Pub. L. No. 100-360, 102 Stat. 683 (1988).

58. Pub. L. No. 101-234 (1989); N.Y. TIMES, Nov. 23, 1989, at 10.

59. Pub. L. No. 98-21, 97 Stat. 65 (1983), *as amended by* Pub. L. No. 98-369, 98 Stat. 1073 (1984); 42 C.F.R. §§ 405.470–405.477.

60. Parrish v. Lamm, 758 P.2d 1356 (Colo. 1988); Annotation, *Validity of state statute prohibiting health providers from the practice of waiving patients' obligation to pay health insurance deductibles or copayments, or advertising such practice*, 8 A.L.R. 5TH 855.

61. 42 C.F.R. § 1001.952(k).

62. *E.g.*, 42 U.S.C.A. § 1395u(b).

63. 42 U.S.C.A. § 1395w-4.

64. American Academy of Ophthalmology v. Sullivan, 998 F.2d 377 (6th Cir. 1993) [demonstration project paying single negotiated global fee for cataract surgery permissible].

65. 42 U.S.C.A. §§ 1395g, 1395u(b)(6); 42 C.F.R. §§ 424.73, 424.66.

66. 42 U.S.C.A. § 1395l(q).

67. 42 U.S.C.A. § 1395x(s)(2)(A).

68. United States v. Krizek, 859 F. Supp. 5 (D. D.C. 1994) [although physician barred from participation until he could abide by coding rules, criticism of government for confusing coding requirements]; Practice Management Info. Corp. v. American Med. Ass'n, 877 F. Supp. 1386 & 1394 (C.D. Cal. 1994) [copyright for CPT coding system not lost by use for Medicare purposes].

69. Heckler v. Community Health Servs., 467 U.S. 51 (1984).

70. *E.g.*, United States v. Blue Cross & Blue Shield of Mich., No. L93-1794 (D. Md. Settlement Jan. 10, 1995), *complaint reprinted in* M.M.G. ¶43,019.

71. 42 U.S.C.A. § 1395x(e); 42 C.F.R. pt. 482, *amended by* 59 FED. REG. 64141 (Dec. 13, 1994) [discharge planning required]. There are also conditions of participation for other providers, *e.g.*, 42 C.F.R. §§ 405.1101–405.1137 [skilled nursing facilities]. All hospitals that participate in Medicare must also participate in CHAMPUS. 32 C.F.R. § 199.6(a)(8)(ii).

72. 42 U.S.C.A. §§ 1395aa, 1395bb; Cospito v. Heckler, 742 F.2d 72 (3d Cir. 1984), *cert. denied*, 471 U.S. 1131 (1985) [not improper delegation to Joint Commission because HHS retains ultimate authority].

73. *E.g.*, Garelick v. Sullivan, 987 F.2d 913 (2d Cir.), *cert. denied*, 114 S. Ct. 78 (U.S. 1993) [fee limits not a taking].

74. 42 U.S.C.A. § 1395u(b)(3)(G), 1395u(j).

75. *E.g.*, Medical Soc'y of N.Y. State v. Cuomo, 976 F.2d 812 (2d Cir. 1992) [no pre-emption of state statute forbidding balanced billing of Medicare]; Pennsylvania Med. Soc'y v. Marconis, 942 F.2d 842 (3d Cir. 1991).

76. *E.g*, In re Westchester County Med. Ctr., No. 91-504-2 (H.H.S. Sept. 29, 1992), *as discussed in* 2 H.L.R. 61 (1993) [revocation of participation of hospital ordered for violation of Rehabilitation Act by restricting HIV-positive worker, but case settled].

77. *E.g.*, Our Lady of Mt. Carmel Hosp. v. Secretary of HEW, Civ. No. 72 CA 84 (W.D. Tex. Oct. 4, 1973), *reprinted in* M.M.G. ¶26,778 [noncompliance with conditions of participation]; Milo Commun. Hosp. v. Weinberger, 525 F.2d 144 (1st Cir. 1975) [noncompliance with Life Safety Code]; Summit Health, Ltd. v. Inspector Gen., No. C-108, dec. 1173 (HHS D.A.B., App. Div. June 29, 1990), *reprinted in* M.M.G. ¶38,653 [exclusion of convalescent hospital after guilty plea to criminal patient neglect].

78. Pub. L. No. 98-21, 97 Stat. 65 (1983).

79. Pub. L. No. 98-21, 97 Stat. 65 (1983) (*codified as amended primarily at* 42 U.S.C.A. § 1395ww); 42 C.F.R. pt. 412.

80. For a list of the DRGs as of October 1, 1994, *see* Table 5, 59 FED. REG. 45447-57 (Sept. 1, 1994). CHAMPUS uses a modified DRG system. 32 C.F.R. § 199.14(a)(1).

81. 42 U.S.C.A. § 1395ww(d)(7); *e.g.*, Little Co. of Mary Hosp. v. Shalala, 24 F.3d 984 (7th Cir. 1994) [no right to hearing after hospital failed to correct its own DRG assignment within 60 days].

82. *See* discussion in 59 FED. REG. 45341 (Sept. 1, 1994).

83. 42 C.F.R. § 412.2(c)(5), *first printed in* 59 FED. REG. 1654 (Jan. 12, 1994).

84. *Close to 4,600 hospitals may face civil prosecution for Medicare claims*, 4 H.L.R. 13 (1995); *Letters to 4,600 hospitals on hold pending federal review, new agreements*, 4 H.L.R. 199 (1995).

85. 42 U.S.C.A. § 1395ww(d)(5)(A); 42 C.F.R. §§ 412.80–412.86.

86. 42 C.F.R. §§ 412.115(a), 413.80; Shalala v. St. Paul-Ramsey Med. Ctr., 50 F.3d 522 (8th Cir. 1995) [independent verification of income and assets of patients not required to qualify for bad debt payment].

87. 42 C.F.R. §§ 412.115(c), 466.78.

88. 42 U.S.C.A. § 1395ww(d)(5)(B), 42 C.F.R. § 413.85 [direct medical education costs]; 42 C.F.R. § 412.100 [kidney acquisition costs].

89. 42 C.F.R. §§ 412.300–412.352, *first printed in* 56 FED. REG. 43358 (Aug. 30, 1991).

90. 42 U.S.C.A. § 1395ww(h); 42 C.F.R. § 412.105.

91. 42 U.S.C.A. § 1395ww(d)(l)(B); 42 C.F.R. § 412.23.

92. 42 U.S.C.A. § 1395ww(d)(5)(F); 42 C.F.R. § 412.106.

93. 42 U.S.C.A. § 1395ww(d)(5)(D), 42 C.F.R. § 412.92; *e.g.*, Macon County Samaritan Mem. Hosp. v. Shalala, 7 F.3d 762 (8th Cir. 1993) [affirming sole community provider criteria].

94. 42 U.S.C.A. § 1395ww(d)(5)(C); 42 C.F.R. § 412.96.

95. 42 U.S.C.A. §1 395ww(d)(5)(D)(v); 42 C.F.R. § 412.109.

96. 42 C.F.R. § 412.4; *see discussion in* 59 FED. REG. 45362-66 (Sept. 1, 1994); and *see Medicare hospital patient transfers improperly reported and paid as hospital discharges*, OIG Report. No. A-06-93-00095 (Feb. 1995), *reprinted in* M.M.G. ¶43139.

97. Sec. of HHS, Report to Congress, *Medicare hospital outpatient prospective payment* (Mar. 1995), *reprinted in* M.M.G. No. 847, pt. 2.

98. Summary, *1995 Annual Reports of the Social Security and Medicare Boards of Trustees*, *reprinted in* M.M.G. ¶43149.

99. 42 U.S.C.A. § 1395mm; 42 C.F.R. pt. 417.

100. *See Medicare risk program payment policy*, in Physician Payment Review Commission, ANNUAL REPORT TO CONGRESS 1995, at 87–112, *reprinted in* M.M.G., No. 847 (1995).

101. *E.g.*, National Kidney Patients Ass'n v. Sullivan, 294 U.S. App. D.C. 269, 958 F.2d 1127 (1992), *cert. denied*, 113 S. Ct. 966 (U.S. 1993).

102. 42 U.S.C.A. §§ 405(h), 1395ff, 1395ii; Michigan Ass'n of Independent Clinical Labs. v. Shalala, 52 F.3d 1340 (6th Cir. 1994).

103. Good Samaritan Hosp. v. Shalala, 113 S. Ct. 2151 (U.S. 1993).

104. Shalala v. Guernsey Mem. Hosp., 115 S. Ct. 1232 (U.S. 1995).

105. 42 U.S.C.A. §§ 1396–1396t.

106. 42 U.S.C.A. § 1396b(w).

107. *E.g.*, Revenue Cabinet v. Smith, 875 S.W.2d 873 (Ky. 1994), *cert. denied*, 115 S. Ct. 509 (U.S. 1994).

108. *U.S. demands repayments from 9 states*, N.Y. TIMES, Jan. 31, 1995, at A9.

109. 42 U.S.C.A. §§ 1381–1383c.

110. 42 U.S.C.A. §§ 601–613.

111. *E.g.*, Norwood Hosp. v. Comm'r of Pub. Welfare, 417 Mass. 54, 627 N.E.2d 914 (1994); *but see* Lewis v. Grinker, 794 F. Supp. 1193 (C.D. N.Y. 1991) [due to status of fetus as citizen, cannot deny Medicaid coverage for prenatal care to financially eligible undocumented aliens], *aff'd*, 965 F.2d 1206 (2d Cir. 1992); *Lewis* criticized in Douglas v. Babcock, 990 F.2d 875 (6th Cir.),

cert. denied, 114 S. Ct. 86 (U.S. 1993) [pregnant women denied Medicaid for noncooperation in determining paternity of previous children].

112. Schweiker v. Wilson, 450 U.S. 221 (1981) [strict scrutiny not applied to Medicaid coverage in public health institutions only under 21 and over 64].

113. Salgado v. Kirschner, 179 Ariz. 301, 878 P.2d 659 (1994), *cert. denied*, 115 S. Ct. 1102 (U.S. 1995).

114. *E.g.*, Evelyn V. v. Kings County Hosp. Ctr., 819 F. Supp. 183 (E.D. N.Y. 1993) [Medicaid Act requirement that state plan provide for maintaining health standards of providers did not authorize suit by recipients against city for deficiencies at municipal hospital]; *contra* Fulkerson v. Comm'r, Maine Dep't of Human Services, 802 F. Supp. 529 (D. Me. 1992) [Medicaid recipients may enforce equal access to care provision]; *see* Chapter 1, note 10.

115. Pub. L. No. 97-35, § 2173 (1981) (*codified as amended* in 42 U.S.C.A. § 1395a(a)(13)(A)).

116. Wilder v. Virginia Hosp. Ass'n, 496 U.S. 498 (1990).

117. *Suits force U.S. and states to pay more for Medicaid*, N.Y. TIMES, Oct. 29, 1991, at A1; R.A. Ringler, *Boren Amendment litigation: An analysis*, 27 J.H.H.L. 65 (1994).

118. *E.g.*, Abbeville Gen. Hosp. v. Ramsey, 3 F.3d 797 (5th Cir. 1993), *cert. denied*, 114 S. Ct. 1542 (U.S. 1994).

119. *E.g.*, Folden v. Washington State Dep't of Social & Health Servs., 981 F.2d 1054 (9th Cir. 1992); Connecticut Hosp. Ass'n v. Weicker, 46 F.3d 211 (2d Cir. 1995).

120. Alexander v. Choate, 469 U.S. 287 (1985).

121. Charleston Mem. Hosp. v. Conrad, 693 F.2d 324 (4th Cir. 1982).

122. *E.g.*, Michigan, M.M.G. ¶15,600; *see also* Presbyterian-Univ. of Pa. Med. Ctr. v. Commonwealth, Dep't of Pub. Welfare, 553 A.2d 1027 (Pa. Commw. Ct. 1989) [Medicaid DRG payment system upheld].

123. Minnesota Ass'n of Health Care Facilities, Inc. v. Minnesota Dep't of Pub. Welfare, 742 F.2d 442 (8th Cir. 1984), *cert. denied*, 469 U.S. 1215 (1985); Highland Chateau, Inc. v. Minnesota Dep't of Pub. Welfare, 356 N.W.2d 804 (Minn. Ct. App. 1984).

124. LaZalla v. Minnesota, 366 N.W.2d 395 (Minn. Ct. App. 1985); *accord* Catir v. Comm'r of Dep't of Human Servs., 543 A.2d 356 (Me. 1988).

125. *NGA report finds 23 states using cost-based reimbursement*, 3 H.L.R. 21 (1994).

126. *E.g.*, Haven Home, Inc. v. Dep't of Pub. Welfare, 216 Neb. 731, 346 N.W.2d 225 (1984). These formulas do not require states to take steps to furnish the specified occupancy, Humphrey v. State, Dep't of Mental Health, 14 Ohio App. 3d 15, 469 N.E.2d 981 (1984).

127. 42 U.S.C.A. § 1396a(a)(23).

128. 42 U.S.C.A. § 1396n(a)(1)(A); *see also* Lackner v. Department of Health Servs., 29 Cal. App. 4th 1760, 35 Cal. Rptr. 2d 482 (1st Dist. 1994), *rev. denied*, 1995 Cal. LEXIS 398 (Jan. 25, 1995) [permissible to enroll persons in managed care if they did not choose an alternative within 30 days of joining].

129. 42 U.S.C.A. § 1396n [§ 1915 of the Social Security Act], which authorizes waivers for two-year periods; 42 U.S.C.A. § 1315 [§ 1115], which authorizes broader waivers for longer time periods for demonstration projects.

130. *E.g.*, Hawaii Health QUEST, Oregon Reform Demonstration, and TennCare Demonstration Project, M.M.G. ¶¶ 41580, 41313, 41908.

131. *E.g.*, Pub. L. No. 100-485, § 507 (1988) [Minnesota].

132. *E.g.*, 60 FED. REG. 4418 (Jan. 23, 1995), 16481 (Mar. 30, 1995), 17791 (April 7, 1995).

133. *Medicaid: Restructuring approaches leave many questions*, No. GAO/HEHS-95-103 (April 1, 1995), *reprinted in* M.M.G. ¶43,153.

134. Jordano v. Steffen, 787 F. Supp. 886, 891 (D. Minn. 1992).

135. *New Jersey plans to cut payments for Medicaid 20%*, N.Y. TIMES, Nov. 23, 1994, at A1; *S&P, New Jersey hospital to discuss Medicaid cuts*, WALL ST. J., Nov. 25, 1994, at A5.

136. 42 U.S.C.A. § 1320a–7b.

137. United States v. Larm, 824 F.2d 780 (9th Cir. 1987), *cert. denied*, 484 U.S. 1078 (1988).

138. 42 U.S.C.A. § 1320a–7a; 42 C.F.R. pt. 1003.

139. Mayers v. United States Dep't of Health & Human Servs., 806 F.2d 995 (11th Cir. 1986), *reh'g denied (en banc)*, 813 F.2d 411 (11th Cir.), *cert denied*, 484 U.S. 822 (1987); *see also* Chapman v. United States Dep't of Health & Human Servs., 821 F.2d 523 (10th Cir. 1987) [$156,318 penalty affirmed]; Scott v. Bowen, 845 F.2d 856 (9th Cir. 1988).

140. United States v. Halter, 490 U.S. 435 (1989).

141. *E.g.*, 18 U.S.C.A. § 286 [conspiracy to defraud the government with respect to a claim]; 18 U.S.C.A. § 287 [fictitious or fraudulent claims]; 18 U.S.C.A. § 371 [conspiracy to commit offense or defraud]; 18 U.S.C.A. § 494 [contractors, bonds, bids, public accords]; 18 U.S.C.A. § 495 [contracts, deeds, and powers of attorney]; 18 U.S.C.A. § 1001 [statements or entries generally]; 18 U.S.C.A. § 1002 [possession of false papers to defraud U.S.], *see* United States v. Radetsky, 535 F.2d 556 (10th Cir.), *cert. denied*, 429 U.S. 820 (1976) [conviction for false Medicare billing under 18 U.S.C.A. §§ 1001, 1002] *overruled in part on other grounds*, United States v. Dailey, 921 F.2d 994 (10th Cir. 1990), *cert. denied*, 502 U.S. 952 (1991); 18 U.S.C.A. § 1341 [mail fraud]; 18 U.S.C.A. §§ 1961–1963 [racketeer influenced, corrupted organizations (RICO)]; 18 U.S.C.A. § 1018 [official certificates, writings]; 18 U.S.C.A. § 1505 [obstruction of proceedings before departments, agencies, committees]; 31 U.S.C.A. § 231 [liability of persons making false claims]; *see also* Brown, *Civil sanctions for Medicare and Medicaid fraud*, 5 HOSP. L. NEWSLETTER, (Pt. 1) Sept. 1988, at 1, (Pt. 2) Oct. 1988, at 1.

142. United States v. Campbell, 845 F.2d 1374 (6th Cir.), *cert. denied*, 488 U.S. 908 (1988) [conviction under 18 U.S.C.A. §§ 287, 1341].

143. *E.g.*, Washoe Med. Ctr., Inc. v. Churchill County, 108 Nev. 622, 836 P.2d 624 (1992) [hospital not entitled to summary determination of county liability where question whether notice given].

144. *E.g.*, University of Utah Hosp. v. Bethke, 101 Id. 245, 611 P.2d 1030 (1980) [Idaho county ordered to pay for emergency services to two indigent county residents].

145. *E.g.*, St. Paul Ramsey County Med. Ctr. v. Pennington County, 857 F.2d 1185 (8th Cir. 1988) [hospital could not collect from county when it had not filed statement of costs]; University of Utah Hosp. v. Minidoka County, 115 Id. 406, 767 P.2d 249 (1989) [claim properly denied because administrative remedies not exhausted]; Middlesex Mem. Hosp. v. Town of North Haven, 206 Conn. 1, 535 A.2d 1303 (1988) [hospital must prove eligibility of recipient]; *but see* Sioux Valley Hosp. Ass'n v. Yankton County, 424 N.W.2d 379 (S.D. 1988) [patient's noncooperation in giving information for application did not justify county denial].

146. *E.g.*, Emanuel Hosp. v. Umatilla County, 314 Or. 393, 840 P.2d 56 (1992); Lutheran Med. Ctr. v. City of Omaha, 229 Neb. 802, 429 N.W.2d 347 (1988); *see also* Borgess Hosp. v. County of Berrien, 114 Mich. App. 385, 319 N.W.2d 354 (1982) [no obligation to pay for care of former prisoner after discharge from jail].

147. *E.g.*, Dade County v. Hospital Affiliates Int'l, Inc., 378 So.2d 43 (Fla. 3d DCA 1979); *but see* Susan B. Allen Mem. Hosp. v. Board of County Comm'rs, 12 Kan. App. 2d 680, 753 P.2d 1302 (1988) [county liable for cost of care of intoxicated person taken into protective custody];

Albany Gen. Hosp. v. Dalton, 69 Or. App. 204, 684 P.2d 34 (1984), *rev. denied*, 298 Or. 68, 688 P.2d 846 (1984) [county responsible for cost of care of person injured in gunfight with police].

148. *E.g.*, *More trouble than he's worth, law says*, N.Y. TIMES, Nov. 26, 1992, at A8 [prosecutor says man accused of theft should be cleared because medical care while in custody costing county too much]; Texas Dep't of Corrections v. Sisters of St. Francis of St. Jude Hosp., 836 S.W.2d 719 (Tex. Ct. App. 1992) [governor's proclamation granting inmate six-month medical reprieve, provided all financial arrangements for care made by inmate or family did not excuse state from responsibility for medical care; inmate did not sign acceptance until after care rendered; hospital did not know of payment condition before rendering services; unconscionable to require waiver of right to medical care as condition of seeking care away from prison; waiver coerced].

149. See *AHA, AMA jointly warn members of billing scam by "silent PPOs,"* 3 H.L.R. 1779 (1994) ["Special membership alert" distributed in Sept. 1994]; B. McCormick, *Where are your discounts?* AM. MED. NEWS, Feb. 6, 1995, at 1.

150. *E.g.*, St. Charles v. Kender, 38 Mass. App. Ct. 155, 646 N.E.2d 411, *rev. denied*, 420 Mass. 1102, 648 N.E.2d 1286 (1995).

151. *E.g.*, *Blue Cross collapse in West Virginia puts many in dire straits*, WALL ST. J., Mar. 8, 1991, at 1A [first collapse of Blue Shield plan, leaving $50 million in unpaid medical bills].

152. *E.g.*, Washington Physicians Serv. v. Marquardt, 67 Wash. App. 650, 838 P.2d 142 (1992).

153. *E.g.*, St. Elizabeth Hosp. Med. Ctr. v. Moliterno, 1991 Ohio App. LEXIS 6040 (Ohio Ct. App. Dec. 11, 1991), *as discussed in* 25 J.H.H.L. 274 (1992), *app. dismissed*, 65 Ohio St.3d 1437, 600 N.E.2d 680 (1992).

154. *E.g.*, 11 U.S.C.A. § 109.

155. *See* discussion in Bankruptcy section of Chapter 6.

156. *E.g.*, In re International Med. Ctrs., Inc., 604 So.2d 505 (Fla. 1st DCA 1992), *rev. dismissed*, 624 So.2d 267 (Fla. 1993).

157. *See supra*, note 150.

158. *E.g.*, Hermann Hosp. v. MEBA Med. & Benefits Plan, 845 F.2d 1286 (5th Cir. 1988); Kennedy v. Deere & Co., 118 Ill. 2d 69, 514 N.E.2d 171 (1987), *cert. denied*, 484 U.S. 1064 (1988); Misic v. Building Serv. Employees Health & Welfare Trust, 789 F.2d 1374 (9th Cir. 1986).

159. *E.g.*, Pritt v. Blue Cross, 699 F. Supp. 81 (S.D. W. Va. 1988).

160. *E.g.*, St. Francis Reg. Med. Ctr. v. Blue Cross & Blue Shield, 49 F.3d 1460 (10th Cir. 1995) [upheld ban on assignment of claims to providers that had not signed contracts with Blue Cross]; Obstetricians–Gynecologists, P.C. v. Blue Cross & Blue Shield, 219 Neb. 199, 361 N.W.2d 550 (1985) [prohibition of assignment enforceable]; Blue Cross Hosp. Serv. v. Frappier, 698 S.W.2d 326 (Mo. 1985) *(en banc)* [state law requiring insurers to accept assignment upheld].

161. Oakland Neurosurgical Arts, P.C. v. Blue Cross & Blue Shield, 135 Mich. App. 798, 356 N.W.2d 267 (1984).

162. Kartell v. Blue Shield, 749 F.2d 922 (1st Cir. 1984), *cert. denied*, 471 U.S. 1029 (1985).

163. *E.g.*, Pro Cardiaco Pronto Socorro Cardiologica S.A. v. Trussell, 863 F. Supp. 135 (S.D. N.Y. 1994).

164. *E.g.*, Allianz Life Ins. Co. v. Riedl, 264 Ga. 395, 444 S.E.2d 736 (1994).

165. *E.g.*, Morehead v. Conley, 75 Ohio App. 3d 409, 599 N.E.2d 786 (1991).

166. *E.g.*, IOWA CODE § 597.14 [both spouses liable for necessary care provided to family members]; St. Francis Reg. Med. Ctr., Inc. v. Bowles, 251 Kan. 334, 836 P.2d 1123 (1992) [both spouses liable for necessary care provided to spouses]; Richland Mem. Hosp. v. Burton, 282 S.C. 159, 318 S.E.2d 12 (1984) [both spouses liable for necessary care provided to spouses]; Richland

Mem. Hosp. v. English, 295 S.C. 511, 369 S.E.2d 395 (Ct. App. 1988) [common-law wife also obligated for necessary care to husband]; Schilling v. Bedford County Mem. Hosp., 225 Va. 539, 303 S.E.2d 905 (1983) [unconstitutional to require husband to pay for wife, but not wife for husband, so neither obligated; ruling partially reversed by VA. CODE § 55-37 (1986)]; *contra* Shands Teaching Hosp. & Clinics, Inc. v. Smith, 497 So.2d 644 (Fla. 1986) [wife not obligated to pay for husband's expenses, but husband obligated to pay for wife's].

167. *E.g.*, Ex parte Odem, 537 So.2d 919 (Ala. 1988) [minor mother may contract for care of her minor child as necessary service, but not bound by attorney fee provision of contract].

168. *E.g.*, Sentry Investigations, Inc. v. Davis, 841 P.2d 732 (Utah Ct. App. 1992) [noncustodial parent not responsible for cost of care arranged by custodial parent]; Inter Valley Health Plan v. Blue Cross/Blue Shield, 16 Cal. App. 4th 60, 19 Cal. Rptr. 2d 782 (4th Dist. 1993), *rev. denied*, 1993 Cal. LEXIS 4438 (Cal. Aug. 19, 1993), *cert. denied*, 114 S. Ct. 881 (U.S. 1994) [father's plan primarily responsible for cost of bone marrow transplant, chemotherapy because divorce decree required father to maintain child as beneficiary under his employment policy].

169. Wagoner v. Joe Mater & Assocs., Inc., 461 N.E.2d 706 (Ind. Ct. App. 1984) [noncustodial parent not required to pay despite support order because willing to pay for care at other location, but opposed particular provider]; *but see* Ex parte Davila, 709 S.W.2d 15 (Tex. Ct. App. 1986) [noncustodial father could be imprisoned for contempt for failure to pay hospital for child's treatment].

170. *E.g.*, Trinity Medical Ctr., Inc. v. Rubbelke, 389 N.W.2d 805 (N.D. 1986) [secondary liability of adult children, so release of patient, spouse released adult children].

171. *E.g.*, Service Fin. Corp. v. Hall, No. CA 86-123 (Ark. Ct. App. Oct. 22, 1986), *as discussed in* 20 HOSP. L. 79 (1987) [financial responsibility agreement not valid when signer believed it to be general consent form]; Memorial Hosp. v. Baumann, 100 A.D.2d 701, 474 N.Y.S.2d 636 (3d Dep't 1984) [daughter not bound by signed commitment to pay because no evidence she intended to be personally bound]; Rohrscheib v. Helena Hosp. Ass'n, 12 Ark. App. 6, 670 S.W.2d 812 (1984) [brother-in-law who signed admission form not personally responsible for bill because it did not contain express promise to pay]; McCarthy v. Weaver, 99 A.D.2d 652, 472 N.Y.S.2d 64 (4th Dep't 1984) [form ambiguous because it contained both promise to pay expenses not covered by insurance and promise to pay all expenses]; Texas County Mem. Found., Inc. v. Ramsey, 677 P.2d 665 (Okla. Ct. App. 1984) [promise by son to pay for nursing home care for indefinite term could be revoked with 30 days' notice]; *see also* Orthopedic & Reconstructive Surgery, S.C. v. Kezelis, 146 Ill. App. 3d 227, 496 N.E.2d 1112 (1st Dist. 1986) [payment contract between hospital and patient did not encompass surgical corporation].

172. 42 U.S.C.A. § 1395dd(d)(2)(B).

173. In re Senior Care Properties, Inc., 161 Bankr. 294 (Bankr. N.D. Fla. 1993).

174. 29 U.S.C.A. § 1144(a).

175. 29 U.S.C.A. § 1144(b)(2)(A).

176. 29 U.S.C.A. § 1144(b)(2)(B).

177. *E.g.*, Gemini Physical Therapy & Rehab. v. State Farm Mut. Auto. Ins. Co., 40 F.3d 63 (3d Cir. 1994).

178. *E.g.*, Swerhun v. Guardian Life Ins. Co., 979 F.2d 195 (11th Cir. 1992).

179. *E.g.*, Bolding v. Prudential Ins. Co., 841 P.2d 628 (Okl. Ct. App. 1992) [policy covering "local" transportation covered air ambulance to out-of-state clinic; "local" not defined in contract]; Davis v. Selectcare, Inc., 834 F. Supp. 197 (E.D. Mich. 1993) ["investigational" in FEHBP was ambiguous as applied to HBCT/ABMT].

180. Winters v. Costco Wholesale Corp., 49 F.3d 550 (9th Cir. 1995).

181. Saltarelli v. Bob Baker Group Med. Trust, 35 F.3d 382 (9th Cir. 1994).

182. *E.g.*, Brown v. Snohomish County Physicians Corp., 120 Wash. 2d 747, 845 P.2d 334 (1993) [exclusion of services covered by uninsured motorist coverage against public policy].

183. *E.g.*, Time Ins. Co. v. Bishop, 245 Va. 48, 425 S.E.2d 489 (1993).

184. *E.g.*, Ramsey v. Colonial Life Ins. Co., 12 F.3d 472 (5th Cir. 1994).

185. *E.g.*, Gilley v. Protective Life Ins. Co., 17 F.3d 775 (5th Cir. 1994) [insured under single person policy sought coverage of baby, but under policy no coverage until day baby released from hospital].

186. 29 U.S.C.A. §§ 1161–1168; Branch v. G. Bernd Co., 955 F.2d 1574 (11th Cir. 1992) [election of COBRA coverage retroactively covers intervening care].

187. *E.g.*, Decatur Mem. Hosp. v. Connecticut Gen. Life Ins. Co., 990 F.2d 925 (7th Cir. 1993).

188. *E.g.*, Bullwinkel v. New England Mut. Life Ins. Co., 18 F.3d 429 (7th Cir. 1994).

189. *E.g.*, American Republic Ins. Co. v. Superintendent of Ins., 647 A.2d 1195 (Me. 1994), *cert. denied*, 115 S. Ct. 1399 (U.S. 1995).

190. Chapter v. Monfort of Colo., Inc., 20 F.3d 286 (7th Cir. 1994); *Drunken drivers may find insurance won't pay the bills for their injuries*, WALL ST. J., July 6, 1995, at B1.

191. *E.g.*, Blair v. Metropolitan Life Ins. Co., 974 F.2d 1219 (10th Cir. 1992) [treatment of traumatic temporal mandibular joint injury by dentist not excluded].

192. *E.g.*, Tabor v. Prudential Ins. Co., 830 F. Supp. 510 (E.D. Mo. 1993) [coverage for out-of-network cancer surgery performed where dependent student was in college properly denied because not an emergency].

193. *E.g.*, Farley v. Benefit Trust Life Ins. Co., 979 F.2d 653 (8th Cir. 1992) [Denial affirmed. Not medically necessary]; Annotation, *What services, equipment, or supplies are "medically necessary" for purposes of coverage under medical insurance*, 75 A.L.R. 4TH 763.

194. *E.g.*, Blue Cross & Blue Shield of Va. v. Keller, 450 S.E.2d 136 (Va. 1994) [proper exercise of administrative discretion in medical necessity review of psychiatric hospitalization].

195. *E.g.*, Florence Nightingale Nursing Serv., Inc. v. Blue Cross & Blue Shield, 41 F.3d 1476 (11th Cir.), *cert. denied*, 115 S. Ct. 2002 (U.S. 1995).

196. C. Culhane, *Medicare denial rates vary widely: Carriers inconsistent in judging medical necessity*, AM. MED. NEWS, Apr. 18, 1994, at 3.

197. Barnett v. Kaiser Found. Health Plan, Inc., 32 F.3d 413 (9th Cir. 1994).

198. 60 FED. REG. 6537 (Feb. 2, 1995); *HCFA announces new lung transplant payment policy*, AM. MED. NEWS, Mar. 20, 1995, at 5.

199. Annotation, *Propriety of denial of medical or hospital benefits for investigative, educational, or experimental medical procedures pursuant to exclusion contained in ERISA-covered health plan*, 122 A.L.R. FED. 1.

200. *E.g.*, Loyola Univ. of Chicago v. Humana Ins. Co., 996 F.2d 895 (7th Cir. 1993) [upholding denial of insurance coverage for all treatment associated with artificial heart implant, Jarvik-7]; *contra* Doe v. Group Hospitalization & Med. Servs., 3 F.3d 80 (4th Cir. 1993) [proper to exclude coverage of transplant, but not related chemotherapy].

201. *E.g.*, *Health insurers embrace eye-of-newt therapy*, WALL ST. J., Jan. 30, 1995, at B1.

202. Texas v. The Prudential Ins. Co., No. CA A-93-CV-658-SS (W.D. Tex. settlement Mar. 21, 1994), *as discussed in* 3 H.L.R. 384 (1994); *see also Disability law used to order treatment*, WALL ST. J., July 28, 1995, at B3 [federal appellate court found employer in violation of Americans with Disabilities Act for adopting health plan that excluded experimental breast cancer treatment; company, not insurer, ordered to pay for treatment].

203. *E.g.*, Mire v. Blue Cross & Blue Shield, 43 F.3d 567 (11th Cir. 1994) [policy covered procedure for specific diseases not including this disease].

204. Lubeznik v. Healthchicago, Inc., 268 Ill. App. 3d 953, 644 N.E.2d 777 (1994).

205. Easley by Easley v. Snider, 36 F.3d 297 (3d Cir. 1994) [requirement complies with Americans with Disabilities Act because allowing surrogates would not be reasonable accommodation].

206. *E.g.*, J. Johnsson, *California governor signs managed care protections*, AM. MED. NEWS, Oct. 3, 1994, at 8 [criteria disclosure].

207. *E.g.*, L. Oberman, *Aetna opens its review criteria to doctors for inspection*, AM. MED. NEWS, Dec. 13, 1993, at 9.

208. G. Borzo, *Illinois Blues: If you sign contract, you follow guidelines*, AM. MED. NEWS, Dec. 6, 1993, at 8.

209. *E.g.*, B. McCormick, *When coverage decisions threaten care*, AM. MED. NEWS, Feb. 20, 1995, at 1 [disciplinary case against Ariz. HMO medical director stopped by lawsuit filed by HMO against licensing board; first attempt to sanction doctor who denied coverage for a service in managed care setting]; J. Johnsson, *Dad's protests lead to record fine against California HMO*, AM. MED. NEWS, Dec. 12, 1994, at 1 [$500,000 state fine for quality violations, endangering life of patient by denying specialty referral].

210. *E.g.*, Taylor v. Hender, 116 Or. App. 142, 840 P.2d 1331 (1992) [insurers retained experts to evaluate chiropractors to assist in controlling costs; no state RICO claim stated against experts, no inference of fraudulent scheme or artifice].

211. *E.g.*, Colleton Regional Hosp. v. MRS Medical Review Systems, Inc., 866 F. Supp. 896 (D. S.C. 1994) [hospitals cannot sue utilization review firm for allegedly inducing plan not to pay for services due to ERISA preemption].

212. *E.g.*, *External appeal of UR decisions seems headed for enactment in Virginia*, 4 H.L.R. 227 (1995) [R.I. enacted external review in 1992, effective Jan. 1, 1993, but only 20–25 reviews in 1994]; *State senate sends bill to governor that permits review of UR decisions*, 4 H.L.R. 285 (1995) [Virginia is second state with external review process for treatment denials].

213. Gulf South Med. & Surgical Inst. v. Aetna Life Ins. Co., 39 F.3d 520 (5th Cir. 1994).

214. McGann v. H. & H. Music Co., 946 F.2d 401 (5th Cir. 1991), *cert. denied sub nom.* Greenberg v. H. & H. Music Co., 113 S. Ct. 482 (U.S. 1992) [ERISA does not bar employer from reducing AIDS benefits from $1,000,000 to $5,000 where plan allowed changes].

215. Carparts Distribution Ctr., Inc. v. Automotive Wholesaler's Ass'n, 37 F.3d 12 (1st Cir. 1994).

216. *E.g.*, Bankers Life & Casualty Co. v. Peterson, 263 Mont. 156, 866 P.2d 241 (1993) [exclusion of normal pregnancy from individual major medical insurance policy violates state sex discrimination law].

217. *E.g.*, Rosen v. Blue Cross, No. C93-843 Z (W.D. Wash. Apr. 28, 1994), *as discussed in* 3 H.L.R. 601 (1994) [settlement of suit alleging insurer did not pass on savings from rates negotiated with providers in calculating copayments]; In re Humana Health Ins. Co. of Fla. (D.O.I. Case No. 92-L-013JEH, order to show cause filed 1/10/92; Dept. of Legal Affairs Investigative Case No. 92-H-14-91), *as discussed in* 3 H.L.R. 764 (1994) [$6.25 million settlement of overcharges to patients treated at Humana hospitals due to copayments being calculated based on gross, not net, hospital bill].

218. *E.g.*, Parrish v. Lamm, 758 P.2d 1356 (Colo. 1988) [upholding law]; Annotation, *Validity of state statute prohibiting health providers from the practice of waiving patient's obligation to pay health insurance deductibles or copayments, or advertising such practice*, 8 A.L.R. 5TH 855.

219. *E.g.*, Principal Health Care v. Lewer Agency, Inc., 38 F.3d 240 (5th Cir. 1994).

220. 42 U.S.C.A. § 1395dd(h).

221. Inman v. HMO Colo., Inc., No. 88-1625 (10th Cir. Jan. 3, 1989), *as discussed in* 17 HEALTH L. DIG., Mar. 1989, at 13.

222. *E.g.*, St. Joseph's Hosp. v. Reserve Life Ins. Co., 154 Ariz. 307, 742 P.2d 808 (1987); *accord* Hermann Hosp. v. Nat'l Standard Ins. Co., 776 S.W.2d 249 (Tex. Ct. App. 1989).

223. Crown Life Ins. Co. v. McBride, 517 So.2d 660 (Fla. 1987).

224. *E.g.*, Thomas v. Gulf Health Plan, Inc., 688 F. Supp. 590 (S.D. Ala. 1988) [precertification of bone marrow harvesting did not estop denial of coverage for high-dose chemotherapy with bone marrow transplantation].

225. *E.g.*, Decatur Mem. Hosp. v. Connecticut Gen. Life Ins. Co., 990 F.2d 925 (7th Cir. 1993).

226. *E.g.*, Vershaw v. Northwestern Nat'l Life Ins. Co., 979 F.2d 557 (7th Cir, 1992).

227. Lordmann Enters., Inc. v. Equicor, Inc., 32 F.3d 1529 (11th Cir. 1994).

228. The Meadows v. Employers Health Ins. Co., 47 F.3d 1006 (9th Cir. 1995).

229. *E.g.*, Eugenia Hosp. v. Young Ja Kim, 844 F. Supp. 1030 (E.D. Pa. 1994); *accord* Faith Hosp. Ass'n v. Blue Cross & Blue Shield, 857 S.W.2d 352 (Mo. Ct. App. 1993).

230. McDaniel v. Blue Cross & Blue Shield, 780 F. Supp. 1360 & 1363 (S.D. Ala. 1991), *aff'd*, 977 F.2d 599 (11th Cir. 1992).

231. *E.g.*, Mimbs v. Commercial Life Ins. Co., 832 F. Supp. 354 (S.D. Ga. 1993) [deny dismissal of claim that insurer breached its duty by refusing to confirm coverage, so that patient delayed opportunity for cardiac bypass surgery].

232. Lozier v. Leonard, 173 Ga. App. 697, 327 S.E.2d 815 (1985).

233. Children's Hosp. v. Crum, No. 94APE01-88, 1994 Ohio App. LEXIS 4078 (Ohio Ct. App. Sept. 13, 1994), *as discussed in* 28 J.H.H.L. 125 (1995).

234. *E.g.*, FLA. STAT. § 395.015.

235. 31 U.S.C.A. §§ 3729–3731; *see* J.C. West, *The False Claims Act: Potential liability for health care providers for fraud and abuse and beyond*, 28 J.H.H.L. 15 (1995).

236. *E.g.*, United States v. Lorenzo, 768 F. Supp. 1127 (E.D. Pa. 1991); United States v. Krizek, 859 F. Supp. 5 (D. D.C. 1994).

237. 31 U.S.C.A. § 3730(b).

238. *E.g.*, Cooper v. Blue Cross & Blue Shield of Florida, Inc., 19 F.3d 562 (11th Cir. 1994).

239. 18 U.S.C.A. § 1341; United States v. Woodely, 9 F.3d 74 (9th Cir. 1993) [mail fraud conviction for Medicare claims by nursing home]; United States v. Migliaccio, 34 F.3d 1517 (10th Cir. 1994) [conviction of doctors for mail fraud for sending false CHAMPUS claims reversed and new trial ordered. Alleged misrepresentation of surgical procedures performed. Inadequate jury instructions].

240. *E.g.*, United States v. Hooshmand, 931 F.2d 725 (11th Cir. 1991).

241. United States v. Milligan, 17 F.3d 177 (6th Cir.), *cert. denied*, 115 S. Ct. 211 (U.S. 1994); *Health-care system is issue in jailing of uninsured patient*, N.Y. TIMES, Jan. 8, 1993, at A7.

242. Lara v. Kern County Bd. of Supervisors, 59 Cal. App. 3d 399, 130 Cal. Rptr. 668 (5th Dist. 1976).

243. *E.g.*, Stein v. Feingold, 629 So.2d 998 (Fla. 3d DCA 1993); *see also* Harris v. Stein, 615 N.Y.S.2d 703 (A.D. 2d Dep't 1994) [malpractice suit barred by judgment in prior suit].

244. *E.g.*, Hale v. Blue Cross & Blue Shield, 862 S.W.2d 905 (Ky. Ct. App. 1993) [one-year limit on lawsuits to recover benefits in group health benefits contract valid].

245. FLA. STAT. § 95.03, *but see* Burroughs Corp. v. Suntogs of Miami, Inc., 472 So.2d 1166 (Fla. 1985) [permitting contractual choice of law of state permitting shortening].

246. 15 U.S.C.A. §§ 1671–1677.

247. Wells v. St. Luke's Mem. Hosp. Ctr., 129 A.D.2d 952, 515 N.Y.S.2d 335 (3d Dep't), *appeal denied*, 70 N.Y.2d 605, 519 N.Y.S.2d 1029, 513 N.E.2d 1309 (1987).

248. Stafford v. Neurological Med., Inc., 811 F.2d 470 (8th Cir. 1987).

249. 15 U.S.C.A. §§ 1692–1692o.

250. *E.g.*, Forsyth Mem. Hosp. Inc. v. Contreras, 107 N.C. App. 611, 421 S.E.2d 167 (1992), *rev. denied*, 333 N.C. 344, 426 S.E.2d 705 (1993 [collection letter by hospital holding company sent on letterhead of attorney did not violate state collection law].

251. Venes v. Professional Serv. Bureau, Inc., 353 N.W.2d 671 (Minn. Ct. App. 1984); *see also* United States v. ACB Sales & Serv., Inc., 683 F. Supp. 734 (D. Ariz. 1987) [each officer fined $25,000, home office fined $150,000 for collection violations after Federal Trade Commission compliance order]; Bieber v. Associated Collection Servs., 631 F. Supp. 1410 (D. Kan. 1986).

252. *E.g.*, Heintz v. Jenkins, 115 S. Ct. 1489 (U.S. 1995) [FDCPA applies to lawyer even when engaged in litigation for creditor client].

253. 15 U.S.C.A. §§ 1681–1681t.

254. *E.g.*, Ippolito v. WNS, Inc., 864 F.2d 440 (7th Cir. 1988), *cert. dismissed*, 490 U.S. 1061 (1989).

255. *E.g.*, In re Estate of Cooper, 125 Ill. 2d 363, 532 N.E.2d 236 (1988) [hospital lien attached to money used to obtain structured settlement annuity]; Woods v. Baptist Med. Ctr., 890 P.2d 1367 (Okl. Ct. App. 1995) [foreclosure of hospital lien].

256. 11 U.S.C.A. § 362(a), (h).

257. 11 U.S.C.A. § 524(a).

258. Medico-Dental Adjustment Bureau v. Ruiz, No. MC-44033 (Cal. Mun. Ct. San Luis Obispo County Aug. 31, 1993), *as discussed in* "Year in Review" from 1994 Annual Meeting of American Academy of Hospital Attorneys.

259. 15 U.S.C.A. §§ 1601–1667e; 12 C.F.R. pt. 226.

260. Hahn v. Hank's Ambulance Serv., Inc., 787 F.2d 543 (11th Cir.), *reh'g denied*, 792 F.2d 1126 (11th Cir. 1986) [$5 ambulance charge for not paying at time of service was not "credit," not subject to Act].

261. 42 U.S.C.A. §§ 291a–291o-1.

262. 42 C.F.R. pt. 124; American Hosp. Ass'n v. Schweicker, 721 F.2d 170 (7th Cir. 1983), *cert denied*, 466 U.S. 958 (1984).

263. 42 C.F.R. § 124.603.

264. *E.g.*, U.S. v. Coweta County Hosp. Auth., 777 F.2d 667 (11th Cir. 1985).

265. *E.g.*, Falmouth Hosp. v. Lopes, 376 Mass. 580, 382 N.E.2d 1042 (1978) [not a defense]; *contra* Creditors Protective Ass'n, Inc. v. Flack, 93 Or. App. 719, 763 P.2d 756 (1988) [defense permitted].

266. *Nonprofit hospitals see increase in gifts*, AM. MED. NEWS, June 13, 1994, 26 [$1.92 billion in cash in 1993; $3.3 billion total]; *Cash donations to hospitals increase 22%*, 19 MOD. HEALTHCARE, June 16, 1989, at 14 [$1.9 billion in cash gifts in 1988, a 22 percent increase over 1987].

267. 26 U.S.C.A. § 170(f)(8).

268. For an example of trouble selling bonds for a health facility, *see* Ford v. First Mun. Leasing Corp., 838 F.2d 994 (8th Cir. 1988) [prospective bond purchasers' failure to purchase not a breach of contract].

269. 26 U.S.C.A. § 103.

270. 26 U.S.C.A. §§ 141, 145, 147–149.

271. Rev. Proc. 93-17, 93-19 [limits on term of contract and compensation arrangements]; *IRS issues proposed regulations on private activity bond restrictions*, 59 FED. REG. 67658 (Dec. 30, 1994) [to replace Rev. Proc. 93-17, 93-19].

272. 26 U.S.C.A. § 141(b); IRS Notice 87-69, 1987-2 C.B. 378.

273. *E.g.*, Manning v. Sevier County, 30 Utah 2d 305, 517 P.2d 549 (1973); *contra* Board of County Comm'rs v. Idaho Health Care Facilities Auths., 96 Id. 498, 531 P.2d 588 (1975).

274. 26 U.S.C.A. § 149(a).

275. 15 U.S.C.A. § 77c(a)(2), (4); Securities & Exch. Comm'n v. Children's Hosp., 214 F. Supp. 883 (D. Ariz. 1963) [exemption does not apply when substantial purpose of hospital is profit for promoters].

276. S.B. Kite, *SEC mandates secondary market disclosure for 501(c)(3) bonds*, 4 H.L.R. 256 (1995) [effective July 3, 1995, ongoing disclosure requirements by beneficiaries of tax-exempt bonds, including annual information and notices of designated events].

277. *E.g.*, PLR No. 9427025 (Apr. 11, 1994); *Hospital sale to for-profit firm requires bond redemption in 90 days*, 3 H.L.R. 971 (1994); *but see* PLR No. 9419022 (Feb. 10, 1994); *Hospital's lease to private entity does not change county bonds' status*, 3 H.L.R. 675 (1994).

278. Trepel v. Pontiac Osteopathic Hosp., 135 Mich. App. 361, 354 N.W.2d 341 (1984).

279. *E.g.*, Travelers Ins. Co. v. Liljeberg Enters., Inc., 38 F.3d 1404 (5th Cir. 1994) [suit by Travelers seeking seizure, judicial sale of St. Jude Medical Office Building].

280. 12 U.S.C.A. § 1715z–7.

281. 7 U.S.C.A. §§ 1926, 1932.

282. Shapiro v. American Home Assur. Co., 584 F. Supp. 1245 (D. Mass. 1984); *accord* INA Underwriters Ins. Co. v. D.H. Forde & Co., 630 F. Supp. 76 (W.D. N.Y. 1985); *but see* Shapiro v. American Home Assur. Co., 616 F. Supp. 900 (D. Mass. 1984) [innocent directors protected under policy that had severability clause].

283. *E.g.*, FLA. STAT. § 395.041.

284. Joint Commission on Accreditation of Healthcare Organizations, 1995 Comprehensive Accreditation Manual for Hospitals, at 240–42.

285. *E.g.*, Revenue Cabinet v. Smith, 875 S.W.2d 873 (Ky.), *cert. denied*, 115 S. Ct. 509 (U.S. 1994).

286. New York State Conf. of Blue Cross & Blue Shield Plans v. Travelers Ins. Co., 115 S. Ct. 1671 (U.S. 1995).

287. *E.g.*, Benton County v. Allen, 170 Or. 481, 133 P.2d 991 (1943) [reorganized hospital not tax exempt].

288. Utah County by County Bd. of Equalization v. Intermountain Health Care, Inc., 709 P.2d 265 (Utah 1985); Rammell & Parsons, *Utah County v. Intermountain Health Care: Utah's unique method for determining charitable property tax exemptions—A review of its mandate and impact*, 22 J.H.H.L. 73 (1989); Howell v. County Bd. of Cache County, 881 p.2d 880 (Utah 1994), [upholding Utah State Tax Comm'n standards for charitable property tax exemption].

289. School Dist. v. Hamot Med. Ctr., 144 Pa. Commw. 668, 602 A.2d 407 (1992), *applying standard adopted in* Hospital Utilization Project v. Commonwealth, 507 Pa. 1, 487 A.2d 1306 (1985); *Challenge to Erie hospital's tax status gains attention of cash-poor U.S. cities*, WALL ST. J., Feb. 16, 1990, at B4A.

290. Missouri Pac. Hosp. Ass'n v. Pulaski County, 211 Ark. 9, 199 S.W.2d 329 (1947).

291. *E.g.*, Callaway Community Hosp. Ass'n v. Craighead, 759 S.W.2d 253 (Mo. Ct. App. 1988); Downtown Hosp. Ass'n v. Tennessee State Bd. of Equalization, 760 S.W.2d 954 (Tenn. Ct. App. 1988).

292. Georgia Osteopathic Hosp. v. Alford, 217 Ga. 663, 124 S.E.2d 402 (1962); Utah County by County Bd. of Equalization v. Intermountain Health Care, Inc., 709 P.2d 265 (Utah 1985).

293. St. Joseph Hosp. v. Bohler, 229 Ga. 577, 193 S.E.2d 603 (1972).

294. *E.g.*, Department of Revenue v. Gallatin Outpatient Clinic, Inc., 234 Mont. 425, 763 P.2d 1128 (1988) [equipment in outpatient clinic not eligible for hospital exemption from personal property tax].

295. *E.g.*, Cole Hosp., Inc. v. Champaign County Bd. of Review, 113 Ill. App. 3d 96, 446 N.E.2d 562 (4th Dist. 1983) [sale-and-leaseback as a financing device did not destroy exemption]; *see* Annotation, *Property tax: exemption of property leased by and used for purposes of otherwise tax-exempt body*, 55 A.L.R. 3D 430.

296. City of Louisville v. Presbyterian Orphans Home Soc'y, 299 Ky. 566, 186 S.W.2d 194 (1945).

297. *E.g.*, FLA. STAT. § 196.192(2).

298. *E.g.*, Appeal of Lanchester Med. Ctr. Ass'n, 23 Pa. Commw. 596, 353 A.2d 75 (1976) [physician office not exempt]; North Shore Med. Ctr., Inc. v. Bystrom, 461 So.2d 167 (Fla. 3d DCA 1984) [physician office not exempt]; *but see* Calais Hosp. v. City of Calais, 138 Me. 234, 24 A.2d 489 (1942) [physician office exempt].

299. Dade County Taxing Auth. v. Cedars of Lebanon Hosp. Corp., Inc., 355 So.2d 1202 (Fla. 1978) [building must be in use]; Cleveland Mem. Med. Found. v. Perk, 10 Ohio St. 2d 72, 225 N.E.2d 233 (1967) [property exempt when plans complete]; *see* Annotation, *Prospective use for tax-exempt purposes as entitling property to tax exemption*, 54 A.L.R. 3d 9.

300. Presbyterian–Univ. of Pa. Medical Ctr. v. Board of Revision, 24 Pa. Commw. 461, 357 A.2d 696 (1976) [tennis court, nurse housing, open area between exempt]; MINN. STAT. § 272.02(3) [recreational facilities not exempt]; Sioux Valley Hosp. v. South Dakota State Bd. of Equalization, 513 N.W.2d 562 (S.D. 1994), [hospital-sponsored wellness center not entitled to property tax exemption].

301. Allegheny Gen. Hosp. v. Board of Property Assessment, 207 Pa. Super. 266, 217 A.2d 796 (1966) [parking building exempt]; Lynn Hosp. v. Board of Assessors, 383 Mass. 14, 417 N.E.2d 14 (1981) [portion of parking building used for private practice not exempt].

302. Evangelical Hosp. Ass'n v. Novak, 125 Ill. App. 3d 439, 465 N.E.2d 986 (2d Dist. 1984).

303. Community Hosp. Linen Servs., Inc. v. Commissioner of Taxation, 309 Minn. 447, 245 N.W.2d 190 (1976).

304. *E.g.*, *Philadelphia non-profits asked to make voluntary payments in lieu of taxes*, 3 H.L.R. 971 (1994) [for payment of 40 percent of taxes that would otherwise be owed, city will not challenge exemption of hospitals that sign up]; Larkin, *Financial success may invite local tax scrutiny*, 62 HOSPS., Oct. 5, 1988, at 30.

305. *E.g.*, FLA. STAT. § 212.08; *see* Annotation, *Exemption of charitable or educational organization from sales or use tax*, 53 A.L.R. 3D 748.

306. *E.g.*, FLA. STAT. § 212.08(2); *but see* Medcat Leasing Co. v. Whiley, 253 Ill. App. 3d 801 (4th Dist. 1993), [upholding denial of exemption for CT scanner from use tax as not being within medical appliance exemption]; Mississippi State Tax Comm'n v. Medical Devices, 624 So.2d 987 (Miss. 1993) [sale of enteral feeding systems to Medicare patient not exempt from sales tax]; *see* Annotation, *Sales and use tax exemption for medical supplies*, 30 A.L.R. 5TH 494.

307. *E.g.*, M.S. Osher, M.D. & R.S. Kerstine, M.D., Inc. v. Limbach, 65 Ohio St.3d 312, 603 N.E.2d 997 (1992) [sale of intraocular lens by manufacturer to ophthalmologist for implantation is not retail sale subject to excise tax; exemption for articles sold for resale in same form received].

308. Carle Found. v. United States, 611 F.2d 1192 (7th Cir. 1979), *cert. denied*, 449 U.S. 824 (1980); Rev. Rul. 85-109, 1985-2 C.B. 165; *but see* PLR 83-49006 [profits from drug sales to patients of hospital-based group practice integrally part of hospital operations not unrelated business income].

309. *E.g.*, PLR No. 9445024 (Aug. 16, 1994); *Hospital's respiratory care contracts do not generate taxable business income*, 3 H.L.R. 1730 (1994) [contracts with skilled nursing facilities to provide services directly through hospital employees].

310. *E.g.*, Curtis v. C.I.R., No. 8310-91 (U.S. Tax Court Jan. 11, 1994), *as discussed in* 22 HEALTH L. DIG., Feb. 1994, at 68 ["salary" paid to key organizer of psychiatric evaluation practice

exceeded reasonable compensation and thus corporate earnings distribution]; Klamath Med. Serv. Bureau v. C.I.R., 29 T.C. 339 (1957), *aff'd*, 261 F.2d 842 (9th Cir. 1958), *cert. denied*, 359 U.S. 966 (1959).

311. IRS Tech. Adv. Mem. No. 9412002 (Dec. 17, 1993).

312. Rev. Rul. 68-27, 1968-1 C.B. 315.

313. *E.g.*, United States v. Wisconsin Power & Light Co., 38 F.3d 329 (7th Cir. 1994) [discussion of weight given to various levels of IRS pronouncements].

314. *E.g.*, Rev. Rul. 73-417, 1973-2 C.B. 332 [pathologist/hospital laboratory director with guaranteed minimum salary who cannot work for other hospitals is employee]; Rev. Rul. 70-629, 1970-2 C.B. 228 [full-time associate physician providing services in office furnished by partnership and under their control was employee]; Tech. Adv. Mem. No. 9508004 (Nov. 17, 1994) [mental health worker performing crisis intervention for local government an employee for federal employment tax purposes]; PLR No. 9149001 (TAM) (July 23, 1991) [physician can be employee of hospital for tax purposes even when state law forbids employment of physicians]; *Are you your own boss? Only if the I.R.S. says so*, N.Y. TIMES, Mar. 19, 1995, at F13.

315. 26 U.S.C.A. § 3403.

316. 26 U.S.C.A. § 501(c)(3).

317. *See* Jeddeloh, *Physician contracts audits: A hospital management tool*, 21 J.H.H.L. 105 (1988).

318. *E.g.*, *GAO investigating hospital executives' compensation at Rep. Dingell's request*, 2 H.L.R. 38 (1993); *see also* Lowry Hosp. Ass'n v. C.I.R., 66 T.C. 850 (1976) [retroactive revocation of hospital's tax exemption due to private inurement to benefit of founding physician].

319. *Healthcare update*, MOD. HEALTHCARE, Feb. 20, 1995, at 28; *see also* Maynard Hosp. v. C.I.R, 52 T.C. 1006 (1969), *supp. op.*, 54 T.C. 1675 (1970) [retroactive revocation of tax exemption of hospital and liability of stockholder–trustees for distributions they received on sale of hospital and related pharmacy that had been transferred to them several years before].

320. Rev. Rul. 69-545, 1969-2 C.B. 117.

321. Eastern Ky. Welfare Rights Org. v. Simon, 165 U.S. App. D.C. 239, 506 F.2d 1278 (1974).

322. Simon v. Eastern Ky. Welfare Rights Org., 426 U.S. 26 (1976).

323. Rev. Rul. 83-157, 1983-2 I.R.B. 94.

324. *E.g.*, PLR 84-42-064 (July 18, 1984).

325. *E.g.*, PLR 88-07-081 (Nov. 30, 1987), *as discussed in* 16 HEALTH L. DIG., Apr. 1988, at 54.

326. Bob Jones Univ. v. Simon, 416 U.S. 725 (1974).

327. *See* K.L. Levine, *IRS application of health care laws: An analysis of IRS enforcement techniques*, 25 J.H.H.L. 334 (1992).

328. Gen. Couns. Mem. 39,326 (Jan. 17, 1985); PLR 9333046 (May 27, 1993).

329 Gen. Couns. Mem. 39,326 (Jan. 17, 1985), IRS POSITIONS REPORTS (CCH) ¶1608.

330. *E.g.*, PLR 85-19-037 (Feb. 12, 1985), *as discussed in* 8 HEALTH L. VIGIL, Aug. 9, 1985, at 10.

331. *See* Gen. Couns. Mem. 39,862 (Nov. 21, 1991) [benefit to hospital not sufficient to justify certain joint ventures that also benefit physicians].

332. PLR # not available (Sept. 29, 1994), 3 H.L.R. 1553 (1994); *Hospital's exempt status not jeopardized by proposed PHO, IRS says*, 3 H.L.R. 1550 (1994) [first PLR on PHOs]; *IRS official clarifies agency view on PHO board representation conditions*, 4 H.L.R. 151 (1995) [for-profit PHOs not subject to 20 percent physician–representation limit; up to 50 percent control probably acceptable if proportional to their investment].

333 *E.g.*, *IRS' Thrasher outlines problems uncovered in audits of hospitals*, 3 H.L.R. 609 (1994).

334. *IRS-HHS agreement calls for caution, experts warn*, 19 MOD. HEALTHCARE, June 2, 1989, at 10; Homer, *Feds staging tag-team attack on physician-hospital ties*, 19 MOD. HEALTHCARE, Oct. 6, 1989, at 56.

335. Geisinger Health Plan v. C.I.R., 985 F.2d 1210 (3d Cir. 1993).

336. Geisinger Health Plan v. C.I.R., 30 F.3d 494 (3d Cir. 1994).

337. 2 H.L.R. 253 (1993) [foundation-type IDS affiliated with a university medical center].

338. 2 H.L.R. 429 (1993) [foundation-type IDS affiliated with a tax-exempt parent of a multihospital system].

339. *Entity operating physician clinic gets tax exemption in third IDS ruling*, 3 H.L.R. 55 (1994); J. Johnsson, *Montana foundation 1st to test new IRS safe harbor*, AM. MED. NEWS, Feb. 7, 1994, at 6 [direct employment model IDS affiliated with hospital].

340. 3 H.L.R. 498 (1994) [direct employment model IDS affiliated with hospital].

341 *IRS issues landmark determinations on creation of regional health network*, 2 H.L.R. 1191 (1993) [Sept. 1, 1993, letter to Northwestern Healthcare Network, Chicago granting tax exemption to superparent as an integral part, unusual example of double derivative exempt status].

342. J. Somerville, *California foundation calling it quits*, AM. MED. NEWS, Sept. 26, 1994, at 3.

343. *IRS official outlines factors that help determine tax-exempt status of systems*, 3 H.L.R. 1550 (1994); more detailed essays concerning requirements appear in IRS EXEMPT ORGANIZATION CONTINUING PROFESSIONAL EDUCATION TECHNICAL INSTRUCTION PROGRAM textbooks for 1994, 1995.

344. *IRS official clarifies agency view on PHO board representation conditions*, 4 H.L.R. 151 (1995) [for-profit PHOs not subject to 20 percent physician–representation limit, with up to 50 percent control probably acceptable if proportional to their investment].

345. IRS Determination Letter to University Affiliated Health Care, Inc., Feb. 17, 1995, *as discussed in* 23 HEALTH L. DIG. (May 1995), at 79 [approval of § 501(c)(3) exemption for PHO with 11 directors, 2 from hospital, 4 from nonprofit group practice associations, 5 from employed physicians, where quorum and voting requirements gave hospital effective veto].

346. *E.g.*, University of Mass. Med. School Group Practice v. C.I.R., 74 T.C. 1299 (1980), *acq.* 1980-2 C.B. 2; B.H.W. Anesthesia Found., Inc. v. C.I.R., 72 T.C. 681 (1979), *nonacq*, 1980-2 C.B. 2.

347. 26 U.S.C.A. § 501(e).

348. HCSC-Laundry v. United States, 450 U.S. 1 (1981) [statutory list is exclusive, laundry not exempt].

349. 26 U.S.C.A. § 115.

5

Antitrust

Antitrust law has become an increasing concern to hospitals and other health care organizations. Federal and state antitrust laws are designed to preserve the private competitive market system by prohibiting various anticompetitive activities. Antitrust suits challenge mergers, exclusive contracts, medical staff privilege denials and terminations, exchanges of price information, and many other actions of hospitals. These suits are generally very complex and expensive to litigate, so even courtroom victory can be costly. Hospitals need to be aware of potential antitrust problems so that questionable conduct can be either avoided or structured to provide the strongest possible defense.

The primary federal antitrust laws are the Sherman Anti-Trust Act,[1] the Clayton Act,[2] the Federal Trade Commission Act,[3] and the Robinson-Patman Act.[4]

Federal antitrust laws apply to only actions affecting interstate and foreign commerce, but interstate commerce has been broadly defined by the U.S. Supreme Court to include intrastate or local activities that have a substantial economic effect on interstate commerce. For example, in 1976 the Court ruled that Mary Elizabeth Hospital, a 49-bed proprietary hospital operated by Hospital Building Company, was involved in interstate commerce because it purchased $100,000 worth of medicines and supplies from out-of-state vendors and received considerable revenues from out-of-state insurance companies and federal payers.[5] Hospital Building Company had sued a competing hospital, Rex Hospital, which had opposed expansion of Mary Elizabeth Hospital. The Court ruling allowed the trustees of Rex Hospital to be sued under the antitrust laws for an alleged conspiracy to restrain trade by blocking the expansion. However, Rex Hospital ultimately won the suit because a jury found that its actions had been reasonable and good-faith participation in the health planning process.[6] In 1991, the Court established a standard for determining effect on interstate commerce, which means that virtually all health care cases affect interstate commerce.[7] A plaintiff does not have to allege an actual effect on interstate commerce. The court has to look at the impact on other participants and potential participants in the market, not just the impact on the plaintiff. Thus, the revocation of the clinical privileges of an ophthalmologist at one hospital was found to affect interstate commerce.

Some of these laws are aimed at relationships among competitors, called "horizontal" relationships. Other laws are aimed at relationships among different levels of production and distribution, called "vertical" relationships. Most states have parallel antitrust laws that apply to intrastate activities.

One unique aspect of the federal antitrust laws is the existence of two independent federal agencies, the Antitrust Division of the Department of Justice (DOJ) and the Federal Trade Commission (FTC), with overlapping authority to evaluate and attack actions as antitrust violations. As more attention has been focused on this anomaly, these two organizations have developed joint guidelines and taken other steps to coordinate their activities,[8] but these competing agencies retain their independent authority.

One of the positive aspects of federal antitrust enforcement is that the involved agencies will give binding advance rulings approving proposed actions. This is very unlike HCFA and OIG, discussed in the previous chapter, which refuse to give advance rulings, requiring providers to act at their own peril. The DOJ Antitrust Division issued 17 review letters from September 1993 to December 1994, and the FTC issued 8 review letters.[9] However, even a settlement with one of these federal agencies does not bar a private action by anyone with standing who is dissatisfied with the settlement.[10]

SHERMAN ANTI-TRUST ACT

The Sherman Anti-Trust Act is aimed at eliminating restraints of both trade and monopolies. Violations of the Act are federal crimes. The federal government and private parties can also obtain injunctive relief from violations. Any person who is injured in business or property by a violation can recover three times his or her actual damages, "treble damages," in a civil suit.[11] The effect of trebling damages is illustrated by an Ohio case in which 1,800 physicians brought a class action against an HMO. In 1988, a jury found the HMO had engaged in price fixing and other violations, causing over $34 million in damages. After trebling, the jury award was over $100 million. The parties settled the suit, with the HMO paying $37.5 million and agreeing not to appeal.[12]

Section 1

Section 1 of the Sherman Anti-Trust Act forbids "every contract, combination . . . or conspiracy, in restraint of trade" in interstate or foreign commerce.[13]

Rule of Reason

The U.S. Supreme Court has recognized that a literal reading of this section would forbid virtually all commercial contracts, so the Court has interpreted this section to forbid only unreasonable restraints. This "rule of reason" standard looks at challenged agreements on a case-by-case basis to determine whether they promote or suppress competition.[14] Courts examine the structure of the industry, the defendant's operation in that industry, the history and duration of the restraint, and the reasons for its adoption.

Geographic/Product Market

A plaintiff has the burden of proof to prove what the relevant market geographic and product markets are. The relevant geographic market in hospital cases generally includes the facilities that referring physicians and patients would perceive as attractive alternatives. For many health care services, this market usually includes an area of several counties,[15] but can be a smaller or larger area and is generally determined on a case-by-case basis. Where a company presently competes does not necessarily determine the relevant market for antitrust purposes.[16] The DOJ, FTC, and courts are cognizant that attempts by one company to engage in anticompetitive behavior, such as raising prices too high, will lead consumers to look more widely for alternatives.[17]

The relevant product market varies depending on the action being challenged. In many hospital merger cases, the relevant product market is acute care hospital services.[18] When individual professionals bring antitrust actions, the services they provide determine the product market. Thus, when an anesthetist challenged an exclusive agreement with an anesthesiology group, the patient market for individual anesthesia services constituted the relevant product market.[19] In some cases, a single brand of a product or service can constitute the relevant product market.[20]

Market Power

In addition to proving the relevant market, a plaintiff must prove the defendant has significant market power, which means the ability to injure customers by curtailing output or raising prices. When this is not proven, Section 1 claims fail.[21]

Antitrust Injury

The plaintiff must also prove an "antitrust injury." In 1990, the U.S. Supreme Court ruled that to be an "antitrust injury" the injury must be attributable to an anticompetitive aspect of the practice under scrutiny and cannot merely be a loss stemming from continued competition.[22] Another way of saying this is that the antitrust law is designed to protect competition in the relevant market, not to protect competitors. Some antitrust cases in the health care area have been rejected based on the failure of the plaintiff to allege or show more than harm to the plaintiff as an individual competitor. For example, when a radiologist challenged exclusion from an IPA providing services to an HMO and from a hospital staff, the case was dismissed because there was no antitrust injury since there was no harm to competition. The court found pro-competition reasons for the exclusion and that there was no duty to aid the plaintiff who was a competitor.[23]

In 1994, in a challenge to the termination of a contract with nurse anesthetists, the Seventh Circuit Court of Appeals ruled that staffing decisions at a single hospital generally do not constitute an antitrust injury.[24] "Before we enlist this court in the micromanagement of the staffing arrangements at Passavant under the aegis of the antitrust laws, we need better reasons than the plaintiffs have given us." The court listed many of the cases dealing with staffing decisions at a single hospital. Although the courts used a variety of different reasons, with only a few exceptions the cases found no violation of Section 1. The court could find only one case in which the plaintiff actually prevailed in establishing antitrust liability for the staffing decision at a single hospital and that was due to the finding that the relevant market in a remote area of Montana was only two hospitals.[25]

Per se *Violations*

When the relevant market, significant market power, and antitrust injury are shown then the rule of reason is applied, except for the business agreements that courts have identified as *per se* unreasonable because they are not viewed as having potential redeeming competitive benefits. Courts presume that these agreements are unreasonable, so the plaintiff does not have to prove unreasonableness, which shortens and simplifies some trials. *Per se* violations include price fixing, market division, tie-ins, and boycotts. Losses flowing from *per se* violations are not automatically "antitrust injuries."[26]

Price Fixing

Price-fixing agreements among competitors for the purpose of raising, lowering, or stabilizing prices are *per se* violations. No defense or justification is recognized except for a governmental mandate. In 1982, the U.S. Supreme Court ruled that a maximum fee schedule for physicians set by physicians was price fixing and, thus, a *per se* violation.[27] Most requirements of sellers concerning the price at which their products may be resold are *per se* violations. A seller's nonprice restrictions on resale, such as territorial limits, are generally examined under the rule of reason.[28] One federal court ruled that a discharged anesthesiologist lacked standing to claim that a hospital and anesthesiology department were engaged in price fixing because the only injury claimed from the alleged price fixing was the inability to participate in the scheme.[29] In 1994, the American Medical Association requested approval from the FTC for a proposed program of advisory peer review of physicians' fees. The FTC did not object to some aspects of the proposed program, but rejected some aspects as price fixing.[30]

Market Division

Any agreement among competitors to divide up the market is a *per se* violation.[31] For example, if two competing hospitals agree that one will provide obstetrical services, while the other will provide open heart surgery services, this would be a *per se* violation.

Tying Arrangements

Under a "tying" arrangement, the seller refuses to sell product A to a customer unless that customer agrees to buy product B from the seller. If three conditions are present, a tying arrangement is generally a *per se* violation: (1) products A and B must be separate, (2) the seller must have sufficient market power to restrain competition in product B, and (3) the arrangement must sufficiently affect commerce.[32] In 1984, in *Jefferson Parish Hospital District v. Hyde,* the U.S. Supreme Court found an exclusive hospital contract with an anesthesia group not to be a *per se* violation.[33] Similarly, in 1988 a federal appellate court ruled that an exclusive pathology contract was not an unlawful arrangement because pathology services are not a separate product, but part of hospital services.[34] However, another federal appellate court in the same year found there was a separate demand for anesthesia services, making them a separate product, so that a nurse anesthetist could successfully challenge an exclusive hospital contract with a group of anesthesiologists.[35] The case was viewed as different from *Hyde* because it involved a conspiracy to eliminate the availability of nurse anesthetist services in the hospital.

There is no illegal tying as long as the buyer is free to choose to buy the two products separately. Discount packages are permitted as long as the products are offered separately.[36] This is especially true when there is also a market for discount packages in which there is also competition.[37] When auto sound dealers challenged the inclusion of the sound systems in the price of vehicles, a federal court ruled that there was insufficient market power to trigger the *per se* rule and that the seller could take advantage of market failure due to inadequate consumer information. As long as the seller does nothing to stop comparison shopping, the seller has no duty to promote comparison shopping.[38]

Boycotts

Any agreement among competitors not to deal with anyone outside the group or to deal with them only on certain terms is considered a boycott and a *per se* violation. For example, in a 1942 decision a federal appellate court found the American Medical Association ethics rules against salaried practice to be a *per se* violation.[39]

Hospitals have been on both sides of boycott claims. Hospitals and others have accused physicians of boycotts of hospitals. An Arizona medical staff settled a claimed boycott of a hospital in 1994 by agreeing not to combine to restrict services to the hospital.[40] In 1994, a federal court ruled that a hospital was not engaged in an illegal boycott by having a policy of sending its patients for radiology services to only another Joint Commission accredited facility, where the former chief of radiology who operated a freestanding radiology clinic failed to show any anticompetitive effects in a relevant market.[41] The chief's contract with the hospital had been terminated when he refused to enter a new agreement limiting his right to compete. In 1993, a federal court ruled that it was not an illegal boycott for an HMO to pay a contracting physician more if he did not do work for competing HMOs, where the exclusivity was not mandatory and could be ended with thirty (30) days' notice.[42]

Joint Ventures

Usually when two competitors enter a joint venture, the courts will apply a rule of reason analysis because the integration of resources in a joint venture can produce efficiencies and new products. Courts determine whether the restraints on competition resulting from the joint venture are necessary to achieve the permitted purpose. For example, in 1988 a federal district court dismissed a physician's price-fixing antitrust suit against an HMO because (1) the HMO was a legitimate joint venture with a shared risk of loss and a new product and (2) the price agreement was necessary to distribute the revenues and control costs to remain competitive.[43] There has been increasing attention on the minimum characteristics necessary to demonstrate sufficient integration.[44]

Information Exchange

Exchange of information, especially price information, among competitors can be a violation. Exchange of past price information is less likely to be a violation. In 1993, the DOJ approved a salary survey by an independent contractor that was voluntary and only reported aggregated data at least three months old.[45] Current and prospective salary information generally cannot be directly exchanged. The DOJ successfully challenged exchange of current and prospective nursing salary information among Utah hospitals, resulting in a consent decree in 1994 specifying what conduct would be permitted.[46] Nonprice information has been viewed more leniently except where it appears to be aimed at suppressing competition.

Trade Associations

"Self-regulation" by trade associations must be carefully structured. Any suppression or destruction of competition can be a violation. In 1994, an association of hospitals in Des Moines, Iowa, agreed to a consent decree with the DOJ ending an agreement that limited competitive advertising by the hospital members.[47]

Agreement

Many violations require the showing of an "agreement" among competitors. An actual agreement need not always be shown. Courts have stated that "interdependent conscious parallelism" among competitors can provide the basis for inferring an agreement.[48] For example, if the dominant health insurer in the area announced that it would not send patients to any hospital unless the hospital stopped accepting patients covered by a competing health insurer and if all the hospitals in the area stopped accepting the competing insurer's patients, an agreement could be inferred from this parallel behavior that cannot be justified by independent business judgment. It would not be necessary to prove any actual communications among the hospitals. However, parallel business behavior is not sufficient when independent business judgment can justify the decisions. For example, if all the hospitals in an area decide independently to stop dealing with a nursing agency that charges more than any other agency or provides unresponsive service, the parallel business behavior could be justified by independent business judgment.

Conspiracy/Intracorporate Immunity

Section 1 of the Sherman Anti-Trust Act requires a conspiracy between separate economic entities. An unincorporated association of otherwise competing physicians can constitute a conspiracy.[49] Usually a corporation cannot conspire with itself or its employees. There is disagreement among the federal circuit courts whether the hospital and medical staff are a single entity for antitrust conspiracy purposes or multiple entities that can conspire. At least four circuits have ruled that, when engaged in peer review, the hospital and medical staff are a single entity protected by the intracorporate conspiracy doctrine.[50] One of these circuits has recognized an exception to intracorporate immunity when a physician is acting pursuant to an independent personal stake,[51] while one of the circuits has rejected any such exception.[52] One court indicated that while the hospital could not conspire with its medical staff, the members could conspire among themselves, but since the ultimate decision was by the board of directors, any conspiracy among the medical staff could not cause antitrust injury.[53] At least two other circuits have ruled that hospitals and their medical staffs are separate entities capable of conspiracy.[54] Other circuits have declined to rule on the issue.[55] To avoid the personal stake exception and to avoid the appearance of a conspiracy, hospitals should limit the involvement of physicians in decisions and recommendations concerning those involved in the same or competing specialties. For example, when a medical staff committee is hearing or considering charges against a cardiac surgeon, other competing cardiac surgeons should not serve on the committee.

Section 2

Section 2 of the Sherman Act prohibits monopolizing, attempts to monopolize, and combinations or conspiracies to monopolize any part of interstate or foreign commerce.[56]

Like Section 1, a relevant geographic and product market must be proved.

Monopoly Power

To establish a monopolization claim under Section 2, it must also be shown that defendants possess monopoly power in the relevant market.[57] However, mere possession of monopoly power is not a violation if it resulted from a superior product, business acumen, or historical accident. For example, it is not an illegal monopoly to be the sole community hospital when by historical accident only one hospital has been founded or the only competitors have experienced business failure without illegal help from the survivor. Monopoly power is the power to control prices or exclude competition. Courts usually look to market share as a sign of monopoly power.

Purposeful Act

Monopolizing requires possession of monopoly power in a relevant market, plus a "purposeful act." A purposeful act is the willful acquisition or maintenance of monopoly power.

Elements of a Claim

In 1993, the U.S. Supreme Court ruled that to demonstrate attempted monopolization a plaintiff must prove (1) use of unfair or predatory means, such as boycotts or discriminatory pricing, (2) specific intent to monopolize, and (3) a dangerous probability of achieving monopoly power. In determining the third element, courts consider (1) the relevant market, both the product and the geographic markets, and (2) market power, the defendant's ability to lessen or destroy competition in that market.[58]

Medical Staff

Physicians frequently bring antitrust suits under Sections 1 and/or 2 of the Sherman Act to challenge exclusive hospital contracts with other physicians and other adverse hospital actions concerning their membership on the medical staff or clinical privileges in the hospital. These suits are discussed in Chapter 7.

CLAYTON ACT

Section 2

Section 2 of the Clayton Act, as amended by the Robinson-Patman Act, forbids certain price discrimination.[59] It is unlawful to discriminate in price between different purchasers when selling commodities of like grade or quality where the effect may be to substantially lessen competition or to injure, destroy, or prevent competition. At least one of the two comparative transactions must cross state lines. The section applies only to commodities, so sales of services and intangibles are not affected, and the section applies only to sales, so leases and consignments are not affected.

Section 2 also prohibits indirect price discrimination through seller-supplied facilities, services, or payments. For example, if the seller provides special promotional advertising for one buyer, this service is indirect price discrimination in favor of that buyer.

The seller is not the only possible violator. A buyer who knowingly induces or receives discriminatory prices also violates Section 2.

Exemptions

Nonprofit institutions have an exemption for purchases "for their own use."[60] As a result, hospital pharmacies in nonprofit hospitals usually buy drugs from manufacturers at a discount not available to commercial pharmacies. These drugs can be used only "for their own use." In 1976, the U.S. Supreme Court defined "use" in "for their own use" to be limited to the following:

1. treatment of inpatients at the hospital;
2. treatment of admitted emergency patients in the hospital;
3. personal use by outpatients on the hospital premises;

4. personal use away from the premises by inpatients or emergency patients upon their discharge;
5. personal use away from the premises by outpatients;
6. personal use by hospital employees, students, and their immediate dependents; and
7. personal use by medical staff members and their immediate dependents.[61]

Thus, hospitals must confine their sales of drugs purchased at a discount to these groups to avoid possible civil liability, including treble damages and loss of the valuable discount.

Purchasers who do not qualify include (1) former patients who wish to renew prescriptions given when they were inpatients, emergency facility patients, or outpatients; (2) physicians who are medical staff members and who intend to dispense the drugs in the course of their private practices away from the hospital; and (3) walk-in customers who are not hospital patients. Hospitals should refuse to sell to these groups or should set up a separate purchase order system to fill their requests.

In 1987, a federal court ruled that drug companies and a hospital could be sued for the hospital's alleged transfer of drugs between its in-house pharmacy and its retail pharmacy.[62]

Governmental entities are also generally exempt from the price discrimination prohibition. However, in 1983 the U.S. Supreme Court ruled that governmental hospitals must observe the same restrictions on resale of discount drugs that nonprofit hospitals do.[63] In 1984, a federal appellate court ruled that resales of drugs by HMOs to their own members are "for their own use."[64]

There is no exemption for for-profit hospitals, so their purchases must be on the same volume discount basis as generally available to other consumers.

In 1989, a federal appellate court upheld the fraud conviction of an operator of a shared services organization for obtaining pharmaceuticals at lower prices in excess of the amount needed by qualified member hospitals and selling the surplus to wholesale drug companies.[65]

Section 3

Section 3 of the Clayton Act[66] prohibits sales of commodities that are conditioned on the buyer not dealing with competitors of the seller. Examples include tie-in sales and exclusive dealing arrangements where the effect "may be substantially to lessen competition or tend to create a monopoly" in any line of commerce. Section 1 of the Sherman Anti-Trust Act prohibits the same conduct not only for commodities but also for services, intangibles, and real property. Examples of the prohibited conduct are included in the discussion of that section earlier in this chapter.

Section 7

Section 7 of the Clayton Act[67] prohibits acquisitions or mergers where the effect "may be substantially to lessen competition or tend to create a monopoly in any line of commerce in any section of the country." With the rapid growth in some national hospital companies and the consolidation of providers, this section has increasingly been applied to hospitals.

Relevant product and geographic markets must be identified in a manner similar to the analysis under Section 2 of the Sherman Act.

Section 7 is preventive, not merely corrective. A reasonable likelihood of substantially lessening competition is sufficient to establish a violation.

Merger Guidelines

The DOJ and FTC have issued merger guidelines in 1992 that are not binding on courts, but give some direction.[68] In 1994, the DOJ and the FTC issued further guidelines that created a "safety zone" for mergers with older hospitals with fewer than 100 beds and an average census of fewer than 40 patients.[69]

Herfindahl-Hirschman Index

One of the tools that is used is a formula, the Herfindahl-Hirschman Index (HHI), which is a measure of market concentration. The HHI is calculated by adding the squares of the percentage market shares of the entities in the market. For example, if each of 20 competing hospitals had 5 percent of the market, the HHI would be 500. If a merger results in an HHI less than 1,000, the government generally will not challenge the merger, so 4 of the 20 hospitals in the example could merge into one hospital (HHI = 800). There are potentially significant federal competitive concerns depending on other factors stated in the 1992 guidelines (but there is no presumption of violation), if (1) the resulting HHI is from 1,000 to 1,800 and is more than 100 points above the premerger HHI or (2) the resulting HHI is over 1,800 and is 50 to 100 points above the premerger HHI. If the resulting HHI is over 1,800 and is more than 100 points above the premerger HHI, there is a presumption the merger will create or enhance market power.[70] This would occur if the 20 hospitals in the example merged into 4 hospitals with equal market shares of 25 percent (HHI = 2,500). This presumption can be overcome by showing efficiencies and other factors.

Hospital Mergers

Section 7 has been used by both the FTC and the DOJ to attack mergers of hospitals. Section 7 clearly applies to for-profit hospital mergers. For example, in 1986 a federal appellate court upheld an FTC order that a for-profit hospital chain divest itself of two of three hospitals that it owned in the Chattanooga, Tennessee, area and notify the FTC in advance of any plan to make a similar acquisition.[71]

Generally, when large chains combine, the resulting entity finds itself with too many hospitals in one or more local markets, so the entity has to divest itself of one or more hospitals in those areas. An example is the divestiture related to the Columbia/HCA acquisition of Healthtrust Inc.–The Hospital Company in 1995.[72]

There is still a question whether Section 7 applies to nonprofit hospitals. Section 7 applies to (1) persons who acquire shares of stock or capital and (2) persons subject to the jurisdiction of the FTC. Nonprofit companies do not have shares of stock or capital, so Section 7 applies to nonprofit hospitals only if they are subject to the jurisdiction of the FTC. There is a question whether nonprofit hospitals are subject to the jurisdiction of the FTC within the meaning of Section 7; the FTC takes the position that they are. In 1988, the FTC ordered two nonprofit hospitals in Reading, Pennsylvania, to separate.[73] Some courts have agreed. One federal appellate court ruled in 1991 that Section 7 does apply to asset acquisitions by nonprofit hospitals.[74]

The DOJ challenged the proposed merger of two nonprofit hospitals in Rockford, Illinois. In 1989, a federal district court in Illinois enjoined the proposed merger. It found that the merger violated Section 7.[75] The appellate court found Section 7 not applicable to the merger of two nonstock nonprofit hospitals, but upheld barring the merger because it violated Section 1 of the Sherman Act.[76] The appellate court indicated that its decision on Section 7 was limited by the way the parties framed the issues. The court indicated its belief that Section 7 would be applicable if the government presented its case correctly.

One other court has found that Section 7 does not apply. The DOJ challenged the proposed merger of two hospitals in Roanoke, Virginia. A federal district court in Virginia ruled in 1988 that Section 7 did not apply to affiliations of nonprofit entities where there was no exchange of stock or share capital and then in 1989 ruled that the merger did not violate Section 1 of the Sherman Act under the rule of reason.[77] In 1989, a federal appellate court affirmed the decision, but did not issue an opinion.[78]

In 1989, the FTC began challenging the acquisition of a small hospital in Ukiah, California, by a large hospital chain that owned the other small hospital in the town.[79] The hospitals tried to stop the FTC from proceeding with its complaint on the grounds that the FTC lacked jurisdiction under Section 7, but the federal court refused to rule until after the FTC had made a final ruling on jurisdiction.[80] In 1990, an Administrative Law Judge (ALJ) dismissed the complaint on the grounds of lack of jurisdiction, but the FTC reversed. In 1992, the ALJ again dismissed, but on the basis that the acquisition was not likely to substantially lessen competition when the proper geographic market was considered.[81] In 1994, the FTC affirmed, dismissing the complaint on the basis that there was insufficient evidence to establish the relevant geographic market.[82] Thus, it is unlikely that the jurisdictional issue will protect hospitals from the expense of responding to the

FTC. The FTC continues to aggressively challenge acquisitions of nonprofit hospitals.[83]

Section 4 Remedies

Section 4 of the Clayton Act[84] gives any person the right to sue for treble damages when injured by violations of the Sherman Act or Clayton Act. There are no criminal sanctions for violations of the Clayton Act, but violations can be enjoined.

FEDERAL TRADE COMMISSION ACT

Section 5(a) of the Federal Trade Commission Act[85] prohibits "unfair methods or competition in or affecting commerce and unfair or deceptive acts or practices in or affecting commerce." The FTC has exclusive authority to enforce this section, so private individuals cannot use it as a basis for suits. The FTC can also take action to enforce the Sherman Act or the Clayton Act, but its authority is not exclusive. Examples of FTC action are included in the discussion of Section 7 of the Clayton Act.

The FTC may (1) issue an order to cease and desist from violating antitrust laws, (2) seek a court-imposed fine for a violation of a cease and desist order, (3) seek injunctions of prohibited conduct, and (4) seek court-ordered restitution to consumers and others from violations.

EXEMPTIONS

The U.S. Supreme Court has made it clear that health care providers are treated in the same way as other industries for antitrust purposes. For example, in 1975 the Court ruled that the learned professions, such as law and medicine, were not excepted from the antitrust laws.[86]

Health Care Quality Improvement Act of 1986

The Health Care Quality Improvement Act (HCQIA) extends protection from monetary liability in private suits under the antitrust laws for professional review activities that meet its procedural standards.[87] HCQIA does not protect from suit, governmental actions, or injunctions.[88] HCQIA is discussed in Chapter 7.

State Action

The law has recognized an exemption from antitrust liability for state action. In 1943, the U.S. Supreme Court ruled that state-compelled activities were immune from antitrust liability to preserve the state's authority to supervise economic activity within the state.[89] The state action doctrine was clarified in 1980 when the Court ruled that state authorization is not enough. The actions must be pursuant to a clearly articulated and affirmatively expressed state policy actively supervised by the state.[90] The doctrine was further defined in 1985 when the Court ruled that the clearly defined state policy did not have to compel the actions to bring them within the state action immunity.[91] Collective rate making by motor carriers was found to be protected as state action because the states expressly permitted the rate making and actively supervised it. On the same day the Court ruled that active state supervision is not a requirement for exemption when the actor is a municipality, rather than a private individual.[92]

One area of dispute has been whether state medical peer review laws provide the requisite state action to protect hospitals from antitrust liability for their peer review activities. Prior to 1988, several courts found various such laws did provide the requisite state action.[93] In 1988, in a medical peer review case, the U.S. Supreme Court tightened the active supervision requirement to require that "state officials have and exercise power to review particular anticompetitive acts of private parties and disapprove those that fail to accord with state policy."[94] The case dealt with an Oregon law that did not include any state administrative review of hospital peer review decisions. The defendants argued that the availability of state judicial review was sufficient active supervision. Applying the new standard, the Court decided that the judicial review available in Oregon was not sufficient without ruling that state judicial review could never provide sufficient state supervision. The efforts to obtain state action immunity for these activities has been reduced since it has become clearer that the HCQIA provides significant protection from antitrust liability for medical peer review actions.[95]

Numerous actions by governmental hospitals have been found to be immune under this standard. Statutory authority to acquire other hospitals is sufficient to immunize acquisitions.[96] Statutory authority to own and operate hospitals immunizes acquisitions of other hospitals.[97] In 1994, a federal appellate court found that state action immunity protected the proposed purchase of Cape Coral Hospital by a health care authority created by Florida as a special purpose unit of local government that already owned another hospital in the county, Lee Memorial Hospital, and that had authority to acquire other hospitals.[98] However, authority to do business is not alone sufficient to demonstrate a state intent to displace competition.[99] Governmental hospitals can also have state action immunity from physician challenges to peer review and staffing decisions.[100]

In 1991 the Supreme Court ruled that there was no conspiracy exception to the state action immunity.[101]

The Local Government Antitrust Act of 1984[102] extends statutory immunity from antitrust damage claims to local governmental agencies and their employees and agents. This applies to local government hospitals.[103] The law does not provide protection from antitrust suits seeking injunctions, but many of those will be precluded by the state action doctrine.[104]

Several states have passed laws providing a mechanism by which health care providers can apply to obtain state approval and, thus, antitrust immunity.[105] Some state approvals have been given under these laws.[106] They have not had a significant impact yet and have not been addressed in any published court decision.

Petitioning Government

In two cases in 1961 and 1965, the U.S. Supreme Court ruled that the antitrust laws do not apply to most activities intended to induce governmental action, such as lobbying.[107] This concept is called the *Noerr-Pennington doctrine* and is based on the right under the First Amendment to petition the government and on a judicial interpretation that lobbying activities are not a restraint of trade. The petitioning must be conducted honestly and for the legitimate purpose of influencing governmental policy. For example, a federal appellate court ruled in 1986 that the Noerr-Pennington doctrine protected a hospital's full use of the administrative process (including delaying tactics and appeals) to challenge a competing hospital's application for a certificate of need for a cardiac surgery program, but the doctrine did not protect misrepresentations to the governmental agency.[108] Efforts that are considered a "mere sham" to suppress competition are not protected. For example, repetitive insubstantial lawsuits may be a mere sham to tie up the competitor so that it cannot make financing or other business arrangements.[109] However, an objectively reasonable effort to litigate is not a sham, regardless of the plaintiff's subjective intent.[110]

Business of Insurance

The McCarran-Ferguson Act created a statutory exemption for the "business of insurance" when it is regulated by state law and does not constitute coercion, boycott, or intimidation.[111] The U.S. Supreme Court has taken a restrictive view of what constitutes the business of insurance entitled to this exemption. For example, in 1979 the Court limited the exemption to the business of insurance, not the business of insurers.[112] It defined the business of insurance as limited to the procedures and activities related to the spreading of risk among policyholders. The Court held that special reimbursement arrangements between Blue Shield and participating pharmacies were not within the business of insurance, but instead were merely the business of insurers.

Implied Exemptions

In 1981, the U.S. Supreme Court ruled that implied exemptions to antitrust laws are not favored and will be applied only to the limited extent necessary to fulfill the purposes of other laws.[113] The Court ruled that the national health planning law, which was then in effect, did not provide implied protection for an insurer from antitrust law liability for refusing to deal with a hospital that did not obtain approval from a planning agency for its new building. State law did not require approval. This principle was applied by a federal appellate court in 1984 when it ruled that a certificate of need does not protect a provider from being charged with monopolization.[114] The provider must still comply with all other laws, including antitrust laws.

Scope of Exemptions

When an exemption is found from one antitrust law, other antitrust laws still must be complied with. In 1988, a federal district court ruled that "Conduct which is specifically exempted from a particular antitrust law may nonetheless be prohibited by another statute. If that same conduct violates another law, the exemption does not follow."[115]

NOTES

1. 15 U.S.C.A. §§ 1–7.
2. 15 U.S.C.A. §§ 12–27, 44.
3. 15 U.S.C.A. §§ 41–58.
4. 15 U.S.C.A. § 13c.
5. Hospital Bldg. Co. v. Trustees of Rex Hosp., 425 U.S. 738 (1976).
6. Hospital Bldg. Co. v. Trustees of Rex Hosp., No. 4048 (E.D. N.C. Dec. 5, 1984), aff'd, 791 F.2d 288 (4th Cir. 1986).
7. Summit Health, Ltd. v. Pinhas, 500 U.S. 322 (1991).
8. E.g., Revised Justice/FTC Enforcement Guidelines for Health Care Industry (Sept. 27, 1994), reprinted in 3 HEALTH L. REP. 1376 (1994) [hereinafter HEALTH L. REP. will be cited as H.L.R. and the Guidelines will be cited as 1994 DOJ/FTC Guidelines].

9. 4 H.L.R. 116 (1995) [list of letters].

10. *E.g.*, *Physicians' group clashes with hospital over standing*, 3 H.L.R. 1646 (1994) [after hospital settled with federal government, physicians sued Santa Cruz, CA, hospital that had acquired the other hospital in town]; Santa Cruz Med. Clinic v. Dominican Santa Cruz Hosp., No. C93 20613 RMW (N.D. Cal. Mar. 28, 1995), *as discussed in* 23 HEALTH L. DIG. (May 1995), at 18 [physicians have antitrust standing to sue over hospital acquisition].

11. 15 U.S.C.A. § 1, 2, 4, 15.

12. Thompson v. Midwest Found. Indep. Physicians Ass'n, No. C-1-86-744 (S.D. Ohio Mar. 14, 1988) [jury verdict]; 124 F.R.D. 154 (S.D. Ohio 1988) [settlement approved], *as discussed in* 16 HEALTH L. DIG. (Apr. 1988) at 1, (Dec. 1988) at 15, 17 HEALTH L. DIG. (Mar. 1989) at 13. Note that not all IPA–HMO arrangements are antitrust violations, *e.g.*, Hassan v. Independent Practice Assocs., P.C., 698 F. Supp. 679 (E.D. Mich. 1988).

13. 15 U.S.C.A. § 1.

14. *E.g.*, Westchester Radiological Assocs., P.C. v. Empire Blue Cross & Blue Shield, 707 F. Supp. 708 (S.D. N.Y. 1989), *aff'd*, 884 F.2d 707 (2d Cir. 1989), *cert. denied*, 493 U.S. 1095 (1990).

15. *E.g.*, Cogan v. Harford Mem. Hosp., 843 F. Supp. 1013, 1019 (D. Md.1994); Morgenstern v. Wilson, 29 F.3d 1291 (8th Cir. 1994), *cert. denied*, 115 S. Ct. 1100 (U.S. 1995); N. Hershey, *Geographic market definition critical to monopolization claim*, 12 HOSP. L. NEWSLETTER (July 1995), at 5 [discussing *Morgenstern*].

16. *E.g.*, Morgan, Strand, Wheeler & Biggs v. Radiology, Ltd., 924 F.2d 1484 (9th Cir. 1991).

17. *E.g.*, DOJ & FTC 1992 Horizontal Merger Guidelines (Apr. 2, 1992), § 1.21, 57 FED. REG. 41552 (Sept. 10, 1992), reprinted in 4 TRADE REG. REP. (CCH) ¶ 13,103 (1992) [hereinafter *1992 DOJ/ FTC Guidelines*]; In re Adventist Health System/West, FTC No. 9234 (Apr. 1, 1994) [FTC dismissal of complaint due to failure sufficiently to address where services would be sought in the event of anticompetitive behavior].

18. *E.g.*, FTC v. University Health, Inc., 938 F.2d 1206 (11th Cir. 1991); *see also* Forsyth v. Humana, Inc., 827 F. Supp. 1498 (D. Nev. 1993) [rejecting attempt to limit market to large for-profit hospitals].

19. Oltz v. Saint Peter's Community Hosp., 861 F.2d 1440 (9th Cir. 1988).

20. *E.g.*, Eastman Kodak Co. v. Image Technical Servs. Inc., 504 U.S. 451 (1992).

21. *E.g.*, Flegel v. Christian Hosp., Northeast-Northwest, 4 F.3d 682 (8th Cir. 1993); Cogan v. Harford Mem. Hosp., 843 F. Supp. 1013, 1019 (D. Md. 1994).

22. Atlantic Richfield Co. v. USA Petroleum Co., 495 U.S. 328 (1990).

23. Williamson v. Sacred Heart Hosp., 41 F.3d 667 (without op.) (11th Cir. Nov. 18, 1994), *as discussed in* 4 H.L.R. 309 (1995); *see also* Cogan v. Harford Mem. Hosp., 843 F. Supp. 1013 (D. Md. 1994).

24. BCB Anesthesia Care v. Passavant Mem. Area Hosp. Ass'n, 36 F.3d 664 (7th Cir. 1994).

25. Oltz v. Saint Peter's Community Hosp., 861 F.2d 1440 (9th Cir. 1988).

26. Atlantic Richfield Co. v. USA Petroleum Co., 495 U.S. 328 (1990).

27. Arizona v. Maricopa County Med. Soc'y, 457 U.S. 332 (1982).

28. Continental T.V. v. GTE Sylvania Inc., 433 U.S. 36 (1977).

29. Purgess v. Sharrock, 806 F. Supp. 1102 (S.D. N.Y. 1992).

30. FTC Advisory Opinion Letter to General Counsel of AMA and Chicago Medical Society, No. P923506 (Feb. 14, 1994), *as discussed in* 22 HEALTH L. DIG. (Mar. 1994) at 6; B. McCormick, *FTC gives qualified OK to medicine's fee-review plan*, AM. MED. NEWS, Mar. 7, 1994, at 3.

31. *E.g.*, Palmer v. BRG of Georgia, Inc., 498 U.S. 46 (1990).

32. *See* Eastman Kodak Co. v. Image Technical Servs., Inc., 504 U.S. 451 (1992).

33. Jefferson Parish Hosp. Dist. No.2 v. Hyde, 466 U.S. 2 (1984).

34. Collins v. Associated Pathologists, Ltd., 844 F.2d 473 (7th Cir.), *cert. denied*, 488 U.S. 852 (1988).

35. Oltz v. Saint Peter's Commun. Hosp., 861 F.2d 1440 (9th Cir. 1988).

36. *E.g.*, Northern Pacific Ry. Co. v. United States, 356 U.S. 1 (1958).

37. *E.g.*, Nobel Scientific Indust., Inc. v. Beckman Instruments, Inc., 670 F. Supp. 1313 (D. Md. 1986), *aff'd*, 831 F.2d 537 (4th Cir. 1987), *cert. denied*, 487 U.S. 1226 (1988).

38. Town Sound & Custom Tops, Inc. v. Chrysler Motors Corp., 959 F.2d 468 (3d Cir.), *cert. denied*, 113 S. Ct. 196 (U.S. 1992).

39. American Med. Ass'n v. United States, 76 U.S. App. D.C. 70, 130 F.2d 233 (1942), *aff'd*, 317 U.S. 519 (1943).

40. In re Med. Staff of Good Samaritan Med. Ctr., FTC File No. 901 0032 (settlement 9/7/94), *as discussed in* 3 H.L.R. 1257 (1994); B. McCormick, *Doctors settle FTC boycott case*, AM. MED. NEWS, Oct. 3, 1994, at 10.

41. Cogan v. Harford Mem. Hosp., 843 F. Supp. 1013 (D. Md. 1994).

42. U.S. Healthcare, Inc. v. Healthsource, Inc., 986 F.2d 589 (1st Cir. 1993).

43. Hassan v. Independent Practice Assocs., P.C., 698 F. Supp. 679 (E.D. Mich. 1988).

44. *See 1994 DOJ/FTC Guidelines*; *Capitation seen as brightest line in quest for sufficient integration*, 4 H.L.R 269 (1995).

45. Business Review Letter from Assistant Attorney General Anne K. Bingaman to Counsel for the New Jersey Hospital Ass'n, DOJ, Antitrust Div. (Feb. 18, 1994) *as discussed in* 22 HEALTH L. DIG. (Mar. 1994) at 9; *New Jersey hospital salary survey satisfies antitrust enforcement guidelines*, 3 H.L.R. 237 (1994).

46. United States v. Utah Soc'y for Healthcare Human Resources Admin., No. 94C282G (D. Utah consent decree Mar. 14, 1994), *as discussed in* 3 H.L.R. 333 (1994).

47. United States v. Hospital Ass'n of Greater Des Moines, No. 4-92-70648 (S.D. Iowa settlement Sept. 22, 1992); *Hospitals settle suit alleging anti-competitive ad rules*, AM. MED. NEWS, Oct. 12, 1992, at 12.

48. Interstate Circuit, Inc. v. United States, 306 U.S. 208 (1939).

49. Anesthesia Advantage, Inc. v. Metz Group, 708 F. Supp. 1180 (D. Colo. 1989), *rev'd on other grounds*, 912 F.2d 397 (10th Cir. 1990).

50. Oksanen v. Page Mem. Hosp., 945 F.2d 696 (4th Cir. 1991) *(en banc), cert. denied*, 502 U.S. 1074 (1992); Weiss v. York Hosp., 745 F.2d 786 (3d Cir. 1984), *cert. denied*, 470 U.S. 1060 (1985); Nanavati v. Burdette Tomlin Mem. Hosp., 857 F.2d 96 (3d Cir. 1988), *cert. denied*, 489 U.S. 1078 (1989); Potters Med. Ctr. v. City Hosp. Ass'n, 800 F.2d 568 (6th Cir. 1986); Nurse Midwifery Assocs. v. Hibbett, 918 F.2d 605 (6th Cir. 1990), *modified on reh'g*, 927 F.2d 904 (6th Cir.), *cert. denied*, 502 U.S. 952 (1991); Pudlo v. Adamski, 789 F. Supp. 247 (N.D. Ill. 1992), *aff'd without op.*, 2 F.3d 1153, 1993 U.S. App. LEXIS 20,442 (7th Cir. 1993), *cert. denied*, 114 S. Ct. 879 (U.S. 1994).

51. Oksanen v. Page Mem. Hosp., *supra*, note 50.

52. Nurse Midwifery Assocs. v. Hibbett, *supra*, note 50.

53. Pudlo v. Adamski, *supra*, note 50.

54. Bolt v. Halifax Hosp. Med. Ctr., 851 F.2d 1273 (11th Cir.), *vacated*, 861 F.2d 1233 (11th Cir. 1988), *reinstated in part*, 874 F.2d 755 (11th Cir. 1989) *(en banc), after remand*, 891 F.2d 810

(11th Cir.), *cert. denied*, 495 U.S. 924 (1990); Oltz v. Saint Peter's Community Hosp., 861 F.2d 1440 (9th Cir. 1988).

55. *E.g.*, Willman v. Heartland Hosp., 34 F.3d 605 (8th Cir. 1994), *cert. denied*, 115 S. Ct. 1361 (U.S. 1995); Okusami v. Psychiatric Inst. of Washington, Inc., 959 F.2d 1062 (D.C. Cir. 1992).

56. 15 U.S.C.A. § 2.

57. *E.g.*, United States v. Grinnell Corp., 384 U.S. 563 (1966).

58. Spectrum Sports, Inc. v. McQuillan, 113 S. Ct. 884 (U.S. 1993); Copperweld Corp. v. Independence Tube Corp., 467 U.S. 752 (1984).

59. 15 U.S.C.A. § 13.

60. 15 U.S.C.A. § 13c.

61. Abbott Labs. v. Portland Retail Druggists Ass'n, Inc., 425 U.S. 1 (1976).

62. Rudner v. Abbott Labs., 664 F. Supp. 1100 (N.D. Ohio 1987).

63. Jefferson County Pharmaceutical Ass'n, Inc. v. Abbott Labs., 460 U.S. 150 (1983).

64. De Modena v. Kaiser Found. Health Plan, Inc., 743 F.2d 1388 (9th Cir. 1984), *cert. denied*, 469 U.S. 1229 (1985).

65. United States v. Stewart, 872 F.2d 957 (10th Cir. 1989).

66. 15 U.S.C.A. § 14 .

67. 15 U.S.C.A. § 18.

68. *1992 DOJ/FTC Guidelines, supra,* note 17.

69. 1994 DOJ/FTC Guidelines, statement 1.

70. *E.g.*, FTC v. University Health, Inc., 938 F.2d 1206 (11th Cir. 1991) [HHI would increase by over 630 to 3,200].

71. Hospital Corp. of Am. v. FTC, 807 F.2d 1381 (7th Cir. 1986), *cert. denied*, 481 U.S. 1038 (1987).

72. *E.g., Columbia, Health Trust will sell 3 Utah sites amid FTC discussions*, WALL ST. J., Feb. 17, 1995, at B6.

73. McGinn, *A first: FTC tells two non-profit hospitals to separate*, AM. MED. NEWS, Oct. 7, 1989, at 3.

74. FTC v. University Health, Inc., 938 F.2d 1206 (11th Cir. 1991).

75. United States v. Rockford Mem. Corp., 717 F. Supp. 1251 (N.D. Ill. 1989).

76. United States v. Rockford Mem. Corp., 898 F.2d 1278 (7th Cir. 1990), *cert. denied*, 498 U.S. 920 (1990).

77. United States v. Carilion Health Sys., 707 F. Supp. 840 (W.D. Va. 1989).

78. United States v. Carilion Health Sys., 892 F.2d 1042, *(without op.)*, 1989 U.S. App. LEXIS 17,911, 1989-2 TRADE CASES (CCH) ¶68,859 (4th Cir. 1989), *reh'g denied (en banc)*, 1990 U.S. App. LEXIS 2657 (4th Cir. 1990).

79. Burda, *FTC files complaint against hospital merger*, 19 MOD. HEALTHCARE, Nov. 17, 1989, at 4 [challenge to merger in Ukiah, California].

80. Ukiah Valley Med. Ctr. v. F.T.C., 911 F.2d 261 (9th Cir. 1990).

81. In re Adventist Health Sys./West, FTC No. 9234 (A.L.J. Dec. 9, 1992).

82. In re Adventist Health Sys./West, FTC No. 9234 (Apr. 1, 1994).

83. *E.g.*, FTC v. Freeman Hosp., No. 95-5015-CV-SW-1 (W.D. Mo. June 9, 1995), *as discussed in* 4 H.L.R. 902 (1995) [injunction of hospital merger denied].

84. 15 U.S.C.A. § 15.

85. 15 U.S.C.A. § 45.

86. Goldfarb v. Virginia State Bar Ass'n, 421 U.S. 773 (1975).

87. 42 U.S.C.A. § 11111(a)(1); *see* Annotation, *Construction and application of Health Care Quality Improvement Act of 1986*, 121 A.L.R. FED. 255.

88. *Id.*

89. Parker v. Brown, 317 U.S. 341 (1943).

90. California Retail Liquor Dealers Ass'n v. Midcal Aluminum, Inc., 445 U.S. 97 (1980).

91. Southern Motor Carriers Rate Conference, Inc. v. United States, 471 U.S. 48 (1985).

92. Town of Hallie v. City of Eau Claire, 471 U.S. 34 (1985).

93. *E.g.*, Marrese v. Interqual, Inc., 748 F.2d 373 (7th Cir. 1984), *cert. denied*, 472 U.S. 1027 (1985).

94. Patrick v. Burget, 486 U.S. 94, 101 (1988); *see also* Shahawy v. Harrison, 875 F.2d 1529 (11th Cir. 1989) [judicial supervision in Florida insufficient to provide state action immunity for medical staff actions]; FTC v. Ticor Title Ins. Co., 504 U.S. 621 (1992) [state regulatory scheme insufficient to provide immunity for setting prices for title insurance].

95. *E.g.*, Bryan v. James E. Holmes Reg. Med. Ctr., 33 F.3d 1318 (11th Cir. 1994), *cert. denied*, 115 S. Ct. 1363 (U.S. 1995).

96. FTC v. University Health, Inc., 938 F.2d 1206 (11th Cir. 1991).

97. Askew v. DCH Reg. Health Care Auth., 995 F.2d 1033 (11th Cir. 1993), *cert. denied*, 114 S. Ct. 603 (U.S. 1993).

98. F.T.C. v. Hospital Bd. of Directors, 38 F.3d 1184 (11th Cir. 1994), *reh'g denied (en banc)*, 50 F.3d 1040 (11th Cir. 1995).

99. *E.g.*, Lancaster Community Hosp. v. Antelope Valley Hosp. Dist., 940 F.2d 397 (9th Cir. 1991), *cert. denied*, 502 U.S. 1094 (1992).

100. *E.g.*, Cohn v. Bond, 953 F.2d 154 (4th Cir. 1991), *cert. denied*, 112 S. Ct. 3057 (U.S. 1992); Todorov v. DCH Healthcare Auth., 921 F.2d 1438 (11th Cir. 1991); Shaw v. Phelps County Reg. Med. Ctr., 858 F. Supp. 954 (E.D. Mo. 1994); Crosby v. Hospital Auth. of Valdosta, 873 F. Supp. 1568 (M.D. Ga. 1995) [government hospital, its officials protected in medical staff privilege case by state action immunity, Local Government Antitrust Act, and HCQIA].

101. City of Columbia v. Omni Outdoor Advertising, Inc., 499 U.S. 365 (1991); Bolt v. Halifax Hosp. Med. Ctr., 980 F.2d 1381 (11th Cir.), *reh'g denied (en banc)*, 988 F.2d 1220 (11th Cir. 1993).

102. 15 U.S.C.A. §§ 34–36.

103. *E.g.*, Sandcrest Outpatient Servs., P.A. v. Cumberland County Hosp. Sys., Inc., 853 F.2d 1139 (4th Cir. 1988).

104. Bloom v. Hennepin County, 783 F. Supp. 418 (D. Minn. 1992) [challenge by physician whose privileges were terminated when he ceased to be employed by group with exclusive contract. Act protected hospital from liability, state action doctrine protected from injunction].

105. *E.g.*, Antitrust Immunity and Competitive Oversight, Substantive Rules and Procedural Rules (Washington Health Services Comm'n Jan. 26, 1995), *as discussed in* 23 HEALTH L. DIG. (May 1995) at 19; *Little activity seen under state laws granting antitrust immunity*, 4 H.L.R. 303 (1995) [20 states adopted laws offering protection from federal antitrust laws, but only Minnesota, Maine have received, approved applications to Dec. 1994; table of laws at 333]; *Health department drafts rules to implement new antitrust immunity*, 4 H.L.R. 434 (1995) [Wyo.]; D. Burda, *Mont. hospitals asking state for immunity*, 25 MOD. HEALTHCARE, Mar. 6, 1995, at 36.

106. *E.g.*, In re Inland Northwest Health Services (Washington Health Services Comm'n Mar. 1995), In re Inland Northwest Health Services (Wash. Att'y Gen.) (informal opinion), *as discussed in* 23 HEALTH L. DIG. (May 1995) at 20.

107. Eastern RR. President's Conference v. Noerr Motor Freight, Inc., 365 U.S. 127 (1961); United Mine Workers v. Pennington, 381 U.S. 657 (1965); Boulware v. State, 960 F.2d 793 (9th Cir. 1992) [opposition to physician construction of MRI facility].

108. St. Joseph's Hosp. v. Hospital Corp. of Am., 795 F.2d 948 (11th Cir.), *reh'g denied (en banc)*, 801 F.2d 404 (11th Cir. 1986).

109. Otter Tail Power Co. v. United States, 410 U.S. 366 (1973).

110. Professional Real Estate Inv., Inc. v. Columbia Pictures Indus., Inc., 113 S. Ct. 1920 (U.S. 1993).

111. 15 U.S.C.A. § 1012(b).

112. Group Life & Health Ins. Co. v. Royal Drug Co., 440 U.S. 205 (1979).

113. National Gerimedical Hosp. v. Blue Cross, 452 U.S. 378 (1981).

114. North Carolina ex rel. Edmisten v. P.I.A. Asheville, Inc., 740 F.2d 274 (4th Cir. 1984), *cert. denied*, 471 U.S. 1003 (1985).

115. American Academic Suppliers, Inc. v. Beckley-Cardy, Inc., 699 F. Supp. 152 (N.D. Ill. 1988).

6

Reorganization and Closure

Some hospitals are in circumstances that will not permit them to continue to function as independent entities. Declining and shifting utilization, reimbursement constraints, other market forces, and governmental initiatives are threatening the existence of some hospitals and leading others to join into larger groups.

In the early 1980s, an average of 40 hospitals closed each year.[1] This rate approximately doubled by the late 1980s,[2] but by the early 1990s the rate had dropped back to the 40–50 range.[3] Each hospital should reevaluate its long-term mission in light of increasing constraints on resources for health care and changing utilization patterns.

Inpatient hospital utilization has declined, while outpatient utilization has grown. Some services have been regionalized to assure efficient use of expensive facilities and equipment and to facilitate better outcome rates by enabling hospital staff to gain and maintain specialized skills that develop through treatment of a larger number of patients with related conditions. Regionalization has reduced the utilization of some local hospitals.

Hospitals are joining into larger groups. Large organizations of many hospitals have formed and those chains are acquiring more hospitals and combining together. On a local scale, two or more hospitals are combining, often without closing any of the hospitals. Even when hospitals do not completely combine, there are many joint ventures and other cooperative efforts[4] to the extent permitted by the antitrust laws discussed in Chapter 5.

Hospitals are also joining with physicians and other providers to form a variety of different organizational relationships including (a) hospitals purchasing physician practices with the physicians becoming hospital employees; (b) physician-hospital organizations (PHOs), medical service organizations (MSOs), and the like (see Chapter 7); (c) selling limited partnership interests in the hospital to the physicians (see Chapter 2); (d) physician foundations purchasing the hospital; and (e) other arrangements.

Managed care is rapidly changing the health care environment. Its effectiveness was demonstrated by the fact that health care costs paid by employers in 1994 were less than in 1993.[5] This reduction was achieved through aggressive use of health maintenance organizations (HMOs) and other managed care entities to control utilization and to negotiate prices.

An increasing percentage of the population is in health care plans that pay only if a network of approved providers are used. Most people cannot afford to seek much of their care, especially hospital care, outside the network. The power to approve providers gives the payers bargaining power in negotiating payment amounts. This has led to reducing payment and to restructuring payment to create incentives for providers to promote efficient utilization. Ultimately in many areas this has led to increased capitation payments, where the provider agrees to provide certain types of health care for an entire population for a fixed price. The provider assumes all or most of the risk of overutilization.

These trends lead hospitals to become part of larger organizations for several reasons.

1. Larger groups have better access to better managed care contracts on a geographic basis. Employers, government, and other ultimate payers generally need networks that cover larger regions than the service area of an individual hospital. If the hospital is not part of an organization that can provide that geographic coverage, the ultimate payers will either contract with a competing organization that can provide the geographic coverage or use an intermediate organization to put together the network that will consume part of the monies that would go to the provider.

2. Larger groups have better access to better managed care contracts on a price basis. For example, only larger organizations are big enough to accept the risks of capitation and other innovative payment systems on a sound actuarial basis. Capitation can work if the population is large enough so that health care needs occur in a statistically predictable fashion. Variations in small populations can be devastating to any capitated budget. Some of these risks are usually insured, but as more of the risks are insured, a greater portion of the payment goes to the insurer. In addition, a larger organization can capitate a wider range of services, reducing the need for an intermediate organization to piece together coverage for the various services covered by the plan.

3. Groups that include hospitals, physicians, and other providers have the potential to manage utilization better, which is attractive to payers and permits the group to provide care within the resources permitted by the payment amount. Groups can have coherent and consistent practice principles and incentives. Not all Integrated Delivery Systems (IDSs) do this effectively, but it is almost impossible for a non-IDS to do it.

4. Larger groups often have better access to capital.

5. Larger groups can purchase supplies and equipment at a greater discount in the national market. Some of the benefits of volume purchasing can be

achieved through joint purchasing organizations without actual merger into a larger system.

6. Larger groups can achieve some savings through centralization of some functions. However, in some cases, this savings can be difficult to achieve[6] or can be offset by the diversion of attention and extra costs of dealing with the central authority.

These trends and others are leading hospitals to reevaluate their future missions. They must consider their capacities, the needs of their communities, and their other responsibilities in evaluating the available options. These options include

1. continuing their present missions and intensifying their relationships with their patients and community, their efforts to contain costs, and their efforts to seek new revenue sources;
2. retaining their independence, but changing their focus in either minor or major ways (a few hospitals may be in a position to expand their individual role to sufficient size, but for many hospitals this is not a realistic option and its pursuit will make the hospital more vulnerable);
3. seeking outside assistance through consultants, shared services, affiliations, or even management contracts;
4. combining with others in multihospital systems or in a single merged hospital[7] and/or in an IDS;
5. relocating;
6. dissolving and closing; and
7. declaring bankruptcy.

Frequently a combination of elements of several of these options will be employed.

The vast majority of hospitals will continue to operate in some form to provide important services to society.[8] However, some institutions will not be able to continue if the present trends persist. As pressure increases, the most responsible course for some hospitals will be to pursue orderly change while the hospital still has substantial bargaining power that can be used to preserve the interests of community and staff to the greatest extent possible, rather than waiting for involuntary reorganization, closure, or a decline in the quality of services provided to the community. The problems of delay are illustrated by one hospital that had to quickly arrange a sale in 1988 before its license expired.[9]

This chapter addresses some of the legal issues involved in merger, consolidation, and sale of assets; dissolution; relocation and closure; bankruptcy; and eminent domain.

MERGER, CONSOLIDATION, AND SALE OF HOSPITALS

Merger occurs when two or more hospitals combine, and one hospital is the surviving organization. Consolidation (sometimes also called a *merger* in nonlegal contexts) occurs when two or more hospitals combine, and the result is an entirely new organization.[10] In a merger or consolidation, the resulting organization assumes the assets and liabilities of the former hospitals.

Without any merger or consolidation, a hospital can be sold, so that it has a new owner. Sometimes the new owner is a large organization[11] and sometimes it is another local organization. Usually the hospital is sold as an ongoing entity with the buyer assuming the assets and liabilities. Sometimes only the assets are sold and the liabilities are not assumed,[12] but this is often not feasible if the intention is to continue to operate the hospital, due to requirements for new licenses, certificates of need, and Medicaid contracts.

The proper procedures must be followed in a merger, consolidation, or sale, including the procedures required by statutes applicable to the constituent hospitals, by their articles of incorporation, and by their bylaws. Some governmental hospitals have special requirements that may include a vote of the residents of the governmental unit, such as a county. When one or more of the hospital organizations is dissolved in the process, the applicable procedures for dissolution must also be followed.

The selection of the proper approach requires a careful analysis that is beyond the scope of this book.[13] Combination or sale of hospitals is often difficult in practice[14] due to (1) philosophical differences, especially religious orientations[15]; (2) reduction in the number of leadership positions; (3) necessary changes in established relationships with physicians, employees, suppliers, the community, and others; and (4) the technical complexity of developing an acceptable approach and obtaining necessary approvals.

Some of the legal considerations in developing the proper approach are restrictions in state statutes, articles of incorporation, bylaws, deeds, grants, gifts, loans, collective bargaining agreements,[16] and other legal documents. For example, if certain changes are made, Hill-Burton hospital construction grants must be repaid to the government,[17] some loans may require accelerated repayment,[18] and some depreciation may be recaptured by governmental payers.[19] There are also complex tax and reimbursement implications. One hospital had to take its case to the California Supreme Court to establish that it did not have to pay sales tax on the sale of its furnishings and equipment as part of the sale of all the assets of the hospital.[20] Proper notification must be given to licensure, certificate of need (CON), and other regulatory authorities, and in some cases licenses, certificates, or permits must be obtained. Some types of changes may even involve federal securities law.

In 1950, the attorney general of Missouri challenged a proposed affiliation of Barnard Free Skin and Cancer Hospital with Washington University Medical Center that involved relocation of Barnard Hospital.[21] The attorney general asserted that the proposal violated several provisions of the gifts and will of Mr. Barnard, which established and supported Barnard Hospital. The Missouri Supreme Court found the affiliation contract to be a reasonable exercise of board powers that did not violate any conditions imposed by gifts and bequests of Mr. Barnard.

In any merger, consolidation, or sale, consideration must be given to antitrust implications (see Chapter 5).

DISSOLUTION

A hospital organization may dissolve as part of a reorganization, merger, or consolidation. The facility may continue to operate under another organization, or the services of the facility may be relocated or discontinued. Proper procedures must be followed in any dissolution, including the procedures in applicable statutes, articles of incorporation, and bylaws. The procedures usually include (1) an approval mechanism, which may involve a state administrative official, a court, or a vote of a specified percentage of the stockholders, members of the corporation, or others; (2) a notification of creditors and others; and (3) clearance by governmental tax departments. Some governmental hospitals have special requirements, including a vote of the residents of the district, city, or county that supports the hospital.

Usually there are not significant questions concerning authority to dissolve a corporation, but such questions are possible. When a Missouri nonprofit hospital association, chartered to provide hospital services to employees of a railroad company, sold its hospital and was distributing the assets to members, several members challenged the dissolution of the association.[22] The court found the dissolution to be beyond the authority of the board under Missouri law because it was not expressly authorized by the articles of incorporation, not approved by a sufficient percentage of the membership, and not of imperative necessity because there was a reasonable prospect of successfully continuing the business.

Dissolution may be voluntarily initiated by the hospital. In appropriate circumstances, dissolution of a hospital corporation may be involuntarily initiated by outside parties, such as the state attorney general, shareholders, directors, and creditors. A person called a *receiver* can be appointed to operate the hospital during the process of involuntary dissolution.

The hospital corporation continues for a period of time after it ceases to operate the hospital so that the affairs of the organization can be concluded. After satisfying any debts and liabilities that have not been assumed by other organizations, the assets of the corporation must be distributed. Some assets may have to be returned to those who gave them to the hospital or to others designated by the giver because of restrictions imposed on the grants or gifts. All other assets are distributed under a plan of distribution that may have to be approved by an administrative agency or court. Assets of for-profit corporations are distributed to their shareholders. Assets designated for charitable purposes must usually be distributed to a corporation or organization engaged in activities that are substantially similar to those of the dissolving corporation.

Some nonprofit hospital corporations choose not to dissolve after selling their assets. They continue as independent foundations and use the proceeds of the sale of the hospital for other charitable purposes, such as paying for indigent patient care.[23]

RELOCATION AND CLOSURE

A hospital building can close (1) as part of a relocation of functions or (2) without transfer or replacement of the functions because they are viewed as excess capacity or are otherwise not viable. Some communities have challenged planned closures, causing costly delays. Although courts have seldom found the plans illegal, some of the challenges have resulted in voluntary modifications of the plans. It is important to determine community concerns when planning relocations and closures and to consider reasonable accommodations to avoid protracted challenges.[24]

The wide variety of theoretically possible legal challenges to the closure of all or part of a hospital is illustrated by the Wilmington Medical Center cases. Two private inner-city hospitals in Wilmington, Delaware, planned to replace a large portion of their inner-city facilities with one suburban hospital, and they obtained approval of the project under section 1122 of the Social Security Act. Neighborhood groups, the National Association for the Advancement of Colored People (NAACP), the Center for Law and Social Policy, and others conducted an extensive legal challenge to the relocation. The plaintiffs claimed that section 1122[25] had been violated, that the relocation discriminated against minorities in violation of Title VI of the Civil Rights Act[26] and against the disabled in violation of section 504 of the Rehabilitation Act of 1973,[27] and that an environmental impact statement was required under the National Environmental Policy Act of 1969.[28] The first reported court order required the Secretary of the Department of Health, Education, and Welfare (HEW) to determine whether there had been any violation and report to the court.[29] In the second reported order the court ruled that an environmental impact statement was not required because no major federal action was involved.[30] In the third reported order the court ruled that it was constitutional to provide different administrative appeal procedures for recipients and complainants under Title VI and section 504.[31] In the next reported order the court ruled that the decision of the secretary of HHS concerning section 1122 approval was not subject to judicial review and that it was constitutional not to provide an appeal mechanism for opponents.[32] In the next reported decision the court ruled that there was a private right of action to challenge discrimination that violated Title VI or section 504 and ordered a trial.[33] After the trial the court ruled that the evidence was adequate to justify the reorganization and relocation plans, so they did not violate Title VI or section 504.[34]

Some courts find that neither patients nor citizens have a right to challenge decisions to close public hospitals.[35] However, when a court ordered a consultation with a community board, failure to do so was contempt of court.[36]

In the 1960s, a New Jersey city sought to enjoin a hospital from relocating outside city limits.[37] The court denied the injunction because the hospital had legally amended its articles of incorporation to give the board authority to relocate and the board had found relocation to be in the hospital's best interests.

Public hospitals frequently must obtain voter approval before closing. Some consumer groups have attempted to use these requirements to preclude the hospital from changing its services. For example, a group in Texas sought to bar the closure of an emergency room of a public hospital. The group asserted that closing the emergency room was equivalent to closing the hospital, so the requirement of a vote before the hospital could be closed should apply. In 1984, a Texas appellate court ruled that they were not equivalent, so no vote was required.[38]

Contractual barriers to closure can also arise. In 1984, an Arkansas court ordered a corporation to continue to operate a nursing home on certain property because it had promised to do so in the lease to the property.[39] In many circumstances federal law requires that employees be given 60 days' notice of closings or large layoffs.[40] Employee challenges to closure have generally been unsuccessful.[41] However, a closing hospital was required to give a union representing its employees copies of some transactional documents so the union could determine worker rights and union responsibilities.[42]

Care must be taken in carrying out the closure. In 1994, all patients were discharged from a small Florida hospital, but the hospital did not relinquish its license or its CON while it pursued sale or consolidation. The city sued to stop the closure. After the hospital refused to treat an emergency patient, the state initiated proceedings to revoke the hospital license. The owner settled with the state, agreeing to transfer ownership or lose the license by a specified date.[43]

BANKRUPTCY

In the past the question of insolvency and bankruptcy of hospitals did not arise often. Generally if a hospital was in a rundown condition physically and financially, funds could be found to bail out or rebuild the hospital. Increased constraints on expansion and modernization of hospitals, higher costs of doing business, changed access to capital, and reduced occupancies have caused the question of insolvency and bankruptcy to be raised more frequently.[44]

For bankruptcy purposes the Federal Bankruptcy Reform Act of 1978 (called the *Bankruptcy Code*) defines an entity as being

> "insolvent" . . . when the sum of such entity's debts is greater than all of such entity's property, at fair evaluation, exclusive of (i) property transferred, concealed, or removed with intent to hinder, delay or defraud such entity's creditors, and (ii) property that may be exempted. . . .[45]

When a hospital discovers that it is insolvent and cannot work out other arrangements with creditors, it may need to consider bankruptcy to settle its accounts and obligations on an equitable and final basis. Since bankruptcy proceedings are entirely a matter of federal law, they are conducted in the federal district courts under the provisions of the Bankruptcy Code. A petition for bankruptcy may be voluntary (by the debtor) or involuntary (by creditors).

Nonprofit corporations, including charitable hospitals, are not subject to involuntary bankruptcy, so they cannot be forced into bankruptcy by creditors. Domestic insurance companies are not subject to bankruptcy. This restriction has led to numerous cases addressing whether HMOs and life care facilities are insurance companies and, thus, not subject to federal bankruptcy. The answer depends on how they are treated under state law.[46] The only remedy available to creditors of a nonprofit organization or insurance company is through applicable state law proceedings. Nonprofit corporations, but not insurance companies, may voluntarily petition to be adjudicated bankrupt. Petitions may be filed with the federal court even after state insolvency proceedings have been instituted.

Bankruptcy does not necessarily require the hospital corporation to dissolve. While bankruptcy under Chapter 7 of the Bankruptcy Code does include dissolution, bankruptcy under Chapter 11 may permit the corporation to continue to operate through modification of its operations and debt structure. Most lawsuits and other actions against a debtor must stop when the petition for bankruptcy is filed. This is called the *automatic stay*.[47] There are some exceptions,[48] and there are procedures creditors can follow to seek permission from the bankruptcy court to pursue their suits, which is generally called "relief from stay."[49]

When the hospital is a creditor, it is important to promptly file in the bankruptcy court most claims against the debtor, or the claims may be lost. In bankruptcy proceedings the debtor or bankruptcy trustee has an opportunity to either assume or reject most ongoing contracts.[50] This has been most controversial when debtors have sought to reject collective bargaining agreements, so the Bankruptcy Code was amended to permit rejections of collective bargaining agreements only after a court finds that certain conditions exist and approves the rejection or modification.[51] Limits have also been placed on the modification of insurance benefits to retired employees.[52] The bankruptcy court has broad powers to undo many transactions that occurred before the filing if they are considered to be preferences that favor one creditor improperly or fraudulent transfers that tried to place assets improperly beyond the reach of creditors.[53]

When a provider continues to operate after filing for bankruptcy, the state Medicaid agency may recoup prior overpayments by reducing current payments. Even though this would be forbidden if done by a private payer, in 1989 the U.S. Supreme Court ruled that a state agency may do so because the Eleventh Amendment to the Constitution grants states immunity from money judgments, even those handed down by bankruptcy courts. The bankruptcy court cannot order the state to make full payment unless the state waives its immunity by filing a claim against the provider.[54]

While a debtor is in the bankruptcy process, it must obtain court approval for some major business transactions.[55] In some cases the bankruptcy court appoints a trustee to operate the business.[56]

For the debtor to successfully leave Chapter 11 bankruptcy, the bankruptcy court must approve a plan for the debtor's reorganization.[57] The debtor has the first opportunity to propose a plan. If the plan is not approved, the creditors may develop a plan. In a Chapter 7 bankruptcy the assets of the debtor are sold, and the proceeds are distributed to the creditors in a priority order specified by the Bankruptcy Code. An important aspect of either Chapter 7 or Chapter 11 of the code is that the court may discharge some debts, so that the debtor is protected from personal liability on those debts.[58]

Hospitals facing insolvency need to evaluate their options to avoid personal liability for directors and to use the available bankruptcy proceedings to optimize the outcome. Directors can be personally liable for voting to authorize improper distribution of corporate assets when the corporation is insolvent.[59] Bankruptcy proceedings can often be used to implement changes that permit the institution to survive.

EMINENT DOMAIN

Federal and state governments have the power to take property for public uses. This is called the power of *eminent domain*. States may authorize local governmental entities to exercise eminent domain. The Fifth Amendment to the Constitution requires the payment of just compensation in exchange for the property. When there is no agreement on compensation, generally courts set the compensation. Eminent domain can be used to take ongoing businesses as well as land.[60]

In the past, hospitals usually confronted eminent domain only when highway authorities took a strip of land to widen a bordering road or when a public hospital authority took neighboring land for expansion. In 1985, the city and county of St. Louis, Missouri, decided that they needed to replace their inner-city public hospitals. Instead of building a new hospital, they proposed to use eminent domain to take a hospital from a for-profit chain and convert it to a public hospital. Faced with the takeover, the chain sold the hospital to a new nonprofit corporation organized by the city and the county to operate the hospital.[61] In 1991, there was a proposal in Miami, Florida, to use eminent domain to take a hospital for public use, but the proposal was abandoned.[62]

NOTES

1. Gallivan, *Trends and Topics*, 59 HOSPS., June 1, 1985, at 29.

2. The exact number of closings was disputed. Pickney, *Hospital closings set record for second consecutive year*, AM. MED. NEWS, Feb. 10, 1989, at 8; Burda & Greene, *AHA closure list questioned*, 19 MOD. HEALTHCARE, Mar. 3, 1989, at 6 [74 ceased acute care operations in 1988]; Office of Inspector General, *Hospital Closure: 1987*, Report No. OAI-04-89-00740, *as reprinted in* MEDICARE & MEDICAID GUIDE (CCH), ¶ 37,864 (May 1989).

3. *Fifty hospitals closed in 1992, report says*, 3 HEALTH L. RPTR. [BNA] 542 (1994) [OIG report] [hereinafter HEALTH L. RPTR. cited as H.L.R.]; *Hospital closure rate falling, IG reports*, 4 H.L.R. 214 (1995) [42 hospitals closed in 1993].

4. *E.g.*, *Thirteen cancer hospitals are forging network in bid to compete for patients*, WALL ST. J., Feb. 1, 1995, at B10.

5. *Health costs paid by employers drop for first time in a decade*, N.Y. TIMES, Feb. 14, 1995, at A1 [1.1 percent decline in 1994]; *Employer costs slip as workers shift to HMOs*, WALL ST. J., Feb. 1, 1995, at A3 [21percent jump in HMO enrollment; 63 percent of eligible employees signed for managed care plans].

6. *E.g.*, *Duplication hard to limit despite hospital mergers*, 25 MOD. HEALTHCARE, Mar. 13, 1995, at 42.

7. *E.g.*, *Hospitals to join in Boston, be largest in U.S.*, WALL ST. J., Dec. 9, 1993, at B7; N.Y. TIMES, Dec. 9, 1993, at A16 [Massachusetts General Hosp. & Brigham and Women's Hosp.].

8. *E.g.*, *Study of market concentration finds distressed hospitals often stay open*, 2 H.L.R. 1573 (1993) [AHA's Hospital Research and Education Trust. tracked 340 hospitals identified as distressed in 1983–1985, 91.2 percent survived through 1990].

9. *St. Anne's out on the auction block*, 18 MOD. HEALTHCARE, Nov. 25, 1988, at 10 [international auction scheduled before closed hospital's license expired].

10. *E.g.*, Larkin, *Financial woes force L.A. hospitals to merge*, 63 HOSPS., July 5, 1989, at 28.

11. *E.g.*, *Hospital corp. completes sale of 104 hospitals*, WALL ST. J., Sept. 18, 1987, at 20 [sale of 104 hospitals by Hospital Corporation of America to Heathtrust, Inc.].

12. *But see* United States v. Vernon Home Health, Inc., 21 F.3d 693 (5th Cir.), *cert. denied*, 115 S. Ct. 575 (U.S. 1994) [asset purchaser liable to United States for Medicare overpayments to prior owner. State law preempted].

13. *See* Greene, *Administrators, attorneys have different approaches to mergers*, 19 MOD. HEALTH-CARE, July 21, 1989, at 38.

14. *E.g.*, D. Burda, *Iowa merger off as boards disagree*, 25 MOD. HEALTHCARE, Feb. 20, 1995, at 8.

15. *E.g.*, *Methodist ministers reviewing proposed sale of Wesley to HCA*, 15 MOD. HEALTHCARE, Jan. 18, 1985, at 9; *Wesley trustees, church approve sale*, 15 MOD. HEALTHCARE, Feb. 15, 1985, at 35

[358 to 252 vote by United Methodist Church. Church to get payments from part of interest income on proceeds. Church to get some control over Foundation]; L. Kertesz, *Community voices concern over hospital's Catholic affiliation*, 25 MOD. HEALTHCARE, Feb. 13, 1995, at 40; *ACLU may sue over dropped services*, MOD. HEALTHCARE, Feb. 13, 1995, at 41 [elimination of contraceptive services after merger with Catholic hospital]; M.C. Jaklevic, *Market forces hospital to lose Catholic status*, 25 MOD. HEALTHCARE, Mar. 6, 1995, at 40 [abandoning religious status so it can be sold to non-Catholic system]; *As health mergers rise, standards of Catholics face a new challenge*, N.Y. TIMES, Mar. 8, 1995, at A11.

16. *E.g.*, Asseo v. Hospital San Francisco, Inc., No. 88-1101 (D. P.R. Oct. 7, 1988), *as discussed in* 16 HEALTH L. DIG., Dec. 1988, at 28 [acquiring hospital found to be successor corporation obligated to bargain with nurses' union].

17. *E.g.*, 15 U.S.C.A. § 291i; United States v. St. John's Gen. Hosp., 875 F.2d 1064 (3d Cir. 1989); United States v. Coweta County Hosp. Auth., 603 F. Supp. 111 (N.D. Ga.1984), *aff'd*, 777 F.2d 667 (11th Cir. 1985); *see also* National Med. Enterprises, Inc. v. United States, 28 Fed. Cl. 540 (1993), *appeal dismissed*, 14 F.3d 612 (Fed. Cir. 1993) [20-year lease is transfer of hospital triggering Hill-Burton recovery].

18. *E.g.*, IRS PLR No. 9427025 (Apr. 11, 1994); *Hospital sale to for-profit firm requires bond redemption in 90 days*, 3 H.L.R. 971 (1994).

19. *E.g.*, Sandpoint Convalescent Servs., Inc. v. Idaho Dep't of Health & Welfare, 114 Idaho 281, 756 P.2d 398 (1988) [recapture of Medicaid depreciation payments not unconstitutional].

20. *E.g.*, Creighton Omaha Regional Health Care Corp. v. Sullivan, 950 F.2d 563 (8th Cir. 1991) [recapture of Medicare depreciation]; Bethesda Found. v. Nebraska Dep't of Social Servs., 243 Neb. 130, 498 N.W.2d 86 (1993) [state recapture of Medicaid depreciation on sale to for-profit organization].

21. Taylor v. Baldwin, 362 Mo. 1224, 247 S.W.2d 741 (1952).

22. McDaniel v. Frisco Employees' Hosp. Ass'n, 510 S.W.2d 752 (Mo. Ct. App. 1974).

23. *E.g.*, J. Greene, *Are foundations bearing fruit?* 25 MOD. HEALTHCARE, Mar. 20, 1995, at 53; Coady, *Not-for-profits, beware—Foundation formed by sale could be short lived*, 15 MOD. HEALTHCARE, Mar. 29, 1985, at 138; Carland, *Computer model used to evaluate foundation had flawed assumptions*, 15 MOD. HEALTHCARE, June 7, 1985, at 177; D.W. Coyne & K.R. Kas, *The not-for-profit hospital as a charitable trust: To whom does its value belong?* 24 J. HEALTH & HOSP. L. 48 (1991); *see also Big charities born of nonprofit-to-profit shifts*, WALL ST. J., Apr. 4, 1995, at B1 [conversions of Blue Cross, other nonprofit health plans].

24. *E.g.*, Mussington v. St. Luke's–Roosevelt Hosp. Ctr., 18 F.3d 1033 (2d Cir. 1994), *aff'g*, 824 F. Supp. 427 (S.D. N.Y. 1993) [individuals, three churches sued to stop transfer of hospital services from minority low-income neighborhood, but all claims barred by laches or statute of limitations]; Greenpoint Hosp. Community Bd. v. New York City Health & Hosps. Corp., 114 A.D.2d 1028, 495 N.Y.S.2d 467 (2d Dep't 1985) [hospital found in contempt of court for violating order on consultations with community board].

25. 42 U.S.C.A. § 1320a-1, which is not being enforced, 53 Fed. Reg. 10,431 (Mar. 31, 1988).

26. 42 U.S.C.A. §§ 2000d–2000d-6.

27. 29 U.S.C.A. § 794.

28. 42 U.S.C.A. § 4332.

29. NAACP v. Wilmington Med. Ctr., Inc., 426 F. Supp. 919 (D. Del. 1977).

30. NAACP v. Wilmington Med. Ctr., Inc., 436 F. Supp. 1194 (D. Del. 1977), *aff'd*, 584 F.2d 619 (3d Cir. 1978).

31. NAACP v. Wilmington Med. Ctr., Inc., 453 F. Supp. 330 (D. Del. 1978).

32. Wilmington United Neighborhoods v. United States, Dep't of HEW, 458 F. Supp. 628 (D. Del. 1978), *aff'd*, 615 F.2d 112 (3d Cir. 1980), *cert. denied*, 449 U.S. 827 (1980).

33. NAACP v. Med. Ctr., Inc., 599 F.2d 1247 (3d Cir. 1979), *rev'g*, 453 F. Supp. 280 (D. Del. 1978).

34. NAACP v. Wilmington Med. Ctr., Inc., 491 F. Supp. 290 (D. Del. 1980), *aff'd*, 657 F.2d 1322 (3d Cir. 1981).

35. *E.g.*, Citizens for State Hosp. v. Commonwealth, 123 Pa. Commw. 150, 553 A.2d 496, *mot. dismissed*, 522 Pa. 137, 560 A.2d 140 (1989), *cert. denied*, 494 U.S. 1017 (1990) [citizens]; Punikaia v. Clark, 720 F.2d 564 (9th Cir. 1983), *cert. denied*, 469 U.S. 816 (1984) [patient residents of leprosarium had no property interest in continued operation of facility, so were not entitled to hearing before closure].

36. Greenpoint Hosp. Commun. Bd. v. N.Y.C. Health & Hosps. Corp., 114 A.D.2d 1028, 495 N.Y.S.2d 467 (2d Dep't 1985).

37. City of Paterson v. Paterson Gen. Hosp., 97 N.J. Super. 514, 235 A.2d 487 (Ch. Div. 1967).

38. Jackson County Hosp. Dist. v. Jackson County Citizens for Continued Hosp. Care, 669 S.W.2d 147 (Tex. Ct. App. 1984).

39. Lonoke Nursing Home, Inc. v. Wayne & Neil Bennett Family Partnership, 12 Ark. App. 282, 676 S.W.2d 461, *adhered to (en banc)*, 12 Ark. App. 286, 679 S.W.2d 823 (1984).

40. 29 U.S.C.A. §§ 2101–2109; *but see* Jurcev v. Central Commun. Hosp., 7 F.3d 618 (7th Cir. 1993), *cert. denied*, 114 S. Ct. 1830 (U.S. 1994) [hospital closure with two weeks' notice did not violate WARN because foundation's decision to stop making payments to hospital was unforeseeable business circumstance that caused hospital to close].

41. *E.g.*, Brindle v. West Allegheny Hosp., 406 Pa. Super. 572, 594 A.2d 766 (1991) [dismissed claim by six nurses of fraud in closure of hospital].

42. Mary Thompson Hosp. v. NLRB, 943 F.2d 741 (7th Cir. 1991).

43. City of Destin v. Columbia/HCA Healthcare Corp., No. 94-17015-CA (Fla. Cir. Ct. Okaloosa County filed June 15, 1994) [city suit]; Agency for Health Care Admin. v. Fort Walton Beach Med. Ctr., HQA No. 01-094-005-HOSP (complaint filed Aug. 22, 1994, settled Aug. 30, 1994) [license revocation proceeding], *as discussed in* 3 H.L.R 877, 1207, 1280 (1994).

44. *E.g., Philadelphia system seeks protection from creditors*, 19 MOD. HEALTHCARE, July 21, 1989, at 14; Larkin, *Town buys bankrupt hospital and turns it around*, 63 HOSPS., June 20, 1989, at 22; Lutz & Kim, *Six Gateway Medical Systems hospitals file for protection in bankruptcy court*, 19 MOD. HEALTHCARE, June 2,1989, at 4; Dine, *Clash between mission and money results in bankruptcy for Catholic hospital*, 18 MOD. HEALTHCARE, Sept. 2, 1988, at 72.

45. 11 U.S.C.A. § 101(31).

46. 11 U.S.C.A. § 109; *e.g.*, In re Estate of Medcare HMO, 998 F.2d 436 (7th Cir. 1993) [HMO not subject to bankruptcy]; In re Family Health Servs., 143 Bankr. 232 (C.D. Cal. 1992) [HMO not subject to bankruptcy]; In re Mich. Master Health Plan, Inc., 90 Bankr. 274 (E.D. Mich. 1985) [HMO subject to bankruptcy because not insurance company under state law]; In re Portland MetroHealth, Inc., 15 Bankr. 102 (Bankr. D. Or. 1981) [HMO is insurance company under state law]; In re Florida Brethren Homes, 88 Bankr. 445 (Bankr. S.D. Fla. 1988) [life care facility subject to bankruptcy because not insurance company, under state law].

47. 11 U.S.C.A. § 362.

48. *E.g.*, In re Grau, 172 Bankr. 686 (Bankr. S.D. Fla. 1994) [not violation of automatic stay for malpractice creditor to have communication with state licensing board concerning failure of debtor doctor to pay judgement where first report filed pre-petition].

49. 11 U.S.C.A. § 362(c), (d); *e.g.*, In re Corporacion de Servicos, 60 Bankr. 920 (D. P. R. 1986), *aff'd*, 805 F.2d 440 (1st Cir. 1986) [exemption from automatic stay for state regulatory actions does not

apply when effort to revoke hospital license is subterfuge to force termination of management contract]; In re Bel Air Chateau Hosp., Inc., 611 F.2d 1248 (9th Cir. 1979) [NLRB proceedings not subject to automatic stay, but can be stayed if assets threatened].

50. 11 U.S.C.A. § 365.

51. 11 U.S.C.A. § 1113; *e.g.*, In re Sierra Steel Corp., 88 Bankr. 337 (Bankr. D. Colo. 1988) [approval of modifications in collective bargaining agreement].

52. 11 U.S.C.A. § 1114.

53. *E.g.*, 11 U.S.C.A. §§ 544, 547, 548, 553; In re Sheppard's Dental Ctrs., Inc., 65 Bankr. 274 (Bankr. S.D. Fla. 1986) [transfer of management agreement can be voidable transfer].

54. 11 U.S.C.A. § 106, as amended by Pub. L. No. 103-394, § 113, 108 Stat. 4117 (1994); Hoffman v. Connecticut Dep't of Income Maintenance, 492 U.S. 96 (1989). For an example of waiver by filing a claim, *see* In re St. Joseph Hosp., 103 Bankr. 643 (Bankr. E.D. Pa. 1989).

55. *E.g.*, *AMH seeks court approval for sale of Calif. facility*, 18 MOD. HEALTHCARE, Oct. 14, 1988, at 8.

56. *E.g.*, *Care creditors ask court to remove chain's owners*, 19 MOD. HEALTHCARE, June 2, 1989, at 7.

57. *E.g.*, In re Community Hosp. of the Valleys, 51 Bankr. 231 (Bankr. 9th Cir. 1987), *aff'd*, 820 F.2d 1097 (9th Cir. 1987) [confirmation of reorganization plan]; In re Medical Equities, Inc., 39 Bankr. 795 (Bankr., S.D. Ohio 1984) [denial of confirmation]; *Judge says plan to reopen hospital is unworkable*, 18 MOD. HEALTHCARE, Sept. 2, 1988, at 14 [bankruptcy court rejected community group reorganization plan].

58. *E.g.*, 11 U.S.C.A. §§ 523, 524, 727, 1141(d).

59. Renger Mem. Hosp. v. State, 674 S.W.2d 828 (Tex. Ct. App. 1984).

60. *E.g.*, Long Island Lighting Co. v. Cuomo, 666 F. Supp. 370 (N.D. N.Y. 1987) [upholding state law authorizing eminent domain to take over power company], *vacated*, 888 F.2d 230 (2d Cir. 1989) [moot due to settlement]. Mandating hospital governing board composition is not considered taking of hospital. *See* American Hosp. Ass'n v. Hansbarger, 600 F. Supp. 465 (N.D. W.Va. 1984), *aff'd*, 783 F.2d 1184 (4th Cir.), *cert. denied*, 479 U.S. 820 (1986).

61. Punch, *Faced with takeover, Charter officials will sell St. Louis hospital for $15 million*, 15 MOD. HEALTHCARE, July 19, 1985, at 24; *New corporation purchases Charter hospital in St. Louis*, 15 MOD. HEALTHCARE, Nov. 8, 1985, at 11.

62. *Dade may force hospital to sell to ease crowding at Jackson*, MIAMI [FL] HERALD, Mar. 4, 1991, at 1B [proposal to take Cedars Medical Center]; *Cedars to fight bid to take over hospital*, MIAMI [FL] HERALD, Mar. 23, 1991, at 4B.

7

Medical Staff

Physicians and other independent practitioners who practice in each hospital are organized into a medical staff. Only members are permitted to admit patients to and practice in the hospital. A physician is appointed to the medical staff and granted clinical privileges by the hospital governing board. A physician is permitted to provide only services for which clinical privileges have been granted. The board has the responsibility to exercise discretion in deciding whether to grant an appointment and what scope of clinical privileges to grant. The board also assures that the physician is periodically reviewed and that clinical privileges are adjusted when needed. The board nearly always relies on the medical staff to conduct reviews and recommend board action.

This chapter is divided into three parts. The first part discusses the present status of the medical staff, appointment to the medical staff, delineation of clinical privileges, periodic review, modification and termination of clinical privileges, hearing rights of physicians, the potential liability of those involved in the process of making medical staff appointment and clinical privilege decisions, and contracts between hospitals and physicians. The second part provides a historical background on the development of the medical staff. The last part discusses possible future directions for the relationship of hospitals and physicians.

RELATIONSHIP OF MEDICAL STAFF AND HOSPITAL

Physicians are organized into a medical staff in order to comply with Joint Commission on Accreditation of Healthcare Organizations (Joint Commission) standards, Medicare conditions of participation, and state hospital licensing rules. The organized medical staff has a collective accountability to the governing board for the quality of care delivered by the medical staff.

The board has ultimate authority over the hospital; this authority must be exercised in a manner consistent with satisfactory patient care. Through bylaws, the board delegates to the medical staff the authority and duty to carry out medical aspects of patient care. The board retains authority and responsibility to approve appointments to the medical staff, to grant and decrease clinical privileges, and to assure that there is a procedure for monitoring quality of care. The board normally looks to the medical staff to monitor quality of care and to provide expert advice on appointment and clinical privilege decisions. The medical staff organization usually includes officers; an executive committee to act in matters that do not require approval of the entire staff; and other committees to address specific issues, such as infection control, pharmaceutical utilization, and credentials review. In smaller hospitals these functions are frequently performed by the entire medical staff as a committee of the whole. In larger hospitals several specialty departments with their own organizations are often coordinated by the overall medical staff organization. Functions of the organized medical staff include (1) facilitating communication among the medical staff members and with the hospital, (2) implementing hospital and medical staff policies and procedures, (3) recommending appointments to the medical staff and scope of clinical privileges, (4) providing continuing medical education, and (5) taking other actions necessary to govern the medical staff and relate to the hospital board.

Liability

The board cannot abdicate its responsibility by relying completely on the medical staff. Joint Commission accreditation standards, Medicare conditions of participation, and most hospital licensing rules require board involvement. Hospitals have been found liable for physician actions when they failed to evaluate the physicians properly prior to appointment or failed to monitor physician performance properly after appointment. The Wisconsin Supreme Court found a hospital liable for injuries to a patient by a physician because the hospital should never have appointed him to the medical staff.[1] The hospital had not checked his professional credentials and references. A check would have uncovered discrepancies and misrepresentations that would have led to denial of appointment. An Arizona court found a hospital liable for failing to curtail the clinical privileges of a physician who had several bad results with a procedure, resulting in suits.[2] The absence of a medical staff recommendation to curtail privileges was not an effective excuse. The court considered the organized medical staff to be the hospital's agent, so the hospital was legally considered to know everything the organized medical staff knew. Most states find liability if a hospital fails to act when it has actual knowledge of, or reason to suspect, serious problems.

External Review

Sometimes the board employs outside experts to assist in medical care review. Usually this is done with the advice and concurrence of the medical staff. Outside experts often review specialists when other staff members do not feel able to review them or when those who are able to conduct the review appear to be biased. Some specialty societies have established programs to provide this consultation.

Medical Staff Bylaws

Since 1985, the Joint Commission has required that medical staff bylaws be adopted and changed only with the mutual consent of the medical staff and hospital.[3] Previously some courts had recognized the legal right of the hospital board to change the medical staff bylaws unilaterally when necessary.[4] In some states, hospitals probably continue to have this legal authority and, in some circumstances, the legal duty to make required changes. However, exercising that authority may jeopardize Joint Commission accreditation. Even when the board has authority to make unilateral changes, hospitals generally seek mutually acceptable changes even when this requires prolonged negotiations. The resulting changes are more likely to be implemented fully when commitment to them is mutual. Unilateral changes are an extraordinary last resort, usually adopted at great cost to deal with impasses.

Cooperation

Hospital and organized medical staff efforts generally should not be focused on defining ultimate legal rights; they should be focused on minimizing misunderstandings and conflicts, seeking mutually acceptable solutions, and resolving impasses without resort to the judicial process. A Joint Task Force on Hospital–Medical Staff Relationships of the AMA and the AHA published a report in 1985 outlining ways to achieve this focus.[5] However, while it is important to be fair to individual medical staff applicants and members, the same effort to reach mutually acceptable solutions to problems with individuals is not required. The hospital and medical staff must take appropriate steps to maintain standards within the hospital.

Boycotts

Unfortunately, some hospital medical staffs or segments of medical staffs have chosen to boycott hospitals.[6] Some hospitals have been reluctant to use the antitrust laws to challenge such boycotts, but increasingly hospitals, other affected entities, and government agencies have initiated action. Most of these enforcement actions have been settled with the boycotting physicians agreeing not to engage in boycotts.[7]

Officers

One area of dispute has been the selection of medical staff officers. Sometimes physicians object when the hospital appoints officers or rejects the officers they prefer. The Joint Commission does not require a particular selection procedure. The Joint Commission requires only that all officers be medical staff members and that they be selected in accordance with hospital bylaws.[8] In 1989, a California court approved rejection by a hospital board of the medical staff's choice for president because the bylaws reserved this authority, but the board later settled the suit and accepted the elected president.[9] In 1985, a Florida appellate court refused to order a hospital to hold a medical staff election.[10] The hospital had appointed temporary officers due to disruption of operations. However, the court indicated that if the medical staff held its own election, a court could decide which set of officers should preside. Hospitals should review individual contracts with physicians as well as bylaws before considering these actions.

In most jurisdictions, if an impasse occurs, the hospital can probably remove medical staff officers.[11] If this results in a breach of contract, the hospital may have to pay damages, but it is unlikely that a court will order the person reinstated to the office. It is rare for circumstances to arise where such removal is appropriate, but such circumstances can occur. In 1994, a Wisconsin court refused to reinstate a chief of staff who had been removed by a hospital.[12] Such hospital actions are often disruptive to the relationship between the hospital and other medical staff members.

Department Structure

In most hospitals, the medical staff is divided into departments along specialty lines. Disputes sometimes arise when the departmental structure is changed.

Medical departments have heads. The selection and removal of heads sometimes leads to disputes. Generally courts will not order the reinstatement of removed department heads,[13] but there have been exceptions.[14] When there is a contract between the hospital and the department head, removal can also lead to a claim for damages for breach of contract.[15]

Joint Commission standards require each department to perform a variety of administrative functions.[16] Thus, it is important to have a head who will actually perform the required functions. Most physicians who accept such positions conscientiously perform their duties, but when one fails to do so due to time pressures, conflicting loyalties, or other factors, the medical staff and ultimately the hospital must be able to put someone in the position who will do the job.

Joint Commission standards also require department heads to make recommendations concerning all applicants for clinical privileges in the departments.[17] In single specialty departments, this means that the head can be an economic competitor of the applicant, so that any negative recommendation may lead to an antitrust claim. If the department head stays out of the later steps of the application process and those steps do not automatically defer to the department head, the risk of a successful antitrust claim may not be great.

To reduce the administrative burden created by departments and reduce the antitrust risk, it has been suggested that the number of departments should be reduced.[18] Some courts have recognized broad discretion to reorganize departments.[19] However, many physicians associate prestige value with departmental positions, so many hospitals may not change the department structure.

Departmental rules have led to litigation. For example, a federal appellate court upheld a departmental rule requiring 24-hour notice of desire to use a particular anesthesiologist.[20] A New York court ruled that the head of a medical department could be sued by a patient injured through treatment by another member of the department based on the head's failure to develop and implement appropriate rules.[21]

Committee Structure

In the past, the Joint Commission and Medicare conditions of participation required an elaborate medical staff committee structure, but now only the medical executive committee is required.[22] The functions that were performed by committees can now be performed in other ways. Many hospitals still have a complex committee structure. It is likely that many medical staffs will simplify the committee structure to reduce the time demands and refocus responsibility for the functions.[23]

RELATIONSHIP OF INDIVIDUAL PHYSICIANS AND HOSPITALS INSIDE THE MEDICAL STAFF STRUCTURE

In most hospitals, physician relationships with the hospital are usually defined through the medical staff structure. The physician is appointed to membership on the medical staff and is granted clinical privileges that define what the physician may do within the hospital. Following is a discussion of

1. the difference between the legal requirements for public and private hospitals,
2. medical staff appointment,
3. delineation of clinical privileges,
4. review and reappointment,

5. modification and termination of clinical privileges,
6. review procedures, and
7. liability issues concerning these actions.

Difference Between Public and Private Hospitals

Lawsuits arising out of board decisions concerning appointments and clinical privileges of physicians usually focus on (1) the right of the board to impose the rules applied or (2) the procedures followed in reaching the decision. In most states, public hospital boards have less discretion than do private hospital boards. Many states have also limited the discretion of private hospitals.

Public Hospitals

Due Process. Public hospitals must satisfy the Fourteenth Amendment to the United States Constitution, which says that no state shall "deprive any person of life, liberty, or property, without due process of law." An action by a public hospital is considered a state action. The interest of a physician in practicing in a hospital can be a liberty or property interest, entitling the physician to "due process of law" when a public hospital makes a decision concerning medical staff appointment or clinical privileges. However, a physician does not have a constitutional right to practice in any public hospital.[24] Physicians must demonstrate that they satisfy valid hospital rules before they may practice in the hospital.

Some federal courts have ruled that an applicant does not have a property or liberty interest in being appointed or being granted privileges.[25] Usually the property right is in continuation of membership or privileges that have been granted.[26]

To provide physicians with due process, hospital rules must be reasonable and adequately express the intent of the hospital. Rules that are too arbitrary or vague may be unenforceable. Physicians must be offered fair procedures when they are being deprived of a liberty or property interest.

In some states, it may be possible to structure clinical privileges in a public hospital so that no property interest is created, if there is no understanding not to revoke the privileges without due process.[27]

Equal Protection. The Fourteenth Amendment also says that no state shall "deny to any person within its jurisdiction the equal protection of the laws." Equal protection means that like persons must be dealt with in like fashion. The equal protection clause is concerned with the justifiability of classifications used to distinguish persons for various legal purposes. Determining whether a particular difference between persons can justify a particular difference in rules or procedures can be difficult. Courts generally require government agencies to justify differences with a *rational reason*. The major exception to this standard is the *strict scrutiny* courts apply to distinctions based on *suspect classifications*, such as race, and the intermediate level of scrutiny applied to sex-based classifications. Because of comprehensive legislation prohibiting discrimination based on many characteristics, most challenges to alleged discriminatory actions are based on legislation, rather than directly on this constitutional principle. Nondiscrimination legislation is discussed in Chapter 9.

Public Hospital Immunities. Public hospitals have some protections from suits. The Eleventh Amendment to the Constitution forbids many private suits in federal courts against states and their agencies. This has been applied to bar some suits against hospitals that are considered agencies of the state,[28] but not against local governmental hospitals.[29] Moreover, Congress may abrogate the immunity to permit suits against states and their instrumentalities.[30]

The Local Government Antitrust Act of 1984[31] protects public hospitals from most antitrust damage claims, and the state action doctrine discussed in Chapter 5 protects public hospitals from many other antitrust suits.

Sovereign immunity protects public hospitals in some states from many claims under state common law (see Chapter 10).

Private Hospitals

Medical staff actions of most private hospitals are subject to fewer legal constraints than are actions by public hospitals. The Fourteenth Amendment does not apply to private hospitals except in the unusual circumstance when the hospital activity is found to be state action. In some states, private hospitals are required to follow only their own rules in medical staff actions. In other states, legislatures and courts require some procedures in medical staff decisions.

Private hospitals are rarely found to be engaged in state action and, thus, subject to the Fourteenth Amendment. Prior to 1974, some courts ruled that private hospitals were engaging in state action because they were heavily regulated by the state and received governmental funds, including Medicare and Medicaid payments.

In 1974, the U.S. Supreme Court ruled that regulation or funding did not establish state action. The Court said that there must be a "sufficiently close nexus between the state and the challenged action of the regulated entity so that the action of the latter may be fairly treated as that of the state itself." The Court gave the following examples of such a connection: (1) when the private entity exercises powers traditionally reserved for the state, (2) when the state directly benefits by sharing in the rewards and responsibilities of the private venture, and (3) when the state directs or encourages the particular act.[32]

In rare circumstances private hospitals can engage in state action. If a majority of the governing board is appointed by a governmental agency, the courts will be likely to find the hospital to be engaged in state action.[33] Appointment of a minority of the governing body is not likely to be sufficient.[34] If the hospital leases from a governmental entity, it may be found to be engaged in state action,[35] but some courts do not consider this sufficient.[36] However, a public hospital that is managed by a private corporation is generally still public, so the actions of the management corporation are state actions.[37]

Hospital Rules

Most hospitals have rules concerning the criteria and procedures to be followed in making decisions concerning medical staff membership and clinical privilege delineation. These rules usually appear in the medical staff bylaws and are required for Joint Commission accreditation.[38] Most courts require hospitals to follow their own rules,[39] but often overlook minor deviations that do not significantly affect the fundamental interests of the physician.[40] A few courts have indicated that hospital rules do not have to be followed if due process is actually provided through other procedures.[41] Most hospitals strive to comply with their own rules, so that they do not have to risk having a court fail to accept deviations from hospital rules.

Some courts have ruled that a physician must be a medical staff member before having a right to seek court enforcement of medical staff and hospital bylaws.[42] This parallels the federal court determinations concerning public hospitals. In those states, applicants cannot use violation of the bylaws as a basis to challenge appointment denial.

State Law Requirements

There is a great range of state law requirements concerning the relationship of public and private hospitals with physicians. Some states have not imposed any requirements, but most states will enforce hospital rules. By statute or court decision some states have limited the latitude of all hospitals.[43] For example, New York requires hospitals to process all applications for membership or clinical privileges from physicians, podiatrists, and dentists.[44] Membership or clinical privileges may be denied, curtailed, or terminated only after reasons have been stated. The only permissible reasons are "standards of patient care, patient welfare, the objectives of the institution or the character or competency of the applicant." The Public Health Council is authorized to investigate complaints alleging violations and to order a hospital to review actions if the council finds "cause exists for the crediting of the allegations." The New York courts require physicians to pursue review by the council before they will permit suits against hospitals.[45]

Some state courts require private hospitals to provide some procedural protections for medical staff members, including notice of alleged shortcomings and an opportunity to be heard.[46] New Jersey requires the right to be represented by a lawyer.[47]

One physician challenged the legality of public hospital bylaws that had been adopted without following the formal rule-making procedures of the state administrative procedure act. The Hawaii Supreme Court ruled that bylaws were internal procedures and, thus, not subject to the act.[48]

Medical Staff Appointment

An identified, competent practitioner must be responsible for the care of each hospital patient to satisfy most definitions of a hospital and of a medically necessary admission. The practitioners will usually be physicians, but in some situations they may be dentists and other practitioners. The following discussion concerning physicians also applies to other practitioners who are permitted to admit patients. Hospitals must screen physicians before appointment to the medical staff and allow only medical staff members to admit patients. The admitting physician then assumes continuing responsibility for medical care of that patient until responsibility is transferred to another medical staff member or until the patient is discharged. Since most physicians practice in groups or have other coverage arrangements to permit some time off duty, in practice, such transfers of responsibility are common.

A medical license does not give a physician the right to practice in a particular hospital. Each physician must apply for medical staff appointment. Each physician must prove that he or she satisfies the hospital appointment criteria or that the criteria are not permitted. The burden of proof is on the applying physician, especially if the medical staff bylaws so provide. Many court cases have involved such medical staff issues. Procedural issues are discussed later in this chapter. This section reviews judicial decisions concerning some criteria for initial appointment, reappointment, and termination.

Permitted Criteria

In addition to the obvious criteria of licensure, education, training, and experience, some of the permitted criteria for review of applicants include

1. a complete and accurate application,
2. verification of credentials,
3. references,
4. a demonstrated ability to work with others,
5. board certification or equivalent training and experience,
6. payment of dues and assessments,
7. geographic proximity to the hospital,
8. agreement to provide indigent care,
9. malpractice insurance,
10. the need for additional staff in the specialty,

11. economic credentialing,
12. an M.D. degree or approved medical residency, and
13. health status.

Some of these criteria are subject to limitations and are not permitted in all states. The same standards should apply to all applicants.[49]

Application. Hospitals require a complete and accurate application form, including an agreement to abide by hospital and medical staff rules.[50] Courts have upheld termination or denial of appointment based on false and incomplete applications.[51] Physicians should be required, along with providing other information, to (1) present evidence of medical education, training, experience, current competence, current licensure, and health status; and (2) disclose professional liability actions and pending and completed governmental, institutional, and professional disciplinary actions against them.[52] In some cases the health status information may need to be collected later in the process, as discussed later in this section. Some states will suspend or revoke a physician's medical license for false answers on an application for hospital clinical privileges.[53]

Refusal to release information concerning discipline at other hospitals may be grounds for denial of an application.[54]

One important aspect of most applications is a waiver of liability. Waivers are discussed in the Liability section of this chapter.

Verification. Hospitals need to carefully check information supplied by applicants.[55] One study indicated that up to five percent of applications contain false information.[56] Hospitals can be liable for injuries to patients by physicians who would have been denied membership if application information had been properly checked.[57] Generally hospitals are liable for failing to check applications only when a reasonable check would have led to rejection of the applicant.[58] At least one state hospital association established a statewide credentials verification system.[59]

Hospitals must make an inquiry to the National Practitioner Data Bank concerning each applicant and, at least every two years, concerning each member in order to qualify for the antitrust immunity discussed later in this chapter.[60] Hospitals are presumed to know information they would have obtained by making such inquiries.[61]

References. Satisfactory references may be required,[62] but not from the present medical staff.[63] Some states require references.[64]

Ability To Work With Others. Courts in many states have accepted a requirement that applicants and members demonstrate ability to work harmoniously with other physicians and hospital staff.[65] Most states have not limited the degree of inability to work with others that justifies denial, but a few states have placed limits. In 1967, a New Jersey court accepted that "prospective disharmony" was a reasonable basis for denial if "valid and constructive criticism of hospital practice" is not equated with disharmony.[66] The court noted that "a person has a right to disagree with the policy or practice, but he does not have a right to be disagreeable in doing so." In 1980, the California Supreme Court accepted inability to work with others as a basis for denial when it presents "a real and substantial danger that patients treated by him might receive other than a 'high quality of medical care' at the facility."[67] A few states have forbidden use of this criterion.[68]

Board Certification. Many hospitals require that physicians be board eligible or board certified before being granted specialty privileges. Some hospitals require board certification to be obtained within a specified time.

Most courts have upheld hospital requirements of board certification or completion of an approved residency before specialty clinical privileges are granted.[69] In 1986, a California appellate court upheld a hospital requirement that limited dilation and curettage privileges to physicians who had completed a residency in obstetrics and gynecology.[70] A few courts have invalidated board certification requirements of public hospitals.[71]

One way to avoid controversy is to require board certification or equivalent training and experience.[72] This requirement permits the hospital to avail itself of the strengths of a private certification system while leaving open a channel to deal with individual applicants on a case-by-case basis.

A workable exceptions process also avoids facing the threat of disqualification from participation in Medicare. The Medicare conditions of participation specifically forbid basing clinical privilege decisions solely on board status.[73] It is doubtful that individual physicians can use this as a basis for judicial relief from such requirements.[74] It is probable that only the federal government can enforce the Medicare rules and its only sanction is to terminate Medicare participation.

Joint Commission states that board certification is an excellent benchmark for specialty privileges, but does not make it a requirement.[75] Joint Commission does state that heads of departments should be board certified in the specialty or prove comparable competence.[76]

Some managed care entities require board certification for participation.[77]

Dues. Physicians may be required to pay dues, fees, and assessments to apply for and retain medical staff membership.[78] For example, in 1984 a Michigan appellate court upheld the suspension of a physician who refused to pay a $100 assessment levied by the medical staff executive committee to furnish a medical library.[79]

Geographic Proximity. Some courts have upheld geographic criteria that require an applicant to live or practice within a certain distance of the hospital, stated in terms of miles, travel time, or location close enough that the applicant is reasonably able to provide continuity of care.[80] These rules are intended to assure response to patient needs, especially during emergencies. The Joint Commission recognizes geographic location as an appropriate criterion.[81] Geographic limits based on political boundaries or utilization control objectives have been successfully challenged.[82]

Since the goal of geographic criteria is to assure timely coverage of patient needs, some hospitals accept coverage arrangements as an alternative means of compliance. For example, (1) a nearby individual or group may agree to provide coverage for a more distant applicant or (2) a group of more distant applicants may agree to have one person on duty at the hospital or on call nearby at all times.

Indigent Care. Physicians may be required to provide uncompensated indigent care.[83]

Malpractice Insurance. Since 1975, appellate courts have consistently upheld reasonable requirements of malpractice insurance as a condition of medical staff membership.[84] In a malpractice suit both the hospital and the physicians are generally sued. If one defendant is not adequately insured, the burden of any payment will fall disproportionately on the others. Thus, there is a legitimate business interest in assuring adequate malpractice protection. The Joint Commission recognizes adequate professional liability insurance as an appropriate criterion.[85] Some courts have required flexibility in enforcing such rules because they can become unreasonable when, for example, no malpractice insurance is available.[86] Some states have imposed statutory requirements for coverage,[87] but generally hospitals are still free to impose stricter requirements.

Staff Size Limitations. Hospitals may limit the size of the medical staff in some circumstances. The limits should be adopted by the board with documentation of the reasons. Courts are concerned that these limits not be used to protect the economic interests of present medical staff members. Limitations on the number of staff members in certain specialties have been upheld in several court decisions.[88] However, in 1976 a New Jersey court invalidated a moratorium on new staff appointments because inadequate evidence had been presented that the moratorium was needed to assure appropriate patient care.[89] In 1986, the New Jersey Supreme Court disapproved closed staff arrangements that permitted only new physicians who associated with current members[90] or who had not practiced in the area for the past two years.[91] In 1985, a North Carolina appellate court ruled that a hospital could close a part of its medical staff if the moratorium was reasonable for the hospital and community and was fairly administered but that the challenging podiatrist was entitled to a trial in which he could attempt to show the moratorium was unreasonable.[92] The Joint Commission recognizes the appropriateness of criteria related to the ability of the hospital to provide facilities and support services.[93]

When a hospital has entered an exclusive contract with one physician or group for a specialty or procedure, others will not be eligible to be granted privileges for that specialty or procedure. Courts have generally permitted hospitals to start a new exclusive contract and terminate the privileges of other physicians to perform the specialty or procedure.[94] In 1994, Illinois passed a law that requires a notice and hearing before privileges of others are terminated due to an exclusive contract.[95]

One of the factors that the IRS uses for determining whether a hospital qualifies for tax exemption is whether it has an open medical staff.[96] Such factors are not enforceable by private parties, such as other applying physicians. However, the IRS could use the absence of this factor as the basis for considering revocation of the hospital tax exemption. The minimum characteristics necessary to assure tax exemption are not yet clear (see discussion in Chapter 4). The purpose behind the open staff requirement was to demonstrate that the hospital was "operated to serve a public rather than a private interest," so the focus appears to have been on assuring that the general public could gain access to the hospital, not to assure that physicians could use the hospital for their private practices. There was also a concern that a closed staff could result in insider benefit to the physicians on the staff.[97] Again the focus appears to be on avoiding benefit to insiders, not on providing benefit to other physicians. Thus, it is possible that the IRS would accept a closed staff if there were contractual commitments and hospital policies that assured public access and effective nonphysician control of the benefits received by those on the closed staff. Such an arrangement could provide the public with better access than an open staff. Tax exemption has been approved for entities that include closed departments in other contexts without addressing the impact on hospital tax exemption.[98]

Economic Credentialing. Several different criteria are lumped together under the label of economic credentialing. Three of these criteria are (1) promoting efficient practice, (2) requiring participation in hospital managed care and related arrangements, and (3) avoiding economic competition with the hospital. Some persons also call exclusive contracts economic credentialing, but they are addressed separately in this book. Although still controversial, many of these criteria have been upheld by courts.

These issues usually arise in the context of nonrenewal or termination of clinical privileges, so they will be discussed in that section of this chapter. One case of the third type did arise in the application context. In 1992, a Florida court upheld denial of surgical privileges to the head of the open heart surgery program at the competing hospital.[99]

M.D. Degree or Medical Residency. Due to antitrust rulings, the Joint Commission no longer restricts the scope of practitioners that a hospital may permit to practice. However, except where state law requires that others be permitted on the staff, a hospital is generally free to limit its staff to those with an M.D. degree.[100] Hospitals that impose such limits should avoid doing so in a manner that could be construed as a conspiracy with the medical staff.[101] Many states have required hospitals to permit dentists, osteopathic physicians, podiatrists, and others on their staffs.[102] One state has ruled that chiropractors may not have hospital privileges.[103]

State statutes that merely authorize a hospital to admit certain practitioners do not require the hospital to do so. In 1994, a North Carolina court ruled that its law authorizing hospital privileges for chiropractors did not require any hospital to admit chiropractors to its staff.[104] However, there are hospitals that have opened chiropractic departments.[105]

Health Status. The Joint Commission requires that health status be a criteria.[106] The Americans with Disabilities Act (ADA) regulates when inquiries can be made concerning health status in situations related to employment (see Chapter 9). Even though most physicians are not employees, the ADA restrictions may apply to some medical staff applicants due to the impact of the medical staff membership decision on their other employment relationships.[107] If a hospital determines that the ADA applies, it should limit application inquiries concerning health status to questions permitted by the ADA. Any offer of membership can then be contingent on ascertainment of health status. The ADA permits consistently applied inquiries and examinations after the employment-related decision has otherwise been made.

Unacceptable Criteria

Some criteria are unacceptable, including (1) violations of nondiscrimination laws, (2) required kickbacks and other illegal contracts, (3) medical society membership, and (4) nonstandardized tests.

Nondiscrimination Laws. Hospitals cannot base their refusal to appoint a physician on the applicant's race, creed, color, sex, national origin, or disability. Alleged violations are often addressed under the antidiscrimination laws discussed in Chapter 9.[108] These laws generally apply to all institutions receiving federal funds, whether the institutions are public or private. Some of these laws also apply to some entities not receiving federal funds.

Citizenship probably cannot be used as a criteria.[109] Thus, legal aliens with appropriate licenses and an immigration status permitting medical practice probably cannot be excluded on the basis of lack of citizenship. Exclusion of undocumented aliens is probably permitted and may be required.[110]

Illegal Contracts. In most states there are limits on the contracts that facilities can require physicians to enter. In 1986, a New York appellate court questioned a nursing home that had required a physician to enter a fee-splitting arrangement before allowing practice in the facility.[111]

Medical Society Membership. Hospitals cannot require membership in a medical society.[112] Courts view such requirements as an abdication of the hospital's responsibility to screen applications and are concerned that medical society membership could be denied for discriminatory reasons. A few older court decisions accepted this criterion for private hospitals,[113] but it is doubtful that courts will permit this criterion today except in states that do not review any private hospital criteria.

Nonstandardized Tests. A California public hospital adopted a requirement that applicants be given "such tests, oral and written, as the credentials committee shall in its discretion determine." A California appellate court invalidated the requirement because it was vague and ambiguous and provided no standards for what the examinations would be.[114] The Alaska Supreme Court also found an oral examination to be prohibited where there was no disclosure of the standards or what was inadequate in the answers.[115] Courts will probably uphold a reasonable, relevant examination uniformly given to all applicants for certain clinical privileges.

Confirmation of Membership

Hospitals can be liable for not promptly responding to requests for confirmation of present or past membership and privileges.[116]

Waiting Period

Hospitals may impose a reasonable waiting period before accepting another application from a person who has lost membership or privileges or had a prior application denied. In 1989, a federal appellate court upheld a hospital rule that a physician must wait one year after a summary suspension before reapplying for staff membership.[117] An Oklahoma court ruled that a public hospital could refuse to consider the application of a physician previously removed for good cause until he offered evidence that the past problems no longer existed.[118]

Delineation of Clinical Privileges

Hospitals must also determine the scope of practice for each physician on the medical staff. A licensed physician can act within the entire scope of medical practice without violating the medical licensing laws of some states. However, no physician is actually competent to perform all medical procedures. The hospital protects patients and physicians by examining physician credentials and granting clinical privileges limited to a defined scope of clinical practice. A physician who acts outside the granted scope, except in an emergency, is subject to discipline, including termination of medical staff membership. The board usually looks to the organized medical staff for expert advice in delineating clinical privileges.

There are many ways to delineate clinical privileges.[119] The key element is a written definition that the medical staff understands. Some hospitals grant clinical privileges for individual procedures. Some hospitals group broad categories of patient conditions and procedures into levels, and physicians are granted clinical privileges to perform everything in the appropriate group. Other hospitals grant clinical privileges by specialty, defining what each specialty is permitted to do. Combinations of these approaches are also used.

Some hospitals require documentation of prior performance of a specified number of certain procedures before privileges are granted. Such requirements are generally acceptable if the numbers are reasonably attainable. In 1992, New York adopted official guidelines requiring surgeons to perform at least 15 laparoscopies under supervision before hospitals could credential them to perform the operation independently.[120]

Hospitals should require appropriate licensure. For example, it is appropriate for hospitals to require dentists to have a medical license before permitting them to provide anesthesia services for nondental patients.[121]

Hospitals may condition clinical privileges for certain procedures on such requirements as having (1) a consultation, (2) assistants, or (3) supervision. Physicians may be disciplined for violating these conditions. Hospitals may change their requirements so that all physicians must begin to meet new conditions. Generally such universal changes would not be viewed as a reduction in clinical privileges, so no right to hearing or report to a data bank would be triggered. However, in the past, some courts have viewed such changes as a clinical privilege reduction, requiring that each affected staff member be given the same opportunity for a hearing as offered for other reductions.[122] When establishing a consultation requirement, hospitals should consider that at least one court has ruled that a hospital with a consultation requirement must assist physicians in obtaining consultations.[123]

Review and Reappointment

After physicians are appointed to the medical staff and granted clinical privileges, their performance should be reviewed periodically as part of the process to determine whether to grant reappointment. Both the Joint Commission and the Medicare conditions of participation require review and reappointment.[124]

Liability

Failure to review performance and take appropriate action can result in hospital liability. For example, a California appellate court ruled that a hospital could be liable for failing to review periodically the performance of those persons granted clinical privileges.[125] However, at least one state has passed a statute that bars hospital liability for professional services of professionals who are not employees or agents, so there is no hospital liability in that state for negligent review.[126]

Provisional

Initial appointments to many medical staffs are provisional. During this period the practice of the new medical staff member is observed.[127] In 1994 a federal appellate court ruled that a holder of provisional privileges in an army hospital did not have a property interest in obtaining full privileges.[128] The Joint Commission has deleted its requirement of a provisional period.

Periodic Review

After the provisional period, hospitals and their medical staffs use several different methods to review performance of individual medical staff members.[129] Ongoing review is conducted by medical staff committees or by an administrative process established to replace the committees.

The Joint Commission requires hospitals to have an approach to improving organizational performance,[130] sometimes still called a *quality improvement program*, but the terminology appears to continue to change. The Joint Commission requires that relevant findings of the assessment process be considered in peer review and periodic evaluations of licensed independent practitioners.[131] The Joint Commission also requires that practitioner-specific information be collected for licensed independent practitioners to support the performance improvement functions.[132]

If problems are discovered through this formalized review or through day-to-day interaction, hospitals have a responsibility to determine what action is appropriate and to initiate that action. Educational efforts will often be adequate, but sometimes steps such as suspension or termination of all or some clinical privileges may be necessary.

Periodic individual review is also necessary to determine whether each medical staff member is still fulfilling the responsibilities of membership and any clinical privileges granted. Medical staff appointments are for a limited time period, usually one or two years.[133] Before appointment expiration, each member is reviewed. The review includes clinical performance, judgment, and skills; licensure; health status; compliance with hospital and medical staff policies; and fulfillment of other medical staff responsibilities, such as active involvement in assigned committees.[134] In 1987, an Ohio appellate court confirmed that review and denial of reappointment could be based on factors other than patient care, such as disruptive behavior and conflicting business interests.[135] In 1987, a federal appellate court confirmed that review did not have to be limited to the period after the previous review, so denial of reappointment could be based on prior miscon-duct.[136] Based on this review, a decision is made whether to reappoint the person to the medical staff and whether to maintain present clinical privileges or to modify them.

Economic Credentialing

Most hospitals attempt to promote cost-effective practices by physicians. One California hospital tried financial incentives in 1985,[137] but the reaction led to a federal law that forbids the use of financial incentives to control services to Medicare or Medicaid patients.[138]

Some hospitals use efficiency criteria in clinical privilege decisions. Courts have generally upheld these criteria if they are properly developed and fairly applied.[139]

Some hospitals try to remove physicians who are competing economically with the hospital. Courts have generally upheld these actions.[140]

Hospitals have generally not yet attempted to require participation in managed care plans as a condition of medical staff membership, except in hospital-based specialties. The requirement for hospital-based specialists to participate is usually found in a contract between the physician and hospital rather than in the medical staff requirements.

Bylaws that forbid economic credentialing may be an antitrust violation.[141]

Activity Requirements

Some hospitals require medical staff members to meet minimum utilization requirements in order to be reappointed.[142] Some commentators have expressed a concern that this could be construed as a referral requirement in violation of Medicare anti-kickback provisions.[143] Others have pointed out that, unless there is a baseline of clinical activity at the hospital, it is impossible to conduct a meaningful review of the physician's continuing performance. Thus, there are good quality reasons for requiring minimum utilization. Some hospitals have adopted an activity requirement that can be satisfied by either clinical utilization or other activities, such as consultations, committee work, and teaching.

Abusive Behavior

Some physicians are occasionally physically or verbally abusive of staff, patients, or visitors.[144] Hospitals need to take prompt action to investigate reports of such actions and take appropriate action when the reports are substantiated. See Chapter 9 for responsibilities concerning sexual harassment.

Declining Capability

Difficult situations sometimes arise when a physician does not recognize declining capabilities. Often physicians will recognize changes when they are approached tactfully and will agree to adjust their scope of practice to fit their capabilities. Often this can be done at the time of reappointment. Some hospitals have an emeritus staff category. If the physician will not agree to needed adjustments, the hospital and medical staff have the duty to protect patients by reducing the physician's clinical privileges to the appropriate scope.

Modification or Termination of Clinical Privileges

Clinical privileges must sometimes be modified or terminated because of changes in the physician's capabilities, violation of hospital or medical staff policies, changes in hospital standards, or other reasons. When physicians challenge modification or termination of privileges, they challenge the adequacy of procedures followed and the reasons given for the action. Procedural issues are discussed in the due process section of this chapter.

Evidence of poor performance or violation of policies should be carefully reviewed before deciding to take adverse action. The hospital should be prepared to justify the action in court.

Medical Records

Clinical privileges are frequently temporarily suspended when physicians fail to complete medical records within time limits established by hospital policy.[145] Suspension of admitting privileges usually continues until overdue records are completed. Physicians who do not have time to complete records do not have time to accept responsibility for additional patients. Courts have generally upheld disciplinary actions for failure to complete records.[146] See Chapter 14 for a discussion of the importance of completion of medical records.

Subjective Standards

Some physicians have challenged adverse actions by claiming that the standards by which they were judged were too vague. Vague standards can violate due process by failing to give notice of what conduct is expected or prohibited. However, courts have generally upheld actions taken on the basis of subjective standards when the standards are applied in a reasonable way.[147] For example, in 1972 the Nevada Supreme Court upheld a clinical privilege termination based on the general standard of "unprofessional conduct."[148] The court recognized that it was not feasible to specify the variety of unprofessional conduct. The physician had not used gloves when touching a spinal needle before using it and had appeared for surgery in no condition to perform it, requiring cancellation of the surgery. The court found that the standard was properly applied. In 1979, a New Jersey appellate court affirmed a physician's suspension based on a bylaws provision that permitted suspension "for cause."[149] The physician had negligently treated a patient. The court found sufficient evidence, so that "for cause" was not too vague. The situation leading to suspension demonstrated that all grounds for suspension could not be specified in advance.

Modifying Standards

When hospitals modify standards, clinical privileges of some physicians may be reduced. Reasonable changes will generally be upheld. The Ohio Supreme Court upheld a hospital's new requirement that a physician be board certified, be board eligible, be a fellow in the American College of Surgery, or have 10 years' experience to qualify for major surgical privileges.[150] In 1975, an Illinois appellate court refused to enjoin a hospital's new requirement that surgeons with general surgery clinical privileges consult with a gynecologist before doing major gynecological surgery. The court ruled that the physician was entitled to a hearing concerning the reasonableness of the rule.[151] Some courts have permitted suits concerning the application of new rules.[152]

When a New Mexico hospital adopted a new rule forbidding all hip-pinnings because it lacked the proper equipment, the New Mexico Supreme Court ruled against a physician who lost his hip-pinning privileges.[153]

Changing to a Full-Time or Exclusive Staff Arrangement

Generally courts have been supportive of hospitals that change staffing arrangements. When a full-time staff approach is adopted, generally the privileges of those who choose not to be full time can be terminated.[154] When an exclusive contract approach is adopted, generally the privileges of those who do not get the full-time contract can be terminated, especially if they had a fair opportunity to get the exclusive contract. In 1992, the Maine Supreme Court upheld a hospital that terminated an emergency medicine contract with a group, offered the physicians individual direct contracts, and terminated those who chose not to sign.[155]

There are exceptions where substantial amounts have been awarded to physicians who are excluded,[156] but generally there are extenuating circumstances of misconduct beyond the termination of privileges.[157] These kinds of changes in staffing arrangements need to be carefully planned to minimize the risk of successful legal challenge.

HIV/AIDS

Hospitals have generally been upheld in restricting privileges of surgeons who are determined to be HIV-positive.[158] The Pennsylvania Supreme Court permitted a hospital to inform patients they may have been exposed to the virus in surgery by an HIV-positive surgeon.[159]

Substance Abuse

The difficult situation of a physician impaired by substance abuse has become easier to address because of the availability of state or medical society programs for rehabilitation[160] and the growing awareness that the first approach should be to promote rehabilitation. Most physicians attempt to cooperate with these efforts, including temporary reductions in clinical privileges as necessary, to protect patients. Unfortunately, it is sometimes extremely difficult to remain rehabilitated, so the hospital must decide how many rehabilitation opportunities to give. If rehabilitation fails, permanent action must eventually be taken to preserve acceptable standards of patient care.

Free Speech in Public Hospitals

Public hospitals usually cannot terminate clinical privileges because of a physician's public criticism of the quality of care. Federal courts have found such criticism can be protected by the First Amendment right of free speech.[161] However, physicians cannot insulate themselves from adverse action by public criticism. In 1986, a federal appellate court upheld the dismissal of a physician who had criticized the hospital.[162] The hospital convinced the court the dismissal was due to patient care concerns, not the public criticism.

Public criticism can also exceed the bounds of protected speech. In 1989, a federal appellate court ruled that a physician's caustic personal attacks were disruptive and unprotected, so termination was justified.[163] In a 1992 hospital case, a federal appellate court applied the general rule that public speech is protected only when it addresses a matter of public concern.[164]

Reporting Requirements

The Health Care Quality Improvement Act of 1986 (HCQIA) requires that all hospitals that want the benefit of the liability limitation provisions of HCQIA must report many of their adverse medical staff actions to the state medical licensing board.[165] The first physician challenge to the data bank was dismissed in 1994.[166]

There are separate state law reporting requirements that are sometimes different from HCQIA requirements.[167]

In 1985, a federal court of appeals ruled that a hospital could not be sued for defamation for filing a required report of suspension of a medical staff member.[168] The hospital was found immune because the report was mandated. In 1994, another federal appellate court decided that a hospital could be liable for defamation for submitting a report that it knew to be false. In that case, a medical chart had been submitted as evidence of a patient incident with knowledge that the reported physician had not been involved in the care of the patient. The court found that bad faith destroyed the qualified immunity.[169]

When reports are required, the hospital no longer has the option of entering an agreement that the physician will resign and the hospital will not disclose the circumstances. The enforceability of such agreements is questionable anyway. In 1989, a federal appellate court ruled that a hospital was not liable for disclosure because the nondisclosure agreement was against public policy.[170] However, it is best not to make any statements concerning nondisclosure. In 1993, the West Virginia Supreme Court ruled that a physician could sue a hospital for reporting to another hospital that his privileges had been summarily suspended, even though they had been so suspended.[171] The physician claimed that he had voluntarily resigned after the suspension pursuant to a promise that his privileges would be reinstated, the suspension would be expunged, and no reports would be made to anyone. The court ruled (1) the agreement would not be against public policy if it were in recognition that the initial suspension was improper and (2) the physician should have an opportunity to prove that was the basis for the agreement.

Review Procedures

Public hospitals are generally required to provide review procedures that satisfy due process requirements. In most states private hospitals are not required to provide the review processes that public hospitals must provide. States that require private hospitals to provide a fair procedure may not include all elements discussed in this section.[172]

Exceptions to Full Review Procedures

Applicants. Public hospitals are usually required by the Fourteenth Amendment to provide due process to medical staff members, but courts disagree on the extent to which applicants have rights. Some courts find that the physician's right to (1) procedures specified in a private hospital's bylaws or (2) constitutional due process in public hospitals is derived from medical staff membership. These courts view actions during an appointment period as interfering with property rights granted to the physician. Unless the hospital has created an entitlement to reappointment, these courts do not consider there to be a similar property right to reappointment. Since an applicant is not yet a member, the applicant does not have a legal right to make claims on the private organization. Thus, in some jurisdictions, hospitals may not be as vulnerable to challenges under federal law when they deny reappointment rather than modify or terminate privileges during an appointment term.[173] In those jurisdictions, hospitals may wait until the reappointment process to address problems with physicians that do not involve immediate risks to patients.

The Joint Commission requires a fair hearing for applicants and members, but does not require the procedures to be identical.[174] Some medical staff bylaws specify that applicants do not have procedural rights. Unless a hospital is in a state that recognizes this difference and the difference is specified in the bylaws, it is prudent to follow the same procedures for both applicants and members.

Substantial Compliance. Most courts do not require technical compliance with every detail of the bylaws procedure. Substantial compliance is usually sufficient.[175]

Informal Investigations. Most courts recognize that review procedures do not have to be provided during the informal investigation of potential medical staff problems that precedes deciding whether to initiate formal proceedings.[176] Although seeking information from the affected physician early in the investigation is almost always helpful, the physician does not have a legal right to notice and an opportunity to present information until formal action is initiated.

Seriousness of Actions. The full scope of due process procedures is usually required only for actions that directly affect the physician's practice, such as decisions concerning the scope of clinical privileges. However, a California court ruled that being on the call roster was a clinical privilege, so that removal entitled the physician to a hearing.[177] Censure usually does not entitle the physician to a hearing.[178]

Waiver by Contract. Even in public hospitals, procedural rights can be waived by contract. Thus, exclusive and other contracts can provide for termination of privileges without a hearing when the contract terminates or other specified events occur.[179]

Arbitration. An alternate procedure that some physicians and hospitals may consider is arbitration.[180] HCQIA authorizes the alternative of using an arbitrator.[181]

Health Care Quality Improvement Act

HCQIA[182] describes procedures for hospital medical staff decisions. Hospitals are not required to follow the procedures,[183] but if they are followed, the Act provides protection from monetary liability in private suits, except under civil rights laws. There is no protection from suits seeking injunctions or from civil rights suits. The antitrust immunity is only from private suits; the state or federal attorney general may still sue. However, most suits concerning medical staff matters are private suits, so this protection can be significant. HCQIA states that the "immunity" applies only when the peer review action was taken "in the reasonable belief that the action was in furtherance of quality health care" and "after a reasonable effort to obtain the facts of the matter." There is a statutory presumption that this standard is met,[184] so it is not easy for a physician to defeat HCQIA immunity.[185]

HCQIA protects hospitals from monetary liability, not from suit. Thus, a refusal by a trial judge to dismiss such a suit cannot be appealed. The hospital must wait until after there is a final judgment against the hospital to obtain appellate review.[186]

Many hospitals have availed themselves of the protection of HCQIA. In 1988, an Indiana court authorized a hospital to substitute HCQIA procedures for the procedures in its bylaws without first amending the bylaws.[187] It is not clear whether other courts will allow this substitution. However, hospitals and affected physicians can agree to change procedures, and some physicians may agree to HCQIA procedures. Refusal to agree may be a waiver by the physician in some contexts.

Originally states could opt out of HCQIA peer review immunity, but that option was deleted in 1989.[188]

Summary Action

Restrictions on clinical privileges may be imposed without prior due process procedures when there is potential immediate risk to patient well-being.[189] Although review procedures must usually be followed before adverse action is taken, courts recognize that summary action can be necessary and appropriate. For example, the Alaska Supreme Court ruled that the fair hearing could be conducted within a reasonable time after the summary suspension of clinical privileges when there was immediate risk to patients.[190]

Courts have issued injunctions prohibiting summary suspension when the risk is not sufficiently immediate.[191] Courts will reconsider an injunction if the physician's conduct during the injunction indicates that summary suspension is needed.[192]

Summary suspension without a hearing is also appropriate when a physician ceases to be licensed to practice medicine or ceases to have a valid DEA registration to prescribe controlled substances.[193]

Reasonable Notice

The first step of due process is to give reasonable written notice of the reasons for the proposed action and of the time and place where the physician may present information. Reasonable notice must include sufficient information to permit preparation of a response, but a detailed and exhaustive listing of each perceived deficiency is not required in most states.[194]

The hospital does not have to cater to the idiosyncrasies of the physician in giving notice.[195] Standard methods such as personal delivery or registered mail are appropriate.

Hearing

The second step is to provide the physician with an opportunity to present information. Often the physician will have had one or more opportunities to present information during the informal investigative steps that precede formal action. However, a formal opportunity to present information is usually required after the formal recommendation of adverse action. Courts vary on the degree of the formality that they require. It is generally agreed the physician is entitled to only one hearing unless the bylaws specify additional hearings.[196]

Physician Presence. Hospitals may require that the physician attend the hearing. Unexcused failure to appear can waive the right to the hearing and the right to object to other defects in the proceedings.[197]

Legal Counsel. There is disagreement on whether the physician should be represented by legal counsel at the hearing. Some attorneys can assist in assuring that information is provided in an orderly fashion and can help the physician understand the outcomes that can be reasonably expected. Some attorneys cannot adapt to the informality of the medical staff hearing and, thus, are disruptive, for example, by attempting to apply formal court rules. As a result, some hospitals do not permit attorneys to be involved; others encourage their involvement.

Courts have disagreed on whether there is a legal right to legal representation. New Jersey requires hospitals to permit representation by an attorney.[198] A federal court ruled that in army hospital proceedings the attorney can be limited to providing advice to the physician and not questioning witnesses or providing argument.[199] California hospitals do not have to permit representation by an attorney, especially when the hospital is not represented by an attorney.[200] Hospitals will have a difficult time convincing any court of the fairness of their procedures if only one side is permitted legal representation.

The safe harbor for HCQIA immunity specifies that the physician be given an opportunity to be represented by a lawyer.[201] This does not create a legal right to an attorney, but denial of an attorney may make it more difficult to maintain HCQIA immunity.

Hearing Body. The committee or individual conducting the hearing should not be biased against the physician. In 1985, the South Carolina Supreme Court found that a physician's due process rights were violated when three of the original accusing physicians were members of the joint conference committee that made the final recommendation to the governing board.[202] A California appellate court ruled that a physician had been denied due process because the committee that recommended his suspension was not impartial.[203] Two committee members depended on the obstetrical expertise of the physician who brought the charges. The HCQIA safe harbor requires that the hearing committee not include physicians who are economic competitors.[204] State law may specify composition. In 1993, an Indiana court ruled that under state law only physicians could serve on a hearing committee.[205]

Courts have recognized the virtual impossibility of complete impartiality because all physicians in a hospital have a collaborative relationship. Some courts require a demonstration of actual bias before a due process violation can be found.[206] In 1986, a California appellate court ruled that the physician should be given an opportunity to examine committee members for possible bias before the hearing.[207] Some courts find that review and approval by an unbiased appeal committee can correct earlier bias,[208] while other courts find no corrective effect.[209]

One federal appellate court ruled that when the applicant falsified his application, any bias in the review process was irrelevant because this applicant would have been denied privileges anyway.[210]

When selecting the hearing body, persons with known biases should be excluded. Persons in the same specialty should generally also be excluded because they may appear to be motivated to remove a competitor. Physicians do not have a right to have persons in the same specialty on a hearing body.[211] To the extent feasible, it is helpful to also exclude those who were involved in earlier stages of the investigation and review process, but this is not essential in all jurisdictions. These steps will assure fairness and minimize the risk of successful challenge. In some cases hospitals with a smaller medical staff may have to arrange for someone from outside the hospital to conduct the hearing.

Opportunity To Present Information. The purpose of the hearing is to give the physician an opportunity to present information on his or her own behalf. Courts have disagreed on which hospital records of patient care and peer review the physician may obtain to prepare the presentation.[212] Access to medical records is discussed in Chapter 14. Another issue is whether the physician is entitled to an opportunity to present witnesses. Some courts have ruled that the bylaws can require all submissions to the hearing body to be in writing.[213] The HCQIA safe harbor includes an opportunity to present witnesses.[214] One federal court has ruled that HCQIA does not require an opportunity for the physician to introduce evidence concerning the performance of other physicians.[215]

Opportunity To Cross-Examine Witnesses. Courts have recognized that hospitals do not have the power to compel witnesses to attend hearings. Due process usually does not require an opportunity to cross-examine all those who have complained about the physician's conduct.[216] However, a few courts have found a right to cross-examine some witnesses.[217] Many hospitals permit cross-examination of witnesses who actually provide information at the hearing. The HCQIA safe harbor includes an opportunity to cross-examine the witnesses who testify.[218]

Record. It is prudent to make a record of hearing proceedings. If the final decision is appealed to the courts, a record will be necessary to prove fairness of the proceedings and evidence of the basis for the decision. A court reporter's transcript of the proceedings is expensive and may not be necessary. However, if the physician requests a court reporter and is willing to share the cost appropriately, a court reporter should be considered. Sometimes a tape recording or, in some situations, detailed notes will be sufficient. The HCQIA safe harbor includes a record of the hearing, but the physician can be required to pay reasonable charges to obtain a copy.[219]

Report. The hearing committee should make a substantive report of its findings, especially when such a report is required by the bylaws. In 1989, a District of Columbia court ruled that a physician who was denied privileges could base a suit on the lack of an adequate hearing report.[220] The bylaws required the medical executive committee to consider a fact-finding report from the hearing committee. Without an adequate report, it could not do so, so the bylaws were violated. The HCQIA safe harbor includes a written recommendation by the hearing entity and a written decision by the hospital, with each to include a statement of the basis for the recommendation or decision.[221]

Internal "Appellate" Review

The Joint Commission requires an internal appellate review mechanism for appealing an adverse decision.[222] Some hospitals seek to comply with this requirement by permitting the practitioner to make a written and/or oral presentation to the board or a board committee after an adverse medical executive committee recommendation, but before the board's decision. This first approach can provide the board with useful information. Other hospitals interpret appellate review to require that an appellate process occur after the board makes an adverse decision. Since the board has the acknowledged authority to make the final decision, such internal appellate review is in essence a reconsideration by the board. It is not clear what useful function this second approach performs that justifies its burden on the board.

One physician sought to disqualify the board from acting as its own appellate tribunal. A Colorado court rejected the challenge.[223]

Judicial Appeal

Courts have permitted only the affected physician to seek judicial review of adverse decisions. Courts have not permitted other medical staff members,[224] patients,[225] or families of patients to challenge decisions to grant or deny medical staff membership or clinical privileges. The spouse of the physician also lacks standing even when the family has to move, causing the spouse to lose his job.[226]

Courts generally require the physician to pursue all procedures available within the hospital before allowing appeal to the courts. If a physician refuses to participate in the hospital hearing, courts will usually not allow an appeal based on denial of procedural due process.[227] However, hospital procedures usually do not have to be exhausted before court review when the hospital procedures clearly do not satisfy applicable due process or fair hearing requirements.[228]

When courts review a hospital action, they usually show great deference to the judgment of the hospital and its medical staff. They limit their review to a determination of whether appropriate procedures were followed[229] and whether the action appears arbitrary or capricious. If credible evidence supports the action and proper procedures have been followed, the judiciary will almost always approve hospital actions. A few states do not follow this principle. For example, in 1983 a Missouri appellate court ruled that Missouri courts do not have to show any deference to public hospitals' medical staff decisions.[230] In some states, courts refuse to review the decisions of governing boards of private hospitals.[231] In states with statutory requirements, courts will review whether there has been compliance with the statutes.[232]

Injunction. Some physicians seek injunctions to require hospitals to keep them on or reinstate them to the medical staff. Generally, any person seeking an injunction must prove at least four elements: (1) substantial likelihood of ultimately winning the lawsuit on the merits, (2) irreparable injury, (3) the threatened injury without the injunction outweighs the injury to the opposing party from an injunction, and (4) the injunction will not be adverse to the public interest.[233] An injury is usually not irreparable if it can be compensated by monetary remedies.[234]

In most states, injunctions are seldom issued concerning medical staff privileges.[235] Often this is because (1) money damages are available or (2) potential injuries to the hospital and patients generally outweigh injuries to the physician.

Occasionally injunctions have been issued requiring reinstatement until the bylaws procedures can be completed.[236] Some state courts are more prone to issue injunctions.

In 1989, a physician was assessed over $50,000 in damages by an Illinois court for wrongfully obtaining an injunction requiring restoration of clinical privileges.[237]

Mandamus. In California, a writ of administrative mandamus can be issued by a court to compel a hospital to reinstate a physician to medical staff membership and privileges.[238] California courts generally require physicians to pursue a mandamus proceeding before permitting a tort suit concerning medical staff decisions.[239] In other states, a *writ of mandamus*[240] is generally not available to private individuals unless they have obligations in the nature of a public or quasi-public duty[241] nor is it available to enforce private rights or to enforce contractual obligations.[242] Employment contracts, even with public entities, are generally not enforceable by mandamus unless a statute sets the terms of the employment.[243] Thus, a writ of mandamus will generally not be available outside California in medical staff matters.[244]

Liability

When physicians challenge adverse hospital actions, they often seek payment of money in addition to reversal of the hospital action. They base their claims on several grounds, including lost earnings or emotional distress during the proceedings, defamation, malicious interference with their business, antitrust violations, and discrimination. Some legal doctrines provide those involved in these determinations with limited immunity from some of these claims.

Refusing to take necessary actions also exposes the medical staff and hospital to liability, so inaction does not avoid liability.

Waiver

Many hospitals require all applicants to sign a waiver protecting those involved from liability. The Joint Commission recognizes this common practice by requiring applicants to sign such waivers.[245] Several courts have upheld these waivers,[246] but some courts have declined to enforce them.[247]

Breach of Contract

When a physician has a contract with the hospital, termination or other breach of the contract can result in assessment of monetary damages for the breach. Some courts view the bylaws as such a contract, permitting a breach of contract claim for violation of the bylaws.[248]

Interference with Business Relationships

Physicians often claim that the actions of the hospital or its staff tortiously interfered with their business relationships with patients, other physicians, hospitals, and others. Generally merely denying or terminating privileges or professional service contracts does not constitute tortious interference. Although tort liability for such action is possible,[249] the greatest exposure of hospitals and their staffs occurs when they take additional steps, such as when they try to deny access to billing information or other records,[250] discriminate in access to equipment or staff necessary to exercise remaining privileges,[251] or create or disseminate false information.[252]

Generally a claim of tortious interference with a business relationship requires a showing of (1) an existing business relationship under which the plaintiff has legal rights,[253] (2) knowledge of that relationship by defendant, (3) an intentional and unjustified interference with the relationship, and (4) damage to the plaintiff as a result of the breach of the relationship.[254] In some jurisdictions, the business relationship does not need to be enforceable, so some expectancies are protected if there is an understanding that would have been completed if the interference had not occurred. In 1995, the Florida Supreme Court ruled that this did not permit a claim based on the "mere hope that some of its past customers may choose to buy again" where there was no ongoing relationship with those customers.[255]

In assessing what interference is justified, some courts recognize a privilege of competition that permits efforts to convince others who are in business relationships that are terminable at will to shift their business, as long as certain prohibited means are not used.[256]

Generally actions by a party to a business relationship cannot constitute tortious interference with that relationship. Generally only an individual or entity that is not a party to the relationship can tortiously interfere with a business relationship. Thus, a director, officer, or employee of a corporation cannot tortiously interfere with a contract between the corporation and someone else.[257] When these people cause a physician's contract with the hospital to be terminated, they generally cannot be sued personally for tortious interference with the physician's relationship with the hospital. In jurisdictions that recognize the medical staff to be within this intracorporate immunity, other medical staff members will generally also be immune from personal suit, except where they are acting out of personal economic interests.

Some jurisdictions permit a claim for tortious interference with the relationship with patients or other physicians arising out of the termination of the relationship with the hospital. The intracorporate immunity may not apply to such claims. However, there are other barriers to prevailing with such claims, especially in jurisdictions that do not permit a claim for a mere expectancy.

In hospitals that have complex corporate structures it is not clear whether the intracorporate immunity will apply to protect an action by one corporation that affects employment by or contracts with a parent, subsidiary, or other related corporation or entity.[258] Risk is minimized if communications and actions affecting employment and contractual relationships are kept in proper channels.

Lost Earnings or Emotional Distress

Courts will sometimes award physicians money for their lost earnings or emotional distress during the hospital review process if it is found that the physician's rights were violated. In 1982, a federal court of appeals affirmed an award for emotional distress, but reversed an award for lost earnings because the physician would have been discharged even if proper procedures had been followed.[259]

Defamation

Wrongful injury to another person's reputation is *defamation*. Defamation is discussed in Chapter 10. One defense to a defamation claim is a qualified privilege, which means that there is no liability for certain privileged communications, even if they injure another's reputation, if the communications were not made with malice. Most courts apply a qualified privilege to communications during medical staff peer review activities, including hospital board review and action.[260] In 1982, a Pennsylvania court dismissed the portion of a defamation suit against the hospital because no malice had been shown, but refused to dismiss the portion against the physicians.[261] It was asserted that the physicians had made their statements because they wanted the financial benefit of keeping a competitor from obtaining clinical privileges. If proved at trial, the financial motive could establish malice. The immunity statutes discussed later in this chapter may provide more protection than the qualified privilege.

Antitrust

Physicians frequently challenge medical staff actions by claiming the actions are a restraint of trade or an attempt to monopolize medical practice, thus violating federal antitrust laws. Four of the reasons for federal antitrust suits are (1) if the physician wins, treble damages can be obtained; (2) suits are expensive to litigate, so hospitals may be more willing to compromise; (3) suits can be tried in federal court; and (4) state laws that protect peer review documents from disclosure do not apply.

Prior to 1991, one of the major barriers that protected hospitals from medical staff antitrust suits was the difficulty in proving the impact on interstate commerce necessary for federal antitrust laws to apply. In 1991, the U.S. Supreme Court established a new standard so that impact on interstate commerce is easy to demonstrate in many medical staff cases.[262]

Antitrust cases against hospitals remain difficult for practitioners to win. HCQIA provides immunity from monetary liability based on antitrust claims for most credentialing actions, as discussed previously in this chapter. Other legal doctrines that limit antitrust exposure are discussed in Chapter 5.

Discrimination

Medical staff decisions should not be based on discriminatory criteria, such as race, creed, color, sex, national origin,[263] or disability. Sometimes medical staff actions are challenged on the basis that they violate federal and state statutes barring discrimination.[264] For example, an African American female physician in the District of Columbia claimed she had been terminated from her position in a health maintenance organization because of her race, violating the federal Civil Rights Act. In 1981, a federal court found sufficient evidence that her termination was based on complaints of African American and Caucasian co-workers and on failure to improve her performance after being warned and not on her race, so no violation was found.[265]

Nondiscrimination statutes are discussed in more detail in Chapter 9.

Other Claims

Physicians have claimed violations of the Racketeer Influenced and Corrupt Organizations Act (RICO), but those claims have generally been dismissed or dropped.[266]

Immunity

In some states, persons involved in medical staff review may be entitled to some immunity from liability for their statements or actions. The common law qualified privilege from liability for defamation previously discussed is an example. Some state statutes provide limited immunity from damages for actions in the peer review process.[267] An Arizona appellate court ruled that the chief of staff and the hospital administrator could not be sued for summarily suspending a surgeon's clinical privileges unless there was a showing that the primary purpose of the action was other than safeguarding patients.[268] Since a patient had died following "serious errors in judgment" by the surgeon and the surgeon had scheduled another patient for the same type of surgery, the court found the primary purpose was safeguarding patients.

Some states have enacted statutes that grant broader immunity for peer review participants. For example, in Florida there is no liability unless intentional fraud is proved.[269] However, the Florida Supreme Court declared unconstitutional an additional requirement that, before suing, a physician must post a bond to pay the defendants' defense costs if liability is not found.[270] In Illinois there is statutory absolute immunity.[271] Louisiana's immunity statute has been interpreted to protect only individuals, not institutions.[272]

State statutes that prohibit the use of certain peer review records as evidence may make it impossible to prove certain claims, effectively granting immunity. For example, the Florida prohibition on introducing testimony and records concerning peer review proceedings effectively bars nearly all defamation claims for statements made in the peer review process.[273]

RELATIONSHIP OF INDIVIDUAL PHYSICIANS AND HOSPITALS OUTSIDE THE MEDICAL STAFF RELATIONSHIP

In most hospitals, most physicians are not hospital employees or agents. However, many physician relationships with the hospital are based on and defined by a contract, as an employee of the hospital, an independent contractor, or an employee of an independent contractor or joint venturer with the hospital.

Physicians increasingly have other relationships with hospitals. Some examples include:

1. owning a limited partnership interest in the hospital or having other ownership interests in an entity that owns the hospital;
2. serving on the governing board;
3. contracting with the hospital or a related medical service organization (MSO) for space, equipment, staff, and other support services; and
4. participating in a physician-hospital organization (PHO) or integrated delivery system (IDS), which may contract with managed care plans on behalf of the hospital and the physicians.[274]

Some of these other relationships involve credentialing and review mechanisms that duplicate many medical staff functions, which is leading to consideration of alternatives to the medical staff structure as discussed in the last section of this chapter.

The structuring of these relationships is constrained by Medicare anti-kickback restrictions; Stark self-referral restrictions; federal tax exemption or other tax considerations; and state anti-kickback, self-referral, and other legal restrictions. Many of these restrictions are discussed in Chapter 4.

Most legal disputes between individual physicians and hospitals concern either denial, restriction, or loss of clinical privileges or contracts. Frequently contracts waive any rights that exist under the medical staff bylaws, so that the relationship can be predominantly defined by individual contract.

Physician-Hospital Organizations

PHOs, sometimes jointly owned by the hospital and physicians, provide a forum for joint analyses of affiliations with third party payers and often seek to contract with managed care entities on behalf of the hospital and physicians, as well as perform other functions.[275] There are many legal issues that need to be considered in structuring a PHO.[276] For example, when the hospital is nonprofit, the IRS has stated that the governing board of the PHO cannot have more than 20 percent physicians, unless the physicians have contributed more than 20 percent of the total investment, and then their representation can be increased to be proportional to their share of the investment, provided the total representation does not exceed 50 percent.[277]

PHOs are generally viewed as transitional organizations that are unlikely to be a viable structure for the future. Some PHOs have little success in obtaining contracts. Some have been valuable forums for planning the next organizational steps, while others have become inactive awaiting dissolution, merger, or conversion into another organizational structure. Some PHOs have been more successful in obtaining contracts, but even successful PHOs generally are planning the next steps.

Practice Acquisition

Hospitals and other entities, for profit and nonprofit, are seeking to acquire physician practices and to employ physicians. More physicians are willing to enter these transactions. There are many legal restrictions that apply to structuring these transactions.[278] Medicare and Medicaid anti-kickback restrictions require that payment for the acquisition of the practice must be fair market value and structured so that payment is not payment for referrals; however, payment to an employed physician for services as an employee is exempt from these restrictions. Stark self-referral restrictions place some limits on the structuring of compensation of physicians, including employees, and may restrict the use of installment payments for the practice. State law imposes additional constraints.[279] In addition, nonprofit hospitals must observe the requirements for retaining tax exemption, including avoiding private inurement. The IRS also takes the position that violation of other laws, such as Medicare anti-kickback restrictions, can result in loss of tax exemption (see Chapter 4). Hospitals that have or plan to have tax-exempt bonds must observe constraints on the length and payment formula for certain service contracts involving the facilities financed with the bonds.[280]

Physician Recruitment and Retention

To attract and keep physicians, many hospitals in the past have offered loans, office space, practice assistance, liability protection, and income guaranties. There is increasing scrutiny of arrangements that tax-exempt hospitals make to recruit and retain physicians.[281] Such arrangements must be properly limited and structured so that they are not (1) private inurement that could cause the loss of the hospital's tax-exempt status or (2) inducements or kickbacks for referrals that violate the Medicare and Medicaid fraud and abuse provisions.[282] Private inurement and the fraud and abuse provisions are discussed in Chapter 4.

Physician-Hospital Contracts

Hospitals and physicians often enter contracts concerning the performing of medical or administrative services in the hospital. Written contracts help to define the relationship to the mutual benefit of hospital and physician. Many questions must be considered in negotiating the contract. Will the contract be with an individual physician or a group of physicians? Will the physicians be hospital employees or independent contractors? This question will affect fringe benefits, applicability of personnel policies, potential liability, and responsibility for withholding taxes and paying workers' compensation. What qualifications must the physician meet? What services will the physician perform? In addition to providing direct patient care, the physician may also participate in professional review and other advisory capacities and may also have some administrative responsibilities, such as budgeting or preparing reports. Space, equipment, and supply issues may be addressed. Who will be responsible for selecting, training, supervising, scheduling, and disciplining professional and technical personnel who work with the physician? What insurance or indemnification agreements should the parties require? How will the physician be compensated? Salary, percentage, and fee-for-service arrangements or combinations of these arrangements are possible. Sometimes the physician is not compensated by the hospital and charges fees to the patient directly. How will the charges be established, and who will be responsible for billing them? How will changes in third party payer requirements, such as the adoption of capitation or other global billing (one bill for both physician and hospital services) be addressed? Will the agreement include restrictions on competition during the term of the agreement or after termination? Some state laws and court decisions limit the scope of enforceable restrictions.[283] How can the agreement be amended or terminated? How are disagreements to be resolved? These and other questions must be considered in contracting with physicians.

The answers to the above questions will be influenced by reimbursement policies of Medicare and other third party payers and by tax implications, such as threats to tax exemption. For example, hospitals that desire to be eligible to raise funds from tax-exempt bonds must limit the length of many contracts with physicians.[284]

A clause concerning access to records should be included in all contracts for services that have a value of $10,000 or more over a year. Medicare will not pay the hospital for services under a contract that does not contain that clause.[285] The clause must allow the Secretary of HHS and the Comptroller General to have access to the subcontractor's books, documents, and records that are necessary to verify the costs of services furnished under the contract. The records must be retained for at least four years after the services are provided. This requirement will apply to many contracts with physicians.

Exclusive Contracts

Hospitals frequently enter contracts with specialists that specify specialists' exclusive right to provide certain types of care, such as radiology, pathology, emergency room services, and cardiac catheterization. These contracts can help hospitals to optimize patient care. Competing physicians have attacked these contracts as violations of equal protection, due process, and antitrust laws. Most courts have upheld these exclusive privilege contracts when it is clear that they are intended to foster good quality patient care.

In 1973, the Pennsylvania Supreme Court upheld a contract that granted exclusive cardiac catheterization privileges to the full-time director of the cardiology laboratory.[286] A physician who had been performing the procedure in the hospital challenged the contract. The court found the arrangement reasonable and related to the hospital's operation because it

1. assured the best training and supervision of the catheterization team,
2. enabled the physician to maintain competence by performing more procedures,
3. centralized responsibility for use and maintenance of the equipment,
4. reduced scheduling problems for patients,
5. improved the ability to monitor quality of care, and
6. assured the presence of a physician in the event of complications.

Antitrust attacks on exclusive contracts have generally been unsuccessful. However, in 1982 one federal appellate court declared an exclusive contract for anesthesia services to be a violation of the antitrust laws and ordered the hospital to permit the physician recommended for appointment by the medical staff to provide anesthesia services.[287] The court found the use of the operating room and the use of anesthesia services to be two separate products that were illegally "tied" by the exclusive contract. An agreement to sell one product only on the condition that the buyer also purchase a different product is a tying arrangement and, thus, a per se violation of antitrust laws if the seller has sufficient market power to coerce purchase of the tied product. The court defined the market area as so small that the hospital had sufficient market power. The court focused on the fact that anesthesia services were predominantly being provided by nurse anesthetists employed by the hospital and supervised by the anesthesiologists, so the court believed the "actual basis for the hospital's actions in this case" was "increasing the hospital's profit." The court rejected the other "business justifications" for the contract because it believed there were less restrictive ways to accomplish the same ends.

The *Hyde* decision led many to question the viability of exclusive contracts. Then, in 1984, the U.S. Supreme Court reversed the decision with an opinion that refined the definition of tying arrangements considered to be per se antitrust violations.[288] The Court concluded that the arrangement did not force purchases that would not otherwise have been made, so it was not a tying arrangement. Applying the rule of reason, the Court found the contract did not unreasonably restrain competition.

The Court's decision was not an endorsement of all exclusive contracts. Exclusive contracts may still be successfully attacked in some circumstances. However, the decision has made it possible in most settings to structure exclusive arrangements that have survived antitrust attack.[289] One of the few successful antitrust attacks was in a suit by nurse anesthetists challenging an exclusive contract with anesthesiologists.[290] These exclusive contract decisions are also discussed in Chapter 5.

At least one hospital has tried to use antitrust laws as an excuse to break an exclusive contract. In 1989, a federal district court ruled that a hospital was not permitted to seek a declaration that a 35-year radiology contract violated the Sherman Act.[291]

In some states, state law may be more restrictive than federal law. For example, when a Texas hospital sought a court determination that it could legally have an exclusive radiology contract, the state counterclaimed on the basis of violation of state law.[292] The hospital entered a consent judgment agreeing to abandon the exclusive arrangement.

Corporate Practice of Medicine

Some states have statutes or court decisions that forbid corporations from employing physicians.[293] This is called the *corporate practice of medicine* doctrine. Most states do not have or do not enforce the doctrine.[294] In the states that do have the doctrine, frequently there are exceptions that permit employment by some types of corporations, such as nonprofit corporations,[295] physician-controlled corporations, HMOs, or hospitals.[296] There are a few states that aggressively enforce the doctrine, especially California, Colorado, and Texas.[297] In those states, unusual business structures are frequently required to achieve integration without violating the doctrine. Hospitals in other states can usually avoid these unusual business structures.

PARALLEL CREDENTIALING MECHANISMS

Many managed care plans have their own credentialing and evaluation system for physicians. This has many significant implications for hospitals and physicians. First, this represents considerable duplication of effort for physicians. Since managed care plans often control access to patients, hospitals need to have their medical staffs participating in plans, so it is important to make the process of qualification as easy as possible for the physician. Hospitals can take some steps to help create this environment and reduce some of the duplication.[298] Second, also due to managed care control over access to patients, unless the physician and hospital are working together in relation to the managed care plans, the relationship of the managed care plan with the physician or with the hospital can become more important to each of them than their relationship with each other. Third, it is becoming more important to both physicians and hospitals to understand the criteria that are being applied by managed care plans.

HISTORY

The relationship between physicians and hospitals has not always been as described above. This section provides a short history to help understand how the present relationship developed.

In the nineteenth century it was common for hospitals to have hospital-based physicians who provided all the care to hospitalized patients. In some hospitals, new staff were nominated by senior staff, but the final decision was by the trustees and their decision was sometimes subject to political influence. Frequently the admission and discharge decisions were not made by the physician, but by a lay administrator or board member. Hospitals began to permit a visiting staff of independent physicians to admit and treat patients, but initially they were generally not permitted to charge for their services.[299] Hospitals began to look to physicians to make admission and discharge decisions.[300]

When workers' compensation was introduced in the late nineteenth century, providing the first broadly applicable third party payment, hospitals began to restructure their charges so that patients became an asset and not just another demand on the charitable or tax resources of the hospital.[301] Visiting physicians were encouraged to admit their paying patients and were permitted to charge for their services.[302]

Medical knowledge, technology, and practice underwent dramatic changes starting near the beginning of the twentieth century. Hospitals ceased to be perceived as solely places for the poor. The middle and upper classes began using hospitals. Physicians had practiced without any hospital connections because few of their patients were ever admitted to a hospital. When more patients were viewed as requiring the services of hospitals, physicians needed hospital connections to provide continuity of care to their patients and to avoid losing their patients to hospital-based physicians. The percentage of physicians with hospital privileges increased from approximately 10 percent in 1907 to over 84 percent in 1933.[303]

American College of Surgeons Standards

Physicians were concerned with the quality of care being provided in hospitals with which they were associated. The American College of Surgeons (ACS), with the cooperation of the American Hospital Association (AHA), introduced the first nationwide system of hospital review in 1919, which was called *hospital standardization*.[304] The ACS review system was a major force toward the significant improvement of the standards of operation of American hospitals and the improvement of the quality of medicine practiced by physicians in those hospitals. Parallel with the ACS standardization process, the AMA maintained a list of hospitals approved for residency programs.[305]

One ACS requirement was that the hospital must have a procedure by which the medical staff reviewed all applicants for admission to the medical staff. While some hospitals had had such review processes before, this was the first attempt to establish it as the standard.

There were several court challenges by physicians who were excluded or subject to restrictions pursuant to ACS or similar standards. Actions of private hospitals were generally upheld,[306] except where there were contrary provisions in the hospital's articles of incorporation or bylaws that were not properly amended prior to adopting the ACS standards. These cases generally addressed whether the standards could be enforced against physicians.[307]

One case addressed whether the standards also gave the physician procedural rights. In 1928, the Wisconsin Supreme Court ruled that a private hospital that had adopted ACS procedures did not have to follow those procedures when excluding or expelling a physician.[308]

Most courts also upheld actions by public hospitals. For example, public hospitals were permitted (1) to exclude osteopathic physicians[309] and (2) to require supervision of surgery until full surgical privileges could be earned.[310]

The Indiana Supreme Court ruled in 1949 that a public hospital could not give its medical staff a veto over appointments.[311] The staff could only review and recommend. The court later ruled that the hospital could require completion of three years of surgical training of the standard approved by the ACS, but the board could not rely on the ACS determination whether that standard had been met; the hospital had to make its own determination to avoid an improper delegation.[312]

A few state courts adopted the minority position that all licensed physicians had a right to practice in public hospitals,[313] but these states later permitted public hospitals to exercise some selectivity.[314]

Other Attempts To Control Access to Hospital Practice

In addition to ACS standards, organized medicine sought to control hospital practice through other initiatives.

There were attempts to make local medical society membership a condition of hospital privileges, which would have given physicians complete control over who practiced in hospitals.[315] This requirement was generally rejected by the courts.[316]

There was a movement that began in the 1930s to establish prepaid health care cooperatives and salaried arrangements with physicians. Organized medicine opposed the movement. Access to hospital facilities for patients and physicians in such cooperatives was obstructed by other physicians. In 1943, the opposition of the AMA was declared a violation of the antitrust laws by the U.S. Supreme Court.[317] The court ruled that the business of the prepaid health care entity was a trade protected by the Sherman Act and that it was a restraint of trade for the AMA to obstruct access to hospital facilities for members and medical staff of these entities. In 1951, the Washington Supreme Court ruled that a public hospital could not exclude a physician because he practiced "contract medicine."[318]

Hospital Licensing and Regulation

In the 1940s, government began to be more involved in the operation of hospitals. Many states adopted hospital licensing laws to be eligible for federal hospital construction money under the federal Hill-Burton program. The federal requirements included state hospital licensing and a state hospital construction plan. Under these licensing laws, a state regulatory agency was generally empowered to adopt licensing rules, which usually reinforced the existing pattern of hospital organization. Thus, most hospital licensing laws still require an organized medical staff, and some specify features of the medical staff organization and procedures. Hospital licensing regulation or statute changes may be required in some states before some changes in the relationship of the hospital and the medical staff.

In the 1950s, courts generally reaffirmed the latitude of private hospitals in medical staff matters,[319] while more states constrained the power of public hospitals. In Wisconsin a public hospital could not suspend a physician from its staff without a notice and hearing.[320] In Arizona a public hospital could not require medical staff members to assist other members on request.[321] A New Jersey court required a public hospital to follow its own rules in restricting the surgical privileges of a physician.[322] However, Wyoming permitted public hospitals to refuse reappointment to a physician who refused to comply with rules for completion of medical records.[323]

These developments culminated in the 1954 Michigan Supreme Court decision that any licensed physician could practice in any county hospital in the state and the governing board could not restrict the scope of practice.[324]

Joint Commission on Accreditation of Hospitals

In 1951, hospital accreditation was transferred from ACS to the Joint Commission on Accreditation of Hospitals (Joint Commission). See Chapter 3 for its composition.

Joint Commission requirements continued to include medical staff standards. These requirements and their implementation have always required a balance of the need to assure that the expertise of physicians is applied to maintain quality of care with the need to avoid allowing physicians to misuse their role to the detriment of the hospital or for their own economic advantage. Usually this balance has been maintained. However, as illustrated by the earlier attempts to place control over medical staff membership in medical societies and to exclude from hospitals salaried physicians and other physicians serving health care cooperatives, the balance has not always been maintained.

The Joint Commission initially required that the medical staff of accredited hospitals be limited to fully licensed medical physicians, so that osteopathic physicians had to be excluded in order for a hospital to be accredited. In 1959, the Joint Commission rescinded the accreditation of a county hospital in West Virginia because it admitted an osteopathic physician to its medical staff. The accreditation was not restored until after his privileges were rescinded in 1960. The West Virginia Supreme Court upheld the exclusion of osteopathic physicians.[325]

The events in one Texas county hospital illustrate the aggressiveness with which some medical staffs sought to enforce the exclusion. The hospital was established in 1940 and established a medical staff in 1950. One osteopathic physician practiced in the hospital from 1940 until 1955. Another osteopathic physician applied for membership in 1955. The medical staff recommended that the two osteopathic physicians not be appointed for 1956. The hospital board had a tie vote, so pursuant to Texas law, a judge joined the board to break the tie. The augmented board voted to admit the osteopathic physicians. The next morning the remainder of the medical staff resigned and the following day all of the registered nurses resigned. Two days later the board suspended the osteopathic physicians and adopted a rule requiring that applicants be graduates of medical schools approved by the AMA. The osteopathic physicians sued. The trial court ruled that they could not be excluded. The appellate court reversed, noting that permitting osteopathic physicians on the staff would preclude Joint Commission accreditation. The antitrust implications of the collective resignation were not mentioned.

In the early 1960s, many of the barriers to osteopathic physicians were removed.[326] In some states there was a movement to merge osteopathic societies and medical societies.[327] When Medicare was enacted in 1966, osteopathic physicians were included in the definition of physicians.[328]

Medicare

The enactment of Medicare resulted in the first federal standards for the operation of hospitals. Hospitals have to satisfy conditions of participation to be eligible to receive Medicare payments. The Medicare law provides that Joint Commission–accredited hospitals are deemed to meet the conditions of participation (see Chapter 3).

The original 1966 conditions of participation required that the medical staff be organized under bylaws approved by the governing body that met detailed standards, including a complex committee structure and a mechanism to appeal decisions regarding medical staff membership and privileges.[329] Membership and privileges could not be "dependent solely upon certification, fellowship, or membership in a specialty body or society."[330] Simplified conditions were adopted in 1986,[331] deleting the requirement of the committee structure and appeals mechanism, but retaining the prohibition on sole use of specialty certification.

Joint Commission Standards Changed

In its 1970 Accreditation Manual for Hospitals, the Joint Commission for the first time permitted dentists to be on the medical staff of accredited hospitals.[332] In 1977, the standard was revised to provide that medical staff should be limited to fully licensed physicians and dentists, "unless otherwise provided by law," so that the decision whether to permit other practitioners on the staff was a matter for local law.[333] The medical staff standards were completely rewritten for the 1985 accreditation manual, permitting membership and privileges for limited license practitioners.[334] The standards have been further changed periodically, including a complete reorganization of the standards for 1995.[335] The standards continue to be a significant constraint on attempts to fundamentally change the relationship of hospitals and physicians. In the late 1980s, the Joint Commission changed its name to the Joint Commission on Accreditation of Healthcare Organizations.

Judicial Deference

Courts have continued to generally defer to the medical staff decisions of private hospitals.[336] Some courts have found enforceable contract rights under the medical staff bylaws,[337] so that private hospitals must comply with the notice and hearing procedures in the medical staff bylaws. Some courts have rejected all contract rights under the bylaws.[338]

Quasi-Public Hospitals/State Action

In the 1960s there was an effort to subject private hospitals to the same principles as those public hospitals were subject to, by virtue of governmental regulation and the receipt of government money. As discussed previously, in 1974 the U.S. Supreme Court ultimately ruled that regulation and funding were not sufficient to transform a private entity's actions into state action.[339] By that time there were civil rights laws that prohibited much discrimination by private institutions including hospitals.

Common Law and Statutory Standards

A few courts have found a common law right to exercise some judicial review over medical staff decisions. Several states have enacted statutes or adopted regulations that require a fair hearing procedure in private hospitals.

In states where courts will review medical staff decisions, courts will usually require physicians to exhaust internal remedies before they can sue.[340] This has led many hospitals to adopt exhaustive remedies that assure an opportunity for a complete airing of available information about the physician before a final decision is made and that also deter frivolous challenges. However, these exhaustive remedies are also a burden on the hospital and its medical staff, so such remedies have probably also deterred the initiation of action against physicians.

Liability

Another motivation for increased medical staff credentialing activity has been the related liability exposure. From the earliest days of the visiting staff, hospitals were not liable for wrongful acts of visiting physicians since they were neither employees nor agents of the hospital.[341] In the 1960s, some courts began to impose a duty on hospitals to review the practice of physicians and take action in some circumstances. This was expanded to include a duty to check a physician's application and qualifications before granting clinical privileges.

As discussed in the next section, the changing relationship of the physician and hospital may change the effect of liability on decisions concerning credentialing.

Using History To Prepare for the Future

As physicians, hospitals, and other health care entities develop new relationships, they need to understand the concerns and forces that shaped the present relationships. Understanding how and why alternative relationships were rejected may facilitate reexamination of the full range of alternatives, while avoiding unintentional reopening of resolved conflicts.

THE FUTURE OF THE MEDICAL STAFF

In some settings, especially where there is less managed care penetration, the present medical staff structure may survive indefinitely. However, in many areas it is possible that the pressure of managed care and other market forces will make the traditional medical staff structure a luxury that neither hospitals nor physicians will be able to afford.[342]

Physicians and hospitals are under increasing pressure to make more efficient use of their time and other resources. Extensive time must be devoted to perform the medical staff functions in the complex medical staff committee and procedural structure. In the past this time commitment performed a bonding function. However, in some institutions it is increasingly difficult to find physicians who are willing to provide the time. The burdensome procedural requirements for action through the medical staff structure can deter addressing important issues which can in turn threaten the survival of the hospital in the competitive market. In addition, the medical staff organization may experience reduced influence, as managed care and other entities duplicate many of its traditional roles.

It is not yet clear what will replace the medical staff organization. It is likely that there will be a variety of approaches, varying due to the histories, economics, personalities, and other factors in each jurisdiction and each hospital. In some settings, hospitals and medical staffs will completely integrate, for example, by the hospital purchasing the physician practices and employing the physicians or by a physician organization purchasing the hospital.

It may be that physician administrative structures will develop analogous to the kinds of administration that are used by large medical groups or other professional service providers, such as accountants and lawyers. Physician group practices seldom have the kind of procedural protections for their members that medical staff organizations have provided for physicians. Administration by other physicians is apparently compatible with professional standards. Thus, it is possible that there is a chief medical officer (CMO) in the future of some hospitals.

The relationship of each physician to the hospital may be established by an employment contract or a job description. Goals of the parties and their relative bargaining power will determine the structure of the relationship. Disputes that cannot be resolved between the parties will be resolved under employment law and/or contract law.

The introduction of employment law and the reliance on contract law has many implications. A wider range of nondiscrimination laws and other employee protection laws will apply. Requirements of equal benefits for all employees will need to be addressed. Hospitals that do not want a medical staff union will need to consider labor relations laws when structuring employment relations. Hospitals will need to review their employment disciplinary procedures and determine whether to apply those procedures or different procedures to physician employees. Employment issues are discussed in Chapter 9.

When the physician becomes an employee or agent of the hospital, it becomes liable for the malpractice of the physician. A plaintiff does not have to prove deficient credentialing to impose liability on the hospital. A malpractice suit would focus on whether there was malpractice, not on whether there was proper credentialing. Except to the extent that accreditation and legal standards continued to impose specific credentialing requirements, hospitals would be able to allocate their resources to the areas that would do the most to minimize malpractice, which may or may not be the type of credentialing generally performed now. There would still be some credentialing, but it might be more like the review of other prospective professional employees.

Clearly, there is a wide range of expertise that only physicians can bring to important decision making, so ways will need to be found to assure that expertise is solicited and considered. It is likely that this will be accomplished by placing physicians in administrative positions with responsibility for various functions or at least the responsibility of providing a professional review component for the functions. It is unlikely that many committees will be used, except for special projects. When broader consultation is needed, it will generally be sought through noncommittee approaches.

It is questionable that many hospitals can afford to continue to accommodate the unique demands of every physician. To achieve the provision of service at a price the market is willing and able to pay, some practices will no longer be acceptable. Such boundaries can (1) improve practice and outcomes, (2) be neutral in their impact, or (3) curtail the availability of needed services and impair outcomes. The process of defining and assessing the impact of those boundaries will determine the shape of health care services. Hospitals and physicians need to find ways to assure that physicians have appropriate input into those decisions.

NOTES

1. Johnson v. Misericordia Comm. Hosp., 99 Wis. 2d 708, 301 N.W.2d 156 (1981); *see also* Sheffield v. Zilis, 170 Ga. App. 62, 316 S.E.2d 493 (1984) [hospital not liable because it demonstrated adequate review of physician's credentials]; Annotation, *Hospital's liability for negligence in selection or appointment of staff physician or surgeon*, 51 A.L.R. 3D 981.

2. Purcell v. Zimbelman, 18 Ariz. App. 75, 500 P.2d 335 (1972); *see also* Pedroza v. Bryant, 101 Wash. 2d 226, 677 P.2d 166 (1984) [hospital can be liable for granting privileges to physician who is not competent, but liability does not extend to treatment provided off hospital premises].

3. Joint Commission on Accreditation of Healthcare Organizations, 1995 COMPREHENSIVE ACCREDITATION MANUAL FOR HOSPITALS [hereinafter cited as 1995 Joint Commission CAMH], at 463.

4. *E.g.*, Weary v. Baylor Univ. Hosp., 360 S.W.2d 895 (Tex. Civ. App. 1962); *contra* St. John's Hosp. Med. Staff v. St. John Reg. Med. Ctr., 90 S.D. 674, 245 N.W.2d 472 (1976).

5. American Medical Association & American Hospital Association, THE REPORT OF THE JOINT TASK FORCE ON HOSPITAL–MEDICAL STAFF RELATIONSHIPS (Feb. 1985).

6. *E.g.*, Duson v. Poage, 318 S.W.2d 89 (Tex. Civ. App. 1958).

7. *E.g.*, In re Med. Staff of Good Samaritan Med. Ctr., FTC, File No. 901 0032 (settlement 9/7/94), *as discussed in* 3 HEALTH L. RPTR. [BNA] 1257 (1994) [agreement of medical staff not to combine to prevent or restrict services of hospital or multispecialty clinic] [hereinafter HEALTH L. RPTR. cited as H.L.R.]; B. McCormick, *Doctors settle FTC boycott case*, AM. MED. NEWS, Oct. 3, 1994, at 10 [Good Samaritan]; S. Lutz, *Antitrust concerns pit Texas hospital against staff doctors in legal fight*, MOD. HEALTHCARE, Mar. 6, 1995, at 18 [hospital accusing eight doctors of conspiring to fix prices, boycott hospital, pay bribe to CEO]; *See also* P. Guinta, *District sees admissions drop after irking MDs*, FLA. MED. BUSINESS (S. FLA. ED.), Mar. 28, 1989, at 6 [drop in admissions at North Broward Hospital District hospitals after privileges granted to Cleveland Clinic physicians]; D.A. Gilmore, *The antitrust implications of boycotts by health care professionals: Professional standards, professional ethics and the First Amendment*, 14 LAW, MED. & HEALTH CARE 221 (1988).

8. 1995 Joint Commission CAMH, at 463.

9. *Eisenhower medical staff to appeal court decision*, 19 MOD. HEALTHCARE, Apr. 14, 1989, at 24; Staver, *Hospital board settles, OKs staff president*, AM. MED. NEWS, Nov. 10, 1989, at 6.

10. Lawnwood Med. Ctr., Inc. v. Cassimally, 471 So.2d 1346 (Fla. 4th DCA 1985).

11. *See* R.D. Miller, *Removing physicians from medical staff offices*, 1 MEDSTAFF NEWS (Winter 1995), at 1.

12. *E.g.*, Keane v. St. Francis Hosp., 186 Wis. 2d 637, 522 N.W.2d 517 (Ct. App. 1994) [removal of chief of staff].

13. *E.g.*, Hrehorovich v. Harbor Hosp. Ctr., 93 Md. App. 772, 614 A.2d 1021 (1992), *cert. denied*, 330 Md. 319, 624 A.2d 490 (1993).

14. Shoemaker v. Los Angeles County, No. BC096101 (Cal. Super. Ct. Jan. 31, 1994), *as discussed in* 3 H.L.R. 186 (1994) [injunction of county hospital from removing chief of emergency medicine, based on due process, civil service requirements despite threatened loss of accreditation of emergency medicine residency because chief not board certified]; *Agency restores Drew Medical School emergency residency accreditation*, 3 H.L.R. 317 (1994) [on Feb. 23, appellate court granted stay of injunction, so board certified interim chair, program director were appointed and accreditation was restored the next day]; Shoemaker v. Los Angeles County, No. B081963 (Cal. Ct. App. 2d Dist. Aug. 4, 1995), *as discussed in* 4 H.L.R. 1261 (1995) [injunction lifted].

15. *E.g.*, Finley v. Giacobbe, 827 F. Supp. 215 (S.D. N.Y. 1993) [bylaws may be contract of employment], *later op.*, 848 F. Supp. 1146 (S.D. N.Y. 1994) [partial summary judgment for defendant on contract claim].

16. 1995 Joint Commission CAMH, at 287–93, 473–76.

17. 1995 Joint Commission CAMH, at 506.

18. *See* R.D. Miller & J.A. Farrell, *The future of the medical staff: Part I—What can be done today*, 1 MEDSTAFF NEWS (Summer 1995), at 1.

19. *E.g.*, Anne Arundel Gen. Hosp. v. O'Brien, 49 Md. App. 362, 432 A.2d 483 (1981) [combined radiology and nuclear medicine, entered exclusive contract].

20. Faucher v. Rodziewicz, 891 F.2d 864 (11th Cir. 1990).

21. Maxwell v. Cole, 126 Misc. 2d 597, 482 N.Y.S.2d 1000 (1984).

22. 1995 Joint Commission CAMH, at 463; Medicare conditions of participation require a Utilization Review Committee, but it can be a hospital committee, 42 C.F.R. § 482.30(b).

23. *See* note 18, *supra*.

24. *E.g.*, Hayman v. Galveston, 273 U.S. 414 (1927) [state medical license does not give constitutional right to practice in public hospital].

25. *E.g.*, Shahawy v. Harrison, 778 F.2d 636 (11th Cir. 1985), *corrected*, 790 F.2d 75 (11th Cir. 1986); *see also* Randall v. United States, 30 F.3d 518 (4th Cir. 1994), *cert. denied*, 115 S. Ct. 1956 (U.S. 1995) [provisional privileges in army hospital created no property interest in request for full privileges].

26. *E.g.*, Shahawy v. Harrison, 875 F.2d 1529 (11th Cir. 1989) [property interest in continuation of privileges].

27. *See* Lowe v. Scott, 959 F.2d 323, 335–36 (1st Cir. 1992).

28. *E.g.*, Atascadero State Hosp. v. Scanlon, 473 U.S. 234 (1985); Sullivan v. University of Miss. Med. Ctr., 617 F. Supp. 554 (S.D. Miss. 1985).

29. *E.g.*, Laje v. R.E. Thomason Gen. Hosp., 665 F.2d 724 (5th Cir. 1982); Howard v. Liberty Mem. Hosp., 752 F. Supp. 1074 (S.D. Ga. 1990); Magula v. Broward Gen. Med. Ctr., 742 F. Supp. 645 (S.D. Fla. 1990).

30. *E.g.*, Fitzpatrick v. Bitzer, 427 U.S. 445 (1976); Brinkman v. Department of Corrections, 21 F.3d 370 (10th Cir. 1994), *cert. denied*, 115 S. Ct. 315 (U.S. 1994) [Fair Labor Standards Act]; Davidson v. Board of Governors, 920 F.2d 441 (7th Cir. 1990) [Age Discrimination in Employment Act].

31. 15 U.S.C.A. §§ 34–36; Sandcrest Outpatient Servs., P.A. v. Cumberland County Hosp. Sys., Inc., 853 F.2d 1139 (4th Cir. 1988).

32. Jackson v. Metropolitan Edison Co., 419 U.S. 345 (1974).

33. *E.g.*, Downs v. Sawtelle, 574 F.2d 1 (1st Cir.), *cert. denied*, 439 U.S. 910 (1978).

34. *E.g.*, Aasum v. Good Samaritan Hosp., 395 F. Supp. 363 (D. Or. 1975), *aff'd*, 542 F.2d 792 (9th Cir. 1976).

35. *E.g.*, Jatoi v. Hurst-Euless-Bedford Hosp. Auth., 807 F.2d 1214 (5th Cir.), *modified & reh'g denied (en banc)*, 819 F.2d 545 (5th Cir. 1987), *cert. denied*, 484 U.S. 1010 (1988).

36. *E.g.*, Greco v. Orange Mem. Hosp., 513 F.2d 873 (5th Cir.), *cert. denied*, 423 U.S. 1000 (1975).

37. *E.g.*, Milo v. Cushing Mun. Hosp., 861 F.2d 1194 (10th Cir. 1988).

38. 1995 Joint Commission CAMH, at 463–64, 486–89.

39. *E.g.*, Bricker v. Sceva Speare Mem. Hosp., 111 N.H. 276, 281 A.2d 589, *cert. denied*, 404 U.S. 995 (1971).

40. *E.g.*, Owens v. New Britain Gen. Hosp., 229 Conn. 592, 643 A.2d 233 (1994) [substantial compliance with bylaws is sufficient]; Friedman v. Memorial Hosp., 523 N.E.2d 252 (Ind. Ct. App. 1988); Rhee v. El Camino Hosp. Dist., 201 Cal. App. 3d 477, 247 Cal. Rptr. 244 (6th Dist. 1988).

41. *E.g.*, Kaplan v. Carney, 404 F. Supp. 161 (E.D. Mo. 1975).

42. *E.g.*, Bello v. South Shore Hosp., 384 Mass. 770, 429 N.E.2d 1011 (1981).

43. *E.g.*, CAL. BUS. & PROF. CODE § 809.05; Nicholas v. North Colo. Med. Ctr., Inc., 1995-1 Trade Cases ¶ 70,899 (Colo. Ct. App. Feb. 2, 1995) [upholding decision of Board of Medical Examiner's Committee on Anticompetitive Conduct that hospital peer review decision to restrict staff privileges of cardiologist motivated by personal animosity of opposing cardiologist, those acting in concert with him].

44. N.Y. PUB. HEALTH LAW § 2801-b.

45. *E.g.*, Guibor v. Manhattan Eye, Ear & Throat Hosp., Inc., 56 A.D.2d 359, 392 N.Y.S.2d 628 (1st Dep't 1977), *aff'd*, 46 N.Y.2d 736, 413 N.Y.2d 638, 386 N.E.2d 247 (1978); Johnson v. Nyack Hosp., 964 F.2d 116 (2d Cir. 1992) [applies to claims in federal court, including federal antitrust claims].

46. Sussman v. Overlook Hosp. Ass'n, 95 N.J. Super. 418, 231 A.2d 389 (App. Div. 1967); Anton v. San Antonio Comm. Hosp., 19 Cal. 3d 802, 140 Cal. Rpt. 442, 567 P.2d 1162 (1977); Silver v. Castle Mem. Hosp., 53 Haw. 475, 563, 497 P.2d 564, *motion denied*, 53 Haw. 675, 501 P.2d 60, *cert. denied*, 409 U.S. 1048 (1972).

47. Garrow v. Elizabeth Gen. Hosp., 79 N.J. 549, 401 A.2d 533 (1979).

48. Rose v. Oba, 68 Haw. 422, 717 P.2d 1029 (1986).

49. *E.g.*, Weiss v. York Hosp., 745 F.2d 786, 821 (3d Cir. 1984), *cert. denied*, 470 U.S. 1060 (1985).

50. *E.g.*, Evers v. Edward Hosp. Ass'n, 247 Ill. App. 3d 717, 617 N.E.2d 1211 (2d Dist.), *app. denied*, 153 Ill. 2d 559, 624 N.E. 2d 806 (1993) [declined to evaluate application because deemed incomplete]; Smith v. Cleburne County Hosp., 870 F.2d 1375 (8th Cir.), *cert. denied*, 493 U.S. 847 (1989) [failure to submit papers for reappointment was voluntary withdrawal].

51. *E.g.*, Huellmantel v. Greenville Hosp. Sys., 303 S.C. 549, 402 S.E.2d 489 (Ct. App. 1991) [misrepresentation on application]; Pariser v. Christian Health Care Sys., Inc., 816 F.2d 1248 (8th Cir. 1987), *after remand*, 859 F.2d 78 (8th Cir. 1988) [falsely denied prior denial of privileges]; Lapidot v. Memorial Med. Ctr., 144 Ill. App. 3d 141, 494 N.E.2d 838 (4th Dist. 1986) [false denial of prior suspension of privileges]; Brooks v. Arlington Hosp. Ass'n, 850 F.2d 191 (4th Cir. 1988) [failure to complete delineation of privileges form]; Unterthiner v. Desert Hosp. Dist., 33 Cal. 3d 285, 656 P.2d 554, 188 Cal. Rptr. 590 (1983), *cert. denied*, 464 U.S. 1068 (1984); Yeargin v. Hamilton Mem. Hosp., 225 Ga. 661, 171 S.E.2d 136 (1969), *cert. denied*, 397 U.S. 963 (1970) [exception to agreement to abide by rules].

52. Many of these items are required by the Joint Commission. 1995 Joint Commission CAMH, at 491–95.

53. *E.g.*, Abdelmessih v. Board of Regents, 205 A.D.2d 983, 613 N.Y.S.2d 971 (3d Dep't 1994); Radnay v. Sobol, 175 A.D. 2d 432, 572 N.Y.S.2d 489 (3d Dep't 1991); *contra* Elmariah v. Department of Prof. Reg., 574 So.2d 164 (Fla. 1st DCA 1990).

54. *E.g.*, Scott v. Sisters of St. Francis Health Servs., Inc., 645 F. Supp. 1465 (N.D. Ill. 1986), *aff'd without op.*, 822 F.2d 1090 (7th Cir. 1987).

55. For a discussion of verification difficulties, *see* Reade & Ratzan, *Access to information—Physicians' credentials and where you can't find them*, 321 N. ENGL. J. MED. 466 (1989).

56. Schaffer, Rollo & Holt, *Falsification of clinical credentials by physicians applying for ambulatory-staff privileges*, 318 N. ENGL. J. MED. 356 (1988).

57. Rule v. Lutheran Hosps. & Homes Soc'y, 835 F.2d 1250 (8th Cir. 1987).

58. *E.g.*, Ferguson v. Gonyaw, 64 Mich. App. 685, 236 N.W.2d 543 (1975), *leave denied*, 396 Mich. 817 (1976).

59. Perry, *Statewide system lifts hospitals' burden of verifying credentials of physicians*, 19 MOD. HEALTHCARE, Sept. 8, 1989, at 38 [Maryland].

60. 42 U.S.C.A. § 1135(a).

61. 42 U.S.C.A. § 1135(b).

62. *E.g.*, Truly v. Madison Gen. Hosp., 673 F.2d 763 (5th Cir.) *cert. denied*, 459 U.S. 909 (1982).

63. *E.g.*, Ascherman v. St. Francis Mem. Hosp., 45 Cal. App. 3d 507, 119 Cal. Rptr. 507 (1st Dist. 1975).

64. *E.g.*, Johnson v. Misericordia Comm. Hosp., 99 Wis. 2d 708, 301 N.W.2d 156 (1981).

65. Landefeld v. Marion Gen. Hosp, Inc., 994 F.2d 1178 (6th Cir. 1993) [stealing internal mail indicated inability to work with others].

66. Sussman v. Overlook Hosp. Ass'n, 95 N.J. Super. 418, 231 A.2d 389 (App. Div. 1967).

67. Miller v. Eisenhower Med. Ctr., 27 Cal. 3d 614, 166 Cal. Rptr. 826, 614 P.2d 258 (1980); *applied in* Pick v. Santa Ana-Tustin Comm. Hosp., 130 Cal. App. 3d 970, 182 Cal. Rptr. 85 (4th Dist. 1982) [sufficient danger shown to justify denial].

68. *E.g.*, McElhinney v. William Booth Mem. Hosp., 544 S.W.2d 216 (Ky. 1976).

69. *E.g.*, Khan v. Suburban Comm. Hosp., 45 Ohio St. 2d 39, 340 N.E.2d 398 (1976).

70. Hay v. Scripps Mem. Hosp., 183 Cal. App. 3d 753, 228 Cal. Rptr. 413 (4th Dist. 1986).

71. *E.g.*, Armstrong v. Board of Directors, 553 S.W.2d 77 (Tenn. Ct. App. 1976).

72. *E.g.*, Sarasota County Pub. Hosp. Bd. v. Shahawy, 408 So.2d 644 (Fla. 2d DCA 1981) [public hospital may require board certification or unusual qualifications for cardiac catheterization privileges] [partially superseded by statute, Fla. Stat. § 395.0191(3), that requires acceptance of equivalent osteopathic training].

73. 42 C.F.R. § 482.12(a)(7); *see* Regional Survey and Certification Letter No. 94-48 (Dec. 9, 1994) [Regional Office VI advisory to state survey agencies that board certification requirements violate conditions of participation].

74. *See, e.g.*, Evelyn V. v. Kings County Hosp. Ctr., 819 F. Supp. 183 (E.D. N.Y. 1993) [Medicaid Act requirement that state plan provide for maintaining health standards of providers did not authorize suit by recipients against city for deficiencies at municipal hospital]; *contra* Fulkerson v. Comm'r, 802 F. Supp. 529 (D. Me. 1992) [Medicaid recipients may enforce equal access to care provision].

75. 1995 Joint Commission CAMH, at 488, 507.

76. 1995 Joint Commission CAMH, at 472.

77. H. Larkin, *All aboard?* AM. MED. NEWS, Mar. 13, 1995, at 11 [options for those without board certification to deal with managed care, where 35–40 percent of physicians not board certified]; S. McIlrath, *Board-certified only need apply*, AM. MED. NEWS, Dec. 12, 1994, 1 [medical groups seeking to block requirement of board-certification for managed care participation].

78. Rev. Rul. 65-264, 1965-2 C.B. 53 [nondiscriminatory fees do not jeopardize federal tax exemption]; *see also* Brooks & Morrisey, *Credentialing: Say good-bye to the "rubber stamp,"* 59 HOSPS., June 1, 1985, at 50, 52.

79. Chapman v. Peoples Comm. Hosp. Auth., 139 Mich. App. 696, 362 N.W.2d 755 (1984).

80. *E.g.*, Kennedy v. St. Joseph Mem. Hosp., 482 N.E.2d 268 (Ind. Ct. App. 1985) [moved personal residence too far away], *disapproved on other grounds*, Pepple v. Parkview Mem. Hosp., 536 N.E. 2d 274 (Ind. 1989); *but see* Quinn v. Kent Gen. Hosp., Inc., 617 F. Supp. 1226 (D. Del. 1985) [factual issue of whether 15-mile rule reasonable precluded summary judgment in antitrust case].

81. 1995 Joint Commission CAMH, at 488.

82. *E.g.*, Sams v. Ohio Valley Gen. Hosp. Ass'n, 413 F.2d 826 (4th Cir. 1969) [county boundary not valid geographic limit], *disapproved on other grounds*, Modaber v. Culpeper Mem. Hosp., 674 F.2d 1023 (4th Cir. 1982) [private hospital medical staff decisions not state action so no review under 42 U.S.C.A. § 1983]; Berman v. Valley Hosp., 103 N.J. 100, 510 A.2d 673 (1986)

[geographic limits to control utilization unenforceable under unique New Jersey review of private hospitals as quasi-public entities].

83. Clair v. Centre Comm. Hosp., 317 Pa. Super. 25, 463 A.2d 1065 (1983); *accord* Coker v. Hunt Mem. Hosp., No. CA-3-86-1200-H (N.D. Tex., July 29, 1986), *as discussed in* 14 HEALTH L. DIG., Sept. 1986, at 4; Rooney v. Medical Ctr. Hosp. of Chillicothe, Ohio, No. C2-91-110, 1994 U.S. Dist. LEXIS 7420 (S.D. Ohio, Mar. 30, 1994).

84. *E.g.*, Backlund v. Board of Comm'rs, 106 Wash. 2d 632, 724 P.2d 981 (1986), *appeal dismissed*, 481 U.S. 1034 (1987) [religious objections to insurance do not excuse compliance]; Scales v. Memorial Med. Ctr., 690 F. Supp. 1002 (M.D. Fla. 1988) [insurance with risk retention group not approved by state is not compliance]; Pollock v. Methodist Hosp., 392 F. Supp. 393 (E.D. La. 1975); Wilkinson v. Madera Comm. Hosp., 144 Cal. App. 3d 436, 192 Cal. Rptr. 593 (5th Dist. 1983) [hospital can require insurance to be with company approved by state]; Annotation, *Propriety of hospital's conditioning physician's staff privileges on his carrying professional liability or malpractice insurance*, 7 A.L.R. 4TH 1238; *see also* Schwartz & Mendelson, *Physicians who have lost their malpractice insurance*, 262 J.A.M.A. 1335 (1989) [analysis of their characteristics].

85. 1995 Joint Commission CAMH, at 488.

86. *E.g.*, Holmes v. Hoemako Hosp., 117 Ariz. 403, 573 P.2d 477 (1977).

87. *E.g.*, FLA. STAT. § 458.320.

88. *E.g.*, Hackett v. Metropolitan Gen. Hosp., 465 So.2d 1246 (Fla. 2d DCA 1985); Guerrero v. Burlington County Hosp., 70 N.J. 344, 360 A.2d 334 (1976); Davis v. Morristown Mem. Hosp., 106 N. J. Super. 33, 254 A.2d 125 (Ch. Div. 1969); *see also* Oliver v. Board of Trustees, 181 Cal. App. 3d 824, 227 Cal. Rptr. 1 (4th Dist. 1986) [requirement of specialty not represented on staff or renowned reputation].

89. Walsky v. Pascack Valley Hosp., 145 N.J. Super. 393, 367 A.2d 1204 (Ch. Div. 1976), *aff'd*, 156 N.J. Super. 13, 383 A.2d 154 (App. Div. 1978).

90. Desai v. St. Barnabas Med. Ctr., 103 N.J. 79, 510 A.2d 662 (1986).

91. Berman v. Valley Hosp., 103 N.J. 100, 510 A.2d 673 (1986).

92. Claycomb v. HCA-Raleigh Comm. Hosp., 76 N.C. App. 382, 333 S.E.2d 333 (1985), *rev. denied*, 315 N.C. 586, 341 S.E. 2d 23 (1986).

93. 1995 Joint Commission CAMH, at 480.

94. *E.g.*, Anne Arundel Gen. Hosp. v. O'Brien, 49 Md. App. 362, 432 A.2d 483 (1981) [even when bylaws are viewed as contract]; Holt v. Good Samaritan Hosp. & Health Ctr., 69 Ohio App. 3d 439, 590 N.E.2d 1318 (1990) [employee of former exclusive provider of emergency medical services not entitled to hearing when clinical privileges lost due to awarding of contract to new group].

95. *Governor signs bill that requires fair hearing for excluded providers*, 3 H.L.R. 1330 (1994).

96. Rev. Rul. 69-545, 1969-2 C.B. 117.

97. Sound Health Ass'n v. C.I.R., 71 T.C. 158 (1978), *acq.* 1981-2 C.B.2.

98. *E.g.*, B.H.W. Anesthesia Found., Inc. v. C.I.R., 72 T.C. 681 (1979) *nonacq.*, 1980–2 C.B.2 [closed anesthesia department granted tax exemption]; *see also* Rev. Rul. 73-417, 1973–2 C.B. 332 [pathologist/hospital laboratory director with apparently exclusive contract was found to be employee of hospital]; Kiddie v. C.I.R., 69 T.C. 1055 (1978) [pension plan issues concerning pathologist who apparently had exclusive contract with hospital].

99. Rosenblum v. Tallahassee Mem. Reg. Med. Ctr., No. 91-589 (Fla. Cir. Ct. June 18, 1992), *as discussed in* 26 J. HEALTH & HOSP. L. 61 (1993).

100. New Hampshire Podiatric Med. Ass'n v. New Hampshire Hosp. Ass'n, 735 F. Supp. 448 (D. N.H. 1990) [not violation of equal protection to deny podiatrists privileges]; Petrocco v. Dover Gen. Hosp., 273 N. J. Super. 501, 642 A.2d 1016 (App. Div.), *cert. denied*, 138 N.J. 264, 649 A.2d 1284 (1994) [exclusion of chiropractors from hospital privileges upheld].

101. *E.g.*, Cohn v. Bond, 953 F.2d 154 (4th Cir. 1991), *cert. denied*, 112 S. Ct. 3057 (U.S. 1992) [denial of privileges to chiropractor at municipal hospital, but no conspiracy because intracorporate immunity applied]; Nurse Midwifery Assocs. v. Hibbett, 918 F.2d 605 (6th Cir. 1990), *op. modified on reh'g*, 927 F.2d 904 (6th Cir.), *cert. denied*, 502 U.S. 952 (1991) [intracorporate conspiracy doctrine protected pediatricians, but not obstetricians, who recommended against nurses' privileges; could find conspiracy between obstetricians, hospital]; Lee v. Chesterfield Gen. Hosp., 289 S.C. 6, 344 S.E.2d 379 (App. 1986) [conspiracy to exclude PAs from hospital stated].

102. *E.g.*, FLA. STAT. § 395.0191(1); Stern v. Tarrant County Hosp. Dist., 755 F.2d 430 (5th Cir.) [Texas law requires admitting osteopathic physicians], *modified on reh'g (en banc)*, 778 F.2d 1052 (5th Cir. 1985) [state law violation is not Federal Constitution violation], *cert. denied*, 476 U.S. 1108 (1986); Dooley v. Barbarton Citizen's Hosp., 11 Ohio St. 3d 216, 465 N.E.2d 38 (1984) [state law requires admitting podiatrists].

103. Ogrodowczyk v. Tennessee Bd. for Licensing Health Care Facilities, 886 S.W.2d 246 (Tenn. Ct. App. 1994) [affirming state board decision that hospitals cannot grant clinical privileges to chiropractors based on evidence patients too ill to tolerate manipulation; high percentage of admissions deemed inappropriate; chiropractors receive little training, experience in hospital protocol, practice].

104. Cohn v. Wilkes Reg. Med. Ctr., 113 N.C. App. 275, 437 S.E.2d 889, *rev. denied*, 336 N.C. 603, 447 S.E. 2d 387 (1994); *see related case*, Cohn v. Bond, 953 F.2d 154 (4th Cir. 1991) [medical staff immune from antitrust liability for denying privileges to chiropractor at municipal hospital].

105. *E.g.*, *Easing into the medical mainstream: Chiropractors gain acceptance at hospitals*, THE HERALD (Miami, FL), Feb. 18, 1995, at 1C [hospital adding chiropractic department].

106. 1995 Joint Commission CAMH, at 487–89.

107. Medical Staff and Physician Relations Committee of American Academy of Hospital Attorneys, PEER REVIEW GUIDEBOOK (1995) [hereinafter cited as AAHA GUIDEBOOK], at 28–31; *but see* Elbrecht v. HCA Health Servs. of Fla., Inc., No. 93-10113 (N.D. Fla. Sept. 26, 1994), *as discussed in* 22 HEALTH L. DIG., Nov. 1994, at 62 [neurologist sought exemption from emergency call on disability grounds, but ADA did not apply because hospital was not employer; employment relationship between physician, her patients not sufficient to trigger coverage].

108. *E.g.*, Chowdhury v. Reading Hosp., 677 F.2d 317 (3d Cir. 1982), *cert. denied*, 463 U.S. 1229 (1983).

109. Duane v. Government Employees Ins. Co., 37 F.3d 1036 (4th Cir. 1994), *cert. dismissed*, 115 S. Ct. 2272 (U.S. 1995) [42 U.S.C.A. §1981 prohibits private discrimination against aliens in making contracts]; *contra*, Bhandari v. First Nat'l Bank, 829 F.2d 1343 (5th Cir. 1987) *(en banc)*, *vacated*, 492 U.S. 901, *reinstated on remand*, 887 F.2d 609 (5th Cir. 1989), *cert. denied*, 494 U.S. 1061 (1990) [with dissent by Justices White, O'Connor], but note *Bhandari* was decided before 1991 amendment to § 1981 (see discussion of amendment in Chapter 9); Annotation, *Application of 42 USCS sec. 1981 to private discrimination against aliens*, 99 A.L.R. FED. 835; *see also* 8 U.S.C.A. § 1324b [prohibition of employment discrimination against protected noncitizens]; Espinoza v. Farah Mfg. Co., 414 U.S. 86 (1973) [Title VII does

not prohibit discrimination on basis of citizenship]; *accord*, Fortino v. Quasar Co., 950 F.2d 389 (7th Cir. 1991).

110. 8 U.S.C.A. § 1324a [prohibition of employment of unauthorized aliens, with subsection (a)(4) including contracts for labor in definition of employment].

111. Hauptman v. Grand Manor Health Related Facility, Inc., 121 A.D.2d 151, 502 N.Y.S.2d 1012 (1st Dep't 1986).

112. *E.g.*, Greisman v. Newcomb Hosp., 40 N.J. 389, 192 A.2d 817 (1963).

113. *E.g.*, Natale v. Sisters of Mercy, 243 Iowa 582, 52 N.W.2d 701 (1952).

114. Martino v. Concord Comm. Hosp. Dist., 233 Cal. App. 2d 51, 43 Cal. Rptr. 255 (1st Dist. 1965).

115. Kiester v. Humana Hosp. Alaska, Inc., 843 P.2d 1219 (Alaska 1992).

116. *E.g.*, Purgess v. Sharrock, 33 F.3d 134 (2d Cir. 1994); *see also* Mishler v. Nevada State Bd. of Med. Examiners, 896 F.2d 408 (9th Cir. 1990) [right to confirmation of license]; *contra* Chuz v. St. Vincent's Hosp., 186 A.D.2d 450, 589 N.Y.S.2d 17 (1st Dep't 1992) [liability only if delay due to malice]; Humana Med. Corp. v. Peyer, 155 Wis. 2d 714, 456 N.W.2d 355 (1990) [hospital may refuse to release information until physician repaid money hospital loaned him to establish practice].

117. Leach v. Jefferson Parish Hosp. Dist., 870 F.2d 300 (5th Cir.), *cert. denied*, 493 U.S. 822 (1989); *accord*, Huellmantel v. Greenville Hosp. Sys., 303 S.C. 549, 402 S.E.2d 489 (Ct. App. 1991) [one-year wait].

118. Theissen v. Watonga Mun. Hosp. Bd., 550 P.2d 938 (Okla. 1976).

119. 1995 Joint Commission CAMH, at 483–84.

120. *Surgical injuries lead to new rule*, N.Y. TIMES, June 14, 1992, at 1.

121. *E.g.*, Paravecchio v. Memorial Hosp., 742 P.2d 1276 (Wyo. 1987), *cert. denied*, 485 U.S. 915 (1988).

122. *E.g.*, Fahey v. Holy Family Hosp., 32 Ill. App. 3d 537, 336 N.E.2d 309 (1975), *cert. denied*, 426 U.S. 936 (1976).

123. Johnson v. St. Bernard Hosp., 79 Ill. App. 3d 709, 399 N.E.2d 198 (1st Dist. 1979).

124. 1995 Joint Commission CAMH, at 497–99, 506; 42 C.F.R. § 482.22(a)(1).

125. Elam v. College Park Hosp., 132 Cal. App. 3d 332, 183 Cal. Rptr. 156 (4th Dist. 1982); *see also* Annotation, *Hospital liability for negligence in failing to review or supervise treatment given by doctor, or to require consultation*, 12 A.L.R. 4TH 57.

126. McVay v. Rich, 255 Kan. 371, 874 P.2d 641 (1994), *aff'g*, 18 Kan. App. 2d 746, 859 P.2d 399 (1993).

127. One court ruled that patient cannot sue monitoring physician who is proctoring surgery during probationary period, Clarke v. Hoek, 174 Cal. App. 3d 208, 219 Cal. Rptr. 845 (1st Dist. 1985). For use of unfavorable proctor report, *see* Nicholson v. Lucas, 21 Cal. App. 4th 1657, 26 Cal. Rptr. 2d 778 (5th Dist. 1994).

128. Randall v. United States, 30 F.3d 518 (4th Cir. 1994), *cert. denied*, 115 S. Ct. 1956 (U.S. 1995).

129. For a summary of some of the methods, *see* D.S. Wakefield, C.M. Helms, L. Helms, *The peer review process: The art of judgment*, 17 J. HEALTHCARE QUALITY (May/June 1995), 11.

130. 1995 Joint Commission CAMH, at 219–66.

131. *Id.*, at 252–53, 497.

132. *Id.*, at 418.

133. *Id.*, at 504 [no longer than two years].

134. *Id.*, at 497–99.

135. Siegel v. St. Vincent Charity Hosp., 35 Ohio App. 3d 143, 520 N.E.2d 249 (1987).

136. Yashon v. Hunt, 825 F.2d 1016 (6th Cir. 1987), *cert. denied*, 486 U.S. 1032 (1988); *accord* Bhatnagar v. Mid-Maine Med. Ctr., 510 A.2d 233 (Me. 1986).

137. *Kickback plan by hospital hit*, AM. MED. NEWS, June 28–July 5, 1985, at 1 [Paracelsus Corp. cash reward for minimizing services to Medicare patients]; *Investigation into hospital pledged*, AM. MED. NEWS, June 28–July 5, 1985, at 34; *Plan to cut costs by rewarding doctors assailed*, N.Y. TIMES, Sept. 24, 1985, at 12; *For-profit chain admits mail fraud*, AM. MED. NEWS, Dec. 12, 1986, at 2 [mail fraud plea unrelated to physician bonus, but arose out of IG bonus investigation].

138. 42 U.S.C. § 1320a-7a(b).

139. *E.g.*, Friedman v. Delaware County Mem. Hosp., 672 F. Supp. 171 (E.D. Pa. 1987), *aff'd without op.*, 849 F.2d 600, 603 (3d Cir. 1988) [overutilization of bronchoscopies]; Knapp v. Palos Comm. Hosp., 125 Ill. App. 3d 244, 465 N.E.2d 554 (1st Dist. 1984) [termination of privileges for overutilization of lung scans, other tests]; J.D. Blum, *Evaluation of medical staff using fiscal factors: Economic credentialing*, 26 J. HEALTH & HOSP. L. 65 (1993); Miller, *Use of hospital data in medical staff discipline*, 1 TOPICS IN HOSP. L., Dec. 1985, at 37; *see also* Hassan v. Independent Practice Assocs., P.C., 698 F. Supp. 679 (E.D. Mich. 1988) [upholding decision of IPA to exclude physicians because of indications of unjustified use of tests; cost containment objectives procompetitive].

140. Huhta v. Children's Hosp. of Phila., No. 93-2765 (E.D. Pa. May 31, 1994), *as described in* 3 H.L.R. 793 (1994) [dismissal of antitrust suit by former chief of division of pediatric cardiology who had resigned to open multispecialty group practice at competing hospital after denied access to certain hospital-owned pediatric cardiology equipment, facilities]; Tarabishi v. McAlester Reg. Hosp., 951 F.2d 1558 (10th Cir. 1991), *cert. denied*, 112 S.Ct. 2996 (U.S. 1992) [rejecting antitrust challenge to termination after attempted to open outpatient surgical clinic]; Katz v. Children's Hosp. Corp., 33 Mass. App. Ct. 574, 602 N.E.2d 598 (1992) [hospital may restrict subspecialties to persons who practice full time at hospital].

141. FTC letter to Georgia Hosp. Ass'n, May 28, 1993, *as discussed in* 2 H.L.R. 1161 (1993).

142. *E.g.*, Jackaway v. Northern Dutchess Hosp., 139 A.D.2d 496, 526 N.Y.S.2d 599 (2d Dep't 1988); *see also* St. Louis v. Baystate Med. Ctr., Inc., 30 Mass. App. Ct. 393, 568 N.E.2d 1181 (1991) [group lost exclusive contract, terminated for lack of admissions].

143. *E.g.*, J.D. Blum, *Evaluation of medical staff using fiscal factors: Economic credentialing*, 26 J. HEALTH & HOSP. L. 65, 70 (1993).

144. *E.g.*, Ross v. Beaumont Hosp., 687 F. Supp. 1115 (E.D. Mich. 1988) [verbal abuse by physician]; *Nurse gets $65,000 for a pulled ponytail*, N.Y. TIMES, July 24, 1988, at 10 [out-of-court settlement with doctor].

145. *E.g.*, *Hospital suspends 300 Tampa doctors slow on paper work*, MIAMI [FL] HERALD, May 18, 1988, at 1A.

146. *E.g.*, Peterson v. Tucson Gen. Hosp., 114 Ariz. 66, 559 P.2d 186 (Ct. App. 1976).

147. *E.g.*, Jackson v. Fulton-DeKalb Hosp. Auth., 423 F. Supp. 1000 (N.D. Ga. 1976), *aff'd without op.*, 559 F.2d 1214 (5th Cir. 1977).

148. Moore v. Board of Trustees, 88 Nev. 207, 495 P.2d 605, *cert. denied*, 409 U.S. 879 (1972).

149. Pagliaro v. Point Pleasant Hosp., No. A-3932-75 (N.J. Super. Ct. App. Div. Jan. 19, 1979), *as discussed in* 12 HOSP. L., Apr. 1979, at 5.

150. Khan v. Suburban Comm. Hosp., 45 Ohio St. 2d 39, 340 N.E.2d 398 (1976).

151. Fahey v. Holy Family Hosp., 32 Ill. App. 3d 537, 336 N.E.2d. 309 (1975), *cert. denied*, 426 U.S. 936 (1976).

152. *E.g.*, Cooper v. Delaware Valley Med. Ctr., 654 A.2d 547 (Pa. 1995).

153. Clough v. Adventist Health Sys., 780 P.2d 627 (N.M. 1989).

154. *E.g.*, Katz v. Children's Hosp. Corp., 33 Mass. App. Ct. 574, 602 N.E.2d 598 (1992).

155. Bartley v. Eastern Me. Med. Ctr., 617 A.2d 1020 (Me. 1992).

156. *E.g.*, B. McCormick, *Hospital loses over economic credentialing*, AM. MED. NEWS, Mar. 28, 1994, at 4 [radiologist awarded $12.7 million due to exclusive contract].

157. *E.g.*, American Med. Int'l v. Scheller, 590 So.2d 947 (Fla. 4th DCA 1991), *rev. denied*, 602 So.2d 533 (Fla. 1992).

158. *E.g.*, Estate of Behringer v. Med. Ctr. at Princeton, 249 N.J. Super. 597, 592 A.2d 1251 (1991) [upholding suspension of surgical privileges of physician with AIDS]; *HIV-infected surgeons: Behringer v. Medical Center*, 266 J.A.M.A. 1134 (1991); Scoles v. Mercy Health Corp., 887 F. Supp. 765 (E.D. Pa. 1994) [HIV-positive surgeon's practice was justifiably restricted, was not violation of Rehabilitation Act or ADA because not otherwise qualified]; Scoles v. Mercy Health Corp., No. 92-6712 (E.D. Pa. Feb. 7, 1995), *as discussed in* 4 H.L.R 230 (1995) [confidential settlement of federal employment discrimination case by orthopedic surgeon against hospital that restricted his practice when it learned of his HIV-positive status]; *Court: Hospital may bar HIV-positive doctor from surgery*, AM. MED. NEWS, Jan. 16, 1995, at 11 [Scoles may pursue claims of wrongful removal from occupational programs where he did not perform invasive procedures]; Doe v. University of Md. Med. Sys. Corp., 50 F.3d 1261 (4th Cir. 1995) [affirming judgment in favor of hospital on claims under Rehabilitation Act, ADA by resident suspended from surgery when tested HIV positive; was offered nonsurgical residency which he refused; court ruled he posed significant risk to patients that could not be eliminated by reasonable accommodation; hospital may elect to restrict activities of only those known to be HIV positive].

159. In re Milton S. Hershey Med. Ctr., 535 Pa. 9, 634 A.2d 159 (1993).

160. *E.g.*, FLA. STAT. § 455.261; Goetz v. Noble, 652 So.2d 1203 (Fla. 4th DCA 1995) [absolute immunity from state law claims, qualified immunity from federal civil rights claims for medical director of program under § 455.261].

161. *E.g.*, Malak v. Associated Physicians, Inc., 784 F.2d 277 (7th Cir. 1986); Schwartzman v. Valenzuela, 846 F.2d 1209 (9th Cir. 1988) [jury question whether discharge was retaliation]; Cohen v. County of Cook, 677 F. Supp. 547 (N.D. Ill. 1988).

162. Zaky v. Veterans Admin., 793 F.2d 832 (7th Cir.), *cert. denied*, 479 U.S. 937 (1986); *accord* Setliff v. Memorial Hosp., 850 F.2d 1384 (10th Cir. 1988).

163. Smith v. Cleburne County Hosp., 870 F.2d 1375 (8th Cir.), *cert. denied*, 493 U.S. 847 (1989).

164. DiMarco v. Rome Hosp., 952 F.2d 661 (2d Cir. 1992).

165. 42 U.S.C.A. § 11133; 45 C.F.R. pt. 60, *first published in* 54 FED. REG. 42722 (Oct. 17, 1989); U.S. DEP'T OF HHS, NATIONAL PRACTITIONER DATA BANK GUIDEBOOK (1990); I.S. Rothschild, *Operation of National Practitioner Data Bank*, 25 J. HEALTH & HOSP. L. 225 (1992); American Dental Ass'n v. Shalala, 303 U.S. App. D.C. 231, 3 F.3d 445 (1993) [HCQIA does not require reports of payments by individual practitioners]; *National Practitioner Data Bank now accepting physician rebuttal statements*, 3 H.L.R. 495 (1994) [announcement 3/31/94]; N.J. Schendel, *Banking on confidentiality: Should consumers be allowed access to the national practitioner data bank?* 27 J. HEALTH & HOSP. L. 289 (1994); L. Oberman, *Data bank exempts self-paid claims*, AM. MED. NEWS, Dec. 26, 1994, at 1 [self-paid malpractice claims exempted from reporting, previous reports purged from files]; OIG Report: *Hospital reporting to the National Practitioner Data Bank*, Feb. 1995; L. Oberman, *IG asks why more hospitals don't report adverse actions*, AM. MED. NEWS, Feb. 13, 1995, at 4.

166. Doe v. United States D.H.H.S., 871 F. Supp. 808 (E.D. Pa. 1994) [no private right of action under HCQIA, no liberty or property interest in having mail fraud conviction excluded from data bank]; *see also* Randall v. United States, 30 F.3d 518 (4th Cir. 1994), *cert. denied*, 115 S. Ct. 1956 (U.S. 1995) [entry in national data base that physician's privileges had been restricted due to incompetence did not deprive of constitutional liberty interest].

167. *E.g.*, FLA. STAT. §§ 395.011(7), 395.0115(4); Weirton Med. Ctr., Inc. v. West Va. Bd. of Med., 450 S.E.2d 661 (W. Va. 1994) [hospital must report disciplinary action against physician within 60 days of completion of formal disciplinary proceedings, again after completion of legal action, if any, but hospital fine of $7,500 reversed due to ambiguity in statute].

168. Cuatico v. Idaho Falls Consol. Hosps., Inc., 753 F.2d 1081 (9th Cir. 1985) (mem.), *as described in* 18 HOSP. L., Mar. 1985, at 6; *accord* Dorn v. Mendelzon, 196 Cal. App. 3d 933, 242 Cal. Rptr. 259 (1st Dist. 1987).

169. Purgess v. Sharrock, 33 F.3d 134 (2d Cir. 1994); *MD gets $5.1 million from hospital in defamation suit*, AM. MED. NEWS, Sept. 12, 1994, at 13.

170. Walton v. Jennings Comm. Hosp., 875 F.2d 1317 (7th Cir. 1989), *appeal after remand*, 999 F.2d 277 (7th Cir. 1993) [affirming judgment for defendants]; *see also* Salaymeh v. St. Vincent Mem. Hosp. Corp., 706 F. Supp. 643 (C.D. Ill. 1989).

171. Garrison v. Herbert J. Thomas Mem. Hosp. Ass'n, 190 W.Va. 214, 438 S.E.2d 6 (1993).

172. For a more detailed analysis of procedural approaches to medical staff matters, see AAHA GUIDEBOOK (1995). For examples of disputes and techniques for addressing them, *see* American Hospital Association, Office of Legal and Regulatory Affairs, Legal Memorandum #13, *The Report of the Task Force on Dispute Resolution in Hospital-Medical Staff Relationships* (August 1988).

173. *E.g.*, Jit Kim Lim v. Central DuPage Hosp., 871 F.2d 644 (7th Cir. 1989).

174. 1995 Joint Commission CAMH, at 463–64, 469, 503–04.

175. *E.g.*, Owens v. New Britain Gen. Hosp., 229 Conn. 592 643 A.2d 233 (1994); Everhart v. Jefferson Parish Hosp. Dist., 757 F.2d 1567 (5th Cir. 1985).

176. *E.g.*, Setliff v. Memorial Hosp., 850 F.2d 1384 (10th Cir. 1988).

177. Bergeron v. Desert Hosp. Corp., 221 Cal. App. 3d 146, 270 Cal. Rptr. 397 (4th Dist. 1990), *rev. denied*, 1990 Cal. LEXIS 3961 (Aug. 30, 1990).

178. *E.g.*, Chaudhry v. Prince George's County, 626 F. Supp. 448 (D. Md. 1985); Hoberman v. Lock Haven Hosp., 377 F. Supp. 1178 (M.D. Pa. 1974) [hearing not required for censure]; *contra* Grodjesk v. Jersey City Med. Ctr., 135 N.J. Super. 393, 343 A.2d 489 (Ch. Div. 1975) [censure requires notice, opportunity to respond].

179. *E.g.*, Bloom v. Hennepin County, 783 F. Supp. 418 (D. Minn. 1992).

180. *E.g.*, International Med. Ctrs., Inc. v. Sabates, 498 So.2d 1292 (Fla. 3d DCA 1986), *rev. denied*, 508 So.2d 14 (Fla. 1987) [confirming arbitrator award for physician].

181. 42 U.S.C.A. § 11112(a).

182. Pub. L. No. 99-660, 100 Stat. 3784 (1986) (*codified at* 42 U.S.C.A. §§ 11101–11152).

183. *E.g.*, Gill v. Mercy Hosp., 199 Cal. App. 3d 889, 245 Cal. Rptr. 304 (5th Dist.), *cert. denied*, 488 U.S. 892 (1988).

184. 42 U.S.C.A. § 11112(b)(3)(A)(i).

185. *E.g.*, Imperial v. Suburban Hosp. Ass'n, Inc., 37 F.3d 1026 (4th Cir. 1994) [affirming summary judgment for hospital]; Bryan v. James E. Holmes Reg. Med. Ctr., 33 F.3d 1318 (11th Cir. 1994), *cert. denied*, 115 S. Ct. 1363 (U.S. 1995) [determination of immunity by judge, not jury; $4.2 million jury verdict for physician reversed based on HCQIA immunity]; Smith v. Ricks, 31 F.3d 1478 (9th Cir. 1994), *cert. denied*, 115 S. Ct. 1400 (U.S. 1995) [affirming summary

judgment for hospital; peer review proceedings need not be like trial]; Austin v. McNamara, 979 F.2d 728 (9th Cir. 1992).

186. *E.g.*, Decker v. IHC Hosp., Inc., 982 F.2d 433 (10th Cir. 1992), *cert. denied*, 113 S. Ct. 3041 (U.S. 1993); Manion v. Evans, 986 F.2d 1036 (6th Cir.), *cert. denied sub nom.* Lima Mem. Hosp. v. Manion, 114 S. Ct. 71 (U.S. 1993).

187. Van Kirk v. Trustees of White County Mem. Hosp., No. 91C01-8809-CP-128 (Ind. Cir. Ct. White County Nov. 9, 1988), *as discussed in* 16 HEALTH L. DIG., Dec. 1988, at 67.

188. 42 U.S.C.A. § 11111(c)(2)(B) (1988), *deleted by* P.L. 101-239, 103 Stat. 2208, § 6103(e)(6)(A).

189. *E.g.*, Caine v. Hardy, 943 F.2d 1406 (5th Cir. 1991), *cert. denied*, 503 U.S. 936 (1992).

190. Storrs v. Lutheran Hosps. & Homes Soc'y, 609 P.2d 24 (Alaska 1980), *appeal after remand*, 661 P.2d 632 (Alaska 1983); *accord* Darlak v. Bobear, 814 F.2d 1055 (5th Cir. 1987).

191. *E.g.,* Poe v. Charlotte Mem. Hosp., 374 F. Supp. 1302 (W.D. N.C. 1974) [two-year-old incidents were insufficient basis for summary action].

192. *E.g.*, Conley v. Brownsville Med. Ctr., 570 S.W.2d 583 (Tex. Civ. App. 1978) [injunction dissolved after mistreatment of patient].

193. *E.g.*, Paskon v. Salem Mem. Hosp. Dist., 806 S.W.2d 417 (Mo. Ct. App.), *cert. denied*, 502 U.S. 908 (1991).

194. *E.g.*, Woodbury v. McKinnon, 447 F.2d 839 (5th Cir. 1971).

195. Arizona Osteopathic Med. Ass'n v. Fridena, 105 Ariz. 291, 463 P.2d 825, *cert. denied*, 399 U.S. 910 (1970).

196. *E.g.*, Sywak v. O'Connor Hosp., 199 Cal. App. 3d 423, 244 Cal. Rptr. 753 (6th Dist. 1988), *op. withdrawn*, 1988 Cal. LEXIS 177 (May 19, 1988).

197. *E.g.*, Randall v. United States, 30 F.3d 518 (4th Cir. 1994), *cert. denied*, 115 S. Ct. 1956 (U.S. 1995); In re Corines, 149 A.D. 2d 591, 540 N.Y.S.2d 273 (2d Dep't 1989), *appeal dismissed*, 75 N.Y. 2d 850, 552 N.Y.S.2d 923, 552 N.E.2d 171 (1990); Suckle v. Madison Gen. Hosp., 499 F.2d 1364 (7th Cir. 1974).

198. Garrow v. Elizabeth Gen. Hosp., 79 N.J. 549, 401 A.2d 533 (1979).

199. Randall v. United States, 30 F.3d 518 (4th Cir. 1994), *cert. denied*, 115 S. Ct. 1956 (U.S. 1995).

200. Anton v. San Antonio Comm. Hosp., 19 Cal. 3d 802, 140 Cal. Rptr. 442, 567 P.2d 1162 (1977); *accord* Yashon v. Hunt, 825 F. 2d 1016 (6th Cir. 1987); Wright v. Southern Mono Hosp. Dist., 631 F. Supp. 1294 (E.D. Cal. 1986), *aff'd without op.*, 924 F.2d 1063 (9th Cir. 1991).

201. 42 U.S.C.A. § 11112(b)(3)(C)(i).

202. In re Zaman, 285 S.C. 345, 329 S.E.2d 436 (1985).

203. Applebaum v. Board of Directors, 104 Cal. App. 3d 648, 163 Cal. Rptr. 831 (3d Dist. 1980).

204. 42 U.S.C.A. § 11112(b)(3)(A).

205. Mann v. Johnson Mem. Hosp., 611 N.E.2d 676 (Ind. Ct. App. 1993).

206. *E.g.*, Laje v. R.E. Thomason Gen. Hosp., 564 F.2d 1159 (5th Cir. 1977), *reh'g denied*, 568 F.2d 1367 (5th Cir.), *cert. denied*, 437 U.S. 905 (1978).

207. Lasko v. Valley Presbyterian Hosp., 180 Cal. App. 3d 519, 225 Cal. Rptr. 603 (2d Dist. 1986).

208. *E.g.*, Ladenheim v. Union County Hosp. Dist., 76 Ill. App. 3d 90, 394 N.E.2d 770 (5th Dist. 1979).

209. Applebaum v. Board of Directors, 104 Cal. App. 3d 648, 163 Cal. Rptr. 831 (3d Dist. 1980).

210. Pariser v. Christian Health Care Sys., 859 F.2d 78 (8th Cir. 1988).

211. Ezpeleta v. Sisters of Mercy Health Corp., 800 F.2d 119 (7th Cir. 1986).

212. *E.g.*, Rosenblit v. Superior Court, 231 Cal. App. 3d 1434, 282 Cal. Rptr. 819 (4th Dist. 1991), *rev. denied*, 1991 Cal. LEXIS 4251 (Sept. 19, 1991) [new medical staff hearing ordered for several reasons including failure to give physician copies of 30 charts].

213. *E.g.*, Ezekial v. Winkley, 20 Cal. 3d 267, 142 Cal. Rptr. 418, 572 P.2d 32 (1977).

214. 42 U.S.C.A. § 11112(b)(3)(C)(iii); Smith v. Ricks, 798 F. Supp. 605 (N.D. Cal. 1992), *aff'd*, 31 F.3d 1478 (9th Cir. 1994), *cert. denied*, 115 S. Ct. 1400 (U.S. 1995) [HCQIA does not require opportunity to present evidence of other physicians' performance].

215. Smith v. Ricks, 798 F. Supp. 605 (N.D. Cal. 1992), *aff'd*, 31 F.3d 1478 (9th Cir. 1994), *cert. denied*, 115 S. Ct. 1400 (U.S. 1995).

216. *E.g.*, Woodbury v. McKinnon, 447 F.2d 839 (5th Cir. 1971); Kaplan v. Carney, 404 F. Supp. 161 (E.D. Mo. 1975).

217. *E.g.*, Poe v. Charlotte Mem. Hosp., 374 F. Supp. 1302 (W.D. N.C. 1974).

218. 42 U.S.C.A. § 11112(b)(3)(C)(iii).

219. 42 U.S.C.A. § 11112(b)(3)(C)(ii).

220. Balkissoon v. Capitol Hill Hosp., 558 A.2d 304 (D.C. 1989).

221. 42 U.S.C.A. § 11112(b)(3)(D).

222. 1995 Joint Commission CAMH, at 463, 503–04.

223. Leonard v. Board of Directors, Prowers County Hosp. Dist., 673 P.2d 1019 (Colo. Ct. App. 1983).

224. *E.g.*, Ad Hoc Exec. Comm. v. Runyan, 716 P.2d 465 (Colo. 1986) [committee cannot challenge governing board rejection of suspension it recommended]; Forster v. Fishermen's Hosp., Inc., 363 So.2d 840 (Fla. 3d DCA 1978), *cert. denied*, 376 So.2d 71 (Fla. 1979) [chief of hospital staff cannot challenge privileges granted after he recommended denial].

225. *E.g.*, Brindisi v. University Hosp., 131 A.D.2d 667, 516 N.Y.S.2d 745 (2d Dep't 1987) [patient cannot challenge denial of privileges to use laser]; Bello v. South Shore Hosp., 384 Mass. 770, 429 N.E.2d 1011 (1981).

226. Hurst v. Beck, 771 F. Supp. 118 (E.D. Pa. 1991).

227. *E.g.*, Yaeger v. Sisters of St. Joseph, No. 87-6427-E (D. Or. Aug. 9, 1988), *as discussed in* 16 HEALTH L. DIG., Oct. 1988, at 78; Suckle v. Madison Gen. Hosp., 499 F.2d 1364 (7th Cir. 1974); *but see* Qasem v. Kozarek, 716 F.2d 1172 (7th Cir. 1983) [failure to pursue hospital procedures does not bar suit seeking only payment of damages by credentials committee member].

228. *E.g.*, Christhilf v. Annapolis Emergency Hosp. Ass'n, Inc., 496 F.2d 174 (4th Cir. 1974).

229. *E.g.*, Pepple v. Parkview Mem. Hosp., Inc., 511 N.E.2d 467 (Ind. Ct. App. 1987), *aff'd*, 536 N.E.2d 274 (Ind. 1989).

230. Long v. Bates County Mem. Hosp., 667 S.W.2d 419 (Mo. Ct. App. 1983) [injunction of 21-day suspension for test without patient authorization].

231. *E.g.*, Hottentot v. Mid-Maine Med. Ctr., 549 A.2d 365 (Me. 1988); Barrows v. Northwestern Mem. Hosp., 123 Ill. 2d 49, 525 N.E.2d 50 (1988); Lakeside Comm. Hosp. v. Levenson, 101 Nev. 777, 710 P.2d 727 (1985).

232. *E.g.*, Medical Ctr. Hosps. v. Terzis, 235 Va. 443, 367 S.E.2d 728 (1988) [review limited to determination whether written reasons for adverse action are in list of permitted reasons in statute].

233. *E.g.*, United States v. Jefferson County, 720 F.2d 1511, 1519 (11th Cir. 1983).

234. *E.g.*, Deerfield Med. Ctr. v. Deerfield Beach, 661 F.2d 328 (5th Cir. 1981).

235. *E.g.*, Prakasam v. Popowski, 566 So.2d 189 (La. Ct. App.), *cert. denied*, 569 So.2d 986 (La. 1990) [error to issue injunction]; J. Sternberg, S. Schulman & Assocs., M.D., P.A. v. Hospital Corp. of Am., 571 So.2d 1334 (Fla. 4th DCA 1989) [affirming denial of injunction].

236. *E.g.*, Porter Mem. Hosp. v. Malak, 484 N.E.2d 54 (Ind. Ct. App. 1985); Lawler v. Eugene Wuesthoff Mem. Hosp. Ass'n, 497 So.2d 1261 (Fla. 5th DCA 1986); *see also* notes 191–192, *supra.*

237. Knapp v. Palos Comm. Hosp., 176 Ill. App. 3d 1012, 531 N.E.2d 989 (Ill. Ct. App. 1988), *cert. denied*, 493 U.S. 847 (1989).

238. *E.g.*, Rosenblit v. Superior Court, 231 Cal. App. 3d 1434, 262 Cal. Rptr. 819 (4th Dist. 1991), *rev. denied*, 1991 Cal. LEXIS 4251 (Sept. 19, 1991) [writ granted]; Bollengier v. Doctors Med. Ctr., 222 Cal. App. 3d 1115, 272 Cal. Rptr. 273 (5th Dist. 1990) [writ denied for failure to exhaust administrative remedies within hospital]; Bonner v. Sisters of Providence Corp., 194 Cal. App. 3d 437, 239 Cal. Rptr. 530 (1st Dist. 1987) [writ reversed because evidence supported finding that doctor did not meet hospital's reasonable standards]; Hay v. Scripps Mem. Hosp., 183 Cal. App. 3d 753, 228 Cal. Rptr. 413 (4th Dist. 1986) [affirming denial of writ because reasonable to require Ob-Gyn residency for D & C privileges].

239. Westlake Comm. Hosp. v. Superior Court, 17 Cal. 3d 465, 131 Cal. Rptr. 90, 551 P.2d 410 (1976) [physician whose privileges are terminated cannot sue hospital or involved individuals in tort without first having hospital action overturned in mandamus proceeding].

240. *See also* Fed. R. Civ. P. 81(b) [writ of mandamus abolished in federal courts].

241. AM. JUR. 2D, *Mandamus* § 104.

242. AM. JUR. 2D, *Mandamus* § 104; Green v. Board of Directors of Lutheran Med. Ctr., 739 P.2d 872 (Colo. Ct. App. 1987) [physician denied privileges not entitled to mandamus relief]; State ex rel. St. Joseph Hosp. v. Fenner, 726 S.W.2d 393 (Mo. Ct. App. 1987) [mandamus not appropriate relief for contract dispute between physician and hospital, not appropriate for breach of contract]; Lawnwood Med. Ctr. v. Cassimally, 471 So.2d 1346 (Fla. 4th DCA 1985) [not appropriate to use mandamus to compel election of medical staff officers].

243. AM. JUR. 2D, *Mandamus* § 69.

244. R.D. Miller, *Removing physicians from medical staff offices*, 1 MEDSTAFF NEWS (Winter 1995), at 1, *discussing* Keane v. St. Francis Hosp., 186 Wis. 2d 637, 522 N.W.2d 517 (Ct. App. 1994) [mandamus available to reinstate medical staff officer, but denied due to circumstances].

245. 1995 Joint Commission CAMH, at 503.

246. *E.g.*, Everett v. St. Ansgar Hosp., 974 F.2d 77 (8th Cir. 1992); DeLeon v. Saint Joseph Hosp., 871 F.2d 1229 (4th Cir.), *cert. denied*, 493 U.S. 825 (1989) [application release barred defamation claim]; Stitzell v. York Mem. Osteopathic Hosp., 768 F. Supp. 129 (M.D. Pa. 1991); King v. Bartholomew County Hosp., 476 N.E.2d 877 (Ind. Ct. App. 1985) [immunity provision on application upheld].

247. *E.g.*, Westlake Comm. Hosp. v. Superior Court., 17 Cal. 3d 465, 131 Cal. Rptr. 90, 551 P.2d 410 (1976); Keskin v. Munster Med. Research Found., 580 N.E.2d 354 (Ind. Ct. App. 1991) [release signed as part of application for privileges did not preclude action challenging exclusive anesthesia contract, but hospital found to be within its rights in entering contract]; Rees v. Intermountain Health Care, Inc., 808 P.2d 1069 (Utah 1991) [immunity provisions in bylaws only precluded defamation action, not action for violating bylaws].

248. *E.g.*, Bass v. Ambrosius, 185 Wis. 2d 879, 520 N.W.2d 625 (Ct. App. 1944).

249. *See* Annotation, *Liability in tort for interference with physician's contract or relationship with hospital*, 7 A.L.R. 4TH 572.

250. *E.g.*, Scheller v. American Med. Int'l, Inc., 502 So.2d 1268 (Fla. 4th DCA 1987), *rev. denied*, 513 So.2d 1068 (Fla.), *appeal after remand*, 590 So.2d 947 (Fla. 4th DCA 1991), *rev. dismissed*, 602 So.2d 533 (Fla. 1992) [affirming punitive damage award of $19 million]; *Doctor, lawyer feud over $15.5 million settlement*, PALM BEACH [FL] POST, June 29, 1992, at 1B [case settled].

251. *Id.*

252. *E.g.*, Purgess v. Sharrock, 33 F.3d 134 (2d Cir. 1994); Chakrabarti v. Cohen, 31 F.3d 1 (1st Cir. 1994).

253. *E.g.*, Scheller v. American Med. Int'l, 583 So.2d 1047 (Fla. 4th DCA 1991), *rev. denied*, 598 So.2d 78 (Fla. 1992) [no enforceable agreement for perpetual agreement].

254. *E.g., id.*

255. Ethan Allen, Inc. v. Georgetown Manor, 647 So.2d 812 (Fla. 1994).

256. *E.g.*, Greenberg v. Mount Sinai Med. Ctr., 629 So.2d 252 (Fla. 3d DCA 1993).

257. Annotation, *Liability of corporate director, officer, or employee for tortious interference with corporation's contract with another*, 72 A.L.R. 4TH 492.

258. *E.g.*, Hospital Corp. of Am. v. Jarvinen, 624 So.2d 303 (Fla. 4th DCA 1993), *rev. denied*, 634 So.2d 624 (Fla. 1994) [issue mentioned but not decided].

259. Laje v. R.E. Thomason Gen. Hosp., 665 F.2d 724 (5th Cir. 1982).

260. *E.g.*, DeLeon v. Saint Joseph Hosp., 871 F.2d 1229 (4th Cir.), *cert. denied*, 493 U.S. 825 (1989); Sibley v. Lutheran Hosp., 709 F. Supp. 657 (D. Md. 1988), *aff'd*, 871 F.2d 479 (4th Cir. 1989); Guntheroth v. Rodaway, 107 Wash. 2d 170, 727 P.2d 982 (1986); Spencer v. Community Hosp., 87 Ill. App. 3d 214, 408 N.E.2d 981 (1st Dist.1980).

261. Baldwin v. McGrath, No. 76-5-336 (Pa. C.P. Ct. York County Mar. 18, 1982), *as discussed in* 10 HEALTH L. DIG., Apr. 1982, at 17.

262. Summit Health v. Pinhas, 500 U.S. 322 (1991).

263. 1995 Joint Commission CAMH, at 501.

264. *E.g.*, Fobbs v. Holy Cross Health Sys. Corp., 29 F.3d 1439 (9th Cir. 1994), *cert. denied*, 115 S. Ct. 936 (U.S. 1995) [race]; Johnson v. Hills & Dales Gen. Hosp., 40 F.3d 837 (6th Cir. 1994), *cert. denied*, 115 S.Ct. 1698 (U.S. 1995) [race].

265. Harris v. Group Health Ass'n, Inc., 213 U.S. App. D.C. 313, 662 F.2d 869 (1981).

266. *E.g.*, Smith v. Our Lady of the Lake Hosp., 960 F.2d 439 (5th Cir. 1992); Jackson v. Radcliffe, 795 F. Supp. 197 (S.D. Tex. 1992).

267. *E.g.*, ARIZ. REV. STAT. ANN. § 36-445.02; Harris v. Bellin Mem. Hosp., 13 F.3d 1082 (7th Cir. 1994).

268. Scappatura v. Baptist Hosp., 120 Ariz. 204, 584 P.2d 1195 (Ct. App. 1978); *accord* Rodriguez-Erdman v. Ravenswood Hosp. Med. Ctr., 163 Ill. App. 3d 464, 516 N.E.2d 731 (1st Dist. 1987), *appeal denied*, 118 Ill. 2d 551, 520 N.E.2d 392 (1988).

269. FLA. STAT. §§ 395.011(8), (10), 395.0115(2), (5).

270. Psychiatric Assocs. v. Siegel, 610 So.2d 419 (Fla. 1992).

271. Cardwell v. Rockford Mem. Hosp. Ass'n, 136 Ill. 2d 271, 555 N.E.2d 6, *cert. denied*, 488 U.S. 998 (1990).

272. Smith v. Our Lady of the Lake Hosp., 639 So.2d 730 (La. 1994).

273. Holly v. Auld, 450 So.2d 217 (Fla. 1984).

274. *See generally*, American Academy of Hospital Attorneys, HOSPITAL-AFFILIATED INTEGRATED DELIVERY SYSTEMS: FORMATION, OPERATION, AND CONTRACTS HANDBOOK (1995) [AAHA Practice Guide Series/Vol. 2] [cited hereinafter as AAHA IDS HANDBOOK].

275. AAHA IDS HANDBOOK, at 31–2.

276. *See generally*, AAHA IDS HANDBOOK.

277. B. McCormick, *AMA delegates see IRS rulings as a threat to PHOs*, AM. MED. NEWS, Dec. 26, 1994, 4 [limit of 20 percent physician representation on boards criticized by physicians]; *IRS official clarifies agency view on PHO board representation conditions*, 4 H.L.R. 151 (1995) [for-profit PHOs not subject to 20 percent physician representation limit; up to 50 percent control probably acceptable if proportional to their investment]; M. Mitka, *More doctors on PHO boards*, AM. MED. NEWS, Feb. 13, 1995, 3 [IRS announces no limit on physicians on boards of taxable PHOs, but representation must reflect investment]; AAHA IDS HANDBOOK, at 93–4.

278. *See generally*, AAHA IDS HANDBOOK, *especially* 103–14, 169.

279. *E.g.*, In re: Petition for Declaratory Statement of C. Robert Crow, M.D. (Fla. Bd. of Med. Draft Final Order Feb. 10, 1995) [bonus to employed physician based on fees generated for ancillary services would violate state anti-kickback law]; *Hospital resolves Missouri concerns over practice acquisitions*, 4 H.L.R. 9 (1995) [settlement between hospitals, state concerning practice acquisitions, related issues].

280. Rev. Proc. 93-19, 1993-1 C.B. 526.

281. *E.g.*, *IRS closing agreement with Hermann Hospital with IRS' physician recruitment guidelines* (Sept. 16, 1994), *reprinted in* 3 H.L.R. 1519 (1994).

282. *See* AAHA IDS HANDBOOK, *especially* 114–18.

283. *E.g.*, Vencor, Inc. v. Webb, 33 F.3d 840 (7th Cir. 1994) [when operator of long-term acute-care hospitals sought to enjoin competition by former employee contrary to noncompete agreement, agreement unenforceable under applicable Kentucky law].

284. Rev. Proc. 93-19, 1993-1 C.B. 526.

285. 42 U.S.C.A. § 1395x(v)(1)(I); 42 C.F.R. § 420.300–420.304.

286. Adler v. Montefiore Hosp. Ass'n, 453 Pa. 60, 311 A.2d 634 (1973), *cert. denied*, 414 U.S. 1131 (1974); *see also* Annotation, *Validity and construction of contract between hospital and physician providing for exclusive medical services*, 74 A.L.R.3D 1268 (1976).

287. Hyde v. Jefferson Parish Hosp. Dist. No. 2, 686 F.2d 286 (5th Cir. 1982).

288. Jefferson Parish Hosp. Dist. No. 2 v. Hyde, 466 U.S. 2 (1984). On remand the appellate court rejected Dr. Hyde's other challenges to the denial of his application, 764 F.2d 1139 (5th Cir. 1985).

289. *E.g.*, White v. Rockingham Radiologists, 820 F.2d 98 (4th Cir. 1987); Collins v. Associated Pathologists, 676 F. Supp. 1388 (C.D. Ill. 1987), *aff'd*, 844 F.2d 473 (7th Cir.), *cert. denied*, 488 U.S. 852 (1988).

290. Oltz v. Saint Peter's Comm. Hosp., 861 F.2d 1440 (9th Cir. 1988).

291. Community Hosp. v. Tomberlin, 712 F. Supp. 170 (M.D. Ala. 1989).

292. Medical Ctr. Hosp. v. Texas, No. 374,830 (Tex. Dist. Ct. Travis County, Oct. 17, 1985), *as discussed in* 18 HOSP. L., Dec. 1985, at 4.

293. *See* AAHA IDS HANDBOOK, at 178–81.

294. *E.g.,* Rush v. City of St. Petersburg, 205 So.2d 11 (Fla. 2d DCA 1967).

295. *E.g.*, Mich. Op. Att'y Gen. No. 6770 (1993).

296. *E.g.*, St. Francis Reg. Med. Ctr. v. Weiss, 254 Kan. 728, 869 P.2d 606 (1994).

297. *Id.*, at 179; TEX. REV. CIV. STAT. ANN. art. 4495b; Garcia v. Texas State Bd. of Med. Examiners, 384 F. Supp. 434 (W.D. Tex. 1974), *aff'd*, 421 U.S. 995 (1975) [constitutional]; Parker v. Board

of Dental Examiners, 216 Cal. 285, 14 P.2d 67 (1932); People ex rel. State Bd. of Med. Examiners v. Pacific Health Corp., 12 Cal. 2d 156, 82 P.2d 429 (1938), *cert. denied*, 306 U.S. 633 (1939).

298. *See* R. Miller, J. Farrell, *The medical staff of the future: Part I—What can be done today*, 1 MEDSTAFF NEWS (Spring 1995), at 1.

299. *See* A.M. Chesney, THE JOHNS HOPKINS HOSPITAL AND THE JOHNS HOPKINS UNIVERSITY SCHOOL OF MEDICINE: A CHRONICLE, VOL. II 1893–1905 (Johns Hopkins Press, 1958), 246–50.

300. M.J. Vogel, THE INVENTION OF THE MODERN HOSPITAL (Univ. of Chicago Press, 1980), 45–46, 68–69, 116 [hereinafter cited as VOGEL]; P. Starr, THE SOCIAL TRANSFORMATION OF AMERICAN MEDICINE (Basic Books 1982), 163–64 [hereinafter cited as STARR].

301. VOGEL, 121–23.

302. STARR, 163–64, 165–67; VOGEL, 69, 121.

303. STARR, 162, 167.

304. STARR, 167; P. Stevens, AMERICAN MEDICINE AND THE PUBLIC INTEREST (Yale Univ. Press paper ed. 1971), 91, 129 [hereinafter cited as STEVENS].

305. STEVENS, 129.

306. *E.g.*, Harris v. Thomas, 217 S.W. 1068 (Tex. Civ. App. 1920); State ex rel. Wolf v. La Crosse Lutheran Hosp. Ass'n, 181 Wis. 33, 193 N.W. 994 (1923); Hughes v. Good Samaritan Hosp., 289 Ky. 123, 158 S.W.2d 159 (1942) [upholding termination of surgical privileges until he obtained the "indorsement" of ACS so that hospital could continue its accreditation]; *see also the following cases not involving ACS standards*, Van Campen v. Olean Gen. Hosp., 210 A.D. 204, 205 N.Y.S. 554 (1924), *aff'd*, 239 N.Y. 615, 147 N.E. 219 (1925); Strauss v. Marlboro County Gen. Hosp., 185 S.C. 425, 194 S.E. 65 (1937) [private hospital free to forbid physician from practicing surgery in hospital]; Levin v. Sinai Hosp. of Baltimore City, 186 Md. 174, 46 A.2d 298 (1946) [private hospital may exclude any physician; power to appoint includes power to remove, subject to constitution, bylaws of hospital].

307. Stevens v. Emergency Hosp. of Easton, 142 Md. 526, 121 A. 475 (1923).

308. State ex rel. Wolf v. La Crosse Lutheran Hosp. Ass'n, 181 Wis. 33, 193 N.W. 994 (1923).

309. *E.g.*, Hayman v. City of Galveston, 273 U.S. 414 (1927); Richardson v. City of Miami, 144 Fla. 294, 198 So. 51 (1940); Harris v. Thomas, 217 S.W. 1068 (Tex. Civ. App. 1920); Newton v. Board of Comm'rs of Weld County, 86 Colo. 446, 282 P. 1068 (1929); Munroe v. Wall, 66 N.M. 15, 340 P.2d 1069 (1959); *contra*, Stribling v. Jolley, 241 Mo. App. 1123, 253 S.W.2d 519 (1952) [note that osteopathy started in Missouri].

310. *E.g.*, Selden v. City of Sterling, 316 Ill. App. 455, 45 N.E.2d 329 (1942); Green v. City of St. Petersburg, 154 Fla. 339, 17 So.2d 517 (1944).

311. Hamilton County Hosp. v. Andrews, 227 Ind. 217, 84 N.E.2d 469, *reh'g denied*, 227 Ind. 228, 85 N.E.2d 365, *cert. denied*, 338 U.S. 831 (1949).

312. Hamilton County Hosp. v. Andrews, 227 Ind. 228, 85 N.E.2d 365, *cert. denied*, 338 U.S. 831 (1949).

313. Henderson v. City of Knoxville, 157 Tenn. 477, 9 S.W.2d 697 (1928); Albert v. Board of Trustees, 341 Mich. 344, 67 N.W.2d 244 (1954).

314. *E.g.*, State ex rel. Carpenter v. Cox, 61 Tenn. App. 101, 453 S.W.2d 69 (1969); Armstrong v. Board of Directors, 553 S.W.2d 77 (Tenn. Ct. App. 1976) [still cannot require board certification]; *see also* note 324.

315. STARR, 168.

316. *E.g.*, Ware v. Benedikt, 225 Ark. 185, 280 S.W.2d 234 (1955); Hamilton County Hosp. v. Andrews, 227 Ind. 217, 84 N.E.2d 469 (1949).

317. American Med. Ass'n v. United States, 317 U.S. 519 (1943), *aff'g* 76 U.S. App. D.C. 70, 130 F.2d 233 (1942).

318. Group Health Coop. v. King County Med. Soc'y, 39 Wash. 2d 586, 237 P.2d 737 (1951).

319. *E.g.*, Natale v. Sisters of Mercy, 243 Iowa 582, 52 N.W.2d 701 (1952) [hospital not required to follow procedure in bylaws].

320. Johnson v. City of Ripon, 259 Wis. 84, 47 N.W.2d 328 (1951).

321. Findlay v. Board of Sup'rs, 72 Ariz. 58, 230 P.2d 526 (1951).

322. Jacobs v. Martin, 20 N.J. Super. 531, 90 A.2d 151 (Ch. Div. 1952).

323. Board of Trustees v. Pratt, 72 Wyo. 120, 262 P.2d 682 (1953).

324. Albert v. Board of Trustees, 341 Mich. 344, 67 N.W.2d 244 (1954). Later Michigan statutes authorized public hospitals to establish qualifications for medical staff membership, *see* Milford v. People's Comm. Hosp. Auth., 380 Mich. 49, 155 N.W.2d 835 (1968); Touchton v. River Dist. Comm. Hosp., 76 Mich. App. 251, 256 N.W.2d 455 (1977).

325. Wallington v. Zinn, 146 W. Va. 147, 118 S.E.2d 526 (1961).

326. *See* F. Helminski, *"That peculiar science": Osteopathic medicine and the law*, 12 LAW, MED. & HEALTH CARE, Feb. 1984, 32.

327. *See* Osteopathic Physicians & Surgeons v. California Med. Ass'n, 224 Cal. App. 2d 378, 36 Cal. Rptr. 641 (2d Dist. 1964).

328. Pub. L. No. 89-97, § 102(a), 79 Stat. 313 (1965) [*codified as amended at* 42 U.S.C.A. § 1395x(r)].

329. 42 C.F.R. § 405.1023, *as adopted in* 31 FED. REG. 13424 (Oct. 18, 1966) *and corrected* 32 FED. REG. 136 (Jan. 7, 1967).

330. 42 C.F.R. § 405.1023(e)(4), *as adopted in* 31 FED. REG. 13424 (Oct. 18, 1966).

331. 51 FED. REG. 22010 (June 17, 1986) (*codified as amended at* 42 C.F.R. pt. 482).

332. Wilk v. American Medical Ass'n, 671 F. Supp. 1465, 1490 (N.D. Ill. 1987), *aff'd*, 895 F.2d 352 (7th Cir.), *cert. denied*, 496 U.S. 927 (1990).

333. *Id.*, 671 F. Supp., at 1491.

334. *Id.*, 671 F. Supp., at 1492–93; Joint Commission, 1985 ACCREDITATION MANUAL FOR HOSPITALS.

335. 1995 Joint Commission CAMH.

336. *E.g.*, West Coast Hosp. Ass'n v. Hoare, 64 So.2d 293 (Fla. 1953); Hughes v. Good Samaritan Hosp., 289 Ky. 123, 158 S.W.2d 159 (1942); Edson v. Griffin Hosp., 21 Conn. Super. 55, 144 A.2d 341 (1958); Akopiantz v. Board of County Comm'rs, 65 N.M. 125, 333 P.2d 611 (1958).

337. *E.g.*, Rees v. Intermountain Health Care, 808 P.2d 1069 (Utah 1991).

338. *E.g.*, Robles v. Humana Hosp. Cartersville, 785 F. Supp. 989 (N.D. Ga. 1992).

339. Jackson v. Metropolitan Edison Co., 419 U.S. 345 (1974).

340. *E.g.*, Westlake Comm. Hosp. v. Superior Court, 17 Cal. 3d 465, 131 Cal. Rptr. 90, 551 P.2d 410 (1976).

341. *E.g.*, Schloendorff v. Society of N.Y. Hosp., 211 N.Y. 125, 105 N.E.92 (1914), *overruled on other grounds*, Bing v. Thunig, 2 N.Y.2d 656, 16 N.Y.S.2d 3, 143 N.E.2d 3 (1957).

342. *See, e.g.*, J. Johnsson, *Hospital medical staffs: Next managed care casualty?* AM. MED. NEWS, Oct. 17, 1994, at 1.

8

Individual Licensure and Credentialing

Licensing and credentialing are an attempt to assure that qualified people are engaged in health care practice. The primary purpose is to protect the public health by helping the public identify qualified providers and by prohibiting unqualified persons from providing services that require expertise. Some persons criticize all licensing and credentialing as a barrier to those who want to enter practice and, thus, a restriction on competition. There are many public and private credentialing methods. The public method is individual licensure. The private methods include accreditation of educational programs, certification of individuals, and credentialing by institutions.

INDIVIDUAL LICENSURE

The public method of credentialing is licensure, which can be either mandatory or permissive. A mandatory licensing law requires that individuals obtain licenses before practicing within the scope of practice reserved for those with licenses, unless the individual is eligible under an exception in the law. A permissive licensing law usually regulates use of titles; an individual cannot use the title without a license but can perform the functions. In the past, some licensing laws, both mandatory and permissive, provided for registration with no required special qualifications. Today registration laws are rare. Nearly all licensing laws have educational and examination requirements.

States have discretion to determine which professions to license. In 1889, the U.S. Supreme Court upheld mandatory licensure of physicians.[1] The scope of discretion is illustrated by a 1966 Supreme Court decision that states may choose not to recognize naturopathy as a discipline distinct from orthodox medical practice.[2] Thus, naturopaths must qualify for a full medical license unless the state chooses to license them separately.

Physicians and dentists were generally the first health professionals to be licensed. All states now have mandatory licensing laws for them. Nursing was usually the next profession to be licensed, and all states now license nurses. Pharmacists are another professional group licensed in all states. Most other health professionals, including physical therapists, psychologists, speech pathologists, audiologists, occupational therapists, and podiatrists, are licensed in many states. Some states license technical personnel, such as emergency medical technicians and radiologic technologists.

States have discretion in determining the requirements for licensing. Some states impose requirements in addition to education and testing. For example, some states require physicians to participate in Medicare and accept its payment as payment in full.[3] The Illinois Supreme Court ruled that the state can require good moral character and place the burden on the applicant to prove it.[4] However, the Americans with Disabilities Act may limit inquiries into physical and mental health.[5]

Unless the licensing statute authorizes waiver of requirements, generally the licensing agency does not have the discretion to waive requirements that are set by statute.[6]

When the state does license a health professional, the property right that is thereby conferred includes the right to prompt official verification of the license.[7]

Failure to renew licenses in a timely manner not only violates the licensing law, but can increase liability exposure. The Virginia Supreme Court ruled that the state statutory cap on malpractice damages does not apply to services provided while a physician has an expired license.[8]

In some states, hospitals and other health care organizations have the responsibility to determine that certain professional and technical personnel meet government-imposed qualifications,[9] instead of having a governmental agency evaluate the qualifications and issue a license.

Hospitals need a system to determine that all staff have the required qualifications and licenses. Use of unqualified staff can have adverse consequences. In some states if a patient is harmed by a staff member who is practicing illegally, the hospital may be liable in situations where it would not be liable if the staff member were practicing legally.[10] However, in liability cases involving unlicensed staff, most states focus on whether the employee was competent, rather than on lack of a license.[11] Hospitals can be subject to administrative and criminal penalties for using unlicensed staff. For example, a New Jersey hospital was ordered to pay an administrative fine for aiding and abetting the illegal practice of medicine because it employed an unlicensed physician in its emergency room.[12] The agency that licenses all or part of the hospital could suspend the hospital license or put the hospital on probation.

Courts generally understand that hospitals must take action against employees who fail to maintain necessary licenses. For example, a Pennsylvania court ruled in 1984 that a nurse who was terminated for failure to renew her license was not entitled to unemployment compensation.[13] The failure was considered "willful misconduct."

Some hospital staff are exempt from some licensure requirements. Exemption gives hospitals more flexibility in determining qualifications of those staff.

The federal government also licenses some individual health care providers. For example, professionals who manufacture, prescribe, distribute, or dispense controlled substances must be registered with the Drug Enforcement Administration.[14]

Scope of Practice

Mandatory licensing laws reserve a scope of practice for those who obtain licenses. The definition and evolution of the scope of practice for physicians, nurses, and others have been controversial. The controversy has focused on two issues. Who may make the judgment that certain procedures will be performed? Who may perform the procedures?

Although courts will uphold almost all restrictions on scope of practice adopted under the state police power, occasionally courts will find that some laws have gone too far. In 1992, the Georgia Supreme Court declared a statute unconstitutional that permitted only physicians, dentists, podiatrists, and veterinarians to perform any surgery, operation, or invasive procedure in which human or animal tissue was cut, pierced, or altered.[15] The court concluded that there was no rational basis for this statute, which did not permit nurses to give injections or diabetics to inject themselves with insulin.

In general, medical diagnoses and orders for most diagnostic and therapeutic procedures are reserved for physicians. Other professionals are increasingly being permitted to make some diagnoses and order some treatments. States vary concerning which procedures may be ordered by physicians' assistants and nurse practitioners. Nursing diagnosis has gained recognition. Generally nurses determine what nursing care is needed and when nursing care is insufficient, so that medical attention or instructions must be sought. In some states, nurses are permitted to make some judgments traditionally reserved for physicians when the nurses act under standing orders or established protocols.[16]

Most medical procedures are restricted to physicians when they are first introduced. As experience with the procedures grows and they become better defined, nurses tend to be permitted to perform the procedures, and in some situations technical personnel are permitted to perform them. This evolution has varied from state to state and has been recognized in several ways. Some licensing statutes have been changed to list permitted procedures. Some procedures have been declared to be permitted or prohibited by state attorney general opinions. In some states, the medical and/or nursing licensing board has issued rules or statements concerning the permitted scope of practice.[17] Another approach has been joint statements of private professional organizations, such as state medical societies and nurses' associations. Judicial decisions have defined the scope in some states. Many sources need to be examined to determine the scope of practice in a particular state.

The positions of interested agencies and organizations should also be considered. If they disagree and a court can be convinced that the recognized scope is not permitted by statute, these announcements, opinions, and even agency determinations can be declared invalid. For example, the Iowa Supreme Court affirmed an injunction prohibiting a chiropractor from performing acupuncture, drawing blood specimens, and giving advice on diet and nutrition even though the Board of Chiropractic Examiners had issued a declaratory ruling that these practices were permitted.[18] The board's ruling probably protected individual practitioners from prosecution for acts performed prior to the court ruling.

Some specific practices that have been addressed for nurses include administering anesthesia, giving injections, starting intravenous (IV) fluids and medications, and inserting various tubes. These issues generally have been answered for registered nurses. Some of these issues are now being addressed for licensed practical nurses.

Some states have given physicians broad authority to delegate functions to nurses. For example, Michigan permits physicians to delegate functions under proper supervision if permitted by standards of acceptable and prevailing practice.[19] The Michigan attorney general has interpreted this to permit physicians to delegate to nurses the prescribing of any drugs except controlled substances if the prescription identifies the supervising physician.[20] Other states have given licensing boards broad authority to expand nursing functions. For example, Iowa gives the Board of Nursing authority to expand nursing roles by rule when the expanded roles are recognized by the medical and nursing professions.[21] Oregon has gone one step further and permitted nurse practitioners to be selected as the "attending physician" of an injured worker under the workers' compensation law.[22]

Physicians should not assume that they can delegate functions. A physician's assistant was convicted for prescribing a controlled substance without statutory authority when he authorized refilling a prescription for Tylenol with codeine in accordance with written instructions from the supervising physician. The physician and the physician's assistant were excluded from participation in Medicare for five years as a result of the conviction.[23]

Licensed professionals who act outside their permitted scope of practice are unlicensed practitioners when performing those acts, with the potential adverse consequences for the hospital discussed above.

Rule Making

Some rules promulgated by licensing boards have been challenged on the basis that they are believed to be beyond the boards' authority. Licensing boards generally have broad authority, but occasionally specific controversial rules have been found to exceed their authority.

A New Jersey appellate court upheld a rule requiring licensed radiologists who provide diagnostic services for other physicians to also provide those services for licensed chiropractors.[24] Although this service was inconsistent with the practice of many radiologists, the court ruled that it was reasonable, within the board's authority, and promulgated using proper procedures. The Ohio Supreme Court upheld a rule prohibiting the prescription of anabolic steroids for the enhancement of athletic ability.[25] In 1990, the New Jersey Supreme Court upheld a Board of Physical Therapy rule that reduced physician supervision and permitted therapists to modify the prescribed treatment.[26]

A Florida appellate court ruled that the licensing board did not have authority to prohibit chelation therapy for arteriosclerosis unless the board found the therapy was harmful or hazardous to patients.[27] The prohibition was not justified by the lack of proof of effectiveness or the limited number of physicians who used it. An Illinois appellate court invalidated a rule that excluded from the dental licensing examination all persons who were not graduates of schools approved by the American Dental Association or schools with a curriculum equivalent to that of the University of Illinois College of Dentistry.[28] The statute limited the examination to graduates of "reputable" schools, and the board could not arbitrarily determine that a school was not reputable; it had to evaluate the school. A Florida appellate court ruled that a Board of Optometry rule authorizing optometrists to use certain drugs was beyond the authority of the board.[29] A Pennsylvania court invalidated a rule requiring physicians to obtain permission from the board on a patient-by-patient basis before prescribing amphetamines.[30] The preceding cases illustrate some of the kinds of rules that licensing boards are promulgating. It is important to be familiar with the current positions of the boards that license hospital personnel. Some rules can be successfully challenged in some states even though courts in other states might uphold similar rules.

Discipline and Due Process

Licensing boards have broad authority to discipline licensed professionals when they violate professional standards specified in licensing laws or board rules.[31] The discipline may be license revocation, suspension, a fine,[32] or a probationary period during which conditions must be met.[33] Most licensing boards have authority to impose various conditions, including prohibiting types of practice, requiring substance abuse rehabilitation efforts, consulting about or supervising specified procedures, or completing education programs. Before imposing disciplinary sanctions, licensing boards must provide due process to licensed professionals, including notice of the wrongful conduct, and an opportunity to present information.[34]

Many states impose stricter requirements that must be followed for the board's action to be valid. For example, the Colorado Supreme Court ordered a nurse's license to be reinstated, in part because the statute required the full licensing board to attend the revocation hearing and the full board had not done so.[35] Most licensing laws do not require the presence of the full board, but if this is required, the law must be followed. In some states, the licensing board cannot attend the evidentiary hearing.[36]

To provide due process, licensed professionals must have two types of notice. They must have individualized notice of the specific questioned acts and omissions, which form the basis for discipline.[37] In addition, the statute and regulations must provide generalized advance notice that conduct of that type will lead to discipline. Courts usually rule that prohibition of "unprofessional conduct" gives adequate notice that a wide range of inappropriate behavior is prohibited. "Unprofessional conduct" is not considered too vague when it is applied to conduct widely recognized as unprofessional. The Oregon Supreme Court upheld the revocation of a nurse's license for "conduct derogatory to the standards of professional nursing."[38] She had instructed, recommended, and permitted her daughter to serve as a registered nurse, knowing that her daughter had no nursing license. However, "unprofessional conduct" is not adequate notice for all possible violations. The Idaho Supreme Court ordered reinstatement of a nursing license that had been suspended for six months for unprofessional conduct.[39] The Board of Nursing found that the nurse had discussed laetrile treatment with a hospitalized leukemia patient without physician approval, interfering with the physician–patient relationship. The board considered this to be unprofessional conduct. The court ruled that the board could have prohibited this conduct by rule, but that a prohibition of unprofessional conduct did not give nurses adequate warning that this conduct was prohibited.

Many licensing boards are now specifying by rule more detailed grounds for discipline, but some courts have considered the statutory criteria to be sufficiently clear, so that no rules are needed.[40] Hospitals and health professionals should monitor these efforts closely and participate in the rule-making process to assure that the rules do not inadvertently prohibit appropriate existing practices.

When licensed professionals prevail in challenges to board actions, they usually cannot get payment from the state or the board members.[41] They are limited to reversal of improper discipline and invalidation of improper rules. In most states, board members have broad immunity from monetary liability.[42]

Competition

States have broad authority to determine which professions to license.[43] The state is confronted with a difficult cost-benefit analysis whenever it is requested to license a health discipline.

Many professional and technical disciplines seek to be licensed. They claim that licensing is necessary to protect the public from unqualified practitioners.

Licensure is also sought because it provides status and often is accompanied by expansion of the scope of practice into areas previously reserved for other licensed professionals. Licensure can be an economic benefit to those licensed, by reducing the number of people permitted to perform specific tasks. The educational and testing requirements designed to protect the public increase the time and expense of becoming qualified and reduce the number of people available to provide the service. This can have a detrimental effect if the cost increase is too great. It can have a catastrophic effect if too few people meet the requirements, since some members of the public then receive no service. Licensure can be a barrier to innovation because of the difficulty in changing statutes and rules that define what licensees may do.

The barriers to entry imposed by licensing are widely accepted for some health professions, especially for professionals who often function independently, such as physicians, dentists, and nurses. The appropriateness of state licensure of dependent practitioners who function under the supervision of other licensed practitioners has been questioned. Some commentators believe that the public health could be adequately protected through placing responsibility on the institution and supervising independent health professionals and that the public interest in innovative, cost-effective health services could be advanced by more flexibility in the use of dependent health personnel. However, the trend appears to continue toward licensure of more health disciplines.

PRIVATE CREDENTIALING

Many private credentialing methods have been developed. Educational programs are accredited, individuals are certified, and hospitals and other institutions investigate the credentials of prospective staff members before permitting them to practice in the institution.

Accreditation of Educational Programs

Private professional organizations have established criteria to evaluate educational programs. Periodically an individual or a team investigates programs that desire to be accredited. Programs that meet the criteria are accredited. Although accreditation is voluntary, most educational programs strive to obtain and retain accreditation from established accrediting bodies because students prefer accredited programs. Graduates of accredited programs often find it easier to obtain permission to take licensing examinations or to be admitted for advanced study because their degrees are generally accepted without additional proof of their education. Graduates of accredited programs also find it easier to convince employers that they are prepared for employment in the discipline. Graduates of other programs will usually have to provide more information concerning their training programs to demonstrate the adequacy of their training.

Not all accrediting bodies have earned the wide acceptance given to the longer-standing bodies that accredit medicine and nursing programs. Hospitals should not automatically assume that accreditation assures high standards. If the hospital is not familiar with the accrediting body, it should make inquiries before relying on its accreditation.

There have been legal challenges to denial of accreditation. Most courts defer to the accrediting bodies. A Pennsylvania hospital that lost accreditation of a general surgery residency program attacked the action in state and federal court. The state attack started with a petition to the state medical licensing board to review the accrediting body's action. The board denied review. A lower state court ordered the board to review the action, but the Pennsylvania Supreme Court reversed, finding the board did not have authority to review individual residency accreditation decisions.[44] A lower federal court granted an injunction of withdrawal of accreditation of a residency program, which the federal appellate court vacated, finding that the accreditation decision was not state action.[45] A Maryland Roman Catholic hospital lost accreditation of its obstetrics-gynecology residency program because it failed to provide training in family planning. Another federal court found that the loss of accreditation did not violate any constitutional or statutory rights of the hospital.[46]

Certification

Private professional organizations sponsor programs to certify that individuals meet certain criteria and are considered prepared to practice in the discipline. Individual certification is generally related to performance, usually including passing a test. Some certifications, especially certifications by medical specialty boards, have become so widely accepted that it may be difficult to practice without them. However, as discussed in Chapter 7, Medicare-participating hospitals cannot adopt an absolute requirement of board certification for specialty clinical privileges. Instead, hospitals can avail themselves of the value of certification, while avoiding the absolute requirement, by requiring "board certification or equivalent training and experience."

Some managed care plans require board certification.[47] Some structuring may be necessary to address this controversial requirement while complying with the requirements for Medicare participation.

Certifying bodies have proliferated, resulting in a certifying body for virtually every professional and technical discipline practicing in the hospital.[48] Not all of these bodies have earned the same acceptance as the longer-standing certification bodies. There is also variation in the acceptance of medical specialties. The American Board of Medical Specialties recognizes 23 medical specialty boards, while another 105 exist that it has not recognized.[49] Hospitals should be familiar with a certifying body before giving it substantial weight in evaluating applications. One advantage of the private certification system is that the hospital generally has the discretion to use its own evaluation system.

States can require private certification as a condition of state licensure.[50]

Individuals who challenge denial of certification are generally unsuccessful.[51] Courts will generally enforce the releases that boards require as part of the application process, except as to antitrust claims.[52] Unsuccessful applicants have generally been unable to state antitrust claims.[53]

HOSPITAL CREDENTIALING

As discussed in Chapter 7, hospitals have an elaborate system for evaluating the credentials of physicians and determining appropriate clinical privileges to grant physicians. Hospitals also have a responsibility to evaluate credentials of others working in the hospital and to delineate what they may do.

For most hospital staff, this responsibility is fulfilled through the hiring process, hospital or department rules concerning practice patterns, the supervisory system, performance evaluation, and verification of relicensure. In the hiring process, qualifications of individuals should be checked, including verification of licensure or other credentials. This process helps to determine professional competence and to detect other problems that could interfere with proper patient care. A Georgia appellate court ruled that a hospital could be liable for the molesting of an infant by an orderly because the hospital had not checked his past, which would have disclosed a criminal conviction for being a "peeping Tom."[54] A Texas appellate court found a hospital liable to a patient who was injured when an orderly attempted to remove a catheter from the patient's bladder without first deflating a bulb that held it in place.[55] The court upheld an additional assessment against the hospital, called *punitive* or *exemplary damages*, because the hospital had failed to check the employment and personal references of the orderly before hiring him. A check would have indicated that the orderly had been expelled from Naval Medical Corps School with a serious drug problem and criminal record. After staff members are hired, their practice is delineated by hospital and departmental rules and by the supervisory system. There should be a system for assuring that staff members maintain required licensure by appropriate renewals.

Hospitals need to address professionals who are involved in patient care but who are not hospital employees. Traditionally, physicians, some dentists, and a few private-duty nurses were the only nonemployees involved in patient care. Today, many physicians and dentists seek authorization for their employees to assist in patient care. In addition, many other professionals seek authorization to practice in the hospital on an independent or quasi-independent basis. These groups include chiropractors, clinical psychologists, nurse anesthetists, other nurse practitioners, physical therapists, and podiatrists.

In many states, hospitals have authority to decide whether to permit these services in the hospital and, if so, whether they will be provided by nonemployees. For example, an Oregon appellate court ruled that hospitals do not have to admit any chiropractors or naturopaths to their staffs or provide a procedure for reviewing their applications.[56] In 1980, however, a federal appellate court ruled that a public hospital must provide a podiatrist who applies for clinical privileges with due process procedures, but does not have to admit any podiatrists to its staff.[57] The only apparent function of the due process procedures is to give the applicant an opportunity to urge that the hospital rules be changed, since the hospital may decide that no podiatrists will be admitted.

In some states, the hospital's discretion has been limited by statute or court decision. For example, in some states, hospitals have been prohibited from discriminating against an applicant solely on the basis that the practitioner is a podiatrist or psychologist.[58] Hospitals are still permitted to deny admission on the basis of competence or other factors related to quality of care. One state promulgated a regulation that forbade hospitals to admit psychologists to their medical staffs.[59]

When a Maryland hospital challenged a requirement that it grant privileges to qualified podiatrists, a state appellate court ruled that the statute was constitutional.[60] The court viewed the statute as a justified exercise of the state police power, so that the hospital was not entitled to compensation for the state-ordered use of its facilities.

Court decisions have limited the hospital's discretion in some states. For example, a New York court ordered a hospital to permit a *mohel*, a Jewish official who performs ritual circumcisions, to perform a circumcision on hospital premises because the parents' religion required completion on a certain day; no mohel had been granted clinical privileges, and it was not practical to remove the child from the hospital.[61]

If the hospital decides to permit or is required to permit nonemployees to practice on hospital premises, there should be procedures for verifying their qualifications, obtaining their commitment to abide by all applicable hospital and departmental rules, defining their scope of practice, assuring appropriate supervision and evaluation of their performance, and terminating their permission to practice. These procedures are necessary even when the person is an employee of a physician member of the medical staff. In 1973, a federal appellate court ruled that a hotel could be liable for the actions of a treating nurse employed by an independent contractor physician because the hotel did not check her qualifications and determine she was not licensed.[62] One aspect of policies for physicians' employees should be different from policies for other nonemployees. Permission for the physician employee should be contingent on continuation of the physician's clinical privileges. If the physician ceases to have clinical privileges, permission for the physician employee to practice should automatically cease.

NOTES

1. Dent v. West Virginia, 129 U.S. 114 (1889); St. George's School of Med. v. Dep't of Registration & Educ., 640 F. Supp. 208 (N.D. Ill. 1986) [authority to license doctors belongs to state].

2. Beck v. McLeod, 240 F. Supp. 708 (D. S.C. 1965), *aff'd*, 382 U.S. 454 (1966); *see also* Peckmann v. Thompson, 745 F. Supp. 1388 (C.D. Ill. 1990) [state has broad police power to regulate healing arts; no constitutional right to have midwives recognized or licensed].

3. *E.g.*, Massachusetts Medical Soc'y v. Dukakis, 637 F. Supp. 684 (D. Mass.1986), *aff'd*, 815 F.2d 790 (1st Cir.), *cert. denied*, 484 U.S. 896 (1987); McGinn, *R.I. mandates Medicare assignment for all claims*, AM. MED. NEWS, Sept. 22/29, 1989, at 3; *but see* Hennessey v. Berger, 403 Mass. 648, 531 N.E.2d 1268 (1988) [nonparticipating physician may refuse to treat Medicaid recipient].

4. Abrahamson v. Illinois Dep't of Prof. Reg., 153 Ill. 2d 76, 606 N.E.2d 1111 (1992).

5. *E.g.*, Medical Soc'y of N.J. v. Jacobs, Civ. 93-3670 (D. N.J. Sept. 26, 1994), *as discussed in* 3 HEALTH L. RPTR. [BNA] 1459 (1994) [in ADA challenge to license questions concerning mental illness, substance abuse, settlement agreed to drop questions, pay legal fees] [hereinafter HEALTH L. RPTR. cited as H.L.R.]; *but see* Colorado State Bd. of Med. Examiners v. Davis, 893 P.2d 1365 (Colo. Ct. App. 1995) [ADA does not bar revocation of license of physician with recent history of illegal prescription drug use]; Ramachandar v. Sobol, 838 F. Supp. 100 (S.D. N.Y. 1993) [Rehabilitation Act does not preclude license revocation of physician for mental illness].

6. *E.g.*, Department of Prof. Reg. v. Florida Dental Hygienist Ass'n, Inc., 612 So.2d 646 (Fla. 1st DCA 1993) [licensing agency exceeded its delegated authority by permitting practice by dental hygienists who had graduated from programs with lower standards than required by legislature]; *but see* Abramson v. Florida Psychological Ass'n, 634 So.2d 610 (Fla. 1994) [state must honor settlement with applicants for psychology license even though settlement granted psychology license to person who did not meet statutory licensing requirements].

7. Mishler v. Nevada State Bd. of Med. Examiners, 896 F.2d 408 (9th Cir. 1990) [17-month delay in verification too long].

8. Taylor v. Mobil Oil Corp., 444 S.E.2d 705 (Va. 1994).

9. *E.g.*, Roach v. Kelly Health Care, Inc., 87 Or. App. 495, 742 P.2d 1190, *rev. denied*, 304 Or. 437, 746 P.2d 1166 (1987) [home health agency violated regulations by using certified nursing assistant who had not received required additional 60 hours of training with emphasis on home care].

10. *E.g.*, Central Anesthesia Assocs., P.C. v. Worthy, 173 Ga. App. 150, 325 S.E.2d 819 (1984), *aff'd*, 254 Ga. 728, 333 S.E.2d 829 (1985) [hospital liable for injuries caused by student nurse anesthetist under supervision of physician's assistant when law required physician supervision].

11. *E.g.*, Turek v. St. Elizabeth Community Health Ctr., 241 Neb. 467, 488 N.W.2d 567 (1992); Leahy v. Kenosha Mem. Hosp., 118 Wis. 2d 441, 348 N.W.2d 607 (Ct. App. 1984).

12. State Bd. of Med. Examiners v. Warren Hosp., 102 N.J. Super. 407, 246 A.2d 78 (Dist. Ct. 1968), *aff'd*, 104 N.J. Super. 409, 250 A.2d 158 (App. Div.), *certif. denied*, 54 N.J. 100, 253 A.2d 548 (1969).

13. Adams v. Commonwealth, Unemployment Comp. Bd. of Review, 86 Pa. Commw. 238, 484 A.2d 232 (1984).

14. 21 U.S.C.A. § 823; Pearce v. United States Dep't of Justice, DEA, 867 F.2d 253 (6th Cir. 1988) [example of revocation of DEA license].

15. Miller v. Medical Ass'n of Ga., 262 Ga. 605, 423 S.E.2d 664 (1992).

16. *E.g.,* Sermchief v. Gonzales, 660 S.W.2d 683 (Mo. 1983).

17. *E.g.,* State ex rel. Lakeland Anesthesia Group, Inc. v. Ohio State Med. Bd., 74 Ohio App. 3d 643, 600 N.E.2d 270 (1991).

18. State ex rel. Iowa Dep't of Health v. Van Wyk, 320 N.W.2d 599 (Iowa 1982).

19. MICH. COMP. LAWS § 333.16215(1).

20. Opinion No. 5630, Jan. 22, 1980.

21. IOWA CODE ANN. § 152.1(2)(d).

22. Cook v. Workers' Compensation Dep't, 306 Or. 134, 758 P.2d 854 (1988).

23. Mullen v. Inspector General, HHS D.A.B., Civil remedies Div. No. C-94-299, Dec. No. CR227 (Oct. 5, 1994), *as reprinted in* MEDICARE & MEDICAID GUIDE (CCH) ¶43,008.

24. Brodie v. State Bd. of Med. Examiners, 177 N.J. Super. 523, 427 A.2d 104 (App. Div.), *cert. denied,* 87 N.J. 386, 434 A.2d 1068 (1981).

25. State Med. Bd. v. Murray, 66 Ohio St. 3d 527, 613 N.E.2d 636 (1993).

26. Medical Soc'y of N.J. v. New Jersey Dep't of Law & Pub. Safety, 120 N.J. 18, 575 A.2d 1348 (1990).

27. Rogers v. State Bd. of Med. Examiners, 371 So.2d 1037 (Fla. 1st DCA 1979), *aff'd,* 387 So.2d 937 (Fla. 1980).

28. Garces v. Dep't of Registration & Educ., 118 Ill. App. 2d 206, 254 N.E.2d 622 (1st Dist. 1969).

29. Board of Optometry v. Florida Med. Ass'n, Inc., 463 So.2d 1213 (Fla. 1st DCA), *rev. denied,* 475 So. 2d 693 (Fla. 1985).

30. Pennsylvania Med. Soc'y v. Commonwealth, State Bd. of Med., 118 Pa. Commw. 635, 546 A.2d 720 (1988).

31. *Punishing of doctors increased in 1994,* N.Y. TIMES, Apr. 6, 1995, at A8 [3,685 doctors disciplined in U.S.]; *More physicians disciplined in '94 by state boards,* WALL ST. J., Apr. 6, 1995, at B4 [1,498 revocations, suspensions].

32. *E.g., Boca doctor fined for surgery mistake,* PALM BEACH [FL] POST, Feb. 14, 1995, at 1B [neurosurgeon fined $5,000 for operating on wrong side of skull].

33. *E.g.,* Birchard v. Louisiana State Bd. of Med. Examiners, 609 So. 2d 980 (La. Ct. App. 1992), *cert. denied,* 612 So. 2d 83 (La. 1993) [physician on probation with condition he obtain board approval for changes of employment not entitled to hearing on denial of approval].

34. Annotation, *Rights as to notice and hearing in proceeding to revoke or suspend license to practice medicine,* 10 A.L.R. 5TH 1; Fleury v. Clayton, 847 F.2d 1229 (7th Cir. 1988) [right to notice, hearing applies when only sanction is censure].

35. Colorado State Bd. of Nurse Examiners v. Hohu, 129 Colo. 195, 268 P.2d 401 (1954); *see also* In re Grimm, 138 N.H. 42, 635 A.2d 456 (1993) [violation of due process for some members of hearing panel, acting in fact-finding capacity, to fail to attend all testimony, especially cross-examination of respondent]; Pet v. Dep't of Health Servs., 228 Conn. 651, 638 A.2d 6 (1994) [remand where no board member attended all hearings, record did not indicate whether voting members had read entire record].

36. *E.g.,* Virginia Bd. of Med. v. Fetta, 244 Va. 276, 421 S.E.2d 410 (1992) [proceedings against chiropractor dismissed because board violated law when 4 of 16 members sat with hearing officer at evidentiary hearing].

37. *E.g.,* Devous v. Wyoming State Bd. of Med. Examiners, 845 P.2d 408 (Wyo. 1993) [violation of due process not to notify physician of facts, nature of charges against him].

38. Ward v. Oregon State Bd. of Nursing, 266 Or. 128, 510 P.2d 554 (1973).

39. Tuma v. Board of Nursing, 100 Idaho 74, 593 P.2d 711 (1979).

40. *E.g.*, Kibler v. State, 718 P.2d 531 (Colo. 1986).

41. *But see* Burns v. Board of Psychologist Examiners, 116 Or. App. 422, 841 P.2d 680 (1992) [no tort damages against licensing board for testing irregularities, but statute authorized ancillary relief, which could include repayment for direct losses].

42. *E.g.*, Watts v. Burkhart, 978 F.2d 269 (6th Cir. 1992) [quasi-judicial immunity for licensing board members in suspension of physician's license]; Horwitz v. State Bd. of Med. Examiners, 822 F.2d 1508 (10th Cir.), *cert. denied*, 484 U.S. 964 (1987) [absolute immunity from civil rights liability]; Ivancie v. State Bd. of Dental Examiners, 678 F. Supp. 1496 (D. Colo. 1988).

43. *E.g.*, Sutker v. Illinois State Dental Soc'y, 808 F.2d 632 (7th Cir. 1986) [state need not offer separate license to denturists].

44. McKeesport Hosp. v. Pennsylvania State Bd. of Med., 652 A.2d 827 (Pa. 1995), *rev'g*, 628 A.2d 476 (Pa. Commw. Ct. 1993).

45. McKeesport Hosp. v. A.C.G.M.E., 24 F.3d 519 (3d Cir. 1994).

46. St. Agnes Hosp. v. Riddick, 748 F. Supp. 319 (D. Md. 1990).

47. H. Larkin, *All aboard?* AM. MED. NEWS, Mar. 13, 1995, at 11 [options for those without board certification to deal with managed care, since 35–40 percent of physicians are not board certified].

48. *E.g.*, J.L. Fickeissen, *56 ways to get certified*, AM. J. NURSING, Mar. 1990, at 50.

49. Koska, *Specialty board proliferation causes confusion*, 63 HOSPS., Aug. 5, 1989, at 58; Page, *Should there be regulations on use of MD specialties?* AM. MED. NEWS, Sept. 8, 1989, at 1.

50. Gilliam v. National Comm'n for Certification of Physicians Assistants, 727 F. Supp. 1512 (E.D. Pa. 1989), *aff'd*, 898 F.2d 140 (3d Cir.), *cert. denied*, 495 U.S. 920 (U.S. 1990).

51. *E.g.*, Patel v. American Bd. of Psychiatry & Neurology, Inc., 975 F.2d 1312 (7th Cir. 1992); Goussis v. Kimball, 813 F. Supp. 352 (E.D. Pa. 1993).

52. *E.g.*, Sanjuan v. American Bd. of Psychiatry & Neurology, Inc., 40 F.3d 247 (7th Cir. 1994), *amend'g, reh'g denied (en banc)*, 1995 U.S. App. LEXIS 565 (7th Cir. Jan. 11, 1995).

53. *E.g., Id.*; Marrese v. American Acad. of Orthopaedic Surgeons, 977 F.2d 585 (*without op.*), 1992 U.S. App. LEXIS 25530 (7th Cir. 1992).

54. Hipp v. Hospital Auth., 104 Ga. App. 174, 121 S.E.2d 273 (1961).

55. Wilson N. Jones Mem. Hosp. v. Davis, 553 S.W.2d 180 (Tex. Civ. App. 1977).

56. Samuel v. Curry County, 55 Or. App. 653, 639 P.2d 687, *rev. denied*, 292 Or. 863, 648 P.2d 850 (1982); *accord* Ft. Hamilton-Hughes Mem. Hosp. Ctr. v. Southard, 12 Ohio St. 3d 263, 466 N.E.2d 903 (1984); *but see* Wilk v. American Med. Ass'n, 719 F.2d 207 (7th Cir. 1983), *cert. denied*, 467 U.S. 1210 (1984).

57. Shaw v. Hospital Auth., 614 F.2d 946 (5th Cir.), *cert. dismissed*, 449 U.S. 955 (1980).

58. *E.g.*, NEV. REV. STAT. §§ 450.005, 450.430 [podiatrists, psychologists]; CAL. HEALTH SAFETY CODE § 1316 [podiatrists]; FLA. STAT. § 395.011 [podiatrists, psychologists, nurse practitioners].

59. Illinois Psychological Ass'n v. Falk, 818 F.2d 1337 (7th Cir. 1987).

60. State v. Good Samaritan Hosp., 299 Md. 310, 473 A.2d 892, *app. dismissed*, 469 U.S. 802 (1984).

61. Oliner v. Lenox Hill Hosp., 106 Misc. 2d 107, 431 N.Y.S.2d 271 (Sup. Ct. 1980).

62. Stahlin v. Hilton Hotels Corp., 484 F.2d 580 (7th Cir. 1973).

9

Staff Relations

Hospitals and other health care organizations provide patient care through their staff. The quality and performance of the staff and the relationship between the organization and its staff determine whether satisfactory, compassionate care can be provided to patients. Health care organizations should carefully select, train, supervise, and discipline staff members. Many aspects of staff relations are now subject to detailed state and federal regulation, including equal employment opportunities, compensation and benefits, occupational safety, labor-management relations, and other matters.

This chapter discusses some general concerns regarding staff relations and then reviews the pertinent federal laws. Some state laws are mentioned, but a detailed state-by-state analysis is not attempted. Three aspects of staff relations are not addressed here because they are covered in other chapters: (1) the relationship with the hospital administrator (Chapter 2), (2) the relationship with the medical staff (Chapter 7), and (3) the credentialing of other staff (Chapter 8).

GENERAL STAFF RELATIONS ISSUES

Selection

Health care organizations must exercise care in selecting their employees.[1] As discussed in Chapter 8, the organization should verify any required licenses and should check references and other information provided by the applicant to confirm that it is reasonable to believe the applicant is qualified.[2] The Immigration Reform and Control Act of 1986 requires all employers to verify the identity and work authorization of each employee hired on or after November 6, 1986.[3] Selection must also be in compliance with applicable equal employment opportunity laws that are discussed later in this chapter.

In 1990, however, a federal appellate court ruled that an employer does not have a duty to a prospective employee to determine whether that individual is qualified before planning to hire, so the hospital employer was not liable to the prospective physician who was not permitted to start the job because of a lack of qualifications.[4] Employers should be truthful in their promises during recruitment. Some courts will impose liability for breaches of such promises.[5]

One controversial area is the extent to which an employer should or may make inquiries concerning the criminal record of applicants and use the information in employment decisions. Some states do not permit collection or use of such information. In states where it is permitted, employers have been held liable for crimes by employees when no background check has been made,[6] and employees have been discharged for failing to disclose their criminal record on the employment application form.[7]

Health Screening

Employers should screen employees to identify conditions, such as contagious diseases, that may constitute a risk to patients and take appropriate steps to assure that persons who constitute risks do not have contact with patients or objects that could transmit their condition. However, employers should be prepared to defend their policies, especially when national guidelines have been adopted, such as the guidelines for AIDS.[8]

Employers that choose to perform health screening of applicants must postpone it until after a contingent offer of employment has been made and must require it for all applicants for covered positions.[9]

In some states, the examining physician or other professional owes no patient care duties to examined candidates or employees. In other states, the professional can be liable for negligent examinations or failure to disclose results to the person examined.[10]

Training and Supervision

As discussed in Chapter 10, employers are liable for injuries caused by negligent or intentional acts of their employees in the course of employment. To optimize patient care and minimize liability exposure, health care providers must assure that employees receive necessary training and supervision. Employees should participate in continuing education to maintain and improve their skills. While employers should facilitate continuing education, in most states there is no obligation to provide it without cost to employees or during compensated time.

In 1993, a Texas court ruled that there was a qualified privilege for performance appraisals, so the hospital was not liable for defamation for the contents of the appraisal of a nurse.[11]

Staffing

As hospitals respond to the pressures to reduce costs from government, employers, and other purchasers of hospital services, hospitals are reexamining present staffing patterns.[12] In most areas, they have considerable latitude to make changes. However, nurses unions and others have filed law suits and made political appeals seeking legally mandated nurse-patient ratios.[13] Some courts have protected individual employees who objected to staffing decisions.[14]

Discipline and Dismissal

Health care providers have a responsibility to take appropriate steps to enforce institutional policies to maintain appropriate patient care and institutional integrity. Proper procedures should be followed, and actions should be based on legally permissible grounds.[15] Generally employees are considered to be employees at will unless they have contracts for a specified time period. Employers may terminate employees at will at any time without cause[16] unless (1) the employer is bound by contract or statute to follow certain procedures or standards in terminations or (2) the termination violates public policy.

Many courts view some personnel policy manuals and other procedures for discipline or dismissal to be contracts with the employees that the employer must follow.[17] However, courts have disagreed on what constitutes an enforceable policy or procedure. The Delaware Supreme Court ruled that statements in employee handbooks do not change an employee's at-will status unless they specify a definite term of employment.[18] In 1986, the Idaho Supreme Court found a hospital employee manual to be a contract.[19] Several courts have ruled that handbooks or manuals are not contracts when they contain disclaimers or other clear indications they are not intended to be contracts.[20]

Some public health care employees are covered by civil service laws that require certain procedures. Absent statutory or contractual requirements, public employees are generally not entitled to a formal hearing prior to termination. For example, in 1985 the U.S. Supreme Court ruled that public employees must be given oral or written notice of the charges, an explanation of the employer's evidence, and a pretermination opportunity to present their side of the story, but a formal hearing was not required.[21] Employees do not have a constitutional right to due process concerning termination by private employers.[22]

When staff members are covered by individual employment contracts or collective bargaining agreements, procedures specified in the contract or agreement should be followed.[23] Usually employees will be required to exhaust contractual remedies before being allowed to sue.[24] Such contracts do not have to be in writing to be enforceable. In 1979, a Louisiana court found a hospital liable for breaching an oral promise to five certified registered nurse anesthetists that they would be given a six-month notice of termination. The court awarded payment of salary for six months, less the amount the anesthetists actually earned during the six months.[25] However, if the oral contract is for a specified period of more than one year, instead of at will, it will not be enforceable in most states because the Statute of Frauds requires that such contracts be in writing to be enforceable.[26]

As the 1979 Louisiana case illustrates, courts generally will not order employees reinstated unless authorized by statute; instead, former employees who are wrongfully discharged are awarded payment of lost wages and other damages. Some statutes do authorize reinstatement.[27]

Employees have protection from retaliatory discharge in some situations. Some statutes forbid retaliatory discharge for making certain reports to governmental agencies,[28] and some courts have extended such protection to employees who make other reports,[29] who refuse to testify untruthfully in malpractice cases,[30] who refuse to handle radioactive materials in violation of federal regulations,[31] who refuse to prepare or file false claims with the government,[32] or who refuse to work with inadequate staffing.[33]

Employees of public institutions who are discharged for exercising their right of free speech have some protection under the First Amendment.[34] Employee grievances that are not matters of public concern are not protected.[35] This right does not extend to employees of private employers.[36] For example, an Illinois appellate court ruled that even if a nurse had been terminated solely in retaliation for reporting incidents to a newspaper, she would not be entitled to any more protection than that afforded other at-will employees of private employers.[37]

When an employer conducts an investigatory interview of an employee that the employee reasonably believes might result in discipline and the employee is part of a unit represented by a union, the employee has a right to have a representative present during the interview if the employee so requests.[38] The employer does not have to advise the employee of that right, and the employer may decide not to conduct the interview if the right is invoked. In a collective bargaining agreement, a union can waive the right to representation in such interviews.[39] Nonunion employees do not have a right to representatives.[40]

Some provisions of the National Labor Relations Act also apply when employees are not represented by a union. The equal employment opportunity laws apply to all aspects of employment, including discipline and dismissal, so the provisions of these laws also must be considered. Employers must also be aware of what grounds for dismissal will be considered "just cause" by the unemployment compensation agency in their state so that they are not required to pay unemployment compensation to a dismissed staff member. These regulatory aspects of dismissal decisions are discussed in more detail later in this chapter.

Supervision and discipline must be handled in a civilized manner. In 1986, the Alabama Supreme Court upheld an award to a nurse from a physician who struck her and yelled at her to turn on a suction machine.[41] Some employee terminations and other discipline must be reported to state agencies.[42]

Drug Testing

In a 1989 U.S. Supreme Court case, Customs Service workers challenged a requirement that employees applying for promotion to positions involving interdicting drugs or carrying firearms submit to drug analysis of urine specimens. Since the employer was the government, the Fourth Amendment protected the employees from unreasonable searches.[43] The Court concluded that the urine-testing requirement was a reasonable search, even without suspicion of wrongful conduct by the individual, for persons in these sensitive positions, especially since the procedures for collection and analysis minimized intrusion on privacy interests. The government interest in the integrity and capacity of persons in these positions outweighed the employees' privacy rights. In a companion case, the Court ruled that the Fourth Amendment protections also applied to private employer testing that was mandated or authorized by governmental regulations.[44] The regulations required tests of railway employees after certain train accidents and incidents and authorized tests after violations of certain safety rules. The Court concluded that the tests were reasonable without individualized suspicion of impairment because of the government's interest in the safety of the traveling public. The Court did not address whether the government could require testing of health care employees, but the factors the Court viewed as important to justify testing, such as the need for unimpaired employees to assure public safety and the highly regulated nature of the industry, appear to apply in the health care context.

When an employer wants to begin a drug-testing program in a situation where there is no governmental mandate for the program, the employer may do so if there is no collective bargaining agreement and no law forbidding the program. In 1989, the National Labor Relations Board (NLRB) ruled that drug tests of union workers are a mandatory subject of bargaining, so employers without a governmental mandate cannot, without union concurrence, start testing union workers.[45] On the same day the Court ruled that when the existing collective bargaining agreement can be construed to permit drug testing, the employer is not obligated in some situations to bargain with the union before starting the program, but the union can challenge the contract interpretation through the arbitration provisions of the contract after the program is initiated.[46] Also on the same day the NLRB ruled that a program to test job applicants is not a mandatory subject of bargaining, but unions are entitled to information concerning the program to monitor employer practices.[47] If there is no collective bargaining agreement, the employer may start a program within any limitations imposed by state and local laws.[48]

Polygraph Testing

The Employee Polygraph Protection Act of 1988[49] prohibits most uses of polygraph tests on employees. There are some limited exemptions where such tests may still be used, but most employers will avoid using the exemptions because (1) the situations that justify a polygraph generally justify adverse action against the employee without the polygraph and (2) tested employees can bring federal lawsuits in which the employer must prove the exemption applied.

Communications about Former Staff

Employers have been sued for libel or slander by former staff members based on unfavorable evaluations, termination notices, and responses to inquiries from prospective employers.[50] Some supervisory personnel have been reluctant to communicate deficiencies accurately because of liability concerns.

In general, communicating the truth cannot result in liability for libel or slander.[51] However, since absolute truth is often difficult to prove, certain communications have a *qualified privilege*. This means there is liability only if the communication was made with malice. The qualified privilege applies to communications to persons who have a legitimate interest in the information given, but such communications must be limited in scope commensurate with that interest and must be made in a proper manner so that others do not also learn of it inappropriately. Courts have recognized that an employer or prospective employer has a legitimate interest in employment-related information.[52] The best way to avoid exceeding the qualified privilege is to limit the communication to factual statements and avoid statements concerning personality or personal spite. Neutral factual statements can communicate the deficiencies that need to be communicated without creating the appearance of malice. Knowing communication of false information indicates malice and can lead to liability.[53]

Most former employers require a written authorization from the former employee before releasing information. This authorization provides some additional protection, but care must still be taken in the wording of any information released.[54]

Employee Liability

Employees can be liable criminally and civilly for their conduct. For example, a 1988 federal appellate court decision addressed an employee who had arranged for his employer to purchase laser paper at $14.25 per thousand sheets and for the vendor to pay him a kickback of $2.00 per thousand sheets. The court upheld the conviction of the employee for engaging in a conspiracy to defraud.[55] Civil liability is discussed in Chapters 10 and 11.

EQUAL EMPLOYMENT OPPORTUNITY LAWS

The federal government has enacted several laws to expand equal employment opportunities by prohibiting discrimination on various grounds. These laws include Title VII of the Civil Rights Act of 1964, the Equal Pay Act of 1963, the Age Discrimination in Employment Act, sections 503 and 504 of the Rehabilitation Act of 1973, and the Americans with Disabilities Act. In addition, numerous state laws address equal employment opportunities.

The older Civil Rights Acts from the 1860s and 1870s provide remedies for a broad range of discrimination, which includes employment discrimination. These older acts are applied in several other contexts involving health care organizations, including some hospital medical staff cases. These older acts are discussed first.

42 U.S.C.A. § 1981

Section 16 of the Civil Rights Act of 1870,[56] codified at 42 U.S.C.A. § 1981, as amended, guaranties individuals equal rights under the law, including the right to make and enforce contracts. Since employment is based on contract, this law provides a remedy for some kinds of employment discrimination.

Section 1981 has been interpreted to apply only to discrimination that is based on race. In 1988, a federal appellate court upheld a judgment under § 1981 against a hospital for discharging an African American hospital employee due substantially to racial motivation even though there were nondiscriminatory reasons for the discharge. The employee had been a security guard. He failed three polygraph tests concerning thefts. However, Caucasian guards who had also failed had not been fired.[57]

Due to the impossibility of developing a satisfactory definition of race, the U.S. Supreme Court in 1987 decided that § 1981 protects against discrimination based on being a member of an ethnically or physiognomically distinctive subgroup of humans, but that distinctive physiognomy is not essential.[58] Section 1981 does not apply to discrimination based on such factors as age, sex, and religion.

In 1989, the Court narrowly interpreted making and enforcing contracts, so that § 1981 did not apply, for example, to discriminatory conditions of continuing employment.[59] In the same year, the Court also decided another case limiting the reach of § 1981.[60] In an effort to reverse these decisions and to make certain other traditional interpretations expressly part of the statute, the Civil Rights Act of

1991 was passed.[61] It amended § 1981 to (1) expand the definition of "make and enforce contracts" to include the enjoyment of the benefits of the contractual relationship and (2) extend express protection from nongovernmental discrimination. The Court had interpreted § 1981 to apply to nongovernmental racial discrimination prior to the amendment.[62]

42 U.S.C.A. § 1983

Section 1 of the Civil Rights Act of 1871,[63] codified at 42 U.S.C.A. § 1983, as amended, addresses deprivation "under color of state law" of "rights, privileges or immunities" secured by the Constitution or laws. Thus, a plaintiff must show (1) the existence of some right secured by the Constitution or law, (2) deprivation of that right, and (3) that the deprivation is under color of state law. Purely private action cannot be remedied under § 1983.

Actions of public health care entities are generally under color of state law. For example, a discharged quality assurance director was able to sue a county hospital under § 1983 due to the alleged (1) lack of pretermination notice of charges and opportunity to respond and (2) arbitrary, capricious, and improperly motivated basis for discharge.[64]

Private health care providers are generally considered not to act under color of state law; receiving Medicare and Medicaid funds is not sufficient.[65] Being designated by the state as the emergency receiving facility for the mentally ill was held not to be sufficient in one 1994 case.[66] When a nurse sued to challenge her termination, a federal appellate court ruled that the lease of a public hospital to a private corporation did not make the actions of that corporation under color of state law.[67]

Private individuals and entities can act under color of state law when they act in concert with governmental officials. Thus, private hospital paramedics were found to be acting under color of state law when they acted in concert with police to detain a person under the emergency detention state statute.[68]

42 U.S.C.A. § 1985

The Civil Rights Act of 1861,[69] codified at 42 U.S.C.A. § 1985, as amended, forbids conspiracies to interfere with civil rights, including deprivation of equal protection of the laws or equal privileges and immunities under the laws.

A conspiracy needs to be shown, which means that two or more entities must be acting together. Some courts recognize an intracorporate conspiracy exception so that all of the employees and agents of a corporation generally are treated as one entity,[70] similar to the exception recognized for antitrust (see Chapter 7).

The conspiracy does not have to involve state action or be under color of state law to violate § 1985.[71] However, when the conspiracy is aimed at interfering with a right that protects only against state interference, the conspiracy must involve state action in order to state a claim under § 1985. For example, the Fourteenth Amendment creates the right to be free from state action that interferes with equal protection or due process, so a purely private conspiracy would not interfere with Fourteenth Amendment rights. Thus, state action would have to be shown to state a claim under § 1985 for a conspiracy to interfere with Fourteenth Amendment rights. A federal appellate court applied this rule to conclude that a physician had failed to state a claim under § 1985 for the termination of his clinical privileges by a private hospital; there was no state involvement and he based his claim on the Fourteenth Amendment.[72] On the other hand, some federal laws create rights to be free from private action, so no state action would need to be shown.

There generally must be a racial or other class-based invidiously discriminatory animus behind the conspiracy.[73]

Title VII of the Civil Rights Act of 1964

Title VII of the Civil Rights Act of 1964[74] prohibits disparate employment treatment based on race, color, religion, sex, national origin, or pregnancy. It applies to hiring, dismissal, promotion, discipline, terms and conditions of employment,[75] and job advertising. It applies to nearly all employers; governmental agencies were included by the 1972 amendments.

The primary enforcement agency is the Equal Employment Opportunity Commission (EEOC).[76] In some situations the EEOC can defer to enforcement by local or state agencies or through individual suits. Generally, employees must exhaust the administrative remedies from the EEOC before they can sue under Title VII.

Three legal theories are used as the basis for finding employment discrimination. First, violations can be found on the basis of disparate treatment when work rules or employment practices are not applied in a consistent fashion due to a discriminatory motive. Second, violations can be found on the basis of disparate impact when an employment practice, such as a written employment test, has an adverse impact on minorities and cannot be justified as job related. In 1988, the U.S. Supreme Court ruled that an employee had to present more than statistics to establish a disparate impact case.[77] The employee must prove specific employment practices that caused the disparate impact. If such practices are proved, then the employer has the burden of presenting legitimate nondiscriminatory reasons for the practices, but need not present formal studies validating the practices. The burden then returns to the employee to prove that the reasons are just a pretext for discrimination. Third, carryover from past discrimination can constitute a violation when minorities are in a disadvantageous position because of prior discriminatory practices.

Employees can waive Title VII rights in private settlements, but the release must be knowingly and voluntarily entered.[78] Employees can agree to arbitration of Title VII claims,[79] but a federal court in 1995 ruled that an employer could not require mandatory arbitration of discrimination complaints.[80]

Title VII overlaps with the older civil rights acts. Thus, for example, most claims of ethnic-based discrimination in employment can be made under either § 1981 or Title VII. Frequently, claims are made under both statutes. Some courts have considered the elements of the claims to be identical. There are procedural differences; a plaintiff does not have to pursue the EEOC administrative procedure before filing a § 1981 suit. There are some differences in the remedies granted. Some claims can be brought under only Title VII. For example, a religion discrimination claim against a private hospital that could be brought under Title VII probably could not be brought under the older civil rights acts.

Who Is an Employee?

Courts apply several different tests to determine whether a person is an employee and, thus, entitled to the protection of these employment nondiscrimination laws. Clearly, if the employer withholds employment taxes from the person's income, the person is an employee. In less clear cases the courts apply either or both the common law control test and the economic realities test. Under the control test, persons are employees if the employer controls the details and means by which the work is performed. Under the economic realities test, persons are employees if they are dependent on the business to which they render service.[81] Some courts use a hybrid test that combines elements of these two tests.[82]

Title VII also applies to interference with employment opportunities. Thus, some physicians who have been denied or lost medical staff membership have been able to use Title VII to sue hospitals even when they clearly are not employees of the hospital.[83]

However, Title VII and the other federal nondiscrimination laws do not apply to discharge of a chaplain from a church-affiliated facility because such interference would constitute a violation of the First Amendment freedom of religion.[84]

Who Is an Employer?

In most cases the answer to this question is clear. Co-workers are not employers; they are not liable under Title VII.[85] Generally a parent company of the employer is not liable as employer under Title VII.[86]

Race and National Origin

While most racial discrimination suits are brought by persons of African descent, the courts have recognized that other races are protected, including Arabs and Orientals.[87] In addition, reverse discrimination suits have been brought by Caucasian persons.[88]

Many racial and national origin discrimination suits are based on both Title VII and § 1981.[89]

Employers can require experience as a qualification when it is needed,[90] but a neutral requirement of experience for promotion can become discriminatory when the employer discriminates in opportunities to gain experience.[91] The Immigration Reform and Control Act[92] also forbids some employment discrimination based on national origin or citizenship status, but citizens may be preferred over equally qualified aliens.

Religion

Employers must make reasonable accommodations for employee religious observances, short of incurring undue hardship.[93] This includes accommodating religious practices that preclude working on certain days. The offering of a reasonable accommodation satisfies the requirement even if it is not the accommodation the employee prefers.[94] Not everything that is claimed to be a religious observance is given this protection. In 1986, a federal district court rejected a woman's claim that her belief in adultery was religious, so it ruled that her discharge was not religious discrimination.[95]

Not all religious practices have to be accommodated. In 1986, a federal appellate court upheld the termination of a Veterans Administration psychiatric hospital chaplain.[96] The court accepted the hospital's explanation that the chaplain's evangelical approach was inappropriate in the hospital and antithetical to its philosophy of care.

Religious employers are exempt from the religious discrimination laws.[97] In 1987, the U.S. Supreme Court ruled that this exemption was constitutional, including its application to secular nonprofit activities, such as hospitals.[98] In 1988, a federal court ruled that a religious hospital does not forfeit its exemption from the religious discrimination statutes by accepting Medicare payments.[99]

Sex

In addition to the unjustified preference of one sex for certain jobs, sex discrimination can also take the form of sexual harassment. The two forms of sexual harassment are (1) *quid pro quo* sexual harassment when job conditions are altered due to refusal to submit to sexual demands and (2) *hostile environment* sexual harassment when the employer's conduct unreasonably interferes with performance or creates an intimidating or offensive environment. Employers are generally liable for any quid pro quo sexual harassment by supervisors.[100] In some situations employers may be liable for harassment of employees by third parties such as patients and suppliers.[101] Harassment by medical staff members can lead to hospital liability.[102]

In 1986, the U.S. Supreme Court held that sexual harassment that created a hostile or offensive working environment could violate Title VII.[103] It is not necessary to show that the sexual harassment is tied to the granting or denial of an economic benefit. Employers are not strictly liable for hostile environment sexual harassment by supervisors, but employers are not always shielded from suit by lack of knowledge of the behavior. If the employer has a policy against sexual harassment and has implemented a reasonable procedure to resolve harassment claims, the employer will usually be shielded from liability absent actual knowledge of misconduct. The procedure should not require that the first step be a complaint to the supervisor who is the source of the harassment.

In 1993, the U.S. Supreme Court made it easier to prove sexual harassment by determining that it was not necessary to prove injury or a serious effect on the employee's psychological well-being.[104]

Most courts have held that preferential treatment of an employee on the basis of a consensual romantic relationship between a supervisor and employee is not sexual discrimination.[105]

In 1994, a federal appellate court dismissed a sex discrimination charge against the navy on the grounds that the claimant had rejected an offer of full relief, so there was a failure to exhaust administrative remedies. However, in 1995 the court withdrew its opinion and sent the case back to the lower court, so the effect of rejecting relief is again unclear.[106]

Some groups have sought to convince courts that Title VII requires adoption of a *comparable worth doctrine*. This doctrine would require employers to revise wage scales so that pay is based on a comparison of the work done by persons in different job classifications without regard to the labor market. This doctrine goes beyond the Equal Pay Act (discussed in the following section) that requires equal pay for essentially identical work. Courts generally have ruled that Title VII does not require wage scales based on comparable worth.[107]

Pregnancy

In 1978, Title VII was amended to prohibit discriminatory treatment of pregnant women for all employment-related purposes. No special considerations are required. However, for example, if leaves are offered for disability, similar leaves must be offered for disabling maternity. Mandatory maternity leaves not based on inability to work violate Title VII.[108] Pregnancy itself is not considered a disability, but if a pregnant worker becomes unable to work, then disability benefits must be offered the pregnant worker. Some states require employers to offer a leave of absence for pregnancy.

One federal court found that job absences for infertility treatment were protected.[109]

In 1991, the U.S. Supreme Court ruled that Title VII was violated by fetal protection programs that prohibit female employees capable of childbearing from some jobs, such as those that expose workers to toxic chemicals or contribute to high blood lead levels.[110] In 1994, a federal appellate court ruled that a pregnant home health nurse could be terminated for refusal to treat an AIDS patient.[111]

Employer health plans that cover employee's spouses must cover pregnancy-related disabilities of spouses.[112]

Bona Fide Occupational Qualifications

In some circumstances, sex or factors related to religion or national origin are bona fide occupational qualifications (BFOQ) reasonably necessary to the normal operation of a particular business. When employers can demonstrate this necessity, the use of the qualification is not a violation of the law. For example, in 1981 a federal district court ruled that it was not illegal sex discrimination for a hospital to employ only female nurses in its obstetrics-gynecology department.[113] The court noted that the policy was based on the privacy rights of the patients, not just patient preference. An appellate court vacated the decision because the case became moot when the male nurse voluntarily quit his job.[114] In 1981, a federal appellate court ruled that it was not illegal discrimination based on national origin for a hospital to require all employees to have some facility in communication in the English language.[115] The court recognized that ability to communicate in English was a BFOQ for virtually every position in a sophisticated medical center. However, requiring employees to speak only English on the job can be national origin discrimination unless the employer can demonstrate business necessity.[116]

Retaliation

Employers are prohibited from retaliating against employees who oppose discrimination by engaging in reasonable activities.[117] In 1984, a federal appellate court found that a hospital had violated this provision when it fired an African American registered nurse who had complained about African American patient care.[118] However, filing a discrimination complaint does not shield an employee from all adverse actions. Employees may be disciplined or discharged, even after a complaint has been filed, if there are sufficient nonpretextual reasons for the action.[119]

Firing Discriminating Employees

Since employers can sometimes be found liable for discriminatory acts of employees, it is fortunate that most courts recognize such discriminatory acts to be grounds for discipline and even termination of the offending employees. For example, in 1987 a federal district court ruled that an employer's reasonable belief that an African American employee was making unwelcome sexual overtures to female employees was a legitimate, nondiscriminatory reason to terminate the offending employee, so there was no racial discrimination in the discharge.[120] However, some courts have ruled that discrimination is not good cause for termination of a physician's contract, so there may be liability for breach of contract.[121] If an employer wishes to avoid such liability, it should structure its contracts to permit appropriate action to deal with discrimination.

State Law

Title VII does not preempt the entire field of equal employment opportunity. While state law cannot permit something prohibited by Title VII, state law can assure more opportunities. Thus, many state laws that limit the types of work women may perform are superseded, but state laws requiring employers to offer pregnancy leaves are not suspended.[122]

Equal Pay Act of 1963

The Equal Pay Act[123] is designed to prohibit discriminatory compensation policies based on sex. It requires equal pay for equal work. Equal work is defined as work requiring equal skill, equal effort, and equal responsibility that is performed under similar working conditions. In 1985, a federal district court in Georgia upheld paying physicians' assistants more than nurse practitioners because of the greater training and skills required even though they provided substantially similar services.[124] The payment of higher wages to male orderlies than to female aides has been challenged in several cases.[125] In general the courts have required equal pay except when the hospital has been able to prove actual differences in the work performed during a substantial portion of work time.

Age Discrimination in Employment Act

The Age Discrimination in Employment Act[126] prohibits discriminatory treatment of persons 40 years of age and older for all employment-related purposes.[127] Mandatory retirement is prohibited except for certain exempted executives. The law applies to employers of 20 or more persons. There are exceptions for BFOQs,[128] bona fide seniority systems, and reasonable factors other than age, such as physical fitness. In 1984, a federal appellate court found a hospital guilty of age discrimination because its medical director had fired a 56-year-old secretary and replaced her with a 34-year-old individual.[129] The replacement testified that the medical director told her she was selected for her appearance. Violations can also be found for discriminating in favor of those who are older. An Oregon appellate court found a retirement home guilty of age discrimination under a state nondiscrimination law because it had refused to hire a beautician, saying she was too young for its residents.[130]

The employer is not liable for termination of a protected person if the employer presents valid reasons, such as reduction in force or inability to do the job, that are not pretexts.[131]

Employers must be careful not to give the impression of age discrimination. After a 62-year-old day-shift nurse supervisor resigned, she sued the hospital for age discrimination[132]; a federal appellate court ruled in 1985 that a jury should decide whether the CEO's statements concerning the need for "new blood" and her "advanced age" created intolerable working conditions in violation of the Act that forced her to resign.

Some hospitals have tried to settle age discrimination suits and have obtained from the employee a signed waiver of the right to sue for damages. These unsupervised waivers may not be effective. Waivers must satisfy statutory standards.[133] Thus, prior approval from the enforcement agency or a court may be necessary to make such waivers binding.

Americans with Disabilities Act

The Americans with Disabilities Act (ADA)[134] prohibits discrimination on the basis of disabilities in employment, transportation, and public accommodations. Title I provides that employers of 15 or more employees may not "discriminate against a qualified individual with a disability because of the disability in regard to job application procedures, the hiring, job assignment, advancement, or discharge of employees, employee compensation or fringe benefits, job training, and other terms, conditions, and privileges of employment."[135]

Employees and applicants who are "qualified" individuals with "disabilities" are protected. A *disability* is (1) having a physical or mental impairment that substantially limits one or more major life activities, (2) having a record of such an impairment, or (3) being regarded as having a substantially limited impairment.[136] *Major life activities* include self-care, performing manual tasks, walking, seeing, hearing, speaking, breathing, sitting, standing, lifting, reaching, learning, and working. A *qualified person with a disability* means "an individual with a disability who meets the skill, experience, education, and other job-related requirements of a position held or desired, and who, with or without reasonable accommodation, can perform the essential functions of the positions."[137] An individual who poses a "direct threat" to the health or safety of others is not "qualified."[138] A person currently engaged in the illegal use of drugs is not qualified.[139] An employer may prohibit the use of alcohol and illegal drugs in the workplace, may prohibit employees from being under the influence of illegal drugs in the workplace, and may require compliance with the Drug Free Workplace Act of 1988.[140]

As part of nondiscrimination, covered employers must provide "reasonable accommodations" that do not involve undue hardship on the employer. The law imposes numerous restrictions on the hiring process. While inquiries can be made about the ability to perform job-related functions, no inquiry can be made about whether the applicant has a disability or has any history of workers' compensation. Job criteria and employment tests are scrutinized to determine that they are job related and consistent with business necessity; in addition, tests that screen out disabled people are not permitted when alternative tests are available that disabled people can pass. The use of medical examinations is limited. They cannot be used until after a job offer is made and then only if they are required for all entering employees for the job regardless of disability and if access to and use of the resulting information is limited.

In 1993, a federal appellate court ruled that reassignment of an HIV-positive surgical technician to be a procurement technician did not violate the ADA. The person was not otherwise qualified for the surgical job.[141] In 1993, a federal appellate court ruled that requiring fire fighters to be clean shaven did not violate ADA rights of persons with a skin condition that precluded shaving. There was business necessity to safely use respirators and no showing that a reasonable accommodation was available.[142] In 1994, another federal appellate court decided that insulin-dependent diabetics cannot be accommodated as school bus drivers.[143] In 1994, a federal court ruled that a health maintenance organization did not violate the ADA by firing an internist with a shoulder injury that precluded him from performing his duties. The employer was not required to create a position with just supervision and administration and was not required to hire an assistant to perform the physical tasks of the job.[144]

Generally when the condition of the employee results in frequent absences without warning, the courts recognize that no reasonable accommodation can be made without undue hardship.[145]

Rehabilitation Act of 1973

The Rehabilitation Act of 1973[146] prohibits discrimination on the basis of handicap. Section 503 prohibits discrimination by government contractors, while section 504 prohibits discrimination by entities that receive federal financial assistance.[147] This law overlaps the ADA, but remains as an independent requirement. Because of the overlap in terminology, court decisions under this law are often considered in deciding ADA cases, but the detailed requirements of the Rehabilitation Act and the ADA are different. Hospitals are generally subject to both laws and need to comply with both.

In 1984, the U.S. Supreme Court ruled that any entity receiving federal financial assistance may not discriminate in either services or employment.[148] In 1990, the law was amended to prohibit the entire health care facility from disciminating, not just the program receiving federal financial assistance.[149] Medicare and Medicaid reimbursement have been interpreted to be federal financial assistance.[150]

When the Rehabilitation Act applies, the institution is prohibited from discriminating against any qualified person with disabilities who, with reasonable accommodation, can perform the essential functions on the job in question.[151] Pre-employment inquiries about disabilities are prohibited except that applicants can be asked if they are able to perform the job. Pre-employment physical examinations may be required only if all applicants for similar positions must undergo the same examination.

In 1994, a federal appellate court ruled against a blood bank administrator who was terminated after stating she was unable to work because the ventilation system made her asthma worse. She was not handicapped because she was not substantially limited in any major life activity where her condition was exacerbated in only this one setting.[152]

In 1987, the U.S. Supreme Court ruled that a discharged teacher with a history of tuberculosis was otherwise qualified to teach and must be reasonably accommodated.[153] The Department of Justice ruled in 1989 that persons with HIV infections were handicapped and protected.[154] In 1995, a federal appellate court decided that the FBI violated the Act when it asked a physician under contract to examine a FBI agent for AIDS and then terminated the agent's contract based on reports he had AIDS. The court ruled that the contract could not be terminated for his evasiveness about AIDS. The FBI should have focused its inquiries on the character and effectiveness of infection control procedures.[155] Numerous other conditions have been ruled to be protected handicaps.[156]

When a handicap precludes a function, the courts look closely to determine whether that function is needed for the job. Thus, a federal appellate court questioned whether heavy lifting was really necessary for a postal job for a person with a back injury.[157] However, generally standards do not have to be lowered, and the nature of the job does not have to be changed. The *Federal Register* was not required to lower its accuracy standards to accommodate an editor with cerebral palsy.[158] The FBI was not required to change the role of special agents to accommodate an insulin-dependent diabetic.[159]

An employer may refuse to hire or retain a person on the basis of behavioral manifestations of the handicap, such as sleeping on the job by a diabetic[160] or excessive absenteeism.[161] Employers may also refuse to hire or retain persons whose current use of alcohol or drugs prevents them from performing job duties or constitutes a direct threat to property or the safety of others. Employers may strictly enforce rules prohibiting possession or use of alcohol or drugs in the workplace.

In 1985, the U.S. Supreme Court ruled that state agencies could not be sued for violating section 504 because of their Eleventh Amendment sovereign immunity from being sued.[162] Thus, sanctions for violations by state agencies must be initiated by administrative agencies, not the courts.

COMPENSATION AND BENEFITS

Compensation and benefits of employees are regulated by several federal laws, including the Fair Labor Standards Act, the Federal Wage Garnishment Law, the Employee Retirement Income Security Act, the Family and Medical Leave Act of 1993, and the Internal Revenue Code. In addition, numerous state laws address these issues.

Fair Labor Standards Act

The Fair Labor Standards Act[163] establishes minimum wages, overtime pay requirements, and maximum hours of employment. Employees of all nonprofit and for-profit health care employers are covered by this Act. Bona fide executive, administrative, and professional employees are exempt from the wage and hour provisions when they are salaried. While physicians and administrators are clearly exempt, Department of Labor regulations must be consulted to determine the status of other employee classifications.[164] The 1974 amendments to the Fair Labor Standards Act extended minimum wage and overtime coverage to almost all employees of state and local governments. The coverage of governmental employees was declared constitutional by the U.S. Supreme Court in 1985.[165]

Most employers are required to pay overtime rates for work that exceeds 40 hours in 7 days. However, hospitals may enter agreements with employees to establish an alternative work period of 14 consecutive days. If this option is chosen, the hospital pays the overtime rate for hours worked in excess of 80 hours during the 14-day period. Even with this option, the hospital must pay overtime rates for hours worked in excess of eight in any one day.

In 1988, a federal appellate court ruled that a hospital could pay "on-premises-on-call" operating room technicians and nurses at one and one-half times minimum wage for periods in which they did no work, instead of at one and one-half times their regular hourly wage.[166] Also in 1988 a federal district court ruled that security staff in one hospital were not entitled to compensation for lunch breaks.[167] The possibility of being called to duty did not make the time compensable.

The Fair Labor Standards Act also addresses child labor by regulating the hours and conditions of employment of children. The Fair Labor Standards Act does not preempt more protective state or local laws that establish a higher minimum wage, a shorter minimum work week, or more protection for children. There are other federal rules that regulate hours and conditions of employment for specific jobs. For example, the Federal Aviation Administration requires flight crew members, including crews of emergency medical helicopters, to have 8 consecutive hours of rest every 24 hours.[168]

Federal Wage Garnishment Law

One way to enforce a court judgment against another person is to impose garnishment of the debtor's wages. Garnishment is a court order to an employer to pay a portion of the debtor's paycheck to the creditor until the debt is paid. The Federal Wage Garnishment Law[169] and various state laws restrict how much of a paycheck may be garnisheed. When there are multiple garnishments, proper priorities must be observed not to exceed the limit on aggregate garnishments. Federal law prohibits employers from discharging employees because of garnishment for one indebtedness. The limits on garnishment do not apply to certain bankruptcy court orders or debts due for state or federal taxes.

Employee Retirement Income Security Act of 1974

The Employee Retirement Income Security Act of 1974 (ERISA)[170] regulates nearly all pension and benefit plans for employees, including pension, profit sharing, bonus, medical or hospital benefit, disability, death benefit, unemployment, and other plans. The law applies to all employers except for governmental agencies and to all plans except for some plans of churches. The law regulates many features of these plans, including nondiscrimination, benefit accrual, vesting of benefits, coverage, responsibilities of plan managers, termination of plans, descriptions of plans, and required reports. ERISA requirements should be considered before changing any pension or benefit plan that is not exempt.

Some health benefit plans have attempted to use ERISA to attack state laws that mandate certain benefits. In 1985, the U.S. Supreme Court ruled that neither ERISA nor the National Labor Relations Act preempts state laws that mandate that insured plans provide certain benefits, such as mental illness coverage.[171] However, states cannot require self-insured or uninsured health plans to provide the specific benefits because such plans are not covered by the savings clause in ERISA that allows state regulation of insurance.

Furnishing false information to a health or welfare fund subject to ERISA is a federal crime. The administrator of a provider of outpatient services was convicted of this crime because he did not report actual costs in a utilization report to a fund, but instead reported the estimated value of the services based on charges.[172]

ERISA forbids retaliation against employees for exercising their rights under a benefit plan. Thus, it is a violation of ERISA to discharge an employee to prevent coverage under a medical benefits plan.[173] In 1993, a federal appellate court held it a violation to fire an employee who refused to become an independent contractor where more than an incidental reason for the change was to eliminate health coverage.[174] However, it is not a violation of ERISA for the employer to change a welfare benefit plan to the extent permitted by the plan. A discriminatory change that reduces benefits for one disease, such as AIDS, does not violate ERISA,[175] but generally will violate the ADA.

The Family and Medical Leave Act of 1993

The Family and Medical Leave Act of 1993 requires that eligible employees be provided with 12 work weeks of leave during any 12-month period for purposes of care of a serious health condition of the employee, spouse, child, or parent, or for birth or adoption. The leave need not be compensated, but health care benefits must be continued during the leave.[176]

Internal Revenue Code

The Internal Revenue Code requires employee benefit plans to meet certain standards to qualify as deductible business expenses. Some of the most onerous provisions were eliminated when Congress repealed the section 89 qualification and nondiscrimination requirements in 1989. However, the repeal did not eliminate all requirements.[177]

The Internal Revenue Service (IRS) is more closely scrutinizing the classification of workers as employees or independent contractors in an effort to require employers to pay employment taxes on more workers. This is discussed in Chapter 4.

The IRS is also scrutinizing pension plans, deferred compensation, and other benefits.

OCCUPATIONAL SAFETY AND HEALTH

Congress enacted the Occupational Safety and Health Act (OSHA) of 1970[178] to establish standards for occupational health and safety and to enforce the standards. Standards developed for various industries are mandatory for all covered employers. When no federal standard has been established, some state safety rules remain in effect.

The Act mandates that each state enact legislation to implement the standards and procedures promulgated by the Department of Labor. Litigation has arisen over the issue of inspections used by federal and state officials to enforce OSHA standards. Courts have ruled that an employer may refuse an inspection unless the inspector obtains consent from an authorized agent of the employer or the inspector has a valid search warrant. The U.S. Supreme Court ruled unconstitutional an OSHA provision that permitted "spot checks" by OSHA inspectors without a warrant.[179]

OSHA regulations prohibit employers from discriminating against employees who refuse to expose themselves to conditions presenting a real danger of death or serious injury in urgent situations where there is insufficient time to pursue correction through OSHA.[180] This regulation was upheld by the U.S. Supreme Court in 1980.[181] However, in 1988 an Indiana appellate court ruled that a laboratory technician could be terminated for refusing to test vials of bodily fluids with AIDS warnings because the laboratory had provided appropriate safety manuals and precautions, so there was insufficient danger to justify the refusal.[182]

OSHA preempts all state occupational safety and health regulation. In 1992, the U.S. Supreme Court decided that states must obtain the approval of the Secretary of Labor for any such state regulations. There is no public safety exception. A non-occupational impact is not sufficient to defeat preemption.[183]

In 1991, OSHA adopted rules to protect health care employees from blood-borne diseases.[184] In 1993, a federal appellate court upheld the blood-borne disease regulations, except as to sites not controlled by the employer or another entity subject to the employer's rules.[185] Thus, the regulations could not be applied to home care by home health workers.

There is a general duty clause in OSHA. Under it, hospitals have been cited for not protecting workers from tuberculosis[186] and for failure to protect workers from patient violence.[187]

Employers have a statutory duty in some states to furnish employees with a safe place to work. Even in states that do not have such statutes, employers are liable for most injuries suffered by employees as a result of employment unless the employers are protected by governmental immunity. In most situations employees may pursue compensation only through the workers' compensation system, not through courts.

Other state statutes require that specific facilities be provided to employees. These facilities, such as lavatories, must be provided for the convenience and safety of employees. Local governmental ordinances and laws may also include requirements, such as sanitary and health codes, to promote and safeguard the health and safety of employees and others. In most states, state institutions are exempt from local regulation unless state laws grant local governments the authority to encompass state institutions.

LABOR-MANAGEMENT RELATIONS

Unions are a significant factor in the employee relations of health care providers in some parts of the United States. Various labor organizations have been recognized as collective bargaining representatives for groups of health care employees. There are craft unions that devote their primary organizing efforts to skilled employees, such as carpenters and electricians; industrial unions and governmental employee unions that seek to represent large groups of relatively unskilled or semiskilled employees; and professional and occupational associations and societies, such as state nurses associations, that represent their members and sometimes others.

Labor-Management Relations Act

The Labor-Management Relations Act,[188] which defines certain conduct of employers and employees as unfair labor practices and provides for hearings on complaints that such practices have occurred, explicitly exempts governmental hospitals from its coverage. This Act consists of the National Labor Relations Act of 1935,[189] the Taft-Hartley amendments of 1947,[190] and numerous other amendments, including the Labor-Management Reporting and Disclosure Act of 1959.[191] The Act is administered by the NLRB. The NLRB (1) investigates and adjudicates complaints of unfair labor practices[192] and (2) conducts secret ballot elections among employees to determine whether they wish to be represented by a labor organization and, if so, to determine which organization.

The exemption for governmental hospitals has been interpreted by the NLRB to apply to only hospitals that are owned and operated by governmental agencies. For example, a municipal hospital operated under contract may be considered a private entity subject to the NLRB if a private contractor exercises overall daily control. Exempt governmental hospitals are usually subject to state laws concerning governmental employees.

Nonprofit hospitals were exempt until the amendments of 1974[193] eliminated the exemption. The 1974 amendments attempted to deal with some of the unique aspects of health care by providing legislative direction about collective bargaining, mediation, conciliation, and strikes.

Some religious hospitals have challenged these laws. Federal appellate courts have found that it is not a violation of First Amendment religious freedoms to apply these laws to hospitals owned and operated by religious organizations.[194]

The law directs the NLRB to give hospitals some special consideration because of their sensitive mission, but individual NLRB rulings will continue to be made on the basis of many factors in addition to the uniqueness of health care.

Exempt Staff

Several groups of staff members are excluded from the NLRB's jurisdiction, including independent contractors, supervisors, managerial employees, confidential employees, and some students. Each of these groups has been defined by numerous NLRB and court decisions, so familiarity with those decisions is necessary to determine whether a particular staff member is exempt.

In 1994, the U.S. Supreme Court decided that nurses who direct other employees are supervisors, striking down the stricter test for supervisor status used by the NLRB.[195] Nursing groups are seeking legislation to change this rule. Some nurses are negotiating collective bargaining agreements that preclude assignment of supervisory jobs to nurses.[196]

Unfair Labor Practices

Section 7 of the National Labor Relations Act (NLRA) established four fundamental rights of employees: (1) the right to self-organize, (2) the right to engage in concerted activities for the purpose of collective bargaining or other mutual aid or protection, (3) the right to engage in collective bargaining, and (4) the right to refrain from union activities.

Employer Unfair Labor Practices

An employer commits an unfair labor practice through

1. interference with any of the four rights recognized in section 7;
2. domination of a labor organization;
3. discouragement or encouragement of union activity;
4. discrimination against employees who file charges or testify in an NLRB proceeding; or
5. violation of the other obligations, including good faith bargaining, specified in section 8(a) of the NLRA.

The NLRA also applies to employers that do not have employees represented by a labor organization. The employee's right to engage in concerted activities for the purposes of mutual aid or protection can apply to isolated incidents, so employers should obtain legal advice before disciplining employees who may be engaged in protected activities. For example, in 1978 the NLRB ruled that a small group of unorganized staff was protected by the NLRA when members of the group left their workstation to complain to hospital officials concerning work conditions.[197] Not all employee actions are protected. In 1982, the NLRB upheld the dismissal of two hospital employees for continual criticism of the program director.[198] The NLRB found this activity unprotected because it was aimed at influencing administration of the program, rather than at working conditions.

In 1994, a federal appellate court found that an employer had violated the NLRA by discharging a supervisor in retaliation for refusing to engage in unfair labor practice.[199]

Permanent replacement workers have been a contentious issue. In 1991, a federal appellate court found that a hospital had committed an unfair labor practice by refusing to reinstate striking nurses to pre-strike positions and preferring nonstriking nurses for positions. During the strike, the hospital had closed until it was compelled by community needs to open two units and later to open the whole hospital with supervisory personnel, new hires, and striking nurses who crossed picket lines. The hospital had guaranteed returning nurses they could keep their new positions. The court ruled that those who had actually worked in the new positions could have permanent replacement status, but that others were nonpermanent and not entitled to keep positions they were promised.[200]

There is frequently litigation over what information the union is entitled to. For example, in 1993 a federal appellate court ruled on the scope of information about nonunit employees that the union could access.[201] The NLRB ruled that a hospital had committed an unfair labor practice by not giving information on its benefit plans.[202]

In 1994, a federal appellate court refused to enforce a nationwide NLRB cease and desist order directed at a nursing home chain. The court ruled that the order had to be directed at specific facilities that had engaged in unfair labor practices, since there was no showing of unlawful acts at a substantial number of facilities.[203]

Employers should also obtain legal advice before working with employee advisory committees. If their role is not appropriately limited, such committees may be considered labor organizations, and many of the employers' interactions with them could be interpreted as unfair labor practices. For example, in 1977 the NLRB ruled that a hospital had engaged in the unfair labor practice of management domination of a labor organization because the hospital ran the election for an employee committee and wrote its bylaws.[204] In 1994, a federal appellate court found that an employer-formed forum for nurses to discuss and consider professional nursing practice issues was not a "labor organization" because it did not deal with the employer on matters affecting employment. There was no pattern or practice of making proposals to which the hospital responded, and isolated instances did not constitute "dealing."[205]

In 1995, a federal appellate court ruled that a hospital had committed an unfair labor practice by unilaterally deciding to stop supplying surgical garbs without bargaining with the union, but that the hospital's decision to reduce to zero the number of teams receiving 80 hours' pay for 70 hours' work was within its authority under the collective bargaining agreement.[206]

Labor Organization Unfair Labor Practices

A labor organization commits an unfair labor practice through

1. restraining or coercing interference with the exercise of the four rights recognized in Section 7 or interfering in management's selection of its representative,
2. attempting to cause the employer to discriminate through encouraging or discouraging membership in a labor organization,
3. failing to bargain in good faith,
4. engaging in prohibited secondary boycotts,
5. charging excessive union initiation fees,
6. causing employers to pay for services not performed, or
7. picketing solely to compel an employer to recognize a union (recognitional picketing) or persuading employees to join the union (organizational picketing) without filing a petition for an election within the appropriate time limit.

In 1985, the U.S. Supreme Court ruled that a union committed an unfair labor practice by prohibiting members from resigning from the union during a strike or when a strike was imminent.[207]

In 1995, a federal appellate court affirmed an order that a union not picket a nursing home for one year following its defeat in a decertification election.[208]

Employee Representation

A labor organization seeking representation rights for employees may petition the NLRB for a secret ballot election. The petition must make a "showing of interest" supporting the petition. At least 30 percent of the workers who will ultimately make up the bargaining unit must support it and show their interest by signing union authorization cards.

Bargaining Unit Designation

The employer may take the position that certain persons (supervisors, confidential employees, temporary employees) should be excluded from the unit as inappropriate because of the hospital's organization. The NLRB will then conduct a representation hearing to determine the appropriate bargaining unit. The NLRB must implement the congressional intent in the 1974 amendments to avoid "proliferation of bargaining units" in the health care industry.[209] In addition, section 9 of the NLRA forbids including professional employees in bargaining units with nonprofessionals unless a majority of the included professionals vote in favor of inclusion.

Until 1984, the NLRB determined whether the proposed unit was appropriate by applying a "community of interest" test. That is, a proposed unit was appropriate if its members had a community of interest. This resulted in the recognition of five basic units in health care institutions:

1. clerical,
2. service and maintenance,
3. technical,
4. professional, and
5. registered nurses.

In 1984, the NLRB abandoned the "community of interest" test, replacing it with a "disparity of interest" test.[210] Under this test, the NLRB began with the broadest possible unit and excluded only those groups that were shown to have disparate interests. No unit was automatically assumed to be appropriate; all were examined on a case-by-case basis.

In 1989, the NLRB abandoned the disparity of interest test and case-by-case determination. The NLRB published rules that eight units were presumed to be appropriate in acute care hospitals:

1. registered nurses;
2. physicians;
3. professionals, except registered nurses and physicians;
4. technical employees;
5. skilled maintenance employees;
6. business office clerical employees;
7. guards; and
8. other nonprofessional employees.[211]

In 1991, the U.S. Supreme Court upheld the rules.[212] However, in 1993 the NLRB ruled that it would not upset pre-existing appropriate units based on the new rules.[213]

Solicitation and Distribution

Most health care institutions have rules concerning solicitation of employees and distribution of materials in the facility to avoid interference with patient care. These rules become especially important during campaigns to organize employees, so they should be written to be enforceable under the NLRA. Each policy is examined on a case-by-case basis by the NLRB.[214] Some general guidelines can be derived from past decisions. Nonemployees may generally be prohibited access to the facility for solicitation or distribution. Employees can be prohibited from these activities during work time. Work time does not include mealtimes or work breaks.[215] Solicitation or distribution can be limited to nonpatient care areas at all times. In 1979, the U.S. Supreme Court ruled that solicitation and distribution could be prohibited in areas devoted to patient care.[216] Areas to which visitors have general access, such as cafeterias and lounges, usually cannot be prohibited because a genuine likelihood of patient disturbance cannot be shown. Another important factor in the exclusion of certain areas is whether reasonable alternative space is designated. In 1993, a federal appellate court decided that a hospital could enforce its nonsolicitation rule in a cafeteria because no nonemployees had been permitted to solicit there and the presumption of access to the union's message elsewhere had not been rebutted.[217]

However, selective enforcement of such rules will generally preclude enforcement against unions.[218]

Election

A labor organization can become the exclusive bargaining agent for a bargaining unit by winning a secret ballot election conducted by the NLRB. After an election, the employer or the labor organization can challenge the outcome by filing an objection.[219] If misconduct is found, the election can be set aside with a new election ordered.

Recognition without an Election

An employer can voluntarily recognize a labor organization as the exclusive bargaining agent without an election.[220] Some employer actions, such as checking union authorization cards or polling employees, can sometimes constitute recognition of a labor organization. Recognition without an election can constitute an unfair labor practice in some circumstances, especially when other labor organizations are also seeking to represent the employees. Most employers avoid all actions that could be interpreted as voluntary recognition. A second way that a labor organization can be recognized without an election is by NLRB order. When the NLRB finds serious unfair labor practices, it may order the extraordinary remedy of recognition. A third way is accretion.[221] If a labor organization has negotiated a contract with an employer that later acquires a new facility, under some circumstances the new facility is considered to be accreted to the existing one, and new unit employees are automatically covered by the preexisting contract. However, where there is a history of separate bargaining at the two sites, they can sometimes remain separate.[222] A fourth way is a successor corporation being required to continue to recognize a union in some circumstances.[223]

Collective Bargaining and Mediation

After a labor organization has been recognized as the exclusive bargaining agent, the employer and labor organization have a duty to negotiate in good faith. They must bargain concerning mandatory subjects, including wages, hours, and other terms and conditions of employment. They may bargain concerning other permissive subjects, but are not legally obligated to do so. It is unlawful to bring negotiations to an impasse, to strike, or to lock out employees over permissive subjects.

Several special notice, mediation, and conciliation safeguards were built into the law to help the health care industry avoid strikes when possible. For example, 90 days' notice is required if a party intends to terminate or modify a bargaining agreement, and the Federal Mediation and Conciliation Service (FMCS) must be given 60 days' notice.[224] When notified, the FMCS is required to attempt to bring about an agreement, and all parties must participate fully and promptly in meetings called by the FMCS for the purpose of aiding settlement. If a strike is threatened, the FMCS can, under certain conditions, establish an impartial board of inquiry to investigate issues and provide a cooling-off period of up to 30 days.[225]

Another special provision for health care institutions is a 10-day advance notice of intention to engage in concerted economic activities, including strikes, picketing, or any other concerted refusal to work.[226] This provision is designed to allow a hospital to make plans for continuity of patient care. Hospitals that use this opportunity to take "extraordinary steps" to stock up on ordinary supplies for an unduly extended period of time may, however, be engaging in an unfair labor practice that would permit the union to strike without notice or during the ten-day period. In 1984, a Minnesota court ruled that nurses were entitled to unemployment compensation during a layoff where the hospital had laid them off when the union gave the 10-day notice of intent to strike.[227]

Some courts have ruled that individual unorganized employees do not have to give a 10-day notice of work stoppage. In 1980, a federal appellate court ruled that two physicians who walked out of the hospital and joined the picket line of a lawful strike by other employees did not have to give the notice.[228] The court noted that the action was inconsiderate and ethically suspect, but protected.

In some circumstances, the ally doctrine allows a union to strike against a secondary employer not involved in the original dispute. The strike is permitted when the secondary employer loses its neutrality by performing work during the course of the labor dispute that would have been performed by striking employees of the primary employer. The legislative history of the 1974 amendments modifies the ally doctrine by permitting a hospital to accept the critically ill patients of a struck hospital without losing its status as a neutral employer. In an advice memorandum issued by the NLRB in September 1977, a union was said to violate the Act when it threatened to picket two neutral hospitals because they received critically ill patients and 46 pregnant women transferred from the struck hospital.[229]

Administering the Contract

After negotiating a labor agreement, the employer and labor organization should spend no less care on its administration. Managerial rights that have been established at the bargaining table, sometimes at a high price, can be eroded or entirely lost through inattention. The entire managerial team, especially supervisors, should know the aspects of the contract applicable to their responsibilities. Managers must be trained to ensure that discipline is administered for proper reasons and by appropriate procedures under the contract.

Frequently, collective bargaining agreements provide for arbitration of grievances. Courts defer to arbitration decisions unless they violate public policy, but courts seldom find superseding public policies. For example, in 1988 two federal district courts refused to overturn arbitration decisions ordering reinstatement of (1) a nursing attendant who changed an intravenous bag in violation of the state nursing practice act and (2) a nurse who failed to notify a physician of a sudden change in a patient's blood pressure and who committed other violations of proper nursing practice.[230] In 1988, the Illinois Supreme Court confirmed an arbitration award reinstating two mental health workers whose patient had died while they were on an unauthorized errand.[231] In 1987, the U.S. Supreme Court upheld an arbitrator's reinstatement of an employee who had been found with traces of marijuana in his automobile.[232] This did not violate public policy because there was insufficient connection with use of the drug. However, sometimes a superseding public policy is found. In 1991, a New York court reversed an arbitrator's reinstatement of a respiratory therapist who, after being warned several times, continued to engage in the life-threatening practice of reusing a single syringe to draw blood from multiple patients.[233] In 1991, the Ohio Supreme Court reversed an arbitrator's reinstatement of an aide terminated for abuse of a mentally retarded patient.[234] A federal district court in 1989 vacated an arbitration decision ordering reinstatement of a nurse discharged for negligent administration of medication because reinstatement would violate state "public policy in favor of providing safe and competent nursing care."[235] In 1990, a Minnesota court ruled that an arbitrator had improperly reinstated a paramedic. Where all of the paramedic's functions were under the medical director's license and the director was responsible for quality of care, the decision concerning competence was for the medical director.[236]

There are frequently disputes over the scope of arbitration.[237] At least one court has ruled that the duty to arbitrate can continue beyond the end of the collective bargaining agreement.[238]

Reporting and Disclosure

The Labor-Management Reporting and Disclosure Act of 1959[239] places controls on labor unions and their relationship with their members. It also requires employers to report payments and loans made to representatives of labor organizations. Payments to employees for the purpose of persuading them or causing them to persuade other employees to exercise or not to exercise their rights to organize and bargain collectively must also be reported. Many of these payments are illegal, and the reporting requirement does not make them legal. Reports must also be made of (1) expenditures to interfere with employee rights to organize and bargain collectively and (2) certain agreements with labor relations consultants. Reports are made public. Failure to report and false reports can lead to substantial penalties. Governmental entities are not subject to these provisions.

STATE LAWS

While federal laws have preempted many state labor laws,[240] state laws still apply in at least two situations. First, when federal law does not cover an activity, states may regulate it. Second, when courts rule that state law does not conflict with federal law, the state law will be enforceable. Despite the broad scope of federal preemption, states may regulate labor relations activity that also falls within the NLRB jurisdiction when the regulated conduct touches interests deeply rooted in local feeling and responsibility. Thus, violence, threats of violence, mass picketing, and obstructing streets may be regulated by states.

In some states, there are no labor relations statutes, but in others two types directly affect the rights of employees to organize and bargain collectively: (1) anti-injunction acts and (2) laws regulating union security agreements. Other state labor laws deal with equal employment opportunity, child labor, safety, workers' compensation, and unemployment compensation. Many states have laws concerning the relationship between public employees and governmental employers that apply to governmental hospitals.

Anti-Injunction Acts

The federal government and many states have enacted anti-injunction acts that narrowly define the circumstances in which courts may enjoin strikes, picketing, and related activities in labor disputes. The federal statute is the Norris-LaGuardia Act.[241] Some aspects of state anti-injunction statutes may be preempted. Anti-injunction acts generally apply to health care providers.[242]

Union Security Contracts and Right To Work Laws

Labor organizations frequently seek union security contracts with employers in the form of either (1) the *closed shop contract*, which provides that only members of a particular union may be hired,[243] or (2) the *union shop contract*, which makes continued employment dependent on union membership, but does not require the employee to become a member until after being hired. Many states have constitutional provisions or statutes, generally called *right to work laws*, making such contracts unlawful.[244] Other states have statutes or decisions that restrict such contracts or specify procedures that must be followed before such agreements may be made. Some states require an employee election. Some states permit a union shop agreement, but not a closed shop. State right to work laws are not preempted by the NLRA because section 14(b) of the NLRA explicitly authorizes them.[245] In states where such agreements are illegal, any request for such a contract must be refused, and the employer can obtain an injunction to stop a strike or picketing designed to induce such agreements. In states that permit such agreements, there is no legal obligation to agree. It is one of the matters on which there may be bargaining.

Workers' Compensation

Every state has workers' compensation legislation to compensate employees for accidental on-the-job injuries. These acts replace the employee's common law remedy of suing the employer for negligence, which was usually an unsuccessful process. Most employers are subject to these acts. Many employers purchase workers' compensation insurance, although self-insurance is an option. An employee must give written notice of injury to the employer. In cases not routinely paid, the matter will be heard by a state commission to determine liability. State statutes define employee, injury, and other terms and have schedules of payment amounts for types of injuries. When the workers' compensation law applies, the employee is barred from suing the employer for the injury. Courts become involved only when there is an appeal concerning a decision of the state commission.

Several issues are frequently litigated. One issue is whether the injury arose out of and occurred in the course of employment. A related issue is whether the injury was caused by an accident. Numerous exclusions are stated for pre-existing or congenital physical conditions and for injuries caused by horseplay or other nonemployment causes.

Workers' compensation laws generally do not bar suits against persons who are not employers. A nurse anesthetist was permitted to sue a psychiatrist for injuries she received while administering electroconvulsive therapy because he was not the employer or a fellow employee.[246] States vary on when fellow employees may be sued.

In 1994, a California court held that a child could sue for in utero injuries that occurred when the mother, a psychiatric nurse, was kicked in the abdomen by a psychiatric patient in the hospital where she was employed. Since there was direct injury to the child separate from the injury to the mother and the child was not an employee, the court ruled that under California law the workers' compensation law did not bar the suit.[247]

Workers' compensation acts and other benefit programs under which injured workers may seek compensation are often complex. Familiarity with applicable state law is necessary to appropriately address employee injuries.

Unemployment Compensation

State law generally provides for payment of unemployment compensation to many unemployed individuals. Generally persons who have been discharged for misconduct forfeit all or part of the compensation they would have otherwise received. There is considerable litigation concerning what constitutes misconduct. For example, in 1981 the Pennsylvania Supreme Court found a nursing assistant guilty of misconduct for smoking in a patient's room contrary to hospital rules, so she was denied compensation.[248] In 1981, the Vermont Supreme Court ruled that a nurse who had been discharged for giving a patient medications by IV push instead of IV drip was entitled to unemployment compensation because her error had been in good faith.[249] In 1985, the Nebraska Supreme Court ruled that a change of hours from the 3 P.M.- to 11 P.M.-shift to the 11 P.M.- to 7 A.M.-shift was not good cause for a licensed practical nurse to resign, so she was not entitled to compensation.[250] In 1988, the Florida unemployment agency ruled that a hospital laboratory technologist who resigned due to fear of AIDS was not entitled to compensation.[251] In 1992, a Pennsylvania court decided that it was willful misconduct for a phlebotomist to mislabel a blood sample after three prior reprimands for mislabeling, so compensation was denied.[252] In 1993, a North Carolina court ruled that a hospital employee was disqualified from compensation for violating the hospital policy against fighting with co-workers.[253]

However, due to the peculiar features of the unemployment compensation process in some states, strange results do occur. In 1991, the Michigan Supreme Court ruled that under Michigan law a nurse who failed the state licensing examination and, thus, could not legally function as a nurse, was entitled to unemployment compensation because the court viewed that she had not lost her job voluntarily.[254]

An employer's contribution to the state unemployment compensation fund often depends on the amount the state has paid to its former employees, so employers should be prepared to substantiate discharges for misconduct.

Public Employees

Since the NLRA does not apply to employees of state and local governmental agencies, the relations between these public employees and their governmental employers are controlled by state law. Some states prohibit collective bargaining by public employees, so employee rights are determined by state civil service laws and individual agency policies. Many states authorize representation by a labor organization and collective bargaining. A state agency similar to the NLRB is usually established to administer the law. State laws frequently limit the subjects that may be determined by collective bargaining, and they are different from the NLRA in other ways. Many states prohibit strikes by all or some public employees and require that bargaining impasses be resolved by arbitration.

NOTES

1. *See* American Hospital Association, *The Wrongful Discharge of Employees in the Health Care Industry*, Legal Memorandum No. 10,13-28 (Aug. 1987) [hereinafter *Wrongful Discharge*] [suggested preventive measures].

2. *As value of diplomas grows, more people buy bogus credentials*, WALL ST. J., Apr. 2, 1987, at 1.

3. 8 U.S.C.A. § 1324a; see *Calif. hospital assessed largest immigration fine*, 19 MOD. HEALTHCARE, June 23, 1989, at 12 [$183,200 fine for 259 violations].

4. Carlson v. Arnot-Ogden Mem. Hosp., 918 F.2d 411 (3d Cir. 1990).

5. *Employers face new liability: Truth in hiring*, WALL. ST. J., July 9, 1993, at B1.

6. Tallahassee Furniture v. Harrison, 583 So. 2d 744 (Fla. 1st DCA 1991), *rev. denied*, 595 So. 2d 558 (Fla. 1992); *Court ruling may increase record checks on workers*, PALM BEACH POST, Aug. 8, 1991, at 11B.

7. *E.g.*, Curry v. Almance Health Servs., No. 2:92CV00351 (M.D. Ga. April 1, 1994), *as discussed in* 3 HEALTH L. RPTR. [BNA] 519 (1994) [judgment for hospital in race, sex bias suit by employee fired for failing to disclose criminal record on employment application] [hereinafter HEALTH L. RPTR. cited as H.L.R.].

8. Centers for Disease Control [hereinafter CDC], *Guidelines for prevention of transmission of human immunodeficiency virus and hepatitis B virus to health-care and public-safety workers*, 38 M.M.W.R., June 23, 1989, No. S-6; CDC, *Update: Universal precautions for prevention of transmission of human immunodeficiency virus, hepatitis B virus, and other bloodborne pathogens in health care settings*, 37 M.M.W.R 377 (June 24, 1988), *reprinted in* 260 J.A.M.A. 462 (1988); CDC, *Recommendations for prevention of HIV transmission in health care settings*, 36 M.M.W.R. 25 (Aug. 21, 1987), *reprinted in* 258 J.A.M.A. 1293, 1441 (1987); Leckelt v. Board of Comm'rs, 909 F.2d 820 (5th Cir. 1990), *aff'g*, 714 F. Supp. 1377 (E.D. La. 1989) [not a violation of Rehabilitation Act to discharge LPN who refused to disclose her HIV test results; under CDC guidelines employer needed information to make job assignment]; Bradley v. University of Tex. M.D. Anderson Cancer Ctr., 3 F.3d 922 (5th Cir. 1993), *cert. denied*, 114 S. Ct. 1071 (U.S. 1994) [hospital properly reassigned surgical technician with HIV to purchasing department; not retaliation for newspaper report of HIV status]; *see also* Fedro v. Reno, 21 F.3d 1391 (7th Cir. 1994) [need not create new position for employee with hepatitis B].

9. 42 U.S.C.A. §§ 12101–12117; 29 C.F.R. pt. 1630.

10. *E.g.*, Daly v. United States, 946 F.2d 1467 (9th Cir. 1991) [examining physician has duty to disclose abnormal results]; Baer v. Regents of Univ. of Cal., 118 N.M. 685, 884 P.2d 841 (Ct. App. 1994) [provider performing periodic employee exam for employer owes duty of care to employee].

11. Schauer v. Memorial Care Sys., 856 S.W.2d 437 (Tex. Ct. App. 1993).

12. See *Hospitals' RX for high costs: Fewer nurses, more aides*, WALL ST. J., Feb. 10, 1995, at B1.

13. *E.g.*, California Nurses Ass'n v. Alta Bates Med. Ctr., No. 74079-5 (Cal. Super. Ct. Alameda County filed Sept. 13, 1994), *as discussed in* 3 H.L.R. 1319 (1994) [hospital charged with consumer fraud, deception by implementing work restructuring for nurses, censoring employees who speak out]; California Nurses Assoc. v. Alta Bates Med. Ctr., No. C94-03555 CW (N.D. Cal. Mar. 13, 1995), *as discussed in* 4 H.L.R. 484 (1995) [remand to state court of lawsuit alleging staffing proposal endangers public health because case does not require interpretation of collective bargaining agreement]; *Health care unions developing strategy on clinical restructuring*, 4 H.L.R. 93 (1995); *Nurses rally in Washington to protest hospital practices of restructuring*, 4 H.L.R. 521 (1995) [seeking legally mandated nurse–patient ratios].

14. *E.g.*, Dabbs v. Cardiopulmonary Management Servs., 188 Cal. App. 3d 1437, 234 Cal. Rptr. 129 (4th Dist. 1987) [respiratory therapist could not be discharged for refusing to work night shift as only experienced therapist], *disapproved*, Gantt v. Sentry Ins., 1 Cal. 4th 1083, 4 Cal. Rptr. 2d 874, 824 P.2d 680 (1992) [wrongful discharge action must be based on public policy expressed in constitution or statutes].

15. *See Wrongful Discharge, supra* note 1, at 47–55, 70–78, 104–11.

16. *E.g.*, Burrell v. Carraway Methodist Hosp., 607 So. 2d 193 (Ala. 1992) [employee at will fired for failing to report private work for supervisor on hospital time]; Lampe v. Presbyterian Med. Ctr., 590 P.2d 513 (Colo. Ct. App. 1978) [head nurse terminated for inability to follow staffing procedures, stay within budget].

17. *E.g.*, Jones v. Central Peninsula Gen. Hosp., 779 P.2d 783 (Alaska 1989); Duldulao v. St. Mary of Nazareth Hosp. Ctr., 115 Ill. 2d 482, 505 N.E.2d 314 (1987) [employee handbook can create contract in certain situations]; Annotation, *Right to discharge allegedly "at-will" employee as affected by employer's promulgation of employment policies as to discharge*, 33 A.L.R. 4TH 120.

18. Heideck v. Kent Gen. Hosp., 446 A.2d 1095 (Del. 1982) [dismissal for failure to heed patient plea for privacy on bedside commode]; *see also* Mursch v. Van Dorn Co., 851 F.2d 990 (7th Cir. 1988) [guidelines in employee handbook not contract under Wisconsin law].

19. Watson v. Idaho Falls Consol. Hosps., 111 Idaho 44, 720 P.2d 632 (1986) [employee handbook can be contract].

20. *E.g.*, Bowe v. Charleston Area Med. Ctr., Inc., 428 S.E.2d 773 (W. Va. 1993) [disclaimer in employee handbook precluded it from being binding]; Lee v. Sperry Corp., 678 F. Supp. 1415 (D. Minn. 1987) [disclaimer added to employee handbook terminated claim of contract]; *see* Annotation, *Effectiveness of employer's disclaimer of representations in personnel manual or employee handbook altering at-will employment relationship*, 17 A.L.R. 5TH 1; *but see* Robinson v. Ada S. McKinley Community Servs., Inc., 19 F.3d 359 (7th Cir. 1994) [new employee handbook with disclaimer did not modify contract formed by old manual].

21. Cleveland Bd. of Educ. v. Loudermill, 470 U.S. 532 (1985); *see also* Bradley v. Colonial Mental Health & Retardation Servs. Bd., 856 F.2d 703 (4th Cir. 1988) [terminated substance abuse employees given adequate due process]; Phares v. Gustafsson, 856 F.2d 1003 (7th Cir. 1988) [terminated medical records technician given adequate due process].

22. *E.g.*, Simpkins v. Sandwich Comm. Hosp., 854 F.2d 215 (7th Cir. 1988).

23. *E.g.*, Musgrave v. HCA Mideast, Ltd., 856 F.2d 690 (4th Cir. 1988) [jury question under Virginia law whether written contract intended to require cause for termination]; Jackam v. Hospital Corp. of Am. Mideast, Ltd., 800 F.2d 1577 (11th Cir. 1986) [cause of action stated against employer for termination of written contract].

24. *E.g.*, Dearden v. Liberty Med. Ctr., Inc., 75 Md. App. 528, 542 A.2d 383 (1988).

25. Hebert v. Woman's Hosp. Found., 377 So.2d 1340 (La. Ct. App. 1979), *cert. denied*, 379 So.2d 254 (La. 1980).

26. 72 AM. JUR. 2D *Statute of frauds* (1974); *e.g.*, Santa Monica Hosp. v. Superior Ct., 204 Cal. App. 3d 28, 218 Cal. Rptr. 543 (1985), *review granted*, 222 Cal. Rptr. 224, 711 P.2d 520 (Cal. 1986) [not citable in Cal.].

27. *E.g.*, 29 U.S.C.A. § 626(b) [age discrimination].

28. *E.g.*, Fla. Stat. § 440.205 [no retaliation for workers' compensation claims]; *but see* Allan v. SWF Gulf Coast, Inc., 535 So.2d 638 (Fla. 1st DCA 1988) [employee may be terminated for other reasons even after claim].

29. Shores v. Senior Manor Nursing Ctr., 164 Ill. App. 3d 503, 518 N.E.2d 471 (5th Dist. 1988) [report of patient abuse to administrator]; Palmer v. Brown, 242 Kan. 893, 752 P.2d 685 (1988)

[report of fraudulent Medicaid billing]; Kelsay v. Motorola, Inc., 74 Ill. 2d 172, 384 N.E.2d 353 (1978) [worker's compensation claim]; *contra* Washington v. Union Carbide Corp., 870 F.2d 957 (4th Cir. 1989) [no recovery in West Virginia for discharge for reporting safety violations to company].

30. Sides v. Duke Hosp., 74 N.C. App. 331, 328 S.E.2d 818, *rev. denied*, 314 N.C. 331, 335 S.E.2d 13 (1985).

31. Wheeler v. Caterpillar Tractor Co., 108 Ill. 2d 502, 485 N.E.2d 372 (1985), *cert. denied*, 475 U.S. 1122 (1986).

32. *E.g.*, Webb v. HCA Health Servs. of Midwest, 300 Ark. 613, 780 S.W.2d 571 (1989); *see also* Godwin v. Visiting Nurse Ass'n Home Health Servs., 831 F. Supp. 449 (E.D. Pa. 1993), *aff'd without op.*, 39 F.3d 1173 (3d Cir. 1994) [violation of False Claims Act to discharge bookkeeper for refusing to participate in false Medicare claims].

33. *See supra* note 14; *but see* Fineman v. New Jersey Dep't of Human Servs., 640 A.2d 1161 (N.J. App. Div. 1994) [physician could be terminated for refusing to provide temporary medical care to 300 nursing home patients].

34. *E.g.*, Waters v. Churchill, 114 S. Ct. 1878 (U.S. 1994) [remand of case in which employee had criticized nurse cross-training]; Roth v. Veterans Admin., 856 F.2d 1401 (9th Cir. 1988) [physician's criticism of wastefulness, violations, risks to patients was protected free speech]; Jones v. Memorial Hosp. Sys., Inc., 746 S.W.2d 891 (Tex. Ct. App. 1988) [nurse's newspaper article on prolongation of life was protected free speech]; Hitt v. North Broward Hosp. Dist., 387 So.2d 482 (Fla. 4th DCA 1980) [private duty nurse put flyers concerning nursing group on public hospital bulletin board]; Annotation, *First Amendment protection for public hospital or health employees subjected to discharge, transfer, or discipline because of speech*, 107 A.L.R. FED. 21; *but see* Pilarowski v. Macomb County Health Dep't, 841 F.2d 1281 (6th Cir.), *cert. denied*, 488 U.S. 850 (1988) [insufficient evidence that budget cuts resulting in layoff were retaliation for letters to local newspaper]; Black v. City of Wentzville, 686 F. Supp. 241 (E.D. Mo. 1988) [no liability for discharge of policeman after public statements due to documented poor work performance].

35. *E.g.*, Rahn v. Drake Ctr., 31 F.3d 407 (6th Cir. 1994), *cert. denied*, 115 S. Ct. 2578 (U.S. 1995).

36. *E.g.*, Wright v. Shriners Hosp. for Crippled Children, 412 Mass. 469, 589 N.E.2d 1241 (1992) [reversing award of $50,000 to nurse for dismissal after critical remarks to internal survey team because termination did not violate public policy]; Willis v. University Health Servs., 993 F.2d 837 (11th Cir), *cert. denied*, 114 S. Ct. 468 (U.S. 1993) [private entity managing county hospital that fired nurse allegedly for free speech was not public employer].

37. Rozier v. St. Mary's Hosp., 88 Ill. App. 3d 994, 411 N.E.2d 50 (5th Dist. 1980); *see also* Maus v. National Living Ctrs., Inc., 633 S.W.2d 674 (Tex. Ct. App. 1982) [discharge of nurse's aide by nursing home for complaints to superiors concerning patient care].

38. NLRB v. J. Weingarten, Inc., 420 U.S. 251 (1975); see *Wrongful Discharge*, *supra* note 1, at 102–03.

39. Prudential Ins. Co., 275 N.L.R.B. 208 (1985).

40. Slaughter v. NLRB, 876 F.2d 11 (3d Cir. 1989).

41. Peete v. Blackwell, 504 So.2d 222 (Ala. 1986).

42. *See Wrongful Discharge*, *supra* note 1, at 63–70, 129–33.

43. National Treasury Employees Union v. Von Raab, 489 U.S. 656 (1989).

44. Skinner v. Ry. Labor Executives' Ass'n, 489 U.S. 602 (1989).

45. Johnson-Bateman Co., 295 N.L.R.B. No. 26 (June 19, 1989); *see also, e.g.*, Utility Workers v. Southern Cal. Edison Co., 852 F.2d 1083 (9th Cir. 1988), *cert. denied*, 489 U.S. 1078 (1989).

46. Conrail v. Railway Labor Executives' Ass'n, 491 U.S. 299 (1989); *see also, e.g.*, Laws v. Calmat, 852 F.2d 430 (9th Cir. 1988); Utility Workers v. Southern Cal. Edison Co., 852 F.2d 1083 (9th Cir. 1988), *cert. denied*, 489 U.S. 1078 (1989).

47. Cowles Media Co., Star Tribune Div., 295 N.L.R.B. No. 63 (June 19, 1989).

48. *E.g.*, Greco v. Halliburton Co., 674 F. Supp. 1447 (D. Wyo. 1987); Stevenson v. Panhandle E. Pipe Line Co., 680 F. Supp. 859 (S.D. Tex. 1987); *see also* Green, *Drug testing becomes corporate minefield*, WALL ST. J., Nov. 21, 1989, at B1 [discussion of state, local laws, court decisions]; American Hospital Association, *The Law of Substance Abuse for Healthcare Providers*, Legal Memorandum No. 11 (Sept. 1987) [discussion of drug testing of employees]; Annotation, *Liability for discharge of at-will employee for refusal to submit to drug testing*, 79 A.L.R. 4TH 105; *but see* CONN. GEN. STAT. ANN. § 31-51x [prohibition of employee drug testing without showing good cause for suspected drug use].

49. 29 U.S.C.A. §§ 2001-2009.

50. Stickler & Nelson, *Defamation in the workplace: Employer rights, risks, and responsibilities*, 21 J. HEALTH & HOSP. L. 97 (1988).

51. *E.g.*, Mayer v. Morgan Stanley & Co., 703 F. Supp. 249 (S.D. N.Y. 1988).

52. *E.g.*, Gengler v. Phelps, 92 N.M. 465, 589 P.2d 1056 (Ct. App.), *cert. denied*, 92 N.M. 353, 588 P.2d 554 (1979) [communication concerning nurse anesthetist].

53. *E.g.*, Burger v. McGilley Mem. Chapels, Inc., 856 F.2d 1046 (8th Cir. 1988); *see also* Annotation, *Defamation: loss of employer's qualified privilege to publish employee's work record or qualification*, 24 A.L.R. 4TH 144.

54. *E.g.*, Kellums v. Freight Sales Ctrs., Inc., 467 So.2d 816 (Fla. 5th DCA 1985) [release form did not preclude liability for deliberate falsehood].

55. United States v. Kibby, 848 F.2d 920 (8th Cir. 1988); *see also Ex-Provident employees face wire fraud charges*, 18 MOD. HEALTHCARE, Oct. 21, 1988, at 15 [information sent by wire in obtaining alleged kickbacks from contractors]; Johnson v. United Airlines, 680 F. Supp. 1425 (D. Haw. 1987) [solicitation of tips by airline skycap legitimate basis for termination].

56. Act of May 31, 1879, ch. 114, § 16, 16 Stat. 144.

57. Edwards v. Jewish Hosp., 855 F.2d 1345 (8th Cir. 1988); *see also* Roberts v. Gadsden Mem. Hosp., 835 F.2d 793 (11th Cir. 1988), *amended on reh'g*, 850 F.2d 1549 (11th Cir. 1988) [violation not to give promoted African American county maintenance employees same raise as Caucasians who were promoted]; *but see* Armstrong v. Turnage, 690 F. Supp. 839 (E.D. Mo. 1988), *aff'd without op.*, 873 F.2d 1448 (8th Cir. 1989) [disparate treatment of African American, Caucasian hospital pharmacists after errors insufficient to prove motive where rules consistently applied].

58. St. Francis College v. Al-Khazraji, 481 U.S. 604 (1987).

59. Patterson v. McLean Credit Union, 491 U.S. 164 (1989).

60. Wards Cove Packing Co. v. Atonio, 490 U.S. 642 (1989).

61. Pub. L. No. 102-166, 105 Stat. 1071 (1991).

62. Runyon v. McCrary, 427 U.S. 160 (1976).

63. Act Apr. 20, 1871, ch. 22, § 1, 17 Stat. 13.

64. Anglemyer v. Hamilton County Hosp., 848 F. Supp. 938 (D. Kan. 1994), *aff'd*, 58 F.3d 533 (10th Cir. 1995).

65. *E.g.*, Wheat v. Mass, 994 F.2d 273 (5th Cir. 1993).

66. Trimble v. Androscoggin Valley Hosp., 847 F. Supp. 226 (D.N.H. 1994); *but see* Snyder v. Albany Med. Ctr. Hosp., 206 A.D. 2d 816, 615 N.Y.S.2d 139 (3d Dep't 1994) [holding involuntarily committed patient at private hospital was under color of state law].

67. Willis v. University Health Servs., Inc., 993 F.2d 837 (11th Cir.), *cert. denied,* 114 S. Ct. 468 (U.S. 1993).

68. Moore v. Wyoming Med. Ctr., 825 F. Supp. 1531 (D. Wyo. 1993).

69. Acts July 31, 1861, ch. 33, 12 Stat. 284; Acts Apr. 20, 1871, ch. 22, § 2, 17 Stat. 13.

70. *E.g.,* Travis v. Gary Community Mental Health Ctr., Inc., 921 F.2d 108 (7th Cir, 1990), *cert. denied,* 502 U.S. 812 (1991); *but see* Fobbs v. Holy Cross Health Sys. Corp., 29 F.3d 1439 (9th Cir. 1994), *cert. denied,* 115 S.Ct. 936 (U.S. 1995) [claim stated against hospital, 27 individual staff physicians]; Saville v. Houston County Healthcare Auth., 852 F. Supp. 1512 (M.D. Ala. 1994) [intracorporate conspiracy exception not available in Eleventh Circuit in § 1985 (3) suit].

71. Griffin v. Breckenridge, 403 U.S. 88 (1971).

72. Wong v. Stripling, 881 F.2d 200 (5th Cir. 1989).

73. United Brotherhood v. Scott, 463 U.S. 825 (1983).

74. 42 U.S.C.A. §§ 2000e–2000e-17.

75. *E.g.,* Judie v. Hamilton, 872 F.2d 919 (9th Cir. 1989) [restrictions on supervisory responsibilities of African American hospital food manager could be violation].

76. *Backlog of cases is overwhelming jobs-bias agency,* N.Y. TIMES, Nov. 26, 1994, at 1; *EEOC is making sweeping changes in handling cases,* WALL ST. J., Apr. 20, 1995, at B8 [categorization, prioritization of complaints].

77. Watson v. Ft. Worth Bank & Trust, 487 U.S. 977 (1988).

78. *E.g.,* Beadle v. City of Tampa, 42 F.3d 633 (11th Cir.), *cert. denied,* 115 S. Ct. 2600 (U.S. 1995).

79. *E.g.,* Metz v. Merrill Lynch Pierce Fenner & Smith, 39 F.3d 1482 (10th Cir. 1994).

80. EEOC v. River Oaks Imaging & Diagnostic, No. H-95-755 (S.D. Tex. Apr. 19, 1995), *as discussed in* 4 H.L.R. 647 (1995) [preliminary injunction of employer's alternative dispute resolution policy, retaliation against employees who refused to sign agreement].

81. *E.g.,* Diggs v. Harris Hosp.-Methodist, Inc., 847 F.2d 270 (5th Cir.), *cert. denied,* 488 U.S. 956 (1988); Amiable v. Long & Scott Farms, 20 F.3d 434 (11th Cir.), *cert. denied,* 115 S. Ct. 351 (U.S. 1994).

82. *E.g.,* Deal v. State Farm County Mut. Ins. Co., 5 F.3d 117 (5th Cir. 1993).

83. *E.g.,* Zaklama v. Mt. Sinai Med. Ctr., 842 F.2d 291 (11th Cir. 1988) [hospital can be liable for adverse recommendation by employee physician that resulted in another hospital discharging resident physician]; Pardazi v. Cullman Med. Ctr., 838 F.2d 1155 (11th Cir. 1988) [physician stated Title VII claim when hospital's denial of medical staff membership led to loss of employment opportunity with medical group that depended on membership]; Doe on behalf of Doe v. St. Joseph's Hosp., 788 F.2d 411 (7th Cir. 1986), *on remand,* 113 F.R.D. 677 (N.D. Ind. 1987) [physicians terminated from medical staff may sue under Title VII if they can show interference with employment by others]; Gomez v. Alexian Bros. Hosp., 698 F.2d 1019 (9th Cir. 1983) [rejection of contract proposal by emergency medical professional corporation can violate Title VII as to Hispanic physician employee of corporation]; Sibley Mem. Hosp. v. Wilson, 160 U.S. App. D.C. 14, 488 F.2d 1338 (1973) [hospital can violate Title VII by interfering with private duty nurse's employment opportunities]; LeMasters v. Christ Hosp., 777 F. Supp. 1378 (D. Ohio 1991); Annotation, *Who is "employee" as defined in sec. 701(f) of the Civil Rights Act of 1964,* 72 A.L.R. FED 522; *but see* Diggs v. Harris Hosp.-Methodist, Inc., 847 F.2d 270 (5th Cir. 1988) [physician's "employment" relationship with patients not sufficient to permit Title VII action against hospital for termination of medical staff membership]; Mitchell v. Frank R. Howard Mem. Hosp., 853 F.2d 762 (9th Cir. 1988), *cert. denied,* 489 U.S. 1013 (1989) [relationship with patients, with wholly-owned professional corporation insufficient]; Shrock v. Altru Nurses Registry, 810 F.2d 658 (7th Cir. 1987) [nurse referral agency not employer, not liable under Title VII].

84. Scharon v. St. Luke's Episcopal Presbyterian Hosp., 929 F.2d 360 (8th Cir. 1991).

85. *E.g.*, Smith v. St. Bernards Reg. Med. Ctr., 19 F.3d 1254 (8th Cir. 1994).

86. *E.g.*, Garcia v. Elf Atochem N.Am., 28 F.3d 446 (5th Cir. 1994).

87. St. Francis College v. Al-Khazraji, 481 U.S. 604 (1987) [Arabs are a race for purposes of 42 U.S.C.A. § 1981 suits; "distinctive physiognomy is not essential"]; Jatoi v. Hurst-Euless Bedford Hosp. Auth., 807 F.2d 1214 (5th Cir.), *as modified*, 819 F.2d 545 (5th Cir. 1987) [East Indians]; Doe on behalf of Doe v. St. Joseph's Hosp.,788 F.2d 411 (7th Cir. 1986), *on remand*, 113 F.R.D. 677 (N.D. Ind. 1987) [Orientals]; MacDissi v. Valmont Indust., Inc., 856 F.2d 1054 (8th Cir. 1988) [Lebanese]; Janko v. Illinois State Toll Highway Auth., 704 F. Supp. 1531 (N.D. Ill. 1989) [Gypsies].

88. *E.g.*, Harding v. Gray, 9 F.3d 150 (D.C. Cir. 1993) [hospital shop foreman; allegations of superior qualifications, if supported by facts, can constitute sufficient background circumstances to establish prima facie case]; McNabola v. Chicago Transit Auth., 10 F.3d 501 (7th Cir. 1993) [affirming reverse discrimination judgment for Caucasian physician terminated as per diem medical examiner].

89. *E.g.*, Williams v. Health Maintenance Org. of Fla., 689 F. Supp. 1082 (M.D. Fla. 1988).

90. *E.g.*, Mosley v. Clarksville Mem. Hosp., 574 F. Supp. 224 (M.D. Tenn. 1983).

91. *E.g.*, Walker v. Jefferson County Home, 726 F.2d 1554 (11th Cir. 1984).

92. 8 U.S.C.A. § 1324b.

93. Trans World Airlines, Inc. v. Hardison, 432 U.S. 63 (1977).

94. *E.g.*, Brener v. Diagnostic Ctr. Hosp., 671 F.2d 141 (5th Cir. 1982); Mathewson v. Florida Game & Fresh Water Fish Comm'n, 693 F. Supp. 1044 (M.D. Fla. 1988), *aff'd without op.*, 871 F.2d 123 (11th Cir. 1989); Murphy v. Edge Mem. Hosp., 550 F. Supp. 1185 (M.D. Ala. 1982).

95. McCrory v. Rapides Regional Med. Ctr., 635 F. Supp. 975 (W.D. La. 1986), *aff'd without op.*, 801 F.2d 396 (5th Cir. 1986).

96. Baz v. Walters, 782 F.2d 701 (7th Cir. 1986).

97. 42 U.S.C.A. § 2000e-1.

98. Corporation of Presiding Bishop v. Amos, 483 U.S. 327 (1987).

99. Young v. Shawnee Mission Med. Ctr., No. 88-2321-S (D. Kan. Oct. 21, 1988), *as discussed in* 22 J. HEALTH & HOSP. L. 160 (1989).

100. *E.g.*, Steele v. Offshore Shipbuilding, Inc., 867 F.2d 1311 (11th Cir), *reh'g denied (en banc)*, 874 F.2d 821 (11th Cir. 1989); Sparks v. Pilot Freight Carriers, Inc., 830 F.2d 1554 (11th Cir. 1987).

101. *Harassment of workers by 'third parties' can lead into maze of legal, moral issues*, WALL ST. J., Oct. 26, 1992, at B1.

102. *E.g.*, Kopp v. Samaritan Health Sys., Inc., 13 F.3d 264 (8th Cir. 1993) [hospital could be liable for hostile environment sexual harassment based on conduct of cardiologist where (1) hospital required physician to take short leave or get counseling but did not show it had checked on physician, (2) employee relocated to avoid contact with doctor, losing many supervisory tasks]; *but see* Sparks v. Regional Med. Ctr. Bd., 792 F. Supp. 735 (N.D. Ala. 1992) [hospital's prompt response to sexual harassment by pathologist prevented hospital liability for physician conduct].

103. Meritor Sav. Bank v. Vinson, 477 U.S. 57 (1986), *on remand*, 255 U.S. App. D.C. 397, 801 F.2d 1436 (1986). For EEOC regulations, *see* 29 C.F.R. § 1604.11. For examples, *see* Ross v. Twenty-Four Collection, Inc., 681 F. Supp. 1547 (S.D. Fla. 1988), *aff'd without op.*, 875 F.2d 873 (11th Cir. 1989) [liability for sexual harassment]; Dockter v. Rudolf Wolff Futures, Inc., 684 F. Supp. 532 (N.D. Ill. 1988), *aff'd,* 913 F.2d 456 (7th Cir. 1990) [hostile working environment not shown]; *see also* Scott v. Western State Hosp., 658 F. Supp. 593 (W.D. Va.

1987) [duty to investigate racial harassment charges, take steps]; Powell, *Comment: Sexual harassment in the health care environment*, 22 J. HEALTH & HOSP. L. 42 (1989).

104. Harris v. Forklift Sys., Inc., 114 S. Ct. 367 (U.S. 1993).

105. *E.g.*, De Cintio v. Westchester County Med. Ctr., 807 F.2d 304 (2d Cir. 1986), *cert. denied*, 484 U.S. 965 (1987) [writing job description to favor girlfriend not sex discrimination]; Autry v. North Carolina Dep't of Human Resources, 820 F.2d 1384 (4th Cir. 1987); Miller v. Aluminum Co. of Am., 679 F. Supp. 495 (W.D. Pa. 1988), *aff'd*, 856 F.2d 184 (3d Cir. 1988); *contra* King v. Palmer, 598 F. Supp. 65 (D. D.C. 1984), *rev'd on other grounds*, 250 U.S. App. D.C. 257, 778 F.2d 878 (1985).

106. Greenlaw v. Garrett, 1994 U.S. App. LEXIS 36, 450 (9th Cir. 1994), *opinion withdrawn*, 43 F.3d 463 (9th Cir. 1995).

107. *E.g.*, Lemons v. City of Denver, 620 F.2d 228 (10th Cir.), *cert. denied*, 449 U.S. 888 (1980); Briggs v. City of Madison, 536 F. Supp. 435 (W.D. Wis. 1982); American Nurses Ass'n v. Illinois, 783 F.2d 716 (7th Cir. 1986) [case settled in 1989, 19 MOD. HEALTHCARE, Mar. 10, 1989, at 14]; AFSCME v. Washington, 770 F.2d 1401 (9th Cir. 1985), *reh'g denied (en banc)*, 813 F.2d 1034 (9th Cir. 1987) [case settled in 1985, N.Y. TIMES, Jan. 2, 1986, at 7].

108. *E.g.*, Floca v. Homcare Health Servs., 845 F.2d 108 (5th Cir. 1988) [violation to terminate pregnant director of nursing]; Carney v. Martin Luther Home, Inc., 824 F.2d 643 (8th Cir. 1987) [violation to force unpaid medical leave while still able to work]; *but see* McKnight v. North Charles Gen. Hosp., 652 F. Supp. 880 (D. Md. 1986) [hospital hired replacement head nurse for CCU when return from pregnancy delayed; not discrimination to place returning nurse in staff position in same unit].

109. Pacourek v. Inland Steel Co., 858 F. Supp. 1393 (N.D. Ill. 1994); *but see* Tyndall v. National Educ. Ctrs., 31 F.3d 209 (4th Cir. 1994) [discharge for health-related absences not protected by ADA]; Zatarain v. WDSU-Television, Inc., 1995 WL 16777 (E.D. La.) [employer not required by ADA to accommodate employee's infertility treatment].

110. International Union United Auto Workers v. Johnson Controls, Inc., 499 U.S. 187 (1991); *Decision poses dilemma for employers*, WALL ST. J., Mar. 21, 1991, at B1.

111. Armstrong v. Flowers Hosp., 33 F.3d 1308 (11th Cir. 1994).

112. Newport News Shipbuilding & Dry Dock Co. v. EEOC, 462 U.S. 669 (1983).

113. Backus v. Baptist Med. Ctr., 510 F. Supp. 1191 (E.D. Ark. 1981); *accord* Jones v. Hinds Gen. Hosp., 666 F. Supp. 933 (S.D. Miss. 1987); *Hospitals can ban male nurses from delivery room*, AM. MED. NEWS, Oct. 3, 1994, at 19 [Cal. Fair Employment and Housing Comm'n]; *see also* Jennings v. N.Y. State Office of Mental Health, 977 F.2d 731 (2d Cir. 1992) [state mental health facility could require at least one security treatment assistant assigned to each ward to be of same gender as patients]; *but see* Little Forest Med. Ctr. of Akron v. Ohio Civil Rights Comm'n, 61 Ohio St. 3d 607, 575 N.E.2d 1164 (1991), *cert. denied*, 503 U.S. 906 (1992) [gender not BFOQ for nurse's aide].

114. Backus v. Baptist Med. Ctr., 671 F.2d 1100 (8th Cir. 1982).

115. Garcia v. Rush-Presbyterian-St. Luke's Med. Ctr., 660 F.2d 1217 (7th Cir. 1981).

116. 29 C.F.R. § 1606.7; Dimaranan v. Pomona Valley Hosp. Med. Ctr., 775 F. Supp. 338 (C.D. Cal. 1991) [hospital rule restricting use of Tagalog language by Filipino nurses was not prohibited English-only rule in violation of Title VII where shift-specific directive addressed conflicts among identified nurses]; McNeil v. Aguilos, 831 F. Supp. 1079 (S.D. N.Y. 1993) [nonFilipino nurse did not state claim for hospital policy of allowing nurses to communicate in workplace in

Tagalog]; Reed v. Driftwood Convalescent Hosp., EEOC Charge No. 377-93-0509 (July 13, 1994) [Calif. Dep't of Health Services policy; employees may speak other languages away from patients, but not to patients].

117. 42 U.S.C.A. § 2000e-3.

118. Wrighten v. Metropolitan Hosps., Inc., 726 F.2d 1346 (9th Cir. 1984); *see also* Sparrow v. Piedmont Health Sys. Agency, 593 F. Supp. 1107 (M.D. N.C. 1984) [refusal to give reference letter was prohibited retaliation for filing charge with EEOC].

119. *E.g.*, Vislisel v. Turnage, 930 F.2d 9 (8th Cir. 1991) [VA did not retaliate for discrimination complaint by requesting physical, mental exams after peculiar behavior]; Davis v. State Univ. of N.Y., 802 F.2d 638 (2d Cir. 1986) [African American nurse fired after filing discrimination charges, but sufficient reasons that were not pretexts, e.g., low productivity, inability to accept supervision, angry response to conflict]; Jackson v. St. Joseph State Hosp., 840 F.2d 1387 (8th Cir.), *cert. denied*, 488 U.S. 892 (1988) [harassing subordinate to change her complaint was not pretextual reason for discharge]; Klein v. Trustees of Ind. Univ., 766 F.2d 275 (7th Cir. 1985) [refusal to reschedule private practice hours to accommodate student health service hours was nonpretextual reason for discharge].

120. Baker v. McDonald's Corp., 686 F. Supp. 1474 (S.D. Fla. 1987), *aff'd without op.*, 865 F.2d 1272 (11th Cir. 1988), *cert. denied*, 493 U.S. 812 (1989); *accord* Stroehmann Bakeries Inc. v. Local 776, 969 F.2d 1436 (3d Cir. 1992), *cert. denied*, 113 S. Ct. 660 (U.S. 1992) [violated public policy for arbitrator to order reinstatement of accused sexual harasser]; Anderson v. Hewlett-Packard Corp., 694 F. Supp. 1294 (N.D. Ohio 1988) [personnel manager's constant sexual remarks, innuendos, suggestions to female subordinates created hostile or offensive work environment justifying termination]; *see also* Davis v. Monsanto Chem. Co., 858 F.2d 345, 350 (6th Cir. 1988), *cert. denied*, 490 U.S. 1110 ["In essence, while Title VII does not require an employer to fire all 'Archie Bunkers' in its employ, the law does require that an employer take prompt action to prevent such bigots from expressing their opinions in a way that abuses or offends their co-workers."]; Stockley v. AT&T Information Sys., Inc., 687 F. Supp. 764 (E.D. N.Y. 1988) [since employer obligated to investigate sexual harassment claims, report of investigation protected by qualified privilege in defamation action].

121. Flanagan v. Aaron E. Henry Comm. Health Servs. Ctr., 876 F.2d 1231 (5th Cir. 1989) [termination of Caucasian physician for race discrimination was not good cause under employment contract]; Szczerbaniuk v. Memorial Hosp. for McHenry County, 180 Ill. App. 3d 706, 536 N.E.2d 138 (2d Dist.), *appeal denied*, 545 N.E.2d 132 (Ill. 1989) [action by radiologist for termination of three-year exclusive contract by CEO after allegations of sexual harassment by hospital employees]; Charter Southland Hosp., Inc. v. Eades, 521 So.2d 981 (Ala. 1988) [psychologist independent contractor made sexual advances to hospital employees; termination of contract not justified because contract permitted termination for only death, disability, or conviction for felony].

122. *E.g.*, California Fed. Sav. & Loan Ass'n v. Guerra, 479 U.S. 272 (1987) [state statute requiring pregnancy leave, reinstatement not preempted by Title VII].

123. 29 U.S.C.A. § 206(d); *see* Lambert v. Genesee Hosp., 10 F.3d 46 (2d Cir. 1993), *cert. denied*, 114 S. Ct. 1612 (U.S. 1994) [female hospital employee in duplicating services department failed to establish Equal Pay Act claim]; Jones v. Westside-Urban Health Center, Inc., 760 F. Supp. 1575 (S.D. Ga.) [employed male physician stated prima facie case under Equal Pay Act].

124. Beall v. Curtis, 603 F. Supp. 1563 (M.D. Ga. 1985).

125. *E.g.*, Marshall v. St. John Valley Security Home, 560 F.2d 12 (1st Cir. 1977) [no violation]; Brennan v. Prince Williams Hosp., 503 F.2d 282 (4th Cir. 1974), *cert. denied*, 420 U.S. 972 (1975) [violation]; EEOC v. Harper Grace Hosps., 689 F. Supp. 708 (E.D. Mich. 1988) [violation].

126. 29 U.S.C.A. §§ 621–634, 663(a).

127. *E.g.*, Stamey v. Southern Bell Tel. & Tel. Co., 859 F.2d 855 (11th Cir.), *reg'h denied (en banc)*, 867 F.2d 1431 (11th Cir.), *cert. denied*, 490 U.S. 1116 (1989); Stickler & Nelson, *Liability for age discrimination in the health care workplace*, 21 J. HEALTH & HOSP. L. 185 (1988).

128. *E.g.*, Trans World Airlines, Inc. v. Thurston, 469 U.S. 111 (1985) [age of less than 60 years not bona fide occupational qualification for flying engineers].

129. O'Donnell v. Georgia Osteopathic Hosp., Inc., 748 F.2d 1543 (11th Cir. 1984).

130. Ogden v. Bureau of Labor, 68 Or. App. 235, 682 P.2d 802 (1984), *aff'd in part/rev'd in part*, 299 Or. 98, 699 P.2d 189 (1985).

131. *E.g.*, Gehring v. Case Corp., 43 F.3d 340 (7th Cir. 1994), *cert. denied*, 115 S. Ct. 2612 (U.S. 1995) [theory of disparate impact of reduction in force not an ADEA theory]; Rhodes v. Guiberson Oil Tools, 39 F.3d 537 (5th Cir. 1994) [reduction in force nonpretexual; to show pretext must show reason false, discrimination was real reason], *reh'g granted (en banc)*, 49 F.3d 127 (5th Cir. 1995); Anderson v. Baxter Healthcare Corp., 13 F.3d 1120 (7th Cir. 1994) [goal of reducing salary costs is not age discrimination]; Myers v. Glynn-Brunswick Mem. Hosp., 683 F. Supp. 1387 (S.D. Ga. 1988) [reduction in force was nonpretextual]; Grohs v. Gold Bond Bldg. Prods., 859 F.2d 1283 (7th Cir. 1988), *cert. denied*, 490 U.S. 1036 (1989) [difficulty getting along with peers was nonpretextual].

132. Buckley v. Hospital Corp. of Am., 758 F.2d 1525 (11th Cir. 1985).

133. 29 U.S.C.A. § 626(f), as amended by Pub. L. No. 101–433, § 201, 104 Stat. 983 (1990).

134. 42 U.S.C.A. §§ 12101-12117; 29 C.F.R. pt. 1630, first published in 56 FED. REG. 35727 (July 26, 1991) [employment rules]; see M.A. Dowell, *The Americans with Disabilities Act: The responsibilities of health care providers, insurers, and managed care organizations*, 25 J. HEALTH & HOSP. L. 289 (1992).

135. 42 U.S.C.A. § 12112(a).

136. 42 U.S.C.A. § 12102(2).

137. 42 U.S.C.A. § 12111(8); 29 C.F.R. § 1630.2(m).

138. 42 U.S.C.A. §§ 12111(3), 12113.

139. 42 U.S.C.A. §§ 12110(a), 12114(a).

140. 42 U.S.C.A. § 12114(c); 29 C.F.R. § 1630.16(b).

141. Bradley v. University of Tex. M.D. Anderson Cancer Ctr., 3 F.3d 922 (5th Cir. 1993), *cert. denied*, 114 S. Ct. 1071 (U.S. 1994).

142. Fitzpatrick v. City of Atlanta, 2 F.3d 1112 (11th Cir. 1993).

143. Wood v. Omaha School Dist., 25 F.3d 667 (8th Cir. 1994).

144. Reigel v. Kaiser Found. Health Plan, 859 F. Supp. 963 (E.D. N.C. 1994).

145. *E.g.*, Carr v. Reno, 306 U.S. App. D.C. 217, 23 F.3d 525 (1994); Tyndall v. National Educ. Ctrs., 31 F.3d 209 (4th Cir. 1994).

146. 29 U.S.C.A. §§ 701–794.

147. 29 U.S.C.A. § 793 [section 503]; 29 U.S.C.A. § 794 [section 504].

148. Conrail v. Darrone, 465 U.S. 624 (1984).

149. Pub. L. No. 100–259, § 4, 102 Stat. 29 (1988).

150. United States v. Baylor Univ. Med. Ctr., 736 F.2d 1039 (5th Cir. 1984), *cert. denied*, 469 U.S. 1189 (1985).

151. *E.g.*, Tuck v. HCA Health Servs., 7 F.3d 465 (6th Cir. 1993) [hospital violated act by terminating nurse].

152. Heilweil v. Mount Sinai Hosp., 32 F.3d 718 (2d Cir. 1994), *cert. denied*, 115 S. Ct. 1095 (U.S. 1995).

153. *E.g.*, School Bd. of Nassau County v. Arline, 480 U.S. 273 (1987), *on remand*, 692 F. Supp. 1286 (M.D. Fla. 1988) [discharged teacher with history of tuberculosis otherwise qualified, entitled to reinstatement, back pay].

154. Opinion by Douglas W. Kmeic, Oct. 6, 1988; *see* AM. MED. NEWS, Oct. 21, 1988, at 11.

155. Doe by Lavery v. Attorney General, 1995 U.S. App. LEXIS 16,264 (9th Cir. June 28, 1995), *rev'g on reconsideration*, 44 F.3d 715 (9th Cir. 1995), *reissuing withdrawn opinion*, 34 F.3d 781 (9th Cir. 1994), *aff'g*, 814 F. Supp. 844 (N.D. Cal.), *after remand from*, 941 F.2d 780 (9th Cir.), *vacating*, 723 F. Supp. 452 (N.D. Cal.); *Court: FBI wrong to stop using doctor*, AM. MED. NEWS, July 24, 1995, at 23.

156. Carter v. Casa Cent., 849 F.2d 1048 (7th Cir. 1988) [director of nursing at nursing home with multiple sclerosis handicapped, otherwise qualified]; Chalk v. United States Dist. Ct., 840 F.2d 701 (9th Cir. 1988) [teacher with AIDS was handicapped, otherwise qualified to teach; discrimination to assign to administrative job]; Harrison v. Marsh, 691 F. Supp. 1223 (W.D. Mo. 1988) [surgical removal of part of muscle of arm made typist handicapped; inadequate efforts to accommodate handicap]; Hall v. Veterans Admin., 693 F. Supp. 546 (E.D. Mich. 1988), *aff'd*, 1991 U.S. App. LEXIS 26,046 (6th Cir. Oct. 28, 1991) [denial of dismissal of suit seeking smoke-free environment as accommodation of obstructive lung disease]; Wallace v. Veterans Admin., 683 F. Supp. 758 (D. Kan. 1988) [recovering addict could not be denied nursing position because authority to administer narcotics had been restricted; otherwise qualified].

157. *E.g.*, Hall v. U.S. Postal Serv., 857 F.2d 1073 (6th Cir. 1988) [on-the-job back injury precluded heavy lifting; lower court should decide whether lifting requirement essential, whether employee could perform function, if essential, whether reasonable accommodation possible, if not essential].

158. Bruegging v. Burke, 696 F. Supp. 674 (D. D.C. 1987) [*Federal Register* not required to lower standards of accuracy to accommodate editor with cerebral palsy], *aff'd without op.*, 298 U.S. App. D.C. 97, 976 F.2d 95 (1988), *cert. denied*, 488 U.S. 1009 (1989).

159. Davis v. Meese, 692 F. Supp. 505 (E.D. Pa. 1988), *aff'd*, 865 F.2d 592 (3d Cir. 1989) [insulin-dependent diabetic applicant for FBI special agent position not otherwise qualified; employer not required to make fundamental alteration in nature of job as accommodation]; *accord* Serrapica v. City of New York, 708 F. Supp. 64 (S.D. N.Y.), *aff'd without op.*, 888 F.2d 126 (2d Cir. 1989) [diabetic not otherwise qualified for sanitation worker job because of heavy vehicles]; *see also* Matzo v. Postmaster Gen., 685 F. Supp. 260 (D. D.C. 1987), *aff'd without op.*, 274 U.S. App. D.C. 95, 861 F.2d 1290 (1988) [discharged postal service legal secretary manic-depressive, not otherwise qualified because disruptive and had poor attendance, and good-faith efforts had been made to accommodate her handicap]; Bailey v. Tisch, 683 F. Supp. 652 (S.D. Ohio 1988) [postal service applicant not otherwise qualified where heart condition never diagnosed as stable, exercise-related extra heartbeats made him unsuitable].

160. *E.g.*, Reese v. U.S. Gypsum Co., 705 F. Supp. 1387 (D. Minn. 1989) [state Human Rights Act not violated by discharge of diabetic who slept on job].

161. *E.g.*, Jackson v. Veterans Admin., 22 F.3d 277 (11th Cir.), *reh'g denied (en banc)*, 30 F.3d 1500 (11th Cir. 1994) [housekeeping aide not otherwise qualified because did not satisfy presence requirement for job, no duty to accommodate unpredictable absences]; Lemere v. Burnley, 683

F. Supp. 275 (D. D.C. 1988) [alcoholic employee lost status as qualified handicapped employee by pattern of unscheduled absences].

162. Atascadero State Hosp. v. Scanlon, 473 U.S. 234 (1985).

163. 29 U.S.C.A. §§ 201–219.

164. *E.g.*, Klein v. Rush-Presbyterian–St.Luke's Med. Ctr., 990 F.2d 279 (7th Cir. 1993) [hospital staff nurse not exempt as professional from FLSA, so entitled to overtime]; *but see* Reich v. Newspapers of New England, Inc., 44 F.3d 1060 (1st Cir. 1995) [listing nursing as example of exempt professional].

165. Garcia v. San Antonio Metro. Transit Auth., 469 U.S. 528 (1985), *rev'g*, National League of Cities v. Usery, 426 U.S. 833 (1976).

166. Townsend v. Mercy Hosp., 862 F.2d 1009 (3d Cir. 1988), *aff'g* 689 F. Supp. 503 (W.D. Pa. 1988).

167. Kaczmerak v. Mount Sinai Med. Ctr., No. 86-C-0472 (E.D. Wis. Feb. 24, 1988), *as discussed in* 16 HEALTH L. DIG., June 1988, at 23.

168. *E.g.*, United States v. Rocky Mountain Helicopters, 704 F. Supp. 1046 (D. Utah 1989).

169. 15 U.S.C.A. §§ 1671–1677.

170. Pub. L. No. 93-406, 88 Stat. 829 (1974) (codified as amended in scattered sections of 5, 18, 26, 29, 31, 42 U.S.C.); 29 C.F.R. pt. 2509–2677.

171. Metropolitan Life Ins. Co. v. Massachusetts, 471 U.S. 724 (1985).

172. United States v. Martorano, 767 F.2d 63 (3d Cir. 1985), *cert. denied*, 474 U.S. 949 (1985).

173. *E.g.*, Kross v. Western Electric Co., 701 F.2d 1238 (7th Cir. 1983).

174. Seaman v. Arvida Realty Sales, 985 F.2d 543 (11th Cir.), *reh'g denied (en banc)*, 993 F.2d 1556 (11th Cir.), *cert. denied*, 114 S. Ct. 308 (1993).

175. McGann v. H. & H. Music Co., 742 F. Supp. 392 (S.D. Tex. 1990), *aff'd*, 946 F.2d 401 (5th Cir. 1991), *cert. denied*, 115 S. Ct. 482 (1992).

176. Pub. L. No. 103-3, 107 Stat. 6 (1993) [codified as amended at 29 U.S.C.A. §§ 2611–2619 and in scattered sections of 2, 5, and 29 U.S.C.]; 60 FED. REG. 2180 (Jan. 6, 1995) [final regulations].

177. *E.g.*, 26 U.S.C.A. §§ 401–425; Rosenthal, *Sobering thoughts intrude on eulogy of section 89*, 45 TAX NOTES 930 (1989); Lawrie, Singerman, & Goetz, *The hidden employee benefit dangers in hospital-physician joint ventures*, 22 J. HEALTH & HOSP. L. 304 (1989). Pub. L. No. 101-140 (1989) repealed 26 U.S.C.A. § 89 (1989 Supp.).

178. Pub. L. No. 91-596, 84 Stat. 1590 (1970) (codified as amended at 29 U.S.C.A. §§ 651–678 (1985) and in scattered sections of 5, 15, 29, 42, 49 U.S.C.).

179. Marshall v. Barlow's Inc., 436 U.S. 307 (1978).

180. 29 C.F.R. § 1977.12(b)(2).

181. Whirlpool Corp. v. Marshall, 445 U.S. 1 (1980).

182. Stepp v. Review Bd., 521 N.E.2d 350 (Ind. Ct. App. 1988).

183. Gade v. National Solid Waste Mgmt. Ass'n, 505 U.S. 88 (1992).

184. 26 C.F.R. § 1910.1030, *first printed in* 56 FED. REG. 64004 (Dec. 6, 1991) [adoption of universal precautions]; E. Gregory, *Bloodborne pathogens—Is OSHA one step over the line?* 26 J. HEALTH & HOSP. L. 225 (1993).

185. American Dental Ass'n v. Secretary of Labor, 984 F.2d 823 (7th Cir. 1993) [dissent questioned OSHA's involvement in an area already addressed by CDC and its competence to do so], *cert. denied*, 114 S. Ct. 172 (U.S. 1993).

186. *E.g.*, *TB control plans focus of settlements between OSHA, two Wisconsin hospitals*, 2 H.L.R. 1342 (1993) [hospitals cited under general duty clause for not protecting workers from hazard

of TB infection through contact with patients at high risk for TB; failure to record on occupational illness and injury logs workers who tested positive for TB; allowed unapproved respirators, allowed facial hair, skull cap with respirators]; *see also* 59 FED. REG. 54242 (Oct. 28, 1994) [CDC guidelines on TB].

187. *Psychiatric hospital in Chicago cited by OSHA for workplace violence,* 2 H.L.R. 1479 (1993) [cited for failure to protect workers from patient violence; abatement program worked out].

188. 29 U.S.C.A. §§ 141–187.

189. Act of July 5, 1935, ch. 372, 49 Stat. 449.

190. Act of June 23, 1947, ch. 120, 61 Stat. 136.

191. Pub. L. No. 86-257, 73 Stat. 519.

192. See *Federal labor board gets more aggressive, to employers' dismay,* WALL ST. J., June 1, 1995, at A1.

193. 29 U.S.C.A. §§ 152(2), 158.

194. St. Elizabeth Comm. Hosp. v. NLRB, 708 F.2d 1436 (9th Cir. 1983); St. Elizabeth Hosp. v. NLRB, 715 F.2d 1193 (7th Cir. 1983).

195. NLRB v. Health Care & Retirement Corp. of Am., 114 S. Ct. 1778 (U.S. 1994).

196. *E.g., Illinois nurses negotiate language dealing with restructuring at hospital,* 4 H.L.R. 162 (1995).

197. Mercy Hosp. Ass'n, Inc., 235 N.L.R.B. 681 (1978).

198. Good Samaritan Hosp. & Richey, 265 N.L.R.B. 618 (1982).

199. Marshall Durbin Poultry Co. v. NLRB, 39 F.3d 1312 (5th Cir. 1994).

200. Waterbury Hosp. v. NLRB, 950 F.2d 849 (2d Cir. 1991).

201. East Tenn. Baptist Hosp. v. NLRB, 6 F.3d 1139 (6th Cir. 1993).

202. Swedish Hosp. Med. Ctr., NLRA Cases 19-CA-22412, 22823 (Oct. 14, 1993), *as discussed in* 2 H.L.R. 1419 (1993).

203. Torrington Extend-A-Care Employee Ass'n v. NLRB, 17 F.3d 580 (2d Cir. 1994).

204. Rideout Mem. Hosp., 227 N.L.R.B. 1338 (1977).

205. NLRB v. Peninsula Gen. Hosp. Med. Ctr., 36 F.3d 1262 (4th Cir. 1994).

206. Gratiot Comm. Hosp. v. N.L.R.B., 51 F.3d 1255 (6th Cir. 1995).

207. Pattern Maker's League v. NLRB, 473 U.S. 95 (1985).

208. NLRB v. 1115 Nursing Home & Serv. Employees Union, 44 F.3d 136 (2d Cir. 1995).

209. S. Rep. No. 93-766, 93d Cong., 2d Sess. 5, *reprinted in* 1974 U.S. CODE CONG. & ADMIN. NEWS 3,946, 3,950.

210. St. Francis Hosp. & Int'l Bhd. of Elec. Workers, 271 N.L.R.B. 948 (1984). Direct versus indirect patient care is not factor in this analysis, Health-Care Enters., 275 N.L.R.B. No. 194 (1985).

211. 29 C.F.R. § 103.30, *as added by* 54 FED. REG. 16,347–48 (Apr. 21, 1989); *see also* American Hospital Association, *The New NLRB Bargaining Unit Rules: Hospitals Prepare Yourselves,* Legal Memorandum No. 14 (May 1989).

212. American Hosp. Ass'n v. NLRB, 499 U.S. 606 (1991).

213. Kaiser Found. Hosps., 312 N.L.R.B. No. 139 (Sept. 30, 1993).

214. *E.g.,* Manchester Health Ctr. v. NLRB, 861 F.2d 50 (2d Cir. 1988) [rule upheld].

215. *E.g.,* Cooper Tire & Rubber Co. v. NLRB, 957 F.2d 1245 (5th Cir. 1992); *see also* Our Way, Inc., 268 N.L.R.B. 394 (1983) [policy can refer to "worktime," but not to "work hours"].

216. NLRB v. Baptist Hosp., 442 U.S. 773 (1979).

217. Oakwood Hosp. v. NLRB, 983 F.2d 698 (6th Cir. 1993).

218. Fairfax Hosp. v. NLRB, 14 F.3d 594 (*without op.*), 1993 U.S. App. LEXIS 31,936 (4th Cir. 1993), *cert. denied*, 114 S. Ct. 2674 (U.S. 1994).

219. *E.g.*, Dacas Nursing Support Sys., v. NLRB, 7 F.3d 511 (6th Cir. 1993) [where union stipulated per diem nurses could vote, it could not object to inclusion of per diem nurse, so the NLRB erred in sustaining its objection to ballot; union did not prevail in ballot, so employer not required to bargain]; Indiana Hosp. v. NLRB, 10 F.3d 151 (3d Cir. 1993) [hospital asserted NLRB misconduct during election by giving misleading information to voters; NLRB denied hospital discovery of its records, NLRB certified union, so hospital refused to bargain; court found prejudice by denial of records, granted hospital's petition for review of NLRB order].

220. *E.g.*, Exxel/Atmos, Inc. v. NLRB, 307 U.S. App. D.C. 376, 28 F.3d 1243 [new president committed unfair labor practice by refusal to bargain with union that predecessor had voluntarily recognized within prior year], *reh'g denied (en banc)*, 308 U.S. App. D.C. 411, 37 F.3d 1538 (1994).

221. *E.g.*, Local 144 v. NLRB, 9 F.3d 218 (2d Cir. 1993).

222. *E.g.*, Staten Island Univ. Hosp. v. NLRB, 24 F.3d 450 (2d Cir. 1994).

223. *E.g.*, NLRB v. Hospital San Rafael, Inc., 42 F.3d 45 (1st Cir. 1994); United Steelworkers v. St. Gabriel's Hosp., 871 F. Supp. 335 (D. Minn. 1994) [state law requiring business purchaser to honor existing labor contract until expiration conflicts with federal labor law, so preempted; successor liability under federal law only if continuity of work force].

224. 29 U.S.C.A. § 158(d).

225. 29 U.S.C.A. § 183; 29 C.F.R. pt. 1420.

226. 29 U.S.C.A. § 158(g); *see also* NLRB v. Stationary Eng'rs, 746 F.2d 530 (9th Cir. 1984) [notice must specify date].

227. Metropolitan Med. Ctr. v. Richardville, 354 N.W.2d 867 (Minn. Ct. App. 1984).

228. Montefiore Hosp. v. NLRB, 621 F.2d 510 (2d Cir. 1980); *see also, e.g.*, East Chicago Rehab. Ctr., Inc. v. NLRB, 710 F.2d 397 (7th Cir. 1983), *cert. denied*, 465 U.S. 1065 (1984) [wildcat strike by 17 nurse's aides].

229. Memorandum from Dietz, Associate General Counsel, NLRB, to Siegel, Director, Region 31 (Sept. 2, 1977) [concerning cases No. 31-CC-820, -821, 31-CG-7, -8].

230. Flushing Hosp. v. Local 1199, 685 F. Supp. 55 (S.D. N.Y. 1988) [nursing attendant]; Brigham & Women's Hosp. v. Massachusetts Nurses Ass'n, 684 F. Supp. 1120 (D. Mass. 1988) [nurse].

231. AFSCME v. Illinois, 124 Ill. 2d 246, 529 N.E.2d 534 (1988).

232. United Paperworkers v. Misco, Inc., 484 U.S. 29 (1987).

233. State Univ. of N.Y. v. Young, 170 A.D.2d 510, 566 N.Y.S.2d 79 (2d Dep't 1991), *appeal denied*, 80 N.Y.2d 753, 587 N.Y.S.2d 905, 600 N.E.2d 632, *cert. denied*, 113 S. Ct. 815 (U.S. 1992).

234. Ohio Office of Collective Bargaining v. Ohio Civil Srvc. Employees Ass'n, 59 Ohio St. 3d 177, 572 N.E.2d 71 (1991).

235. Russell Mem. Hosp. Ass'n v. United Steelworkers, 720 F. Supp. 583 (E.D. Mich. 1989).

236. County of Hennepin v. Hennepin County Ass'n of Paramedics & Emergency Med. Technicians, 464 N.W.2d 578 (Minn. Ct. App. 1990).

237. *E.g.*, Fairview Southdale Hosp. v. Minnesota Nurses Ass'n, 943 F.2d 809 (8th Cir. 1991) [arbitrator did not exceed his authority in determining hospital could not terminate free parking without bargaining about termination despite contract silence on parking]; Trustees of Columbia Univ. v. Local 1199, 805 F. Supp. 216 (S.D. N.Y. 1992) [suit claiming breach of no-strike clause was dismissed, referred to arbitration under broad arbitration clause in contract, despite employer claim arbitration clause intended to apply only to employee grievances]; Clark

County Pub. Employees Ass'n v. Pearson, 106 Nev. 587, 798 P.2d 136 (1990) [elimination of nursing clinical ladder program subject to binding arbitration].

238. Luden's Inc. v. Local Union No. 6, 28 F.3d 347 (3d Cir. 1994).

239. 29 U.S.C.A. §§ 401–531; *see* International Union v. Dole, 276 U.S. App. D.C. 178, 869 F.2d 616 (1989) [scope of reportable activities defined].

240. *E.g.,* United Steelworkers v. St. Gabriel's Hosp., 871 F. Supp. 335 (D. Minn. 1994) [state law requiring business purchaser to honor existing labor contract until expiration conflicts with federal labor law, so preempted].

241. 29 U.S.C.A. §§ 101–111; *e.g.,* Modeste v. Local 1199, 38 F.3d 626 (2d Cir. 1994) [dismissal of suit against union for alleged intentional torts during strike; Norris-LaGuardia Act does not preempt state law requirement of showing liability of each member of union in order to hold union liable].

242. *E.g.,* District 1199E v. Johns Hopkins Hosp., 293 Md. 343, 444 A.2d 448 (1982).

243. *E.g., Alta Bates Medical Center nurses approve four-year contract,* 3 H.L.R. 925 (1994) [includes closed shop provision].

244. *E.g.,* Fla. Const. art. I, § 6.

245. 29 U.S.C.A. § 164(b).

246. Salih v. Lane, 244 Va. 436, 423 S.E.2d 192 (1992).

247. Agnew-Watson v. County of Alameda, 30 Cal. App. 4th 626, 36 Cal. Rptr. 2d 196 (1st Dist. 1994), *rev. denied & op. withdrawn,* 1995 Cal. LEXIS 1103 (1995) [not citable in Cal].

248. Selan v. Unemployment Comp. Bd., 495 Pa. 338, 433 A.2d 1337 (1981).

249. Porter v. Department of Employment Sec., 139 Vt. 405, 430 A.2d 450 (1981).

250. Montclair Nursing Ctr. v. Wills, 220 Neb. 547, 371 N.W.2d 121 (1985); *accord* Baptist Med. Ctr. v. Stolte, 475 So.2d 959 (Fla. 1st DCA 1985), *rev. denied,* 486 So.2d 598 (Fla. 1986) [nurse who refuses to accept offered 3–11 position is not "available for work" and, thus, ineligible for unemployment compensation].

251. Vinokurov v. Mt. Sinai Hosp., No. 88-3158U (Fla. Dep't of Labor & Employment Sec. Apr. 1, 1988); *see also* Gagliano, *When health care workers refuse to treat AIDS patients,* 21 J. HEALTH & HOSP. L. 255 (1988).

252. Holly v. Unemployment Compensation Bd. of Review, 151 Pa. Commw. 450, 617 A.2d 80 (1992), *appeal denied,* 534 Pa. 643, 626 A.2d 1160 (1993).

253. Fair v. St. Joseph's Hosp., 113 N.C. App. 159, 437 S.E.2d 875 (1993), *rev. denied,* 336 N.C. 315, 445 S.E.2d 394 (1994).

254. Clarke v. North Detroit Gen. Hosp., 437 Mich 280, 470 N.W.2d 393 (1991).

10

General Principles of Civil Liability

Everyone involved in health care delivery is acutely aware of the potential for patients or their families to make legal claims for money because of injuries they believe were caused by malpractice or other wrongful conduct. This chapter outlines liability principles and the legal process. A basic understanding of liability principles can help minimize claims and facilitate proper handling of claims.

Civil liability is the liability imposed other than through criminal law. Civil liability can be divided into liability that is based on contract, tort liability, and other liability that is based on governmental statutes and regulations. *Tort liability* is the liability that is imposed by the common law and some statutes for injuries caused by breaches of duties not based on contractual agreement. This chapter reviews contract law and then tort law. The review of tort law includes (1) the three basic types of tort liability—liability for intentional torts, liability for negligent torts, and strict liability; (2) the basis for personal and institutional liability; and (3) the range of attempts to reform tort law. Cases illustrating tort liability of hospitals and various staff members are surveyed in Chapter 11.

CONTRACTS

A *contract* is a legally enforceable agreement. Health care providers have many contracts involving all areas of operations, including employment contracts, contracts to purchase supplies and equipment, construction contracts, sales contracts, contracts to purchase services, leases, loans, and others. The primary purpose of a written contract is to set forth the agreement to facilitate compliance, not to prepare for litigation. All elements of contracts should be carefully thought through and clearly articulated. This section outlines some of the legal problems associated with contracts. The law of contracts is complex, and there are exceptions to these general rules, so contracts should be reviewed with the assistance of legal counsel. Health care administrators are expected to be sophisticated at business and will be bound by many disadvantageous contracts that might not be enforced for less sophisticated consumers.

Usually agreements to agree in the future are not enforceable. Generally there is no contract until the agreement itself is reached. However, sometimes courts find that a contract exists before the formal contract is signed, so administrators should be circumspect with promises, negotiations, correspondence, and letters of intent.

Some agreements are not enforceable. Courts usually require all participants, often called *parties*, to pay a price in order for a contract to exist and be binding. This price, called the *consideration* for the contract, can be an act, forbearance, change of legal relationship, or promise. When one party has not provided any consideration, the courts usually will not let that party enforce the contract. One exception is that most written sales contracts are enforceable against merchants without consideration because of state laws called the *Uniform Commercial Code* (UCC). Courts will not enforce many other contracts, such as illegal contracts, contracts that are viewed by the court as against public policy, oral contracts of the type the law requires to be written, and unconscionable contracts. The public policy rule was applied by a federal appellate court in 1994 to declare a contract with an unlicensed nursing agency unenforceable.[1] The agency could not sue to enforce the contract because it did not have the license required by state law. *Unconscionable contracts* are contracts that shock the conscience of the court, usually by being extortionate. Since courts usually apply the unconscionability doctrine to only consumer contracts, health care providers are seldom protected by the doctrine in dealings with other businesses. However, some contracts with patients, such as exculpatory contracts purporting to limit the patient's right to sue, could be found to be unconscionable and, thus, unenforceable.

Courts occasionally refuse to enforce part of an agreement. For example, courts will generally not enforce penalty provisions. Many contracts specify that if the agreement is found partly invalid, the remainder is still enforceable. This provision can create problems when the invalid portion was of central importance but it can also save advantageous arrangements when the invalid portion is less significant.

Courts tend to review only the words in the written contract by applying the *parol evidence rule*, under which oral promises made during negotiations that are not included in the final written agreement are assumed to have been negotiated away.[2] Health care providers cannot rely on oral statements made prior to signing a written contract. If these statements are important to the agreement, they should be in the written contract.

In some circumstances a court will add terms to contracts. First, when a written contract is ambiguous or missing critical elements, the court will sometimes consider testimony concerning oral understandings. The court will try to avoid this, but sometimes oral understandings must be considered. The court then must sift through the usually conflicting recollections of the parties and decide what to believe. Second, sometimes it is clear that no agreement, written or oral, was reached concerning critical elements, such as the delivery date. The court will sometimes fill these gaps with a provision the court considers to be reasonable. However, courts will not always fill the gaps, which forces the parties to solve the problem on their own. Third, the law will routinely imply some elements in contracts if an issue is not otherwise addressed. For example, the UCC specifies that certain sales contracts will be interpreted as having certain provisions unless the contract provides otherwise. One such provision is an *implied warranty of merchantability*, which means that the goods are fit for the ordinary purposes for which such goods are normally used. In addition, another provision is an *implied warranty of fitness for a particular use*, meaning that the goods are fit for the specific use the seller has reason to know the buyer intends for the goods. There are many exceptions to these warranties. One of the clearest is when the contract explicitly disclaims warranties. Courts will sometimes imply additional elements—for example, that the person signing the contract has the authority to do so. Administrators should be cautious about making promises or concessions, especially in writing. Other employees should be instructed not to sign documents without proper authority and review.

The purpose of the contract is to document plans for completing the agreement and for dealing with contingencies that preclude completion. As a last resort, litigation can be required to deal with breach of contract. The courts will compel performance of some contracts, such as contracts to transfer land or unique goods. Courts will also sometimes issue an injunction prohibiting another party from violating a restrictive covenant, such as an agreement not to compete or not to disclose a trade secret. However, in most situations the only remedy the court will award is money, called *damages*. When it will be difficult to calculate the damages from breach of a contract, the parties sometimes agree in advance what the amount of damages will be. This agreed amount is called *liquidated damages*. Although courts will usually not enforce contract provisions that are considered penalties, courts will frequently enforce liquidated damages provisions when the amounts are reasonable.

Contracts can address other issues concerning dispute resolution. They can specify which state's law will govern the contract and where litigation can be brought. Some contracts specify that disputes will be resolved by arbitration, rather than by court litigation.

There are several defenses to contract suits, including waiver and default. Sometimes courts interpret conduct of the parties, such as regular acceptance of late delivery without complaint, as implying a modification to the agreement, waiving rights under the agreement. The defense of default arises from the recognition that some promises are dependent on others and that some events must occur in a sequence. A party that fails to perform an earlier step in the sequence can be found to be in default, excusing the other parties from carrying out subsequent steps. Vendors sometimes claim that their delay is due to failure of the hospital to provide needed data or material. Sequences should be carefully structured so that this defense is available only when it is appropriate.

Sometimes courts will permit persons called *third party beneficiaries*, who are not parties to contracts, to enforce the part of the contract that affects them. Sometimes this is intended. For example, where a contract between a hospital and health maintenance organization (HMO) states that the hospital will not bill the patient even if the HMO does not pay, the patient generally can use that contract to oppose billing efforts by the hospital. Generally a third party beneficiary must take the limitations in the contract along with the benefits. In a 1988 Colorado case, a physician claimed to be a third party beneficiary to a hospital purchase contract. The court ruled that the claim had to be arbitrated under the arbitration clause in the contract because third party beneficiaries have to take the burdens with the benefits.[3]

One ambiguous area of the law is the extent to which relationships with governmental agencies are governed by contract law principles. In some areas, contract law principles are applied. In other areas, the government retains the power to make unilateral changes which a party to a private contract could not do. In some areas, the government claims that contract principles do not apply. For example, in 1994 a federal appellate court ruled that the relationship between the federal government and a physician in the National Health Service Corps is a statutory relationship, not a contractual relationship, so no contractual defenses were available.[4]

PROMISE TO CURE OR TO USE A CERTAIN PROCEDURE

Most malpractice suits against physicians, hospitals, and other health care providers are based on tort law, not on contract law. One type of malpractice case based on contract law is the claim that the physician promised a certain outcome that was not achieved. Absent a specific promise to cure, a physician is not an insurer of a particular outcome. However, if the physician is incautious enough to make a promise, the law will sometimes enforce it. One of the most publicized cases was *Guilmet v. Campbell*,[5] in which the Michigan Supreme Court upheld a jury finding that a physician had promised to cure a bleeding ulcer and on that basis imposed liability for the unsuccessful outcome even though the physician was not negligent in providing the care. The Michigan legislature later passed a law[6] making promises to cure unenforceable unless they are in writing, in effect overruling *Guilmet*. In states that do not have these laws, a consent form that disavows any assurance of results may provide protection from these claims.[7]

A breach of contract suit can also arise from failure to use a promised procedure. In a 1957 Michigan case, the patient had been promised that her child would be delivered by a cesarean operation.[8] The physician failed to arrange for the operation, and the baby was stillborn. The physician was found liable for breaking his promise to arrange for the operation.

In 1994, a New York appellate court ruled that when a physician orally agreed to deliver a baby for a Jehovah's Witness mother without using transfusions, obtaining a court order and giving a transfusion could constitute a breach of contract.[9]

Cases based on oral promises are unusual, but they demonstrate that physicians and other health care providers should be careful in what they say to patients so that their efforts to reassure do not become promises they cannot fulfill.

GENERAL PRINCIPLES OF TORT LIABILITY

A tort is a civil wrong that is not based on the violation of a contract. Tort liability is almost always based on fault; that is, something was done incorrectly or something that should have been done was omitted. This act or omission can be intentional or can result from negligence. In some exceptional circumstances there is strict liability for all consequences of certain activities regardless of fault.

INTENTIONAL TORTS

Intentional torts include assault and battery, defamation, false imprisonment, invasion of privacy, intentional infliction of emotional distress, malicious prosecution, and abuse of process.

Assault and Battery

An *assault* is an action that puts another person in apprehension of being touched in a manner that is offensive, insulting, provoking, or physically injurious without lawful authority or consent. No actual touching is required; the assault is the credible threat of being touched in this manner. If actual touching occurs, then the action is called *battery*. Liability for assault and battery compensates persons for violations of their right to be free from unconsented invasions of their person. Assault or battery can occur when medical treatment is attempted or performed without consent or lawful authority.[10] Assault or battery can occur in other circumstances, such as during attempts to restrain patients without lawful authority.

Defamation

Defamation is wrongful injury to a person's reputation. *Libel* is written defamation, and *slander* is spoken defamation. The defamatory statement must be communicated to a third person; a statement is not defamatory if made only to the person impugned. A defamation claim can arise from inappropriate release of inaccurate medical information or from untruthful statements about other staff members.

The defenses to a defamation claim include truth and privilege. A true statement is not defamatory even if it injures another's reputation. Some communications, although otherwise defamatory, are privileged because the law recognizes a higher duty to disclose the particular information to certain persons. Courts have recognized the importance of communicating information concerning a staff member's performance to appropriate supervisors and officials. Such communications are protected by a "qualified privilege" when they are made in good faith to persons who need to know. This protection means that liability will not be imposed for communications later proved to be false if they were made without malice. Malice is usually found when the communication was made with knowledge of its falsity or with reckless disregard of whether it was false. An example of the qualified privilege is a 1988 New York appellate court decision in which a hospital official's statements to other officials concerning a physician were found to be privileged.[11] Another example is a 1991 Ohio case resulting from a nurse's statements at a nursing technician's predisciplinary hearing.[12] The communication must be made within appropriate channels because discussions with others will not be protected by the qualified privilege. As discussed in Chapter 7, many states have enacted broader statutory privileges or immunities for participants in some peer review activities. These statutes may provide protection from some defamation claims. As discussed in Chapter 14, many states prohibit use of some peer review committee proceedings and reports in any civil suit, which in effect may make it impossible to pursue most defamation cases for statements within the peer review process.[13]

Many courts have also recognized a qualified privilege for assessments provided by a former employer to a prospective employer. For example, in 1979 a Michigan court found the director of a department of health not liable for providing a prospective employer with information concerning a former nursing employee's abilities.[14] The court ruled that the qualified privilege applied and that no malice had been shown. Most institutions do not release information regarding any former employee until they receive a written request signed by the former employee, so they do not need to rely on the court to decide that the qualified privilege applies. There still could be liability for untruthful information released with malice.

False Imprisonment

False imprisonment is the unlawful restriction of a person's freedom. Holding persons against their will by physical restraint, barriers, or even threats of harm can constitute false imprisonment if not legally justified. Claims of false imprisonment can arise from patients who are being detained inappropriately or from patients who are challenging their commitment for being mentally ill. Health care institutions generally have common law authority to detain patients who are disoriented. All states have a legal procedure to obtain authorization to detain some categories of persons who are mentally ill, engage in substance abuse, or are infected with contagious diseases. When patients are oriented, competent, and not legally committed, staff should avoid detaining them unless authorized by institutional policy or by an institutional administrator. There are few situations in which institutions are justified in authorizing detention of such patients.

Invasion of Privacy

Claims for *invasion of privacy* can arise from unauthorized release of information concerning patients. Not all releases of information violate the right of privacy. For example, in 1982 the Minnesota Supreme Court found that even though the patient had requested that information not be released, it was not an invasion of privacy to disclose orally that the patient had been discharged from the hospital and that she had given birth when the information was disclosed in response to a direct inquiry concerning that patient at a time near her stay in the hospital.[15] However, laws and regulations in some states may not permit this disclosure. The better practice would be to attempt to avoid release of discharge and birth information when the patient requests nondisclosure.

Sometimes information such as a child abuse or contagious disease report is required to be disclosed by law. These disclosures (discussed in Chapter 14) are not an invasion of privacy because they are legally authorized. Institutional policies concerning confidentiality should be followed; some courts will impose liability for failure to follow institutional rules. One exception to the general rule permitting disclosure of admission and discharge information concerns information about substance abusers. With few exceptions, federal regulations[16] prohibit disclosure of information concerning patients being treated for substance abuse or related conditions. Disclosing whether the patient is in the institution is also prohibited. Staff who are involved with substance abusers should be familiar with these regulations and know how to comply with them. They are discussed in more detail in Chapter 14.

Intentional Infliction of Emotional Distress

Intentional infliction of emotional distress is another intentional tort that includes outrageous conduct causing emotional trauma. This tort is easy to avoid by remembering to treat patients and their families in a civilized fashion, but such treatment was apparently forgotten in the following examples of this tort.

In a 1988 Kentucky case, a nurse intentionally deactivated a patient's bedside buzzer.[17] In a 1975 Tennessee case, a hospital staff member gave a woman the body of her newborn baby preserved in a jar of formaldehyde.[18] In a 1973 Ohio case, a physician sent repeated checkup reminders to a deceased patient's family who had sued him for malpractice in her death.[19]

Malicious Prosecution and Abuse of Process

Some unjustifiable or harassing litigation and other misuses of the legal system constitute intentional torts, called *malicious prosecution* and *abuse of process*, respectively.

A plaintiff alleging malicious prosecution must prove that (1) the other person filed a suit against the plaintiff, (2) the suit ended in favor of the plaintiff, (3) there was no probable cause for filing the suit, and (4) the other person filed the suit because of malice. In 1995, a Michigan appellate court found Blue Cross liable for malicious prosecution of a provider.[20] Blue Cross initiated prosecution of the provider for billing as a technician surgical assistant in violation of a 1979 physician manual provision. Its investigator knew the provision no longer applied because it had been deleted in 1984. Blue Cross did not tell state law enforcement authorities that the provision no longer applied. However, absent such egregious circumstances, claims of malicious prosecution are seldom successful.[21] In 1990, a New York court found that a hospital had not committed malicious prosecution by having a patient's son arrested for criminal trespass after he became disruptive. Dismissal of the prosecution by the prosecutor in the interest of justice did not constitute the suit ending in favor of the son, so the second requirement for a malicious prosecution suit was not met.[22]

A plaintiff alleging abuse of process must prove that (1) a legal process (e.g., notice of suit, subpoena, notice of deposition, or garnishment) was used against the plaintiff, (2) the use was primarily to accomplish a purpose for which it was not designed, and (3) the plaintiff was harmed by this misuse. Abuse of process actions are rarely successful.

Some physicians who have successfully defended malpractice suits have sued the patient and the patient's attorney for malicious prosecution. Generally, public policy favors giving people an opportunity to present their cases to the courts for redress of wrongs, so the law protects them when they act in good faith upon reasonable grounds in commencing either a civil or a criminal suit. Thus, few countersuits have been successful.[23]

NEGLIGENT TORTS

The most frequent basis for liability of health care professionals and institutions is the negligent tort. Fortunately, negligence by itself is not enough to establish liability. The negligence must cause an injury. Four elements must be proved to establish liability for negligent torts: (1) duty (what should have been done); (2) breach of duty (deviation from what should have been done); (3) injury; and (4) causation (injury directly and legally caused by the deviation from what should have been done).

There is a "fifth element" that the courts do not discuss, but that health care providers should remember: someone must be willing to make a claim. Health care providers who maintain good relationships with their patients before and after incidents are less likely to be sued. If a staff member suspects that an incident has occurred, the persons responsible for institutional risk management should be notified promptly so that steps can be taken to minimize the chance of a claim.

Duty

The first element that must be proved in any negligence suit is the *duty*. Duty has two aspects. First, it must be proved that a duty was owed to the person harmed. Second, the scope of that duty, sometimes called the *standard of care*, must be proved.

In general the common law does not impose a duty on individuals to come to the rescue of persons for whom they have no other responsibility.[24] Under the common law rule, a person walking down the street has no legal obligation to come to the aid of a heart attack victim unless (1) the victim is the person's dependent; (2) the person contributed to the cause of the heart attack; (3) the person owns or operates the premises where the attack occurred; or (4) the person has a contractual obligation to come to the victim's aid, for example, by being on duty as a member of a public emergency care team. In most health care cases it is not difficult to establish a duty based on the patient's admission to the institution or relationship with the individual practitioner. When a person is denied admission, there may be a question whether a duty was ever created. This issue is discussed in Chapter 12.

Complex questions can arise concerning when there are duties to third parties. For example, the Illinois Supreme Court ruled in 1990 that a hospital had no duty to a nonpatient bystander in the emergency room unless the person had been invited to participate in the treatment.[25] In 1993, an Oregon appellate court ruled that the entity that negligently prescribed the drug Xanax could be liable for the death of two children in an automobile accident with a driver under the influence of the drug.[26]

After existence of a duty is established, the scope of the duty must be established. This aspect is sometimes called the obligation to conform to the standard of care. The standard of care for health care institutions is usually the degree of reasonable care the patient's known or apparent condition requires. Some states extend the standard to include the reasonable care required for conditions the institution should have discovered through exercise of reasonable care. Usually the standard for individual health care professionals is what a reasonably prudent health care professional engaged in a similar practice would have done under similar circumstances. A judge or jury will make the determination based on one or more of the following: (1) expert testimony, (2) common sense, or (3) written standards.

In 1994, the California Supreme Court decided an important case that concluded that in California there is no difference between professional and ordinary negligence.[27] It is not yet clear what the effect of this will be on liability determinations in California.

Expert Testimony

The technical aspects of care must be proved through expert testimony, usually by other health professionals. As part of tort reform, some states have limited who may testify as experts.[28] Sometimes the health care provider's out-of-court statements can be used against the provider as an admission, so caution must be exercised in what is said or written after an incident.[29]

Common Sense

Nontechnical aspects of care can be proved by nonexperts. Some courts will permit juries to use their own knowledge and common sense when the duty is considered common knowledge. For example, some courts consider protecting a disoriented patient from falling to be a nontechnical aspect.[30] In 1992, a Texas court ruled that expert testimony was not required to establish negligence in assigning a nurse to duty where evaluation forms disclosed unsatisfactory performance including sleeping on the job.[31]

Written Standards

Some courts will look to written standards, such as licensure regulations, accreditation standards, and institutional rules, to determine the duty. Courts have permitted these written standards to be used in three ways: (1) as evidence the jury can consider in determining the standard of care without any supporting expert testimony[32]; (2) as evidence the jury can consider in determining the standard of care, but only if there is also expert testimony confirming that the published standard states the actual standard of care[33]; and (3) as presumptively the standard of care the jury must accept unless the defendant can prove otherwise.[34]

Accreditation standards have been used to establish the standard of care for accredited hospitals. For example, a Texas court found a hospital liable for injuries due to failure to employ a licensed pharmacist. Joint Commission on the Accreditation of Healthcare Organizations (Joint Commission) standards that required a licensed pharmacist were used to establish the standard of care.[35]

Institutional rules and policies can also be used to establish the standard of care. For example, in 1975 the highest court of New York ruled that the hospital could be liable for injuries due to failure to raise the patient's bedrails when the hospital had a rule requiring bedrails to be raised for all patients over the age of 50.[36] Thus, it is important for staff members to be familiar with and act in compliance with the institutional rules and policies applicable to their areas of practice. If the rules are impossible to follow, steps should be taken to modify them instead of ignoring them.

Eliminating all rules is not a solution because failure to adopt necessary rules can be a violation of the standard of care. In Michigan a hospital was found liable for an infection transmitted by a transplanted cornea because the hospital did not have a procedure to assure that the relevant medical records of the proposed donor were reviewed prior to the transplant.[37] In 1990, a federal court found that failure to have procedures for determining if products had been recalled was an administrative issue that did not require expert testimony.[38]

The development of medical practice guidelines, practice parameters, clinical protocols, and other guidelines for clinical decision making has introduced a new dimension to the role of written standards.[39] Maine has led in the experimentation with these guidelines as a way to reduce medical malpractice claims,[40] but the effects on medical malpractice cases are still inconclusive.[41] The goal is for compliance with the guidelines to preclude suits or assure their successful defense. At least one medical society-sponsored insurer is requiring compliance with guidelines by its insured physicians.[42] Others are developing guidelines for a variety of purposes,[43] including the promotion of more efficient practice.[44] Physicians have expressed concerns that guidelines are of varying quality, are sometimes contradictory, and may not be sufficiently sophisticated to deal with complex situations. Medical groups are developing processes to assess guidelines.[45] Some studies indicate that guidelines can help physicians to avoid selecting traditional tests or treatments that are ineffective.[46] Efforts to stop the release of guidelines have generally been unsuccessful.[47] In 1994, one state medical society challenged the process that a managed care entity was using for development of guidelines and was able to reach an agreement for more medical society input.[48]

Negligence Per Se

Statutes or governmental regulations can be used to establish the standard of care. When a law requires an action in order to benefit other individuals or forbids an action in order to protect others, a violation is generally considered *negligence per se*. An individual who is harmed by a violation need only prove (1) the law was intended to benefit the class of persons of which the individual is a member, (2) the law was violated, (3) the injury is of the type the law was intended to prevent, and

(4) the injury was caused by the violation. Some states limit the defenses that may be used.[49] A Maryland court found a hospital liable for injuries that resulted from failure to comply with a hospital licensing regulation requiring segregation of sterile and nonsterile needles.[50] The patient had a liver biopsy with a needle that was suspected to be nonsterile, requiring postponement of other therapy and immediate treatment to prevent infection from the needle. This was the type of patient and harm the regulation was designed to address.

Respected Minority Rule

The proof of what should have been done can become confused when there are two or more professionally accepted approaches. The *respected minority* or *two schools of thought* rule addresses this situation. If a health professional follows the approach used by a respected minority of the profession, then the duty is to follow that approach properly. Liability cannot be based on the decision not to follow the majority approach.[51] In 1992, the Pennsylvania Supreme Court limited the use of the doctrine to situations where the alternative has been adopted by a considerable number of respected physicians.[52]

Since part of the informed consent process is the disclosure of alternative treatments, the physician generally should disclose the alternative treatment to the patient before pursuing a minority approach. Failure to disclose the alternative majority approach could result in liability under the informed consent doctrine discussed in Chapter 13.

Locality Rule

In the past some courts limited the standard of care of health care institutions and professionals to the practice in the same or similar communities. Under this locality rule, experts testifying on the standard of care had to be from the same or similar communities. The rule was designed to avoid finding rural providers liable for not following the practices of urban medical centers. The rule sometimes made it difficult to obtain expert testimony. Most courts have abandoned the rule, so that any experts generally can testify if they are familiar with the relevant standard of care. The jury is usually permitted to consider the expert's degree of familiarity with the community in deciding what weight to give the testimony.

Several states as part of their tort reform efforts have enacted statutes that have reinstated some aspects of the locality rule, restricting which physicians may testify as experts.[53]

Legally Imposed Standards

Courts sometimes impose a more stringent legal standard not previously recognized by the profession when they find the professional standards to be deficient. For example, in 1974 the Washington Supreme Court established a legal standard that glaucoma tests must be given to all ophthalmology patients, although the universal practice of ophthalmologists was to administer such tests to only patients over age 40 and to patients with possible symptoms of glaucoma.[54] The court disregarded the evidence that so few cases would be discovered that expanded testing would not be cost effective. The court found the ophthalmologist liable for failing to administer the test to a patient under age 40 with no symptoms of glaucoma. In another case, in which a woman was killed by a psychiatric patient, the California Supreme Court found liability for the psychiatrist's failure to warn the woman that his patient had threatened to kill her, even though other psychiatrists would have acted in the same manner.[55]

The national standard of peer review of physicians in hospitals was changed by a 1973 California trial court decision.[56] A hospital was found liable for injuries resulting from treatment provided by an independent staff physician because the hospital had not made use of available information that would have alerted it to the surgeon's propensity to commit malpractice. The hospital met all of the Joint Commission standards in effect at the time the patient was injured, but the court ruled that the hospital should have had a better system of becoming aware of available information and acting on it.

Breach of Duty

After the duty is proved, the second element that must be proved is the breach of this duty—that is, a deviation in some manner from the standard of care. Something was done that should not have been done, or something was not done that should have been done.

Injury

The third element of the proof of negligence is injury. The person making the claim must demonstrate physical, financial, or emotional injury. In many malpractice cases, the existence of the injury is very clear by the time of the suit, although there still may be disagreement concerning the dollar value of the injury.

Most courts allow suits based solely on negligently inflicted emotional injuries only in limited situations. These injuries usually are compensated only when they accompany physical injuries. Intentional infliction of emotional injury is generally compensated without proof of physical injury. Negligently inflicted emotional injuries are sometimes compensable without accompanying physical injuries. For example, compensation is available in some states when the plaintiff was in the "zone of danger" created by the defendant's negligence—that is, when the plaintiff was actually exposed to risk of injury. A few states also compensate plaintiffs who witness injury to close relatives. A California court permitted a father to sue for his emotional injuries from being present in the delivery room when his wife died and from placing his hands on her body after her death and feeling the unborn child die.[57] There is a trend toward compensation for negligently inflicted emotional injuries without requiring physical injury.

This issue has been presented in several cases where persons either have been exposed to HIV infection without evidence of having been infected or have been erroneously told that they have AIDS or are HIV-positive. Courts have reached different conclusions on whether such persons have a compensable injury.[58]

Causation

The fourth element is causation. The breach of duty must be proved to have legally caused the injury. For example, a treatment may be negligently administered (which is a breach of duty), and the patient may die (which is an injury), but the person suing must still prove a substantial likelihood that the patient would have lived if the treatment had been administered properly. Causation is often the most difficult element to prove.[59]

Another example is a Texas case concerning a nurse who gave a patient solid food immediately after colon surgery (which is a breach of duty), and eight days later the ends of the sutured colon came apart (which is an injury).[60] Because of the time lag, the patient was not able to prove causation. Causation can be proved in many cases, as illustrated by an Iowa case involving a baby born with Rh blood incompatibility.[61] An outdated reagent was used for blood tests for bilirubin, so the tests erroneously indicated a safe level. When the error was discovered, the high bilirubin level had caused severe permanent brain damage. The hospital and pathologists were liable because accurate tests would have led to timely therapy that probably would have prevented brain damage.

Some courts have adopted a new standard of causation, the *loss of chance* of recovery, that makes it easier for plaintiffs to win suits.[62] Under this standard the plaintiff need only show that the breach of the standard led to a loss of chance of recovery, rather than that the breach caused the injury. Other courts have rejected this change, retaining the traditional proximate cause standard.[63] Virginia has adopted a hybrid approach under which a showing of loss of a substantial possibility of survival is sufficient to create a jury question, but the jury must be instructed using the traditional proximate cause instruction.[64]

Sometimes subsequent providers' errors can break the chain of causation.[65] A New York case arose from the suicide of a patient after a transfer.[66] The referring hospital breached its duty by failing to note the patient's suicidal tendencies in the transfer documents sent with the patient. The referring hospital avoided liability because the receiving hospital did not look at the transfer documents until after the patient was discharged. Thus, the transferring hospital's breach had no impact on the outcome.

In 1993, the U.S. Supreme Court established a stricter standard for the admissibility of scientific testimony on causation.[67] This has made it more difficult to pursue products liability suits claiming that products caused adverse conditions.[68]

Res Ipsa Loquitur

One exception to the requirement that the four elements be proved is the doctrine of *res ipsa loquitur*, "the thing speaks for itself." The doctrine was created in an 1863 English case that arose from a barrel flying out of an upper story window and smashing a pedestrian.[69] When the pedestrian tried to sue the building owner, the owner claimed that the four elements had to be proved. The pedestrian could not find out what went wrong in the building, so the case would have been lost. The court ruled that there should be liability when someone has clearly done something wrong, so the court developed the *res ipsa loquitur* doctrine.

The doctrine applies when the following elements can be proved:

1. the accident is of a kind that does not happen without negligence,[70]
2. the apparent cause is in the exclusive control of the defendants,
3. the person suing could not have contributed to the difficulties,
4. evidence of the true cause is inaccessible to the person suing, and
5. the fact of injury is evident.

Courts have frequently applied this rule to two types of malpractice cases: (1) sponges and other foreign objects unintentionally left in the body[71] and (2) injuries to parts of the body distant from the site of treatment, such as nerve damage to a hand during a hysterectomy.[72] Some courts have extended the applicability of the rule to some other types of malpractice cases.[73] Liability is not automatic in these cases. The defendants are permitted to explain why the injury was not the result of negligence.[74] For example, a physician could establish the absence of negligence by proving the sponge was left in the body because the patient had to be closed quickly on an emergency basis to save the patient's life and there was no time for a sponge count. The evidence necessary to avoid liability varies among states because of variation in the degree to which the burden of proof shifts to the defendant in *res ipsa loquitur* cases.

Defenses

Res Judicata and Collateral Estoppel

As discussed in Chapter 1, sometimes lawsuits are barred by the fact that they deal with matters that have been litigated before. For example, in 1992 a Maryland court ruled that a physician's unsuccessful defamation suit against a hospital barred a new suit against nurses for the same conduct.[75] In 1994, the Ohio Supreme Court ruled that a successful malpractice claim during life does not bar a wrongful death claim after death.[76]

Statute of Limitations

All states have laws called *statutes of limitations,* which limit the time in which suits may be filed. Suits are barred after the time has expired. The time limit varies depending on the nature of the suit and the applicable state law. States have adopted different definitions of when the time starts, including (1) the time the incident occurs,[77] (2) the time the injury is discovered,[78] (3) the time the cause of the injury is or should have been discovered, and (4) the time the patient ceases receiving care from the negligent provider.[79] Some courts have had trouble accepting formulas that can result in the claim being cut off before the potential plaintiff is aware of the injury,[80] but other courts have accepted this result.[81]

The rules are complicated in many states. For example, in Florida, medical malpractice cases must be filed within two years from when the incident should have been discovered, but no more than four years after the incident unless fraudulent concealment or intentional misrepresentation by the provider prevents discovery within the four years, which extends the time to within two years from when the incident should have been discovered, but no more than seven years after the incident.[82] Other states extend the time when there is fraudulent concealment or intentional misrepresentation.[83]

The time limit can be quite long, especially for injuries to children. In many states the time period for suits by minors does not start until they become adults.[84] This means that suits arising out of care of newborns may be filed 18 or more years later.

Immunity

Sovereign immunity, charitable immunity, and various statutory immunities may be available in some situations.

Governmental health care institutions are generally protected by *sovereign immunity* and cannot be sued unless the immunity has been waived. Some state courts have ruled that only governmental functions, not proprietary functions, are protected by sovereign immunity. Most courts have ruled that governmental hospitals are governmental functions.[85]

The federal government and many states have enacted laws, usually called *tort claims acts,* that partially waive sovereign immunity and permit claims against governmental entities, but only if certain procedures are followed. These laws often also place limits on the liability.[86] If a governmental hospital purchases liability insurance or establishes a liability trust fund, most courts find that sovereign immunity is waived to the extent of the insurance or trust fund.[87] In 1991, a Minnesota court decided that the waiver applied even when the insurer was insolvent and unable to pay, but the Minnesota Supreme Court reversed the decision, limiting the waiver to collectible insurance.[88] In some states, sovereign immunity also protects employees.[89]

As discussed in Chapter 1, the common law doctrine of *charitable immunity* has been overruled by nearly all courts. However, a few states have reestablished some charitable immunity by statute.[90] This charitable immunity is generally waived to the extent of any liability insurance.[91]

Some states have extended statutory immunity to other activities. Good Samaritan laws that protect some emergency services are an example. In a few states these laws also protect physicians who provide some emergency care in hospitals.[92]

Release

Another defense is release. When a claim is settled, the claimant usually signs a release. When a release has been signed, it will generally bar a future suit based on the same incident. Sometimes release of one defendant will release other defendants. In 1994, a Maryland court ruled that release of a pathologist released the hospital.[93]

In the past some courts permitted so-called "Mary Carter" agreements where a settling defendant retained a financial interest in the plaintiff's recovery and remained a party in the trial. In 1992–93, the Texas and Florida Supreme Courts declared such agreements to be void as violations of public policy.[94]

Exculpatory Contract

An exculpatory contract is an agreement not to sue or an agreement to limit the amount of the suit. This is different from a release because it is signed before the care is provided. While some courts will enforce these agreements in other contexts,[95] they have consistently refused to enforce these contracts concerning health care services on the grounds that such contracts are against public policy.[96]

Arbitration Agreement

In some states, a patient can sign a valid agreement to arbitrate any claims, instead of taking them to court, as long as the agreement does not place other limits on the claim. If a patient has signed a valid agreement to arbitrate, courts will generally refuse to accept the case except for limited review of the completed arbitration process. However, in 1995 the Supreme Court ruled that, unless the parties clearly agree to arbitrate the scope of the arbitration, courts should determine whether the parties agree to arbitrate the issues in dispute.[97] Arbitration agreements concerning health care are discussed in the tort reform section of this chapter.

In many states, arbitration agreements with employees, vendors, and others concerning contract issues are generally enforceable.[98] When a contract involves interstate commerce, federal law provides for enforcement of such arbitration agreements, preempting contrary state law.[99]

Contributory Negligence

When the patient does something wrong that contributes to the injury to such a degree that the health care provider is not responsible for the damage, the patient is said to be contributorily negligent. This is a defense to a claim of a negligent tort in some states. Examples of contributory negligence include the following:

1. the patient fails to follow clear orders and does not return for follow-up care,[100]
2. the patient fails to seek follow-up care when the patient knows of or suspects a problem,[101]
3. the patient walks on a broken leg,[102]
4. the patient gets out of bed and falls,[103]
5. the patient lights a cigarette in bed when unattended,[104]
6. the patient deliberately gives false information that leads to the wrong antidote being given for a drug overdose,[105] and
7. the patient refuses to take antibiotics during the hospital admission.[106]

The success of this defense depends on the intelligence and degree of orientation of the patient. A patient who does not appear able to follow orders cannot be relied on to follow orders, so contributory negligence is not a successful defense against a claim by such a patient.[107]

Comparative Negligence

A majority of the states have abandoned the all-or-nothing contributory negligence rule. Instead, they apply comparative negligence, which means that the percentage of the cause due to the patient is determined and the patient does not collect that percentage of the total amount of the injury. Some states that have adopted the comparative negligence rule have retained one feature of the contributory negligence rule, so the patient cannot collect anything if the patient is determined to be responsible for 50 percent or more of the cause.[108] While the majority rule is that negligent actions cannot be used to reduce liability for intentional torts,[109] there are cases where such a comparison has been permitted.[110]

BREACH OF IMPLIED WARRANTIES AND STRICT LIABILITY

The major exception to the requirement that liability be based on fault occurs when liability is based on breach of implied warranties or on strict liability in tort. In this area of the law, liability based on contract and liability based on tort overlap. The implied warranties of merchantability and fitness for a particular use are based on contract and are discussed in the section of this chapter on con-tracts.[111] These warranties form the basis for finding liability without fault for many of the injuries caused by the use of goods and products. Normally the seller is liable for the breach of the warranties, but in some situations persons who lease products to others have also been found liable.

Strict liability applies to injuries caused by the use of a product that is unreasonably dangerous to a consumer or user and that reaches the user without substantial change from the condition in which it was sold. Usually the manufac-turer or seller of the product is liable. Strict liability in tort does not require a contractual relationship between the seller and the person injured to establish the liability of the seller. Some courts have extended strict liability to persons who furnish goods or products without a sale. Health care providers are generally considered to be providing services, not selling or furnishing products, so health care providers have seldom been found liable for breach of warranties or strict liability. However, plaintiffs have made numerous efforts to convince courts to apply these principles to make it easier to establish liability. These efforts have arisen out of services involving blood transfusions, drugs, radiation, and medical devices.

Blood Transfusions

One known risk of a blood transfusion is the transmission of diseases such as serum hepatitis. In 1954, a New York court ruled that blood transfusions were a service, not a sale, so that hospital liability for diseases conveyed by the blood could not be based on breach of warranties or strict liability.[112] However, courts in several other states began applying these product liability principles to blood transfusions.[113] Legislatures in nearly all states enacted statutes intended to reverse these court decisions.[114] Some of the statutes state that providing blood is a service, not a sale. Other statutes expressly forbid liability based on implied warranty or strict liability. The second type of statute provides somewhat greater protection because a court that chooses to ignore the public policy decisions of the legislature embodied in the first type of statute could still impose liability on the hospital by extending the applicability of strict liability to services. These immu-nity statutes have been found constitutional.[115] Health care providers can still be liable for negligence in administering blood transfusions. Immunity statutes in many states also apply to some other services, such as tissue transplantation.

Drugs

Efforts to use implied warranties or strict liability to impose liability on health care providers for the administration of drugs have generally been unsuccessful. For example, a Texas appellate court refused to apply these product liability principles to the administration of a contaminated drug.[116] In 1992, a Pennsylvania court ruled that a hospital was not a merchant when it dispensed a drug incidental to the service of healing, so it was not liable under implied warranties for an allergic reaction.[117]

Radiation

In 1980 the Illinois Supreme Court reversed a lower court's application of strict liability principles to X-ray treatment.[118] The court ruled that the issue in the case was the decision to use a certain dosage. The X-rays themselves were not a defective product, so strict liability in tort was not applicable.

Medical Devices

Most courts have not applied implied warranties or strict liability in tort to health care providers for injuries due to medical devices.[119] For example, a California court ruled that the hospital was the user, not the supplier, of a surgical needle that broke during an operation.[120] Similarly, in 1994 an Indiana court ruled that products liability law does not apply to a hospital where a pacemaker is implanted.[121] However, this position is not unanimous. In 1984, the Alabama Supreme Court ruled that a hospital was liable based on the implied warranty of fitness for intended use when a suturing needle broke and remained in a patient's body.[122] The court viewed the hospital as a merchant, not a user. In 1994, a Missouri court ruled that a hospital could be sued based on strict liability for a defective jaw implant.[123] Even when the health care provider is viewed as only a user, the provider may still be liable based on negligence, and the manufacturer of the equipment may be liable based on implied warranties or strict liability in tort.

Some courts may not view certain items supplied by health care providers as integral to the provider's service. In 1981, a Texas court found that a hospital could be strictly liable for supplying a hospital gown that was not flame-retardant because the gown was not integrally related to supplying services.[124]

Some implied warranty and strict liability claims concerning medical devices are preempted by the federal medical device laws.[125] Courts disagree on the scope of the preemption. Some courts have limited the preemption to issues for which the Food and Drug Administration (FDA) had adopted regulations.[126]

PAYMENT OF AWARD

When a judgment is entered against a health care provider, the provider should either make arrangements to pay the award or take appropriate steps to prohibit collection of the award during appeals. Otherwise, traditional means of collecting debts may be used against the provider. In 1989, an attorney who had won a $1.7 million malpractice award against a hospital and had not been paid arranged for police to seize computers, desks, and other hospital property not involved in direct patient care. After the property was loaded on trucks, the hospital promptly paid.[127]

WHO IS LIABLE?

Liability can be divided into personal liability, liability for employees and agents, and institutional liability. Individual staff members are personally liable for consequences of their own acts. Individual liability is nearly always based on the principle of fault. To be liable, the person must have done something wrong or must have failed to do something he or she should have done. Employers can be liable for the consequences of the job-related acts of their employees or agents even when the employer is not at fault personally. Institutions can also be liable for the consequences of breaches of duties owed directly to patients and others, such as the duties to maintain buildings, grounds, and equipment and select and supervise employees and medical staff.

Respondeat Superior

Employers are liable for the consequences of their employees' activities within the course of employment for which the employee is liable. This legal doctrine is called *respondeat superior*, which means "let the master answer." The employer need not have done anything wrong. For example, if a nurse employed by a hospital injures a patient by giving the wrong medication, the hospital can be liable even if the nurse was properly selected, properly trained, and properly assigned the responsibility.

The supervisor is not the employer. *Respondeat superior* does not impose liability on the supervisor. Supervisors are liable only for the consequences of their own acts or omissions. The employer can also be liable for those acts or omissions under *respondeat superior*.

This employer liability is for the benefit of the injured person, not for the benefit of the employee. The employer does not have to provide the employee with liability protection. *Respondeat superior* permits the plaintiff to sue the employer, the employee, or both. If the employee is individually sued and found liable, the employee must pay. If, as often occurs, the employee is not individually sued, then the employer must pay. The employer may sue the employee to get the money back.[128] The repayment is called *indemnification*. As part of settlements, hospitals sometimes assign their right of indemnity against physicians or others to the plaintiff.[129] However, indemnification is seldom sought except from employees with substantial insurance.

Many employers provide individual liability protection for their employees. Some governmental employers are required to provide employees with liability protection. Some employers choose to provide liability protection through self-insurance. Before deciding what additional protection, if any, to obtain, an employee should determine the coverage provided by the employer. Most employers who provide liability protection cover only job-related activities, so some employees elect to purchase coverage for outside activities not covered by institutional insurance arrangements.

Employers are liable under *respondeat superior* only for actions of employees within the scope of their employment. Courts differ on what acts are within the scope of employment. Many courts follow the rule that intentional torts are not within *respondeat superior* unless the employee is acting in the furtherance, no matter how misguided, of the employer's business.[130] In 1993, a Georgia court ruled that a hospital was not liable for the lethal injection of five patients by a nurse employee because the nurse was pursuing her own interests.[131] In 1994, a federal court ruled that an employing physician was not liable for the disclosure of confidential medical information by a nurse and her daughter nurse assistant where they were not authorized to make the disclosure and did not make it in work time or space.[132] Courts disagree on when an employer is liable for sexual misconduct by employees.[133]

Borrowed Servant and Dual Servant

In some situations health care providers may not be liable for the consequences of the negligent acts of nurses and other employees because of the *borrowed servant doctrine*. In some states, when an employer delegates its right to direct and control the activities of an employee to an independent staff physician who assumes responsibility, the employee becomes a borrowed servant. The physician, rather than the employer, is then liable under *respondeat superior* for the acts of the employee.[134] Courts in many states do not apply the doctrine when an employee continues to receive substantial direction from the employer through its policies and rules. Thus, the trend appears to be toward abandoning the borrowed servant doctrine[135] or replacing it with a *dual servant doctrine* under which both the physician and the employer are liable under *respondeat superior* for the acts of the employee.[136]

Physician-Employees and Agents

Usually hospitals and other health care institutions are not liable for the negligent acts of independent staff physicians.[137] When the physician is an employee of the hospital, the hospital can be liable under *respondeat superior* for the physician's acts. The trend is for courts to find more hospital-physician relationships to be employment relationships. The criteria for finding an employment relationship focus on whether the hospital has a right to control the time, manner, and method of the physician's work. Some courts require significant control to find an employment relationship. For example, a Georgia appellate court declined to find an emergency room physician to be an employee despite scheduling, billing, and other control features of the agreement between the physician and the hospital.[138] The court focused on the contract provision that the hospital would exercise no control over the physician's methods of running the emergency room. However, other courts are more liberal in applying the criteria. For example, an Arizona court found a hospital to be the employer of a nonsalaried radiologist, based on the hospital's legal right to control the professional performance of medical staff members, the exclusiveness of the contract, the hospital's role as billing agent, and the patient's lack of choice in selecting a radiologist.[139] The court declined to be bound by a statement in the hospital admission form, signed by the patient, acknowledging that the radiologist was an independent contractor and not a hospital employee.

Even when a court finds a physician not to be an employee, it may still find the hospital liable for the physician's acts on the basis of agency, apparent agency, or enterprise liability.

Agency

Hospitals and other health care institutions can be held liable for the consequences of their agents' acts in a fashion similar to their being held liable for their employees' acts. For example, a federal district court found a hospital liable for a radiologist's negligence in not promptly relaying to the treating physician the results of an X-ray examination.[140] The court ruled that prompt reporting was an administrative responsibility and that the physician was functioning as an agent of the hospital when relaying the report.

Partners are considered agents of each other, so partners are liable for the torts committed by other partners in carrying out partnership activities. A *joint venture* is a kind of partnership. Health care institutions are liable for actions of physicians within the scope of partnerships or joint ventures with those physicians. In 1987, a Florida appellate court expanded the definition of joint venture to include a hospital contract with an anesthesiologist, imposing liability on the hospital for the anesthesiologist's malpractice.[141]

Apparent or Ostensible Agency

Some courts refuse to examine the details of the hospital-physician relationship. Instead they consider how the relationship appears to patients. If the hospital appears to be offering physician services, the physician is considered a hospital agent under the doctrine of apparent or ostensible agency. For example, the Michigan Supreme Court found a physician to be the hospital's ostensible agent because the patient did not have a patient-physician relationship with the physician independent of the hospital setting.[142] The physician, who was a member of the medical staff, had assisted in the patient's treatment. The court ruled that there was sufficient evidence that the hospital had appeared to provide the physician for the patient. The court noted that there was no evidence that the patient had been given any notice that the physician was an independent contractor. Thus, hospitals may find it helpful to give patients notice.[143] However, even signed acknowledgments may not be sufficient in some states.[144]

Some hospitals address their liability exposure for physicians' actions by including in physician contracts "hold harmless" clauses in which the physician agrees to indemnify the hospital for such losses. These clauses do not bar patients from collecting from the hospital, but they provide a basis for seeking reimbursement from physicians and their insurers.

Institutional Liability

Institutions can be liable for the consequences of breaches of duties owed directly to the patient.[145] Two examples of these duties—the maintenance of building and grounds and the selection and maintenance of equipment—are discussed in Chapter 11. Proper selection and supervision of employees is a third duty, discussed in Chapters 8 and 9. Proper selecting and monitoring of medical staff are increasingly being recognized as institutional duties. They are discussed in Chapters 7 and 8.

In 1978, a Washington appellate court imposed another form of institutional liability. A hospital was found liable for the treatment provided in an emergency room by an independent professional corporation because the emergency services were an *inherent function* of the hospital's overall enterprise for which the hospital bears some responsibility.[146] Liability was not based on *respondeat superior*, ostensible agency, negligent selection, or negligent monitoring of the medical staff.

Kansas abolished such liability by a statute that bars all liability for licensed medical facilities for professional services of professionals who are not employees or agents.[147]

Off-Premises Liability

Some patients have sought to hold hospitals liable for the actions of medical staff members in their private practice off hospital premises. Nearly all courts have rejected these attempts.[148] One exception is a 1988 Massachusetts decision that a hospital employee could sue the hospital for a rape by a medical staff member during a house call in his private practice.[149] The hospital was aware of prior complaints about the physician's sexual conduct, had given him an oral warning, and had required a chaperone to be present when he visited female patients in the hospital. Apparently the hospital's liability was based on the court's belief that it should have terminated the physician's privileges or taken other disciplinary measures that would have come to the employee's attention.

HMOs and Other Managed Care Entities

Courts are still struggling with the extent to which managed care entities should be liable for the consequences of errors of participating providers, for their selection of participating providers, and for their decisions not to authorize hospitalization or other treatment.[150] Some employer-sponsored plans have sought to avoid all such liability by asserting ERISA preemption.[151] Courts have disagreed on whether ERISA preempts such claims.[152]

Managed care entities have sought to avoid all responsibility for errors by participating providers who are not employees or apparent agents of the managed care entity. Sometimes participating physicians have been found to be apparent agents.[153] At least one court has found that participating physicians who are paid on a capitation basis are actual agents.[154] Other courts have required more than a participating provider agreement to establish apparent agency.[155]

Similar to the evolution of the law concerning hospitals, there has been an effort to impose liability on managed care entities for providers who are neither employees nor apparent agents based on negligent selection or failure to deselect a provider when problems become known or should have been discovered. Managed care entities have sought to avoid all responsibility for selection and retention of providers. In 1989, the Missouri Supreme Court ruled that an HMO had a duty to conduct a reasonable investigation of the credentials and reputation of participating physicians.[156]

Managed care entities have sought to avoid all responsibility for their coverage decisions, generally based on versions of the theory that patients and providers are still free to seek and provide care at their own expense, so the managed care entity's denial did not cause the failure to obtain timely treatment. In 1986, a California court ruled that a state reviewer could not be liable for the complications a patient suffered when the reviewer authorized only half of the additional hospital days requested by the treating physician because the treating physician had the responsibility to make the discharge decision.[157] This theory is increasingly becoming a legal fiction because patients and providers cannot afford care when third party payers refuse payment and those providers who appeal denials in an effort to obtain coverage risk being deselected from the managed care panel of approved providers. The efforts to avoid liability have not been entirely success-ful. A California jury awarded an $89 million verdict against an HMO for denial of coverage for bone marrow transplantation for a breast cancer patient. The case was later settled for $5 million.[158]

Piercing the Corporate Veil

Generally when a corporation is liable, its parent corporation or other share-holder is not also liable due to the limited liability of corporations. However, this corporate "veil" can be pierced, exposing the parent or shareholder to liability, in several circumstances, such as when the corporate formalities are not performed, the corporation is used for an illegal purpose, or the corporation does not have independence and becomes an instrumentality or alter ego of the parent or other shareholder.[159] Thus, when separate corporations are established for liability purposes, care needs to be taken to assure they are properly administered.

Insurance and Other Indemnity

In the past, most professional liability insurance was on an occurrence basis, which means that a policy purchased for a specific year covered all future claims arising out of incidents during the policy period. Since the 1970s, most profes-sional liability insurance is on a claims-made basis, which means that a policy purchased for a specific year covers only the claims that are made during that year that arise from incidents after a retroactive date specified in the policy. Thus, to have coverage for future claims, an additional policy needs to be purchased. This can be a renewal policy with a retroactive date covering incidents in the prior period, or it can be a reporting endorsement, often called a "tail" policy, which covers future claims arising from incidents during the period covered by the prior policy, without covering any new incidents.

Sometimes when providers elect not to buy tail coverage, before expiration of the old policy they send the insurer a list of all the potential claims of which they are aware so that a "claim" will be made during the policy period. In 1992, the New Hampshire Supreme Court ruled that these were valid claims triggering coverage.[160] It was not necessary for the claims to come from the patient.

Faced with the reluctance of physicians to prescribe drugs that frequently lead to litigation, manufacturers have occasionally adopted special programs where they agreed to pay the legal costs and settlements or verdicts against physicians sued for prescribing the drugs.[161]

RISK MANAGEMENT AND QUALITY IMPROVEMENT

Legislatures, accrediting agencies, and health care institutions have sought to reduce injuries to patients and the resulting liability exposure of institutions through risk management programs. Many states[162] require hospital risk management programs. These programs are designed to identify, evaluate, and reduce risks. The state requirements are generally focused on patient injuries, but some hospitals expand their programs to include employee injuries, property loss and damage, and other risks.

The Joint Commission requires hospitals to have an approach to improving organizational performance,[163] sometimes still called a *quality improvement program*, but the terminology appears to continue to change. This includes a requirement that data be collected about risk management activities.[164]

TORT REFORM

The cumulative effect of the number of malpractice cases and the cost of individual cases has resulted in a substantial increase in the cost of malpractice insurance and, in some areas of the country, has occasionally reduced availability of malpractice insurance at any price. This periodic malpractice insurance crisis has led nearly every state to review and revise its laws concerning tort suits. Although some changes have had an effect,[165] in most states it is not clear whether or not they have been a solution. Periodically there are times in which aggregate payments have dropped,[166] but the payments remain substantial and the cause of the drops is difficult to assess. There is still substantial dispute concerning the indirect effect of tort liability on the cost of health care through defensive medicine and other practices.[167]

These tort reforms can be grouped into (1) changes in dispute resolution mechanisms, (2) changes in the amount of the award and how it is paid, (3) changes in the time in which the suit must be brought, and (4) other changes. These reforms have received a mixed reception in the courts. Courts have disagreed on whether they violate various state and federal constitutional provisions.

When reforms are enacted to apply to only health care providers, there is often litigation over whether a particular type of provider is protected by the law.[168] The outcome generally is determined by the wording of the statute.

Dispute Resolution Mechanisms

The two primary changes in the mechanism for dispute resolution have been the introduction of screening panels and the authorization of binding agreements to arbitrate disputes. Administrative systems have also been proposed as substitutes.

Screening Panels

Several states have enacted laws that require all malpractice claims to be screened by a panel before a suit can be filed.[169] These screening panels are designed to promote settlement of meritorious claims and abandonment of frivolous claims.

A few courts have held the panels unconstitutional as an infringement of state constitutional rights to access to the courts.[170] The Florida Supreme Court declared the state's medical mediation requirement unconstitutional on the ground that it violated due process by being arbitrary and capricious in operation because of its ten-month limitation on the mediation process with no procedure to extend the limit.[171]

Most courts have upheld the required use of screening panels since plaintiffs still have the right to sue after the screening process is completed.[172] However, state courts vary in how broadly they interpret the scope of cases subject to screening.[173] The federal courts require plaintiffs to complete any state-required screening process before pursuing a state malpractice claim in federal court.[174]

State law varies on the ways the results of such screening panels can be used in a subsequent suit.[175]

Arbitration

Several states have statutes authorizing binding agreements to arbitrate future malpractice disputes.[176] Under the common law, agreements to arbitrate are not valid unless signed after the dispute arises, so the statutes were necessary to validate agreements to arbitrate future disputes. When there is a valid arbitration agreement, the dispute is submitted to one or more arbitrators who decide whether any payment should be made and, if so, how much. Several states specify that certain elements must be included in arbitration agreements, such as a right to withdraw from the agreement within 30 days after signing or 60 days after discharge. The laws differ on which health care providers are eligible to enter arbitration agreements. Generally courts can set aside arbitration decisions only for limited reasons, such as failure to follow proper procedures or bias of the arbitrator.[177] A valid arbitration decision has the same effect as a court judgment and can be enforced using the same procedures.

Arbitration is favored by some health care providers and patients because it is faster and less costly than litigation. It is a less formal process than litigation, avoiding adverse publicity and the complex rules of litigation that promote adversarial positions. Others are opposed to arbitration because they prefer having their disputes decided by a jury, using procedures with which attorneys are more familiar. Some providers believe they have a better chance of avoiding any payment, while some patients believe that if they win, they will be awarded a larger payment by a jury.

Arbitration agreements have been enforced in many cases. For example, in 1976 the California Supreme Court upheld the application to an individual employee of an arbitration agreement that had been included in a group medical contract negotiated between an employer and a health maintenance organization.[178] In 1985, a California appellate court ruled that an arbitration agreement in a group medical contract also applied to the spouse, children, and heirs of the employee.[179] In 1984, the Michigan Supreme Court declared the state's arbitration act to be constitutional, overruling several lower court decisions that had questioned several aspects of the process.[180] However, in some states the status of arbitration is less clear.

In 1994, the California Supreme Court ruled that the litigation privilege protects a medical expert who is testifying in private arbitration.[181]

Administrative Systems

There have been proposals that an administrative system be created to determine whether there should be payment and, if so, the amount in all malpractice cases.[182] This would replace the courts and arbitration. Appeals to the courts would be allowed only in limited circumstances. No state has enacted such a system yet. Courts in many states would view such a system as a violation of the right, under the state constitution, to access to the courts. In those states an amendment to the state constitution may be necessary before such a law would be possible.

Care will need to be taken in defining the grounds for entitlement to payment under any administrative system. Under the law applicable to Veterans Administration (VA) hospitals, veterans can claim disability through an administrative process. In 1994, the U.S. Supreme Court ruled that a claim for disability benefits from the VA does not require any fault of the VA hospital.[183]

Amount and Payment of the Award

The amount and payment of the award have been modified by

1. imposing ceilings on the amount,
2. abolishing the collateral source rule,
3. creating state payment systems,
4. authorizing periodic payments, and
5. modifying joint and several liability.

Ceilings

Limitations on the amount that can be awarded in a malpractice suit have been one of the most controversial approaches to tort reform. Several states have enacted limits.[184] A 1993 study by the Congressional Office of Technology

Assessment reported that damage caps were one of the most effective means of reducing malpractice costs.[185]

Courts have disagreed on the constitutionality of such limits.[186] In 1976, the Illinois Supreme Court declared ceilings to be a violation of the constitutional requirement of equal protection because it could find no rational justification for treating those injured by medical malpractice differently from those injured by other means.[187] In 1980, the Indiana Supreme Court declared ceilings to be constitutional because it found a rational justification in the need for a risk-spreading mechanism for malpractice liability at a reasonable cost to assure the continued availability of health services.[188] Generally where there is a valid state cap on damages, it applies to most federal suits, including EMTALA suits[189] and Federal Tort Claims Act suits.[190]

There have been repercussions for some courts that have invalidated limits. In May 1988, the Texas Supreme Court struck down the state cap on noneconomic damages.[191] Texas judges must be periodically approved by the voters. In the November 1988 election, the justices that had dismantled the tort reform law were removed.[192] In 1990, the court upheld a cap on damages.[193] In June 1988, the Kansas Supreme Court struck down the state cap on malpractice damages.[194] The legislature scheduled hearings on a state constitutional amendment. In March 1989, the court ruled that it would uphold a cap on noneconomic damages in nonmedical cases, and the constitutional amendment effort was dropped.[195]

Collateral Source Rule

Under the common law the defendant must pay for the entire cost of the plaintiff's injuries even if the plaintiff has already received some compensation from other sources, such as insurance. This is called the *collateral source rule*. Several states abolished the collateral source rule, so the amount of compensation the plaintiff receives from other sources is deducted from the amount the defendant owes. This process has been declared constitutional by several courts,[196] but a few courts have disagreed.[197]

Governmental Payment Systems

Some states have insurance systems that pay part of any malpractice award. These laws have generally been upheld, including the requirement that all health care providers contribute to the fund[198] and the requirement that the administrative procedure associated with the system be followed.[199]

The federal government established the National Childhood Vaccine Injury Act to pay for injuries caused by certain vaccination programs.[200]

Periodic Payments

Under the common law the plaintiff is entitled to payment of court judgments in a single lump sum. One advantage of settling cases involving large liabilities is that the parties can agree to periodic payments that are easier for the defendant to pay. Some states have passed laws authorizing courts to direct that large judgments be paid by periodic payments. The courts have not agreed on whether these laws are constitutional.[201]

Some courts may have inherent authority to structure payout of awards to the beneficiary, provided the full amount has been paid by the person found liable. Thus, a federal appellate court ruled that there was inherent authority to place an award for a child in a reversionary trust over the objections of the parents who had a conflict of interest.[202]

Joint and Several Liability

Under the common law when several defendants are found liable, each is liable for the entire amount. The plaintiff can select from whom to try to collect. Thus, for example, when a rider was injured on a ride at Walt Disney World and the jury allocated responsibility—14 percent to the rider, 85 percent to his accompanying fiance, and 1 percent to Walt Disney World—the rider was permitted to collect 86 percent from Walt Disney World.[203] Under contributory negligence principles, the rider was not permitted to collect the remaining 14 percent due to his personal fault. Moreover, under the common law the defendant who pays is not permitted in most cases to recover reimbursement from the other defendants even if they have greater responsibility.[204] Some states have modified these harsh rules by statute.[205]

Statute of Limitations

The statute of limitations specifies the time in which suits must be filed or forever barred. Some states have shortened this time. Prior to the malpractice crisis amendments, nearly all states permitted minors to wait until they became adults to file suit. Some tort reform acts limit minors to a specific number of years after the right to sue accrues. While some courts have upheld these laws, other courts have found them to violate state constitutions.[206]

Some states have redefined when the time begins, as another way to shorten the time. In most states the time begins when the patient discovers an injury that may be due to someone else's negligence.[207] Courts have disagreed on whether limits that start on the date of the incident are enforceable.[208] Such limits can bar the suit before the patient knows there is a basis to sue. In some cases, such as unwanted births after negligent sterilizations, the injury may not occur until many years after the incident.

Other Tort Reforms

Other tort reform amendments have

1. limited the grounds for suits based on lack of informed consent,[209]
2. restricted contingency fees for lawyers or given courts the authority to modify them,[210]
3. prohibited asking for a specific amount of money in the suit,[211]
4. restricted who could give expert testimony,[212]
5. prohibited punitive damages[213] or required part of punitive damage awards to be paid to the state,[214]
6. required notices of intent,[215] and
7. required an affidavit of merit from an expert to be attached to the suit.[216]

What Law Applies?

State law may not always protect providers. Patients have tried to sue providers in other states under the laws of the patients' home state to avoid provider protections in the providers' home state laws. There are two issues—(1) whether the provider has sufficient contacts with the state in which the suit is brought to be forced to litigate in that state and, if so, (2) whether the laws of the state in which the court is located control or whether the laws of the state where the services were provided control.

Generally only minimum contacts are necessary to force a provider to litigate in the other state. A federal appellate court allowed a hospital to be sued in a state in which the hospital had its telephone number listed and from which the hospital had received payment.[217] Registering as a provider under a state's Medicaid law has also been held to be sufficient.[218] However, merely treating a patient from the state should generally not be sufficient.[219]

Even when the provider can be sued in the other state, generally the laws where the care was provided govern.[220] In a 1985 District of Columbia case, however, a health plan's Virginia facilities were found subject to District of Columbia law because the health plan had contracted with the employer of the patient in the District of Columbia.[221] Thus, the plan's Virginia facilities were not protected by Virginia's cap on malpractice recoveries.

In choice of law situations, courts generally apply their home state's laws whenever they find that the law of the other state is opposed to a strong public policy of the home state. Many tort reform issues address the heart of the courts' power. Some courts view protection of that power as a strong public policy, so they tend to find protections of providers that are different from their home state requirements to be contrary to strong public policies. In 1992, a federal court in Washington state was presented with a suit by an Idaho plaintiff against a

Washington pathologist for services provided in Idaho. The court ruled that the Idaho cap on damages did not apply because of the Washington policy against caps.[222] Similarly, a federal court in Mississippi ruled that Mississippi public policy required applying Mississippi comparative negligence rules rather that Maryland contributory negligence rules in malpractice action by a Mississippi resident against a Maryland health care provider involving treatment while the plaintiff lived in Maryland.[223]

Thus, health care providers in states with tort reform laws cannot be certain that they will be protected by those laws when they seek or serve out-of-state patients.

NOTES

1. United States Nursing Corp. v. Saint Joseph Med. Ctr., 39 F.3d 790 (7th Cir. 1994).

2. *E.g.*, International Business Machines Corp. v. Medlantic Healthcare Group, 708 F. Supp. 417 (D. D.C. 1989).

3. Lee v. Grandcor Med. Sys., Inc., 702 F. Supp. 252 (D. Colo. 1988).

4. United States v. Vanhorn, 20 F.3d 104 (4th Cir. 1994).

5. Guilmet v. Campbell, 385 Mich. 57, 188 N.W.2d 601 (1971); *see also* Bobrick v. Bravstein, 116 A.D.2d 682, 497 N.Y.S.2d 749 (2d Dep't 1986) [contract suit allowed against physician].

6. MICH. COMP. LAWS § 566.132. Some states have similar laws, *e.g.*, FLA. STAT. § 725.01.

7. *E.g.*, Moore v. Averi, 534 So.2d 250 (Ala. 1988).

8. Stewart v. Rudner, 349 Mich. 459, 84 N.W.2d 816 (1957).

9. Nicoleau v. Brookhaven Mem. Hosp. Ctr., 201 A.D.2d 544, 607 N.Y.S.2d 703 (2d Dep't 1994).

10. *E.g.*, Bommareddy v. Superior Court, 222 Cal. App. 3d 1017, 272 Cal. Rptr. 246 (5th Dist. 1990), *rev. denied*, 1990 Cal. LEXIS 4989 (Oct. 30, 1990), *disapproved on other grounds*, Central Pathology Serv. Med. Clinic v. Superior Court, 3 Cal. 4th 181, 10 Cal. Rptr. 2d 208, 832 P.2d 924 (1992).

11. Murphy v. Herfort, 140 A.D.2d 415, 528 N.Y.S.2d 117 (2d Dep't 1988), *appeal denied*, 73 N.Y.2d 701, 535 N.Y.S.2d 595, 532 N.E.2d 101 (1988); *see also e.g.*, Malone v. Longo, 463 F. Supp. 139 (E.D. N.Y. 1979) [nurse report to supervisor about physician order protected]; Kletschka v. Abbott-Northwestern Hosp., Inc., 417 N.W.2d 752 (Minn. Ct. App. 1988) [performance evaluation protected].

12. Bartlett v. Daniel Drake Mem. Hosp., 75 Ohio App.3d 334, 599 N.E.2d 403 (1991).

13. *E.g.*, Feldman v. Glucoft, 522 So.2d 798 (Fla. 1988), *appeal after remand*, 580 So.2d 866 (Fla. 3d DCA) [no evidence extrinsic to proceedings alleged, judgment for defendants affirmed], *rev. denied*, 541 So.2d 181 (Fla. 1991), *cert. denied*, 503 U.S. 960 (1992).

14. Wynn v. Cole, 91 Mich. App. 517, 284 N.W.2d 144 (1979).

15. Koudsi v. Hennepin County Med. Ctr., 317 N.W.2d 705 (Minn. 1982).

16. 42 C.F.R. pt. 2.

17. Seitz v. Humana of Ky., Inc., 1988 Ky. App. LEXIS 164 (Ky. Ct. App. Nov. 4, 1988), *as discussed in* 17 HEALTH L. DIG., Jan. 1989, at 27.

18. Johnson v. Woman's Hosp., 527 S.W.2d 133 (Tenn. Ct. App. 1975).

19. McCormick v. Haley, 37 Ohio App. 2d 73, 307 N.E.2d 34 (1973).

20. Matthews v. Blue Cross & Blue Shield, No. 145934 (Mich. Ct. App. Apr. 13, 1995), *as discussed in* 23 HEALTH L. DIG. (May 1995), at 31.

21. *E.g.*, Nicholson v. Lucas, 21 Cal. App. 4th 1657, 26 Cal. Rptr. 2d 778 (5th Dist. 1994) [dismissal of dentist's claim that initiation of medical staff proceedings was malicious prosecution].

22. Macleay v. Arden Hill Hosp., 164 A.D.2d 228, 563 N.Y.S.2d 333 (3d Dep't 1990), *appeal denied*, 77 N.Y.2d 806, 568 N.Y.S.2d 913, 571 N.E.2d 83 (1991); *but see* Steele v. Breinholt, 747 P.2d 433 (Utah Ct. App. 1987) [nursing home visitor arrested for criminal trespass charges presented jury question on malicious prosecution].

23. Dutt v. Kremp, 894 P.2d 354 (Nev. 1995); Spencer v. Burglass, 288 So.2d 68 (La. Ct. App. 1974); *but see* Bull v. McCuskey, 96 Nev. 706, 615 P.2d 957 (1980); Williams v. Coombs, 179 Cal. App. 3d 626, 224 Cal. Rptr. 865 (3d Dist. 1986) [attorney did not review records or obtain medical opinion before filing suit], *disapproved*, Sheldon Appel Co. v. Albert & Oliker, 47 Cal.3d 863, 254 Cal. Rptr. 336, 765 P.2d 498 (1989) [adequacy of attorney research not relevant to objective determination of probable cause to bring suit]; Taub, *Malpractice countersuits: Succeeding at last?* 9 LAW, MED. & HEALTH CARE, Dec. 1981, at 17.

24. Annotation, *Duty of one other than carrier or employer to render assistance to one for whose initial injury he is not liable*, 33 A.L.R. 3D 301.

25. O'Hara v. Holy Cross Hosp., 137 Ill. 2d 332, 561 N.E.2d 18 (1990); *see* Annotation, *Liability of hospital for injury to person invited or permitted to accompany patient during emergency room treatment*, 90 A.L.R. 4TH 478.

26. Zavalas v. State, Dep't of Corrections, 124 Or. App. 166, 861 P.2d 1026 (1993), *rev. denied*, 319 Or. 150, 877 P.2d 86 (1994).

27. Flowers v. Torrance Mem. Hosp. Med. Ctr., 8 Cal. 4th 992, 35 Cal. Rptr. 2d 685, 884 P.2d 142 (1994).

28. *See* note 212, *infra*.

29. *E.g.*, Brookover v. Mary Hitchcock Mem. Hosp., 893 F.2d 411 (1st Cir. 1990) [father could testify that nurse said after fall of son that son should have been restrained; admissible as vicarious admission].

30. *E.g.*, Cockerton v. Mercy Hosp. Med. Ctr., 490 N.W.2d 856 (Iowa Ct. App. 1992) [fall during X-ray exam; failure to use restraint straps routine nonmedical care].

31. St. Paul Med. Ctr. v. Cecil, 842 S.W.2d 808 (Tex. Ct. App. 1992).

32. *E.g.*, Peacock v. Samaritan Health Servs., 159 Ariz. 123, 765 P.2d 525 (Ct. App. 1988) [internal hospital protocol for safeguarding psychiatric patients].

33. *E.g.*, Van Iperen v. Van Bramer, 392 N.W.2d 480 (Iowa 1986) [Joint Commission drug monitoring standard]; Gallagher v. Detroit-Macomb Hosp. Ass'n, 171 Mich. App. 761, 431 N.W.2d 90 (1988) [internal hospital rules].

34. *E.g.*, Hastings v. Baton Rouge Gen. Hosp., 498 So.2d 713 (La. 1986).

35. Sullivan v. Sisters of St. Francis, 374 S.W.2d 294 (Tex. Civ. App. 1963).

36. Haber v. Cross County Hosp., 37 N.Y.2d 888, 378 N.Y.S.2d 369, 340 N.E.2d 734 (1975).

37. Ravenis v. Detroit Gen. Hosp., 63 Mich. App. 79, 234 N.W.2d 411 (1975).

38. Pearce v. Feinstein, 754 F. Supp. 308 (W.D. N.Y. 1990).

39. National Health Lawyers Ass'n, COLLOQUIUM REPORT ON LEGAL ISSUES RELATED TO CLINICAL PRACTICE GUIDELINES (1995); J.C. West, *The legal implications of medical practice guidelines*, 27 J. HEALTH & HOSP. L. 97 (1994); E.B. Hirshfield, *Practice parameters and the malpractice liability of physicians*, 263 J.A.M.A. 1556 (1990).

40. ME. REV. STAT. ANN. tit. 24, § 2971–79; General Accounting Office, MEDICAL MALPRACTICE, MAINE'S USE OF PRACTICE GUIDELINES TO REDUCE COSTS (Oct. 1993), GAO/HRD-94-8; *GAO report finds broad participation in demonstration of practice guidelines*, 2 HEALTH L. RPTR. [BNA] 1490 (1993) [hereinafter HEALTH L. RPTR. cited as H.L.R.].

41. *Maine's experiment with practice guidelines produces little evidence*, 3 H.L.R. 753 (1994).

42. L. Oberman, *Risk management strategy: Liability insurers stress practice guidelines*, AM. MED. NEWS, Sept. 5, 1994, at 1 [Colorado].

43. *E.g.*, *Internists call clinical practice guidelines effective*, 3 H.L.R. 781 (1994).

44. *E.g.*, *Half of unstable angina cases could be treated outside hospital, AHCPR says*, 3 H.L.R. 339 (1994) [practice guidelines released Mar. 15, 1994].

45. *E.g.*, L. Oberman, *AMA panel on guidelines sorts good from misguided*, AM. MED. NEWS, Jan. 10, 1994, at 1.

46. *E.g.*, I.G. Stiell et al., *Implementation of the Ottawa ankle rules*, 271 J.A.M.A. 827 (1994) [reduced use of ankle radiography].

47. *E.g.*, Sofamor Danek Group Inc. v. Clinton, 870 F. Supp. 379 (D. D.C. 1994) [deny injunction of AHCPR release of clinical practice guidelines for lower back pain].

48. *Illinois Blues, medical society strike agreement over guidelines*, 3 H.L.R. 310 (1994); *see also* L. Oberman, *AMA panel on guidelines sorts good from misguided*, AM. MED. NEWS, Jan. 10, 1994, at 1.

49. 57A AM. JUR. 2D *Negligence* §§ 716–803.

50. Suburban Hosp. Ass'n v. Hadary, 22 Md. App. 186, 322 A.2d 258 (1974).

51. Furey v. Thomas Jefferson Univ. Hosp., 325 Pa. Super. 212, 472 A.2d 1083 (1984); Fraijo v. Hartland Hosp., 99 Cal. App. 3d 331, 160 Cal. Rptr. 246 (2d Dist. 1979) [applied to nursing decision].

52. Jones v. Chidester, 531 Pa. 31, 610 A.2d 964 (1992).

53. *E.g.*, FLA. STAT. § 766.102(2)(c); *see also* cases cited note 212, *infra*.

54. Helling v. Carey, 83 Wash. 2d 514, 519 P.2d 981 (1974).

55. Tarasoff v. Regents of Univ. of Cal., 17 Cal. 3d 425, 131 Cal. Rptr. 14, 551 P.2d 334 (1976).

56. Gonzales v. Nork, No. 228566 (Cal. Super. Ct. Nov.19, 1973), *rev'd on other grounds*, 20 Cal. 3d 500, 573 P.2d 458 (1978).

57. Austin v. Regents of Univ. of Cal., 89 Cal. App. 3d 354, 152 Cal. Rptr. 420 (4th Dist. 1979).

58. *E.g.*, R.J. v. Humana of Fla., Inc., 652 So.2d 360 (Fla. 1995) [impact rule applies to damages claim for negligent HIV diagnosis, so must show emotional distress flows from physical injury of impact; when misdiagnosis results in harmful treatment, treatment may provide impact]; Lubowitz v. Albert Einstein Med. Ctr., 424 Pa. Super. 468, 623 A.2d 3 (1993) [no claim for fear of AIDS due to mistakenly being told exposed to HIV]; Carroll v. Sisters of Saint Francis Health Servs. 868 S.W.2d 585 (Tenn. 1993) [no recovery for negligent infliction of emotional distress based on fear of AIDS without showing exposure to HIV virus]; K.A.C. v. Benson, 527 N.W.2d 553 (Minn. 1995) [patient suing HIV-infected physician who performed gynecological examination must allege actual exposure to HIV to be in zone of danger and claim negligent infliction of emotional distress]; Herbert v. Regents of Univ. of Cal., 26 Cal. App. 4th 782, 31 Cal. Rptr. 2d 709 (2d Dist. 1994), *rev. denied*, 1994 Cal. LEXIS 5607 (1994) [no entitlement to damages for emotional distress for fear of HIV from needlescratch where chance of HIV minimal]; Marchica v. Long Island R. Co., 31 F.3d 1197 (2d Cir. 1994), *aff'g*, 810 F. Supp. 445 (E.D. N.Y.), *cert. denied*, 115 S. Ct. 727 (U.S. 1995) [affirming jury verdict for employee for fear of AIDS after hypodermic puncture wound].

59. *E.g.*, Hodges v. Secretary of DHHS, 9 F.3d 958 (Fed. Cir. 1993) [failure to prove causation of death of infant after DPT vaccination]; Campos v. Ysleta Gen. Hosp., Inc., 836 S.W.2d 791 (Tex. Ct. App. 1992) [failure to prove causation of child's death].

60. Lenger v. Physician's Gen. Hosp., 455 S.W.2d 703 (Tex. 1970).

61. Schnebly v. Baker, 217 N.W.2d 708 (Iowa 1974).

62. *E.g.*, Delaney v. Cade, 255 Kan. 199, 873 P.2d 175 (1994) [may make claim for loss of chance of better recovery, not just loss of chance of survival]; Annotation, *Medical malpractice: "loss of chance" causality*, 54 A.L.R. 4th 10.

63. *E.g.*, McKain v. Bisson, 12 F.3d 692 (7th Cir. 1993) [applying Indiana law]; Kilpatrick v. Bryant, 868 S.W.2d 594 (Tenn. 1993).

64. Blondel v. Hays, 241 Va. 467, 403 S.E.2d 340 (1991).

65. *E.g.*, Dillon v. Medical Ctr. Hosp., 98 Ohio App. 3d 510, 648 N.E.2d 1375 (1993), *appeal dismissed*, 72 Ohio St. 3d 1201, 647 N.E.2d 166 (1995) [hospital not liable, despite negligence of nurses, because causation broken by acts of independent physicians].

66. Rivera v. New York City Health & Hosps. Corp., 72 N.Y.2d 1021, 531 N.E.2d 644, 534 N.Y.S.2d 923 (1988).

67. Daubert v. Merrell Dow Pharmaceuticals, Inc., 113 S. Ct. 2786 (U.S. 1993); E. Gonzalez, Comment: *Whither "junk science"? Daubert v. Merrell Dow and the future of expert testimony*, 26 J. HEALTH & HOSP. L. 296 (1993).

68. *E.g.*, Daubert v. Merrell Dow Pharmaceuticals, Inc., 43 F.3d 1311 (9th Cir. 1995), *upon remand from*, 113 S. Ct. 2786 (U.S. 1993) [expert scientific testimony not admissible to prove Bendectin caused plaintiff's birth defects]; Sorensen v. Shaklee Corp., 31 F.3d 638 (8th Cir. 1994) [affirming summary judgment for manufacturer in suit claiming mental retardation due to alfalfa tablets; proposed expert testimony did not have sufficient scientific validity in light of *Daubert*]; Chikovsky v. Pharmaceutical Corp., No. 92-6628 (S.D. Fla. Sept. 23, 1993), *as discussed in* 2 H.L.R. 1375 (1993) [summary judgment for maker of Retin-A because plaintiff's evidence on causation inadmissible under *Daubert*].

69. Byrne v. Boadle, 2 H. & C. 722 (Exch. 1863).

70. *E.g.*, Robb ex rel. Robb v. Anderton, 864 P.2d 1322 (Utah Ct. App. 1993) [*res ipsa loquitur* not applicable to injuries due to cardiac arrest during surgery because did not show it was kind of injury that in ordinary course of events would not have happened had the physician used due care].

71. *E.g.*, Leonard v. Watsonville Commun. Hosp., 47 Cal. 2d 509, 305 P.2d 36 (1956).

72. *E.g.*, Parks v. Perry, 68 N.C. App. 202, 314 S.E.2d 287, *rev. denied*, 311 N.C. 761, 321 S.E.2d 143 (1984); Wiles v. Myerly, 210 N.W.2d 619 (Iowa 1973); Wick v. Henderson, 485 N.W.2d 645 (Iowa 1992) [damage to ulnar nerve during gallbladder surgery].

73. *E.g.*, Sanchez v. Bay Gen. Hosp., 116 Cal. App. 3d 776, 172 Cal. Rptr. 342 (4th Dist. 1981); Reilly v. Straub, 282 N.W.2d 688 (Iowa 1979).

74. *E.g.*, Mulkey v. Tubb, 535 So.2d 1294 (La. Ct. App. 1988) [adequate explanation of damage to site distant from surgery].

75. Deleon v. Slear, 328 Md. 569, 616 A.2d 380 (1992).

76. Thompson v. Wing, 70 Ohio St. 3d 176, 637 N.E.2d 917 (1994); *accord*, Schwarder v. United States, 974 F.2d 1118 (9th Cir. 1992).

77. *E.g.*, Nelson v. American Nat'l Red Cross, 307 U.S. App. D.C. 52, 26 F.3d 193 (1994) [suit for death from HIV barred by statute of limitations which started when blood given not when AIDS appeared].

78. *E.g.*, Katz v. Children's Hosp., 28 F.3d 1520 (9th Cir. 1994) [under California law, time period started when harm experienced].

79. *See* Tullock v. Eck, 311 Ark. 564, 845 S.W.2d 517 (1993) [limiting continuous treatment doctrine].

80. *E.g.*, McCollum v. Sisters of Charity, 799 S.W.2d 15 (Ky. 1990) [violates state constitution to cut off claim before it could be discovered].

81. *E.g.*, Doe v. Shands Teaching Hosp. & Clinics, Inc., 614 So.2d 1170 (Fla. 1st DCA 1993), *rev. denied*, 626 So.2d 204 (Fla. 1993) [statute of limitations for medical malpractice constitutional even for those who could not have known of injury before time limit].

82. FLA. STAT. § 95.11(4)(b).

83. *E.g.*, McDonald v. United States, 843 F.2d 247 (6th Cir. 1988) [reassurances of complete recovery can extend time]; Muller v. Thaut, 230 Neb. 244, 430 N.W.2d 884 (1988) [fraudulent concealment].

84. *E.g.*, IOWA CODE ANN. § 614.8; Annotation, *Medical malpractice statutes of limitation minority provisions*, 62 A.L.R. 4TH 758; *see also* Barnes v. Sabatino, 205 Ga. App.773, 423 S.E.2d 686 (1992) [17-year-old not covered by special rule for minors which applied only to persons under age 5]; *contra*, FLA. STAT. § 95.11(4)(b) [minors subject to same time limit as adults].

85. *E.g.*, Hyde v. University of Mich. Bd. of Regents, 426 Mich. 223, 393 N.W.2d 847 (1986) [public general hospital is governmental function]. Public hospitals were later removed by statute in Michigan. McCummings v. Hurley Med. Ctr., 433 Mich. 404, 446 N.W.2d 114, 117 n.3 (1989).

86. *E.g.*, Allen v. State, 535 So. 2d 903 (La. Ct. App.), *cert. denied*, 536 So.2d 1201 (La. 1988) [$500,000 cap on damages applied]; Eldred v. North Broward Hosp. Dist., 498 So.2d 911 (Fla. 1986) [$50,000 cap on damages applied]; *but see* Condemarin v. University Hosp., 775 P.2d 348 (Utah 1989) [$100,000 cap on governmental hospital liability unconstitutional].

87. *E.g.*, Fields v. Curators of Univ. of Mo., 848 S.W.2d 589 (Mo. Ct. App. 1993) [sovereign immunity waived by purchase of liability insurance]; Green River Dist. Health Dep't v. Wigginton, 764 S.W.2d 475 (Ky. 1989) [sovereign immunity waived to extent of liability insurance]; *but see* Hillsborough County Hosp. v. Taylor, 546 So.2d 1055 (Fla. 1989) [malpractice trust fund does not waive sovereign immunity]; *contra*, Lawrence v. Virginia Ins. Reciprocal, 979 F.2d 1053 (5th Cir. 1992) [community hospital sovereign immunity protected from punitive damages even when insurance covered such damages].

88. Pirkov-Middaugh v. Gillette Children's Hosp., 479 N.W.2d 63 (Minn. Ct. App. 1991), *rev'd*, 495 N.W.2d 608 (Minn. 1993).

89. *E.g.*, Joplin v. University of Mich. Bd. of Regents, 173 Mich. App. 149, 433 N.W.2d 830 (1988), *aff'd on remand*, 184 Mich. App. 497, 459 N.W.2d 70 (1990) [physicians protected by sovereign immunity]; Jaar v. University of Miami, 474 So.2d 239 (Fla. 3d DCA 1985), *rev. denied*, 484 So.2d 10 (Fla. 1986) [physicians protected]; De Rosa v. Shands Teaching Hosp., 504 So.2d 1313 (Fla. 1st DCA 1987) [resident physicians protected]; Canon v. Thumudo, 430 Mich. 326, 422 N.W.2d 688 (1988) [nurses protected]; *see also* Holthaus, *County agrees to shield ob/gyns from liability*, 62 HOSPS., July 20, 1988, at 42 [physicians made county agents so protected by $500,000 liability limitation]; *but see* Cooper v. Bowers, 706 S.W.2d 542 (Mo. Ct. App. 1986) [physician not protected].

90. *E.g.*, Lazerson v. Hilton Head Hosp., 439 S.E.2d 836 (S.C. 1994) [statutory $200,000 limit on liability of charitable organizations is constitutional]; Endres v. Greenville Hosp. Sys., 439 S.E.2d 261 (S.C. 1993) [after settlement with child at maximum under charitable immunity law, affirmed summary judgment barring parent from collecting derivative maximum again]; Marsella v. Monmouth Med. Ctr., 224 N.J. Super. 336, 540 A.2d 865 (App. Div. 1988) [$10,000

cap on damages against nonprofit hospitals]; English v. New England Med. Ctr., 405 Mass. 423, 541 N.E.2d 329 (1989), *cert. denied*, 493 U.S. 1056 (1990) [statutory $20,000 cap on liability of nonprofit institutions upheld]; *but see* Chandler v. Hospital Auth., 500 So.2d 1012 (Ala. 1986) [charitable immunity statute violated state constitution because it applied to too few hospitals].

91. *E.g.*, Johnese v. Jefferson Davis Mem. Hosp., 637 F. Supp. 1198 (S.D. Miss. 1986) [charitable immunity waived by insurance]; *but see* Ponder v. Fulton-De Kalb Hosp. Auth., 256 Ga. 833, 353 S.E.2d 515, *cert. denied*, 484 U.S. 863 (1987) [self-insurance plan did not waive charitable immunity].

92. *E.g.*, Johnson v. Matviuw, 176 Ill. App. 3d 907, 531 N.E.2d 970 (1st Dist. 1988), *cert. denied*, 125 Ill.2d 566, 537 N.E.2d 810 [applied to gratuitous hospital emergency care with no preexisting duty]; Kearns v. Superior Ct., 204 Cal. App. 3d 1325, 252 Cal. Rptr. 4 (2d Dist. 1988), *rev. denied*, 1988 Cal. LEXIS 499 (1988) [applied to emergency assistance in surgery]; Higgins v. Detroit Osteopathic Hosp., 154 Mich. App. 752, 398 N.W.2d 520 (1986), *appeal denied*, 428 Mich. 911 (1987) [applied to hospital emergency]; Annotation, *Construction and application of "Good Samaritan" statute*, 68 A.L.R. 4TH 294; *but see* Deal v. Kearney, 851 P.2d 1353 (Alaska 1993) [Good Samaritan immunity does not apply when there is preexisting duty to provide aid].

93. Anne Arundel Med. Ctr., Inc. v. Condon, 102 Md. App. 408, 649 A.2d 1189 (1994), *cert. granted*, 338 Md. 33, 655 A.2d 1281 (1995); *contra*, JFK Med. Ctr. v. Price, 647 So.2d 833 (Fla. 1994) [continuation of wrongful death malpractice suit against passive tortfeasor after settlement with active tortfeasor not barred].

94. Elbaor v. Smith, 845 S.W.2d 240 (Tex. 1992); Dosdourian v. Carsten, 624 So.2d 241 (Fla. 1993); Annotation, *Validity and effect of "Mary Carter" or similar agreement setting maximum liability of cotortfeasor and providing for reduction or extinguishment thereof relative to recovery against nonagreeing cotortfeasor*, 22 A.L.R. 5TH 483.

95. *E.g.*, Deboer v. Florida Offroaders Driver's Ass'n, 622 So.2d 1134 (Fla. 5th DCA 1993) [exculpatory contract protected sponsor of racing event from liability to spectator hit by car while crossing track].

96. *E.g.*, Cudnik v. William Beaumont Hosp., 207 Mich. App. 378, 525 N.W.2d 891 (1994) [exculpatory contract unenforceable]; Tatham v. Hoke, 469 F. Supp. 914 (W.D. N.C. 1979), *aff'd without op.*, 622 F.2d 584, 587 (4th Cir. 1980) [agreement to limit all claims to $15,000 unenforceable]; Annotation, *Validity and construction of contract exempting hospital or doctor from liability for negligence to patient*, 6 A.L.R.3D 704. For a discussion of the difference between exculpatory, indemnity, hold harmless, and related clauses under Pennsylvania law, *see* Valhal Corp. v. Sullivan Assocs., Inc., 44 F.3d 195 (3d Cir. 1995), *reh'g denied (en banc)*, 48 F.3d 760 (3d Cir. 1995).

97. First Options of Chicago, Inc. v. Kaplan, 115 S. Ct. 1920 (U.S. 1995).

98. *E.g.*, Einhorn v. Valley Med. Specialists, P.C.,172 Ariz. 571, 838 P.2d 1332 (Ct. App. 1992) [affirming arbitration award of year-end bonus to employee].

99. 9 U.S.C.A. § 1-16.

100. *E.g.*, McGill v. French, 333 N.C. 209, 424 S.E.2d 108 (1993); Gruidl v. Schell, 166 Ill. App. 3d 276, 519 N.E.2d 963 (1st Dist. 1988); Roberts v. Wood, 206 F. Supp. 579 (S.D. Ala. 1962); Annotation, *Medical malpractice: patient's failure to return, as directed, for examination or treatment as contributory negligence*, 100 A.L.R. 3D 723.

101. *E.g.*, Chudson v. Ratra, 76 Md. App. 753, 548 A.2d 172 (1988), *cert. denied*, 314 Md. 628, 552 A.2d 894 (1989).

102. *E.g.*, Shirey v. Schlemmer, 140 Ind. App. 606, 223 N.E.2d 759, *rev'd*, 249 Ind. 1, 230 N.E.2d 534 (1967) [jury must determine whether contributory negligence].

103. *E.g.*, Jenkins v. Bogalusa Commun. Med. Ctr., 340 So.2d 1065 (La. Ct. App. 1976).

104. *E.g.*, Seymour v. Victory Mem. Hosp., 60 Ill. App. 3d 366, 376 N.E.2d 754 (2d Dist. 1978).

105. *E.g.*, Rochester v. Katalan, 320 A.2d 704 (Del. 1974).

106. Elbaor v. Smith, 845 S.W.2d 240 (Tex. 1992).

107. *E.g.*, Cowan v. Doering, 111 N.J. 451, 545 A.2d 159 (1988).

108. *E.g.*, Jensen v. Intermountain Health Care, Inc., 679 P.2d 903 (Utah 1984); *contra* Hoffman v. Jones, 280 So.2d 431 (Fla. 1973).

109. 57A AM. JUR. 2D *Negligence* § 1165.

110. Veazey v. Elmwood Plantation Assocs., Ltd., 625 So.2d 675 (La. Ct. App. 1993), *aff'd*, 646 So.2d 866 (La. 1994), *withdrawn by publisher & reported at*, 1994 La. LEXIS 2889 (La. Nov. 30, 1994), *concurring op.*, 650 So.2d 712 (La. 1995); Comer v. Gregory, 365 So.2d 1212 (Miss. 1978).

111. *E.g.*, Mennonite Deaconess Home & Hosp., Inc. v. Gates Eng'g Co., 219 Neb. 303, 363 N.W.2d 155 (1985) [roof supplier liable for breach of warranties for leaky hospital roof].

112. Perlmutter v. Beth David Hosp., 308 N.Y. 100, 123 N.E.2d 792 (1954).

113. *E.g.*, Shortess v. Touro Infirmary, 520 So.2d 389 (La. 1988) [hospital strictly liable for blood with undetectable form of hepatitis]; Cunningham v. MacNeal Mem. Hosp., 47 Ill. 2d 443, 266 N.E.2d 897 (1970).

114. *E.g.*, IOWA CODE ANN. § 142A.8.

115. *E.g.*, Samson v. Greenville Hosp. Sys., 295 S.C. 359, 368 S.E.2d 665 (1988); McDaniel v. Baptist Mem. Hosp., 469 F.2d 230 (6th Cir. 1972).

116. Shivers v. Good Shepherd Hosp., 427 S.W.2d 104 (Tex. Civ. App. 1968).

117. Stephenson v. Greenberg, 421 Pa. Super. 1, 617 A.2d 364 (1992), *appeal denied*, 535 Pa. 649, 633 A.2d 153 (1993).

118. Dubin v. Michael Reese Hosp., 83 Ill. 2d 277, 415 N.E.2d 350 (1980), *rev'g*, 74 Ill. App. 3d 932, 393 N.E.2d 588 (1979); *see also* Nevauex v. Park Place Hosp., 656 S.W.2d 923 (Tex. Ct. App. 1983) [no strict liability for burns from cobalt radiation therapy].

119. *E.g.*, Rolon-Alvarado v. San Juan, 1 F.3d 74 (1st Cir. 1993) [provider not strictly liable for latent defect in endotracheal tube manufactured by third party]; Cafazzo v. Central Med. Health Servs., Inc., 430 Pa. Super. 480, 635 A.2d 151 (1993), *appeal granted*, 645 A.2d 1311 (Pa. 1994) [neither physician who implanted prosthesis nor hospital was seller of prosthesis]; NME Hosp. v. Azzariti, 573 So.2d 173 (Fla. 2d DCA 1991); Hoff v. Zimmer, Inc., 746 F. Supp. 872 (W.D. Wis. 1990); North Miami Gen. Hosp. v. Goldberg, 520 So.2d 650 (Fla. 3d DCA 1988) [hospital not strictly liable for burn from grounding pad]; Hector v. Cedars-Sinai Med. Ctr., 180 Cal. App. 3d 493, 225 Cal. Rptr. 595 (2d Dist. 1986) [hospital not strictly liable for pacemaker]; Silverhart v. Mt. Zion Hosp., 20 Cal. App. 3d 1022, 98 Cal. Rptr. 187 (1st Dist. 1971); Annotation, *Liability of hospital or medical practitioner under doctrine of strict liability in tort, or breach of warranty, for harm caused by drug, medical instrument, or similar device used in treating patient*, 54 A.L.R. 3D 258; *contra*, Garcia v. Edgewater Hosp., 244 Ill. App. 3d 894, 613 N.E.2d 1243 (1st Dist. 1993), *appeal denied*, 152 Ill.2d 558, 622 N.E.2d 1204 (1993) [hospital can be strictly liable for defective heart valve for which it imposed itemized charge].

120. Silverhart v. Mt. Zion Hosp., 20 Cal. App. 3d 1022, 98 Cal. Rptr. 187 (1st Dist. 1971).

121. St. Mary Med. Ctr., Inc. v. Casko, 639 N.E.2d 312 (Ind. Ct. App. 1994).

122. Skelton v. Druid City Hosp. Bd., 459 So.2d 818 (Ala. 1984).

123. Bell v. Poplar Bluff Physicians Group, 879 S.W.2d 618 (Mo. Ct. App. 1994), *rev. denied*, No. 18933 (Mo. Aug. 15, 1994).

124. Thomas v. St. Joseph Hosp., 618 S.W.2d 791 (Tex. Civ. App. 1981).

125. 21 U.S.C.A. § 360c; King v. Collagen Corp., 983 F.2d 1130 (1st Cir. 1993), *cert. denied*, 114 S. Ct. 84 (U.S.) [product liability claims involving class II devices preempted]; Stamps v. Collagen Corp., 984 F.2d 1416 (5th Cir.), *cert. denied*, 114 S. Ct. 86 (U.S. 1993); Gile v. Optical Radiation Corp., 22 F.3d 540 (3d Cir.), *cert. denied*, 115 S. Ct. 429 (U.S. 1994) [state law claims against manufacturer of experimental optical device preempted]; note that FDA has opposed preemption in at least one case, *see* Talbott v. C.R. Bard, Inc., No. 94-1951 (1st Cir. brief filed Nov. 23, 1994), *as discussed in* 3 H.L.R. 1747 (1994).

126. *E.g.*, Anguiano v. E.I. duPont de Nemours & Co., 44 F.3d 806 (9th Cir. 1995); National Bank of Commerce v. Kimberly-Clark Corp., 38 F.3d 988 (8th Cir. 1994) [Medical Device Amendments did not preempt claims regarding testing, design, manufacture of tampon, but claims regarding compliance with FDA regulations preempted].

127. *Lawyer hauls off hospital assets in dispute over malpractice award*, 19 MOD. HEALTHCARE, July 28, 1989, at 69.

128. *E.g.*, St. John's Reg. Health Ctr. v. American Cas. Co., 980 F.2d 1222 (8th Cir. 1992) [indemnity from nurse's liability insurer].

129. *E.g.*, Deal v. Kearney, 851 P.2d 1353 (Alaska 1993).

130. *E.g.*, Rice v. Nova Biomedical Corp., 38 F.3d 909 (7th Cir. 1994), *cert. denied*, 115 S. Ct. 1964 (U.S. 1995).

131. Lucas v. Hospital Auth. of Dougherty County, 193 Ga. App. 595, 388 S.E.2d 871 (1989).

132. Jones v. Baisch, 40 F.3d 252 (8th Cir. 1994).

133. Thompson v. Everett Clinic, 71 Wash. App. 548, 860 P.2d 1054 (1993), *rev. denied*, 123 Wash. 2d 1027, 877 P.2d 694 (1994) [clinic not liable for sexual misconduct by employee physician with male patient during examination]; P.S. v. Psychiatric Coverage, 887 S.W.2d 622 (Mo. Ct. App. 1994) [sexual relations with patient not within scope of employment, so clinic not vicariously liable]; *contra*, Morin v. Henry Mayo Newhall Mem. Hosp., 29 Cal. App. 4th 473, 34 Cal. Rptr. 2d 535 (2d Dist. 1994), [hospital liable under *respondeat superior* for sexual misconduct of ultrasound technician], *rev. granted*, 37 Cal. Rptr. 2d 259, 886 P.2d 1252 (Cal. 1995) [not citable in Cal.]; Samuels v. Southern Baptist Hosp., 594 So.2d 571 (La. Ct. App. 1992), *cert. denied*, 599 So.2d 316 (La. 1992) [hospital liable for sexual assault by employee nursing assistant during working hours on premises because reasonably incidental to employee's performance of his duty]; Annotation, *Liability of hospital or clinic for sexual relationships with patients by staff physicians, psychologists, and other healers*, 45 A.L.R. 4TH 289.

134. *E.g.*, Krane v. St. Anthony Hosp. Sys., 738 P.2d 75 (Colo. Ct. App. 1987).

135. *E.g.*, Holger v. Irish, 316 Or. 402, 851 P.2d 1122 (1993).

136. *E.g.*, Somerset v. Hart, 549 S.W.2d 814 (Ky. 1977) [surgeon, hospital both liable for nurse's instrument count].

137. *E.g.*, Menzie v. Windham Commun. Mem. Hosp., 774 F. Supp. 91 (D. Conn. 1991); Reed v. Good Samaritan Hosp. Ass'n, 453 So.2d 229 (Fla. 4th DCA 1984).

138. Overstreet v. Doctors Hosp., 142 Ga. App. 895, 237 S.E.2d 213 (1977).

139. Beeck v. Tucson Gen. Hosp., 18 Ariz. App. 165, 500 P.2d 1153 (1972).

140. Keene v. Methodist Hosp., 324 F. Supp. 233 (N.D. Ind. 1971).

141. Arango v. Reyka, 507 So.2d 1211 (Fla. 4th DCA 1987); *contra* Underwood v. Holy Name of Jesus Hosp., 289 Ala. 216, 266 So.2d 773 (1972); *see* R. Miller, *Joint Venture: Another theory of hospital liability for physicians*, 5 HOSP. L. NEWSLETTER, Sept. 1988, at 5; *see also* Suarez Matos v. Ashford Presbyterian Comm. Hosp., 4 F.3d 47 (1st Cir. 1993) [granting staff privileges

along with sharing profits was joint enterprise under Puerto Rican law which could make hospital liable pathologist's reporting of tumor as benign although he knew it was not].

142. Grewe v. Mt. Clemens Gen. Hosp., 404 Mich. 240, 273 N.W.2d 429 (1978); *accord*, Creech v. Roberts, 908 F.2d 75 (6th Cir. 1990), *cert. denied*, 499 U.S. 975 (1991); Gilbert v. Sycamore Mun. Hosp., 156 Ill. 2d 511, 622 N.E.2d 788 (1993) [hospital liable for acts of physician at hospital regardless of status as independent contractor unless patient knew or should have known he was independent contractor]; Clark v. Southview Hosp. & Family Health Ctr., 68 Ohio St. 3d 435, 628 N.E.2d 46 (1994) [same]; *see also* Pamperin v. Trinity Mem. Hosp., 144 Wis. 2d 188, 423 N.W.2d 848 (1988); Boyd v. Albert Einstein Med. Ctr., 377 Pa. Super. 609, 547 A.2d 1229 (1988) [HMO may be liable for ostensible agent].

143. *E.g.*, Holmes v. University Health Serv., Inc., 205 Ga. App. 602, 423 S.E.2d 281 (1992), *cert. denied*, 1992 Ga. LEXIS 959 (Nov. 19, 1992) [residents provided by medical college not apparent agents of hospital, especially where decedent had signed document acknowledging that physician was not an employee or agent of hospital].

144. *E.g.*, Beeck v. Tucson Gen. Hosp., 18 Ariz. App. 165, 500 P.2d 1153 (1972).

145. *E.g.*, Thompson v. Nason Hosp., 527 Pa. 330, 591 A.2d 703 (1991).

146. Adamski v. Tacoma Gen. Hosp., 20 Wash. App. 98, 579 P.2d 970 (1978); *accord* Griffin v. Matthews, 36 Ohio App. 3d 228, 522 N.E.2d 1110 (1987).

147. KAN. STAT. ANN. § 65-442(b); McVay v. Rich, 255 Kan. 371, 874 P.2d 641 (1994) [statute bars patient claim against hospital for negligently extending clinical privileges to nonemployee physician].

148. *E.g.*, Pedroza v. Bryant, 101 Wash. 2d 226, 677 P.2d 166 (1984).

149. Copithorne v. Framingham Union Hosp., 401 Mass. 860, 520 N.E.2d 139 (1988).

150. *See* A.M. Zibelman, *The practice standard of care and liability of managed care plans*, 27 J. HEALTH & HOSP. L. 204 (1994).

151. R. Roth, *The effect of ERISA preemption on tort claims against employers, insurers, health plan administrators, managed care entities, and utilization review agents*, 7 THE HEALTH LAWYER (Wint. 1994–95) 7.

152. *E.g.*, Spain v. Aetna Life Ins. Co., 11 F.3d 129 (9th Cir. 1993), *cert. denied*, 114 S. Ct. 1612 (U.S. 1994) [ERISA preempted wrongful death claim based on delay in approval of third part of autologous bone marrow transplantation]; Kuhl v. Lincoln Nat'l Health Plan, 999 F.2d 298 (8th Cir. 1993) [ERISA preempted surviving family's state law claims after death of plan member due to delay in approving necessary heart surgery], *cert. denied*, 114 S. Ct. 694 (U.S. 1994); Corcoran v. United Healthcare, 965 F.2d 1321 (5th Cir.), *cert. denied*, 113 S. Ct. 812 (U.S. 1992) [ERISA preempts wrongful death action against utilization review provider for death of child when reviewer allegedly refused to approve hospitalization of pregnant mother prescribed by physician to monitor fetus; reviewer authorized only home nursing during time no nurse was present, fetus died]; P.M. Mellette & J.E. Kurtz, *Corcoran v. United Healthcare, Inc.: Liability of utilization review companies in light of ERISA*, 26 J. HEALTH & HOSP. L. 129 (1993); *Courts support health insurers that reject 'unnecessary' care*, WALL ST. J., Nov. 25, 1992, at B8 [Corcoran]; Butler v. Wu, 853 F. Supp. 125 (D. N.J. 1994) [claims against HMO for vicarious liability for participating physician preempted by ERISA]; Ricci v. Gooberman, 840 F. Supp. 316 (D. N.J. 1993) [ERISA preempts malpractice suit against HMO for vicarious liability]; *contra*, Dukes v. United States Healthcare, Inc., 57 F.3d 350 (3d Cir. 1995) [medical negligence action against HMO not completely preempted]; Kearney v. United States Healthcare Inc., 859 F. Supp. 182 (E.D. Pa. 1994) [malpractice claim against plan for actions of physicians contracting with plan not preempted by ERISA]; Dearmas v. Av-Med, Inc., 865 F. Supp. 816 (S.D. Fla. 1994) [ERISA preempts negligence claim for plan administration against HMO, but

vicarious liability claim for malpractice of treating physician not preempted]; Stroker v. Rubin, 1994 U.S.Dist. LEXIS 18,379 (E.D. Pa. Dec. 22, 1993) [ERISA bars direct negligence claims against HMO, but not claims that HMO is vicariously liable].

153. *E.g.*, Schleier v. Kaiser Found. Health Plan, 277 U.S. App. D.C. 415, 876 F.2d 174 (1989) [HMO liable for negligence of consulting physician even though independent contractor]; Boyd v. Albert Einstein Med. Ctr., 377 Pa. Super. 609, 547 A.2d 1229 (1988) [participating physicians may be ostensible agents of HMO].

154. Dunn v. Praiss, 256 N.J. Super. 180, 606 A.2d 862 (A.D. 1992). Physician settled and HMO avoided contribution, 139 N.J. 564, 656 A.2d 413 (1995).

155. *E.g.*, Raglin v. HMO Ill., Inc., 230 Ill. App. 3d 642, 595 N.E.2d 153 (1st Dist. 1992) [physician in IPA model HMO not employee or apparent agent so HMO not liable for alleged malpractice]; Chase v. Independent Practice Ass'n, 31 Mass. App. Ct. 661, 583 N.E.2d 251 (1991) [HMO not liable for negligence of contract physician].

156. Harrell v. Total Health Care, 781 S.W.2d 58 (Mo. 1989).

157. Wickline v. State, 183 Cal. App. 3d 1175, 228 Cal. Rptr. 661 (2d Dist. 1986), *rev. dismissed*, 239 Cal. Rptr. 805, 741 P.2d 613 (Cal. 1987).

158. B. McCormick, *Managed care posing new liability risks, insurers warn*, AM. MED. NEWS, June 13, 1994, at 3.

159. *See* M.W. Peregrine, W.H. Roach, and D.L. Glaser, *Ascending liability and attribution: Corporate concerns for the 1990s*, 26 J. HEALTH & HOSP. L. 33 (1993).

160. Concord Hosp. v. New Hampshire Med. Malpractice Joint Underwriting Ass'n, 137 N.H. 680, 633 A.2d 1384 (1993).

161. *E.g.*, *Upjohn, in move to back halcion drug, will pay physicians' legal costs in suits*, WALL ST. J., Nov. 27, 1991, B2 [promise to pay legal costs, settlements or verdicts of physicians sued for prescribing halcion, similar to Eli Lilly program for prozac in summer of 1991]; *Beware of offers of indemnity*, 327 N. ENGL. J. MED. 819 (1992).

162. *E.g.*, FLA. STAT. § 395.041.

163. 1995 Joint Commission CAMH, at 219–66.

164. *Id.* at 240.

165. *E.g.*, Torry, *Arizona law brings lowering of liability insurance rates*, AM. MED. NEWS, July 21, 1989, at 15.

166. *E.g.*, *Malpractice settlements and awards dropped last year*, AM. MED. NEWS, Feb. 13, 1995, at 9.

167. *See Effect of tort reform on health costs is difficult to pin down, researchers say*, 4 H.L.R. 511 (1995); *Reforms unlikely to affect defensive medicine, OTA says; AMA criticizes report*, 3 H.L.R. 1048 (1994); *Potential savings from reform remains key point of controversy*, 3 H.L.R. 1586 (1994).

168. *See* Annotation, *Medical malpractice: who are 'health providers,' or the like, whose actions fall within statutes specifically governing actions and damages for medical malpractice*, 12 A.L.R. 5TH 1; Weinstock v. Groth, 629 So.2d 835 (Fla. 1993) [psychologist not health care provider under Florida tort reform law]; Perez v. Bay State Ambulance & Hosp. Rental Serv., Inc., 413 Mass. 670, 602 N.E.2d 570 (1992) [ambulance company not health care provider so not subject to panel review].

169. *See* Annotation, *Validity and construction of state statutory provisions relating to limitations on amount of recovery in medical malpractice claim and submission of such claims to pretrial panel*, 80 A.L.R. 3D 583.

170. *E.g.*, Hoem v. State, 756 P.2d 780 (Wyo. 1988); Bernier v. Burris, 113 Ill. 2d 219, 497 N.E.2d 763 (1986); State ex rel. Cardinal Glennon Mem. Hosp. v. Gaertner, 583 S.W.2d 107 (Mo. 1979).

171. Aldana v. Holub, 381 So.2d 231 (Fla. 1980).

172. *E.g.*, Keyes v. Humana Hosp. Alaska, Inc., 750 P.2d 343 (Alaska 1988); Paro v. Longwood Hosp., 373 Mass. 645, 369 N.E.2d 985 (1977); Johnson v. St. Vincent Hosp., Inc., 273 Ind. 374, 404 N.E.2d 585 (1980); Cha v. Warnick, 476 N.E.2d 109 (Ind.), *cert. denied*, 474 U.S. 920 (1985).

173. *E.g.*, Winoma Mem. Found. v. Lomax, 465 N.E.2d 731 (Ind. Ct. App. 1984) [screening not required for slip and fall case]; Brown v. Rabbitt, 300 Md. 171, 476 A.2d 1167 (1984) [screening required for express contract to cure].

174. *E.g.*, Bledsoe v. Crowley, 270 U.S. App. D.C. 308, 849 F.2d 639 (1988); Feinstein v. Massachusetts Gen. Hosp., 643 F.2d 880 (1st Cir. 1981); Woods v. Holy Cross Hosp., 591 F.2d 1164 (5th Cir. 1979); *contra* Seck v. Hamrang, 657 F. Supp. 1074 (S.D. N.Y. 1987); *see also* Jones v. Griffith, 870 F.2d 1363 (7th Cir. 1989) [federal court cannot give instructions to state medical review panel].

175. *See* Daigle v. Maine Med. Ctr., 14 F.3d 684 (1st Cir. 1994) [affirming judgment for hospital after findings of prelitigation hearing panel used in accordance with Maine law]; Wright v. Carter, 622 N.E.2d 170 (Ind. 1993) [unanimous opinion of malpractice panel in favor of surgeon coupled with plaintiff's failure to provide rebutting expert testimony entitled surgeon to judgment as a matter of law].

176. Annotation, *Arbitration of medical malpractice claims*, 24 A.L.R. 5th 1.

177. *E.g.*, Neaman v. Kaiser Found. Hosp., 9 Cal. App. 4th 1170, 11 Cal. Rptr. 2d 879 (2nd Dist. 1992), *modified*, 10 Cal. App. 4th 293, *rev. denied*, 1992 Cal. LEXIS 628 (Dec. 17, 1992) [award in favor of hospital vacated, remanded for new panel of arbitrators because "neutral" third arbitrator failed to disclose prior substantial business relationship with hospital].

178. Madden v. Kaiser Found. Hosps., 17 Cal. 3d 699, 131 Cal. Rptr. 882, 552 P.2d 1178 (1976).

179. Herbert v. Superior Court, 169 Cal. App. 3d 718, 215 Cal. Rptr. 477 (2d Dist. 1985); *accord*, Ling Wo Leong v. Kaiser Found. Hosp., 71 Haw. 240, 788 P.2d 164 (1990) [arbitration provision in father's health plan required malpractice claim of newborn treated under plan to be arbitrated]; *see also* Mormile v. Sinclair, 21 Cal. App. 4th 1508, 26 Cal. Rptr. 2d 725 (4th Dist. 1994) [agreement to arbitrate signed by spouse enforceable against nonsigning spouse making consortium claim].

180. Morris v. Metriyakool, 418 Mich. 423, 344 N.W.2d 736 (1984); *see also* Green v. Gallucci, 169 Mich. App. 533, 426 N.W.2d 693 (1988).

181. Moore v. Conliffe, 7 Cal. 4th 634, 29 Cal. Rptr.2d 152, 871 P.2d 204 (Cal. 1994).

182. *E.g.*, McGinn, *Vermont MDs push tort system revamp: Medical negligence bill calls for administrative system*, AM. MED. NEWS, Apr. 28, 1989, at 3.

183. Brown v. Gardner, 115 S. Ct. 552 (U.S. 1994).

184. *See* Annotation, *Validity and construction of state statutory provisions limiting amount of recovery in medical malpractice claims*, 26 A.L.R. 5TH 245.

185. OTA, IMPACT OF LEGAL REFORMS ON MEDICAL MALPRACTICE COSTS (Oct. 27, 1993); *Damage caps, collateral source offsets succeed in reducing malpractice costs*, 2 H.L.R. 1489 (1993).

186. *See* K.A. Olson, *Survey of constitutional arguments in medical malpractice award limit cases*, 23 J. HEALTH & HOSP. L. 328 (1990).

187. Wright v. Central Du Page Hosp. Ass'n, 63 Ill. 2d 313, 347 N.E.2d 736 (1976); *accord*, Morris v. Savoy, 61 Ohio St.3d 684, 576 N.E.2d 765 (1991) [statutory damage cap unconstitutional];

Sofie v. Fibreboard Corp., 112 Wash. 2d 636, 771 P.2d 711 (1989); Reynolds v. Porter, 760 P.2d 816 (Okla. 1988); Smith v. Department of Ins., 507 So.2d 1080 (Fla. 1987) [unconstitutional].

188. Johnson v. St. Vincent Hosp., 273 Ind. 374, 404 N.E.2d 585 (1980); *accord* Duke Power Co. v. Carolina Environmental Study Group, Inc., 438 U.S. 59 (1978) [Congress may cap damages for nuclear reactor incidents]; Scholz v. Metropolitan Pathologists, P.C., 851 P.2d 901 (Colo. 1993) [statutory cap on noneconomic damages constitutional]; Adams v. Children's Mercy Hosp., 832 S.W.2d 898 (Mo.), *cert. denied*, 113 S. Ct. 511 (U.S. 1992) [statutory cap on damages constitutional]; Butler v. Flint Goodrich Hosp., 607 So.2d 517 (La. 1992), *cert. denied*, 113 S. Ct. 2338 (U.S. 1993) [$500,000 cap on medical malpractice judgments not violation of equal protection]; Samsel v. Wheeler Transp. Servs., Inc., 244 Kan. 726, 771 P.2d 71 (1989), *supp. op.*, 246 Kan. 336, 789 P.2d 541 (1990); Boyd v. Bulala, 877 F.2d 1191 (4th Cir. 1989), *answer to certified question conformed to*, 905 F.2d 764 (4th Cir. 1990) [Virginia cap on damages upheld]; Etheridge v. Med. Ctr. Hosps., 237 Va. 87, 376 S.E.2d 525 (1989) [$750,000 cap on total damages upheld]; Franklin v. Mazda Motor Corp., 704 F. Supp. 1325 (D. Md. 1989) [$350,000 cap on noneconomic damages upheld]; Williams v. Kushner, 524 So.2d 191 (La. Ct. App. 4th Cir. 1988) [$500,000 cap upheld], *amended & aff'd*, 549 So.2d 294 (La. 1989) [future medical care excluded from limit]; Fein v. Permanente Med. Group, 38 Cal. 3d 137, 695 P.2d 665, 211 Cal. Rptr. 368, *appeal dismissed*, 474 U.S. 892 (1985) [$250,000 limit on noneconomic damages upheld]; Fetter v. United States, 649 F. Supp. 1097 (S.D. Cal. 1986) [cap applied in suit against U.S.]; Hoffman v. United States, 767 F.2d 1431 (9th Cir. 1985).

189. *E.g.*, Power v. Arlington Hosp. Ass'n, 42 F.3d 851 (4th Cir. 1994) [EMTALA claim subject to state damages cap]; Lee by Wetzel v. Allegheny Reg. Hosp. Corp., 778 F. Supp. 900 (W.D. Va. 1991) [EMTALA damages subject to state cap].

190. *E.g.*, Lozada v. United States, 974 F.2d 986 (8th Cir. 1992) [$1 million state cap applicable to FTCA suit despite contention hospital did not meet requirements as qualified health care provider]; Carter v. United States, 982 F.2d 1141 (7th Cir. 1992) [U.S. protected in FTCA suit by Indiana malpractice damage cap].

191. Lucas v. United States, 757 S.W.2d 687 (Tex. 1988).

192. Page, *TMA-backed coalition ousts court majority*, AM. MED. NEWS, Nov. 18, 1988, at 7.

193. Rose v. Doctors Hosp., 801 S.W.2d 841 (Tex. 1990).

194. Kansas Malpractice Victims Coalition v. Bell, 243 Kan. 333, 757 P.2d 251 (1988).

195. Hillen, *Kan. backs limits for pain, suffering*, AM. MED. NEWS, Apr. 21, 1989, at 22; McGinn, *Kansas MDs await ruling on award cap*, AM. MED. NEWS, Oct. 13, 1989, at 1 [final ruling may also address cap in medical cases].

196. *E.g.*, Bernier v. Burris, 113 Ill. 2d 219, 497 N.E.2d 763 (1986); Rudolph v. Iowa Methodist Med. Ctr., 293 N.W.2d 550 (Iowa 1980).

197. *E.g.*, Coburn v. Agustin, 627 F. Supp. 983 (D. Kan. 1985).

198. *E.g.*, King v. Virginia Birth-Related Neurological Injury Comp. Program, 242 Va. 404, 410 S.E.2d 656 (1991) [constitutional to require physicians to contribute to fund]; McGibony v. Florida Birth-Related Neurological Injury Comp. Plan, 564 So.2d 177 (Fla. 1st DCA 1990), *approved*, 595 So.2d 943 (Fla.), *cert. denied*, 113 S. Ct. 194 (U.S. 1992) [no-fault compensation plan not violation of due process or equal protection rights of physicians who were required to contribute; lawful to delegate to Department of Insurance power to increase assessments on actuarial sound standard]; Johnson v. St. Vincent Hosp., 273 Ind. 374, 404 N.E.2d 585 (1980); Meier v. Anderson, 692 F. Supp. 546 (E.D. Pa. 1988), *aff'd without op.*, 869 F.2d 590 (3d Cir. 1989).

199. *E.g.*, Turner v. Hubrich, 656 So.2d 970 (Fla. 5th DCA 1995) [Birth-Related Neurological Injury Compensation Act, FLA. STAT. §§ 766.301–766.316, provides exclusive administrative remedy

against participating providers if they give notice of their participation to patients prior to services].

200. *See* Shalala v. Whitecotton, 115 S. Ct. 1477 (U.S. 1995); Schindler v. Secretary of DHHS, 29 F.3d 607 (Fed. Cir. 1994); Patton v. Secretary of DHHS, 25 F.3d 1021 (Fed. Cir. 1994); Weddel ex rel. Weddel v. Secretary of DHHS, 23 F.3d 388 (Fed. Cir. 1994).

201. *E.g.*, Bernier v. Burris, 113 Ill. 2d 219, 497 N.E.2d 763 (1986) [constitutional]; American Bank & Trust Co. v. Community Hosp., 36 Cal. 3d 359, 683 P.2d 670, 204 Cal. Rptr. 671 (1984) [constitutional]; *contra* Galayda v. Lake Hosp. Sys., 71 Ohio St. 3d 421, 644 N.E.2d 298 (1994) [statute requiring periodic payments violated right to due process and jury trial]; Smith v. Myers, 181 Ariz. 11, 887 P.2d 541 (1994) [periodic payment statute unconstitutional limit on remedies]; *No periodic payment of damages in Arizona*, AM. MED. NEWS, Feb. 6, 1995, at 4; Kansas Malpractice Victims Coalition v. Bell, 243 Kan. 333, 757 P.2d 251 (1988).

202. Hull v. United States, 971 F.2d 1499 (10th Cir. 1992).

203. Walt Disney World Co. v. Wood, 515 So.2d 198 (Fla. 1987).

204. *E.g.*, Florida Patient's Compensation Fund v. St. Paul Fire & Marine Ins. Co., 535 So.2d 335 (Fla. 4th DCA 1988), *approved*, 595 So.2d 195 (Fla. 1990).

205. FLA. STAT. § 768.81 [joint and several liability modified], § 768.31 [contribution permitted]; *see also* Smith v. Department of Ins., 507 So.2d 1080 (Fla. 1987) [§ 768.81 constitutional]; Fabre v. Marin, 623 So.2d 1182 (Fla. 1993) [§ 768.81(3) not ambiguous; entry of judgment on basis of percentage fault means judgment must be based on percentage of total fault regardless of whether others responsible could have been joined as defendants].

206. *E.g.*, Crowe v. Humana, 439 S.E.2d 654 (Ga. 1994) [upheld requirement minors injured when less than age five sue by age seven]; Douglas v. Hugh A. Stallings, M.D., Inc., 870 F.2d 1242 (7th Cir. 1989) [upheld requirement that minors injured when less than six years old sue by age eight]; *contra* Mominee v. Scherbarth, 28 Ohio St.3d 270, 503 N.E.2d 717 (1986) [minors have right to wait until adulthood to sue]; Strahler v. St. Luke's Hosp., 706 S.W.2d 7 (Mo. 1986) (*en banc*) [minors have right to wait until becoming adults to sue]; Barrio v. San Manuel Div. Hosp., 143 Ariz. 101, 692 P.2d 280 (1984) [unconstitutional to require minors injured when less than age seven to sue by age ten]; Annotation, *Medical malpractice statutes of limitation minority provisions*, 62 A.L.R. 4TH 758.

207. *E.g.*, Hershberger v. Akron City Hosp., 34 Ohio St. 3d 1, 516 N.E.2d 204 (1987), *as clarified by* Allenius v. Thomas, 42 Ohio St. 3d 131, 538 N.E.2d 93 (1989).

208. *E.g.*, Carr v. Broward County, 541 So.2d 92 (Fla. 1989) [suit can be barred before discovery possible]; McDonald v. Haynes Med. Lab., Inc., 192 Conn. 327, 471 A.2d 646 (1984) [suit can be barred before injury occurs]; *contra* Hardy v. VerMeulen, 32 Ohio St. 3d 45, 512 N.E.2d 626 (1987), *cert. denied*, 484 U.S. 1066 (1988) [suit cannot be barred before discovery]; Shessel v. Stroup, 253 Ga. 56, 316 S.E.2d 155 (1984) [suit cannot be barred before injury occurs].

209. *E.g.*, FLA. STAT. § 768.46.

210. *E.g.*, IOWA CODE ANN. § 147.138; Newton v. Cox, 878 S.W.2d 105 (Tenn.), *cert. denied*, 115 S. Ct. 189 (U.S. 1994) [upholding cap on contingent fees in medical malpractice cases]; *see also* Walters v. National Ass'n of Radiation Survivors, 473 U.S. 305 (1985); National Ass'n of Radiation Survivors v. Derwinski, 994 F.2d 583 (9th Cir.), *cert. denied*, 114 S. Ct. 634 (U.S. 1993) [upholding $10 limit on fees veteran can pay attorney for assistance in VA claim, but note Congress removed $10 limit in 1988 in Pub. L. No. 100-687, 102 Stat. 4105 for later claims]; Beck v. Secretary of HHS, 924 F.2d 1029 (Fed. Cir. 1991) [attorney in successful Vaccine Act claim limited to fees provided in Act].

211. *E.g.*, IOWA CODE ANN. § 619.18; *contra* White v. Fisher, 689 P.2d 102 (Wyo. 1984) [unconstitutional]; *but see* Boothe v. Lawrence Hosp., 188 A.D.2d 435, 591 N.Y.S.2d 412 (1st Dep't 1992) [only sanction for violation was striking offensive reference].

212. *E.g.*, FLA. STAT. § 766.102(2)(c); Payne v. Caldwell, 796 S.W.2d 142 (Tenn. 1990) [upheld requirement that expert be licensed in state or contiguous state for full previous year]; Sutphin v. Platt, 720 S.W.2d 455 (Tenn. 1986) [medical experts must be from Tennessee or contiguous states]; Dekker v. Magic Valley Reg. Med. Ctr., 115 Idaho 332, 766 P.2d 1213 (1988) [expert barred from testifying because statutory standard not met].

213. *E.g.*, Williams v. Chicago Osteopathic Med. Ctr., 173 Ill. App. 3d 125, 527 N.E.2d 409 (1st Dist. 1988); Shackleford v. State, 534 So.2d 38 (La. Ct. App. 1988), *cert. denied*, 536 So.2d 1218 (La. 1989).

214. *E.g.*, FLA. STAT. § 768.73; *Punitive damages tax falls short as New York state revenue source*, WALL ST. J., Nov. 13, 1992, at B10.

215. *E.g.*, Patry v. Capps, 633 So.2d 9 (Fla. 1994) [acknowledged receipt of hand-delivered notice sufficient despite statutory requirement of certified mail]; Boyd v. Becker, 627 So.2d 481 (Fla. 1993) [90-day presuit period began on receipt, so suit timely].

216. *E.g.*, Mosberg v. Elahi, 80 N.Y.2d 941, 590 N.Y.S.2d 866, 605 N.E.2d 353 (1992) [dismissal mandated where affidavit of merit not filed]; Estate of Cassara by Cassara v. Illinois, 853 F. Supp. 273 (N.D. Ill. 1994) [dismissal for failure to comply with state law requirement of attached affidavit of professional attesting to reasonable, meritorious case].

217. Wolf v. Richmond County Hosp. Auth., 745 F.2d 904 (4th Cir. 1984), *cert. denied*, 474 U.S. 826 (1985); *see also* Pijanowski v. Cleveland Clinic Found., 635 F. Supp. 1435 (E.D. Pa. 1986) [mailing solicitations into state].

218. Presbyterian Univ. Hosp. v. Wilson, 99 Md. App. 305, 637 A.2d 486 (1994) [Pennsylvania hospital's registration as Maryland medical assistance provider gave Maryland court jurisdiction over claim on behalf of deceased Maryland resident], *aff'd*, 337 Md. 541, 654 A.2d 1324 (1995).

219. *E.g.*, Rogers v. Furlow, 699 F. Supp. 672 (N.D. Ill. 1988) [dismissal for want of personal jurisdiction; confirmatory letter, phone call not sufficient contact].

220. *E.g.*, Etra v. Matta, 61 N.Y.2d 455, 474 N.Y.S.2d 687, 463 N.E.2d 3 (1984).

221. Kaiser-Georgetown Commun. Health Plan v. Stutsman, 491 A.2d 502 (D.C. 1985); *see also* Scharfman v. National Jewish Hosp., 122 A.D.2d 939, 506 N.Y.S.2d 90 (2d Dep't 1986) [Colorado hospital could be sued in New York because it screened patients there].

222. Workman v. Chinchinian, 807 F. Supp. 634 (E.D. Wash. 1992).

223. Rieger v. Group Health Ass'n, 851 F. Supp. 788 (N.D. Miss. 1994).

11

Examples of Tort Liability

The previous chapter reviewed the general principles of civil liability. This chapter reviews the application of those principles to specific situations that have resulted in suits against hospitals and health care professionals, illustrating the scope of the duty of hospitals and their staff members to patients and others.

HOSPITALS

Hospital liability can be based on (1) a violation by an employee of the employee's duties or (2) a violation of the hospital's duties. Hospital liability for injuries caused by an employee's violation of the employee's duties is based on the doctrine of *respondeat superior*, discussed in Chapter 10.

Whenever individual health professionals function as hospital employees or agents, their liability exposure also constitutes hospital liability exposure. Many hospital duties are not based on *respondeat superior*. To prove liability for injuries caused by breaches of these duties, it is not necessary to show that an individual staff member breached a duty; it is sufficient to show a breach of the hospital's duty. Areas in which hospitals have an independent duty include (1) maintenance of the physical condition of the buildings and grounds, (2) selection and maintenance of equipment, and (3) selection and supervision of staff.

Physical Condition of the Buildings and Grounds

The hospital must exercise reasonable care in maintaining its buildings and grounds in a reasonably safe condition. An accident alone is not enough to establish liability. State or local regulations may establish standards, and injuries resulting from violations of those standards can lead to liability. When regulatory standards have not been violated, hospitals generally are liable only when the plaintiff proves that the hospital's employees or agents created a condition likely to cause injury or that they knew or should have known of a condition likely to cause injury and failed to take action to provide warning or correct the condition.

Hospital buildings and grounds should be designed and maintained to meet the special needs of the infirm and disabled persons using hospital facilities. When these patients are injured, it will not be a sufficient defense to show that hospital facilities were safe for people in ordinary physical condition. The hospital may also be liable for injuries to visitors and others. The hospital must exercise the same reasonable care as any other business that regularly invites the public onto its grounds and into its buildings. The hospital is not liable for injuries caused by a dangerous condition when the injured person was aware of the condition, was able to avoid the risk of injury, and, nevertheless, chose to ignore the risk. For example, in a 1968 Texas case, the antenna wire for a television in a patient's room was in a place where it could be tripped over. The patient had been aware of the wire and had walked around the set to avoid the wire several times during her stay. On the day of her discharge she chose to step over the wire and tripped. The hospital won the suit because the danger was open and obvious and the patient had the ability to avoid it.[1] However, in 1990, the North Carolina Supreme Court ruled that a hospital visitor was not responsible for watching for a three-inch rise in the sidewalk when there were diversions such as low-hanging tree branches and uneven illumination.[2]

Suits have arisen out of accidents involving, for example, elevators,[3] broken steps,[4] slippery materials on the floors,[5] defective carpet,[6] automobiles in the parking lot,[7] and malfunction of automatic gates and doors.[8]

Courts have disagreed on the extent to which a hospital must protect persons on hospital premises from crimes by persons unassociated with the hospital. The California Supreme Court ruled that a hospital had a duty to protect persons in its parking lot in a high crime area, so it could be liable to a physician shot by a robber.[9] A Georgia court ruled in 1991 that injuries to a hospital employee who was attacked in the hospital parking lot arose out of her employment so she could only pursue a claim under the workers' compensation law.[10] In 1992, a Louisiana appellate court ruled that the workers' compensation law did not apply to injuries from an attack on an employee in the parking lot, and the hospital could be liable for breaching a duty to keep parking lot patrons free from physical harm.[11] The Louisiana Supreme Court ruled in 1993 that a nurse's employer was not liable for her injuries from being stabbed by an unknown person as she exited a hospital elevator where there had been no prior similar accidents and nothing could have prevented assault.[12]

Numerous cases have arisen out of sexual assaults on patients and others. Courts have disagreed on the standard for determining when the hospital should be liable. In 1992, the Alabama Supreme Court ruled that hospitals were responsible for protecting anesthetized patients from sexual assault even by trespassers.[13] In 1993, a California court ruled that a hospital could be liable for the sexual assault of a disabled patient if the hospital were shown to have provided inadequate supervision and security.[14] In 1988, the Oregon Supreme Court ruled that a hospital could be liable for the sexual assault of a patient by an employee only if negligent retention or supervision of the employee were shown. The hospital did not have an independent direct duty to the patient in Oregon and the act was outside the scope of employment under state law.[15]

Selection and Maintenance of Equipment

Hospitals have an obligation to furnish reasonably adequate equipment for use in the diagnosis and treatment of patients. Problems can arise when hospitals do not have needed equipment, when needed equipment is not available, or when equipment has not been properly inspected and maintained.

When a hospital does not have the equipment reasonably necessary for the treatment of certain conditions, patients with these conditions should be advised of the hospital's limitations, and arrangements should be made for transfer to another hospital with the necessary equipment unless the patient makes an informed decision to decline the transfer. In a 1977 case, a woman had delivered a stillborn baby because the 14-bed obstetrical clinic she entered for delivery did not have the facilities for a caesarean delivery.[16] The court found the clinic liable because it admitted the woman without having the necessary facilities or warning her of the limited nature of the facilities. In a 1963 California case, a hospital was found liable for injuries to a patient with third-degree burns who was kept for nearly two months in a hospital that did not have the equipment to care for the patient's burns.[17] The court ruled that the hospital had a duty to transfer the patient to another hospital with the necessary equipment. When a patient is reluctant to accept transfer, the most prudent practice is still to encourage transfer, rather than relying on refusal. In 1988, a federal appellate court ruled that a VA hospital was not negligent for failing to have a lung scan machine and that timely arrangements had been made for transfer to a hospital that had the machine, so the United States was not liable for the patient's death.[18]

The hospital is not required to provide the latest equipment. For example, in a Louisiana case, a hospital was found not liable for having older equipment to cut sections of tissue for diagnosis instead of having more modern equipment that could cut thinner sections for a more accurate diagnosis.[19] Several experts testified that the older equipment was widely accepted and produced satisfactory results. A woman whose breast was removed due to misdiagnosis of malignancy was not awarded compensation.

Sometimes equipment may not be available for use due to system design problems or hospital staff failure to plan to have the proper equipment in the area. For example, in a 1993 North Carolina case, a hospital was found liable for the death of a patient due to delay in reintubation because the emergency cart was not stocked with the needed laryngoscope blade.[20] In 1992, the Georgia Supreme Court decided that a hospital could be liable when its employees supplied incorrect parts for cataract equipment which caused a malfunction that injured the eye.[21] In a 1974 Texas case, the hospital was found liable for a patient's death because oxygen was unavailable after she was transferred to a private room.[22] A wall plug in the room supplied oxygen, but the equipment accompanying the patient required a wall plug of a different shape. The design problem was the lack of standardization of wall plugs. Portable oxygen equipment could have supplied the necessary oxygen, but none had accompanied the patient.

A hospital must also exercise reasonable care in inspecting and maintaining equipment. Equipment should be periodically inspected, and discovered defects should be remedied. However, the hospital does not guarantee that the equipment will function properly during customary use. Liability for injuries due to defects in equipment generally depends on whether the defect is latent (hidden) or patent (visible). The user of equipment is generally liable for injuries due to use of equipment with patent defects. The owner of the equipment is generally liable for injuries due to use of equipment with latent defects detectable through reasonable inspections, which were not performed. The manufacturer or seller of the equipment is generally liable when the equipment has a latent defect, such as a flaw in the metal, that the owner could not detect through reasonable inspections.

For example, an Alabama case addressed a patient who was injured because of a defect in an electrical-surgical instrument used in the removal of skin for grafting.[23] A bent spring caused the removal of too thick a patch of skin. The bent spring could have been detected only by dismantling the instrument for inspection. The court found the hospital, but not the surgeon who had used the instrument, liable for the injuries. If the bent spring had been visible to the surgeon without dismantling, the surgeon would have been liable. When equipment users are hospital employees, the hospital can be liable under the doctrine of *respondeat superior* for their failure to detect patent defects. If hospital employees switch equipment that the physician has already inspected, the hospital can also be liable for resultant injuries. An Ohio case concerned a surgeon who examined a cauterizing machine and then left the operating room.[24] While he was gone, a hospital employee substituted another machine that appeared so similar that the surgeon did not notice the switch. The patient was burned during the surgery due to a defect in the machine. The surgeon was found not to be liable.

When the hospital or physician knows that the equipment is defective, it is easier to establish liability because the defect is clearly patent. In an Oklahoma case, the employer was found liable for an employee's use of equipment that was clearly malfunctioning.[25] The employee knew the electrotherapy machine was malfunctioning, but instead of turning off the machine and seeking assistance, she continued to use the machine until the patient was burned. In an Iowa case, a surgeon was found liable for a patient's infection resulting from contaminated sutures because he knew they were contaminated when he used them.[26] An earlier patient had become infected through use of sutures from the same supply.

At least one state has adopted a minority position that hospitals may be liable for some defects that are not detectable. A 1975 New Jersey case involved a surgical device that broke with a piece lodging in the patient's spine.[27] The break was due to either improper twisting by the surgeon or a flaw in the metal that could not be detected by the inspections normally conducted by hospitals. The jury found that neither the physician nor the hospital had been negligent. The appellate court ordered a new trial at which either the physician or the hospital had to be found responsible.

Selection and Supervision of Staff

A hospital can be liable for failing to exercise reasonable care in selecting and supervising its staff and in setting staffing levels.[28] This liability applies to both professional and nonprofessional staff. Hospitals have a responsibility to evaluate the credentials of applicants for jobs. When a state license is required, the hospital should determine that the applicant has the license, but checking the license alone is not a sufficient check of the applicant's background and qualifications. The hospital should also provide appropriate training, supervision, and evaluation. When evaluations indicate problems, appropriate action should be taken. In 1992, a Texas court ruled that expert testimony was not required to establish negligence in the supervising and assigning of a nurse, where the employee evaluation forms indicated an unsatisfactory rating over three months before the incident.[29]

These issues are discussed in more detail in the "Private Credentialing" section of Chapter 8 and in the "General Staff Relations Issues" section of Chapter 9.

The hospital also has a responsibility to exercise reasonable care in selecting and monitoring members of the medical staff, as discussed in Chapters 7 and 8. The potential for hospital liability for acts of physicians is discussed in the "*Respondeat Superior*," "Agency," "Apparent or Ostensible Agency," and "Institutional Liability" sections of Chapter 10.

GOVERNING BODY AND ADMINISTRATOR

Members of the governing body have seldom been found personally liable for the activities of the hospital or for their own activities related to the hospital. Their liability exposure is discussed in the "Liability of Board Members" section of Chapter 2. Administrators have been found liable for negligently supervising their subordinates, for entering contracts outside their authority, and for breaching duties imposed by statute. This liability exposure is discussed in the "Liability of the Administrator" section of Chapter 2 and in the "Supervisors" section of this chapter.

SUPERVISORS

Supervisors are not the employers of staff they supervise. Thus, *respondeat superior* does not impose liability on supervisors for the acts or omissions of staff they supervise. Supervisors are liable only for the consequences of their own acts or omissions. The supervisor is usually a hospital employee, so the hospital can be liable under *respondeat superior* for the acts or omissions of supervisors.

The liability of a supervising nurse for the actions of supervised nurses was discussed in a California case involving a needle left in a patient's abdomen during surgery.[30] The patient sued the physicians, the hospital, and the supervising nurse. The court dismissed the suit against the supervising nurse because she had done nothing wrong. She had assigned two competent nurses to assist with the surgery, and she had not been present. Therefore, she had no opportunity to intervene. The court ruled that *respondeat superior* did not apply to the nursing supervisor because she was not the employer.

The actions that can lead to liability of supervising health professionals are discussed in more detail in a New Jersey court decision.[31] The case involved a surgeon who had ordered a resident physician to remove a tube being used to extract the patient's gastric contents. The patient's esophagus was perforated during the removal. The court ruled that the supervising surgeon was not liable for the resident's acts. The court said that the supervising surgeon could be liable only if (1) it was not accepted medical or hospital practice to delegate that particular function to someone with the resident's level of training, (2) he knew or should have known the individual resident was not qualified to perform the task with the degree of supervision provided, (3) he had been present and able to avoid the injury, or (4) he had a special contract with the patient that he did not fulfill. Since none of these circumstances was present, the supervising surgeon was not liable. In some states the courts apply a different legal doctrine to supervising physicians. The *borrowed servant doctrine* and *dual servant doctrine* are discussed in Chapter 10.

A Canadian case provides another illustration of the potential liability of supervising nurses.[32] The court found both the supervising nurse and her hospital employer liable for injuries to a woman who was not observed often enough in a postanesthesia recovery room. The patient had surgery without complications and was transferred to the postanesthesia recovery room. The hospital had provided two nurses for the area, which the court accepted as adequate staffing, but the supervising nurse permitted the other nurse to leave the area for a coffee break just before three patients were admitted to the area. One of the patients suffered a respiratory obstruction that was not observed until the lack of oxygen caused permanent brain damage. The court ruled that the supervising nurse was liable for permitting the other nurse to leave the area at a time when she knew that the operating schedule would result in several admissions to the unit. The court stated that even if she had not known the operating schedule, she would still be liable for not knowing the aspects of the schedule that applied to the staffing needs of the area she supervised. Since the supervising nurse also provided direct nursing care to the patients in the area, she was also liable for failing to observe the patient more frequently. The court ruled that the nurse who left the area would also have been liable if she had been included in the suit because she should have known the aspects of the operating schedule that applied to the staffing needs of the area in which she worked.[33] The hospital was also liable for the acts of both nurses under the doctrine of *respondeat superior.*

In a New York case, a patient who was disoriented had been found on a balcony outside a second-story window.[34] After the patient was returned to the hospital room, the physician told the staff to arrange to have the patient watched. The charge nurse called the patient's family to tell them to arrange to have someone watch the patient. The family said someone would be at the hospital in 10 to 15 minutes. When the family member arrived, the patient had fallen out of the window and was severely injured. The hospital was found liable for failing to move the patient to a secure room, apply additional restraints, or find someone to watch the patient for 15 minutes. One charge nurse, one new registered nurse in orientation, one practical nurse, and one aide were working in a unit with 19 patients. The court found that all except the aide had been engaged in routine duties that could have been delayed for 15 minutes and that the aide had been permitted to leave for supper during that period. The court said that this finding was evidence that staffing was sufficient to provide continuous supervision for a patient in known danger for 15 minutes. The failure of the supervising nurse to properly allocate the time of the available staff was one of the grounds for hospital liability. The general principles discussed in this section also apply to other supervising health care professionals.

In 1994, a federal court decided that there had been failure to supervise assistants adequately at an air force medical center where the supervision had consisted of a random review of a ten-percent sample of the records of their care.[35]

In summary, a supervisor can be liable if

1. the supervisor assigns a subordinate to do something the supervisor knows or should know the subordinate is unable to do;
2. the supervisor does not supervise a subordinate to the degree the supervisor knows or should know the subordinate needs;

3. the supervisor is present and fails to take action when possible to avoid the injury; or
4. the supervisor does not properly allocate the time of available staff.

NURSES

A professional nurse is held to the standard of care generally observed by other competent nurses under similar circumstances.[36] The standard of care applicable to nursing students is not different from the standard for professional nurses. States vary on the standard of care expected of nurses in specialties that overlap with the scope of practice of physicians. In some states such nurses are held to the standard of physicians. For example, a Louisiana decision ruled that when a person assisting a physician performs a task deemed to be medical in nature, such as removal of a cast with a saw, the person is held to the standard of care applicable to a physician.[37] Other states have recognized a distinct standard of care for such nurses. For example, a Texas ruling held nurse specialists to the standard of care observed by those in the same specialty under similar circumstances.[38] In 1985, the California Supreme Court ruled that nurse practitioners should not be held to the standard of care of a physician even when performing functions that overlap with the physician's scope of practice.[39]

Duty To Interpret and Carry Out Orders

Nurses have a duty to interpret and carry out orders properly. Nurses are expected to know basic information concerning the proper use of drugs and procedures they are likely to be ordered to use. When an order is ambiguous or apparently erroneous, the nurse has a responsibility to seek clarification from the ordering physician. This will almost always result in correction or explanation of the order. In the unusual situation in which the explanation does not clarify the appropriateness of the order, the nurse has a responsibility to inform nursing, hospital, or medical staff officials designated by hospital policy who can initiate review of the order and, if necessary, other appropriate action. Pending review, if the drug or procedure appears dangerous to the patient, the nurse should decline to carry out the order, but should immediately notify the ordering physician. Hospitals should have established procedures for nurses to follow when they are not satisfied with the appropriateness of an order. Frequently this procedure will involve notification of a nursing supervisor who will then contact appropriate medical staff officials. Hospital administration may occasionally need to become involved to resolve individual issues.

A 1988 North Dakota case arose when a child was born with severe brain damage after a nurse's alleged failure to place the mother on a fetal heart monitor in accordance with her physician's instructions.[40] In a 1973 California case, a hospital was found liable for the death of a patient because a nurse had failed to follow the physician's order to check the patient's vital signs every 30 minutes and had failed to notify the physician when the patient's condition became life threatening.[41] In a New York case, a nurse and a hospital were held liable for the scalding of a young tonsillectomy patient by water that was served as part of his meal by a nurse, contrary to the dietary instructions ordered by the attending physician.[42] A hospital was sued in a New York case for the blindness of an infant caused by too much oxygen when a nurse gave six liters per minute instead of the four liters per minute ordered by the physician.[43] The hospital presented evidence that six liters per minute was within the range of permissible dosages. The court found this evidence irrelevant because the nurse had not been given authority to deviate from the physician's order and, thus, had breached her duty to the patient. The court ordered a lower court to reconsider the case to determine whether the blindness had been caused by breach of duty.

A physician must, however, make an order known to the nurse by putting it in the medical records or informing the nurse directly. There can be no liability for not following orders given privately to the patient.[44]

Nurses are sometimes given authority to adjust within guidelines the amounts of some drugs or other substances being given to patients. The nurse then has the added responsibility to exercise appropriate judgment in making those adjustments. In many states there are legal limits on the discretion that can be delegated concerning some drugs and substances. As with all delegations, the physician should provide appropriate guidance and delegate this responsibility only to nurses who are able to make the required judgments. In 1979, a California court recognized the appropriateness of delegating to a nurse the decision concerning when a prescribed pain medication was needed.[45] The patient suffered cardiopulmonary arrest and died soon after pain medication was given. The court ruled that it was appropriate for the trial court to give the jury two special instructions usually used only for physicians because the case involved a nurse who was exercising delegated independent judgment. One instruction emphasized that perfection was not required, so liability could not be based on a mere error in judgment by a nurse who possessed the necessary learning and skill and who exercised the care ordinarily exercised by reputable nurses under similar circumstances. The standard applied was the conduct of nurses, not physicians. The other instruction emphasized that when there is more than one recognized method of treatment, it is not negligent to select one of the approved methods that later turns out to be wrong or not to be favored by certain other practitioners. The court upheld the jury verdict in favor of the nurse and the hospital.

Nurses cannot assume that orders have remained unchanged from previous shifts. They have a duty to check for changes in orders. A Delaware case addressed a female patient who had been receiving a drug by injection.[46] The physician wrote an order changing the mode of administration from intravenous to oral. When a nurse prepared to give an injection, the patient objected and referred the nurse to the physician's new order. The nurse told the patient that the patient was mistaken and gave the medication by injection. The nurse's conduct was held to be negligent. The court permitted the jury to find the nurse negligent by applying ordinary common sense, so expert testimony was not necessary to prove the standard of care.

A Louisiana case focused on the nurse's responsibility to obtain clarification of an apparently erroneous physician order.[47] The order was incomplete and subject to misinterpretation. Believing the dosage to be incorrect, the nurse asked two other physicians whether the medication should be given as ordered. The physicians did not interpret the order as the nurse did, so they said the order did not appear out of line. The nurse did not contact the attending physician and administered the misinterpreted dosage, resulting in the patient's death. The nurse was found liable for failing to contact the attending physician before giving the medication. The physician who wrote the ambiguous order was also found liable.

Duty To Monitor Patients

Nurses have a duty to monitor patients. Nurses are expected to distinguish abnormalities in the patient's condition and determine whether nursing care is a sufficient response or whether a physician or others may be required. The nurse has a responsibility to inform the physician promptly of abnormalities that may require physician attention.[48] In a Kansas case, a nurse and a hospital were sued because a woman was injured during delivery of a baby without physician attendance.[49] The nurse had refused to call the physician despite clear signs of imminent delivery, so the nurse and the hospital were found liable. In a West Virginia case the court ruled that the hospital could be found liable for the death of a patient when the nurse failed to notify the physician of the patient's symptoms of heart failure for six hours.[50] In 1992, a New Mexico court affirmed a jury verdict against a hospital based on a finding that the negligence of the nurses in determining whether a woman was in labor influenced the physician's decision to deliver a baby prematurely.[51]

Observations should be properly documented. In an Illinois case, the hospital was sued for the loss of a patient's leg.[52] The patient had been admitted for treatment for a broken leg. The admitting physician wrote an order to "watch condition of toes" and testified at trial that routine nursing care required frequent monitoring of a seriously injured patient's circulation even in the absence of a physician order. The patient developed irreversible ischemia in his leg, requiring its amputation. The nursing notes for the seven-hour period prior to discovery of the irreversibility of the ischemia did not reflect any observations of circulation. The jury was permitted to conclude that absence of entries indicated absence of observations. Thus, the nurse and the hospital could be liable even if the nurse had actually made the observations. It is as important to document no change as it is to document changes. A hospital and a physician were sued in a 1963 California case for damage to a patient's leg from infiltration of intravenous fluid into tissue.[53] A nurse observed increasing swelling and redness around the intravenous tube that indicated infiltration. She notified the physician several times of the swelling, but he ordered continuation of the intravenous infusions. There was conflicting testimony at the trial concerning (1) whether the nurse had communicated the seriousness of the swelling when it became markedly worse, and (2) whether the nurse had authority to discontinue an intravenous infusion without a physician order. The court overturned the trial court decision in favor of the hospital and the physician and ordered a new trial so that a jury could determine these issues. This case illustrates the importance of clearly communicating changes in the patient's condition and clearly defining the authority of nurses to discontinue harmful therapy.

If the physician fails to respond appropriately when notified that a patient is in a dangerous situation, then the nurse is confronted with the same situation as when the physician has not adequately explained an apparently erroneous order. The nurse has a responsibility to inform nursing, hospital, or medical staff officials designated by hospital policy who can initiate review of the situation and, if necessary, take other appropriate action. This is the way a nurse, if confronted with a situation like that in the 1963 California case, should respond today if the nurse believes the seriousness of the swelling has been communicated, if the physician neither examines the patient nor orders discontinuance of the procedure, and if the nurse does not have clear authority to discontinue the procedure without an order. In *Darling v. Charleston Community Memorial Hospital*,[54] one reason for the hospital's liability for amputation of the patient's leg was the nurses' failure to inform hospital administration of the progressive gangrenous condition of the patient's leg and the inappropriate efforts of the attending physician to address the condition. No effective alternative channel had been established for direct nursing notification of the medical staff and for appropriate medical staff intervention. The court found that hospital administration should have been notified so that it could obtain appropriate medical staff intervention. In most hospitals, direct communication channels have been established between nursing administration and medical staff leadership, so direct hospital administration involvement is less frequent. These channels must be used when necessary. In a 1977 West Virginia case, the hospital was found liable for the failure of nurses to comply with the hospital's nursing manual and report a patient's deteriorating condition to the department chairman when the attending physician failed to respond adequately to the patient's worsening condition.[55]

The fact that the nurse believes the physician will not respond does not justify failure to notify the physician and take other action if the physician does not respond. A California court ruled that two nurses and a hospital could be sued for the death of a woman from severe bleeding from an incision made to assist her in giving birth.[56] Although the nurses believed the patient was bleeding heavily, the physician was not notified until nearly three hours later when the patient went into shock. One nurse explained that she did not call the physician because she did not believe he would respond. The court concluded that she should have notified the attending physician and then notified her superiors if the attending physician did not respond.

Duty To Supervise Patients

When nurses determine that a patient requires supervision, they have a duty to exercise appropriate judgment and provide appropriate supervision within the constraints of proper physician orders and available resources. In 1992, an Oklahoma court decided that a nurse and hospital could be liable for a patient's slip and fall in the shower while unsupervised after a nurse administered a drug known to cause drowsiness.[57] An Iowa case illustrates that hospitals may have a direct duty to supervise patients in some situations.[58] A patient with a history of fainting spells had a seizure and fell during a shower, breaking her jaw and losing several teeth. An aide was outside the shower room, but allowed the patient to enter the shower alone. The court ruled that decisions concerning supervision of patient showers are a matter of routine care, not professional care, so no expert testimony is necessary to establish the standard of care. The jury can apply its common sense to determine the reasonable care the patient's known condition requires. The court noted that absence of physician orders requiring close supervision does not insulate the hospital from liability. If subsequent circumstances show a need for change or action, the hospital should make the changes permitted without a physician order and, if further changes are necessary, seek appropriate orders.

Special Duty Nurses

Special duty nurses are held to the same standard of care as other nurses are. Since they are not employees of the hospital, the hospital is usually not liable for their actions.[59] Even when hospital rules require special duty nurses, they do not become hospital employees. In some situations, nurses who are called special duty nurses may be considered agents or employees of the hospital, so that the hospital can be liable under *respondeat superior*.[60] Agency or employment is likely to be found when special duty nurses are selected by the hospital, not by the patient or the patient's representatives. Collection of the nurse's bills by the hospital has also been interpreted by some courts to indicate agency.

PHARMACISTS

Pharmacies are highly regulated, so standards of practice are frequently found in federal or state statutes, agency regulations, and municipal or county ordinances. These generally require pharmaceutical services to be provided by or under the direction of a licensed pharmacist. Some states require hospitals to have at least one pharmacist with a special pharmacist license.[61] Joint Commission on Accreditation of Healthcare Organizations (Joint Commission) and other accreditation standards may also establish duties.[62] The hospital may be liable for drug-related injuries if it fails to employ a licensed and competent pharmacist.[63]

Court decisions concerning pharmacists also help to define their standard of care. Dispensing the wrong drug clearly can lead to liability. In a 1971 Michigan case, a tranquilizer was dispensed instead of the prescribed oral contraceptive.[64] The patient became pregnant, delivered a child, and sued the pharmacist for damages. Damages were awarded, including child support until the child reached the age of majority.

A hospital must take reasonable steps to assure that drugs are available when they are needed. In a 1969 New York case, the hospital was found liable for the suicide of a patient who exhausted his supply of an investigational psychotropic drug.[65] The drug was not available during a long holiday weekend because it was stored in the research department, which was closed. The drug should have been stored in the pharmacy, which was open during the weekend. Some investigational drugs are not available outside of approved research projects, so subjects can no longer receive the drug after they complete their involvement in the study. In 1989, a federal district court applied this principle to dismiss a challenge by an AIDS patient to loss of access to a drug when a study was terminated.[66] This limited availability should be disclosed to the subject before the subject enters the study. In the above case, the patient was still in the study. At times, certain noninvestigational drugs are not available because of manufacturing, transport, or stocking problems. The hospital is not an insurer that drugs will continue to be available, but it should take reasonable steps to anticipate needs to minimize nonavailability.

Drugs should be properly stored to avoid deterioration and contamination. The skill with which this is ordinarily done is exemplified by the lack of reported cases arising from breaching this duty.

Pharmacists sometimes assume the responsibility to maintain profiles of the drugs patients are being administered, to advise physicians concerning drug selection, and to review the appropriateness of drug orders. Until 1995, the Joint Commission stated that the pharmaceutical department should provide drug monitoring services, which could include a drug profile for each patient and review of each patient's drug regimen for interactions, consonant with available resources.[67] In 1995, the Joint Commission replaced its pharmacy requirements with medication requirements that do not require pharmacists to perform any functions except reviewing prescriptions and orders and performing other duties required by law.[68] The 1995 standards require that the hospital have a mechanism to capture, use, and communicate important patient medication information, including a medication history, and monitor the effects of medication, but there is no requirement that this be done by the pharmacy.[69]

Although pharmacists have avoided liability in some cases arising out of these new responsibilities,[70] pharmacists can be liable for failing to fulfill the professional standard of care associated with the responsibilities assumed.[71] While physicians will remain primarily liable for injuries due to negligent prescriptions, pharmacists can be codefendants when they assume the responsibility of review and carry it out negligently.

PHYSICAL THERAPISTS

Most professional liability cases involving physical therapists have dealt with breaches of the duties (1) to follow the physician's instructions, (2) not to subject the patient to excessive therapy, and (3) to supervise the patient properly.

A physical therapist must follow the prescribing physician's instructions unless they are apparently erroneous and dangerous to the patient. In a Florida case, a hospital was found liable for the injuries to a patient who fell while undergoing physical therapy.[72] The physician had ordered that the patient be attended at all times. The therapist left the patient alone in a standing position while getting her a robe. A fall during that short time resulted in a fractured hip. No expert testimony was required to establish the duty to follow the physician's instructions.

Physical therapists are expected to be familiar with the appropriate application of the procedures they use. If a physician's order is apparently erroneous, the therapist has a duty to seek modification or clarification from the prescribing physician. In most states, the therapist should not unilaterally initiate different treatment. If the orders are still apparently erroneous after discussion with the prescribing physician and if the ordered therapy is dangerous to the patient, the therapist should decline to provide the prescribed therapy and notify both the prescribing physician and the appropriate supervisors, medical staff, or administrative officials, in accord with hospital policy.

The physician's orders often give the physical therapist latitude concerning the therapy to be provided. The physical therapist is then generally held to the duty of acting as other physical therapists in good standing would act under the circumstances. In 1976, a Pennsylvania hospital was sued by a patient who fell in the physical therapy room and fractured her leg and arm.[73] The patient was receiving gait training after multiple hip surgeries and was instructed to walk between parallel bars. The patient fell either while between the parallel bars or while using her cane to take a few steps away from the parallel bars. The court ruled that the duty of the physical therapist must be established by expert testimony and that only ordinary care and skill were required, so the physical therapist was not liable for a mere mistake in judgment. The court affirmed a verdict for the hospital.

Physical therapists have been found liable for subjecting patients to excessive therapy. The Kentucky Supreme Court applied res ipsa loquitur when a femur was fractured during therapy to prepare the stump of a leg for an artificial leg.[74] The court did not believe bones would fracture while a leg was being lifted and lowered unless someone was negligent. Thus, it did not require expert testimony. The court ruled that the physician could also be liable for failing to provide an adequate explanation of the procedure to the therapist.

Falls are a frequent cause of injuries involving patients receiving physical therapy. Some courts tend to apply res ipsa loquitur to cases involving falls, as illustrated by the Kentucky case, while other courts analyze the appropriateness of the attendance given from a professional perspective, as illustrated by the Pennsylvania case. Another example of a professional standard involved an Oregon patient undergoing therapy after hip surgery who became dizzy and fainted just after returning to a tilt table after walking between parallel bars.[75] His total hip replacement became dislocated when he fell. The patient's expert witness testified that he should have been given support, including being strapped to the tilt table, as soon as he became dizzy. The court found the hospital liable for the physical therapist's failure to fulfill this duty.

PATHOLOGY

Liability can arise from injuries due to negligent acts associated with laboratory tests and other pathology services. The error can be committed by a laboratory technician, a pathologist, or other staff members. The hospital can become liable under respondeat superior when the person who made the error is the hospital's employee or agent. As discussed in the "Respondeat Superior" and "Agency" sections of Chapter 10, some courts hold hospitals responsible for the acts of physicians, particularly radiologists, pathologists, and emergency room physicians, by considering the physician to be the agent or apparent agent for the hospital.

Liability has arisen from mishandling specimens.[76] In a 1975 Texas case, the hospital was found liable for a patient's mental anguish when an eyeball that had been removed because of a tumor was lost by a technician.[77] The technician was washing the eyeball and dropped it into the sink. The eyeball went down the drain and could not be removed, so the pathologist could not diagnose whether the tumor was malignant. In a 1974 Florida case, the patient was awarded $100,000 from the hospital and a surgeon because the identities of two specimens were confused, resulting in the unnecessary removal of one of the patient's breasts.[78] The surgeon had removed a biopsy specimen from each breast, and the two specimens were put in the same container without labels to distinguish from which breast each originated. The pathologist did not attempt to distinguish the two specimens. One specimen was malignant, and the other was not. Since it was impossible to determine which breast had the malignancy, both breasts were removed. The surgeon was liable for failing to instruct the nurses to label the specimens. The hospital was liable for the nurses' failure to label the specimens and for the failure of its pathologist employee to segregate the specimens.

Misreading a specimen can lead to liability. An Ohio hospital was found liable because its pathologist-employee misdiagnosed a frozen section as indicating cervical cancer.[79] After a total hysterectomy (removal of the uterus and cervix) was performed, it was discovered the patient did not have cancer. Misdiagnosis alone is not enough to establish breach of duty. A diagnosing physician is not expected to always be correct. Most diagnoses are professional judgments. Thus, for there to be liability, the misdiagnosis must be one that a physician in good standing in the same specialty would not have made in the same circumstances.

Using improper techniques or reagents to conduct a test can be a breach of duty. In 1971, a federal appellate court found a hospital liable because a technician used sodium hydroxide instead of sodium chloride to perform a gastric cytology test.[80] In an Iowa case, a hospital was found liable for using a reagent that was too old.[81] The pediatrician ordered appropriate blood tests for a baby with symptoms of Rh incompatibility, but the old reagent caused the test results to indicate normal blood levels of bilirubin rather than the baby's actual high levels. When the high levels were discovered, it was too late to avoid permanent severe brain damage that probably could have been avoided had therapy been initiated after the initial blood tests.

Errors in testing can also result in liability. A 1992 case involved a military member who had been told that he was HIV-positive as a result of a false-positive test. A federal appellate court ruled that the government could be sued for the failure of the military to inform him after discharge of its discovery of the error.[82] Courts disagree on whether there can be liability for a false-positive HIV test in the absence of receiving unnecessary and harmful treatment in the mistaken belief of having the virus. This is discussed in Chapter 10.

Genetic screening and prenatal genetic tests are also types of frequently employed tests. Both parents and children have sued when negligently conducted tests have led parents to conceive or deliver children with genetic defects. In 1978, a federal district court ruled that the parents of an infant born with Tay-Sachs disease could recover damages because they had been informed, based on a negligently performed prenatal test, that the child could not have Tay-Sachs disease.[83] These wrongful conception, wrongful birth, and wrongful life cases are discussed further in Chapter 15.

Autopsies and other aspects of handling dead bodies are another area of potential liability arising from pathology services. Dead bodies are discussed in Chapter 16.

RADIOLOGY

Three common problem areas of radiology include radiation injuries, falls and other problems with patient positioning, and errors or delays in diagnosis. There can also be liability for performing radiologic procedures of no beneficial value.[84]

Radiation injuries from excessive radiation or radiation to the wrong body part have resulted in several suits. The application and effect of radiation are not within the knowledge of laypersons, so courts generally require expert proof of how the radiation should have been administered. If the injury is to a body part that was not intended to receive radiation, most courts will apply *res ipsa loquitur*. However, some courts apply *res ipsa loquitur* in all cases involving severe radiation injuries. These courts require the defendant to show the patient was hypersensitive or otherwise explain injuries to avoid liability.

Several cases have addressed the duty to disclose the risk of radiation injuries from therapeutic radiologic procedures. One of the earliest court decisions to apply the requirement of informed consent ruled in 1960 that a Kansas physician had a duty to inform the patient of the probable consequences of the radioactive cobalt administered for breast cancer.[85] In a 1976 case, a federal appellate court ruled that the physician had to disclose the probable consequences and the experimental nature of the therapy he proposed when he planned to give extremely large doses that exceeded the accepted range and were justified by only research papers read at conferences.[86] The responsibility to obtain informed consent is discussed in Chapter 13.

When radiologic technologists fail to check patient status adequately, sometimes necessary precautions are not taken for patient protection. When injuries result, liability is likely. In a Louisiana case, the court ruled the hospital could be liable for a patient's broken ankle that was discovered after the patient slumped on an X-ray table.[87] The radiologic technologist had not noticed that the patient was sedated, and the X-ray requisition had not included the brief history required by hospital policy, so the technologist had not strapped the patient to the table before raising it. The technologist had a duty to strap the sedated patient. In a 1972 case, a federal appellate court ruled that the hospital could be sued for the way a radiologic technologist handled a patient.[88] Although the patient was to be X-rayed for suspected neck and spinal injuries from an automobile accident, the radiologic technologist told the patient to scoot onto the table and then twisted the patient's neck to position her, resulting in permanent spinal cord damage. Experts testified the neck should have been immobilized before the patient was moved to the table, and after she was on the table, the machine, not the patient's head, should have been moved to achieve the desired angles.

Misdiagnosis by the physician reading X-ray film or another radiologic test has also led to suits. The radiologist is held to the standard of other physicians. Thus, the misdiagnosis must be more than a mere judgmental error to establish breach of duty. The misdiagnosis must be outside the accepted range of determinations by qualified radiologists under similar circumstances. Even when there is misdiagnosis, liability may be avoided if the misdiagnosis did not cause the injury. In an Iowa case, the court ruled in favor of the radiologists in a suit arising from the loss of a patient's eyesight.[89] The radiologist had not detected a piece of steel in the patient's eye. A second set of X-rays led to the discovery of the piece. The patient was unable to prove that delay in diagnosis had caused the eyesight loss.

Delay in reporting a proper diagnosis can also result in liability. In a 1971 federal district court decision, an Indiana hospital was found liable for the death of a patient due to delay in forwarding a radiologist's report.[90] The patient, who had head injuries from a fight, was examined by a physician in a hospital emergency room and released. Four skull X-rays were taken. After the release, a radiologist read the X-rays and found a skull fracture. He did not call the physician who had ordered the X-rays. He dictated his report, which was transcribed two days later. The patient was found unconscious after the X-rays had been read. The patient was taken to a hospital where emergency surgery was performed, but he died. The court ruled that the forwarding of reports was the hospital's administrative responsibility and that the physician was a hospital agent when performing that function. Hospitals need a system for promptly reading emergency X-rays and reporting critical X-ray findings.

Radiologists may also be liable for not informing the treating physician that the X-rays ordered are too limited in scope, so that the diagnosis cannot be relied on.[91]

INFECTION CONTROL

Hospitals can be liable for some infections acquired in the hospital.[92] This liability has been based on the hospital's independent duty concerning the physical condition of buildings and grounds and the selection and maintenance of equipment, and on the hospital's liability under *respondeat superior* for acts of its employees and agents.

In the past, courts found liability for infections when the patient proved the existence of unsanitary conditions in the hospital. Even with improvements in infection control and in determination of infection sources, courts recognize that hospitals cannot guarantee absence of infection and that infections do occur in hospitals for many reasons other than negligence. Thus, most courts require proof of a causal relationship between the alleged injury and a deviation from proper practices.[93] In 1992, an Ohio court ruled that *res ipsa loquitur* did not apply to a staph infection after a helilaminectomy and no break in sterile technique had been identified, so there could be no liability for the infection.[94]

Some hospital licensing rules specify infection control steps that must be taken, particularly isolation and sterilization procedures. These rules can be used to prove the standard of care. In a Maryland case, a hospital was found liable when it failed to comply with a regulation requiring segregation of sterile and nonsterile needles.[95] A hospital may be held to a higher standard of care than is specified in regulations if other hospitals follow a higher standard.

When hospital employees fail to sterilize equipment properly, the hospital can be liable. In a California case, a hospital was found liable for a nurse's failure to sterilize a needle before using it to give a patient an injection.[96] The use of presterilized supplies has reduced both the risk to the patient and the hospital's liability exposure in these situations. If a patient is infected by a presterilized item, the manufacturer will usually be liable unless the item was contaminated by negligent conduct of hospital staff or there was a pattern of infection that should have led the hospital to discontinue the supplies. The Iowa case discussed in the "Selection and Maintenance of Equipment" section of this chapter is an example of a pattern of infection from presterilized supplies.

Another aspect of infection control is pre-employment and periodic screening of hospital personnel. The Americans with Disabilities Act (ADA), discussed in Chapter 9, limits when pre-employment examinations may be given, but examinations are permitted, so the ADA does not provide an excuse for not performing necessary examinations. In a 1966 federal district court case, liability was found for failing to give an employee a pre-employment examination before she was assigned to a newborn nursery.[97] The employee had a staphylococcus infection of the same type that was transmitted to a baby. If the hospital becomes aware that a staff member may be infected, it must remove the person from direct and indirect patient contact until the condition is diagnosed and, if the condition is infectious, until the condition is no longer infectious or until appropriate procedures are implemented to preclude infecting others. Other aspects of health screening are discussed in Chapter 9.

Some states require special training for hospital employees concerning HIV and other transmissible diseases.[98] The Occupational Safety and Health Administration (OSHA) requires employers to follow certain precautions concerning blood-borne pathogens and the Centers for Disease Control and Prevention has provided considerable guidance for handling various diseases (see Chapter 9).

Hospitals are expected to have a system to monitor their facilities, discover infections, and take appropriate remedial action. The Joint Commission standards require such a system.[99] Failure to have an appropriate system could result in liability if a patient's infection could have been prevented by the type of system other hospitals have.

EMERGENCY SERVICES

Emergency services are a source of substantial liability exposure for hospitals and their staff members. The possible bases of liability of the hospital for acts of a physician in the emergency room are discussed in the *"Respondeat Superior,"* "Agency," "Apparent or Ostensible Agency," and "Institutional Liability" sections of Chapter 10. The hospital's duty to provide assistance to patients who come to the emergency room and the proper handling of transfers are discussed in Chapter 12. Consent issues are discussed in Chapter 13. This section focuses on issues concerning the examination of the patient.

The responsibility for diagnosis rests with the physician. Physicians should not diagnose severely injured patients over the telephone because of the risk of communication errors. It is best for all patients who come to the emergency room to be seen by a physician. However, this is not practical in some small hospitals. Substantial liability exposure occurs whenever a patient is sent home without seeing a physician. Thus, even these hospitals should require the on-call physician to examine the patient personally whenever there is doubt concerning the patient's condition. A Maryland case illustrates the problem.[100] A person who had been drinking was hit by a car and thrown through the air. He was brought to an emergency room, and the on-call surgeon was telephoned. The surgeon told the nurse to admit the patient and X-ray him in the morning. Since the hospital was full, the patient was placed in the hall outside the nursing station. His condition deteriorated, and he died within three hours of entering the hospital. The autopsy found a lacerated liver and a badly fractured leg and pelvic area, with bone fragments penetrating the peritoneal cavity. The physician and nurses contradicted each other concerning the information exchanged over the telephone. The physician was found liable because he failed to examine the patient personally, and the hospital was found liable because the nurses failed to notify the physician of the deterioration of the patient's condition.

Emergencies are not always apparent. All patients should be treated as having emergencies until they are determined not to have emergency problems. The most obvious aspect of the patient's condition frequently is not the most critical.

Several cases have arisen from emergency personnel assuming that drunkenness is the only problem and overlooking more serious problems. In a Florida case, a young man was brought unconscious to an emergency room.[101] A superficial examination indicated he was drunk, so he was turned over to police. He was later found dead in his cell with broken ribs piercing his thoracic cavity. The court ruled that a jury could find responsibility to make a thorough examination of an unconscious patient and to take a history from those accompanying the patient. A history would have uncovered the fact that the patient was found lying on a lawn after a suspected fall of 23 feet.

Existing records should be examined if time permits. In a 1974 Louisiana case, a man had chest pains and called his physician, who advised him to go to the emergency room.[102] The physician alerted the emergency room, ordered an electrocardiogram (EKG), and told the emergency room staff to advise him of the outcome. The emergency room physician was not notified of the call, so he ordered an EKG and, without comparing it to prior EKGs, decided there was no heart attack. He sent the patient home with medication and instructions to call if he got worse. The personal physician was not called. The patient got worse and was later admitted for cardiac care. The court said the emergency room physician could be sued for his misdiagnosis due to failure to compare the EKG to prior EKGs. This case also illustrates the importance of involving a physician, when available, who knows the patient. Another reason to examine prior records is that distraught patients may forget information, such as allergies. However, reliance can generally be placed on a history from a competent patient. This is illustrated by a Michigan case in which the patient had a fatal allergic reaction to morphine.[103] He had denied allergies to any painkilling drugs. Although records of a prior unrelated stay noted the allergy, the court found the hospital not liable. When laboratory and radiologic diagnostic tests are performed on emergency patients, the patients should be advised not to leave until the tests are completed. This point is illustrated by the 1971 federal case discussed in the "Radiology" section of this chapter.

Another problem is falls by patients who are left unattended during examinations. Patients should not be left unattended when they are known to be at risk of falling. The risk of falling is removed for some patients by having them lie down or by restraining them. Appropriate precautions should be taken to reduce the risk of falls.

RESIDENTS AND OTHER STUDENTS

Hospitals are generally liable under *respondeat superior* for the acts of residents and other students because they are considered employees or agents of the hospital. In states where they are not considered employees, they are nevertheless considered agents for purposes of hospital liability. Residents are persons who have graduated from medical school and are pursuing further training in the hospital. Trainees in the first year of training after medical school used to be called *interns*. Since residency programs have been reorganized to begin immediately after medical school, first-year trainees are now called *residents*. The term *intern* is no longer in official use, although it is still used unofficially.

Residents are generally expected to exercise the same degree of skill and knowledge possessed by members of the medical profession. In 1972, a federal appellate court ruled that the trial court must reconsider its decision against the patient because the decision was based on applying a standard of care that accounted for the resident's personal level of knowledge and experience.[104] The court ruled that if the resident could not reasonably be expected to discern subtle abnormalities in electrocardiogram tracings, then he should not have been permitted to make unaided electrocardiogram analyses. However, a few courts have instructed juries that residents should be held to only the standard of others with the same amount of training.[105]

NOTES

1. Charrin v. Methodist Hosp., 432 S.W.2d 572 (Tex. Civ. App. 1968); *accord*, Collum v. Jackson Hosp. & Clinic, Inc., 374 So.2d 314 (Ala. 1979); Spann v. Hospital Auth. of Calhoun County, 208 Ga. App. 494, 430 S.E.2d 828 (1993), *cert. denied*, 1993 Ga. LEXIS 937 (Oct. 5, 1993) [nurse's aide].

2. Pulley v. Rex Hosp., 326 N.C. 701, 392 S.E.2d 380 (1990).

3. *E.g.*, Shoemaker v. Rush-Presbyterian-St.Luke's Med. Ctr., 187 Ill. App. 3d 1040, 543 N.E.2d 1014 (1st Dist. 1989).

4. *E.g.*, De Kalb County Hosp. Auth. v. Theofanidis, 157 Ga. App. 811, 278 S.E.2d 712 (1981); *see* Annotation, *Hospital's liability to visitor injured as result of condition of exterior walks, steps, or grounds*, 71 A.L.R. 2D 427.

5. *E.g.*, Calvache v. Jackson Mem. Hosp., 588 So.2d 28 (Fla. 3d DCA 1991), *rev. denied*, 599 So.2d 654 (Fla. 1992); Burwell v. Easton Mem. Hosp., 83 Md. App. 684, 577 A.2d 394 (1990); Gales v. United States, 617 F. Supp. 42 (W.D. Pa. 1985), *aff'd without op.*, 791 F.2d 917 (3d Cir. 1986); *see* Annotation, *Hospital's liability to visitor injured by slippery, obstructed, or defective interior floors or steps*, 71 A.L.R. 2D 436.

6. Pierson v. Sharp Mem. Hosp., Inc., 216 Cal. App. 3d 340, 264 Cal. Rptr. 673 (4th Dist. 1989).

7. *E.g.*, Lovell v. St. Paul Fire & Marine Ins. Co., 310 Ark. 791, 839 S.W.2d 222 (1992); Chernov v. St. Luke's Hosp. Med. Ctr., 123 Ariz. 521, 601 P.2d 284 (1979); *see* Annotation, *Liability of owner or operator of parking lot for personal injuries caused by movement of vehicles*, 38 A.L.R. 3D 138.

8. *E.g.*, McHenry v. Utah Valley Hosp., 724 F. Supp. 835 (D. Utah 1989), *aff'd*, 927 F.2d 1125 (10th Cir.), *cert. denied*, 502 U.S. 894 (1991) [gate]; McDonald v. Aliquippa Hosp., 414 Pa. Super. 317, 606 A.2d 1218, *appeal denied*, 532 Pa. 646, 614 A.2d 1142 (1992) [doors]; *see* Annotation, *Liability of owner or operator of business premises for injuries from electronically operated door*, 99 A.L.R. 2D 725.

9. Isaacs v. Huntington Mem. Hosp., 38 Cal. 3d 112, 211 Cal. Rptr. 356, 695 P.2d 653 (1985); *see* Annotation, *Parking facility proprietor's liability for criminal attack on patron*, 49 A.L.R. 4TH 1257.

10. Maxwell v. Hospital Auth., 202 Ga. App. 92, 413 S.E.2d 205 (1991), *cert. denied*, 1992 Ga. LEXIS 46 (Jan. 10, 1992); *see* Annotation, *Worker's compensation law as precluding employee's suit against employer for third person's criminal attack*, 49 A.L.R. 4TH 926.

11. Hanewinckel v. St. Paul's Property & Liability Ins. Co., 611 So.2d 174 (La. Ct. App. 1992), *cert. denied*, 619 So.2d 65 (La. 1993).

12. Mundy v. Department of Health & Human Resources, 620 So.2d 811 (La. 1993).

13. Young v. Huntsville Hosp., 595 So.2d 1386 (Ala. 1992); *accord*, K.M.H. v. Lutheran Gen. Hosp., 230 Neb. 269, 431 N.W.2d 606 (1988) [direct hospital duty independent of *respondeat superior*].

14. Andrea N. v. Laurelwood Convalescent Hosp., 13 Cal. App. 4th 1992, 16 Cal. Rptr. 2d 894 (2d Dist. 1993), *rev. dismissed*, 27 Cal. Rptr. 2d 1, 865 P.2d 632 (Cal. 1994) [not citable in Cal.]; *accord*, Gregory by Gregory v. State, 195 A.D.2d 1030, 601 N.Y.S.2d 720 (4th Dep't 1993), *appeal denied*, 82 N.Y.2d 660, 605 N.Y.S.2d 5, 625 N.E.2d 590 (1993) [supervision adequate].

15. G.L. v. Kaiser Found. Hosps., Inc., 306 Or. 54, 757 P.2d 1347 (1988).

16. Hernandez v. Smith, 552 F.2d 142 (5th Cir. 1977); *see* Annotation, *Hospital's liability to patient for injury allegedly sustained from absence of particular equipment intended for use in diagnosis or treatment of patient*, 50 A.L.R. 3D 1141.

17. Carrasco v. Bankoff, 220 Cal. App. 2d 230, 33 Cal. Rptr. 673 (2d Dist. 1963).

18. Ducharme v. United States, 850 F.2d 27 (1st Cir. 1988).

19. Lauro v. Travelers Ins. Co., 261 So.2d 261 (La. Ct. App.), *cert. denied*, 262 La. 188, 262 So.2d 787 (1972).

20. Dixon v. Taylor, 111 N.C. App. 97, 431 S.E.2d 778 (1993).

21. Lamb v. Candler Gen. Hosp., Inc., 262 Ga. 70, 413 S.E.2d 720 (1992).

22. Bellaire Gen. Hosp. v. Campbell, 510 S.W.2d 94 (Tex. Civ. App. 1974).

23. South Highlands Infirmary v. Camp, 279 Ala. 1, 180 So.2d 904 (1965); *see* Annotation, *Hospital's liability to patient for injury sustained from defective equipment furnished by hospital for use in diagnosis or treatment*, 14 A.L.R. 3D 1254.

24. Clary v. Christiansen, 54 Ohio L. Abs. 254, 83 N.E.2d 644 (Ct. App. 1948); *see* Annotation, *Malpractice: Attending physician's liability for injury caused by equipment furnished by hospital*, 35 A.L.R. 3D 1068.

25. Orthopedic Clinic v. Hanson, 415 P.2d 991 (Okla. 1966).

26. Shepherd v. McGinnis, 257 Iowa 35, 131 N.W.2d 475 (1964).

27. Anderson v. Somberg, 67 N.J. 291, 338 A.2d 1, *cert. denied*, 423 U.S. 929 (1975).

28. *See* Annotation, *Medical malpractice: Hospital's liability for injury allegedly caused by failure to have properly qualified staff*, 62 A.L.R. 4TH 692; Annotation, *Hospital's liability for injury resulting from failure to have sufficient number of nurses on duty*, 2 A.L.R. 5TH 286.

29. St. Paul Med. Ctr. v. Cecil, 842 S.W.2d 808 (Tex. Ct. App. 1992).

30. Bowers v. Olch, 120 Cal. App. 2d 108, 260 P.2d 997 (1953).

31. Stumper v. Kimel, 108 N.J. Super. 209, 260 A.2d 526 (App. Div. 1970), *cert. denied*, 55 N.J. 589, 264 A.2d 63 (1970); *see* Annotation, *Liability of one physician or surgeon for malpractice of another*, 85 A.L.R. 2D 889.

32. Laidlaw v. Lions Gate Hosp., 8 D.L.R.3d 730 (B.C. Sup. Ct. 1969).

33. *See also* Husher v. Commissioner of Ed., 188 A.D.2d 739, 591 N.Y.S.2d 99 (3d Dep't 1992) [nurse guilty of professional misconduct by leaving unit without proper coverage after agreeing to stay, knowing of nursing shortage, not giving reasonable notice of leaving].

34. Horton v. Niagara Falls Mem. Med. Ctr., 51 A.D.2d 152, 380 N.Y.S.2d 116 (4th Dep't 1976).

35. MacDonald v. United States, 853 F. Supp. 1430 (M.D. Ga. 1994).

36. *E.g.,* Deese v. Carroll City County Hosp., 203 Ga. App. 148, 416 S.E.2d 127 (1992); *see* Annotation, *Nurse's liability for her own negligence or malpractice,* 51 A.L.R. 2D 970.

37. Thompson v. Brent, 245 So.2d 751 (La. Ct. App. 1971).

38. Webb v. Jorns, 473 S.W.2d 328 (Tex. Civ. App. 1971), *rev'd on other grounds,* 488 S.W.2d 407 (Tex. 1972).

39. Fein v. Permanente Med. Group, 38 Cal. 3d 137, 211 Cal. Rptr. 368, 695 P.2d 665, *appeal dismissed,* 474 U.S. 892 (1985).

40. Nelson v. Trinity Med. Ctr., 419 N.W.2d 886 (N.D. 1988).

41. Cline v. Lund, 31 Cal. App. 3d 755, 107 Cal. Rptr. 629 (1st Dist. 1973).

42. Striano v. Deepdale Gen. Hosp., 54 A.D.2d 730, 387 N.Y.S.2d 678 (2d Dep't 1976).

43. Toth v. Comm. Hosp., 22 N.Y.2d 255, 292 N.Y.S.2d 440, 239 N.E.2d 368 (1968).

44. *E.g.,* Hering v. McShane, 145 A.D.2d 683, 535 N.Y.S.2d 227 (3d Dep't 1988).

45. Fraijo v. Hartland Hosp., 99 Cal. App. 3d 331, 160 Cal. Rptr. 246 (2d Dist. 1979).

46. Larrimore v. Homeopathic Hosp. Ass'n, 54 Del. 449, 181 A.2d 573 (1962).

47. Norton v. Argonaut Ins. Co., 144 So.2d 249 (La. Ct. App. 1962).

48. *E.g.,* Gill v. Foster, 626 N.E.2d 190 (Ill. 1994) [nurse breached duty by failing to tell doctor of patient's complaints of pain at discharge, but not cause of injury because doctor already knew of pain]; McMillan v. Durant, 439 S.E.2d 829 (S.C. 1993).

49. Hiatt v. Groce, 215 Kan. 14, 523 P.2d 320 (1974).

50. Duling v. Bluefield Sanitarium, Inc., 149 W. Va. 567, 142 S.E.2d 754 (1965).

51. Lopez v. Southwest Comm. Health Servs., 114 N.M. 2, 833 P.2d 1183 (Ct. App.), *cert. denied,* 113 N.M. 690, 831 P.2d 989 (1992).

52. Collins v. Westlake Comm. Hosp., 57 Ill. 2d 388, 312 N.E.2d 614 (1974).

53. Mundt v. Alta Bates Hosp., 223 Cal. App. 2d 413, 35 Cal. Rptr. 848 (1st Dist. 1963).

54. Darling v. Charleston Comm. Mem. Hosp., 33 Ill. 2d 326, 211 N.E.2d 253 (1965), *cert. denied,* 383 U.S. 946 (1966).

55. Utter v. United Hosp. Ctr., 160 W.Va. 703, 236 S.E.2d 213 (1977).

56. Goff v. Doctors Gen. Hosp., 166 Cal. App. 2d 314, 333 P.2d 29 (3d Dist. 1958).

57. Pierce v. Mercy Health Ctr., Inc., 847 P.2d 822 (Okla. Ct. App. 1992).

58. Kastler v. Iowa Methodist Hosp., 193 N.W.2d 98 (Iowa 1971).

59. *See also* Robinson v. Faine, 525 So.2d 903 (Fla. 3d DCA 1987) [agency not liable for private duty nurse's negligence where she was independent contractor].

60. Emory Univ. v. Shadburn, 180 Ga. 595, 180 S.E. 137 (1935).

61. *E.g.,* FLA. STAT. § 465.019(5) [consultant pharmacist license].

62. Joint Commission on Accreditation of Healthcare Organizations, 1995 COMPREHENSIVE AC-CREDITATION MANUAL FOR HOSPITALS 139-50 [hereinafter cited as 1995 Joint Commission CAMH].

63. Sullivan v. Sisters of St. Francis, 374 S.W.2d 294 (Tex. Civ. App. 1963).

64. Troppi v. Scarf, 31 Mich. App. 240, 187 N.W.2d 511 (1971); *see* Annotation, *Druggist's civil liability for injuries sustained as a result of negligence in incorrectly filling drug prescription*, 3 A.L.R. 4TH 270.

65. McCord v. State, Nos. 43405, 43406, 43407 (N.Y. Ct. Cl. 1969).

66. De Vito v. HEM, Inc., 705 F. Supp. 1076 (M.D. Pa. 1989).

67. Joint Commission on Accreditation of Healthcare Organizations, 1994 ACCREDITATION MANUAL FOR HOSPITALS, 162.

68. 1995 Joint Commission CAMH, 139–50.

69. *Id.*, at 144, 148–49.

70. *E.g.*, Mielke v. Condell Mem. Hosp., 124 Ill. App. 3d 42, 463 N.E.2d 216 (2d Dist. 1984) [no liability for not notifying physician of drug interaction discovered by monitoring systems]; Walker v. Jack Eckerd Corp., 209 Ga. App. 517, 434 S.E.2d 63 (1993), *cert. denied*, 1993 Ga. LEXIS 1033 (Oct. 24, 1993) [pharmacist has no duty to warn customer or notify physician that drug is being prescribed in dangerous amounts].

71. *E.g.*, Lasley v. Shrake's Country Club Pharmacy, Inc., 179 Ariz. 583, 880 P.2d 1129 (Ct. App. 1994) [duty of pharmacist to warn customer of consequences of prolonged use of prescription drug]; Hooks SuperX, Inc. v. McLaughlin, 642 N.E.2d 514 (Ind. 1994) [pharmacist has duty to cease filling refills when they are being sought at an unreasonably faster rate than prescribed].

72. South Miami Hosp. v. Sanchez, 386 So.2d 39 (Fla. 3d DCA 1980); *see* Annotation, *Liability for injuries or death resulting from physical therapy*, 53 A.L.R. 3D 1250.

73. McAvenue v. Bryn Mawr Hosp., 245 Pa. Super. 507, 369 A.2d 743 (1976).

74. Meiman v. Rehabilitation Ctr., Inc., 444 S.W.2d 78 (Ky. 1969).

75. Forsyth v. Sisters of Charity, 39 Or. App. 851, 593 P.2d 1270 (1979); *accord*, Hodo v. General Hosps., 211 Ga. App. 6, 438 S.E.2d 378 (1993); *but see* Gilles v. Rehabilitation Inst., 262 Or. 422, 498 P.2d 777 (1972) [no liability because of patient's volitional efforts to thwart therapist from preventing fall].

76. *But see* Holdren v. Legursky, 16 F.3d 57 (4th Cir.), *cert. denied*, 115 S. Ct. 106 (U.S. 1994) [handling of blood sample at hospital that precluded DNA test did not violate due process].

77. Mokry v. University of Tex. Health Science Ctr., 529 S.W.2d 802 (Tex. Civ. App. 1975).

78. Variety Children's Hosp. v. Osle, 292 So.2d 382 (Fla. 3d DCA 1974).

79. Lundberg v. Bay View Hosp., 175 Ohio St. 133, 191 N.E.2d 821 (1963); *see* Annotation, *Malpractice in connection with diagnosis of cancer*, 79 A.L.R. 3D 915.

80. Insurance Co. of N. Am. v. Prieto, 442 F.2d 1033 (6th Cir.), *cert. denied*, 404 U.S. 856 (1971).

81. Schnebly v. Baker, 217 N.W.2d 708 (Iowa 1974), *overruled in part on other grounds*, Franke v. Junko, 366 N.W.2d 536 (Iowa 1985).

82. M.M.H. v. United States, 966 F.2d 285 (7th Cir. 1992).

83. Gildiner v. Thomas Jefferson Univ. Hosp., 451 F. Supp. 692 (E.D. Pa. 1978).

84. *E.g.*, Riser v. American Med. Int'l, 620 So.2d 372 (La. Ct. App. 1993).

85. Natanson v. Kline, 187 Kan. 186, 354 P.2d 670 (1960).

86. Ahern v. Veterans Admin., 537 F.2d 1098 (10th Cir. 1976).

87. Albritton v. Bossier City Hosp. Comm'n, 271 So.2d 353 (La. Ct. App. 1972).

88. Modave v. Long Island Jewish Med. Ctr., 501 F.2d 1065 (2d Cir. 1974).

89. Barnes v. Bovenmyer, 255 Iowa 220, 122 N.W.2d 312 (1963).

90. Keene v. Methodist Hosp., 324 F. Supp. 233 (N.D. Ind. 1971); *see also* Davison v. Mobile Infirmary, 456 So.2d 14 (Ala. 1984) [failure to inform treating physician of X-rays showing large number of pills in stomach].

91. *E.g.*, Shuffler v. Blue Ridge Radiology Assocs., P.A., 73 N.C. App. 232, 326 S.E.2d 96 (1985).

92. Annotation, *Hospital's liability for exposing patient to extraneous infection or contagion*, 96 A.L.R. 2D 1205.

93. Helman v. Sacred Heart Hosp., 62 Wash. 2d 136, 381 P.2d 605 (1963) [hospital liable for staphylococcus infection where nurses failed to take necessary precautions, such as handwashing, to avoid cross-infection from other patient in room who was infected with the same staphylococcus organism]; Wilson v. Stilwill, 411 Mich. 587, 309 N.W.2d 898 (1981) [*res ipsa loquitur* not applicable to hospital infection]; Vogt v. Katz, 745 S.W.2d 221 (Mo. Ct. App. 1987) [failure to clean injection site established claim for infection].

94. Mahan v. Bethesda Hosp., Inc., 84 Ohio App. 3d 520, 617 N.E.2d 714 (1992).

95. Suburban Hosp. Ass'n v. Hadary, 22 Md. App. 186, 322 A.2d 258 (1974).

96. Kalmus v. Cedars of Lebanon Hosp., 132 Cal. App. 2d 243, 281 P.2d 872 (2d Dist. 1955).

97. Kapuschinsky v. United States, 248 F. Supp. 732 (D. S.C. 1966).

98. *E.g.*, FLA. STAT. § 381.0035.

99. 1995 Joint Commission CAMH, 437–49.

100. Thomas v. Corso, 265 Md. 84, 288 A.2d 379 (1972).

101. Bourgeois v. Dade County, 99 So.2d 575 (Fla. 1956).

102. Fox v. Argonaut Sw. Ins. Co., 288 So.2d 102 (La. Ct. App. 1974).

103. Howell v. Outer Drive Hosp., 66 Mich. App. 142, 238 N.W.2d 553 (1975).

104. McBride v. United States, 462 F.2d 72 (9th Cir. 1972).

105. Hilyer v. Hole, 114 Mich. App. 38, 318 N.W.2d 598 (1982).

12

Relationship with the Patient

There is some overlap between the physician-patient relationship and the hospital-patient relationship, but they are not identical. Some physician-patient relationships are entirely outside the hospital. Even when hospital care is required, the physician may not be able to initiate a hospital-patient relationship with a particular hospital because the hospital does not have space available or the physician does not have admitting privileges. In some emergency situations the relationship with the hospital may begin before the relationship with the physician. Sometimes a patient changes physicians while in the hospital, establishing a new physician-patient relationship. In most situations, after the relationship with the hospital ends, the physician-patient relationship continues.

This chapter discusses the ways in which physician-patient and hospital-patient relationships begin and end and some aspects of that relationship not covered in other chapters.

PHYSICIAN-PATIENT RELATIONSHIP

Beginning the Relationship

Generally a physician has the right to accept or decline to establish a professional relationship with any person.[1] A physician does not have a legal responsibility to diagnose or treat anyone unless there is an express or implied agreement to do so. Likewise, an individual does not have an obligation to accept diagnosis or treatment from any particular physician unless the situation is one in which the law authorizes the person to be cared for involuntarily.

Of course, there are many situations where an individual's freedom of choice is limited economically. A government or private health plan, such as a health maintenance organization (HMO) or other managed care plan, may cover services from only one physician or a panel of physicians. If the patient declines the covered services, the patient forfeits all or part of coverage. It may not be economically feasible for the patient to seek alternatives.

There are three ways in which a physician can establish a physician-patient relationship: (1) by contracting to care for a certain population and to have one of that population seek care, (2) by entering an express contract with a patient or the patient's representative by mutual agreement, or (3) by engaging in conduct from which a contract can be implied.

Contracts To Care for a Certain Population

A physician who enters a contract to care for members of a certain population must provide care for them to the extent required by the contract. For example, physicians enter contracts with hospitals to care for emergency patients or to provide certain services, such as radiology or pathology. Usually these contracts do not permit the physician to refuse to care for individual hospital patients requiring those services. Physician contracts with HMOs and other managed care entities are often of this type. Physicians frequently enter contracts with other institutions and organizations, such as athletic teams, schools, companies, prisons, jails,[2] and nursing homes, that include an agreement to provide certain kinds of care to all members of certain populations who seek care. In unusual circumstances, other agreements can be interpreted to impose these duties. In 1992, the North Carolina Supreme Court ruled that a physician group that had contracted to provide on-call supervision of residents owed a duty of reasonable care in that supervision to patients treated by those residents in some circumstances.[3]

Express Contract

A physician-patient relationship can be begun by mutual agreement of the physician and the patient or the patient's representative, such as the parent or guardian of a minor or the guardian or next of kin of an incompetent adult. The physician usually limits the scope of the contract and does not assume responsibility for all the patient's medical needs. For example, the services can be limited to a particular specialty, so an internist can refuse to perform surgery.[4] An obstetrician can refuse to participate in home deliveries.[5] Physicians may limit the geographic area in which they practice. A California court ruled that a patient who became ill while visiting out of town could not sue her physician for refusing to come to the other town to see her.[6] A consulting physician who examines a patient at the request of the primary physician can limit involvement with the patient to the consultation and refuse continuing responsibility if this limitation is made clear to the patient and primary physician.

Some limitations on the scope of the contract are not permissible. An admitting physician assumes responsibility to examine the patient and offer appropriate treatment until the physician-patient relationship is terminated. In a Florida case, a physician who was at home recovering from an illness agreed to admit a patient as a favor to a friend but attempted to limit his contract solely to the act of admission by making it clear that he could not treat the patient.[7] The patient died of an undiagnosed brain abscess within a few days. The physician never saw her. The court ruled that there was a physician-patient relationship that included a duty to see the patient, so the patient's father could sue the physician for malpractice.

States have considered requiring physicians to accept certain patients. In 1994, Tennessee proposed a rule that would have required all licensed physicians who were accepting new patients to accept patients in the TennCare program, the state's Medicaid program. If TennCare patients were declined, all new patients would have had to be declined. In response to the strong reaction from physicians, the rule was withdrawn.[8]

Implied Contract

Sometimes a physician-patient relationship is inferred from physician conduct. When a physician commences treatment, courts will generally find a physician-patient relationship. Some courts have found a relationship from lesser contact. In an Iowa case, a relationship was established when a physician told a patient he would perform surgery.[9] A New York court found an implied contract when a physician listened to a recital of the patient's symptoms over the telephone.[10] Physicians who do not wish to assume the responsibility of a relationship should limit telephone calls to advising the caller to seek medical assistance elsewhere.

Although some specialists, such as pathologists and diagnostic radiologists, seldom see their patients, a physician-patient relationship is still established. This relationship does not usually include the responsibility for continuing care that is one of the elements of most relationships, but it does include responsibility for the consequences of intentional or negligent errors in providing pathology or radiology services.

Nondiscrimination

In making decisions concerning whether and how to treat patients, physicians are subject to some nondiscrimination laws. These laws are discussed later in this chapter.

Ending the Relationship

A physician has a duty to continue to provide medical care until the relationship is legally terminated. A physician who discontinues care before the relationship is legally terminated can be liable for abandonment.[11] The physician-patient relationship can be ended if

1. medical care is no longer needed,
2. the patient withdraws from the relationship,
3. the care of the patient is transferred to another physician,
4. ample notice of withdrawal is given by the physician to the patient, or
5. the physician is unable to provide care.

Patient Withdrawal

If the patient withdraws from the relationship, the physician has a duty to attempt to warn the patient if further care is needed, but there is no duty to provide further follow-up.[12] Upon request, the physician should advise the successor physician, if any, of information necessary to continue treatment. If care is still needed, the physician should usually request written confirmation of the withdrawal from the patient, realizing that in many situations the patient will decline to provide it.

Transfer

A patient's care may be transferred to another physician. Physicians attend meetings, take vacations, and have other valid reasons they cannot be available. A physician can fulfill the duties of the physician-patient relationship by providing a qualified substitute.[13]

Physician Withdrawal

A physician can withdraw from the relationship without providing a substitute by giving the patient reasonable notice in writing with sufficient time for the patient to locate another physician willing to accept the patient if continuing care is required.[14] Some of the reasons for withdrawal are noncooperation and failure to pay bills when able to do so.

Unable To Provide Care

A physician can be excused from the responsibilities of the relationship when unable to provide care. A physician who is ill should not accept additional responsibilities and should attempt to arrange for a substitute.[15] Sometimes physicians become too ill to be able to arrange a substitute. Also, a physician cannot be with two patients simultaneously. The necessity for attending another patient may provide a valid excuse if the physician has exercised prudence in determining the priority.[16] The physician cannot entirely give up one patient to attend another. The frequency of attendance to each patient will be an important factor in assessing whether one patient has been abandoned.

Abandonment

A physician who fails to see a patient with whom there is a physician-patient relationship without an acceptable reason may face liability for breach of contract or malpractice if the patient is injured as a result. Physicians do not have to be with the patient continuously to satisfy their responsibility. Physicians can leave orders for others to administer medications or other care if they return at intervals appropriate to the patient's condition. When hospital admission is not indicated, the patient can usually be sent home with instructions to call if further care is needed. The patient has the responsibility to call. However, when the patient and those responsible for the patient are unable to provide the needed care in the home, the physician should have arrangements made for other assistance or placement. The patient or representative can be told to follow certain instructions or to return at a certain time. It is not abandonment if the patient fails to return or follow instructions. However, if the patient has a known debility, it may be necessary to follow up if the patient does not return.

HOSPITAL-PATIENT RELATIONSHIP

This section addresses nondiscrimination laws and restrictions on patient recruiting, followed by the hospital's responsibilities to persons who are not in need of emergency care, the hospital's responsibilities to persons who need emergency care, issues concerning discharge, and allocation of scarce resources.

Nondiscrimination Statutes

Several statutes forbid discrimination in all aspects of patient care, but generally do not grant a right to be admitted.

Title VI

Title VI of the Civil Rights Act of 1964[17] forbids discrimination on the basis of race, color, or national origin in any institution that receives federal financial assistance. A hospital must comply with this statute and its implementing regulations[18] if it receives Medicare or Medicaid reimbursement. There are few published court decisions concerning patient claims under this statute.[19] Prior to 1988, Title VI applied only to the portion of the hospital and its programs that were supported by federal financial assistance. In 1988, the law was amended so that it applies to the entire hospital if any part receives federal financial assistance.[20]

The Americans with Disabilities Act

Title III of the Americans with Disabilities Act (ADA)[21] prohibits discrimination based on disability in the full enjoyment of the goods, services, facilities, privileges, and accommodations of any privately owned place of public accommodation. Hospitals and professional offices of health care providers are in the list of public accommodations covered.[22] There is an exemption for insurers and hospitals concerning some underwriting, classifying, and administering of risks.[23] Otherwise the reach of Title III has been interpreted broadly.[24]

Individual physicians can be liable under the ADA for their acts in their professional offices. In 1995, a federal court decided that an HIV-positive patient could sue his primary care physician in his managed care program for allegedly failing to treat or refer.[25] In 1994, another federal court held that the federal government could sue a dentist for refusing to treat HIV-positive patients in his office.[26] Some courts have found that individual physicians can also be liable for their hospital-related actions in some circumstances. When the on-call admitting physician refused to admit an HIV-positive patient, a federal court ruled in 1994 that, in addition to the hospital being liable, the physician could be individually liable as the "operator" of the hospital.[27] However, physicians who are not in such a position of control are probably not individually liable. In 1994, another federal court ruled that, while the hospital could be sued under the ADA, an emergency room physician who was an independent contractor for the hospital could not be individually sued for the hospital's policy concerning interpreters for the deaf because he lacked power to control that policy.[28]

In 1994, a federal court ruled that a state did not satisfy the ADA by providing mental health services to the deaf through interpreters. It ordered the state to provide deaf counselors who could use sign language.[29] It is doubtful that many service providers are large enough for this outcome to be a reasonable accommodation that must be made.

Similarly, discrimination by public programs and facilities is prohibited by Title II.[30]

The Rehabilitation Act of 1973

The Rehabilitation Act of 1973[31] forbids discrimination on the basis of disability in any institution that receives federal financial assistance. A hospital that receives Medicare and Medicaid reimbursement must comply with this statute and its implementing regulations.[32]

In 1994, a federal district court ruled that a nursing facility did not violate the act by refusing to admit an Alzheimer's patient with psychotic tendencies where the facility did not provide psychiatric services for those with disruptive psychotic disorders.[33] In 1995, a federal appellate court reversed that decision and ruled that the facility had failed to show that accommodating the patient would require fundamental changes in its programs or be an undue burden where the patient was largely immobile so that a jury could determine the patient posed little harm to others.[34] The nursing facility is reported to have sought the transfer of the patient based on a change in medical opinion concerning the patient's status that coincided with expiration of the patient's insurance benefits, so, perhaps, this is just a case of the court not believing the diagnosis.[35] However, more broadly read, this case could be a troublesome precedent for forcing providers to initiate new services for disabled patients whenever a jury concludes that the new service does not constitute a "fundamental change" in the program or an undue burden. However, in 1995, another federal district court ruled that a nursing home that did not offer subacute care did not have to accept a patient seeking that level of care.[36] Thus, courts still appear reluctant to force providers to initiate new levels of services.

In 1992, another federal court ruled that the Act did not require a nursing home to keep a violent and aggressive patient who was abusing the staff and who struck another patient. The court refused to enjoin the facility from discharging the patient after eight days' notice to leave.[37]

Individual physicians can also be sued under this law.[38] In 1994, a federal court decided that a physician could be sued by a deaf patient for allegedly refusing to provide an interpreter in her office.[39] However, this Act cannot be used to force unnecessary care that a disabled person desires. In a 1993 federal case, an HIV-positive patient claimed he had not been seen frequently enough by a physician and HMO. The court found no violation of the Act where he had been seen nine times in ten months and had been referred to specialists three times.[40]

Most substance abusers are considered disabled under this law and the ADA, so hospitals cannot discriminate against alcoholics and drug abusers in the providing of services.

The Age Discrimination Act of 1975

The Age Discrimination Act of 1975[41] forbids discrimination on the basis of age in federally assisted programs. In some circumstances reasonable factors other than age may be used even when they have a disproportionate effect on persons of different ages.[42] Also, in some circumstances, entities may reasonably take into account age as a factor when it is necessary to the normal operation or achievement of the statutory objective of the program or activity.[43] Special benefits to children and elderly persons are permitted.[44]

State Law

State nondiscrimination laws can also apply to both hospitals and physicians. Refusal of individual practitioners to treat HIV-positive patients has also been punished under state law.[45] However, a New York court ruled that it was not discrimination to take extra precautions during dental work on an HIV-positive patient.[46] This decision reversed a state administrative ruling that such treatment had exposed the patient to public humiliation.

In 1993, the highest court of New York ruled that it was a violation of the state human rights law for a hospital to exclude all pregnant women from its inpatient drug detoxification program. The lack of equipment to treat pregnant women, the lack of obstetricians on its staff, and the lack of a license to provide obstetrical care did not justify excluding all pregnant women. These services did not have to be provided, but a case-by-case determination had to be made whether each pregnant woman could be treated safely without the availability of these services on site or through arrangements with nearby off-site facilities.[47]

Required Discrimination

In 1994, California voters adopted Proposition 187, which required health care providers to refuse certain services to undocumented aliens and to report the aliens to authorities. A federal court enjoined implementation.[48]

Patient Recruiting

Federal law and many state laws forbid hospitals to recruit patients through providing kickbacks or other benefits to persons who arrange for admissions.[49]

In 1994, a psychiatric hospital chain pled guilty to making unlawful payments to doctors to induce referrals, agreed to divest itself of its psychiatric and substance abuse facilities, and agreed to pay the federal government $379 million to settle all charges.[50]

In 1993–94, Texas and several other states sued several psychiatric hospitals for recruitment of psychiatric patients. During 1994 most of these cases were settled with substantial payments by the psychiatric hospitals.[51]

Nonemergency Patients

Under common law, a person who does not need emergency care usually does not have a right to be admitted to a hospital. The hospital can legally refuse to admit any person unless one of three exceptions applies: (1) the common law exceptions, (2) contractual exceptions, or (3) statutory exceptions. Several statutes forbid discriminatory admission policies, but generally do not grant a right to be admitted. Rights to be admitted are also contingent on necessity for hospitalization, appropriateness of the hospital for the patient's needs, and availability of space.

Common Law Right to Admission

A person generally has a right to be admitted when the hospital is responsible for the original injury that caused the need for hospitalization. In some circumstances a person who becomes ill or injured in hospital buildings or on hospital grounds may have a right to be admitted even if the hospital is not otherwise responsible for the illness or injury. If a hospital begins to exercise control of a person by examining or beginning to provide care, a hospital-patient relationship may be started, entitling the patient to be admitted.

Contractual Right to Admission

When a hospital contracts to accept members of a certain population, they have a right to be admitted when they need care the hospital is able to provide. Some hospitals have contracts with employers agreeing to provide services to their employees or with managed care entities, such as HMOs, agreeing to accept patients covered by the entity. An Alabama court found a hospital liable for breach of a contract to furnish hospital services to employees of a company because the jury concluded that a decision that hospitalization was unnecessary was not made in good faith.[52] When entering such contracts, hospitals should assure that the contract provides that patients will be entitled to admission only when admitted by a physician with clinical privileges at the hospital.

Hill-Burton Community Service

Hospitals that accepted Hill-Burton construction grants or loans agreed to a "community service" obligation. The regulations defining this obligation specify that no person residing in the area serviced by the hospital will be denied admission to the portion of the hospital financed by Hill-Burton funds on any grounds other than the individual's lack of need for services, the availability of the needed services in the hospital, or the individual's ability to pay.[53] Inability to pay cannot be a basis for denial when the person needs emergency services or when the facility still has a Hill-Burton uncompensated care obligation. Emergency patients who are unable to pay and for whom services are not available under the uncompensated care obligation may be discharged or transferred to another facility that is able to provide necessary services. However, there must be a medical determination that the discharge or transfer does not substantially risk deterioration in the patient's medical condition. Advance deposits can be required if the hospital permits alternative arrangements when patients who are able to pay do not have the necessary cash. Hospitals may require admission by a physician with clinical privileges only if sufficient physicians on the staff are willing to admit the patients who must be admitted under the community service obligation. If insufficient physicians on the medical staff will admit certain types of patients, such as Medicaid patients, the hospital must hire physicians who will admit them, condition appointments to the medical staff on an agreement to admit some of them,[54] or grant temporary admitting privileges to the patient's personal physician. Any hospital that received construction funds after the 1974 amendments must provide this access to persons who work in the area served by the facility, in addition to those who reside in the area. In 1988, one court ruled that the community service obligation only applies to direct admissions, not to attempted transfers from other hospitals.[55]

Statutory Right to Admission

Some hospitals, especially governmental hospitals, are obligated by statute to accept all patients from a certain population that may be defined by geographic area of residence, inability to pay for care, or a combination of both. For example, county hospitals in Iowa are required to provide care and treatment to any resident of the county who is sick or injured and observes the rules of conduct adopted by the governing board.[56]

Antitrust

A hospital's discretion to refuse patients may be further decreased when it has recently been involved in a merger. In 1991, a federal appellate court ruled that an antitrust claim was stated by patients who were denied nonemergency treatment after the merger of a hospital with a clinic that employed a physician whom they had sued.[57]

Reasons for Nonadmission

Even when a person otherwise has a right to be admitted to a hospital, several reasons are generally recognized as justifying nonadmission. First, if hospitalization is not medically necessary, there is no right to admission. A hospital is not a hotel; it is an institution for the provision of necessary medical services. Second, if the hospital does not provide the services the patient needs, it does not have to admit the patient. However, as already discussed in the nondiscrimination section, hospitals need to provide reasonable accommodations to permit the disabled and handicapped to have the benefit of their services. Sometimes it may not be clear whether what is needed is a new service that is not required to be provided or an accommodation that must be provided.[58] Even when the hospital cannot provide the needed definitive diagnosis or treatment, if the patient needs emergency care to prepare for transfer to an appropriate facility, the hospital must provide such care to the extent of its capability.

Generally, when space is not available, the hospital may refuse to admit the patient, but still must provide the emergency care necessary to prepare for transfer.[59] This rule usually applies even when a court orders admission. For example, the South Dakota Supreme Court ruled that the lower court had exceeded its jurisdiction when it ordered a state training school to accept a juvenile when no space was available.[60] Therefore, the superintendent's disobedience was not punishable as contempt. However, not all courts adopt this realistic position, so such court orders should be reviewed with legal counsel when compliance is not contemplated. In 1982, the Washington Supreme Court interpreted state law to require a mental hospital to accept all patients presented to the hospital by mental health professionals within its allocated area even though they would exceed the institutional capacity.[61] It based its analysis in part on the need of these patients for immediate treatment, so perhaps this case should be viewed as an example of the hospital's responsibility for emergency patients.

Emergency Patients

The Emergency Medical Treatment and Active Labor Act

In the past the general rule was that persons did not have a right to emergency hospital care except under the circumstances discussed earlier in this chapter in which they would be entitled to any necessary hospital services. The 1986 Medicare amendments added the requirement that all hospitals that participate in Medicare provide certain services to all patients who seek emergency care.[62] This law was often called either COBRA or the "anti-dumping" statute until the 1989 amendments modified the law and changed its name to EMTALA.[63] EMTALA applies only to hospitals, not to medical clinics[64] or utilization review entities.[65] Physicians cannot be sued by private individuals for violations of EMTALA,[66] but they can be sanctioned by federal government officials,[67] and, when hospitals are found liable due to the acts of a physician, at least one court has permitted the hospital to sue the physician for reimbursement.[68]

Screening. All such patients, whether or not they are eligible for Medicare, must be given an appropriate medical screening to determine if they have an emergency medical condition or are in active labor. Most courts have decided that the patient must come to the hospital to be covered by EMTALA,[69] although not necessarily through the emergency room.[70] Most courts have ruled that EMTALA is not a malpractice act, so misdiagnosis is not a violation of EMTALA, provided that an appropriate screening is given.[71] Generally courts recognize that an appropriate screening can result in a misdiagnosis.[72] Most courts have held that EMTALA does not apply to just patients who are unable to pay; it applies to all patients who seek emergency services at the hospital.[73]

Stabilization. If the screening determines that an emergency medical condition or active labor is present, the hospital must provide services to stabilize the patient or arrange for an appropriate transfer. The responsibility to provide stabilization services and transfers does not apply until the emergency condition is determined.[74] The Act is satisfied if the patient is stabilized at discharge.[75]

However, this standard may create a problem when the patient cannot be stabilized. In 1994, a federal appellate court ruled that a hospital could not discontinue the use of a respirator on an anencephalic baby who had been brought to the hospital as an emergency transfer even if the treatment was futile.[76]

Transfers. The patient may be transferred only if (1) the patient requests the transfer or qualified medical personnel certify that benefits outweigh risks and (2) qualified personnel and equipment are used to transfer the patient to a hospital that has accepted the patient and that has space and staff to treat the patient. If a patient is transferred without approval of the receiving hospital, the sending hospital can be required to reimburse the receiving hospital for the care of the patient.

In some circumstances, transfers by private car may satisfy the requirements.[77]

The 1989 Medicare amendments and some state laws require hospitals to accept emergency transfers when the sending hospital is unable to care for the patient and the receiving hospital is able to benefit the patient.[78] In 1993, the Health Care Financing Administration (HCFA) distributed a letter stating that Medicare hospitals do not have to accept transfers from foreign hospitals.[79]

Penalties. When a patient is refused a screening or emergency services, the hospital can be fined,[80] lose its entitlement to participate in Medicare,[81] and be sued by the patient for resulting injuries.[82] Generally courts have applied state law procedures[83] and liability limits[84] to claims under EMTALA.

State Law

In nearly all states, a hospital is liable for injuries due to refusal of emergency treatment even if the hospital is one of the rare non-Medicare hospitals unaffected by federal law.[85] In Texas it is also a crime for any officer or employee of a general hospital supported with public funds to deny a person emergency services available in the hospital on the basis of inability to pay if a physician has diagnosed that the patient is seriously ill or injured.[86]

Continuing Care

When care is provided under the emergency care obligation to patients the hospital would not otherwise accept, the hospital generally does not have a duty to provide continuing care if arrangements can be made for an appropriate transfer without substantial danger to the patient. This is recognized by the Hill-Burton community service regulations discussed earlier in this chapter. The Alabama Supreme Court ruled that a hospital has no obligation to admit a patient after providing proper emergency care.[87] The hospital fulfilled its responsibility by arranging for transfer to a charitable hospital. However, if the emergency care had created a dangerous condition requiring further care, the hospital would have had a duty to admit the patient under the general common law responsibility that everyone has to assist persons they have put in peril. In some states, financial transfers are permitted in a smaller range of circumstances.[88] If the hospital cannot provide the needed care, it has a duty to attempt to arrange a transfer. A California court found a hospital and the treating physician liable for negligent care of a severely burned patient, in part because the hospital did not have facilities to care for severe burns.[89] However, the hospital is not required to be the best facility providing the needed care. In a 1986 New York case, the patient was upset with a scar from a skin graft and sued the physician for failure to transfer the patient to a burn center. The court found no liability because although the hospital might not be the best, it could give adequate care for burn patients.[90]

Common Law Duties in Transfers

If a transfer is required, the hospital has a duty to prepare the patient for the move and to make arrangements for it. Patient preparation includes appropriate examination and stabilization. In a Mississippi case, a veteran who came to a community hospital emergency room bleeding profusely had been transferred to a Veterans Administration hospital by the emergency nurse without any effort by the nurse to stop the bleeding.[91] The first hospital was found liable for the patient's death because the nurse did not obtain information concerning his condition from the people who brought him to the hospital, did not tell the physician on call of the extent of bleeding, and did not do anything to stop the bleeding. Transfer arrangements include appropriate attendants and speed. When ambulances or helicopters staffed with emergency medical technicians, emergency nurses, or physicians are available, it will be difficult to convince a court of the appropriateness of an interhospital transfer of a critically ill patient in an unequipped vehicle that is not staffed with specially trained personnel.

Emergency room staff can take actions based on reasonably available information. They do not have to be able to foresee the future in the absence of information. For example, a Florida hospital was sued by the wife of a man who had been stabbed by a person seen briefly in its emergency room.[92] A grandmother had taken her grandson to the emergency room because she suspected he had taken LSD, but the hospital did not have the testing facilities to determine the presence of the drug. While the grandmother was driving the grandson to another hospital, he jumped out of the car, ran inside a building, and fatally stabbed the plaintiff's husband. The court found that the hospital was not liable because the patient exhibited no behavior that would have led the personnel at the first hospital to suspect a risk of this outcome. If there had been reasons for suspicion, other arrangements would have had to be made for transport.

Discharge

Hospitals that participate in Medicare are required to have a discharge planning process and to arrange for the initial implementation of the patient's discharge plan.[93]

There is a fundamental tension between the liability that can result from holding a patient too long and the liability that can result from releasing a patient too soon. This section discusses the liability for false imprisonment, *habeas corpus*, and liability for discharge of patients in need of additional care. Refusal to leave, temporary releases, and escapes are also discussed.

False Imprisonment

False imprisonment is holding a person against his or her will without lawful authority.[94] Physical restraints or physical barriers are not necessary. Threats leading to a reasonable apprehension of harm can provide enough restraint to establish false imprisonment.[95]

In the past a few cases of false imprisonment arose when hospitals attempted to hold patients until their bills were paid.[96] There have been no reported decisions concerning this situation in more than 30 years, which indicates that hospitals now understand this practice is unacceptable.

In some cases, hospitals inappropriately restrain patients as part of treatment, leading to liability. An unreported 1970 Michigan Circuit Court decision from Wayne County, *Smith v. Henry Ford Hospital*, is an example. A patient who had been transferred from the coronary care unit to a semiprivate room decided to leave the hospital because he did not like the room. When the patient tried to leave, several staff members returned the patient to the hospital room and restrained him in the bed. He escaped from the restraints and exited through the window. He was injured in his fall to the ground. Since there was no evidence that the patient was disoriented or mentally unsound, the court found the hospital liable.

In many situations it is not only appropriate but also a duty of the hospital to detain or restrain a patient. All states have laws providing procedures for the commitment of persons who are seriously mentally ill, are substance abusers, or are a danger to the public health due to contagious disease.[97] States also have laws that provide procedures for taking custody of minors who are neglected or abused.[98] Generally a hospital can hold these persons while reporting them to authorities and obtaining commitment or custody orders.

When these laws do not apply, the hospital still has a common law duty to protect temporarily disoriented patients. Physicians and hospitals generally have authority under the common law to temporarily detain and even restrain temporarily disoriented medical patients without court involvement. This authority is inferred from the cases in which hospitals have been found liable for injuries to patients who are not restrained during temporary disorientation.[99] This common law authority does not apply when the patient is being detained for treatment for mental illness or substance abuse. The applicable statutory procedures should be followed in those cases. This common law authority does not apply when the patient is fully oriented, as in the *Henry Ford Hospital* case, but the hospital can usually maintain custody long enough for the patient's status to be determined if there is reasonable doubt.

If parents try to discharge a child when removal presents an imminent danger to the child's life or health, most states either authorize the health care provider to retain custody of the child or provide an expeditious procedure for obtaining court authorization to retain custody.[100] Many parents will agree to acceptable treatment or postpone precipitous withdrawal when advised that these procedures will be invoked.

If an adult patient is neither disoriented nor committable, the patient generally has a right to leave unless it is one of the unusual situations in which courts will order treatment, as discussed in Chapter 13. Interfering with this right can lead to liability, as illustrated by the *Henry Ford Hospital* case. Honoring the patient's wishes to leave can cause the patient care staff great distress. For example, nearly all physicians and nurses are distressed when an oriented patient with a spinal fracture insists on leaving the hospital, risking paralysis or even death that could probably be prevented by appropriate care in the hospital. This distress does not change the patient's right to leave. It will affect the staff's efforts to convince the patient to stay and to explain the risks of leaving.

Patients who decide to leave against medical advice should be advised of the risks of leaving, if possible, and should be urged to reconsider, if further care is needed. The explanation should be documented. Patients should be asked to sign a form that they are leaving against medical advice and that the risks have been explained to them. However, patients cannot be forced to sign. If patients refuse to sign, the explanation and refusal should be documented in the medical record by the involved staff.

Habeas Corpus

Federal courts have the power under the U.S. Constitution to review the legality of the confinement of any person.[101] When a federal court issues a *writ of habeas corpus* concerning an individual, the person or entity holding that individual must present the individual to the court and prove the right to continue the confinement. If the right is not proven, the court orders release. This is most commonly used to challenge confinement of persons under the criminal law, but it is also used to challenge involuntary treatment of mentally ill persons[102] and others.[103]

State courts also can issue *writs of habeas corpus*. In at least one case a writ was directed to a hospital for holding a patient until he could pay his bill.[104]

Discharge of Patients Needing Additional Care

A patient should be discharged only as a result of (1) a written order of a physician familiar with the patient's condition or (2) the patient's decision to leave against medical advice. This procedure helps to protect the patient from injury and the hospital from liability for premature discharge. Most premature discharge cases arise from misdiagnosis, but sometimes they arise from discharging patients who are ready to leave, but for whom adequate arrangements have not been made. Children, the infirm aged, and others who are unable to care for themselves should be discharged only to the custody of someone who can take care of them. A California physician was found liable for discharging an abused 11-month-old child to the abusing parents without first giving the state an opportunity to intervene.[105]

Patients do not have to be kept in the hospital until cured. Patients generally may be discharged when the hospital is no longer the appropriate level of care or when the patient becomes sufficiently disruptive.

Level of Care. When patients no longer need the level of care provided in a hospital, they can be transferred to a nursing home or discharged to home care. When they no longer need the level of hospital care in a referral center or begin to need the more specialized level of care in a referral center, interhospital transfer is appropriate.

Disruptive Patients. If a patient becomes sufficiently difficult or disruptive, it is permissible in some situations for the hospital to discontinue providing care. In 1982, a California court refused to order a physician and several hospitals to continue to provide chronic hemodialysis to a noncooperative, disruptive patient who had even refused to comply with the conditions of a court order that provided for continued treatment during the litigation.[106] The physician had given her due notice of his withdrawal from the physician-patient relationship with ample time for her to make other arrangements. The court was clearly troubled by the possibility that she would not be able to receive necessary care, but concluded that several alternatives were available.

Courts are more comfortable with involuntary discharges when the patient's condition is not so severe. An Arizona court ruled that a physician and hospital were not liable for discharging a difficult patient who had been admitted for the treatment of lesions on his lips.[107] The court observed that the patient was uncomfortable, but not helpless and that the hospital staff had done nothing actively to retard his treatment or worsen his condition.

In 1992, a federal court refused to enjoin a nursing home from discharging a violent and aggressive patient who had abused staff and struck another patient. The court ruled that the discharge violated neither the Medicaid law nor the Rehabilitation Act.[108]

A Minnesota court ruled in 1994 that a nursing facility could not involuntarily discharge a patient with mental illness because she refused treatment by mental health professionals. The facility must first meet its obligations to assess the patient's needs and examine treatment alternatives, including an incompetency determination to force the medication.[109]

Recommended Procedure. Any discharge of a patient in need of continued care could be controversial, so it should usually be limited to situations that interfere with the care of other patients or threaten the safety of staff members. Hospital administration should review each case to minimize legal liability and other adverse effects on the hospital. When the attending physician desires an inappropriate discharge, it may be necessary to transfer the care of the patient to another physician or to discuss with the physician the compatibility of the proposed discharge with the hospital's standards for continued membership on the medical staff.

The need for a treating physician's discharge order is especially important to remember when a utilization review committee or a third party reviewer decides that a patient should be discharged but the treating physician believes the patient should stay. While the decision of a physician reviewer may be given some weight, it will not insulate the physician or hospital from liability. An independent judgment must be made by the treating physician. For example, a state physician reviewer in California was sued for the complications a patient suffered when the reviewer authorized only half the additional hospital days requested by the treating physician.[110] The trial court found the reviewer could be liable, but the appellate court reversed, finding that the treating physician had the legal responsibility to make the actual discharge decision. In 1990, a California appellate court ruled that the earlier case applied only to Medi-Cal (California's Medicaid program) patients, so that it did not apply to patients insured under policies issued in the private sector.[111] The case arose when a utilization reviewer determined that hospitalization was not medically necessary and the patient committed suicide after discharge. The case was remanded for trial. If a jury found that the utilization reviewer's actions were a substantial factor in causing the suicide, the reviewer could be liable. Liability was not limited to the treating physician. The liability of managed care entities is discussed in Chapter 10.

Refusal To Leave

Patients and patient representatives do not have the right to insist on unnecessary hospitalization. If the patient refuses to leave or the patient's representatives refuse to remove the patient after the physician's discharge order, the patient is a trespasser, and the hospital can take appropriate steps to have the patient removed. If the situation is a delay in discharge due to difficulties in arranging placement, the hospital will usually take reasonable steps to assist in making arrangements. However, if the patient and the patient's representatives will not cooperate, it may be necessary to use reasonable force to remove the patient or to obtain a court order.[112] In a few states it is a crime to refuse to leave a hospital after discharge.[113] When a patient who is refusing to leave is mentally ill, in some circumstances the patient can be involuntarily transferred to a mental facility if the patient meets the criteria for involuntary hospitalization.[114] As with the discharge of noncooperative and disruptive patients discussed in the previous section, hospital administration should make decisions concerning forcible removal.

Generally patients cannot force programs to provide the treatments that they want. In 1992, a federal court denied an injunction of the planned move of mentally retarded persons to a state-owned regional treatment center. The court ruled that they did not have the right to compel the state to provide community-based residential placement. The court stated:

> Unfortunately, funds available for these programs are finite. Ordering the development of the requested facility, at a cost far above the currently available funding limits, would rob Peter to pay Paul. Society, through its elected representatives and appointed agency administrators, has made the difficult decisions regarding the amount and allocation of these funds.[115]

Temporary Releases

Sometimes children, incompetent adults, cooperative committed patients, or competent adults who need continuing supervision or care ask to leave the hospital for a short time. This is permissible in many situations and may assist in patient care. Since liability is possible, precautions should be taken. A written physician authorization should indicate that temporary release is not medically contraindicated. Written authorization from competent adult patients or from the parent or guardian of other patients should acknowledge that the hospital is not responsible for the care of the patient while out of hospital custody. Except for adult patients who are able to take care of themselves and are not a danger to others, patients should only be released to appropriate adults who have been instructed concerning patient needs during the release, such as medications and wheelchair use, and the way to contact the hospital for information or assistance if needed. If the necessary arrangements are then made for patient needs, the risks associated with temporary releases are minimized.

If patients who are a danger to themselves or others are temporarily released and are harmed or harm others, the hospital could be liable.[116] A Florida court ruled that a hospital could be sued by a person who was injured in an automobile accident caused by a patient on a temporary release because the hospital should have known she would attempt to operate an automobile and could not do so safely.[117] This case illustrates the significance of careful medical review before authorizing release.

A Minnesota hospital's policy concerning passes for the mentally ill was challenged as a violation of the state's commitment law. The Minnesota Supreme Court upheld the policy by ruling that passes were not discharges. The court reviewed the precautions, including monitoring and giving interested individuals an opportunity to comment before the pass was issued, and concluded they were appropriate.[118]

Escape

Hospitals can be sued when patients who have escaped commit suicide, are injured or killed in accidents, or injure or kill others. The courts usually focus on (1) how much those involved in the care of the patient knew or should have known about the dangerousness of the patient to self or others and (2) the appropriateness of the precautions taken to prevent escape in light of that knowledge. Generally if the injury was not foreseeable, there is little likelihood of liability for failure to take additional precautions. If the injury was foreseeable, courts will examine the reasonableness of the precautions, and liability will be more likely. However, many courts have recognized the therapeutic benefits of more open patient care units and have found them to be reasonable even for some patients at risk.[119] In other cases the precautions have been found to be inadequate, and liability has been imposed.

At least one federal court has ruled that there is no legal right to be involuntarily committed, so it is not a violation of the 42 U.S.C.A. § 1983 for a mental health facility to fail to stop someone from leaving the facility who is later injured.[120]

Allocation of Scarce Resources

In addition to the decisions concerning when to admit and discharge patients, there can be difficult decisions concerning the allocation of scarce resources. The institutional decisions determine what resources are available at the hospital. When there are insufficient resources to provide the available services to all who could benefit from them, then decisions must be made concerning which individuals will receive the benefits. Society and most institutions try to avoid having to make these decisions.[121]

Individual allocation decisions can be made through exclusionary criteria that are applied either preadmission or postadmission or through selection procedures, which can include expert decisions (e.g., medical need or benefit), a market (i.e., who is able and willing to pay), a lottery (i.e., by chance), a queue (e.g., first come-first served), or a committee decision.[122]

These decisions must be made regularly in transplantation programs. Hospitals are required by HFCA to have criteria and a procedure for making these decisions to be eligible to be a Medicare participating provider of various transplant services.[123]

In 1993, a drug company announced that it was going to use a computer to randomly select which patients would receive a new drug because it could not produce enough of the drug to meet the entire demand.[124]

NOTES

1. *E.g.*, Salas v. Gamboa, 760 S.W.2d 838 (Tex. Ct. App. 1988).

2. *E.g.*, Carswell v. Bay County, 854 F.2d 454 (11th Cir. 1988).

3. Mozingo v. Pitt County Mem. Hosp., 331 N.C. 182, 415 S.E.2d 341 (1992); *see* Annotation, *What constitutes physician-patient relationship for malpractice purposes*, 17 A.L.R. 4TH 132.

4. *E.g.*, Skodje v. Hardy, 47 Wash. 2d 557, 288 P.2d 471 (1955).

5. *E.g.*, Vidrine v. Mayes, 127 So.2d 809 (La. Ct. App. 1961).

6. McNamara v. Emmons, 36 Cal. App. 2d 199, 97 P.2d 503 (4th Dist. 1939).

7. Giallanza v. Sands, 316 So.2d 77 (Fla. 4th DCA 1975); *see also* Maltempo v. Cuthbert, 504 F.2d 325 (5th Cir. 1974) [physician liable for failing to examine jailed patient after agreeing with his parents to do so even though patient was under care of jail physician].

8. J. Somerville, *Physicians furious at Tennessee rule*, AM. MED. NEWS, Nov. 7, 1994, at 3 [proposed rule]; *Tennessee physicians beat back Medicaid rule*, AM. MED. NEWS, Mar. 13, 1995, at 8; *Tenn. drops patient discrimination ban*, AM. MED. NEWS, Mar. 20, 1995, at 9 [proposed rule withdrawn]; *Rule to ban physicians from limiting their Tenncare patient loads rescinded*, 4 HEALTH L. RPTR. [BNA] 372 (1995) [hereinafter HEALTH L. RPTR. cited as H.L.R.].

9. McGulpin v. Bessmer, 241 Iowa 1119, 43 N.W.2d 121 (1950).

10. O'Neil v. Montefiore Hosp., 11 A.D. 2d 132, 202 N.Y.S.2d 436 (1st Dep't 1960); *contra*, Buttersworth v. Swint, 53 Ga. App. 602, 186 S.E. 770 (1936) [answers to questions in hallway not enough]; St. John v. Pope, 1995 Tex. LEXIS 74 (June 8, 1995), *as discussed in* HEALTH L. DIG., July 1995, at 48 [no physician-patient relationship established with on-call physician by telephone consultation with treating emergency room physician].

11. *See* Annotation, *Liability of physician who abandons case*, 57 A.L.R. 2D 432.

12. *E.g.*, East v. United States, 745 F. Supp. 1142 (D. Md. 1990).

13. *E.g.*, Kearns v. Ellis, 18 Mass. App. Ct. 923, 465 N.E.2d 294, *rev. denied*, 393 Mass. 1102, 469 N.E.2d 830 (1984).

14. *E.g.*, Miller v. Greater Southeast Comm. Hosp., 508 A.2d 927 (D.C. 1986).

15. *E.g.*, Kenney v. Piedmont Hosp., 136 Ga. App. 660, 222 S.E.2d 162 (1975) [not abandonment for ill surgeon to permit associate to operate].

16. *E.g.*, Young v. Jordan, 106 W. Va. 139, 145 S.E. 41 (1928) [another patient is not excuse when physician induced labor in first patient].

17. 42 U.S.C.A. §§ 2000d–2000d-7.

18. 45 C.F.R. pt. 80.

19. *E.g.*, Ibarra v. Bexar County Hosp. Dist., 624 F.2d 44 (5th Cir. 1980) [abstention in suit concerning treatment of aliens]; Bryan v. Koch, 627 F.2d 612 (2d Cir. 1980) [hospital closing];

NAACP v. Med. Ctr., Inc., 657 F.2d 1322 (3d Cir. 1981) [hospital relocation; see discussion in Chapter 6]; *see also* Fobbs v. Holy Cross Health Sys. Corp., 29 F.3d 1439 (9th Cir. 1994), *cert. denied*, 115 S. Ct. 936 (U.S. 1995) [physician challenging summary suspension of clinical privileges lacked standing to assert rights of his minority patients].

20. 42 U.S.C.A. § 2000d-4a(3)(A)(ii), *as added by* Pub. L. No. 100-259, § 6, 102 Stat. 31 (1988).

21. 42 U.S.C.A. §§ 12181–12189; *see* M.A. Dowell, *The Americans with Disabilities Act: The responsibilities of health care providers, insurers and managed care organizations*, 25 J. HEALTH & HOSP. L. 289 (1992).

22. 42 U.S.C.A. § 12181(7)(F).

23. 42 U.S.C.A. § 12201(c).

24. *E.g.,* Carparts Distrib. Ctr., Inc. v. Automotive Wholesaler's Ass'n of N. Eng., 37 F.3d 12 (1st Cir. 1994) [not limited to physical structures; can apply to services]; In re Baby K., 832 F. Supp. 1022 (E.D. Va. 1993) [may require futile respiratory support of anencephalic baby], *aff'd on other grounds*, 16 F.3d 590 (4th Cir. 1994), *cert. denied*, 115 S. Ct. 91 (U.S. 1994); Mayberry v. Von Valtier, 843 F. Supp. 1160 (E.D. Mich. 1994) [interpreter for deaf patient]; Aikens v. St. Helena Hosp., 843 F. Supp. 1329 (N.D. Cal. 1994) [interpreter for deaf patient].

25. Woolfolk v. Duncan, 872 F. Supp. 1381 (E.D. Pa. 1995).

26. United States v. Morvant, 843 F. Supp. 1092 (E.D. La. 1994); *see also* United States v. Jack H. Castle, D.D.S., Inc., No. H-93-31450 (S.D. Tex. Sept. 23, 1994), *as discussed in* 3 H.L.R. 1343 (1994) [dental clinic required to pay $100,000 for refusing to treat HIV patient].

27. Howe v. Hull, 874 F. Supp. 779 (N.D. Ohio 1994); 873 F. Supp. 72 (N.D. Ohio 1994).

28. Aikens v. St. Helena Hosp., 843 F. Supp. 1328 (N.D. Cal. 1994).

29. Tugg v. Towey, 864 F. Supp. 1201 (S.D. Fla. 1994).

30. 42 U.S.C.A. §§ 12131–12134.

31. 29 U.S.C.A. § 794.

32. 45 C.F.R. pt. 84.

33. Wagner v. Fair Acres Geriatric Ctr., 859 F. Supp. 776 (E.D. Pa. 1994).

34. Wagner v. Fair Acres Geriatric Ctr., 49 F.3d 1002 (3d Cir. 1995).

35. *See also* N. Hershey, *Patient's discharge linked to end of insurance coverage*, 12 HOSP. L. NEWSLETTER (July 1995), at 1 [describing Muse v. Charter Hosp., 117 N.C. App. 468, 452 S.E.2d 589, *rev. denied*, 340 N.C. 114, 455 S.E.2d 663 (1995), in which a hospital was held liable for suicide of patient allegedly discharged pursuant to hospital policy to discharge when insurance coverage expired].

36. Grubbs v. Medical Facilities of Am., Inc., 879 F. Supp. 588 (W.D. Va. 1995).

37. Nichols v. St. Luke Ctr., 800 F. Supp. 1564 (S.D. Ohio 1992).

38. *E.g.,* Woolfolk v. Duncan, 872 F. Supp. 1381 (E.D. Pa. 1995).

39. Mayberry v. Von Valtier, 843 F. Supp. 1160 (E.D. Mich. 1994).

40. Tony v. U.S. Healthcare, Inc., 838 F. Supp. 201 (E.D. Pa. 1993), 840 F. Supp. 357 (E.D. Pa. 1993) [summary judgment granted for other defendants].

41. 42 U.S.C.A. §§ 6101–6107; 45 C.F.R. pt. 90 [general], 91 [HHS].

42. 45 C.F.R. § 91.14.

43. 45 C.F.R. § 91.15.

44. 45 C.F.R. § 91.17.

45. *E.g.,* State by Beaulieu v. Clausen, 491 N.W.2d 662 (Minn. Ct. App. 1992).

46. *E.g.,* Syracuse Comm. Health Ctr. v. Wendi A.M., 198 A.D.2d 830, 604 N.Y.S.2d 406 (4th Dep't 1993), *app. granted*, 83 N.Y.2d 752, 611 N.Y.S.2d 135, 663 N.E.2d 490 (1994).

47. Elaine W. v. Joint Diseases North Gen. Hosp., 81 N.Y.2d 211, 597 N.Y.S.2d 617, 613 N.E.2d 523 (1993), *rev'g*, 180 A.D.2d 525, 580 N.Y.S.2d 246 (1st Dep't 1992).

48. Gregoria T. v. Wilson, No. 94-7652 (C.D. Cal. Nov. 22, 1994), *as discussed in* 3 H.L.R. 1731 (1994); *Federal court blocks most of California Proposition 187*, 3 H.L.R. 1830 (1994).

49. 42 U.S.C.A. §§ 1320a-7–1320a-7b; FLA. STAT. § 395.0185.

50. United States v. NME Psychiatric Hosps., Inc., No. 94-0268 (D. D.C. proposed settlement filed June 29, 1994), *as discussed in* 3 H.L.R. 917 (1994); O.I.G., Semi-Annual Report, Apr. 1, 1994–Sept. 30, 1994, *reported in* MEDICARE & MEDICAID GUIDE (CCH) ¶42,947, at 42,747 [hereinafter MEDICARE & MEDICAID GUIDE cited as M.M.G.].

51. *E.g., Texas 'bounty hunting' suit against hospitals settled for $1.75 million*, 3 H.L.R. 306 (1994); *State, psychiatric hospital settle over illegal management contracts*, 3 H.L.R. 306 (1994); *Psychiatric hospital agrees to settle state charges of illegal compensation*, 3 H.L.R. 1009 (1994); *Texas settles psychiatric patient recruitment suits*, 3 H.L.R. 1789 (1994).

52. Norwood Hosp. v. Howton, 32 Ala. App. 375, 26 So.2d 427 (1946).

53. 42 C.F.R §§ 124.601–124.607.

54. *E.g.*, Clair v. Centre Comm. Hosp., 317 Pa. Super. 25, 463 A.2d 1065 (1983) [hospital can suspend physician who does not comply with rule requiring indigent care].

55. Ritter v. Wayne County Gen. Hosp., 174 Mich. App. 490, 436 N.W.2d 673 (1988).

56. IOWA CODE ANN. § 347.16.

57. Nelson v. Monroe Reg. Med. Ctr., 925 F.2d 1555 (7th Cir.), *cert. dismissed*, 502 U.S. 903 (1991).

58. *E.g.*, see text at notes 33–37, *supra*.

59. Davis v. Johns Hopkins Hosp., 86 Md. App. 134, 585 A.2d 841 (1991), *aff'd in pertinent part*, 330 Md. 53, 622 A.2d 128 (1993) [no duty to admit emergency pediatric patient when PICU full]; Ritter v. Wayne County Gen. Hosp., 174 Mich. App. 490, 436 N.W. 2d 673 (1988) [no duty to admit patient when no bed available]; People v. Flushing Hosp., 122 Misc. 2d 260, 471 N.Y.S.2d 745 (Crim. Ct. 1983) [hospital found guilty of misdemeanor, fined when patient died after emergency care refused because hospital was full].

60. People in the Interest of M.B., 312 N.W.2d 714 (S.D. 1981); *see also* Rhode Island Dep't of Mental Health v. Doe, 533 A.2d 536 (R.I. 1987) [trial court cannot specify facility for commitment; department places patients based on resources, priorities]; Dennis v. Redouty, 534 So.2d 756 (Fla. 1st DCA 1988) [hospital administrator, not hearing officer, decides whether committed patient should be discharged early].

61. Pierce County Office of Involuntary Commitment v. Western State Hosp., 97 Wash. 2d 264, 644 P.2d 131 (1982).

62. Pub. L. No. 99-272, § 9121(b) (1986) (*codified as amended at* 42 U.S.C.A. § 1395dd); 42 C.F.R. §§ 489.20, 489.24–489.27, *first published in* 59 FED. REG. 32086 (June 22, 1994).

63. Pub. L. No. 101-239, § 6211 (1989); *see* Annotation, *Construction and application of Emergency Medical Treatment and Active Labor Act*, 104 A.L.R. FED. 166.

64. *E.g.*, King v. Ahrens, 16 F.3d 265 (8th Cir. 1994).

65. *E.g.*, Bangert v. Christian Health Servs., No. 92 613 WLB (S.D. Ill. Dec. 17, 1992), *as reprinted in* M.M.G. ¶41,081.

66. *E.g.*, Palmer v. Hospital Auth., 22 F.3d 1559 (11th Cir. 1994) [although physician cannot be sued individually under EMTALA, can be sued under state law as part of suit against hospital under EMTALA].

67. Burditt v. U.S. DHHS, 934 F.2d 1362 (5th Cir. 1991) [affirming assessment of $20,000 penalty against individual physician].

68. McDougal v. LaForche Hosp. Service, No. 92-2006, M.M.G. ¶41,542 (E.D. La. May 25, 1993) (case dismissed in June 1993 pursuant to settlement).

69. *E.g.*, Miller v. Medical Ctr., 22 F.3d 626 (5th Cir. 1994) [no EMTALA violation to tell doctor over phone not to send child to hospital]; Johnson v. University of Chicago Hosps., 982 F.2d 230 (7th Cir. 1992) [no EMTALA violation from diversion by radio before reaching emergency room].

70. *E.g.*, McIntyre v. Schick, 795 F. Supp. 777 (E.D. Va. 1992).

71. *E.g.*, Williams v. Birkeness, 34 F.3d 695 (8th Cir. 1994); Gatewood v. Washington Healthcare Corp., 290 U.S. App. D.C. 31, 933 F.2d 1037 (1991); Ruiz v. Kepler, 832 F. Supp. 1444 (D. N.M. 1993) [misdiagnosis alone not enough to show screening not appropriate; appropriateness to be judged by hospital's capability; question raised by (a) affidavit of physician expert stating standard was minimum of 12 hours' observation of head trauma patient, (b) lack of documentation of periodic nurse checks]; *see* M.J. Staab, *Is there a private cause of action under COBRA for misdiagnosis?* 28 J. HEALTH & HOSP. L. 1 (1995); *see also* Repp v. Anadarko Mun. Hosp., 43 F.3d 519 (10th Cir. 1994) [minor deviations from institutional policies concerning screening do not establish EMTALA liability].

72. *E.g.*, Nash v. Wilkinson, 1992 U.S. Dist. LEXIS 9458 (D. Kan. June 18, 1992), *as discussed in* 26 J. HEALTH & HOSP. L. 87 (1993) [mistaken diagnosis of lack of emergency not violation].

73. *E.g.*, Collins v. DePaul Hosp., 963 F.2d 303 (10th Cir. 1992); *contra*, Cleland v. Bronson Health Care Group, Inc., 917 F.2d 266 (6th Cir. 1990).

74. *E.g.*, Urban v. King, 43 F.3d 523 (10th Cir. 1994).

75. *E.g.*, Holcomb v. Monahan, 30 F.3d 116 (11th Cir. 1994); Green v. Touro Infirmary, 992 F.2d 537 (5th Cir. 1993).

76. In re Baby K, 16 F.3d 590 (4th Cir.), *cert. denied*, 115 S. Ct. 91 (U.S. 1994); *see* G.J. Annas, *Asking the courts to set the standard of emergency care—The case of Baby K,* 330 N. ENGL. J. MED. 1542 (1994).

77. *E.g.*, Wey v. Evangelical Comm. Hosp., 833 F. Supp. 453 (M.D. Pa. 1993).

78. 42 U.S.C.A. § 1395dd(g), as added by Pub. L. No. 101-239, § 6211(f) (1989); *e.g.*, FLA. STAT. § 395.0142; 25 Tex. Admin. Code Ch. 11, § 133.21; Lutz, *Texas sets response deadline for patient transfer requests,* 18 MOD. HEALTHCARE, Nov. 18, 1988, at 74 [30-minute deadline].

79. Letter from Acting HCFA Administrator Toby to Senator Lloyd Benson (Jan. 19, 1993), M.M.G. ¶41,049.

80. 42 U.S.C.A. § 1395dd(d); *e.g.*, a California hospital paid a $40,000 fine to settle an EMTALA claim in 1994, 3 H.L.R. 1170 (1994).

81. 42 U.S.C.A. § 1395dd(d); *see* HCFA Memorandum Mar. 1992, M.M.G. ¶12,105.20 [detailing fast-track termination procedure for EMTALA violations].

82. 42 U.S.C.A. § 1395dd(d); *see* Reid v. Indianapolis Osteopathic Med. Hosp., 709 F. Supp. 853 (S.D. Ind. 1989) [patient action against hospital under § 1395dd subject to state malpractice liability limits, but not procedures]; Bryant v. Riddle Mem. Hosp., 689 F. Supp. 490 (E.D. Pa. 1988) [suit by patient discharged within 24 hours of admission who claimed she was not yet stabilized]; McGinn, *Texas MD becomes first to be sanctioned for patient "dumping,"* AM. MED. NEWS, Nov. 25, 1988, at 3 [California hospital, physicians paid $105,499 in civil money penalties]; Holthaus, *HCFA eager to crack down in patient dumping,* HOSPS., Nov. 5, 1988, at 82 [two Texas hospitals suspended from Medicare]; McGinn, *Texas MD first to be sanctioned for patient transfer,* AM. MED. NEWS, Aug. 11, 1989, at 1 [physician fined $20,000 for transfer of pregnant woman].

83. *E.g.*, Draper v. Chiapuzio, 9 F.3d 1391 (9th Cir. 1993) [must comply with state one-year notice requirement]; *contra*, Cooper v. Gulf Breeze Hosp., 839 F. Supp. 1538 (N.D. Fla. 1993) [need not comply with state malpractice procedures].

84. *E.g.*, Power v. Arlington Hosp. Ass'n, 42 F.3d 851 (4th Cir. 1994) [EMTALA claim subject to state damage cap]; *see also* Lane v. Calhoun-Liberty County Hosp. Ass'n, 846 F. Supp. 1543 (N.D. Fla. 1994) [state law determines amount of damages].

85. *E.g.*, Guerrero v. Copper Queen Hosp., 112 Ariz. 104, 537 P.2d 1329 (1975); Stanturf v. Sipes, 447 S.W.2d 558 (Mo. 1969); Wilmington Gen. Hosp. v. Manlove, 54 Del. 15, 174 A.2d 135 (1961); *see* Annotation, *Liability of hospital for refusal to admit or treat patient*, 35 A.L.R. 3D 841).

86. TEX. REV. CIV. STAT. ANN. ART. 4438a. The first criminal prosecution of an administrator under this statute resulted in a mistrial; *see* Admitting and discharge, HOSPITAL LAW MANUAL 17 (1980).

87. Harper v. Baptist Med. Ctr.-Princeton, 341 So.2d 133 (Ala. 1976).

88. *E.g.*, Thompson v. Sun City Comm. Hosp., 141 Ariz. 597, 688 P.2d 605 (1984); *see also* Kellerman and Ackerman, *Interhospital Patient Transfer: The case for informed consent*, 319 N. ENGL. J. MED. 643 (1988).

89. Carrasco v. Bankoff, 220 Cal. App. 2d 230, 33 Cal.Rptr. 673 (2d Dist. 1963).

90. Kenigsberg v. Cohn, 117 A.D.2d 652, 498 N.Y.S.2d 390 (2d Dep't), *app. denied*, 68 N.Y.2d 602, 505 N.Y.S.2d 1026 (1986).

91. New Biloxi Hosp. v. Frazier, 245 Miss. 185, 146 So.2d 882 (1962).

92. Nance v. James Archer Smith Hosp., 329 So.2d 377 (Fla. 3d DCA), *cert. denied*, 339 So. 2d. 1171 (Fla. 1976).

93. 42 U.S.C.A. § 1395x(ee); 42 C.F.R. § 482.43(c), *as published in* 59 FED. REG. 64,141 (Dec. 13, 1994). Nursing homes have separate discharge requirements under Medicaid law, 42 U.S.C.A. § 1396r(c)(2); 42 C.F.R. § 483.12, 483.200–483.206; O'Bannon v. Town Court Nursing Ctr., 447 U.S. 773 (1980) [residents have no right to hearing before state revocation of Medicaid participation of nursing home]; Blum v. Yaretsky, 457 U.S. 991 (1982) [private nursing home decisions to transfer to lower level of care not state action, no constitutional right to hearing]; Nichols v. St. Luke Ctr., 800 F. Supp. 1564 (S.D. Ohio 1992) [no private cause of action under Medicaid to challenge discharge by private nursing home, cause of action under Rehabilitation Act, but danger to staff justified discharge]. For other discharge issues, see American Hospital Association, *Discharging Hospital Patients: Legal Implications for Institutional Providers and Health Care Professionals*, Legal Memorandum No. 9 (June 1987).

94. *See False imprisonment in connection with confinement in nursing home or hospital*, 4 A.L.R. 4TH 449.

95. *E.g.*, Williams v. Summit Psychiatric Ctrs. P.C., 185 Ga. App. 264, 363 S.E.2d 794 (1987) [threat of commitment if patient attempted to leave not sufficient to create false imprisonment where patient actually left without incident].

96. *E.g.*, Gadsden Gen. Hosp. v. Hamilton, 212 Ala. 531, 103 So. 553 (1925).

97. *E.g.*, Jarrell v. Chemical Dependency Unit, 791 F.2d 373 (5th Cir. 1986) [chemical dependency].

98. *E.g.*, FLA. STAT. § 415.506; In re J.J., 718 S.W.2d 235 (Mo. Ct. App. 1986).

99. *E.g.*, Boles v. Milwaukee County, 150 Wis. 2d 801, 443 N.W.2d 679 (Ct. App. 1989) [county hospital may be liable for not detaining disoriented mentally ill person even when statutory procedure not available]; Smith v. Louisiana Health & Human Resources Admin., 637 So.2d 1177 (La. Ct. App.), *cert. denied*, 644 So.2d 634 (La. 1994) [liability for death of disoriented patient who took ambulance, crashed into construction barricade].

100. *E.g.*, Kempster v. Child Protective Servs., 130 A.D.2d 623, 515 N.Y.S.2d 807 (2d Dep't 1987).

101. U.S. Const., art. I, § 9, ¶ 2.

102. *See* Pacelli v. deVito, 972 F.2d 871 (7th Cir. 1992) [civil rights action concerning failure to comply with class *writ of habeas corpus* ordered release].

103. *E.g.*, United States ex rel. Siegel v. Shinnick, 219 F. Supp. 789 (E.D. N.Y. 1963) [dismissal of *habeas corpus* petition challenging isolation of person exposed to small pox].

104. Gadsden Gen. Hosp. v. Hamilton, 212 Ala. 531, 103 So. 553 (1925).

105. Landeros v. Flood, 17 Cal. 3d 399, 131 Cal. Rptr. 69, 551 P.2d 389 (1976); *see* Annotation, *Validity, construction, and application of state statutes requiring doctor or other person to report child abuse,* 73 A.L.R. 4TH 782.

106. Payton v. Weaver, 131 Cal. App. 3d 38, 182 Cal. Rptr. 225 (1st Dist. 1982); *see also* Hall v. Biomedical Application, Inc., 671 F.2d 300 (8th Cir. 1982).

107. Modla v. Parker, 17 Ariz. App. 54, 495 P.2d 494, *cert. denied,* 409 U.S. 1038 (1972); *but see* Morrison v. Washington County, 700 F.2d 678 (11th Cir.), *cert. denied,* 464 U.S. 864 (1983) [hospital could be liable for physician's discharge of unruly alcoholic patient].

108. Nichols v. St. Luke Ctr., 800 F. Supp. 1564 (S.D. Ohio 1992).

109. In the Matter of the Involuntary Discharge or Transfer of J.S. by Ebenezer Hall, 512 N.W.2d 604 (Minn. Ct. App. 1994).

110. Wickline v. State, No. NWC 60672 (Cal. Super. Ct.), *rev'd,* 192 Cal. App. 3d 1630, 239 Cal. Rptr. 810 (2d Dist. 1986), *review dismissed,* 239 Cal. Rptr. 805, 741 P.2d 613 (Cal. 1987).

111. Wilson v. Blue Cross of So. Cal., 222 Ca. App. 3d 660, 271 Cal. Rptr. 876 (2d Dist. 1990), *rev. denied,* 1990 Cal. LEXIS 4574 (Oct. 11, 1990),

112. *E.g.*, Jersey City Med. Ctr. v. Halstead, 169 N.J. Super. 22, 404 A.2d 44 (Ch. Div. 1979); Lucy Webb Hayes Nat'l Training School v. Geoghegan, 281 F. Supp. 116 (D. D.C. 1967).

113. *E.g.*, N.C. GEN. STAT. § 131E-90.

114. *E.g.*, Pruessman v. Dr. John T. MacDonald Found., 589 So.2d 948 (Fla. 3d DCA 1991).

115. Jordano v. Steffen, 787 F. Supp. 886, 891 (D. Minn. 1992).

116. *E.g.*, Foster v. Charter Med. Corp., 601 So.2d 435 (Ala. 1992) [facility could be liable for suicide of voluntary mental patient on temporary unsupervised pass]; *but see* Leonard v. State, 491 N.W.2d 508 (Iowa 1992) [psychiatrist did not owe duty to general public for release of patient].

117. Burroughs v. Board of Trustees, 328 So.2d 538 (Fla. 1st DCA 1976).

118. County of Hennepin v. Levine, 345 N.W.2d 217 (Minn. 1984).

119. *E.g.*, Lindsey v. United States, 693 F. Supp. 1012 (W.D. Okla. 1988).

120. Wilson v. Formigoni, 42 F.3d 1060 (7th Cir. 1994).

121. *See* G. Calabresi and P. Bobbitt, TRAGIC CHOICES (New York, N.Y.: W.W. Norton & Co., Inc. 1978).

122. *See* R.D. Miller, *Rationing health care: the legal constraints and some guidelines,* 1 TOPICS IN HOSP. L. (Sept. 1986), at 1.

123. *E.g.*, 60 FED. REG. 6537 (Feb. 2, 1995) [lung transplant]; *see also* Wheat v. Mass, 994 F.2d 273 (5th Cir. 1993) [no private cause of action under Medicaid law to challenge organ allocation by private institutions]; Allen v. Mansour, 681 F. Supp. 1232 (E.D. Mich. 1986) [state could not require two-year history of abstinence for eligibility for Medicaid coverage for liver transplant].

124. *Demand for MS drug may help Chiron Corp. emerge from the pack,* WALL ST. J. (Sept. 1, 1993) at A1; for another drug lottery, *see Roche unit to distribute AIDS drug to some patients for free in lottery,* WALL ST. J., June 21, 1995, at A4.

13

Treatment Authorization and Refusal

Health care providers must obtain appropriate authorization before examining a patient or performing diagnostic or therapeutic procedures. Usually authorization is obtained by the patient or the patient's representative giving express or implied consent. The person giving consent must be given sufficient information concerning available choices so that the consent is an informed consent. If the decision is not to consent, usually the examination or procedure cannot be performed. The law overrides some refusals and authorizes involuntary treatment, such as for some mental illness and for substance abuse.

The requirements of consent and informed consent, the decision-making roles of patients and their representatives, the exceptions to the consent requirement, and the refusal of treatment are discussed in this chapter. Decisions concerning reproductive issues are discussed in Chapter 15.

CONSENT AND INFORMED CONSENT

The common law has long recognized the right of persons to be free from harmful or offensive touching. The intentional harmful or offensive touching of another person without authorization is called *battery* (see the discussion in Chapter 10). When there is no consent or other authorization for a procedure, the physician or other practitioner doing the medical procedure can be liable for battery even if the procedure is properly performed, is beneficial, and has no negative effects.[1] The touching alone leads to liability. When consent is given, but the person consenting does not have sufficient information for an informed decision, the provider can be liable for violating the duty to disclose such information. In some early cases, courts ruled that providing incorrect or insufficient information invalidated the consent, making the physician liable for battery. Today, in most jurisdictions, failure to disclose necessary information does not invalidate consent, so the procedure is not a battery.[2] There is still a minority position that a medical procedure without informed consent is a battery.[3] The majority rule is that failure to disclose is a separate wrong for which there can be liability based on principles applicable to negligent torts discussed in Chapter 10. Uninformed consent protects from liability for battery, but informed consent is necessary to protect from liability for negligence.

Some courts have extended the informed consent doctrine to require informed refusal. In 1980, the California Supreme Court ruled that a physician could be liable for a patient's death from cervical cancer because the physician did not inform the patient of the risks of not consenting to a recommended Pap smear.[4] The Pap smear probably would have discovered her cancer in time to begin life-extending treatment. In 1991, a New Jersey court ruled that an obstetrician could be sued for failing to advise the patient sufficiently of the hazards of leaving the hospital against medical advice.[5] As discussed later in this chapter in the transfusion section, there is an aberrant trend in some courts to reverse the thrust of the informed consent doctrine in cases involving refusal of transfusions in the emergency context. The complete reversal is from a duty of the provider to provide information to a duty of the patient to collect and understand the information. These courts then honor only informed refusals, using the reversal of the informed consent doctrine as the stated rationale for disregarding the patient's directions.

Some aggressive attorneys have tried to convince courts that the scope of disclosure should be subject to consumer protection laws. This has generally been unsuccessful.[6]

Consent

Consent may be either express or implied.

Express consent is consent given by direct words, either oral or written. Written consent is sometimes required. For example, some states require written consent before most HIV tests may be performed.[7] Otherwise, either oral or written consent can be legally sufficient authorization.[8] However, oral consent is difficult to prove, so most providers seek written consent.

Implied consent is (1) inferred from some patient conduct or (2) presumed in most emergencies. Consent is usually implied from voluntary submission to a procedure with apparent knowledge of its nature. The highest court of Massachusetts found that a woman had given her implied consent to being vaccinated by extending her arm and accepting a vaccination without objection.[9] Implied consent is why express consent is usually not obtained for physical examinations or minor procedures performed on competent adults.

Consent is presumed to exist in medical emergencies unless the provider has reason to believe that consent would be refused.[10] When treatment has been refused, there can be no implied consent even in life-threatening situations.[11] An immediate threat to life or health is clearly a sufficient emergency. In an Iowa case, implied consent to removal of a limb mangled in a train accident was presumed because amputation was necessary to save the patient's life.[12] Courts have disagreed on whether pain is a sufficient emergency to imply consent.[13]

When unexpected emergency conditions arise during surgery, especially life-threatening conditions, implied consent is sometimes found to extensions or modifications of surgical procedures beyond the scope expressly authorized.[14] Many surgical consent forms include express consent to these extensions or modifications to preserve life or health, but provide an opportunity for the patient to forbid unwanted changes. However, even when there is express consent to extensions in the consent form, such extensions should be limited to bona fide emergencies.[15]

Consent must be voluntary. Consent can be challenged when it is obtained through coercion or undue inducement.

Medical procedures without express or implied consent constitute a battery unless one of the exceptions to the consent requirement applies. Those exceptions to the consent requirement, in which the law authorizes treatment without consent or despite refusal, are discussed later in the chapter. When express consent is given for one procedure and a different procedure is performed, the procedure performed can be a battery.[16]

Informed Consent

Although unfortunately some providers view the obtaining of informed consent as simply an unnecessary administrative burden, providers who actually engage in the intended communication with their patients find that it not only performs its intended function of respecting individual autonomy, but can also improve compliance, outcomes, and satisfaction.[17]

Required Disclosure

Courts have developed two standards for determining whether disclosure is adequate: the reasonable physician standard and the reasonable patient standard.[18] As with other negligent torts, a claimant must show that the breach of this standard caused the injury. Two standards of causation have developed: the objective standard and the subjective standard.

Reasonable Physician. Some states apply the professional (reasonable physician) standard of accepted medical practice. In those states the professional has a duty to make the disclosure that a reasonable medical practitioner would make under the same or similar circumstances.[19] Expert testimony is necessary to prove what disclosure was required.

Reasonable Patient. Many states apply the reasonable patient standard under which the duty to disclose is determined by the patient's informational needs, not by professional practice.[20] Information that is "material" to the decision must be disclosed. A risk is material "when a reasonable person, in what the physician knows or should know to be the patient's position, would be likely to attach significance to the risk or cluster of risks in deciding whether or not to forgo the proposed therapy."[21] No expert testimony is required on the scope of disclosure, although expert testimony is generally necessary to prove the existence of risks and alternatives.[22]

Elements of Disclosure. The usual elements to be disclosed under either standard are the patient's medical condition, the nature and purpose of the proposed procedure, its consequences and risks, and the feasible accepted alternatives, including the consequences of no treatment.

Only risks that are known or should be known by the physician to occur without negligence are required to be disclosed. Nearly all courts recognize that not all risks can be disclosed. One useful guideline is to disclose the risks of the most severe consequences and the risks that have a substantial probability of occurring.

The alleged failure to disclose alternatives is often the focus of informed consent cases.[23] Courts have not agreed on which alternatives must be disclosed.[24]

When a patient indicates a desire for additional information, there is usually a duty to provide it. For example, a patient told a physician that his ability to work was crucial, so the Arizona Supreme Court ruled that the physician should have provided information concerning risks affecting ability to work.[25] In 1992, a Louisiana appellate court ruled that where the patient's primary motivation for treatment was pain relief, the physician had a duty to disclose that the proposed surgery was unlikely to give such relief.[26] However, there are limits to the scope of information that must be provided even when requested. The California Supreme Court ruled that nonmedical concerns of the patient did not create a more extensive fiduciary duty for the physician, who did not have to become the patient's financial advisor.[27]

Some courts are now requiring physicians to disclose certain information about themselves. In 1991, a Louisiana court found that a surgeon had failed to obtain informed consent when he failed to disclose his chronic alcohol abuse.[28] Despite the professional debate over the necessity of such disclosures, several courts have ruled that surgeons should disclose that they are HIV positive.[29] In 1991, a New Jersey court ruled that a hospital could require an HIV-positive surgeon to disclose his condition as part of the consent process.[30]

Patients have sought to establish a wide variety of additional elements. In 1989, a federal court decided that a hospital's nondisclosure of concerns about a surgeon's competence did not create an informed consent action against the hospital.[31] In 1990, the California Supreme Court decided that a physician could have a fiduciary duty to disclose his economic interest in cells that would be extracted in a procedure, which the physician later developed into a commercially valuable product.[32] In 1992, a North Carolina court found that an attending physician did not have a duty to inform a patient of the identity and qualifications of the individuals who would be assisting him.[33] In 1994, a Wisconsin court ruled that a surgeon did not have to disclose the availability of more experienced surgeons.[34] In the same year, an Iowa court ruled that a physician did not have to disclose the probationary status of his license where it was due to the activity of an assistant.[35] However, this may suggest that some restrictions on licenses may need to be disclosed.

In 1993, the California Supreme Court decided that physicians did not need to disclose the odds of success of procedures.[36] However, in 1994, a Wisconsin court addressed a case in which a surgeon had allegedly volunteered statistics that were significantly wrong. The court ruled that, when a surgeon chooses to disclose statistics, there can be liability for misstating the risks.[37]

Some states have passed statutes or created administrative processes that address what disclosure should be made.[38] In one state the statute requires the physician to ask the patient if a more detailed disclosure is desired. If the physician fails to ask, then the physician has a duty of full disclosure.[39]

Causation. Causation is the most difficult element to prove in an informed consent case. Since informed consent suits are based on negligence principles, the plaintiff must prove that the deviation from the standard caused the injury. Thus, the plaintiff must prove that consent would not have been given if the risk that occurred had been disclosed.

The two standards of causation are the objective standard and the subjective standard. Some states apply an "objective" standard of what a prudent person in the patient's position would have decided if informed of the risk or alternative.[40] Other courts apply a "subjective" standard, so that it must be proved that the patient would have refused to consent if informed of the risk or alternative.[41]

Either standard provides substantial protection for the conscientious health care professional who discloses major risks and then has a more remote risk occur. A patient who consents to a procedure, knowing of the risk of death and paralysis, will find it difficult to convince a court that knowledge of a minor risk would have led to refusal. However, courts may be more easily convinced when there are undisclosed alternatives.

In 1992, one federal court decided no disclosure of risks needed to be made before a polio vaccine was given because under state law the vaccine was legally required, with the permitted exception being for religious objections.[42]

A few jurisdictions do not require proof of causation. The Vermont Supreme Court ruled that even though the vasectomy patient could not prove he would have refused if informed of the risk of recanalization, he could still sue for failure to provide accurate information.[43]

In 1992, the Pennsylvania Supreme Court ruled that it was not necessary to prove causation in any informed consent case.[44] In Pennsylvania, informed consent is required only for operations and surgery.[45] In effect, Pennsylvania considers operations and surgeries without informed consent to be batteries.

Exceptions to the Disclosure Requirement

Courts have recognized four exceptions to the disclosure requirement in circumstances where consent still must be obtained: emergencies, the therapeutic privilege, patient waiver, and prior patient knowledge.

Emergencies. As already mentioned, when in an emergency where there is no time to obtain consent, consent is implied. When there is time to obtain some consent, but insufficient time for the usual disclosure, an abbreviated disclosure is sufficient.[46]

Therapeutic Privilege. Most courts recognize a therapeutic privilege not to make disclosures that pose a significant threat of patient detriment.[47] Courts limit the privilege, so it is not applicable when a physician solely fears that the information might lead a patient to forgo needed therapy. Physicians should rely on the privilege, only when they can document that a patient's anxiety is significantly above the norm. In some states, when the therapeutic privilege permits nondisclosure, the information must be disclosed to a relative and that relative must concur with the patient's consent before the procedure may be performed.[48] However, at least one court ruled that relatives did not need to be informed of withheld information.[49]

Patient Waiver. A patient can waive the right to be informed.[50] However, courts will be skeptical of waivers initiated by providers, so prudent providers should not suggest waivers, but instead should encourage reluctant patients to be informed.

Prior Patient Knowledge. There is no liability for nondisclosure of risks that are common knowledge or that the patient has previously experienced or already knows.[51]

Statutory Exceptions. One state enacted a statute that eliminated the requirement of disclosure of risks. The Georgia Code stated that the physician need only disclose "in general terms the treatment or course of treatment" to obtain an informed consent.[52] The Georgia courts interpreted this section as an elimination of the requirement that risks be disclosed, so they no longer based liability on failure to disclose risks.[53] In 1989, a new Georgia statute reinstated the duty to disclose risks of most surgery and some other procedures.[54]

Responsibility for Obtaining Consent

Physician Responsibility

Physicians have the responsibility to provide necessary information and to obtain informed consent; it is generally not a hospital responsibility. Other independent practitioners who order or perform procedures have the same responsibility concerning their procedures.

Physicians who perform procedures, not referring physicians or consultants, have the responsibility to obtain consent.[55] After giving informed consent to a procedure, some patients have sued when the procedure was performed by a physician other than the one they expected.[56] In 1984, the highest court of Massachusetts ruled that a substitute physician did not commit battery by performing a myelography because the patient had not directed postponement if the requested physician could not perform it.[57] In 1987, an Illinois appellate court adopted the minority position that a hospital must determine that there is consent for a particular physician before carrying out that physician's orders.[58] When a patient directs that a specific physician not perform a procedure and the forbidden physician performs it, both the forbidden physician and those who let that physician perform the procedure can be liable.[59]

Limited Hospital Role

Hospitals are generally not liable for the failure of a physician or other independent practitioner to obtain informed consent unless the professional is the hospital's employee or agent. Both court decisions and state statutes have recognized this principle.[60] Plaintiffs have tried to convince courts to require hospitals to intercede in the professional-patient relationship by imposing institutional liability for inadequate disclosures. These efforts have not been successful except in a few cases.[61] Hospital responsibility for the content of the physician's disclosure would require monitoring that could destroy the physician-patient relationship.

The hospital may be liable for failing to intervene when it knows a procedure is being performed without authorization.[62] In some states this liability may be extended to situations in which the hospital should have known there was no authorization, but it is doubtful that liability will be imposed when the only way the hospital could have known is by monitoring physician-patient communications.

Research. In addition, some courts have interpreted the federal rules governing research to impose hospital responsibility for informed consent for participation in research projects.[63]

Role of Hospital Staff. Hospitals disagree concerning the appropriate role of hospital employees in obtaining consent. Some hospitals permit nurses to obtain signatures on consent forms or to provide some or all of the information. Both practices may impair the physician-patient relationship by reducing the opportunity for adequate communication and negotiation. However, in some settings, due to time demands or other reasons, physicians are not able or willing to engage in this communication and negotiation, so the only way to assure that an informed consent is obtained may be through the nursing or other hospital staff. These practices can shift liability for inadequate disclosures to the hospital as the nurse's employer.[64] However, increasingly, the hospital already has liability for the physician's actions, due to employment of the physician, apparent agency, provision of insurance coverage, or other reasons. Thus, if the physicians are not performing the consent function, using other staff to assure obtaining consent may reduce liability exposure, provided the other staff limit their role to the scope of their knowledge and involve the physician when that scope is exceeded.

When hospitals are not already liable for physicians, some hospitals seek to avoid liability and promote the physician-patient relationship by not permitting nurses to obtain consents. However, liability is not the only factor in this decision. Efficient operation of the hospital requires that consents be obtained in a timely fashion. Surgery or other therapy that must be postponed due to lack of consent can lead to costly gaps in scheduling and can lead to increased length of stay, which may not be approved by managed care or may result in increased costs with no increased payment due to capitated, per discharge, or other payment mechanisms.

Some hospitals compromise by permitting nurses to obtain signatures, but limit their role so that the nurses do not attempt to answer patient questions associated with obtaining consent unless authorized to do so by the hospital and the physician. A physician may legally delegate the information disclosure and documentation,[65] but the physician remains legally responsible for the adequacy of the disclosure and validity of the consent.[66] These hospitals have physicians acknowledge responsibility and liability before permitting employees to accept delegation. In this way, the hospital facilitates the documentation while trying to limit the assumption of responsibility. This procedure still relies on the physician to provide the patient with the information necessary for an informed consent.

Under all these approaches, a hospital employee who becomes aware of a patient's confusion or change of opinion regarding a procedure should notify the responsible physician. If the physician does not respond, appropriate medical staff and hospital officials should be notified so that they can determine whether intervention is necessary.

Documentation

Most hospitals require the use of a standard form before major procedures. This usually helps to reduce the liability exposure for lack of consent.[67] The battery consent form described in the next section is usually used. When the hospital requires consent for a procedure, the procedure should not be permitted until a hospital employee has confirmed that consent is appropriately documented or alternative authorization has been obtained.

Most hospitals require documentation of consent by the signature of the patient or the patient's representative on an appropriate form. If a proper form is signed by the appropriate person, most courts accept it as proof of consent unless the plaintiff can prove the form should be ignored because of special circumstances.

Since most forms do not include all information provided by the physician, the form should include an acknowledgment that other information was given.

The Joint Commission on Accreditation of Healthcare Organizations (Joint Commission) accreditation standards concerning medical records require "evidence of informed consent" for procedures or treatments for which informed consent is required by hospital policy.[68] The Joint Commission does not specify the procedures or treatments and does not specify how the consent must be documented. One list of procedures to use as a starting point for developing a policy includes

1. major or minor surgery involving entry into the body,
2. procedures with anesthesia,
3. procedures involving more than a slight risk of harm or causing change in the patient's body structure,
4. radiological therapy,
5. electroconvulsive therapy,
6. experimental procedures, and
7. other procedures that the medical staff determines require a specific explanation to the patient.

In 1993, the Pennsylvania Supreme Court ruled that the use of forceps in a delivery was not a procedure that required informed consent.[69]

The actual process of providing information to the decision maker and of determining that person's decision is more important than the consent form. The form is evidence of the consent process, not a substitute for the process. Someone should have authority to determine that there is actual consent even when the form has been lost or inadvertently not signed prior to patient sedation or when other circumstances make it difficult to obtain the necessary signature.

Consent Forms

Types of Consent Forms

There are three types of consent forms: (1) blanket consent forms, (2) battery consent forms, and (3) detailed consent forms.

Blanket Consent Forms. Prior to the mid-1960s, many hospitals used blanket consent forms that authorized any procedure the physician wished to perform. Courts have ruled that these forms are not evidence of consent to major procedures because the procedure is not specified on the form.[70] Many attorneys recommend continued use of blanket admission consent forms to cover procedures for which individual special consent is not sought even though implied consent to most of these procedures is inferred from hospital admission and submission to the procedures. Admission forms can serve many other purposes unrelated to consent, such as assigning insurance benefits.[71]

Battery Consent Forms. For major procedures nearly all hospitals now require consent forms that include the name and a description of the specific procedure.

These forms usually also state that (1) the person signing has been told about the medical condition, consequences, risks, and alternatives; (2) all questions have been answered to the person's satisfaction; and (3) no guarantees have been made. These forms will almost always preclude a successful battery claim if the proper person signs the form and if the described procedure is performed.[72] These forms also provide support for the reasonableness of the hospital's lack of suspicion that the person who signed was uninformed, while providing some support for the physician's assertion that the patient was informed.[73] However, courts can still be convinced that the information concerning consequences, risks, and alternatives was not actually given.[74]

Detailed Consent Forms. Some physicians use forms that detail the medical condition, procedure, consequences, risks, and alternatives. Such forms have been mandated for federally funded sterilizations and research.[75] Plaintiffs can seldom prove that the information included in this form was not disclosed. One difficulty with detailed consent forms is the cost and time to prepare them for each individual procedure and to keep them updated. Some physicians use these forms only for procedures, such as cosmetic surgery, that carry a higher risk of misunderstanding and unacceptable results.

Detailed forms may not provide protection from risks not disclosed on the form,[76] but a detailed form may make it more difficult for patients who accepted serious consequences to prove that disclosure of additional risks would have made them or reasonable persons change their minds.

Challenges to Consent Forms

Although consent forms are evidence of informed consent, they are usually not conclusive.[77] The person challenging the adequacy of the consent process will usually have an opportunity to convince the court that informed consent was not actually obtained.

Capacity. The challenger might prove that the person who signed the form lacked capacity due to transient impairment by medication.[78] The explanation should be given and the signature obtained when the person is able to understand.

Readability. Persons are generally presumed to have read and understood documents they have signed. Sometimes courts will not apply this rule when the document is either too technical or in a language foreign to the person. Forms that require too high a level of reading ability have been criticized.[79] Forms should be written so that the person signing can understand them.

Translation. When the person has difficulty understanding English, someone should translate.[80] Forms in other languages are not necessary,[81] but they may be useful when a substantial portion of the patients served by the hospital speak a primary language other than English. Otherwise, it is usually sufficient to translate the form orally. The translator should certify that the form and physician explanation have been orally translated for the person signing the form. In some circumstances it may also be necessary to provide an interpreter for the deaf.[82]

Voluntariness. A consent form can be challenged if the signature was not voluntary. The person signing would have to demonstrate that there had been some threat or undue inducement to prove the signature was not voluntary, so this challenge will apply in few hospital situations.

Withdrawal of Consent. As discussed later in this chapter, a consent form can also be challenged by claiming that the consent was withdrawn after it was signed but before the procedure was performed.[83]

Exculpatory Clauses

Exculpatory clauses state that the person signing waives the right to sue for injuries or agrees to limit any claims to not more than a specified amount. Although courts have enforced these clauses in other contexts, courts have not enforced them in suits on behalf of patients against health care providers. In 1979, a federal court refused to enforce a $15,000 limit on liability in an agreement the patient signed before surgery.[84]

Period of Validity of Consent Forms

There is no limit on the period of validity of a consent or the documentation of that consent. If the patient's condition or available treatments change significantly, earlier consents are no longer informed, and a new consent should be obtained. Otherwise, the consent is valid until it is withdrawn. A claim that consent was withdrawn becomes more credible as time passes.[85] The guideline some hospitals follow is to recommend a new consent at each admission. Some hospitals use a guideline that consent forms should be signed no more than 30 days before the procedure. Hospitals are not legally required to have such guidelines, but they generally are required to follow their own rules. Hospital guidelines should clearly state that they are not requirements or that someone has authority to grant exceptions to deal with repetitive treatments for chronic disease, situations in which the person who gave consent now lacks capacity or is unavailable, and other unusual circumstances.

Consent Statutes

Some states have statutes concerning consent forms.[86] These statutes should be considered when developing consent forms for use in those states. Several states provide that if the consent form contains certain information and is signed by the appropriate person, it is conclusive evidence of informed consent or creates a presumption of informed consent. For example, in Nevada if certain information is on the form, it is conclusive evidence of informed consent.[87] In Iowa if certain information is on the form, informed consent is presumed.[88] Such statutes address how courts will consider forms that contain certain information. They do not address forms that do not contain the information. It is not a violation to use a form that contains different information or to forgo the use of a form. Serious consideration should be given to using forms that qualify, especially when such forms are conclusive evidence.

Supplements to Documentation

Some physicians supplement their explanations with other educational materials, such as booklets and videotapes.[89] Some physicians make audio and visual recordings of the consent process to supplement or substitute for written consent. Some patients are given tests of knowledge or write their own consent forms to document their level of understanding. These steps are not legally required and may not preclude malpractice suits,[90] but they should be given serious consideration for controversial procedures.

RESEARCH

Patients ordinarily expect physicians to use the drugs and procedures customarily used for their condition. When experimental methods are used or when established procedures are used for research purposes, the investigator must disclose this to the subject and obtain the consent of the subject or the subject's representative. Governmental regulations specify review procedures for many types of research and specify disclosures that must be made to obtain informed consent to such research.

All research supported by HHS must comply with regulations for the protection of human subjects.[91] These regulations require that an institutional review board (IRB) approve the research before HHS may support the research. Each institution must submit an acceptable institutional assurance to HHS that it will fulfill its responsibilities under the regulations before HHS will accept the decisions of its IRB.

The HHS regulations require that consent be sought "only under circumstances that provide the prospective subject or the representative sufficient opportunity to consider whether or not to participate and that minimize the possibility of coercion or undue influence." The information must be in a language understandable to the subject or representative. Exculpatory wording cannot be included in the information given. Federal regulations specify numerous basic elements of information that must be included in the consent form.[92]

Several kinds of studies are exempted from these regulations, such as the "collection or study of existing data, documents, records, pathological specimens, or diagnostic specimens, if these sources are publicly available or if the information is recorded by the investigator in such a manner that subjects cannot be identified. . . ."[93] Expedited review is authorized for categories of research that HHS determines involve no more than minimal risk.[94] Examples of such categories are collection of small amounts of blood by venipuncture from certain adults and moderate exercise by healthy volunteers.

The HHS regulations do not preempt other federal, state, or local laws or regulations. Thus, proposals involving investigational new drugs or devices must also satisfy the regulations of the Food and Drug Administration.[95] State and local law must also be reviewed because several states have enacted laws regulating research with human subjects.[96]

Hospitals should take appropriate steps to review research involving human subjects, regardless of the sponsorship of the research, to protect patients and avoid liability. Several courts have decided that, since federal regulations require institutional review of consent for certain research, the hospital can be liable for lack of informed consent for such research.[97]

THE RIGHT TO REFUSE

The right to consent generally implies a right to refuse. Most courts have found that since adults with decision-making capacity have the right to refuse, those making decisions on behalf of incapacitated adults and minors must have the right to refuse on their behalf in appropriate situations. In some situations courts have found that state interests outweigh patient interests and have ordered treatment.

There are three legal bases for the right to refuse treatment: (1) common law rights, (2) statutory rights, and (3) constitutional rights.

Among some providers, there is still a surprising lack of understanding of the broad scope of control that patients and their representatives have to limit the scope of treatment.[98] This is particularly surprising because, since December 1991, federal law has required hospitals to ask all adult patients whether they have made an advance directive concerning their care, so that few providers who care for adult patients have not encountered such directives.[99]

Common Law

The common law has long recognized the strong interest of all people to be free from nonconsensual invasion, including medical invasion, of their bodily integrity.[100] Adults have a broad right to make decisions concerning their own medical care. Medical care without express or implied authority is a battery. The common law requirement of informed consent assures that adequate information is made available to provide an opportunity for a knowledgeable decision to consent or refuse. The right to make decisions concerning medical treatment includes the right to decline medical care. For example, in 1981 the highest court of New York recognized the right of Brother Fox, through his guardian, to decline respiratory support based on these principles.[101]

Statutes

Common law rights can be increased or reduced by statute, but few states have adopted this approach to addressing refusal of medical treatment. Most states have enacted laws—such as living will laws, durable power of attorney laws, and hospice laws—to assist patients and others to implement the right to refuse medical treatment, especially for terminally ill patients. These statutes generally do not change existing common law rights, but instead create an alternative statutory procedure.

All 50 states and the District of Columbia have statutes that authorize advance directives (often called living wills) and/or appointment of health care agents. Only three states, Massachusetts, Michigan, and New York, do not have statutes authorizing advance directives. Only Alabama and Alaska do not have statutes authorizing appointment of a health care agent.[102]

Advance Directive Laws

Generally these laws require that advance directives be followed or that reasonable efforts be made to transfer the patient to the care of another provider who will follow the directive.

These Acts vary in their details. There are two model laws that provide some consistency among a few of the states. Six states adopted the 1985 version of the Uniform Rights of Terminally Ill Act.[103] Three of those states replaced the 1985 Act with the 1989 version. Another four states adopted the 1989 version.[104]

Many advance directive laws authorize only competent adults to sign directives. At least seven states have statutes that authorize parents or others to decline treatment on behalf of minors in some circumstances.[105] At least six other states have court decisions permitting parents or others to make such refusals.[106] At least 24 states have statutes that authorize surrogate decision making for incapacitated adults in the absence of advance directives.[107]

Some of these laws specify the wording or what must be addressed in the directive. In states that specify wording, only patients who agree with and use the state wording can have the benefit of the statute. Other persons must rely on common law and constitutional principles to enforce their different directives. Physicians and hospitals should check the wording of directives to determine the patient's intent and if the state statute applies.

Each advance directive law specifies the formality with which the directive must be signed. All acts require witnesses, and some disqualify certain people from being witnesses. Some states require notarization. Most acts specify how a directive may be revoked. If there is a reasonable basis for believing a patient had a change of mind while still competent, a prior directive should not be followed until the matter is investigated.

A physician who does not wish to follow the directive has a duty to arrange a transfer to another physician. One sanction for failing to arrange transfer is usually medical licensing discipline for unprofessional conduct. All living will laws provide some immunity for those who act or refrain from acting in accordance with a directive that complies with the law. In most states it is not clear how much more protection the immunity provisions offer than do common law and constitutional principles. The primary issues in many controversies will be the patient's diagnosis and prognosis. Since the diagnosis is viewed as a professional responsibility for which physicians should be accountable, no statute provides protection from liability due to negligent diagnosis. However, statutory immunity is often easier to prove than is immunity under common law or constitutional principles, so it is prudent to comply with statutory requirements when possible.

Most advance directive laws specify that they do not affect other rights to refuse treatment.[108] Courts have permitted the directives of patients and families to be followed in accord with common law and constitutional principles even when there is no valid statutory directive.[109]

Health Care Agents

Generally these laws permit competent adults to designate a representative to make decisions for them when they become incapacitated, including medical decisions to refuse treatment. Some states limit who may serve as an agent.

Some providers prefer health care agents to other advance directives because they can deal with a competent decision maker, rather than having to interpret written instructions that may be difficult to apply to the specific situation. The best approach may be to use both the designation of an agent and an advance directive to guide the agent.

Hospice Law

Some terminally ill patients elect to forgo treatment for their illness, but still require nursing care, pain medication, and other support. Special facilities, called hospices, provide this care along with personal support to help patients and families cope with dying. Home hospice programs provide similar support in the patient's home. The federal and some state governments have recognized these programs by authorizing Medicare reimbursement for hospice services and regulating hospices.[110] The Medicare payment criteria and some state licensing regulations limit coverage to persons with a life expectancy of six months or less. This use of this time limit to control expenditures and utilization should not be misinterpreted to indicate that persons with longer life expectancies must accept aggressive treatment.

Constitutional Rights

Courts have also found that the constitutional rights protect some refusals. Constitutional rights are generally stronger than common law rights because they cannot be taken away by statute.

Constitutional rights can be taken away only by a constitutional amendment or a change in the highest court's interpretation of the Constitution.

Liberty Interest Protected by Due Process Clause

In 1990, the U.S. Supreme Court addressed a case from Missouri in which the Missouri Supreme Court refused to permit the father of an adult person who was irreversibly comatose to arrange for her artificial nutrition and hydration to be discontinued. The Missouri court ruled that life-sustaining treatment could be refused only when the patient had designated a surrogate to make the decision or there was clear and convincing evidence of the patient's expressed directive.[111] Many commentators and other courts believed this was contrary to the Equal Protection clause; since competent adults could refuse, the same right should be available to the incapacitated.

On appeal, the U.S. Supreme Court affirmed the Missouri court's ruling.[112] It rejected that the Equal Protection required the availability of procedure to refuse on behalf of persons who had not expressed their wishes. The Court ruled that states could forbid surrogate refusals by persons not designated by the patient and that states could require that the patient's wishes be proved by clear and convincing evidence.

Although it did not formally rule on the issue, the Court stated that from its prior decisions it could be "inferred" that competent adults have "a constitutionally protected liberty interest in refusing unwanted medical treatment."

The U.S. Supreme Court did not require the clear and convincing evidence standard. It merely ruled that individual states could require the standard. The clear and convincing evidence standard makes it easier for courts to disregard the oral directions of patients. In most civil litigation the standard of proof of a "fact" is "preponderance of the evidence," which basically means that there is more credible evidence proving the fact than disproving it. Although few courts have tried to define precisely what "clear and convincing evidence" means, it is intended to require more proof than the preponderance of the evidence and give the courts an opportunity to refuse to find a fact even if there is little to disprove it. In effect, in the patient directive context, it permits a court to disregard virtually any oral directive. In fact, the U.S. Supreme Court ruled that states could forbid consideration of oral directives. However, this is not a necessary consequence of the clear and convincing evidence standard. In New York, which also requires clear and convincing evidence, courts have found sufficient proof of oral directives.[113]

To avoid confusion with other cases, it should be noted that the terminology in the U.S. Supreme Court case is given a meaning different from the meaning used by most commentators and other courts. The Court talked of a "surrogate" applying "substituted judgment" based on the directive of the patient proved by clear and convincing evidence. Most courts have used "substitute judgment" to describe the decision making by someone when the patient has not given a directive and have not used the term "surrogate" to apply to an agent who is carrying out the patient's directives. A surrogate has generally been someone selected by relationship to and/or knowledge of the patient rather than through designation by the patient.

Freedom of Religion

When the refusal of treatment is based on religious beliefs, some courts have found that the First Amendment protection of free exercise of religion protects such refusals for adults. Freedom of religion applies primarily to freedom of belief, not freedom of action, so states may restrain some religious conduct. Freedom of religion has a limited role in medical decisions because few religions command adherents to refuse treatments. Most religions merely permit refusal, so legally required treatment does not violate their religious tenets. The cases in which freedom of religion has been significant have involved Jehovah's Witnesses who refuse blood transfusions and Christian Scientists who refuse all treatment. Many courts have upheld the right of adherents to these religions to refuse treatment that violates their religion. For example, in 1972 a District of Columbia court refused to authorize involuntary transfusion of a 34-year-old man who was a Jehovah's Witness.[114]

The religious rights concerning refusal of treatment for minors are much more limited, as discussed later in this chapter.

Right of Privacy

Some courts have found that the constitutional right of privacy protects some refusals.[115] However, the Supreme Court indicated in a footnote to the 1990 case from Missouri that it had never supported this view.[116] Thus, it is doubtful that the federal constitutional right of privacy provides protection. Federal constitutional rights need to be analyzed under the Due Process Clause.

Some states have a right of privacy under the state constitution. This may provide constitutional protection for treatment refusal in some states. For example, in 1984, the Florida Supreme Court ruled that its state constitutional right of privacy protected such decisions.[117]

INVOLUNTARY TREATMENT

In some cases, state interests outweigh the right to refuse, so involuntary treatment is authorized.[118] Courts have traditionally used an analysis that focuses on four state interests: (1) preservation of life, (2) prevention of irrational self-destruction, (3) protection of dependent third parties, and (4) protection of the ethical integrity of health professionals. However, in practice, few of these interests ever apply to outweigh the right to refuse. The analysis of the involuntary treatment cases in this chapter is based on the grounds courts have actually used to justify involuntary treatment:

1. threats to the community due to contagious disease or physical dangerousness;
2. impaired capacity due to mental illness, substance abuse, or other disorientation;
3. protection of the life of others, especially unborn children;
4. in a few cases, protection of dependents from abandonment by the patient's death;
5. some criminal law enforcement needs; and
6. in unusual cases, management of state institutions.

This is followed by a discussion of the limited use of other interests: (1) preservation of the patient's life, (2) prevention of irrational self-destruction, (3) protection of the ethical integrity of health professionals, and (4) family vetoes.

Threat to the Community

Contagious Disease

Courts have long recognized the power of the state to require individuals to submit to medical treatment when refusal threatens the community. In 1905, the U.S. Supreme Court upheld the power of the state to require an adult to submit to vaccination to help prevent the spread of disease.[119] In 1973, a federal appellate court upheld a Denver ordinance that required prostitutes to accept treatment for venereal disease.[120] In 1988, a federal district court ruled that a prisoner could not sue for the forcible administration of a diphtheria-tetanus inoculation.[121]

With the resurgence of tuberculosis in the 1990s, states returned to holding noncompliant patients against their will.[122]

Dangerousness

Courts have also recognized the power of the state to hospitalize persons who have demonstrated dangerousness to the community due to mental illness or substance abuse.[123]

Impaired Capacity

When adults have sufficient impairment of their decision-making capacity due to mental illness or substance abuse, the state authorizes involuntary hospitalization and treatment, but requires that specific procedures be followed and that the person's condition be proved to a court by clear and convincing evidence. Under the common law, providers may involuntarily treat some temporarily disoriented patients without judicial approval.

Commitment

Most states have statutory procedures for involuntarily committing persons to institutions for treatment for mental illness or substance abuse.[124] In 1975, the U.S. Supreme Court ruled that the Constitution permitted involuntary confinement of mentally ill persons, but that they must be treated when their confinement is not based on dangerousness.[125] Commitment procedures vary from state to state. For adults, a judicial hearing is generally required, after which the judicial officer decides whether the evidence is sufficient to justify commitment. Many states do not permit involuntary commitment unless the person is found to be dangerous to self or others.[126]

Most states permit adults to be held temporarily on an emergency basis until the judicial officer can act. In 1979, the U.S. Supreme Court ruled that states could permit parents to admit their minor children involuntarily for mental treatment without court authorization if the admission is approved as necessary by a qualified physician after adequate inquiry.[127] However, many states require judicial involvement in the commitment of minors.

Commitment is not the same as a court determination of incompetency. In 1986, the Texas Supreme Court ruled that a mentally ill person must be informed of the risks of treatment that would influence the decision of a reasonable person.[128] An involuntarily committed person is still competent to be involved in some or all medical decisions unless a court has determined otherwise. Commitment laws usually authorize involuntary treatment that is necessary to preserve the patient's life or to avoid permanent injury to the patient or others.[129] However, there is variation in the extent to which commitment laws authorize the use of antipsychotic drugs or electroconvulsive therapy for purposes of nonemergency treatment of mental illness.[130] Thus, familiarity with local law is important. Most courts have ruled that the constitutional rights to privacy and due process are violated if medication or electroconvulsive therapy is given involuntarily without a judicial finding of incompetency.[131] Some states have resolved this issue by requiring that the judicial officer find the person unable to make treatment decisions as part of the commitment process.[132] In states that authorize involuntary treatment of committed patients without a judicial determination of inability to make treatment decisions, hospitals should give consideration to this evolving standard in developing their treatment policies.

Some courts have required a judicial determination of the need for antipsychotic medications when a patient who has been adjudicated incompetent refuses the medications in a nonemergency situation.[133]

Disorientation

Disoriented patients are frequently restrained temporarily. Physicians and hospitals have authority under common law to detain and restrain temporarily disoriented medical and surgical patients without court involvement. This authority derives from the hospital's duty to use such reasonable care as the patient's known mental and physical condition requires. Hospitals have been found liable for injuries to patients because they were not restrained during temporary disorientation. This common law authority should not be relied on when a patient is being detained for mental illness or substance abuse. The statutory commitment procedures should be followed for those patients. This common law authority also does not apply when a patient is fully oriented, although custody can be maintained temporarily while the patient's status is adequately determined.

Life of Others

Courts have ordered treatment of pregnant women to protect the lives of their unborn children. Courts have refused to order persons to donate tissue to save the lives of others.

Pregnancy

Some courts will authorize treatments for pregnant women to preserve the life of the unborn child, especially immediately before and during birth. In 1964, the New Jersey Supreme Court authorized transfusions for a woman if necessary to save the life of either the unborn child or herself.[134] Other courts have limited their authorizations to transfusions necessary to save the life of the unborn child.[135]

In 1981, the Georgia Supreme Court authorized a caesarean operation because it was informed of a near certainty the child would not survive a vaginal delivery.[136] In 1983, the highest court of Massachusetts refused to order a pregnant woman to submit to an operation to help postpone premature delivery.[137] In 1987, three judges of the District of Columbia appellate court upheld a court order of a caesarean operation on a terminally ill pregnant woman in extremis, which resulted in the death of the mother and the child.[138] There was widespread criticism of the decision. The full appellate court vacated the 1987 decision and reversed, finding that the order should not have been issued.[139] In 1993, the Illinois courts ruled that a mentally competent pregnant woman could refuse a caesarean operation even when this might harm her child.[140]

Some mothers do decide to take significant medical risks for the benefit of their unborn children in situations where courts clearly could not order such behavior. For example, in 1994–95 a mother delayed chemotherapy for leukemia so that it would not harm her twins. After they were born, it was too late for her to be treated for her leukemia and she died.[141]

Mandatory Donation

Courts have refused to order involuntary donation of tissue to save the life of another.[142] In 1978, a Pennsylvania court refused to order a relative of a patient to donate bone marrow necessary to attempt to save the life of the patient.[143] A similar result has been reached in cases where courts have refused to disclose to patients the names of persons with matching tissues who refuse to be donors.[144]

In 1990, the noncustodial father of three and one-half-year-old twins sought an order compelling them to submit to a blood test and bone marrow donation for the benefit of his other son who was their half brother and had leukemia. The custodial mother of the twins opposed the procedures. The trial court denied the order.[145] The Illinois Supreme Court ordered the trial court to appoint two guardians ad litem, one for the twins and one for the other child, and to permit them to present additional evidence.[146] After a hearing, the trial court again denied the order and the Illinois Supreme Court affirmed.[147]

Dependents

Some states assert an interest in protecting dependents, especially minor children, from the emotional and financial damage of the patient's death. This interest has been discussed in cases in which Jehovah's Witnesses refuse transfusions. For example, in 1964 a federal appellate court in the District of Columbia authorized transfusions for a woman in part because she was the mother of a seven-month-old child.[148] In 1972, another District of Columbia court refused to authorize a transfusion for a father of two minor children because adequate arrangements had been made for their future well-being.[149]

In 1989, the Florida Supreme Court ruled that a lower court had erred in ordering transfusions for a competent adult with minor children when there were other arrangements to care for the child, such as a surviving parent.[150]

In 1992, the Florida Supreme Court reversed a transfusion order directed at a mother where no arrangements had been made for her four other children. The court noted that the children had two living parents and, even though they were separated, the law presumed that as natural guardian the father would assume the responsibilities for the children.[151]

These cases involved patients who could probably be restored to normal functioning by appropriate therapy. It is doubtful whether dependents will be a determinative issue in cases involving the terminally ill or irreversibly comatose because emotional and financial damage will seldom be increased by discontinuing treatment.

Criminal Law Enforcement

Sometimes the state's interest in gathering evidence for criminal law enforcement justifies involuntary medical procedures. Law enforcement officers frequently call on medical personnel to perform such procedures, including examining suspects, taking blood samples, pumping stomachs, removing bullets, and performing other interventions. Courts have addressed these procedures primarily in two contexts—admissibility of the resulting evidence[152] and liability for performing the procedures.

In 1951, the U.S. Supreme Court ruled that police-ordered pumping of a suspect's stomach "shocks the conscience," so the stomach contents were not admissible.[153] In 1957, the Court ruled that blood drawn from an unconscious person after a traffic accident was admissible if the blood was drawn after a proper arrest with probable cause to believe the person was intoxicated while driving.[154] In 1966, the Court ruled that blood drawn from an objecting defendant without a search warrant is admissible if five conditions are satisfied:

1. the defendant is arrested,
2. the blood is likely to produce evidence for the criminal prosecution,
3. delay would lead to destruction of evidence,
4. the test is reasonable and not medically contraindicated, and
5. the test is performed in a reasonable manner.[155]

If these conditions are present and properly documented, hospital personnel can safely cooperate in drawing blood for law enforcement officers to the extent authorized by state law. To minimize liability exposure, hospital staff should comply with all additional state requirements concerning by whom, how, and when blood may be withdrawn involuntarily. In most states, hospitals and health professionals have no legal duty to perform tests requested by law enforcement officers. When providers who perform the tests frequently must testify at criminal trials, some health professionals refuse to perform tests to avoid the disruption of their clinical schedules. When subjects physically resist tests, most professionals refuse to perform the tests to avoid injury to the subject and themselves.

Several cases have involved requests for authorization to remove bullets from suspects. In 1985, the U.S. Supreme Court ruled that the reasonableness and, thus, the constitutionality of court-ordered surgery to remove bullets for evidence is to be decided on a case-by-case basis, weighing the individual's interest in privacy and security against the societal interest in gathering evidence.[156] The Court indicated that the privacy interest was very strong when general anesthesia would be required or other dangers to life and health were present. The Court also indicated that state interests could prevail in few situations. When other evidence demonstrates the surgery is likely to produce helpful evidence, that evidence is likely to be sufficient without consideration of the bullet.

In one case the state sought involuntary treatment to preserve the life of a witness. In 1985, the Mississippi Supreme Court ruled that the state's interest in prosecuting crimes, even murder, was not sufficient to outweigh the right of an adult Jehovah's Witness to refuse life-saving transfusions even though she was the only eyewitness to a murder.[157]

Courts have addressed the steps that can be taken to assure that drugs being smuggled internally are detected and recovered. While suspected carriers intercepted by immigration officials at the borders and other points of entry can be detained, even in a hospital, to be observed until drugs can be expelled, there is disagreement among the courts concerning (1) how soon a court must be involved to authorize continued detention and (2) whether a court order is required before a person may be X-rayed. [158]

Civil Law Discovery

There are many situations where parties to civil litigation seek medical examination and testing of persons as part of the discovery process. Usually examination and testing cannot be forced, but a party who refuses to comply with a proper order may have to waive claims or other benefits and may even lose the lawsuit. Thus, most cases focus on what tests can reasonably be demanded as a condition of preserving rights in the suit.

In 1992, an Illinois court ruled that the lower court should not have ordered a minor to undergo magnetic resonance imaging (MRI) where the child would require sedation and it was not shown that this was minimal risk.[159]

However, in civil cases where the purpose of the case is to gain medical information, courts will order mandatory tests in some cases. The Wisconsin Supreme Court ruled in 1993 that a trial court could order involuntary HIV testing of a person who bit a social worker and shouted she had AIDS after the biting. The court determined that the victim's need for the information for medical planning could not be satisfied in any other way.[160]

Institutional Management

In unusual individual cases, the state's interest in management of its institutions may justify involuntary treatment. In 1979, the highest court of Massachusetts authorized dialysis for a prisoner because he attempted to manipulate his placement by refusing dialysis until he was moved.[161] Although prisoners ordinarily have the same rights as others to decline treatment, the state's interest in orderly prison administration was found to outweigh those rights.[162]

Similarly, in some situations courts have ordered forced feeding of prisoners engaged in hunger strikes, but have denied orders in other cases.[163]

Other Interests

Several other state and family interests have been asserted, but they generally have not been found to outweigh the right of an adult with decision-making capacity to refuse treatment.

Preservation of Life

The state asserts an interest in the preservation of life. Nearly all courts have ruled that this interest does not outweigh the right of terminally ill patients to refuse treatment. The *Quinlan* decision[164] ruled that the state's interest in preserving life decreases as the prognosis dims and the degree of bodily invasion of the proposed procedure increases. In the *Saikewicz* decision,[165] which authorized withholding chemotherapy from a patient with leukemia, the court concluded: "The value of life as so perceived is lessened not by a decision to refuse treatment, but by the failure to allow a competent human being the right of choice." Even when the patient is not terminally ill, courts have generally declined to order life-saving transfusions,[166] amputations of gangrenous limbs,[167] and other procedures.[168] Thus, it is not clear when the state's interest in preservation of life alone could justify involuntary treatment of an adult with decision-making capacity. At least one court has adopted a minority position that this state interest may justify involuntary treatment,[169] but no reported appellate decisions have upheld court-ordered involuntary treatment of an adult with decision-making capacity based on the interest in preservation of life without other state interests being present.

There is a new line of cases that uses the state's interest in preservation of life as grounds for disregarding the directions of adult Jehovah's Witnesses in emergency situations where they can no longer repeat their directions. These cases are discussed with other transfusion issues later in this chapter.

Prevention of Irrational Self-Destruction

The prevention of irrational self-destruction (suicide) is another interest asserted by the state. In 1975, a Pennsylvania trial court authorized transfusions for a bleeding ulcer to prevent self-destruction of a 25-year-old Jehovah's Witness.[170] Other courts have refused to consider refusal of transfusions by adult Jehovah's

Witnesses to be irrational self-destruction. Courts have generally recognized that there can be a competent, rational decision to refuse treatment.

Courts generally do not view refusals as suicidal if the patient is not seeking death but is seeking to live without the particular medical treatment. One California appellate court found that the state interest was not sufficient to overcome the refusal of tube feeding by a competent quadriplegic patient who stated that she wanted to die.[171]

Some courts have declined to intervene when terminal patients have taken active steps to hasten death. In 1984, a Florida court addressed the situation of a 55-year-old patient, terminally ill with cancer and in intense pain. After attempting suicide by stabbing herself, she refused surgery for her stab wounds. Even though the wounds were due to a suicide attempt, the court refused to order the surgery.[172]

There have been efforts to legalize assisted suicide. They are discussed at the end of this chapter.

Protection of the Ethical Integrity of Health Care Providers

Several courts have discussed whether they should recognize a state interest in maintaining the ethical integrity of the medical profession and allowing hospitals the opportunity to care for patients who have been admitted. The courts have concluded that it is not a countervailing interest. Some courts have found that the right of privacy is superior to these professional and institutional considerations. Other courts have concluded that honoring directives of patients or their representatives is consistent with medical ethics, so there is no conflict. The state interest in preserving the ethical integrity of the medical profession should not be interpreted to permit individual professionals to impose their own standards on patients.[173]

This state interest still affects one aspect of court decisions. Some courts have used this interest as a rationale for not forcing the objecting provider to carry out the directive of the patient or representative, so that the patient must be transferred to another institution or professional.[174] Other courts have refused to require transfers, ordering objecting providers to withhold or withdraw refused treatment,[175] especially when no other institution will accept the transfer[176] or the institution gave no notice of its policies prior to admission.[177]

No Family Veto

Numerous courts have emphasized the concurrence of the family or the absence of family in their decisions.[178] This should not be interpreted to mean that the family could veto the directive of a competent adult. Courts that have addressed actual disagreements have ruled in favor of the patient's directive. For example, in 1981 a federal district court ordered a Veterans Administration hospital to honor a competent adult's directive to discontinue his respirator, despite the opposition of his wife and children.[179] In 1994, another federal district court ruled that there was no duty to contact the parents of an 18-year-old adult before performing an embolization procedure to which the patient had consented.[180] Similarly, in 1989, the Alabama Supreme Court ruled that there is no duty to inform the wife or daughters of the patient before obtaining informed consent. The only relevant information is the information given to the competent adult patient.[181]

LIMITS ON THE TREATMENT THAT MUST BE OFFERED

There are limits on the treatments that providers must offer and provide. Some treatments need not be offered and, even if they are demanded by or for patients, need not be provided. In some circumstances, treatments can be discontinued without the consent of the patient or the patient's representative. The scope for proper exercise of this professional judgment is still developing.

Inappropriate Treatment

Physicians have a professional obligation to refuse to provide clearly inappropriate treatment despite patient insistence. Some courts in the 19th century ruled that patient insistence after being informed of the inappropriateness insulated the physician from liability.[182] Courts are unlikely to rule in favor of physicians in such circumstances today. In 1993, a Louisiana court ruled that it was a breach of the standard of care to perform a procedure of no beneficial value. However, the court also ruled that the patient had not given informed consent for the procedure.[183] In 1994, a federal appellate court ruled that a physician had a duty to disclose the illegality of treatments in his bills to third party payers, so the billing without disclosure was fraud.[184]

When patients or their families seek therapies outside the accepted range, the first response is often tactful communications to give them information and support to accept the limitations. It is becoming less economically feasible to give them long periods of time to adjust, so confrontation cannot always be avoided. Physicians have the responsibility and authority to refuse to provide illegal and inappropriate therapies. In 1979, the U.S. Supreme Court ruled that the terminally ill have no special right to treatment that the government has declared illegal.[185] A physician who provided a legal, but inappropriate, treatment might be liable for malpractice, notwithstanding patient consent. When reputable physicians disagree regarding the appropriateness of legal treatment, reasonable efforts should be made to transfer the treatment of the patient to a physician who concurs with the patient. If inappropriate treatment desired by the patient is neither illegal nor dangerous, sometimes it is prudent to acquiesce if the patient is willing to continue other accepted necessary therapy simultaneously.

Medically Unnecessary Treatment

Under the standards of Medicare and most third party payers, physicians and hospitals are supposed to provide only medically necessary services. Billing the payer for unnecessary services can be a false claim subject to civil and criminal penalties. To be sure, these laws do not forbid providing additional services, but under Medicare and most managed care contracts, the patient cannot be billed for the additional services unless the patient has given prior approval for the services after being informed that the third party payer will not pay. In most circumstances, a provider should have the discretion to decide whether to offer or provide such additional services.

Treatment Unlikely To Provide Substantial Therapeutic Benefit

The more difficult question arises when a treatment could temporarily prolong life but is unlikely to improve the patient's condition. Sometimes this is called *futile treatment*, although there has been debate concerning the use of the term and the practice of not providing futile treatment.[186]

There are indications that physicians do forgo futile treatment without involvement of the patient or the patient's representatives in some circumstances.[187] Some institutions have attempted to develop policies.[188] There are also indications that government agencies accept, expect, or require such behavior in some circumstances.[189] In 1995, a Massachusetts jury decided that providers were not liable for discontinuing the respirator for a terminally ill patient after consultation with the hospital Optimum Care Committee, but without patient or family consent, because the treatment was futile.[190] However, when courts have been directly confronted with the question prospectively, they have declined to give their advance approval to forgo life-prolonging therapy when neither the patient nor the family concurs.[191] Few of these cases result in a court decision because either the provider waits so long before applying to the court that the patient dies before a decision or the family agrees to terminate treatment when they learn that a lawsuit has or will be filed.[192]

One decision indicates that, at least in the jurisdiction of the U.S. Fourth Circuit Court of Appeals, withholding futile life-prolonging treatment from patients covered by EMTALA is a violation of EMTALA, if done without appropriate patient or patient representative approval[193] (see Chapter 12 for a discussion of EMTALA). However, in a non-EMTALA case another federal court ruled that failure to obtain informed consent from a mother prior to deciding to administer only supportive care to her son did not cause any injury because, due to the child's anencephaly, it would not have survived with vigorous treatment.[194]

Thus, absent patient or representative concurrence, the legal status of not providing futile treatment is still not clear in many circumstances.

Refusal To Leave

Patients do not have a right to stay in the hospital when hospitalization is no longer required. When patients and their families fail to arrange for transfer to a nursing home or other facility within a reasonable time when hospitalization is no longer required, other remedies, including injunctions, may be sought (see discussion in Chapter 12).

ADULTS WITH DECISION-MAKING CAPACITY

The person who makes the decision concerning medical treatment must (1) be legally competent, (2) have the capacity to make the decision, and (3) be informed, unless one of the exceptions applies. Adults with decision-making capacity and some mature minors make the decisions regarding their own treatment. Someone else must make these decisions for other minors and for adults without decision-making capacity.

Who Is an Adult with Decision-Making Capacity?

The age at which a person becomes an adult is established by statute in each state and is generally 18 years of age. In some states a person can become an adult earlier by certain actions, such as marriage.

An adult has decision-making capacity if (1) not declared incompetent and (2) generally capable of understanding the consequences of alternatives, weighing the alternatives by the degree to which they promote his or her desires, and choosing and acting accordingly. There is a strong legal presumption of continued capacity.[195] For example, a Pennsylvania court found a woman capable of refusing a breast biopsy even though she was committed to a mental institution with a diagnosis of chronic schizophrenia and two of her three reasons for refusal were delusional.[196] In 1978, a Massachusetts court found a woman capable of refusing amputation of her gangrenous leg even though her train of thought sometimes wandered, her conception of time was distorted, and she was confused on some matters.[197] The fact that her decision was medically irrational and would lead to her death did not demonstrate incapacity. The court believed she understood the alternatives and consequences of her decision. In 1987, the Ohio Supreme Court ruled that a psychiatric patient was competent to refuse cancer treatment despite delusions concerning her relationship to a faith healer.[198] However, an Illinois appellate court ruled in 1992 that merely presenting a single nondelusional reason for refusing psychotropic medications did not preclude a finding of incapacity to make reasoned decisions and to order authorizing administration of the medications.[199]

In 1994, a Florida appellate court addressed a case in which a patient whose breathing tube had become dislodged refused reintubation for four hours and when she finally consented she died soon after reintubation. The personal representative of her estate and her husband (who had also refused intubation for her) sued, claiming she was not competent to refuse. Their expert pointed out that she was acutely ill, in intensive care, on medication, sleep deprived, and hypoxemic. However, the undisputed evidence was that she was awake, alert, oriented, and asking appropriate questions when she refused. The court ruled that she was competent.[200]

In 1987, a New York court ruled that a jury should determine whether a patient had been sufficiently incapacitated to justify the providers' disregard of his refusals of surgery and, if so, whether there was a sufficient emergency to justify reliance on implied consent. He arrived in the emergency room with multiple stab wounds and a blood alcohol level that was later found to be more than twice the standard for driving while intoxicated.[201]

Some courts require clear and convincing evidence to overcome the presumption of competence.[202]

The determination of capacity is not necessarily the function of psychiatrists. It is usually a practical assessment that should be made by the physician who obtains the consent or accepts the refusal. When it is difficult to assess capacity, consultation is advisable. If there is suspicion of underlying mental retardation, mental illness, or disorders that affect brain functions, the consultant should be a psychiatrist or appropriate specialist.[203]

A provider cannot wait until a person is temporarily incapacitated and then imply consent or look to others to give consent. In 1992, a Utah court found that a physician could be sued for battery for performing surgery on a patient with only his wife's consent. The patient was incapacitated at the moment the wife's consent was obtained because he had already been given the preoperative medications. A Utah statute authorizing spousal consent applied only in an emergency or when the patient was unable to consent. This did not include the situation where the patient was incapacitated temporarily due to preoperative medications.[204]

Spouses generally do not have authority to consent to surgery for each other, except in some emergencies.[205]

Limits on Authority To Consent

There are limits to what an adult may authorize a provider to do. An adult may not authorize (1) mayhem, (2) suicide, (3) drugs and devices prohibited by law, or (4) other inappropriate treatment (as discussed earlier in this chapter).

Intentional maiming or disfiguring of a person without justification is the crime of *mayhem*, which now is sometimes called *willful injury*. Consent or even the request of the victim is not a defense when there is no medical justification. In 1961, a North Carolina physician was convicted of aiding and abetting mayhem because, at the victim's request, he anesthetized the victim's fingers so they could later be removed by the victim's brother.[206]

Aiding and abetting suicide is a crime in most states. Consent and even the request of the victim are not defenses. However, the issue of whether assisted suicide should be permitted is again being debated (see discussion at end of this chapter). However, withholding and withdrawing treatment pursuant to patient directions is not considered aiding and abetting suicide.[207]

The federal government, through the Food and Drug Administration (FDA), has restricted the use of new drugs and devices until their safety and effectiveness are proved. Drugs and devices generally cannot be used legally outside approved testing projects until they are approved by the FDA, regardless of the patient's desires. Alternate ways have been created to gain legal access to some experimental drugs.[208] After drugs are approved for general distribution, many can be distributed only by prescription. A physician or other authorized health professional can write a prescription only for appropriate medical uses. Inappropriate prescriptions can subject the professional to licensing discipline and to criminal prosecution. Consent of the patient to the prescription is not a defense.

Consequences of Refusal

Patients who refuse often must accept consequences beyond the health consequences. Workers' compensation,[209] disability,[210] and other benefit payments may be denied or reduced in claims concerning the underlying illness if the refused procedure would help diagnose or reduce the injury. In 1981, the Iowa Supreme Court affirmed the denial of payment to a policeman for his medical expenses because he refused to submit to coronary arteriography that was necessary to diagnose his condition.[211] In 1986, when a defendant sought to postpone a criminal trial on the grounds of his ill health, a federal court refused because the defendant was refusing all treatments that could improve his health.[212]

In a 1990 case, Blue Cross denied payment for an entire hospital stay based on a policy provision that excluded coverage if the patient left against medical advice. The Arkansas Supreme Court ruled that the provision was against public policy and ordered payment.[213]

In 1984, a New York court ruled that a patient could be discharged from a nursing home for refusing to take an annual physical examination required by the state. The home had sought a waiver of the requirement that had been denied by the state and the home was facing civil penalties for having a resident who violated the requirement.[214]

Particular Treatments

Transfusions

Jehovah's Witnesses refuse blood transfusions based on a literal interpretation of the biblical prohibition against eating blood. Nearly all courts have refused to order involuntary transfusions for competent adults,[215] except to protect a minor dependent or unborn child. Most courts refuse to authorize transfusions even when there are minor children. Until a Pennsylvania case in 1987, the only other court authorizations involving adult Jehovah's Witnesses had applied to patients who said they would not resist the transfusion if ordered.

The number of cases involving Jehovah's Witnesses should not be misinterpreted as an indication that routine judicial involvement in these cases is necessary. In many areas, transfusion refusals by adult Jehovah's Witnesses are routinely honored without any judicial involvement.[216]

Two developments have the potential for creating uncertainties in some states about the responsibilities of providers in responding to Jehovah's Witnesses' directives that transfusions not be given. Some courts have refused to honor the refusals in two respects. First, they have not given full effect to the directives as waivers of liability for carrying out the refusals. Second, in emergency situations, they have refused to honor advance directives.

Liability. Until 1985 it was thought that health care providers could rely on documents signed by Jehovah's Witnesses releasing the hospital from all liability for not providing blood transfusions. The Washington Supreme Court cast doubt on that reliance in the case of *Shorter v. Drury*.[217] After a Jehovah's Witness patient and her husband signed releases, the patient underwent a dilation and curettage procedure. The surgeon negligently perforated her uterus during the procedure, causing bleeding. The patient would have survived if blood could have been given. However, in accord with her wishes, blood was not given, and she died. Her husband sued the surgeon. The court ruled that the release form did not provide protection from liability for the surgeon's negligence. The jury found the surgeon liable for the patient's death, but allocated 75 percent of the liability to the patient and her husband for refusing blood. Thus, the surgeon had to pay 25 percent of the $412,000 verdict. The dissenting state supreme court judges felt the surgeon should have paid the full amount.

In 1990, an Illinois appellate court adopted the same position, finding that the provider could be sued for the death of the patient despite the religious refusal of transfusions.[218]

This appears to be the wrong outcome because it places any provider who agrees to provide services without transfusions at the risk of having any negligently caused bleeding result in a death for which the provider will be assigned a substantial part of the liability, where absent the agreement not to use transfusions the bleeding would cause only minor consequences. It is not clear why providers would agree to provide services without transfusions in states that adopt this position. Thus, this position in effect may reduce the availability in such jurisdictions of bloodless procedures for people with these beliefs.

At least two courts have rejected this position. In 1989, a federal appellate court held that a negligent driver could not be liable for the death of an accident victim that could have been avoided if the victim had not refused transfusions.[219] In 1993, an Illinois appellate court ruled that a release signed by a Jehovah's Witness was valid. The hospital was not liable for the death of a patient who underwent open heart surgery. The patient died when transfusions could not be given after the surgery was lengthened due to a defective heart valve that had to be removed and replaced with a second valve.[220]

Advance Directives and Emergencies. In 1987, the Pennsylvania Supreme Court upheld a court-ordered transfusion of an adult Jehovah's Witness who had been in an accident and was unable to express his directions at the time.[221] The patient was carrying a card that stated that he was a Jehovah's Witness and directed that he should not be given blood. There was some question whether the card had accompanied the patient when he was transferred to the hospital where the transfusion order was obtained and the transfusion was administered. However, the court did not ground its decision on this uncertainty. It ruled that, even if there was a refusal, the refusal was invalid because it was uninformed in that the patient had not known that refusal of blood could threaten his life. The court stated that there had to be a contemporaneous refusal.

A few other states have adopted the same position. One case involved elective surgery where the patient had expressly conditioned her consent to the surgery on not using transfusions.[222] In another case the court did not permit the patient to sue a doctor who had unilaterally disregarded the patient's expressed directions without even seeking a court order.[223] In these cases the court did not even have the benefit of the possibility that the providers were not aware of the patient's directions. In the past, the emergency exception to the consent requirement was limited to cases where the patient's directions were not known. Here the courts had to go through the two-step process of voiding the express refusals of these patients through the informed refusal doctrine, so that the court could adopt the fiction that the patient's directions were not known, and then invoke the emergency exception to the consent doctrine. These cases represent a significant retreat from the respect for religious and other beliefs of adults that the law has demonstrated in other jurisdictions. Requiring informed refusal stands the informed consent doctrine on its head. The informed consent doctrine was designed (1) to preserve the individual's right to autonomy and to be left alone by not permitting treatment without informed consent and (2) to promote disclosure of information by physicians to facilitate the exercise of that autonomy. This informed refusal doctrine removes the requirement that providers obtain consent to treatment and permits the courts and doctors to force emergency treatment on a person unless the person can meet a strict standard set by the court.

In addition, in states that have adopted this informed refusal doctrine, it is not clear whether there are any emergency situations in which the provider can safely act in accordance with a directive refusing transfusions. Must advance directives always be ignored in those jurisdictions? Does the provider have a duty either to seek a court order or to proceed to give necessary transfusions without an order?

It is not clear how a Jehovah's Witness can make an effective advance refusal of transfusions in these states that will cover emergency situations, since the standard there is a contemporaneous informed refusal. It is also not clear what effect this rejection of advance directives from Jehovah's Witnesses will have on these courts' enforcement of other advance directives, especially directives that are not expressly authorized by statute.

In 1990, one court fully enforced the more traditional view. A Canadian appellate court upheld an award of $20,000 for battery against a doctor who performed an emergency blood transfusion on a Jehovah's Witness who had a card in her wallet directing that she was not to receive a transfusion under any circumstances.[224]

Declining To Perform Surgery on Patients Who Refuse Transfusions. In jurisdictions that impose liability on providers for the death of patients who refuse transfusions after negligently inflicted injuries, some providers will consider declining to perform such surgery. In 1986, a federal district court in Arkansas found that there is no duty to perform surgery on a Jehovah's Witness who refuses blood transfusions and no duty to locate a surgeon who will comply.[225] When physicians decline to perform surgery without transfusions, it appears that these patients can be given the choice of arranging for their own transfer, forgoing surgery, or accepting transfusions.

Of course, due to EMTALA, hospitals cannot refuse to care for emergency patients, but courts have not yet addressed the scope of responsibilities in emergencies when the patient refuses a critical component of definitive care, such as transfusions.

Cardiopulmonary Resuscitation

Cardiopulmonary resuscitation (CPR) is a series of steps used to attempt to reestablish breathing and heartbeat after cardiac or respiratory arrest. Some steps are highly intrusive and even violent in nature. CPR is automatically initiated in most hospitals unless a physician orders "do not resuscitate" (DNR) or "no CPR." This policy has been criticized by some physicians who believe the presumption of automatic CPR should not apply in cases where it is futile.[226] However, the standard of care in virtually all areas is to initiate CPR unless there is a contrary physician order.[227]

Hospitals should have a written policy concerning resuscitative measures. This is required by the Joint Commission.[228] Written DNR orders assure that the responsible physician has approved the decision. Unwritten orders and nonphysician orders have led to grand jury and licensing agency investigations.[229] Appropriate consultation with and concurrence from the patient or patient's representative should also be documented. The nature of the treatment to be withheld should be explained before obtaining the concurrence. A DNR order was challenged in a 1981 Minnesota case.[230] The court was not convinced the patient's parents knew what they were declining, so it ordered the cancellation of the DNR order until the parents gave "knowledgeable approval" to reinstate the order. A court order is generally not required for a DNR order.[231]

At least 24 states have laws that address out-of-hospital DNR orders, with many permitting emergency medical personnel to honor certain orders.[232]

A DNR order is not authorization to withhold all treatment. Other treatment should still be given until there is an order concerning the other treatment. In 1992, the Idaho Supreme Court found that nurses and a hospital could be sued because the nurses discontinued supplemental oxygen to a patient during a transfer and refused to supply it despite urging from the family who were present. During the move the patient's condition suddenly worsened dramatically. The patient was under a DNR order and not expected to live more than 24 hours. He was not resuscitated and died.[233]

Ventilators/Respirators

Courts have generally permitted competent adults to decide to discontinue the use of ventilators and respirators. For example, in 1989 the Georgia Supreme Court decided that a quadriplegic patient could discontinue the use of the respirator and that his physician could give him a sedative to alleviate his pain when the ventilator was disconnected.[234]

Nutrition and Hydration

Nearly all appellate courts that have addressed the issue have agreed that artificial nutrition and hydration (tube feeding) are medical treatments that can be refused in the same situations in which other medical treatments can be refused.[235] While acknowledging the symbolic importance of feeding, which has led some groups to seek to preclude refusal of these treatments, courts have ruled that there is no legal difference between artificial breathing with a respirator and artificial feeding with a tube. Some groups who have opposed refusal of tube feeding have asserted that such feeding is necessary for comfort care. Medical studies tend to show that tube feeding does not contribute to comfort.[236]

The Missouri Supreme Court is the only state supreme court that has suggested that artificial feeding may be a mandatory procedure that cannot be refused.[237] However, Missouri later permitted withdrawal of artificial nutrition and hydration for the same patient, Nancy Cruzan. After the U.S. Supreme Court affirmed the Missouri decision on other grounds (see discussion in the constitution section of this chapter), the Cruzan family initiated new proceedings to prove Nancy's wishes. The state withdrew from the case. A lower court found clear and convincing evidence of Nancy Cruzan's intent and approved withdrawal of her feeding tube. The Missouri Supreme Court declined to review the decision. The feeding tube was withdrawn. Despite protests at the hospital that led to arrests of protestors and despite the protestors' unsuccessful attempts to obtain intervention from several different state and federal courts, the feeding tube was not replaced and Nancy Cruzan died.[238]

The American Medical Association has recognized that refusal of artificial nutrition and hydration is appropriate in some cases.[239]

Courts have enforced refusals of this treatment by competent patients[240] and by patient representatives on behalf of patients who are terminally ill[241] or irreversibly unconscious.[242] Courts have had difficulty in defining when substituted decisions to refuse any treatment, including artificial nutrition, should be permitted on behalf of other patients. In 1985, in *In re Conroy*[243] the New Jersey Supreme Court addressed a patient who was neither terminally ill nor unconscious. After ruling that tube feeding was a treatment like a respirator that could be discontinued in appropriate cases, the court stated that discontinuance would be appropriate pursuant to the clearly articulated wishes of an elderly nursing home patient with severe and permanent mental and physical impairments and a life expectancy of a year or less. Without adequate proof of the patient's wishes, the feeding could be discontinued when either (1) there was trustworthy evidence of the patient's wishes and unavoidable pain caused patient suffering that markedly outweighed any physical pleasure, emotional enjoyment, or intellectual satisfaction the patient still derived from life; or (2) there was no trustworthy evidence of the patient's wishes, the net burdens of the patient's life with treatment markedly outweighed the benefits the patient derived from life, and recurring, unavoidable, and severe pain with treatment made the administering of treatment inhumane. The emphasis that this decision places on pain can be questioned, but it is an important contribution to the legal responses to nutritional technologies.

In 1984, in the only prosecution of physicians for withholding artificial nutrition and hydration from a terminally ill patient, a California appellate court ordered the dismissal of homicide indictments against two physicians.[244] The court ruled that artificial means of feeding are treatment, not natural functions, so there is no duty to continue the treatment when it becomes ineffective. The physicians could not be criminally liable for their professional decision made in concert with the patient's family when the individual was incompetent and terminally ill, with virtually no hope of significant improvement.

INCAPACITATED ADULTS WITH A PRIOR DIRECTIVE

Competent adults who direct that certain treatments be withheld or withdrawn generally lose their decision-making capacity before they die. Their refusal of medical treatment must apply through the period of incapacity, so their right to make decisions regarding their own treatment is not vitiated. Some states have addressed this situation through living will statutes. In situations in which either there is no applicable statute or the statutory procedures have not been followed, common law and constitutional principles require that the patient's directive continue to be followed. At or near the time of admission, patients and families of incapacitated patients should be asked if there is a written directive, so it can be documented, discussed, and implemented.[245]

If, before becoming incapacitated, a patient gives unambiguous directions either orally and directly to the provider or in writing, the directions should generally be followed to the same extent that directions from a patient who still has capacity would be. If time permits, oral directions should be written and signed. If the provider has not discussed a prior written directive with the patient and it does not comply with the state living will law or guidelines from the state courts, prudent providers should talk to family members. If there is no reason to suspect the authenticity of the directive, it should usually be followed, especially when the patient is terminally ill or irreversibly unconscious. In other situations court review may be warranted in some states[246] unless the principles for patients without directives lead to the same treatment decision.

When reviewing written directives, attention should be focused on what event triggers the directive and what treatment is being refused. Some of the triggering events that have been used include (1) terminal illness, (2) imminence of death, and (3) loss of capacity to care for self.[247] Some of the treatments refused include (1) extraordinary procedures, (2) life-prolonging procedures, (3) artificial nutrition and hydration, and (4) all procedures permitted by law.

Prior oral directives to persons other than the provider are more difficult to assess. If such directives do not agree with the treatment decision by representatives, court involvement may be necessary in most states. Courts place substantial weight on such oral directives when they can be proved,[248] but some courts require so much proof of these oral directives that few persons can satisfy the standard.[249]

When a competent patient still is able to communicate or when there is a reasonable likelihood that the patient will again be competent and able to communicate, reliance usually should not be placed on directives made before the condition was known. The patient should be given an opportunity to recover the ability to communicate and express his or her present directive. The major exception is that providers in most jurisdictions should not wait for recovery before following directives based on religious or other strongly held views that are intended to transcend individual conditions. However, as previously discussed in the transfusion section of this chapter, there are some jurisdictions in which the courts apply an informed refusal doctrine to disregard advance directives in some situations, especially emergency care situations.

INCAPACITATED ADULTS WITH NO PRIOR DIRECTIVE

Who Decides?

When patients have not expressed their directives and are no longer able to do so, some individual or group must be able to make surrogate decisions for them. The physician and other professionals involved in patient treatment have an important role and are relatively easy to identify. Identification of the proper person to represent the patient can be more difficult. When a court has declared the patient incompetent and appointed a guardian, the guardian can usually make the required decisions on the patient's behalf.[250] When close family members disagree with the guardian, guidance from a court may be needed. In some states, physicians have been given the power to make some medical decisions for incompetents who have no other surrogate decision maker.[251]

Some patients who do not have decision-making capacity have never been determined to be incompetent by a court, so they do not have guardians. When decisions concerning their treatment cannot be deferred until recovery of capacity, it is common practice to seek a decision from the spouse, next of kin, or others who have assumed supervision of the patient. In many states, laws or court decisions support this practice.[252] Some advance directive laws state who may refuse in the absence of a patient directive.[253] When state law does not specify such a priority of decision makers, disagreement among interested persons should usually be taken to court.

In a 1991 case in Florida, the son sought to discontinue life support of his comatose father, while his stepmother sought to continue life support. The wife would receive an additional $100,000 under a prenuptial agreement if the man lived until the anniversary of their marriage. The trial court authorized discontinuance, but an appellate court stayed the order. The man died, still receiving life support, before the legal dispute could be resolved and before the anniversary.[254]

If the incapacity is temporary, the procedure should usually be postponed until the patient regains capacity and can make his or her own decision, unless the postponement presents a substantial risk to the patient's life or health. Many court decisions concerning terminally ill patients involve guardians because the appointment of a guardian is a procedure courts use to effectuate their judgments. However, generally courts have permitted family members to make these decisions without being legally designated guardians.[255] The decision-making role of the family is limited by the physician's diagnostic role and responsibility to the patient. The family can decide to refuse treatment without court involvement only after the physician has made the appropriate diagnosis of terminal illness, irreversible unconsciousness, or perhaps other conditions and accepts the family's treatment decision. When the physician and family concur in refusing treatment for an incapacitated patient who is terminally ill or irreversibly unconscious and has not expressed contrary directions, the risk associated with carrying out the decision is minimal. Physician nonacceptance is not necessarily a veto; in many cases the patient should be transferred to the treatment of another physician who will accept the family's decision.

When the hospital becomes aware of disagreement among the patient, family, and physician, the hospital administration should remember the hospital's independent duty to the patient; it should become involved to facilitate communication and to determine whether to seek clarification from a court.

When a hospital has determined that a patient lacks capacity, it should treat the patient consistently as incapacitated until it determines that capacity is restored and begins treating the patient consistently as having decision-making capacity. In a 1984 case, the federal district court ruled that when the Veterans Administration issues a "statement of incapacity" and designates the patient's wife or another person to be the one to whom it will turn for decisions on the patient's behalf, the patient's consent is no longer sufficient authorization for treatment; the consent of the person designated must be sought.[256]

Substituted Judgment and Best Interests

Courts have developed two standards for surrogate decision makers to use. Most courts apply the *substituted judgment* standard, which requires the decision maker to strive to make the decision the patient would have made if able.[257] Some courts apply the *best interests* standard, which focuses not on what the patient would want, but on what is best for the patient in the view of the decision maker.[258]

Giving Weight to the Patient's Wishes

In making a treatment decision, appropriate weight should be given to what is known of the patient's wishes even if they do not qualify as a prior directive. Patient wishes expressed after loss of capacity should also be considered. In 1984, a Massachusetts court considered the patient's efforts to pull out tubes in deciding to permit termination of tube feeding.[259] In the same year, despite the guardian's preference for surgery, the Washington Supreme Court honored an incompetent's desire not to have surgery for cancer of the larynx, which would have destroyed her ability to speak.[260]

Limits on Permitted Consents

Any person acting on behalf of an incapacitated adult or a minor does not have the same latitude for consent as in self-treatment decisions. Decision makers cannot authorize two procedures—organ donation and sterilization—for incompetent adults or minors without prior court approval. Courts in a few states will not approve kidney donations by minors and incompetents,[261] but courts in other states have authorized them.[262] Bone marrow donations have been approved.[263] The courts that have approved kidney donations have usually based their approval on the close relationship between the donor and the proposed recipient and on the emotional injury to the donor if the recipient were to die. The issue of sterilization of minors and incompetent adults is discussed in Chapter 15. The limits on consents by adults for their own treatment discussed earlier in this chapter also apply to surrogate decisions.

Permitted Refusals

Nearly all state appellate courts that have addressed treatment refusal have decided that surrogate decision makers may refuse treatment for some incapacitated patients.[264] The minority position rejects this view and allows only self-refusals by patients with decision-making capacity.[265] The discretion to refuse is generally limited to situations in which the treatment is elective or not likely to be beneficial. Life prolongation is not always viewed as beneficial. States that allow surrogate refusals generally agree that they are permitted when the patient is irreversibly unconscious[266] or terminally ill.[267]

There is no widely accepted definition of terminal illness; it remains a diagnosis based on medical judgment. One element is that no available course of therapy offers a reasonable expectation of remission or cure of the condition. Another element is that death is imminent, but there is no consensus on the time period, largely because it is not possible to predict time of death precisely.[268] Some courts have accepted patients as being terminally ill with predicted lives of one to five years.[269] Thus, the range of medical opinion concerning terminal illness appears to be legally acceptable. It is prudent to avoid establishing a specific time period. Some widely publicized institutional systems for classifying patients have not included a definition of terminal illness, but instead have focused on the appropriate therapeutic effort.[270]

A few courts have addressed refusals on behalf of patients who are incapacitated, conscious, and not terminally ill, but there is no consensus.[271] Hospitals should generally take these cases to court unless the issue has been adequately addressed in their states.

MINORS

Consent of the parent or guardian should be obtained before treatment is given to a minor[272] unless it is (1) an emergency, (2) one of the situations in which the consent of the minor is sufficient, or (3) a situation in which a court order or other legal authorization is obtained.

Either parent can give legally effective consent except when there is legal separation or divorce. It is not necessary to seek the wishes of the other parent. When objections are known, either the treatment should not be given, or court authorization should be obtained.[273] When the parents are legally separated or divorced, usually the consent of the custodial parent must be obtained.

Emergency Care

As with adults, consent is implied in medical emergencies when there is an immediate threat to life or health unless the provider has reason to believe that consent would be refused by the parent or guardian. In 1986, one New York trial court ruled that a hospital could not be liable for giving necessary emergency treatment over parental objections when a court would have ordered the treatment.[274] However, prudent providers will not rely on this decision and instead will follow the procedure for seeking court authorization when parents refuse necessary treatment.

Minors Who May Decide for Themselves

Statutes

Many states have minor treatment statutes empowering older minors to consent to medical treatment. The age limits and the scope of the treatments vary from state to state.[275] Many states have special minor consent laws for venereal disease and substance abuse treatment that have no age limits.

Generally these statutes are intended to expand the rights of minors. However, in 1993 a New York appellate court, in order to strike down a program that was planning to provide condoms to minors at school without parental consent as part of an HIV/AIDS prevention program, ruled that the state minor consent statute abrogated all common law rights of minors to consent, so that the exclusive means for minors to consent in the jurisdiction of that court are those listed in the statute.[276] This is probably an aberrant case where the court did not consider the other implications for delivery of medical services to adolescents when trying to respond to the public concerns with the role of the family and the school in addressing adolescent sexual behavior and disease prevention.

Emancipated Minors

Emancipated minors may consent to their own medical care. Minors are emancipated when they are no longer subject to parental control and are not supported by their parents. The specific factors necessary to establish emancipation vary from state to state. Some states require that the parent and the child agree on the emancipation, so self-emancipation is not possible in those states.

Mature Minors

Mature minors may consent to some medical care under common law and constitutional principles and under the statutes of some states. In states that do not have an applicable minor consent statute, the risk associated with providing necessary treatment to mature minors with only their consent is minimal.[277] The oldest minor who underwent a medical procedure with his personal consent and won a reported lawsuit based on lack of parental consent was 15.[278] That 1941 case involved nontherapeutic removal of some skin for donation to another person for a skin graft operation.

When the age of adulthood was 21, the English common law used the Rule of Sevens to assess the decision-making capacity of minors. Minors under age seven did not have capacity. From age 7 through 13 there was a rebuttable presumption of no capacity, so in individual cases capacity might be proved. From age 14 through 20 there was a rebuttable presumption of capacity, so many persons of this age range had capacity, but in individual cases capacity might be disproved. In 1987, the Tennessee Supreme Court recognized the continuing vitality of the Rule of Sevens and upheld the consent to medical treatment of a minor over age 13.[279] However, in 1989, when the Illinois Supreme Court ruled that a mature 17-year-old minor with leukemia could refuse transfusions and that it was not neglect for her mother to acquiesce,[280] the court required proof of maturity with clear and convincing evidence. Thus, it did not apply any rebuttable presumption of maturity.

Failure to consult with a mature minor can lead to liability. In 1992, the West Virginia Supreme Court ruled that suit could be brought challenging a DNR order for a mature minor whose parents had consented to the DNR order without consulting the patient. After the child died, the father as executor brought the suit. The court remanded for a determination whether the son was a mature minor who was entitled to participate in the decision.[281]

In 1994, a federal court held that Georgia does not recognize any right of a mature minor to refuse medical care.[282] However, the case involved a Jehovah's Witness refusing a transfusion in a situation where restoration to health was likely. Similarly, another court, while recognizing the mature minor exception, found that a 17-year-old Jehovah's Witness was not sufficiently mature to understand the fatal consequences of refusing a transfusion seven weeks before his 18th birthday.[283] These cases indicate that courts are reluctant to extend the general right to refuse any medical care to minors, even mature minors, in cases where the minor can be restored to health. However, it is doubtful that the same result will be reached in cases where the mature minor is terminally ill. For example, after a state agency forcibly removed a 15-year-old liver transplant patient from his home and placed him in a hospital to force him to take antirejection drugs, which could cause painful side effects, a Florida trial court authorized the refusal.[284]

The constitutional right of privacy restricts state authority to mandate parental involvement in certain reproductive decisions, such as abortions. Reproductive issues are discussed in Chapter 15.

When treating any minor, the minor should be urged to involve his or her parents. When a mature minor refuses to permit parental involvement, the provider can provide necessary care without substantial risk unless (1) there is likelihood of harm to the minor or others that requires parental involvement to avoid or (2) institutional policy requires parental involvement. When such harm is likely, parents should usually be involved unless state law forbids parental notification.

Limits on Decisions

All limits on consents by adults for their own treatment and for the treatment of incapacitated adults discussed earlier in this chapter apply when parents and guardians consent to the treatment of minors.

In addition, courts tend to require that decisions on behalf of minors be in minors' best interests. Since minors have never had decision-making capacity, substituted judgment seldom applies even though courts often do give weight to minors' preferences. In addition to the state interests, which the state asserts concerning adults, the state asserts an interest in minors and some incapacitated adults under its *parens patriae* power, the general power as "parent" to protect the welfare of incompetent persons.

Parents do still have considerable latitude in decision making concerning their minor children's care.

Refusals by and for Minors

Courts tend to find that since adults with decision-making capacity have the right to refuse, adults making decisions on behalf of minors have a right to refuse on their behalf in some situations. However, because the decision makers have an obligation to act in the best interest of the minor, they must provide necessary treatment. Their discretion to decline treatment is generally limited to situations in which the treatment is elective or not likely to be beneficial. The duty to provide necessary treatment to minors is reinforced in all states by legislation concerning abused or neglected minors that facilitates state intervention to provide needed assistance. The duty is further illustrated by a 1987 New Jersey appellate court decision that providers have no duty to inform parents of the alternative of withholding treatment in cases where withholding is illegal.[285]

However, the state has no constitutional duty to protect children in this fashion, so it is not liable for failing to intervene.[286] The state's responsibilities are limited to those it assumes under its statutes.

Courts have generally permitted the refusal of treatment for irreversibly comatose minors[287] and some terminally ill minors. For example, in 1982 the highest court of Massachusetts approved a decision not to attempt resuscitative efforts if a terminally ill child less than one year of age experienced cardiac or respiratory arrest.[288] In 1992, a Michigan appellate court authorized parents to terminate the life support of an 11-year-old in a persistent vegetative state.[289] These decisions are being made on a regular basis without court involvement. One study of care decisions in pediatric intensive care units (PICUs) in 16 hospitals reported 119 patients who had their care limited during 1990 and 1991. The limitations varied from DNR orders to withdrawal of care. Ninety-four of the patients died in the PICU.[290]

Courts have declined to override parental refusals in several situations in which the benefit did not clearly outweigh the risk. For example, the Washington Supreme Court refused to authorize the amputation of an 11-year-old girl's arm, which was so abnormally large that it was useless and interfered with her association with other people.[291] In 1972, the Pennsylvania Supreme Court refused to authorize transfusions that would permit an operation to correct the severe spinal curvature of the 16-year-old son of a Jehovah's Witness.[292] In 1994, a Florida court reversed an order that a child be treated with chemotherapy and transfusions for acute monocytic leukemia despite the religious objections of the parents. The court found that the state must show a compelling interest to override the liberty interest in the parent-child relationship. The state's interest in preservation of life could provide that interest, but that "interest diminishes as the severity of an affliction and the likelihood of death increase." It was not clear that the trial court had weighed the competing interests of the parents in making such decisions for their children and of the child's right of privacy under the state constitution, so the court was ordered to further consider the case.[293]

In 1991, the Delaware Supreme Court ruled that a 3-year-old child with Burkitt's syndrome was not neglected when his Christian Science parents refused to consent to radical chemotherapy that had only a 40% chance of success, so the court reversed the trial court order that had awarded custody to the state. The Supreme Court applied the "best interests" test and concluded:

> The egregious facts of this case indicate that Colin's proposed medical treatment was highly invasive, painful, involved terrible temporary and potentially permanent side effects, posed an unacceptably low chance of success, and a high risk that the treatment itself would cause death. The State's authority to intervene in this case, therefore, cannot outweigh the Newmarks' parental prerogative and Colin's inherent right to enjoy at least a modicum of human dignity in the short time that is left for him.[294]

Courts will generally decline to intervene when parents or guardians are following the advice of a licensed physician in good standing even if the advice is unorthodox. In 1979, the highest court of New York refused to authorize chemotherapy for a child with leukemia because the parents were following the advice of a physician who had prescribed laetrile even though laetrile was not proven to be effective.[295]

Courts do not have unbridled authority to compel treatment of minors. In 1993, an Illinois court voided a juvenile court order giving police authority to consent to medical exams of minors taken into custody when parents or guardians were unavailable or unwilling to consent because the order was beyond the juvenile court's authority.[296] Courts must follow the proper procedures for their orders to be valid. In 1994, a federal appellate court upheld a $1.95 million award against a physician for the death of a minor after the insertion of a Hickman catheter over the objection of the father.[297] A court order had been obtained but was found to be invalid.[298]

Parents who fail to obtain necessary medical care have been convicted of child abuse and even homicide, but criminal liability has generally not been imposed when there are questions concerning (1) the parents' knowledge of the seriousness of the child's condition or (2) the necessity for or net benefit from the proposed services.[299]

Infants

The treatment of infants with severe deformities that are inconsistent with prolonged or sapient life has been controversial.[300] It has been accepted practice in many hospitals, upon the concurrence of the parents and the treatment team, to provide only ordinary care to these infants so that their suffering is not prolonged through extraordinary efforts. If parents wish heroic measures, they generally are attempted. If parents refuse treatment when the attending physician believes treatment provides a reasonable likelihood of benefit, child neglect laws are invoked to obtain court authorization for treatment.

Health care professionals disagree on whether some conditions are sufficiently severe that treatment offers no reasonable likelihood of benefit. There has been general acceptance of withholding treatment when the condition is anencephaly (the absence of the higher brain) or other conditions that preclude development of sapient life or are inconsistent with prolonged life.[301] In the past, surgical treatment for spina bifida was frequently withheld. With improvements in treatments and outcomes, surgery can now be withheld only in the most severe cases. A New York hospital obtained a court order authorizing surgical repair of a newborn with several of the complications associated with spina bifida.[302]

Neither mental retardation at a sapient level nor physical deformities consistent with prolonged survival are considered to justify withholding treatment from newborns. This is illustrated by the refusal of a Massachusetts probate court in 1978 to approve parental refusal of respiratory support and cardiac surgery, in spite of some degree of mental retardation and multiple medical problems, because the condition was not terminal and the degree of mental retardation had not been established.[303]

The Department of Health and Human Services (HHS) began an effort in 1982 to force aggressive treatment of virtually all severely deformed newborns. HHS sent a letter to many hospitals threatening to withhold federal funding from any hospital that permitted medically indicated treatment to be withheld from a disabled newborn.[304] This letter was a reaction to a widely publicized case in Indiana in which an infant with Down Syndrome (which usually results in mental retardation) was permitted to starve to death when relatively minor surgery would have permitted the newborn to live. A court order was sought to authorize the surgery, but the Indiana courts refused to intervene.[305]

In 1983, HHS published rules (1) creating a hotline in Washington, D.C., for the reporting of suspected violations and (2) requiring notices to be posted in hospitals announcing the hotline.[306] A federal court enjoined the rules,[307] which were widely criticized.[308] HHS published revised rules in 1984 that continued the hotline, required notices to be posted, and recommended the creation of institutional ethics committees.[309] The revised rules were also declared to be beyond the authority of HHS.[310]

In 1983, New York's highest court upheld parental refusal of corrective surgery for a newborn with spina bifida and hydrocephalus.[311] The federal government sought access to the child's medical records, and the parents and the hospital refused to grant access. A federal appellate court refused to order access and ruled that the federal government did not have authority under existing handicapped rights laws to investigate the case.[312] Congress then passed legislation that required states to implement programs within their child abuse prevention and treatment systems to address the withholding of medically indicated treatment from infants with life-threatening conditions.[313] The HHS implementing regulations recommended institutional infant care review committees.[314]

These decisions will continue to be controversial, but the real exposure to potential legal sanctions is minimal if refusals are carefully limited to appropriate cases. Withholding treatment is acceptable only when the deformities are inconsistent with prolonged or sapient life. When these cases are taken to court, courts do approve refusal in appropriate cases.[315] It is important to obtain consultations regarding diagnosis, prognosis, and treatment decisions. Documenting the reasons for the decisions and the decision-making process is essential to ensure that decision makers give principled consideration to all relevant information.

Giving Weight to the Minor's Wishes

Minors are generally treated as incompetents for purposes of medical treatment decisions. When minors are able to participate in decisions, their wishes should be given substantial weight. This presents little difficulty when the minor and the parents or guardian agree,[316] such as when the minor initiates the idea of withholding treatment and the parents agree. These cases seldom require court involvement.[317] When disagreement concerning treatment of an immature minor is irreconcilable and either the minor or a parent or guardian wants to treat, treatment should be pursued. In such cases, court authorization will ordinarily be required only if the minor wants treatment and the parent or guardian will not authorize it. Irreconcilable disagreements concerning treatment of mature minors can require court involvement.

Older minors do not always acquiesce in decisions by others to require them to undergo therapy. In 1994, a 16-year-old cancer patient ran away from home to avoid chemotherapy and did not return until his parents agreed he could stop chemotherapy.[318] Thus, as a practical matter, decision makers need to give due weight to minors' wishes.

Disagreements should not be avoided by completely excluding the minor from the process. The West Virginia Supreme Court held that a hospital could be sued if a DNR order was entered with parental consent, but with no consultation with a mature minor.[319] Thus, in some circumstances, courts have recognized that minors have rights concerning these decisions.

Particular Procedures

Transfusions

Courts generally agree that minors should have an opportunity to mature and make their own decisions concerning their religious beliefs. Thus, courts have authorized blood transfusions for minors in nearly every reported case in which the minor had a life-threatening condition and was not terminally ill.[320] A few courts have permitted mature minors to refuse transfusions with the concurrence of their parents.[321] In nearly all cases where the condition was not life threatening, the courts have also authorized transfusions.[322] One of the few exceptions is a 1972 Pennsylvania case, described earlier in this chapter, where the court declined to order transfusions to permit surgery for spinal curvature.[323]

Major Surgery

Courts have authorized major surgery for minors when it is likely to be beneficial. In 1986, an Ohio appellate court ordered surgery to treat a minor's cancer.[324] In 1981, an Oregon court authorized surgical treatment of an infant's hydrocephalus to prevent mental retardation even though her life was not in immediate danger.[325]

Chemotherapy and Other Medications

When parents are not following reputable medical advice, courts authorize treatment that is likely to be beneficial for life-threatening conditions. In 1979, the highest court of Massachusetts authorized chemotherapy for a child with leukemia despite parental insistence on laetrile treatment[326]; a federal district court refused to intervene.[327] In 1987, a California appellate court ordered continued medical monitoring of a minor after completion of court-ordered chemotherapy for cancer.[328] However, when the probability of success is low and the chemotherapy has major side effects, courts tend to refuse to order treatment.[329]

Hospitalization

Many states have laws that authorize certain health care providers to hold and treat minors in emergencies.[330] For example, Florida authorizes a physician to take custody of a child without a court order when there is imminent danger to the child's life or health and not enough time to obtain a court order.[331] However, the statute does not authorize treatment of the child, so authorization to treat must be obtained from a parent, the Florida Department of Health and Rehabilitative Services,[332] or a court. If there is insufficient time to obtain authorization, apparently the common law emergency exception to the consent requirement must be relied on, notwithstanding parental refusal. North Carolina authorizes the physician, with the concurrence of another physician, to provide necessary care when the parents refuse and there is no time to obtain a court order.[333] Familiarity with local law is essential so that proper procedures can be followed promptly when these situations arise.

Resuscitation

Several courts have approved parental consent to DNR orders.[334] In most jurisdictions court approval for DNR orders for minors are probably not required in most cases. However, concurrence of mature minors is probably required.[335]

PROVIDER LIABILITY IN REFUSAL CASES

Civil Liability

Because they fear liability, physicians and hospitals have sometimes been reluctant to follow the directives of patients and their families. While liability is theoretically possible, it is no more likely that physicians and other health care providers will be held liable for following treatment refusals than for their many other decisions and actions.

Civil liability for withholding or withdrawing medical treatment would have to be based on negligent or deliberate failure to act in accordance with some duty to the patient. The duty to the patient is shaped by the patient's directions and condition. There is no duty to provide properly refused treatment or to treat terminally ill or irreversibly unconscious patients as if they are curable. Explicit refusal by an informed patient with decision-making capacity relieves the physician and hospital of further duty to provide the refused treatment unless it is a situation in which involuntary treatment is authorized. If refused treatment is given without legal authorization, liability for battery is possible. The same principles generally apply to proper refusals by an incapacitated patient's representative.

A medical decision may be questioned in subsequent litigation and be found to have been negligent. The risk for decisions regarding the treatment of terminally ill and irreversibly unconscious patients is no greater than is the risk for the treatment of other patients. Liability is even possible when physicians act pursuant to a court order if they are negligent in implementing the order. Limited statutory immunity has been granted in some circumstances by living will laws, but those laws have broad exceptions that preserve accountability.

One indication of the limited exposure to civil liability is the small number of civil lawsuits brought against physicians and hospitals for withholding or withdrawing medical treatment from terminally ill patients.[336] One case arose after the physician and the patient's husband decided to discontinue the patient's dialysis at a Minnesota hospital.[337] Six months after the wife's death the husband died. Three years later the patient's children sued the physician for her death, but a jury found in favor of the physician. Other courts have found no liability when family have sued because they had no right to participate in a competent patient's decision.[338]

Liability exposure is possible in cases of misdiagnosis of terminal illness or unjustifiable failure to obtain the concurrence of the patient, or, in the case of incapacitated patients, the family, but no reported liability cases address those issues.

Exposure to civil liability is probably greater from refusing to honor the directives of the patient and the family.[339] Several suits have been brought against providers who continued treatment for a prolonged period after refusal.[340]

When the husband of a terminally ill woman requested that she be taken off a respirator, an Ohio hospital refused to permit removal until a court order was obtained. After the court order was obtained,[341] the husband filed suit against the physician and the hospital, claiming that his wife's constitutional right of privacy was violated and seeking payment for her pain, suffering, and medical expenses during the time the order was sought. An Ohio court refused to dismiss the suit, ruling that the providers could be sued for battery for continuing treatment for too long a period after authorization was withdrawn.[342] The hospital settled and the trial judge ruled in favor of the physician.[343] In another more recent Ohio case, a patient sued a hospital for resuscitation after a noncode order had been written. The court ruled that providers could be sued for battery and negligence, but prolonged life was not a compensable injury as "wrongful living."[344]

Another case arose in Massachusetts after a court authorized discontinuance of dialysis.[345] The patient's wife sued the health care institution that had forced the matter to be taken to court. The trial court dismissed several parts of the suit, but the jury awarded $2.5 million on the remaining parts. A new trial was ordered, and a second jury awarded $1 million based solely on a letter, sent to a newspaper by several institutional employees with the approval of the administration, that opposed the court order. The letter was found to violate a statute that prohibited certain releases of personal data. The highest court of Massachusetts reversed the award, finding that the statute did not apply to public institutions such as the defendant in the suit.[346] These cases illustrate that extended delay, pursuit of court orders, and vigorous advocacy of continued treatment may increase exposure to suits.

One reported case affirmed the provider tort liability for providing refused care. In 1990, a federal appellate court ruled that the physicians involved in implanting a Hickman catheter in a minor, pursuant to an ex parte court order, could be sued for the death of the minor two weeks later from a massive pulmonary embolus.[347]

The implantation was a battery because the court order was not valid—it had not been properly obtained. The hospital had been dismissed from the case by agreement of the parties without explanation. At trial the father, who had opposed the implantation, was awarded nearly $2 million, which the appellate court affirmed.[348] It is important to insist that proper procedures be followed when court orders are obtained.

There have been disputes over whether a provider can charge the patient for services that were refused. In 1993, the highest court of New York permitted a nursing home to charge for refused services, due to the uncertain state of the law during the period the services were provided.[349]

Several decisions have required providers to pay the attorney's fees of the patient and the family in seeking court orders.[350]

Criminal Liability

In some decisions involving terminally ill patients, courts have discussed the potential criminal liability for withholding or withdrawing medical treatment. In the *Quinlan* decision, after observing that termination of treatment would accelerate death, the court concluded that "there would be no criminal homicide but rather expiration from existing natural causes." It added as a second reason, "even if it were to be regarded as homicide, it would not be unlawful. . . .The termination of treatment pursuant to the right of privacy is, within the limits of this case, *ipso facto* lawful." The court discussed the constitutional dimensions:

> Furthermore, the exercise of a constitutional right such as we have here found is protected from criminal prosecution. [Citation omitted.] We do not question the State's undoubted power to punish the taking of human life, but that power does not encompass individuals terminating medical treatment pursuant to their right of privacy. [Citation omitted.] The constitutional protection extends to third parties whose action is necessary to effectuate the exercise of that right where the individuals themselves would not be subject to prosecution or the third parties are charged as accessories to an act which could not be a crime.[351]

Thus, there is little risk of criminal liability for these actions.[352] The criminal trials of physicians in the United States for the deaths of unrelated terminally ill patients have involved alleged injections of substances to hasten death. Juries have acquitted the physicians. The results of these cases illustrate the difficulty in obtaining convictions when the patient is terminally ill, even in cases alleging active euthanasia. This is one reason prosecutors seldom pursue cases that involve withholding or withdrawing treatment from the terminally ill. The other reason is that it would be difficult to establish a duty to provide the withheld or withdrawn treatment. One case that did not go to trial supports this position. In 1983, two California physicians were charged with murder for terminating all life support, including intravenous feeding, of an irreversibly comatose patient upon the written request of the family. A California appellate court ordered the charges dismissed because the physicians had no legal duty to continue futile treatment and, thus, they did not unlawfully fail to fulfill a legal duty that could be the basis for a murder charge.[353]

Some investigations into the deaths of terminally ill patients have resulted in the prosecution of hospital personnel. Two nurses were accused of poisoning 11 patients at the Ann Arbor Veterans Administration Hospital by injecting a muscle relaxant into their intravenous tubes. The nurses were convicted on several of the counts in 1977, but when the court ordered a new trial, their indictments were dismissed.[354] A Maryland nurse was accused of unilaterally disconnecting three patients' respirators and turning down the oxygen flow to a fourth. Tried for one of the disconnection cases, she surrendered her license before the trial. The jury deadlocked, and she was not convicted. All charges were then dropped.[355] In 1992, the California Supreme Court upheld the murder conviction of a nurse.[356]

These cases demonstrate the importance of proper documentation of the circumstances under which medical treatment may be withheld or withdrawn so that authorized actions can be distinguished from unauthorized actions. Nurses and other hospital personnel should seek, and hospitals should require, appropriate documentation of decisions by the physician and the patient or family before withholding or withdrawing medical treatment, to assure appropriate treatment and to avoid the risk of investigation or prosecution in the absence of documented medical authorization of actions. As mentioned in the section on DNR orders, hospitals have been investigated for permitting actions to be taken without appropriate written orders.[357]

ASSISTED SUICIDE

There has been a renewed debate on whether individuals, especially those who are terminally ill, should be permitted to have assistance, especially assistance from physicians, in committing suicide.

This is not a new debate.[358] In the 1930s, proposed legislation authorizing assisted suicide was debated and defeated in the British House of Lords.[359] During the same period, a bill was defeated in the Nebraska legislature.[360] In the early 1950s, a bill was prepared for the New York legislature and widely debated in the public, but never formally introduced.[361]

Those who support assisted suicide have pursued four approaches: (1) publishing how-to books, (2) seeking legislation authorizing assisted suicide, (3) seeking judicial recognition of a right, or (4) taking matters into their own hands and assisting with suicides.

Numerous books that include descriptions of methods have been published.[362] In the past there have been attempts to stop the publication of such books, asserting that the publication alone is assisting suicide. These attempts have generally been unsuccessful.[363]

Several attempts were made in the 1990s to enact legislation. Although several bills have been introduced, none has been passed by a legislature. In several states there is a procedure by which laws can be adopted directly by the voters. Attempts have been made in several states to use this procedure to adopt assisted suicide laws. In 1991, Washington voters defeated an assisted suicide initiative.[364] In 1992, California voters defeated Proposition 161, which would have permitted physician-assisted suicide.[365] In 1994, the voters of Oregon approved The Oregon Death with Dignity Act.[366] However, in 1995, a federal judge enjoined the law before it could take effect.[367] At least one other such law has been enacted in another country.[368]

Some states have appointed committees to investigate the issue. Such groups consistently issue reports opposed to assisted suicide.[369]

Attempts have been made to convince courts to permit assisted suicide or to declare laws against assisted suicide unconstitutional or otherwise invalid. These attempts have been unsuccessful.[370] In 1994, a federal district court in Washington declared the state law against assisting suicide to be unconstitutional, but in 1995 that decision was overturned by the Ninth Circuit Court of Appeals.[371] In 1992, a California appellate court upheld a ban on assisted suicide, refusing to permit cryogenic preservation of the bodies of living terminally ill persons.[372]

Many states have laws that make assisting suicide a crime. Despite these laws there have been numerous well-publicized cases of assisting suicide. Frequently law enforcement officials and grand juries have decided not to bring charges.[373] In other cases, when prosecutions were pursued, juries refused to convict.[374] However, there have been several cases in which persons have been convicted for assisting suicide.[375]

No American health care provider has been convicted for assisting suicide. In the early 1990s, the most famous cases involved the efforts of Dr. Kevorkian in Michigan. The first case was in June 1990.[376] In 1991, his Michigan license to practice medicine was suspended.[377] By the end of 1994, Kevorkian allegedly had assisted at least 21 suicides.[378] Some of the cases against him were dismissed on various grounds, but they were reinstated by the Michigan appellate courts.[379] In 1994, a jury acquitted him of one assisted suicide.[380] In 1995, there were still pending charges.[381]

NOTES

1. *E.g.,* Fox v. Smith, 594 So.2d 596 (Miss. 1992) [removal of IUD during laparoscopy could be battery, where express directions not to remove]; Bommareddy v. Superior Court, 222 Cal. App.

3d 1017, 272 Cal. Rptr. 246 (1990), *rev. denied*, 1990 Cal. LEXIS 4989 (Oct. 30, 1990) [punitive damages allowable for battery of cataract surgery without consent when consent only to tear duct surgery]; Gaskin v. Goldwasser, 166 Ill. App. 3d 996, 520 N.E.2d 1085 (4th Dist.), *app. denied*, 121 Ill.2d 569, 526 N.E.2d 830 (1988); Throne v. Wandell, 176 Wis. 97, 186 N.W. 146 (1922); *but see* Gracia v. Meiselman, 220 N.J. Super. 317, 531 A.2d 1373 (App. Div. 1987) [no damages when beneficial surgery without consent properly performed].

2. *E.g.*, Baltzell v. Buskirk, 752 S.W.2d 902 (Mo. Ct. App. 1988); Kohoutek v. Hafner, 383 N.W. 2d 295 (Minn. 1986); Moser v. Stallings, 387 N.W.2d 599 (Iowa 1986).

3. *E.g.*, Fox v. Smith, 594 So.2d 596 (Miss. 1992); Marino v. Ballestas, 749 F.2d 162 (3d Cir. 1984) [battery action permitted]; Hales v. Pittman, 118 Ariz. 305, 576 P.2d 493 (1978) [battery action permitted]; ARIZ. REV. STAT. ANN. § 12-562(B) (1982) [battery action eliminated by statute]; Rubino v. DeFretias, 638 F. Supp. 182 (D. Ariz. 1986) [Arizona statute unconstitutional].

4. Truman v. Thomas, 27 Cal. 3d 285, 165 Cal. Rptr. 308, 611 P.2d 902 (1980).

5. Battenfeld v. Gregory, 247 N.J. Super. 538, 589 A.2d 1059 (App. Div. 1991).

6. *E.g.*, Foflygen v. Zemel, 420 Pa. Super. 18, 615 A.2d 1345 (1992), *app. denied*, 535 Pa. 619, 629 A.2d 1380 (1993) [Pennsylvania Unfair Trade Practices and Consumer Protection Law not applicable to medical services, so cannot claim misrepresentation of stomach stapling procedure under act]; Lareau v. Page, 39 F.3d 384 (1st Cir. 1994) [physician did not violate Massachusetts Consumer Protection Act by arranging for patient to be informed of theoretical risk of brain tumor from previously administered contrast medium, allegedly to trigger statute of limitations period without causing awareness of negligence]; Benoy v. Simons, 66 Wash. App. 56, 831 P.2d 167, *rev. denied*, 120 Wash. 2d 1014, 844 P.2d 435 (1992); *but see* Quimby v. Fine, 45 Wash. App. 175, 724 P.2d 403 (1986), *rev. denied*, 107 Wash. 2d 1032 (1987) [Consumer Protection Act claim can be stated for lack of informed consent resulting from dishonest, unfair practices motivated by financial gain].

7. *E.g.*, ILL. REV. STAT. ch. 111 1/2, § 7304 [required written consent], §§ 7307–7308, 7311 [exceptions].

8. *E.g.*, Kelly v. Gershkoff, 112 R.I. 507, 312 A.2d 211 (1973) [jury can find informed consent without documentary evidence].

9. O'Brien v. Cunard S.S. Co., 154 Mass. 272, 28 N.E. 266 (1891); *see also* Hernandez v. United States, 465 F. Supp. 1071 (D. Kan. 1979) [consent implied from submitting to operation]; Busalacchi v. Vogel, 429 So.2d 217 (La. Ct. App. 1983) [no objection to preoperative medication].

10. *E.g.*, Kozup v. Georgetown Univ., 271 U.S. App. D.C. 182, 851 F.2d 437 (1988) [jury question whether life-threatening emergency existed to justify transfusions that caused AIDS].

11. *E.g.*, Rodriguez v. Pino, 634 So.2d 681 (Fla. 3d DCA), *rev. denied*, 645 So.2d 454 (Fla. 1994); Mulloy v. Hop Sang [1935], 1 W.W.R. 714 (Alberta Sup. Ct.); *but see* discussion of informed refusal doctrine which some courts have used to disregard express refusals, text at notes 220–222.

12. Jackovach v. Yocom, 212 Iowa 914, 237 N.W. 444 (1931); *accord* Stafford v. Louisiana State Univ., 448 So.2d 852 (La. Ct. App. 1984) [no liability for emergency amputation after good-faith attempt to contact family].

13. *E.g.*, Sullivan v. Montgomery, 155 Misc. 448, 279 N.Y.S. 575 (City Ct. 1935) [pain is sufficient emergency]; Cunningham v. Yankton Clinic, 262 N.W.2d 508 (S.D. 1978) [pain is not sufficient].

14. *E.g.*, Douget v. Touro Infirmary, 537 So.2d 251 (La. Ct. App. 1988) [emergency removal of spleen, kidney during anterior lumbar puncture justified]; Kennedy v. Parrott, 243 N.C. 355, 90 S.E.2d 754 (1956).

15. *See* Lipscomb v. Memorial Hosp., 733 F.2d 332 (4th Cir. 1984) [affirming jury award for nonemergency extension despite extension provision in consent form]; Kennis v. Mercy Hosp. Med. Ctr., 491 N.W.2d 161 (Iowa 1992) [battery claim for cystostomy procedure during surgery to reverse intestinal bypass; expert testimony required to show whether totally different type of treatment or inherent complication].

16. *E.g.*, Szkorla v. Vecchione, 231 Cal. App. 3d 1541, 283 Cal. Rptr. 219 (4th Dist. 1991), *rev. dismissed*, 13 Cal. Rptr. 2d 53, 838 P.2d 781 (Cal. 1992) [subcutaneous mastectomy performed instead of breast reduction].

17. F.J. Skelly, *The payoff of informed consent*, AM. MED. NEWS, Aug. 1, 1994, at 11.

18. *See* Annotation, *Modern status of views as to general measure of physician's duty to inform patient of risks of proposed treatment*, 88 A.L.R. 3D 1008.

19. *E.g.*, Culbertson v. Mernitz, 602 N.E.2d 98 (Ind. 1992); Eccleston v. Chait, 241 Neb. 961, 492 N.W.2d 860 (1992); Sherwood v. Carter, 119 Idaho 246, 805 P.2d 452 (1991); Natanson v. Kline, 186 Kan. 393, 350 P.2d 1093 (1960).

20. *E.g.*, Korman v. Mallin, 858 P.2d 1145 (Alaska 1993); Largey v. Rothman, 110 N.J. 204, 540 A.2d 504 (1988); Rook v. Trout, 113 Idaho 652, 747 P.2d 61(1987); Pauscher v. Iowa Methodist Med. Ctr., 408 N.W.2d 355 (Iowa 1987).

21. Canterbury v. Spence, 150 D.C. App. 263, 464 F.2d 772, 787, *cert. denied*, 409 U.S. 1064 (1972).

22. *E.g.*, Moure v. Raeuchle, 529 Pa. 394, 604 A.2d 1003 (1992).

23. *See* Annotation, *Medical malpractice: Liability for failure of physician to inform patient of alternative modes of diagnosis and treatment*, 38 A.L.R. 4TH 900.

24. *E.g.*, Wachter v. United States, 689 F. Supp. 1420 (D. Md. 1988), *aff'd*, 877 F.2d 257 (4th Cir. 1989) [need not disclose alternative not in general use or subject of definitive study]; Smith v. Reisig, 686 P.2d 285 (Okla. 1984); Marino v. Ballestas, 749 F.2d 162 (3d Cir. 1984) [parents must be told alternatives to surgery for child]; Logan v. Greenwich Hosp. Ass'n, 191 Conn. 282, 465 A.2d 294 (1983) [feasible alternatives involving greater risks must also be disclosed].

25. Hales v. Pittman, 118 Ariz. 305, 576 P.2d 493 (1978).

26. Givens v. Cracco, 607 So.2d 727 (La. Ct. App. 1992).

27. Arato v. Avedon, 5 Cal. 4th 1172, 23 Cal. Rptr. 2d 131, 858 P.2d 598 (1993); N. Hershey, *California Supreme Court recognizes limit on physicians' disclosure obligation*, 11 HOSP. L. NEWSLETTER (Apr. 1994), at 5.

28. Hidding v. Williams, 578 So.2d 1192 (La. Ct. App. 1991).

29. *E.g.*, Faya v. Almaraz, 329 Md. 435, 620 A.2d 327 (1993) [jury permitted to determine HIV-infected surgeon negligent in failing to inform patients, could be liable even when they did not get infected]; *see also* Kerins v. Hartley, 17 Cal. App. 4th 713, 21 Cal. Rptr. 2d 621 (2d Dist. 1993) [when patient asked about surgeon's health, she conditioned her consent on being operated on by healthy surgeon, so nondisclosure of HIV-positive status established cause of action for battery], *transferred*, 28 Cal. Rptr. 2d 151, 868 P.2d 906 (Cal. 1994), *on transfer*, 27 Cal. App. 4th 1062, 33 Cal. Rptr. 2d 172 (2d Dist. 1994) [statistically insignificant chance that patient exposed to AIDS during surgery by infected doctor precluded recovery for emotional distress from fear of AIDS].

30. Estate of Behringer v. Medical Ctr., 249 N.J. Super. 597, 592 A.2d 1251 (1991).

31. Wachter v. United States, 877 F.2d 257 (4th Cir. 1989).

32. Moore v. Regents of Univ. of Cal., 51 Cal. 3d 120, 271 Cal. Rptr. 146, 793 P.2d 479 (1990), *cert. denied*, 499 U.S. 936 (1991).

33. Bowlin v. Duke Univ., 108 N.C. App. 145, 423 S.E.2d 320 (1992), *rev. denied*, 333 N.C. 461, 427 S.E.2d 618 (1993) [bone marrow harvest].

34. Johnson by Adler v. Kokemoor, 188 Wis.2d 202, 525 N.W.2d 71 (Ct. App. 1994).

35. Bray v. Hill, 517 N.W.2d 223 (Iowa Ct. App. 1994).

36. Arato v. Avedon, 5 Cal. 4th 1172, 23 Cal. Rptr. 2d 131, 858 P.2d 598 (1993); *but see* J.V. Truhe, Jr., *Quality assessment in the '90s: Legal implications for hospitals*, 26 J. HEALTH & HOSP. L. 171, 176–77 (1993) [posing question whether knowledge of complication rates, other QA/TQM data has to be disclosed for informed consent].

37. Johnson by Adler v. Kokemoor, 188 Wis.2d 202, 525 N.W.2d 71 (Ct. App. 1994).

38. *E.g.,* Jones v. Papp, 782 S.W.2d 236 (Tex. Ct. App. 1989) [consent form met standard established by Texas Medical Disclosure Panel].

39. Zacher v. Petty, 312 Or. 590, 826 P.2d 619 (1992).

40. *E.g.,* Boyd v. Louisiana Med. Mut. Ins. Co., 593 So.2d 427 (La. Ct. App. 1991), *cert. denied*, 594 So.2d 877 (La. 1992); McKinley v. Stripling, 763 S.W.2d 407 (Tex. 1989); Latham v. Hayes, 495 So.2d 453 (Miss. 1986); Pardy v. United States, 783 F.2d 710 (7th Cir. 1986); Canterbury v. Spence, 150 U.S. App. D.C. 263, 464 F.2d 772, *cert. denied*, 409 U.S. 1064 (1972).

41. *E.g.,* Arena v. Gingrich, 305 Or. 1, 748 P.2d 547 (1988); Wilkinson v. Vesey, 110 R.I. 606, 295 A.2d 676 (1972).

42. Snawder v. Cohen, 804 F. Supp. 910 (W.D. Ky. 1992), *aff'd on other grounds*, 5 F.3d 1012 (6th Cir. 1993).

43. Begin v. Richmond, 150 Vt. 517, 555 A.2d 363 (1988).

44. Gouse v. Cassel, 532 Pa. 197, 615 A.2d 331 (1992).

45. *See* Wu v. Spence, 413 Pa. Super. 352, 605 A.2d 395 (1992), *app. dismissed*, 534 Pa. 309, 632 A.2d 1294 (1993) [informed consent not required for drug administration]; *accord* Boyer v. Smith, 345 Pa. Super. 66, 497 A.2d 646 (1985); *but see* Jones v. Philadelphia College of Osteopathic Med., 813 F. Supp. 1125 (E.D. Pa. 1993) [transfusion part of surgery, so informed consent must be obtained].

46. *E.g.,* Shinn v. St. James Mercy Hosp., 675 F. Supp. 94 (W.D. N.Y. 1987), *aff'd without op.*, 847 F.2d 836 (2d Cir. 1988); Crouch v. Most, 78 N.M. 406, 432 P.2d 250 (1967).

47. *E.g.,* Shultz v. Rice, 809 F.2d 643 (10th Cir. 1986); Pardy v. United States, 783 F.2d 710 (7th Cir. 1986).

48. Lester v. Aetna Casualty & Sur. Co., 240 F.2d 676 (5th Cir.), *cert. denied*, 354 U.S. 923 (1957).

49. Nishi v. Hartwell, 52 Haw. 188 and 296, 473 P.2d 116 (1970).

50. Putensen v. Clay Adams, Inc., 12 Cal. App. 3d 1062, 91 Cal. Rptr. 319 (1st Dist. 1970).

51. *E.g.,* Wachter v. United States, 877 F.2d 257 (4th Cir. 1989).

52. GA. CODE ANN. § 31-9-6(d) (1985).

53. *E.g.,* Young v. Yarn, 136 Ga. App. 737, 222 S.E.2d 113 (1975).

54. GA. CODE ANN. § 31-9-6.1 (1988 Supp.).

55. *E.g.,* Inge v. Fernandes, No.1-87-316, 1988 WL 38866 (Ohio Ct. App. Apr. 22, 1988), *as discussed in* 21 J. HEALTH & HOSP. L. 200 (1988); Sangiuolo v. Leventhal, 132 Misc. 2d 680, 505 N.Y.S.2d 507 (Sup. Ct. 1986); Hill v. Seward, 122 Misc. 2d 375, 470 N.Y.S.2d 971 (Sup. Ct. 1983); *but see* Prooth v. Wallsh, 105 Misc. 2d 603, 432 N.Y.S.2d 663 (Sup. Ct. 1980) [duty of referring physician to advise patient concerning treatment by referring physician]; Kashkin v. Mt. Sinai Med. Ctr., 142 Misc. 2d 863, 538 N.Y.S.2d 686 (Sup. Ct. 1989) [referring physician has duty to inform of risks if he orders specific procedure].

56. Annotation, *Recovery by patient on whom surgery or other treatment was performed by other than physician who patient believed would perform it*, 39 A.L.R. 4TH 1034.

57. Forlano v. Hughes, 393 Mass. 502, 471 N.E.2d 1315 (1984).

58. Kenner v. Northern Ill. Med. Ctr., 164 Ill. App. 3d 366, 517 N.E.2d 1137 (2d Dist. 1987).

59. *E.g.*, Johnson v. McMurray, 461 So.2d 775 (Ala. 1984).

60. *E.g.*, Johnson v. Sears, Roebuck & Co., 113 N.M. 736, 832 P.2d 797 (Ct. App.), *cert. denied*, 113 N.M. 744, 832 P.2d 1223 (1992); Pauscher v. Iowa Methodist Med. Ctr., 408 N.W.2d 355 (Iowa 1987); Fiorentino v. Wenger, 19 N.Y.2d 407, 280 N.Y.S.2d 373, 227 N.E.2d 296 (1967); *but see* Creech v. Roberts, 908 F.2d 75 (6th Cir. 1990), *cert. denied*, 499 U.S. 975 (1991) [hospital vicariously liable for failure of staff physician to obtain informed consent where no patient relationship with physician before coming to center for services].

61. *E.g.*, Keel v. St. Elizabeth Med. Ctr., 842 S.W.2d 860 (Ky. 1992) [hospital liable for failing to disclose risks of CT scan with contrast since hospital performed procedure]; Magana v. Elie, 108 Ill. App. 3d 1028, 439 N.E.2d 1319 (2d Dist. 1982).

62. *E.g.*, Urban v. Spohn Hosp., 869 S.W.2d 450 (Tex. Ct. App. 1993); Schloendorff v. Society of N.Y. Hosp., 211 N.Y. 125, 105 N.E. 92 (1914).

63. *See* note 97, *infra*.

64. *But see* Ritter v. Delaney, 790 S.W.2d 29 (Tex. Ct. App. 1990) [hospital, referring physician not responsible for surgeon obtaining informed consent, even where pursuant to physician orders hospital nurse obtained signature on hospital consent form]; Frye v. Medicare-Glaser Corp., 153 Ill.2d 26, 605 N.E.2d 557 (1992) [when pharmacist warned of one side effect of drug, did not assume responsibility to warn of all side effects which was still responsibility of physician].

65. *E.g.*, Smogor v. Enke, 874 F.2d 295 (5th Cir. 1989) [cardiologist may delegate disclosure of risks to laboratory technician].

66. *E.g.*, Barner v. Gorman, 605 So.2d 805 (Miss. 1992) [consent form which did not mention possibility of recurrent disfiguring scar from reconstructive surgery not sufficient to preclude suit, especially where obtained by licensed practical nurse; signature should be obtained by physician where possible]; Hoffson v. Orentreich, 144 Misc. 2d 411, 543 N.Y.S.2d 242 (Sup. Ct. 1989), *aff'd as modified on other grounds*, 168 A.D.2d 243, 562 N.Y.S.2d 479 (1st Dep't 1990).

67. *E.g.*, Graham v. Ryan, 641 So.2d 677 (La. Ct. App. 1994), *cert. denied*, 648 So.2d 403 (La. 1994) [adult children of deceased surgery patient failed to rebut presumption of informed consent from written consent]; Jones v. United States, 720 F. Supp. 355 (S.D. N.Y. 1989) [documentation showed informed consent obtained]; Blincoe v. Luessenhop, 669 F. Supp. 513 (D. D.C. 1987) [required disclosures made, documented in two consent forms]; *but see* Jones v. Philadelphia College of Osteopathic Medicine, 813 F. Supp. 1125 (E.D. Pa. 1993) [claim stated against college and hospital based upon contents of consent form because through preparing form they gratuitously undertook obligation to obtain informed consent].

68. Joint Commission on Accreditation of Healthcare Organizations, 1995 COMPREHENSIVE AC-CREDITATION MANUAL FOR HOSPITALS 397 [cited hereinafter as 1995 Joint Commission CAMH].

69. Sinclair by Sinclair v. Block, 534 Pa. 563, 633 A.2d 1137 (1993).

70. *E.g.*, Cross v. Trapp, 170 W.Va. 459, 294 S.E.2d 446 (1982); Rogers v. Lumbermens Mut. Casualty Co., 119 So.2d 649 (La. Ct. App. 1960).

71. *E.g.*, State Cent. Collection Unit v. Columbia Med. Plan, 300 Md. 318, 478 A.2d 303 (1984) [valid assignment in registration form].

72. *E.g.*, Moser v. Stallings, 387 N.W.2d 599 (Iowa 1986).

73. *E.g.*, Blincoe v. Luessenhop, 669 F. Supp. 513 (D. D.C. 1987).

74. *E.g.*, Barner v. Gorman, 605 So.2d 805 (Miss. 1992) [signed consent not specific to procedure insufficient to bar action]; MacDonald v. United States, 767 F. Supp. 1295 (M.D. Pa. 1991), *award of damages*, 781 F. Supp. 320, *aff'd without op.*, 983 F.2d 1051 (3d Cir. 1992) [failure to obtain informed consent notwithstanding consent form—no risks or alternatives ever described to patient]; Hansbrough v. Kosyak, 141 Ill. App. 3d 538, 490 N.E. 2d 181 (4th Dist. 1986);

Pegram v. Sisco, 406 F. Supp. 776 (W.D. Ark. 1976), *aff'd without op.*, 547 F.2d 1172 (8th Cir. 1976).

75. 42 C.F.R. §§ 441.250–441.259 [sterilization]; 45 C.F.R. pt. 46 [research].

76. *E.g.*, Bedel v. University OB-GYN Assoc., Inc., 76 Ohio App. 3d 742, 603 N.E.2d 342 (1991).

77. *E.g.*, Gordon v. Neviaser, 478 A.2d 292 (D.C. 1984); Siegel v. Mt. Sinai Hosp., 62 Ohio App. 2d 12, 403 N.E.2d 202 (1978).

78. *E.g.*, Zinermon v. Burch, 494 U.S. 113 (1990) [person who signed voluntary admission form for mental hospital could bring 42 U.S.C.A. § 1983 action for deprivation of liberty based on allegation incapacitated due to medication, disorientation when form signed]; Demers v. Gerety, 87 N.M. 52, 529 P.2d 278 (Ct. App.), *cert. denied*, 87 N.M. 47, 529 P.2d 273 (1974) [sedation can render patient incapacitated], *on appeal after remand*, Gerety v. Demers, 92 N.M. 396, 589 P.2d 180 (1978) [jury verdict for physician affirmed]; Grannum v. Berard, 70 Wash. 2d 304, 422 P.2d 812 (1967) [patient had capacity to consent to surgery despite sedatives].

79. *E.g.*, Kaufer et al., *Revising medical consent forms: An empirical model and test*, 11 LAW, MED. & HEALTH CARE 155 (1983).

80. *See* S. Woloshin et al., *Language barriers in medicine in the United States*, 273 J.A.M.A. 724 (1995).

81. *See* Ramirez v. Plough, Inc., 6 Cal. 4th 539, 25 Cal. Rptr. 2d 97, 863 P.2d 167 (1993) [drug manufacturer not liable for labeling nonprescription drug only in English in accordance with FDA regulations].

82. *See* Aikins v. St. Helena Hosp., 843 F. Supp. 1329 (N.D. Cal. 1994) [denial of dismissal of Rehabilitation Act suit for allegedly failing to provide interpreter services to deaf woman while husband was in hospital unconscious and hospital looked to her for decisions].

83. *E.g.*, Fox v. Smith, 594 So.2d 596 (Miss. 1992); Mullany v. Eiseman, 125 A.D.2d 457, 509 N.Y.S.2d 387 (2d Dep't 1986); *see also* Cook v. Highland Hosp., 168 N.C. 250, 84 S.E. 352 (1915) [patient did not waive right to change mind by signing agreement to abide by hospital rules, so free to leave].

84. Tatham v. Hoke, 469 F. Supp. 914 (W.D. N.C. 1979), *aff'd without op.*, 622 F.2d 584, 587 (4th Cir. 1980); *see also* Emory Univ. v. Porubiansky, 248 Ga. 391, 282 S.E.2d 903 (1981) [dental school exculpatory clause invalid].

85. *E.g.*, Busalacchi v. Vogel, 429 So.2d 217 (La. Ct. App. 1983).

86. *E.g.*, Hondroulis v. Schuhmacher, 553 So.2d 398 (La. 1989) [statute establishes rebuttable presumption of consent], *on remand*, 612 So.2d 859 (La. Ct. App. 1992) [judgment against physician affirmed}, *cert. denied*, 615 So.2d 335 (La. 1993).

87. NEV. REV. STAT. § 41A.110; Allan v. Levy, 109 Nev. 46, 846 P.2d 274 (1993) [consent form did not meet requirement of state statute].

88. IOWA CODE ANN. § 147.137.

89. Foard v. Jarman, 326 N.C. 24, 387 S.E.2d 162 (1990) [informed consent claim barred by admission of reading and understanding pamphlet]; *see also* G. Borzo, *CIGNA gives new life to patient empowerment initiative*, AM. MED. NEWS, Sept. 19, 1994, at 1 [sent outcome-based videotapes to patients to educate about treatment options].

90. *E.g.*, Hanson v. Parkside Surgery Ctr., 872 F.2d 745 (6th Cir.), *cert. denied*, 493 U.S. 944 (1989) [claim permitted despite videotape, but jury found for defendant physician].

91. 45 C.F.R. pt. 46 [HHS].

92. 45 C.F.R. § 46.116(a).

93. 45 C.F.R. § 46.101(b).

94. 45 C.F.R. § 46.110; *see* 46 FED. REG. 8,392 (Jan. 26, 1981) for the initial list of approved categories.

95. 21 C.F.R. pts. 50, 56, 312, 314, 812.

96. *E.g.*, N.Y. Pub. Health Law §§ 2440–2446.

97. *E.g.*, Anderson v. George H. Lanier Mem. Hosp., 982 F.2d 1513 (11th Cir. 1993) [use of experimental intraocular lens]; Friter v. IOLAB Corp., 414 Pa. Super. 622, 607 A.2d 1111 (1992) [use of experimental intraocular lens].

98. *See Doctors admit ignoring dying patients' wishes*, N.Y. Times, Jan. 14, 1993, at A12 [survey in Am. J. Pub. Health, Jan. 1993]; J.E. Brody, *The rights of a dying patient are often misunderstood, even by medical professionals*, N.Y. Times, Jan. 27, 1993, at B7.

99. Patient Self-Determination Act of 1990, Pub. L. No. 101-508, § 4206(a)(2), 104 Stat. 1388-116 (*codified in* 42 U.S.C.A. §§ 1395cc(a)(1)(Q), (f) [hospitals], 1395i-3(c)(1)(E) [skilled nursing facilities], 1395l(r) [prepaid plans], 1395mm(c)(8) [HMOs & competitive medical plans], 1395bbb(a)(6) [home health agencies]; 42 C.F.R. §§ 489.100–489.104, *as first published in* 57 Fed. Reg. 8194 (Mar. 6, 1992) *and amended by final regulations in* 60 Fed. Reg. 33,262 (June 27, 1995).

100. *E.g.*, Schloendorff v. Society of N.Y. Hosp., 211 N.Y. 125, 105 N.E. 92 (1914), *overruled in part on other grounds*, Bing v. Thunig, 2 N.Y.2d 656, 163 N.Y.S.2d 3, 143 N.E.2d 3 (1957).

101. In re Storar, 52 N.Y.2d 363, 438 N.Y.S.2d 266, 420 N.E.2d 64, *cert. denied*, 454 U.S. 858 (1981).

102. Choice in Dying, Right-to-Die Law Digest (Mar. 1995); *see also* Annotation, *Living wills: Validity, construction, and effect*, 49 A.L.R. 4th 812.

103. 9B U.L.A. 609 (1987), 145 (1994 Supp.).

104. 9B U.L.A. 127 (1994 Supp.).

105. *Id.*

106. *Id.;* John F. Kennedy Mem. Hosp. v. Bludworth, 452 So.2d 921 (Fla. 1984).

107. *Id.*

108. *E.g.*, Fla. Stat. § 765.15; *contra* Ark. Stat. Ann. §§ 20-17-201–20-17-218.

109. *E.g.*, Camp v. White, 510 So.2d 166 (Ala. 1987) [patient]; In re Grant, 109 Wash. 2d 545, 747 P.2d 445 (1987), *corrected*, 757 P.2d 534 (Wash. 1988) [family]; Corbett v. D'Alessandro, 487 So.2d 368 (Fla. 2d DCA), *rev. denied*, 492 So.2d 1331 (Fla. 1986) [family].

110. 42 U.S.C.A. §§ 1395c, 1395d (a) (4), (d) (1), 1395f(i), 1395y(a)(1)(C), 1395x(dd) [Medicare]; 42 C.F.R. pt. 418 [Medicare hospice conditions of participation]; Fla. Stat. §§ 400.601–400.614 [state licensure]; *see also* Bulkin and Lukashok, *Rx for dying: The case for hospice*, 318 N. Engl. J. Med. 376 (1988).

111. Cruzan v. Harmon, 760 S.W.2d 408 (Mo. *en banc* 1988).

112. Cruzan v. Director, Mo. Dept. of Health, 497 U.S. 261 (1990), *aff'g*, 760 S.W.2d 408 (Mo. 1988) (*en banc*); R.D. Miller, *The Supreme Court speaks on treatment refusal: The* Cruzan *case*, 7 Hosp. L. Newsletter (Oct. 1990), at 1.

113. *E.g.*, In re Storar, 52 N.Y.2d 363, 438 N.Y.S.2d 266, 420 N.E.2d 64, *cert. denied*, 454 U.S. 858 (1981).

114. In re Osborne, 294 A.2d 372 (D.C. 1972); *see also* In re Brown, 478 So.2d 1033 (Miss. 1985) [state interest in preserving life of only witness to murder not sufficient to overcome right of adult Jehovah's Witness to refuse transfusion].

115. *E.g.*, In re Quinlan, 70 N.J. 10, 355 A.2d 647, *cert. denied sub nom.*, Garger v. New Jersey, 429 U.S. 922 (1976).

116. Cruzan v. Director, Mo. Dept. of Health, 497 U.S. 261, 279 n.7 (1990).

117. John F. Kennedy Mem. Hosp. v. Bludworth, 452 So.2d 921 (Fla. 1984); In re Guardianship of Browning, 568 So.2d 4 (Fla. 1989).

118. *See* Annotation, *Power of courts or other public agencies, in the absence of statutory authority, to order compulsory medical care for adult,* 9 A.L.R. 3D 1391.

119. Jacobson v. Massachusetts, 197 U.S. 11 (1905).

120. Reynolds v. McNichols, 488 F.2d 1378 (10th Cir. 1973); *see also Law on AIDS testing of prostitutes is upheld,* N.Y. TIMES, Jan. 2, 1991, at A9 [decision by 1st Dist. of Cal. Ct. App.]; *but see* Hill v. Evans, No. 91-A-626-N (M.D. Ala. Oct. 7, 1993), *as discussed in* 2 HEALTH L. RPTR. (BNA) 1563 (1993) [state law allowing physician to test patient for AIDS without consent when physician thinks patient at risk violates equal protection, but other exceptions to consent upheld where necessary to protect other health workers or may be necessary to change treatment] [hereinafter HEALTH L. RPTR. cited as H.L.R.].

121. Zaire v. Dalsheim, 698 F. Supp. 57 (S.D. N.Y. 1988), *aff'd without op.,* 904 F.2d 33 (2d Cir. 1990).

122. *Some hospitals reviving quarantine to fight spread of new TB strain,* MOD. HEALTHCARE, Nov. 28, 1992, at 4A [holding patients against their will in Mass., N.Y., Cal.]; *Tuberculosis spreads civil rights concerns,* WALL ST. J., Feb. 16, 1993, at B10 [NYC quarantined over 90 people in 2 years]; L.O. Gostin, *Controlling the resurgent tuberculosis epidemic: A 50-state survey of TB statutes and proposals for reform,* 269 J.A.M.A. 255 (1993); *Confinement for TB: Weighing rights vs. health,* N.Y. TIMES, Nov. 21, 1993, at 1 [15 people held in NYC under guard]; *San Joaquin County officials resort to arrests in TB treatment crackdown,* 3 H.L.R. 1702 (1994); *TB control act quarantine provisions include adequate procedural protection,* 4 H.L.R. 58 (1995) [TN]; T. Flowers, *Quarantining the noncompliant TB patient: Catching the "red snapper,"* 28 J. HEALTH & HOSP. L. 95 (1995).

123. *E.g.,* O'Connor v. Donaldson, 422 U.S. 563 (1975); Addington v. Texas, 441 U.S. 418 (1979) [mental illness must be proved by clear, convincing evidence]; Schell v. State Dep't of Mental Health & Mental Retardation, 606 So.2d 1149 (Ala. Civ. App. 1992) [patient mentally ill, dangerous despite control of behavior by drugs, where patient would not comply without supervision]; Glass v. Mayas, 984 F.2d 55 (2d Cir. 1993) [qualified immunity for doctors, nurses in 42 U.S.C.A. § 1983 challenge to involuntary commitment; objectively reasonable belief in dangerousness]; In re Blodgett, 510 N.W.2d 910 (Minn.), *cert. denied,* 115 S. Ct. 146 (U.S. 1994) [state may authorize commitment of persons with "psychopathic personality" even if not medically recognized as "mentally ill"].

124. *E.g.,* Dudley v. State, 730 S.W.2d 51 (Tex. Ct. App. 1987) [involuntary alcoholism treatment].

125. O'Connor v. Donaldson, 422 U.S. 563 (1975).

126. *E.g.,* Thompson v. State Dep't of Mental Health & Mental Retardation, 620 So.2d 25 (Ala. Civ. App. 1992), *cert. denied,* 1993 Ala. LEXIS 455 (Mar. 26, 1993) [dangerousness to self proved by setting fires and assaultive behavior when not taking drugs, which she refused to do outside facility due to lack of insight into illness, and by refusal to stop smoking, comply with diet, or learn to self-administer insulin, despite diabetes and precancerous throat lesion]; In re E.J.H., 493 N.W.2d 841 (Iowa 1992) [mere status as untreated substance abuser did not justify commitment without evidence of dangerousness to self or others].

127. Parham v. J.L. & J.R., 442 U.S. 584 (1979); Secretary of Public Welfare v. Institutionalized Juveniles, 442 U.S. 640 (1979).

128. Barclay v. Campbell, 704 S.W.2d 8 (Tex. 1986).

129. *See* Sherman v. Four County Counseling Ctr., 987 F.2d 397 (7th Cir. 1993) [qualified immunity protected hospital for involuntary medication during emergency commitment].

130. *See* In re C.E., 161 Ill. 2d 200, 641 N.E.2d 345 (Ill. 1994), [law authorizing court ordered involuntary psychotropic drugs is constitutional], *cert. denied,* 115 S. Ct. 1956 (U.S. 1995); *see also* Annotation, *Nonconsensual treatment of involuntarily committed mentally ill persons with*

neuroleptic or antipsychotic drugs as violative of state constitutional guaranty, 74 A.L.R. 4TH 1099.

131. *E.g.*, In re B., 609 P.2d 747 (Okla. 1980); State ex rel. Jones v. Gerhardstein, 141 Wis. 2d 710, 416 N.W.2d 883 (1987).

132. *E.g.*, IOWA CODE ANN. § 229.1(2).

133. *E.g.*, Jarvis v. Levine, 418 N.W.2d 139 (Minn. 1988); In re Guardianship of Roe, 383 Mass. 415, 421 N.E.2d 40 (1981); Rogers v. Commissioner of Dep't of Mental Health, 390 Mass. 489, 458 N.E.2d 308 (1983); *contra* United States v. Charters, 863 F.2d 302 (4th Cir. 1988), *cert. denied*, 494 U.S. 1016 (1990).

134. Raleigh Fitkin-Paul Morgan Mem. Hosp. v. Anderson, 42 N.J. 421, 201 A.2d 537, *cert. denied*, 377 U.S. 985 (1964); *accord* Crouse-Irving Mem. Hosp., Inc. v. Paddock, 127 Misc. 2d 101, 485 N.Y.S.2d 443 (Sup. Ct. 1985).

135. *E.g.*, In re Bentley, Misc. No. 65-74 (D.C. Super. Ct. Apr. 25, 1974); Mercy Hosp., Inc. v. Jackson, 62 Md. App. 409, 489 A.2d 1130 (1985), *vacated as moot*, 306 Md. 556, 510 A.2d 562 (1986).

136. Jefferson v. Griffin Spalding County Hosp. Auth., 247 Ga. 86, 274 S.E.2d 457 (1981); *see also* Nelson and Mulliken, *Compelled medical treatment of pregnant women: Life, liberty, and law in conflict*, 259 J.A.M.A. 1060 (1988).

137. Taft v. Taft, 388 Mass. 331, 446 N.E.2d 395 (1983).

138. In re A.C., 533 A.2d 611 (D.C. 1987), *vacated for reh'g en banc*, 539 A.2d 203 (D.C. 1988).

139. In re A.C., 573 A.2d 1235 (D.C. 1990) (*en banc*); H. Neale, *Mother's rights prevail: In re A.C. and the status of forced obstetrical intervention in the District of Columbia*, 23 J. HEALTH & HOSP. L. 208 (1990).

140. Baby Boy Doe v. Mother Doe, 260 Ill. App. 3d 392, 632 N.E.2d 326 (1st Dist. Dec. 14, 1993 with formal opinion Apr. 5, 1994) [mentally competent pregnant woman has right to refuse caesarean operation even if refusal will harm her child], *rev. denied*, Ill. Sup. Ct. (Dec. 16, 1993), *denial of motion to remand*, 114 S. Ct. 652 (U.S. 1993), *cert. denied*, 114 S. Ct. 1198 (U.S. 1994); *Illinois is seeking to force woman to have caesarean*, N.Y. TIMES, Dec. 14, 1993, at A11; *Baby whose mother refused C-section appears healthy*, MIAMI [FL] HERALD, Dec. 31, 1993, at 6A.

141. *A mother sacrifices life so twins can be born*, N.Y. TIMES, Feb. 13, 1995, at A7.

142. See *Propriety of surgically invading incompetent or minor for benefit of third party*, 4 A.L.R. 5TH 1000.

143. McFall v. Shimp, 10 D. & C.3d 90 (Pa. C.P. Ct. Allegheny County 1978); A. Meisel and L. Roth, *Must a man be his cousin's keeper?* 8 HASTINGS CENTER REPORT, Oct. 1978, at 5.

144. *E.g.*, Head v. Colloton, 331 N.W.2d 870 (Iowa 1983).

145. Bosze v. Curran, No. 87 M1 4599 (Ill. Cir. Ct. Cook County July 18, 1990), *as discussed in* 23 J. HEALTH & HOSP. L. 282 (1990).

146. Curran v. Bosze, No. 70501 (Ill. Aug. 10, 1990), *as discussed in* 23 J. HEALTH & HOSP. L. 282 (1990).

147. Curran v. Bosze, 141 Ill. 2d 473, 566 N.E.2d 1319 (1990); P. Hughes and R. Wood, *Comment: Curran v. Bosze; Disposing of an incompetent donor consent case: The role of parental autonomy and bodily integrity*, 24 J. HEALTH & HOSP. L. 88 (1991).

148. Application of President & Directors of Georgetown College, Inc., 118 U.S. App. D.C. 80, 331 F.2d 1000, *reh'g denied*, 118 U.S. App. D.C. 90, 331 F.2d 1010, *cert. denied*, 377 U.S. 978 (1964).

149. In re Osborne, 294 A.2d 372 (D.C. 1972).

150. Public Health Trust v. Wons, 541 So.2d 96 (Fla. 1989).

151. In re Dubreuil, 629 So.2d 819 (Fla. 1993).

152. *See* Annotation, *Admissibility, in criminal case, of physical evidence obtained without consent by surgical removal from person's body*, 41 A.L.R. 4TH 60.

153. Rochin v. California, 342 U.S. 165 (1951).

154. Breithaupt v. Abram, 352 U.S. 432 (1957).

155. Schmerber v. California, 384 U.S. 757 (1966); Graham v. Connor, 490 U.S. 386 (1989) [force seizing person must meet "objectively reasonable" standard]; *see also* Hammer v. Gross, 932 F.2d 842 (9th Cir.), *cert. denied*, 502 U.S. 980 (1991) [forcible blood sample from suspect in DUI case not objectively reasonable; city liable but individuals escaped liability because standard not clear at the time].

156. Winston v. Lee, 470 U.S. 753 (1985); *see also* People v. Richard, 145 Misc. 2d 755, 548 N.Y.S.2d 369 (1989) [denial of order to surgically remove bullet].

157. In re Brown, 478 So.2d 1033 (Miss. 1985).

158. United States v. Montoya de Hernandez, 473 U.S. 531 (1985) [particularized and objective basis for suspecting alimentary canal smuggling justifies detention at border for observation]; United States v. Vega-Bravo, 729 F.2d 1341 (11th Cir.), *cert. denied*, 469 U.S. 1088 (1984) [search warrant not required for x-ray]; United States v. Esieke, 940 F.2d 31 (2d Cir.), *cert. denied*, 502 U.S. 992 (1991) [in Second Circuit must notify U.S. Attorney within 24 hours of detention, who must notify court]; United States v. Adekunle, 980 F.2d 985 (5th Cir. 1992), *cert. denied*, 113 S. Ct. 2380 & 2455 (U.S. 1993) [X-rays performed pursuant to federal magistrate order; forcible laxatives justified under circumstances], *other parts of opinion vacated & superseded*, 2 F.3d 559 (5th Cir. 1993) [judicial determination must be sought within reasonable time, usually within 48 hours of detention]; United States v. Ibekwe, 760 F. Supp. 1546 (M.D. Fla. 1991), *aff'd without op.*, 990 F.2d 1267 (11th Cir. 1993) [insufficient justification for forced X-rays]; Velez v. United States, 693 F. Supp. 51 (S.D. N.Y. 1988) [X-rays justified, but false imprisonment to delay review by qualified radiologist who would have determined not smuggling].

159. Stasiak v. Illinois Valley Comm. Hosp., 226 Ill. App.3d 1075, 590 N.E.2d 974 (3d Dist. 1992); *accord* State ex rel. Letts v. Zakaib, 189 W.Va. 616, 433 S.E.2d 554 (1993) [denial of order for MRI examination of minor]; *see also* Lefkowitz v. Nassau County Med. Ctr., 94 A.D.2d 18, 462 N.Y.S.2d 903 (2d Dep't 1983) [deny order of test involving radiated material where no proof without danger].

160. Syring v. Tucker, 174 Wis. 2d 787, 498 N.W.2d 370 (1993).

161. Commissioner of Correction v. Myers, 379 Mass. 255, 399 N.E.2d 452 (1979).

162. *E.g.*, Walker v. Shansky, 28 F.3d 666 (7th Cir. 1994) [cruel, unusual punishment claim stated against officials for forced injections of tranquilizing drugs in prisoners]; *but see* Doe v. Dyett, 1993 U.S. Dist. LEXIS 13,450 (S.D. N.Y. Sept. 24, 1993), as discussed in 19 AM. J. LAW & MED. 346 (1993) [not constitutional violation to give involuntary antipsychotic drugs to prisoner in emergency situation where safety of inmate or others threatened].

163. *E.g.*, Commonwealth, Dep't of Public Welfare v. Kallinger, 134 Pa. Commw. 415, 580 A.2d 887 (1990), *app. dismissed*, 532 Pa. 292, 615 A.2d 730 (1992) [forced feeding ordered]; Von Holden v. Chapman, 87 A.D.2d 66, 450 N.Y.S.2d 623 (4th Dep't 1982) [forced feeding ordered]; *contra*, Thor v. Superior Ct., 5 Cal. 4th 725, 21 Cal. Rptr. 2d 357, 855 P.2d 375 (1993) [inmate may refuse life-sustaining treatment; deny application by prison physician to force feed irreversible quadriplegic inmate where no showing it would undermine prison security]; Zant v. Prevatte, 248 Ga. 832, 286 S.E.2d 715 (1982).

164. In re Quinlan, 70 N.J. 10, 355 A.2d 647 (1976).

165. Superintendent of Belchertown State School v. Saikewicz, 373 Mass. 728, 370 N.E.2d 417, 426 (1977).

166. *E.g.*, Public Health Trust v. Wons, 541 So.2d 96 (Fla. 1989); In re Estate of Brooks, 32 Ill. 2d 361, 205 N.E.2d 435 (1965).

167. *E.g.*, Lane v. Candura, 6 Mass. App. Ct. 377, 376 N.E.2d 1232 (1978).

168. *E.g.*, In re Farrell, 108 N.J. 335, 529 A.2d 404 (1987) [respirator]; Bouvia v. Superior Court, 179 Cal. App. 3d 1127, 225 Cal. Rptr. 297 (2d Dist. 1986) [tube feeding]; In re Milton, 29 Ohio St. 3d 20, 505 N.E.2d 255, *cert. denied*, 484 U.S. 820 (1987) [cancer treatment]; In re Lydia E. Hall Hosp., 116 Misc. 2d 477, 455 N.Y.S. 2d 706 (Sup. Ct. 1982) [dialysis]; *see also* Commonwealth v. Konz, 498 Pa. 639, 450 A.2d 638 (1982) [no duty to intervene when competent diabetic husband discontinued insulin].

169. *E.g.*, Cruzan v. Harmon, 760 S.W.2d 408 (Mo. 1988) (*en banc*), *aff'd on other grounds*, 497 U.S. 261 (1990).

170. In re Dell, 1 D. & C.3d 655 (Pa. C.P. Ct. Allegheny County 1975).

171. Bouvia v. Superior Court, 179 Cal. App. 3d 1127, 225 Cal. Rptr. 297 (2d Dist. 1986), *rev. denied*, No. B019134 (Cal. June 5, 1986).

172. MIAMI [FL] HERALD, Oct. 23, 1984, at 1A; Oct. 24, 1984, at 17A; N.Y. TIMES, Oct. 24, 1984, at 11.

173. *E.g.*, Warthen v. Toms River Comm. Mem. Hosp., 199 N.J. Super. 18, 488 A.2d 229 (App. Div.), *cert. denied*, 101 N.J. 255, 501 A.2d 926 (1985) [upholding termination of nurse who refused to dialyze a seriously ill patient due to moral objections].

174. *E.g.*, Gray v. Romeo, 697 F. Supp. 580 (D. R.I. 1988); *see also* Miles et al., *Conflicts between patients' wishes to forgo treatment and the policies of health care facilities*, 321 N. ENGL. J. MED. 48 (1989).

175. *E.g.*, Bouvia v. Superior Court, 179 Cal. App. 3d 1127, 225 Cal. Rptr. 297 (2d Dist. 1986), *rev. denied*, No. B019134 (Cal. June 5, 1986).

176. *E.g.*, In re Rodas, No. 86PR139 (Colo. Dist. Ct. Mesa County Jan. 22, 1987), *damages denied*, Ross v. Hilltop Rehabilitation Hosp., 676 F. Supp. 1528 (D. Colo. 1987).

177. *E.g.*, In re Requena, 213 N.J. Super. 443, 517 A.2d 869 (App. Div. 1986).

178. *E.g.*, John F. Kennedy Mem. Hosp. v. Bludworth, 452 So.2d 921 (Fla. 1984).

179. Foster v. Tourtellottee, No. CV-81-5046-RMT (C.D. Cal. Nov. 18, 1981), *as discussed in* 704 F.2d 1109 (9th Cir. 1983) [denying attorneys' fees]; *accord* In re Yetter, 62 D. & C.2d 619 (Pa. C.P. Ct. Northampton County 1973) [disagreement between patient, brother]; Lane v. Candura, 6 Mass. App. Ct. 377, 376 N.E.2d 1232 (1978) [disagreement between patient, daughter]; *see also* Brooks v. United States, 837 F.2d 958 (11th Cir. 1988) [no duty to involve relatives].

180. Lasley v. Georgetown Univ., 842 F. Supp. 593 (D. D.C. 1994).

181. Dick v. Springhill Hosps., 551 So.2d 1034 (Ala. 1989).

182. *E.g.*, Gramm v. Boener, 56 Ind. 497 (1877).

183. Riser v. American Med. Int'l, 620 So.2d 372 (La. Ct. App. 1993).

184. Trustees of the Northwest Laundry & Dry Cleaners Health & Welfare Trust Fund v. Burzynski, 27 F.3d 153 (5th Cir.), *reh'g denied (en banc)*, 38 F.3d 571 (5th Cir. 1994), *cert. denied*, 115 S. Ct. 1110 (U.S. 1995).

185. United States v. Rutherford, 442 U.S. 544 (1979).

186. *E.g.*, J.R. Curtis et al., *Use of the medical futility rationale in do-not-attempt-resuscitation orders*, 273 J.A.M.A. 124 (1995); L.J. Schneiderman and N.S. Jecker, *Futility in practice,* 153 ARCH. INTERN. MED. 437 (1993); A. Alpers and B. Lo, *When is CPR futile?* 273 J.A.M.A. 156 (1995); R.D. Truog, et al., *The problem with futility*, 326 N. ENGL. J. MED. 1560 (1992); R.M. Veatch and C.M. Spicer, *Medically futile care: The role of the physician in setting limits*, 18 AM. J. LAW & MED. 15 (1992); T. Tomlinson and H. Brody, *Futility and ethics of resuscitation*, 264

J.A.M.A. 1276 (1990); L. J. Schneiderman, et al., *Medical futility: its meaning and ethical implications,* 112 ANN. INTERN. MED. 949 (1990); *see also* T. Tomlinson and H. Brody, *Futility and the ethics of resuscitation,* 264 J.A.M.A. 1276 (1990); J.C. Hackler and F.C. Hiller, *Family consent to orders not to resuscitate,* 264 J.A.M.A. 1281 (1990) [advocating DNR orders despite family objections in some circumstances].

187. *E.g., Study reveals continuing conflicts over end-of-life care,* AM. MED. NEWS, Mar. 13, 1995, at 20 [article in Feb. 1995 issue of AM. J. RESPIRATORY & CRITICAL CARE MED. reports 39% critical care physicians have withdrawn or withheld life-sustaining treatment without consent of patient or family]; Evans v. Salem Hosp., 83 Or. App. 23, 730 P.2d 562 (1986), *rev. denied,* 303 Or. 331, 736 P.2d 565 (1987) [physician allegedly withheld life support without patient or family consent].

188. *E.g., Draft UCLA Medical Center policy would let doctor call halt to care,* 2 H.L.R. 512 (1993) [physician may refuse to provide such treatment in certain cases; distinction made between medically appropriate and "medically inappropriate" treatment which need not be offered, provided, or continued; if patient or surrogate wishes to pursue inappropriate treatment, assistance provided in transferring care to another provider].

189. *See* Norwood Hosp. v. Commissioner of Pub. Welfare, 417 Mass. 54, 627 N.E.2d 914 (1994) [undocumented alien who died at end of seven-week hospitalization not eligible for Medicaid because not considered treatment for emergency medical condition since so compromised at time of admission that lack of immediate attention would not place her in more serious jeopardy]; 60 FED. REG. 6537 (Feb. 2, 1995) [to be covered by Medicare, lung transplant programs must have patient selection criteria for determining suitable candidates based on critical medical need and "strong likelihood of a successful clinical outcome"]; *HCFA announces new lung transplant payment policy,* AM. MED. NEWS, Mar. 20, 1995, at 5; Barnett v. Kaiser Found. Health Plan, 32 F.3d 413 (9th Cir. 1994) [upholding denial of liver transplant on grounds it was not medically appropriate in light of patient's history, including hepatitis B].

190. Gilgunn v. Massachusetts Gen. Hosp., No. 92-4820-H (Mass. Super. Ct. Suffolk County jury decision Apr. 21, 1995), *as discussed in* 4 H.L.R. 698 (1995).

191. *E.g., As family protests, hospital seeks an end to woman's life support,* N.Y. TIMES, Jan. 10, 1991, at A1 [Helga Wanglie; Hennepin County Court, Minnesota]; *Judge rejects request by doctors to remove a patient's respirator,* N.Y. TIMES, July 2, 1991, at A13 [Helga Wanglie]; *Brain-damaged woman at center of lawsuit over life-support dies,* N.Y. TIMES, July 6, 1991, at 8; *Helga Wanglie's ventilator,* HASTINGS CENTER REPORT, July–Aug. 1991, at 23.

192. *E.g., Hospital wants to pull plug on baby,* MIAMI [FL] HERALD, June 10, 1990, at 17A [Leslie Crane]; *Boy in 2½-year coma dies after respirator stopped,* N.Y. TIMES, June 25, 1990, at A11 [Leslie Crane, parents refused termination due to fear mother would be charged with murder, but when hospital announced plans for suit, father agreed to termination].

193. In re Baby "K," 16 F.3d 590 (4th Cir.), *cert. denied,* 115 S. Ct. 91 (U.S. 1994).

194. Johnson v. Thompson, 971 F.2d 1487 (10th Cir. 1992), *cert. denied,* 113 S. Ct. 1255 (U.S. 1993).

195. *See* Annotation, *Mental competency of patient to consent to surgical operation or medical treatment,* 25 A.L.R. 3D 1439.

196. In re Maida Yetter, 62 Pa. D. & C. 2d 619 (C.P. Ct. Northampton County 1973).

197. Lane v. Candura, 6 Mass. App. Ct. 377, 376 N.E.2d 1232 (1978).

198. In re Milton, 29 Ohio St. 3d 20, 505 N.E.2d 255, *cert. denied,* 484 U.S. 820 (1987).

199. In re Jeffers, 239 Ill. App. 3d 29, 606 N.E.2d 727 (4th Dist. 1992), *appeal granted,* 158 Ill.2d 552, 643 N.E.2d 839 (1994), *adhered to,* 272 Ill. App. 3d 44, 650 N.E.2d 242 (4th Dist. 1995).

200. Rodriguez v. Pino, 634 So.2d 681 (Fla. 3d DCA), *rev. denied,* 645 So.2d 454 (Fla. 1994).

201. Oates v. New York Hosp., 131 A.D.2d 368, 517 N.Y.S.2d 6 (1st Dep't 1987).

202. *E.g.*, Grannum v. Berard, 70 Wash. 2d 304, 422 P.2d 812 (1967); In re Romero, 790 P.2d 819 (Colo. 1990).

203. For a discussion of the determination of capacity, *see* Applebaum and Grisso, *Assessing patients' capacities to consent to treatment*, 319 N. ENGL. J. MED. 1635 (1988).

204. Lounsbury v. Capel, 836 P.2d 188 (Utah Ct. App.), *cert. denied*, 843 P.2d 1042 (Utah 1992).

205. *E.g.*, Beck v. Lovell, 361 So.2d 245 (La. Ct. App.), *cert. denied*, 362 So.2d 802 (La. 1978).

206. State v. Bass, 255 N.C. 42, 120 S.E.2d 580 (1961); *but see also Military court acquits sailor who had airman break leg*, PALM BEACH [FL] POST, Sept. 5, 1994, at 6A; Morehead v. State, 556 So.2d 523 (Fla. 5th DCA 1990) [prisoner's intentionally cutting hand to obtain medical treatment off prison grounds where he hoped girlfriend would help him escape not sufficient overt act to support conviction for attempted escape].

207. *E.g.*, Satz v. Perlmutter, 362 So.2d 160, 162–63 (Fla. 4th DCA 1978), *approved*, 379 So.2d 359 (Fla. 1980).

208. *E.g.*, 21 U.S.C.A. § 360dd [open protocols for orphan drugs]; *but see* Kolata, *Innovative AIDS drug plan may be undermining testing*, N.Y. TIMES, Nov. 21, 1989, at 1 [few volunteers for tests when drug otherwise available].

209. Annotation, *What amounts to failure or refusal to submit to medical treatment sufficient to bar recovery of worker's compensation*, 3 A.L.R. 5TH 907.

210. Annotation, *Social Security: Right to disability as affected by refusal to submit to, or cooperate in, medical or surgical treatment*, 114 A.L.R. Fed. 141.

211. McQuillen v. City of Sioux City, 306 N.W.2d 789 (Iowa 1981); *see also* Holt v. Lanes Nursing Home, No. CA86-171 (Ark. Ct. App. Jan. 28, 1987), *as discussed in* 20 HOSP. L. 94 (1987) [workers' compensation suspended while surgery refused]; Annotation, *Duty of injured person to submit to surgery to minimize tort damages*, 62 A.L.R. 3D 9; *Duty of injured person to submit to nonsurgical medical treatment to minimize tort damages*, 62 A.L.R. 3D 70; *but see* Dawkins v. Bowen, 848 F.2d 1211 (11th Cir. 1988) [poverty excused refusal, so disability payments not lost]; Johnson v. Bowen, 866 F.2d 274 (8th Cir. 1989) [failure to take prescribed dose of medication not justified by lack of financial resources].

212. United States v. Goldstein, 633 F. Supp. 424 (S.D. Fla. 1986).

213. Arkansas Blue Cross & Blue Shield v. Long, 303 Ark. 116, 792 S.W.2d 602 (1990).

214. Jagr v. Kubus, 126 Misc. 2d 280, 481 N.Y.S.2d 977 (Just. Ct. 1984).

215. *E.g.*, Fosmire v. Nicoleau, 144 A.D.2d 8, 536 N.Y.S.2d 492 (2d Dep't 1989), *aff'd*, 75 N.Y.2d 218, 551 N.Y.S.2d 876, 551 N.E.2d 77 (N.Y. 1990) [lower court erred in ordering transfusion]. Note that a subsequent suit against attorneys who obtained order dismissed, 181 A.D.2d 815, 581 N.Y.S.2d 382 (2d Dept.), *appeal denied*, 80 N.Y.2d 754, 587 N.Y.S.2d 905, 600 N.E.2d 632 (1992); suit against hospital dismissed, but breach of contract action against physician not dismissed, Nicoleau v. Brookhaven Mem. Hosp., 201 A.D.2d 544, 607 N.Y.S.2d 703 (2d Dep't 1994).

216. *E.g.*, *Jehovah's Witness who refused blood transfusion dies*, PALM BEACH [FL] POST, July 5, 1989, at 2B [Florida]; *Stab victim dies; he refused blood*, MIAMI [FL] HERALD, Mar. 17, 1990, at 2A [California].

217. Shorter v. Drury, 103 Wash. 2d 645, 695 P.2d 116, *cert. denied*, 474 U.S. 827 (1985).

218. Corlett v. Caserta, 204 Ill. App. 3d 403, 562 N.E.2d 257 (1st Dist. 1990).

219. Munn v. Algee, 924 F.2d 568 (5th Cir. 1991), *aff'g*, 719 F. Supp. 525 (N.D. Miss. 1989), *cert. denied*, 502 U.S. 900 (1991); *see also* Annotation, *Refusal of medical treatment on religious grounds as affecting right to recover for personal injury or death*, 3 A.L.R. 5TH 721.

220. Garcia v. Edgewater Hosp., 244 Ill. App. 3d 894, 613 N.E.2d 1243 (1st Dist.), *appeal denied,* 152 Ill.2d 558, 622 N.E.2d 1204 (1993).

221. In re Dorone, 517 Pa. 3, 534 A.2d 452 (1987), *aff'g,* 349 Pa. Super. 59, 502 A.2d 1271 (1985).

222. *E.g.,* In re Hughes, 259 N.J. Super. 193, 611 A.2d 1148 (App. Div. 1992).

223. Werth v. Taylor, 190 Mich. App. 141, 475 N.W.2d 426 (1991).

224. Malette v. Schulman, 72 O.R.2d 417 (Ont. Ct. App. 1990); N. Hershey, *Heeding patient's directive essential,* 9 HOSP. L. NEWSLETTER, Mar. 1992, at 1.

225. Davis v. United States, 629 F. Supp. 1 (E.D. Ark.), *aff'd without op.,* 802 F.2d 463 (8th Cir. 1986).

226. *See* Murphy, *Do-not-resuscitate orders,* 260 J.A.M.A. 2098 (1988); *but see* Schiedermayer, *The decision to forgo CPR in the elderly patient,* 260 J.A.M.A. 2096 (1988).

227. *See* Taffet et al., *In-hospital cardiopulmonary resuscitation,* 260 J.A.M.A. 2069 (1988).

228. 1995 Joint Commission CAMH, at 73–74 [resuscitation policy].

229. *E.g.,* N.Y. TIMES, Mar. 21, 1984, at 17 [grand jury report on unwritten orders]; Nov. 20, 1984, at 16 [civil charges for orders by unlicensed interns].

230. Hoyt v. St. Mary's Rehabilitation Ctr., No. 77455S (Minn. Dist. Ct. Hennepin County Feb. 13, 1981), *as discussed in* HEALTH L. VIGIL, June 12, 1981, at 7; AM. MED. NEWS, Mar. 6, 1981, at 15.

231. *E.g.,* In re Dinnerstein, 6 Mass. App. 466, 380 N.E.2d 134 (1978); *but see* In re Spring, 380 Mass. 629, 405 N.E.2d 115 (1980) [while court order not required, when matter presented to court in Massachusetts, court must decide and not delegate to physician or family].

232. *E.g.,* FLA. STAT. § 401.45; FLA. ADMIN. CODE, § 10D-66.325; D.M. Gianelli, *"Right-to-die" debate turns to out-of-hospital DNR orders,* AM. MED. NEWS, Nov. 7, 1994, at 3; *Maryland school officials must obey DNR order for student with disabilities,* 3 H.L.R. 827 (1994) [Maryland attorney general's opinion May 13, 1994].

233. Manning v. Twin Falls Clinic & Hosp., 122 Idaho 47, 830 P.2d 1185 (1992).

234. State v. McAfee, 259 Ga. 579, 385 S.E.2d 651 (1989); *An angry man fights to die, then tests life,* N.Y. Times, Feb. 9, 1990, at A1 [McAfee decided not to exercise right he had established]; *see also* M. Williams, *Michigan quadriplegic earns right to die,* AM. MED. NEWS, Aug. 4, 1989, at 3 [David Rivlin; same procedure approved]; *Judge rules patient can fulfill her wish to die,* N.Y. TIMES, Apr. 28, 1990, at 6 [Thelma Stussy; Pennsylvania court approved removal of respirator pursuant to blinked directions of paralyzed woman]; *Woman dies, the wish court granted,* N.Y. TIMES, Apr. 29, 1990, at 16 [Stussy]; Bartling v. Superior Court, 163 Cal. App. 3d 186, 209 Cal. Rptr. 220 (2d Dist. 1984); Bouvia v. Superior Court, 179 Cal. App. 3d 1127, 225 Cal. Rptr. 297 (2d Dist. 1986).

235. *E.g.,* Brophy v. New Engl. Sinai Hosp., Inc., 398 Mass. 417, 497 N.E.2d 626 (1986).

236. R.M. McCann et al., *Comfort care of terminally ill patients: The appropriate use of nutrition and hydration,* 272 J.A.M.A. 1263 (1994); *Terminally ill should be allowed to refuse artificial sustenance, report says,* N.Y. TIMES, Oct. 26, 1994, at A7.

237. Cruzan v. Harmon, 760 S.W.2d 408 (Mo. 1988) (*en banc*), *aff'd on other grounds,* Cruzan v. Director, Mo. Dept. of Health, 497 U.S. 261 (1990).

238. *State asks to quit right-to-die case,* N.Y. TIMES, Oct. 12, 1990, at A9; *Missouri family renews battle over right to die,* N.Y. TIMES, Nov. 2, 1990, at A12; *Judge allows removal of woman's feeding tube,* N.Y. TIMES, Dec. 15, 1990, at 1; *Ordeal ending for Nancy Cruzan with removal of feeding tube,* AM. MED. NEWS, Dec. 28, 1990, at 1; *Protestors thwarted in effort to feed comatose woman,* N.Y. TIMES, Dec. 19, 1990, at A14; *Missouri high court upholds right to die in Cruzan case,* N.Y. TIMES, Dec. 21, 1990, at A16; *For Missouri's Webster, '92 gubernatorial*

race appears likely to be a life-and-death campaign, WALL ST. J., Dec. 20, 1990, at A18; *Cruzan's condition worse; court rejects 7th appeal*, PALM BEACH POST (FL), Dec. 26, 1990, at 4A; *Nancy Cruzan dies, outlived by debate over right to die*, N.Y. TIMES, Dec. 27, 1990, at A1.

239. American Medical Association, Council on Ethical and Judicial Affairs, *Withholding or Withdrawing Life-Prolonging Medical Treatment* (Mar. 15, 1986), *quoted in* Corbett v. D'Alessandro, 487 So.2d 368, 371, n.1 (Fla. 2d DCA 1986); *see also* Steinbrook and Lo, *Artificial feeding—Solid ground, not a slippery slope*, 318 N. ENGL. J. MED. 286(1988); Wanzer et al., *The physician's responsibility toward hopelessly ill patients*, 310 N. ENGL. J. MED. 955 (1984); Wanzer et al., *The physician's responsibility toward hopelessly ill patients: A second look*, 320 N. ENGL. J. MED. 844 (1989).

240. *E.g.*, Bouvia v. Superior Court, 179 Cal. App. 3d 1127, 225 Cal. Rptr. 297 (2d Dist. 1986), *rev. denied*, No. B019134 (Cal. June 5, 1986); Application of Plaza Health & Rehabilitation Center (N.Y. Sup. Ct. Onondaga County Feb. 2, 1984); N.Y. TIMES, Feb. 3, 1984, at A1 [describing Plaza case]; Williams, *Michigan quadriplegic earns right to die*, AM. MED. NEWS, Aug. 4, 1989, at 3.

241. *E.g.*, In re Guardianship of Grant, 109 Wash. 2d 545, 747 P.2d 445 (1987), *corrected*, 757 P.2d 534 (Wash. 1988).

242. *E.g.*, Brophy v. New Engl. Sinai Hosp., Inc., 398 Mass. 417, 497 N.E.2d 626 (1986).

243. In re Conroy, 98 N.J. 321, 486 A.2d 1209 (1985); *see also* In re Guardianship of Browning, 568 So.2d 4 (Fla. 1990).

244. Barber v. Superior Court, 147 Cal. App. 3d 1006, 195 Cal. Rptr. 484 (2d Dist. 1983).

245. McCrary and Botkin, *Hospital policy on advance directives*, 262 J.A.M.A. 2411 (1989).

246. *E.g.*, In re Estate of Dorone, 517 Pa. 3, 534 A.2d 452 (1987) [written directive of Jehovah's Witness refusing transfusion may be disregarded in Pennsylvania in some situations].

247. *E.g.*, In re Guardianship of Browning, 568 So.2d 4 (Fla. 1990) [imminence of death]; In re A.K., RJI No. 26796 (N.Y. Sup. Ct. Warren County Feb. 16, 1989), *as described in* 17 HEALTH L. DIG., May 1989, at 17 [loss of capacity to care for self].

248. *E.g.*, In re Severns, 425 A.2d 156 (Del. Ch. 1980).

249. *E.g.*, In re Westchester County Med. Ctr. (O'Connor), 72 N.Y.2d 517, 534 N.Y.S.2d 886, 531 N.E.2d 607 (1988).

250. *E.g.*, In re Blilie, 494 N.W.2d 877 (Minn. 1993) [mentally retarded ward treated involuntarily with neuroleptic drugs entitled to same procedural protections as mentally ill person; consent of public guardian can be substituted for court-appointed guardian ad litem; deny injunction of therapy only on consent of public guardian]; *see also* S.S. Herr and B.L. Hopkins, *Health care decision making for persons with disabilities: An alternative to guardianship*, 271 J.A.M.A. 1017 (1994) [N.Y. Surrogate Decision-Making Committee as provided in N.Y. Mental Hygiene Law, §§ 80.11, 80.07; N.Y. Compilation of Codes, Rules and Regulations, tit. 14, § 710.4; but prohibited from addressing withdrawal of treatment].

251. *E.g.*, CAL. HEALTH AND SAFETY CODE, § 1418.8; Rains v. Belshe, 32 Cal. App. 4th 157, 38 Cal. Rptr. 2d 185 (1st Dist. 1995) [constitutionality of state statute permitting doctor to consent for non-emergency medical treatment of incompetent in long-term care facility without legal surrogate].

252. *E.g.*, Lounsbury v. Capel, 836 P.2d 188 (Utah Ct. App.), *cert. denied*, 843 P.2d 1042 (Utah 1992) [spouse may consent only if patient otherwise unable to consent]; Young v. Oakland Gen. Hosp., 175 Mich. App. 132, 437 N.W.2d 321 (1989), *appeal denied*, 434 Mich. 894 (1990) [consent by adult child]; Farber v. Olkon, 40 Cal. 2d 503, 254 P.2d 520 (1953) [consent by next of kin]; Ritz v. Florida Patient's Compensation Fund, 436 So.2d 987 (Fla. 5th DCA 1983), *rev. denied*, 450 So.2d 488 (Fla. 1984) [consent by parents]; In re Barbara C., 101 A.D.2d 137, 474

N.Y.S.2d 799 (2d Dep't 1984), *appeal dismissed*, 64 N.Y.2d 866, 487 N.Y.S.2d 549, 476 N.E.2d 994 (1985) [consent by parents]; MISS. CODE ANN. §§ 41-41-3, 41-41-5.

253. *E.g.*, FLA. STAT. § 765.07.

254. PALM BEACH [FL] POST, June 20, 1991, at 1A; June 25, 1991, at 1A; July 17, 1991, at 5A; Oct. 2, 1991, at 9.

255. *E.g.*, John F. Kennedy Mem. Hosp. v. Bludworth, 452 So.2d 921 (Fla. 1984).

256. Aponte v. United States, 582 F. Supp. 65 (D. P.R. 1984); *see also* Aikins v. St. Helena Hosp., 843 F. Supp. 1329 (N.D. Cal. 1994) [denial of dismissal of Rehabilitation Act suit for allegedly failing to provide interpreter services to deaf woman while her husband was in hospital unconscious and hospital looked to her for decisions].

257. *E.g.*, Superintendent of Belchertown State School v. Saikewicz, 373 Mass. 728, 370 N.E.2d 417 (1977).

258. *E.g.*, In re Guardianship of Hamlin, 102 Wash. 2d 810, 689 P.2d 1372 (1984).

259. In re Hier, 18 Mass. App. Ct. 200, 464 N.E.2d 959, *rev. denied*, 392 Mass. 1102, 465 N.E.2d 261 (1984).

260. In re Guardianship of Ingram, 102 Wash. 2d 827, 689 P.2d 1363 (1984).

261. *E.g.*, In re Guardianship of Pescinski, 67 Wis. 2d 4, 226 N.W.2d 180 (1975) [incompetent adult]; In re Richardson, 284 So.2d 185 (La. Ct. App. 1973) [minor], *application denied*, 284 So.2d 338 (La. 1973); *see* Annotation, *Propriety of surgically invading incompetent or minor for benefit of third party*, 4 A.L.R. 5TH 1000.

262. *E.g.*, Strunk v. Strunk, 445 S.W.2d 145 (Ky. 1969) [incompetent adult]; Hart v. Brown, 29 Conn. Supp. 368, 289 A.2d 386 (Super. Ct. 1972) [minor].

263. *E.g.*, In re Doe, 104 A. D. 2d 200, 481 N.Y.S.2d 932 (4th Dep't 1984).

264. *E.g.*, John F. Kennedy Mem. Hosp. v. Bludworth, 452 So.2d 921 (Fla. 1984).

265. *E.g.*, Cruzan v. Harmon, 760 S.W.2d 408 (Mo. 1988) (*en banc*), *aff'd*, 497 U.S. 261 (1990); In re Storar, 52 N.Y.2d 363, 438 N.Y.S.2d 266, 420 N.E.2d 64, *cert. denied*, 454 U.S. 858 (1981); *New York rule compounds dilemma over life support*, N.Y. TIMES, May 12, 1992, at A1 [no surrogate decision making in N.Y.].

266. *E.g.*, John F. Kennedy Mem. Hosp. v. Bludworth, 452 So.2d 921 (Fla. 1984); In re Quinlan, 70 N.J. 10, 355 A.2d 647, *cert. denied*, 429 U.S. 922 (1976).

267. *E.g.*, FLA. STAT. § 765.07.

268. *E.g.*, *Survival predictions found imprecise for hospice patients*, AM. MED. NEWS, Dec. 9, 1988, at 40 [predictions tend to be overly optimistic].

269. *E.g.*, In re Spring, 380 Mass. 629, 405 N.E.2d 115, 118 (1980) [five years].

270. *E.g.*, Wanzer et al., *The physician's responsibility toward hopelessly ill patients*, 310 N. ENGL. J. MED. 955 (1984); Grenvik et al., *Cessation of therapy in terminal illness and brain death*, 6 CRITICAL CARE MED. 284 (1978); *Optimal care for hopelessly ill patients*, 295 N. ENGL. J. MED. 362 (1976).

271. *E.g.*, In re Guardianship of Conroy, 98 N.J. 321, 486 A.2d 1209 (1985); In re Guardianship of Browning, 568 So.2d 4 (Fla. 1990).

272. Annotation, *Medical practitioner's liability for treatment given child without parent's consent*, 67 A.L.R. 4TH 511.

273. *E.g.*, In re Rotkowitz, 175 Misc. 2d 948, 25 N.Y.S.2d 624 (Dom. Rel. Ct. 1941) [surgery ordered when parents disagreed].

274. Joswick v. Lenox Hill Hosp., 134 Misc. 2d 295, 510 N.Y.S.2d 803 (Sup. Ct. 1986).

275. For a state-by-state list of minor consent statutes, see *Consents*, HOSPITAL LAW MANUAL.

276. Alfonso v. Fernandez, 195 A. D. 2d 46, 606 N.Y.S.2d 259 (2d Dep't 1993), *appeal dismissed without op.*, 83 N.Y.2d 906, 614 N.Y.S.2d 388, 637 N.E.2d 279 (1994).

277. *But see, id.* [mature minor rule abrogated by statute in N.Y. at least in the jurisdiction of the second appellate department].

278. Bonner v. Moran, 75 U.S. App. D.C. 156, 126 F.2d 121 (1941).

279. Cardwell v. Bechtol, 724 S.W.2d 739 (Tenn. 1987).

280. In re E.G., 133 Ill. 2d 98, 549 N.E.2d 322 (1989).

281. Belcher v. Charleston Area Med. Ctr., 188 W.Va. 105, 422 S.E.2d 827 (1992).

282. *E.g.*, Novak v. Cobb County-Kennestone Hosp. Auth., 849 F. Supp. 1559 (N.D. Ga. 1994) [court could order transfusion for 16-year-old Jehovah's Witness despite objection of patient, mother].

283. In re Long Island Jewish Med. Ctr., 147 Misc. 2d 724, 557 N.Y.S.2d 239 (Sup. Ct. 1990).

284. *Youth who refused a liver transplant drug dies*, N.Y. TIMES, Aug. 22, 1994, at A7 [Benito Agrelo].

285. Iafelice v. Zarafu, 221 N.J. Super. 278, 534 A.2d 417 (App. Div. 1987).

286. DeShaney v. Winnebago County Dep't of Social Servs., 489 U.S. 189 (1989).

287. *E.g.*, In re L.H.R., 253 Ga. 439, 321 S.E.2d 716 (1984); In re Guardianship of Barry, 445 So.2d 365 (Fla. 2d DCA 1984), *approved*, John F. Kennedy Mem. Hosp. v. Bludworth, 452 So.2d 921 (Fla. 1984).

288. Custody of a Minor, 385 Mass. 697, 434 N.E.2d 601 (1982).

289. In re Rosebush, 195 Mich. App. 675, 491 N.W.2d 633 (1992).

290. M. Levetown et al., *Limitations and withdrawals of medical intervention in pediatric critical care*, 272 J.A.M.A. 1271 (1994).

291. In re Hudson, 13 Wash. 2d 673, 126 P.2d 765 (1942).

292. In re Green, 448 Pa. 338, 292 A.2d 387 (1972).

293. M.N. v. Southern Baptist Hosp., 648 So.2d 769 (Fla. 1st DCA 1994).

294. Newmark v. Williams/DCPS, 588 A.2d 1108, 1118 (Del. 1991).

295. In re Hofbauer, 47 N.Y.2d 648, 419 N.Y.S.2d 936, 393 N.E.2d 1009 (1979).

296. In re General Order of October 11, 1990, 256 Ill. App. 3d 693. 628 N.E.2d 786 (1st Dist. 1993).

297. Bendiburg v. Dempsey, 19 F.3d 557 (11th Cir. 1994).

298. Bendiburg v. Dempsey, 909 F.2d 463 (11th Cir. 1990), *cert. denied*, 500 U.S. 932 (1991); *but see* Novak v. Cobb County-Kennestone Hosp. Auth., 849 F. Supp. 1559 (N.D. Ga. 1994) [*Bendiburg* does not mean ex parte orders are invalid in bona fide emergencies].

299. *E.g.*, Martineau v. Angelone, 25 F.3d 734 (9th Cir. 1994) [in *habeas corpus* action court found insufficient evidence to support convictions for child abuse for delay in seeking medical attention; state court had affirmed convictions, King v. State, 105 Nev. 373, 784 P.2d 942 (1989)].

300. *E.g.*, Lantos et al., *Survival after cardiopulmonary resuscitation in babies of very low birth weight. Is CPR futile therapy?* 318 N. ENGL. J. MED. 91 (1988).

301. *E.g.*, In re Guardianship of Barry, 445 So.2d 365 (Fla. 2d DCA 1984), *approved*, John F. Kennedy Mem. Hosp. v. Bludworth, 452 So.2d 921 (Fla. 1984) [approval of termination of ventilatory support of infant who had only minimal brain stem function; court review not required when diagnosis confirmed by two physicians]; In re Baby "K," 16 F.3d 590 (4th Cir.), *cert. denied*, 115 S. Ct. 91 (U.S. 1994) [treatment for anencephalic baby after emergency admission required until parents agreed to termination].

302. In re Cicero, 101 Misc. 2d 699, 421 N.Y.S.2d 965 (Sup. Ct. 1979); *but see* Johnson v. Thompson, 971 F.2d 1487 (10th Cir. 1992), *cert. denied*, 113 S. Ct. 1255 (U.S. 1993) [no cause of action stated under Rehabilitation Act for treatment of infant with myelomeningocele].

303. In re McNulty, 4 Fam. L. Rptr. 2255 (Mass. P.Ct. Essex County Feb. 15, 1978).

304. HHS letter in HASTINGS CENTER REPORT, Aug. 1982, at 6.

305. In re Infant Doe, No. GU 8204-00 (Ind. Cir. Ct. Monroe County Apr. 12, 1982), *writ of mandamus dismissed sub nom.* State ex rel. Infant Doe v. Baker, No. 482 S 140 (Ind. May 27, 1982). For a description of the medical status of Infant Doe, see 309 N. ENGL. J. MED. 664 (1983). The records of the case are not public records, Marzen v. Department of HHS, 825 F.2d 1148 (7th Cir. 1987).

306. 48 FED. REG. 9,630 (1983).

307. American Academy of Pediatrics v. Heckler, 561 F. Supp. 395 (D. D.C. 1983).

308. *E.g.*, Presidents Commission for the Study of Ethical Problems in Medicine and Biomedical and Behavioral Research, DECIDING TO FORGO LIFE-SUSTAINING TREATMENT 227 (Mar. 1983).

309. 49 FED. REG. 1622 (1984).

310. Bowen v. American Hosp. Ass'n, 476 U.S. 610 (1986).

311. Weber v. Stony Brook Hosp., 60 N.Y.2d 208, 456 N.E.2d 1186, 469 N.Y.S.2d 63, *cert. denied*, 464 U.S. 1026 (1983); parents later authorized limited surgery, N.Y. TIMES, Apr. 12, 1984, at 12.

312. United States v. University Hosp., 729 F.2d 144 (2d Cir. 1984).

313. Child Abuse Amendments of 1984, Pub. L. No. 98-457, 98 Stat. 1753.

314. 50 FED. REG. 14,878 (1985); *see* Kopelman et al., *Neonatologists judge the "Baby Doe" regulations*, 318 N. ENGL. J. MED. 677 (1988).

315. *E.g.*, Hillsborough County Hosp. Auth. v. Muller, No. 88-1073 (Fla. Cir. Ct. 13th Cir. Feb. 9, 1988) [ventilator removal authorized for semicomatose infant]; In re Steinhaus, No. J-8692 (Minn. Dist. Ct. Redwood County Oct. 13, 1986) [treatment removal authorized for comatose infant], *as discussed in* AM. MED. NEWS, Oct. 24/31, 1986, at 1.

316. *E.g.*, In re Seiferth, 309 N.Y. 80, 127 N.E.2d 820 (1955) [denial of order for surgery when 14-year-old patient and father both refused]; In re L.D.K., 48 R.F.L. 2d 164 (Ont. Prov. Ct. 1985) [denial of order for chemotherapy, transfusions when 12-year-old leukemia patient and parents both refused]; *but see* In re Hamilton, 657 S.W.2d 425 (Tenn. Ct. App. 1983), *appeal denied* (Tenn. Sept. 29, 1983) [chemotherapy, radiation ordered for 12-year-old bone cancer patient although she and her parents refused]; N.Y. TIMES, Mar. 29, 1985, at 44 [Pamela Hamilton died of bone cancer after receiving therapy].

317. *E.g.*, *'84 MDA poster child dies after halting treatment*, PALM BEACH [FL] POST, Aug. 27, 1994, at 1B [John Ashburn Rodriguez; 14-year-old stopped medications, went home in Florida].

318. *Boy who fled chemotherapy goes home, his wish granted*, N.Y. Times, Nov. 24, 1994, at A10 [Billy Best].

319. Belcher v. Charleston Area Med. Ctr., 188 W.Va. 105, 422 S.E.2d 827 (1992).

320. *E.g.*, In Interest of Ivey, 319 So.2d 53 (Fla. 1st DCA 1975); *see also* Novak v. Cobb County-Kennestone Hosp. Auth., 849 F. Supp. 1559 (N.D. Ga. 1994) [no civil rights liability for properly obtaining court order for transfusion of 16-year-old].

321. *E.g.*, In re E.G., 133 Ill. 2d 98, 549 N.E.2d 322 (1989) [17-year-old].

322. *E.g.*, In re Sampson, 29 N.Y.2d 900, 328 N.Y.S. 2d 686, 278 N.E.2d 918 (1972) [transfusions to permit surgical correction of deformed face, neck].

323. In re Green, 448 Pa. 338, 292 A.2d 387 (1972).

324. In re Willmann, 24 Ohio App. 3d 191, 493 N.E.2d 1380 (1986).

325. In re Jensen, 54 Or. App. 1, 633 P.2d 1302 (1981).

326. Custody of Minor, 378 Mass. 732, 393 N.E.2d 836 (1979).

327. Green v. Truman, 459 F. Supp. 342 (D. Mass. 1978).

328. In re Eric B., 189 Cal. App. 3d 996, 235 Cal. Rptr. 22 (1st Dist. 1987).

329. *E.g.*, Newmark v. Williams/DCPS, 588 A.2d 1108, 1118 (Del. 1991).

330. *See* Annotation, *Validity and application of statute allowing endangered child to be temporarily removed from parental custody*, 38 A.L.R. 4TH 756; Young v. Arkansas Children's Hosp., 721 F. Supp. 197 (E.D. Ark. 1989) [medical hold of child for treatment]; *see also* Williams v. Pollard, 44 F.3d 433 (6th Cir. 1995) [social worker not liable for detaining children for over two hours to investigate alleged child abuse]; Forman v. Pillsbury, 753 F. Supp. 14 (D. D.C. 1990) [providers have no duty to force parents to bring minor to office].

331. FLA. STAT. § 415.506; *see also* IOWA CODE ANN. § 232.79.

332. FLA. STAT. § 415.507(2)(b), (c) [HRS authority to consent].

333. N.C. GEN. STAT. §§ 90-21.1–90-21.3.

334. *E.g.*, In the Interest of C.A., 236 Ill. App.3d 594, 603 N.E.2d 1171 (1992), *appeal denied*, 148 Ill.2d 642, 610 N.E.2d 1264 (1993) [guardian of infant with AIDS has authority to consent to DNR order]; A.R. Crosswaite, *Comment: "Do not resuscitate order" allowed for an infant with AIDS*: In the Interest of C.A., 26 J. HEALTH & HOSP. L. 11 (1993).

335. *See* Belcher v. Charleston Area Med. Ctr., 188 W.Va. 105, 422 S.E.2d 827 (1992) [suit could be brought challenging DNR order for mature minor to which parents had consented where patient had not been consulted].

336. *E.g.*, Payne v. Marion Gen. Hosp., 549 N.E.2d 1043 (Ind. Ct. App. 1990) [patient died after no resuscitation pursuant to DNR order entered at sister's request; in suit by estate, sufficient evidence patient still awake, alert, capable of communicating to require remand to determine whether incapacitated]; Evans v. Salem Hosp., 83 Or. App. 23, 730 P.2d 562 (1986), *rev. denied*, 303 Or. 331, 736 P.2d 565 (1987) [dismissal on procedural grounds of intentional infliction of emotional distress claim for not resuscitating patient where no patient or family approval not to resuscitate].

337. *See* Neu and Kjellstrand, *Stopping long-term dialysis*, 314 N. ENGL. J. MED. 14, 17 (1986).

338. *E.g.*, Brooks v. United States, 837 F.2d 958 (11th Cir. 1988).

339. Annotation, *Tortious maintenance or removal of life supports*, 58 A.L.R. 4TH 222.

340. *E.g.*, Ross v. Hilltop Rehabilitation Hosp., 676 F. Supp. 1528 (D. Colo. 1987); Westhart v. Mule, 213 Cal. App. 3d 542, 261 Cal. Rptr. 640 (4th Dist. 1989), *rev. denied & op. withdrawn*, 1989 Cal. LEXIS 4990 (Nov. 22, 1989) [not citable in Cal.] [dismissal of suit arising from insertion of feeding tube contrary to wife's directions; she never asked to have tube removed]; Bartling v. Glendale Adventist Med. Ctr., 184 Cal. App. 3d 961, 229 Cal. Rptr. 360 (2d Dist. 1986) [refusal to find intentional infliction of emotional injuries]; *see also* Benoy v. Simons, 66 Wash. App. 56, 831 P.2d 167, *rev. denied*, 120 Wash.2d 1014, 844 P.2d 435 (1992) [family challenged putting child on respirator without consent, but did not claim refusal; refusal to recognize wrongful prolongation of life as cause of action; refusal to find intentional infliction of emotional injuries].

341. Leach v. Akron Gen. Med. Ctr., 68 Ohio Misc. 1, 22 Ohio Op. 3d 49, 426 N.E.2d 809 (C.P. Ct. Summit County 1980).

342. Estate of Leach v. Shapiro, 13 Ohio App. 3d 393, 469 N.E.2d 1047 (1984).

343. *Doctor is cleared in death plea case,* N.Y. TIMES, Sept. 19, 1985, at 16.

344. Anderson v. Saint Francis-Saint George Hosp., 83 Ohio App. 3d 221, 614 N.E.2d 841 (1992), *rev. denied*, 66 Ohio St. 3d 1459, 610 N.E.2d 423, *appeal after remand*, 1995 Ohio App. LEXIS 911 (Mar. 15, 1995).

345. In re Spring, 380 Mass. 629, 405 N.E.2d 115 (1980).

346. Spring v. Geriatric Auth., 394 Mass. 274, 475 N.E.2d 727 (1985).

347. Bendiburg v. Dempsey, 909 F.2d 463 (11th Cir. 1990), *cert. denied*, 500 U.S. 932 (1991).

348. Bendiburg v. Dempsey, 19 F.3d 557 (11th Cir. 1994).

349. Grace Plaza v. Elbaum, 82 N.Y.2d 10, 603 N.Y.S.2d 386, 623 N.E.2d 513 (1993); G.J. Annas, *Adding injustice to injury: Compulsory payment for unwanted treatment*, 327 N. ENGL. J. MED. 1885 (1992).

350. *E.g.*, Hoffmeister v. Coler, 544 So.2d 1067 (Fla. 4th DCA 1989); Gray v. Romeo, 709 F. Supp. 325 (D. R.I. 1989); McMahon v. Lopez, 199 Cal. App. 3d 829, 245 Cal. Rptr. 172 (2d Dist. 1988); Bartling v. Glendale Adventist Med. Ctr., 184 Cal. App. 3d 97, 228 Cal. Rptr. 847 (2d Dist. 1986); *see also* Ross v. Hilltop Rehabilitation Hosp., 124 F.R.D. 660 (D. Colo. 1988) [after unsuccessfully seeking damages for continuation of unwanted treatment, plaintiff required to pay costs of hospital and physician].

351. In re Quinlan, 70 N.J. 10, 355 A.2d 647, 669–70 (1976).

352. *See* Annotation, *Homicide: physician's withdrawal of life supports from comatose patient*, 47 A.L.R. 4TH 18.

353. Barber v. Superior Court, 147 Cal. App. 3d 1006, 195 Cal. Rptr. 484 (2d Dist. 1983).

354. United States v. Narciso, 446 F. Supp. 252 (E.D. Mich. 1976); Wiley, *Liability for death: Nine nurses' legal ordeals*, 11 NURSING 81, Sept. 1981, at 34 [hereinafter cited as WILEY].

355. WILEY, at 37; *Nurse admits plug-pulling but is acquitted of murder*, 20 MED. WORLD NEWS, Apr. 30, 1979, at 48.

356. People v. Diaz, 3 Cal. 4th 495 & 757, 11 Cal. Rptr. 2d 353, 834 P.2d 1171 (1992), *cert. denied*, 113 S. Ct. 2356 (U.S. 1993), *related proceeding*, Diaz v. Lukash, 82 N.Y.2d 211, 604 N.Y.S.2d 28, 624 N.E.2d 156 (1993) [convicted nurse permitted to inspect autopsy reports to develop theory that no murder occurred]; *see also* Jones v. State, 716 S.W.2d 142 (Tex. Civ. App. 1986) [conviction of nurse].

357. N.Y. TIMES, Mar. 21, 1984, at 17; Nov. 20, 1984, at 16.

358. See *Consenting to suicide*, 16 LEGAL OBSERVER 491 (1838); C. Bell, *Has the physician ever the right to terminate life?* 14 MEDICO-LEGAL J. 463 (1897).

359. G. Williams, THE SANCTITY OF LIFE AND THE CRIMINAL LAW (Alfred A. Knopf 1968), 331 [hereinafter cited as WILLIAMS]; E.J. Gurney, *Is there a right to die?—A study of the law of euthanasia*, 3 CUMBER.-SAM. L. REV. 235, 251–53 (1972) [hereinafter cited as GURNEY].

360. L.B. 135, 52d Sess., Neb. Legislature (1937), *as cited in* GURNEY at 251 n.85, 252 n.92; WILLIAMS, 331.

361. WILLIAMS, 331.

362. *E.g.*, D. Humphrey, FINAL EXIT (Hemlock Society 1991); *A how to book on suicide surges to top of best-seller list in week*, N.Y. TIMES, Aug. 8, 1991, at A1 [Final Exit].

363. *E.g.*, Attorney General v. Able [1984], 1 All E.R. 277 (Q.B.D. 1983) [denial of declaratory judgement that distribution of book would violate law].

364. *Voters turn down legal euthanasia*, N.Y. TIMES, Nov. 7, 1991, at A10.

365. A.M. Capron, *Even in defeat, Proposition 161 sounds a warning*, 23 HASTINGS CENTER REPORT (Jan.–Feb. 1993), at 32.

366. *Suicide law placing Oregon on several uncharted paths*, N.Y. TIMES, Nov. 25, 1994, at A1; the text is in Kane v. Kulongoski, 318 Or. 593, 871 P.2d 993, 1001–6 (1994), which approved putting the matter on the ballot; *see* A.M. Capron, *Sledding in Oregon*, 25 HASTINGS CENTER REPORT (Jan.–Feb. 1995), at 34; A. Alpers & B. Lo, *Physician-assisted suicide in Oregon: A bold experiment*, 274 J.A.M.A. 483 (1995).

367. Lee v. Oregon, 869 F. Supp. 1491 (D. Or. 1994).

368. *E.g.*, *Australian territory backing euthanasia*, N.Y. TIMES, May 26, 1995, at A4 [Northern Territory].

369. *E.g.*, *Panel tells Albany to resist legalizing assisted suicide*, N.Y. TIMES, May 26, 1994, at A1 [New York State Task Force on Life and the Law].

370. *E.g.*, People v. Kevorkian, 447 Mich. 436, 527 N.W.2d 714 (1994) [*rev'g in part/ aff'g in part* Hobbins v. Attorney General, 205 Mich. App. 194, 518 N.W.2d 487 (1994) *and vacating,* People v. Kevorkian, 205 Mich. App. 180, 517 N.W.2d 293 (1994)], *cert. denied*, 115 S. Ct. 1795 (U.S. 1995); Quill v. Koppell, 870 F. Supp. 78 (S.D. N.Y. 1994), *appealed, see Appeals court hears case for assisting some suicides*, N.Y. TIMES, Sept. 2, 1995, at 12.

371. Compassion in Dying v. Washington, 49 F.3d 586 (9th Cir. 1995) [*rev'g*, 850 F. Supp. 1454 (W.D. Wash. 1994)], *reh'g en banc granted*, 1995 U.S. App. LEXIS 20, 704 (9th Cir. 1995).

372. Donaldson v. Van de Kamp, 2 Cal. App. 4th 1614, 4 Cal. Rptr. 2d 59 (2d Dist. 1992).

373. T.E. Quill, *Doctor, I want to die. Will you help me?* 1993 J.A.M.A. 870 (1993); *Doctor says he agonized, but gave drug for suicide*, N.Y. TIMES, Mar. 7, 1991, at A1 [Quill]; *Jury declines to indict doctor who said he aided in a suicide*, N.Y. TIMES, July 27, 1991, at 1; *State won't press case on doctor in suicide*, N.Y. TIMES, Aug. 17, 1991, at 9 [Quill; no professional misconduct charges]; *see also* B. Rollin, LAST WISH (Linden Press 1985).

374. *E.g., Jurors acquit Dr. Kevorkian in suicide case*, N.Y. TIMES, May 3, 1994, at A1; *Man cleared of murder in aiding wife's suicide*, N.Y. TIMES, May 11, 1991, at 8 [Michigan jury acquitted Betram Harper].

375. *See also* State v. Sexson, 117 N.M. 113, 869 P.2d 301 (Ct. App.), *cert. denied*, 117 N.M. 215, 870 P.2d 753 (1994) [prosecution for second-degree murder, not assisting suicide, when actually held gun to head, pulled trigger].

376. *Doctor tells of first death using his suicide device*, N.Y. TIMES, June 6, 1990, at A1.

377. *Michigan board suspends license of doctor who aided in suicides*, N.Y. TIMES, Nov. 21, 1991, at A14; M. Williams, *Dr. Kevorkian's future without a license is uncertain*, AM. MED. NEWS, Dec. 9, 1991, at 9.

378. *Kevorkian aids in suicide as Michigan's ban expires*, N.Y. TIMES, Nov. 27, 1994, at 12.

379. People v. Kevorkian, 205 Mich. App. 180, 517 N.W.2d 293, *vacated & remanded*, 447 Mich. 436, 527 N.W.2d 714 (1994), *cert. denied*, 115 S. Ct. 1795 (U.S. 1995).

380. *Jurors acquit Dr. Kevorkian in suicide case*, N.Y. TIMES, May 3, 1994, at A1.

381. *Kevorkian faces trial on suicide charges*, N.Y. TIMES, Sept. 1, 1995, at A12.

14

Information Management

Health care organizations and professionals must collect sensitive information about patients to provide appropriate diagnosis, treatment, and care. This chapter discusses the recording of patient information and its uses, the law concerning confidentiality of patient information, and the circumstances in which disclosure of information is prohibited, permitted, or mandated.

In addition to patient information, health care providers have extensive information concerning utilization patterns, costs, and other features of health care delivery. This information is an asset that often determines payment and assists in management and marketing. Others seek access to this asset for business and other purposes.[1] Providers need to manage this asset.

MEDICAL RECORDS

Hospitals are required by both governmental and nongovernmental agencies to have accurate and complete medical records and a functioning medical records library. The licensing laws and regulations of many states include specific requirements with which hospitals and other providers must comply. In addition, nongovernmental agencies, such as the Joint Commission on Accreditation of Healthcare Organizations (Joint Commission), establish medical records standards.[2]

The primary purpose of medical records is to facilitate diagnosis, treatment, and patient care. Records provide a communications link among the team members caring for the patient. Records are also documentation of what was found and what was done so that patient care can be evaluated, billing and collections can be performed, and other administrative and legal matters can be addressed. Medical records are also valuable in hospital educational and research programs.

Contents

Many statutes and regulations require providers to maintain medical records. Hospitals that participate in Medicare must comply with minimum content requirements.[3] State hospital licensing laws and regulations addressing medical records can be divided into three groups: (1) those detailing the information required; (2) those specifying the broad areas of information required; and (3) those stating simply that the medical record shall be adequate, accurate, or complete. Some local governments require additional information to be kept.

To be accredited, hospitals must meet Joint Commission medical records standards, including a long list of items that must be in the medical record to assure identification of the patient, support for the diagnosis, justification for the treatment, and accurate documentation of results.[4] While some items apply only to inpatients, the general standards apply to all patients, including ambulatory care patients, emergency patients, and patients in hospital-administered home care programs.

The medical record consists of three types of data: (1) personal, (2) financial, and (3) medical. Personal information, usually obtained upon admission, includes name, date of birth, sex, marital status, occupation, other items of identification, and the next of kin or other contact person. Some hospitals also collect social data concerning family status, community activities, and other information related to the patient's position in society.

Financial data usually include the patient's employer, health insurance identification, and other information to assist billing. Medical data form the clinical record, a continuously maintained history of patient condition and treatment, including physical examinations, medical history, treatment administered, progress reports, physician orders, clinical laboratory reports, radiological reports, consultation reports, anesthesia records, operation records, signed consent forms, nursing notes, and discharge summaries. The medical record should be a complete, current record of the history, condition, and treatment of the patient.

Incomplete hospital record keeping can be used to infer negligence in treatment.[5] One federal court found a hospital negligent for permitting its nurse to chart by exception in postoperative monitoring.[6] An infection was missed. However, minor variations from hospital standards concerning charting do not automatically prove that an examination or treatment did not meet legal standards. A federal court found that an emergency screening satisfied EMTALA even though the full hospital screening procedure was not followed.[7]

Accuracy and Timely Completion

Accurate and timely completion of medical records is essential to expedite payment, to comply with governmental and accreditation requirements, and to minimize liability exposure.

State licensing statutes and regulations and Joint Commission standards require accurate records.[8] An inaccurate record may increase the hospital's exposure to liability by destroying the entire record's credibility. In a 1974 Kansas case, the court found that one discrepancy between the medical record and what actually happened to the patient could justify a jury finding that the record could also be erroneous in other parts and be considered generally invalid.[9]

Complete records include observations that the patient's condition has not changed, as well as observations of change. If there is no notation of an observation, many courts permit juries to infer that no observation was made. In 1974, the Illinois Supreme Court decided a case involving a patient admitted with a broken leg.[10] The leg suffered irreversible ischemia while in traction and required amputation. The physician had ordered the nurse to observe the patient's toes, and the medical record indicated hourly observations during the first day of hospitalization. No observations were documented during the seven hours prior to finding the foot cold and without sensation. Though the nurse may have observed the foot during that period, the jury was permitted to infer from the lack of documentation that no observations were made, indicating a breach of the nurse's duty. The hospital, as employer, could be liable for resulting injuries.

Complete records can often protect hospital and staff. A Kentucky hospital was found not liable for a patient death approximately 13 hours after surgery because the medical record included documentation of proper periodic nursing observation, contacts with the physician concerning patient management, and compliance with physician directions.[11] As discussed in Chapter 11, compliance with physician directions does not provide protection when the directions are clearly improper. When the directions are within the range of acceptable professional practice, properly documented compliance provides substantial liability protection.

Medical record entries should usually be made when treatment is given or observations are made. Entries made several days or weeks later have less credibility than those made during or immediately after the patient's hospitalization. Medicare conditions of participation require completion of hospital records within 30 days following patient discharge.[12] Joint Commission accreditation standards require medical staff regulations to state a time limit for completion of the record that cannot exceed 30 days after discharge.[13] Persistent failure to conform to this medical staff rule is a basis for suspension of the staff member.[14]

A West Virginia court ruled in favor of a hospital in a case in which a director of social services ordered social workers to review patient charts and complete missing information in master treatment plans for an upcoming accreditation survey. One social worker refused, claiming that it was illegal, and then resigned under pressure. The court ruled that completing the plans based on information in the charts was not unethical altering of records.[15]

Corrections and Alterations

Medical record corrections should be made only by proper methods. Improper alterations reduce record credibility, exposing the hospital to increased liability risk.

Medical record errors can be (1) minor errors in transcription, spelling, and the like, or (2) more significant errors involving test data, orders, omitted progress notes, and similar substantive entries. Persons authorized to make record entries may correct minor errors in their own entries soon after the original entry. Hospital policy should limit who may correct substantive errors and errors discovered at a later date. Those who could have been misled by the error should be notified of changes.

Corrections should be made by placing a single line through the incorrect entry, entering the correct information, initialing or signing the correction, and entering the time and date of the correction. Erasing or obliterating errors may lead jurors to suspect the original entry.

After a claim has been made, changes should not be made without first consulting defense counsel. After some New York physicians won a malpractice suit, it was discovered that a page of the medical record had been replaced before the suit, so the court ordered a new trial.[16] A Maryland court ruled that a malpractice insurer could cancel a physician's coverage for alteration of patient records.[17]

Altering or falsifying a medical record to obtain reimbursement wrongfully is a crime.[18] In some states a practitioner who improperly alters a medical record is subject to license revocation or other discipline for unprofessional conduct.[19] In some states improper alteration of a medical record is a crime regardless of the purpose.

Some patients request modification of medical records. Since records are evidence of what occurred and were relied on in making patient care decisions, hospitals should usually not modify records except to update patient name changes. If a patient disagrees with an entry, some hospitals permit amendments in the same manner as corrections of substantive errors if the physician concurs in the amendment. Such an amendment should note the patient's request as a means of explaining the change if it is questioned later. Instead of changing original entries, some hospitals permit patients to add letters to the record. Staff concurrence, if any, can be noted on the letter. Occasionally courts will order record modifications, especially for records of involuntary evaluation or treatment for mental illness.[20]

A Minnesota court ruled that a jury could decide whether there was malice in entering a notation of suspected child abuse on a chart, when there was a refusal to remove the notation.[21] It is questionable whether courts in other jurisdictions will reach this conclusion, in light of the public policy in favor of the integrity of medical records and in favor of intervention in potential child abuse situations.

Retention of Records

Since records are maintained primarily for patient care purposes, decisions concerning record retention periods should be based on sound hospital and medical practice, as well as on applicable regulations. Some states specify minimum retention periods for some or all records. Medicare requires records to be kept for at least five years.[22] Medicare providers must include in contracts with subcontractors a provision requiring the subcontractor to retain records for at least four years after services are provided and to permit the Department of Health and Human Services (HHS) to inspect them.[23] Several state regulations provide that records be kept permanently, but some require retention for the period in which suits may be filed. Some states provide that records cannot be destroyed without state agency approval.

Where there are no controlling regulations, any retention beyond the time needed for medical and administrative purposes should be determined by hospital administration with advice of legal counsel. In hospitals where extensive medical research is conducted, a longer retention period may be appropriate to facilitate retrospective studies.

The importance of retaining records until the time has passed for lawsuits is illustrated by a 1984 Florida appellate court decision.[24] The anesthesia records concerning a patient were lost, so the proof necessary to sue the anesthesiologist was not available. The court ruled that the hospital could be sued for negligently maintaining its records and that the hospital could avoid liability only by showing that the treatment recorded in the missing records was performed nonnegligently, which would be difficult to do without the records.

Sometimes records are lost due to catastrophe such as fire. One federal court permitted the use in a trial of noncontemporaneous medical records created long after the contemporaneous Veterans Administration (VA) hospital records were destroyed in a fire.[25]

Destruction of Records

The issue of record destruction arises when the retention period has passed or when a patient requests destruction.

Some state hospital licensing regulations specify the methods for destroying records. The method should protect confidentiality by complete destruction. Certificates of destruction should be retained permanently as evidence of record disposal. Some states require creation of a permanent abstract prior to destruction.

Some patients request premature destruction. Some states forbid destruction on an individual basis.[26] In states without specific statutes, it is still prudent not to destroy individual records unless ordered to do so by a court. Courts have generally refused to order destruction. For example, in 1978 the highest court of New York ruled that records could be ordered sealed, but not destroyed.[27] One exception is a 1978 case in which the Pennsylvania Supreme Court ordered destruction of records of the illegal hospitalization of a mental patient.[28]

When Canadian courts began to permit sexual assault defendants to discover records of rape crisis treatment of their victims, some centers providing such treatment began a controversial practice of shredding their records, which led to investigations of the centers for destroying evidence and to some sexual assault charges being dropped.[29]

Ownership

The hospital owns the hospital medical record, which is its business record. Hospital ownership is explicitly stated in the statutes and regulations of some states, and courts have recognized this ownership.[30] If a physician has separate records, they are the physician's property, but the physician is still responsible for maintaining complete hospital records.

The medical record is an unusual type of property because, physically, it belongs to the hospital and the hospital must exercise considerable control over access, but the patient and others have an interest in the information in the record. The hospital owns the paper or other material on which the information is recorded,[31] but it is just a custodian of the information. The patient and others have a right of access to the information in many circumstances, but they do not have a right to possession of original records.[32] Courts have also ruled that patients do not have a right to X-ray negatives.[33] The patient does not purchase a picture; the patient purchases the professional service of interpreting the X-ray. Thus, the patient could not use the physician's retention of the X-ray as a defense to a suit to collect professional fees.

Computers

Many hospitals are developing computerized methods for handling medical record information.[34] Some states require authentication of physician entries and orders by a physician signature which cannot be done when there is no hard copy for the physician to sign or initial. Some states permit authentication with computer codes.[35] Medicare permits computer and facsimile attestations after a hospital's procedures are approved by the Peer Review Organization (PRO).[36] However, there is still variation in the Medicare acceptance of the practice.[37] In some states that require retention of original medical records, computerized records may not suffice. In most states, licensing agencies have the authority to grant waivers. In some states there may be a question of the admissibility in court of information from computerized systems.

Confidentiality questions may arise because more people may have potential access.[38] However, a properly designed security system may provide more protection of confidentiality than traditional records do because (1) there are fewer points of access, (2) each person's access can be restricted to a limited scope of information, and (3) the information sought through individual access codes can be monitored, making misuse easier to detect. The security system depends in part on educating staff that disclosure of personal access codes is equivalent to disclosure of confidential medical information and subject to the same sanctions.

However, attention must be paid to the peculiarities of computers. One hospital sold a surplus computer without completely erasing its backup memory, which contained medical information.[39]

Computers are rapidly moving beyond word processing and data analysis. Computer programs are being developed to assist physicians in making diagnostic and treatment decisions.[40] Hospital or medical staff adoption of such programs is an additional aspect of information management.

CONFIDENTIALITY

The primary rationale for confidentiality is to encourage candor by patients and their associates to optimize diagnosis and treatment. Confidentiality also respects patient privacy; people should not have to broadcast details of their bodily condition to obtain medical treatment. Confidentiality can also promote candor by those treating the patient.

People outside the health care organization often seek to obtain patient information. There is much interest in the condition and treatment of individuals. Family members are interested in their relatives. Some individuals can have a significant effect on affairs of business and state, and their conditions are valuable information. The general interest in unusual health conditions and conditions of those involved in public events focuses media attention on health information.[41] The health condition of individuals is an important element of many insurance coverage determinations and legal proceedings, both criminal and civil.

The tension between access and secrecy has existed since the beginning of medicine. Most health professions have addressed the issue, incorporating confidentiality mandates into their ethical standards. For example, the Hippocratic oath of physicians states: "And whatsoever I shall see or hear in the course of my profession, as well as outside my profession in my intercourse with men, if it be what should not be published abroad, I will never divulge, holding such things to be holy secrets."[42] These ethical standards led to tensions as legal disclosure requirements evolved. For example, some physicians challenged early laws requiring the reporting of births and deaths. However, most modern codes recognize the obligation of professionals to make legally mandated disclosures. The American Medical Association code, adopted in 1980, states: "A physician . . . shall safeguard patient confidences within the constraints of the law."[43]

When hospitals began requiring physicians to document the personal history and physical condition of patients, some physicians objected, but the courts upheld such requirements as reasonable.[44]

ACCESS FOR INTERNAL USES

There are many needs for access to information within the health care organization, including direct patient care, administrative uses, and research uses.

Patient Care

Those who are involved in patient care must have timely access to records to fulfill the patient care functions of the records. Records must be located where they are readily accessible for present and future patient care even when accessibility increases the risk of unauthorized access by others. Although confidentiality is an important goal that health care organizations and health professionals should strive to achieve, unauthorized access results in less liability exposure than does improper patient care due to unavailable records.

However, at least one federal court has adopted the realistic position that there is no duty to review all prior medical records before proceeding with treatment.[45]

Administrative Uses

Medical records are also business records. Many staff members must have access to them to operate the health care organization. The organization has authority to permit internal access by professional, technical, and administrative personnel who need access. Examples of uses requiring access include auditing, filing, billing, replying to inquiries, and defending potential litigation.

These administrative uses are so widely understood that they have seldom been addressed in reported court decisions. The few cases reported have been decided in favor of administrative access. In 1965, the highest court of New York authorized a trustee to examine medical records of patients involved in a controversial research project.[46] The court observed, "Actually, the supposed strict secrecy does not really exist as to qualified persons since these records have been seen, read and copied by numerous staff members and employees of the hospital and co-operating institutions." In 1975, a Missouri court upheld the authority of hospitals to review records for quality assurance purposes.[47] In 1979, a Canadian court ruled that the hospital's insurers and lawyers may have access to prepare to deal with patient claims.[48]

Some plaintiffs' attorneys have attempted to bar hospital attorneys from communicating with physicians and hospital employees involved in the case without the presence of the plaintiffs' attorneys. Courts have generally rejected these attempts.[49] None of these cases have involved attempts to bar access to hospital medical records.

In 1988, a federal appellate court ruled that a public hospital could not permit a chaplain to review records without patient consent.[50]

Research

Research is another major purpose of internal access. Important medical discoveries have been made through researching medical records.[51] A few commentators have questioned records research without patient consent, but the practice is generally recognized as appropriate and permissible. The general practice is to permit staff members to use the medical records for bona fide research. Research by nonstaff members should be subject to a review and approval process. The HHS recognizes this practice in its human studies regulations. Some federally funded research involving only records is exempt from review or eligible for expedited review.[52]

ACCESS BY AUTHORIZATION OF THE PATIENT

The competent patient is one source of authority to release information outside the health care organization.

Patient Access

Competent patients can generally authorize their own access to medical records concerning their care. Some state statutes establish this right of patient access.[53] Most courts have recognized a common law right of access.[54] In 1986, a Pennsylvania court found that denial of access could be intentional infliction of emotional distress.[55] In 1990, the Maryland high court ruled that a hospital could be assessed punitive damages for failing to provide requested medical records within a reasonable time.[56]

The provider may require the patient to pay a reasonable charge for the copy.[57] Courts have disagreed on how much is reasonable.[58] Unless otherwise limited by law, copying charges should be based on hospital costs, including personnel time. In setting copying charges, it is prudent to check the charges of local courts and their libraries because it will be difficult for courts to find comparable charges unreasonable.

In 1994, a Florida appellate court ruled that a health care provider could require that the patient's signature on a release form be notarized.[59] This case should not be interpreted to suggest that notarization is necessary. However, it is clear that courts will accept identity checks that are appropriate to the situation.

Access by Others

When patients may authorize their own access, they may authorize access by others. A federal district court in Oklahoma ruled that insurers have a right to copy hospital records upon proper patient authorization.[60] The court found hospital refusal to provide access to be unlawful interference with the insurer's business. In 1989, a federal appellate court ruled that a physician could be sued by a patient who was denied medical insurance because the physician failed to submit a required report.[61]

There is implied consent to keep the immediate family informed of patient progress unless the patient directs that no information be released or a statutory prohibition applies, such as the federal substance abuse confidentiality rules discussed later in this chapter. In 1963, a Louisiana court ruled that a husband has a right of access to information concerning his wife's care, even though they are separated and he is pursuing divorce.[62] It is doubtful whether many courts would extend the right of access that far today. It is prudent to require patient consent or court authorization before releasing information when estrangement is known.

Consent is usually not implied for other persons unassociated with the health care organization. A Texas court permitted a hospital to be sued for allowing a person assisting a patient's investigations to review her medical records without her express consent.[63]

Release of psychiatric information is subject to special restrictions in some states. In 1982, a New York court stated that a spouse should not be given psychiatric information, even when there is no estrangement, unless (1) the patient authorizes disclosure or (2) a danger to the patient, spouse, or another person can be reduced by disclosure.[64] Some states authorize disclosure of psychiatric information to spouses and others in additional circumstances.[65]

Hospitals can refuse to release records until presented with a release form that complies with their reasonable policies. A Missouri court upheld a hospital's refusal to release records to an attorney who presented a form with an altered date.[66]

Exceptions

Some courts have recognized exceptions to the general rule in favor of access. Release is sometimes against the best interests of the patient's health. Courts have generally insisted that medically contraindicated information be made available to the patient's representative, who is frequently an outside professional acting on behalf of the patient. For example, in 1979 a federal appellate court addressed the withholding of information from patients preparing for hearings challenging their transfer to a lower level of care.[67] The court ruled that it was not enough for the state to offer to release information to a representative when the patient did not have a representative. The state was permitted to withhold medically contraindicated information from patients only when they had representatives, provided by the state if necessary.

Mental health information may be treated differently in some circumstances. In 1995, the Utah Supreme Court ruled that a mental health clinic could assert a privilege not to disclose its records even after the patient executed a release document.[68] In a 1983 case, a New York mental hospital attempted to enforce its policy of releasing records only to physicians.[69] The court ruled that the records could be protected from disclosure only if the hospital proved release would cause detriment (1) to the patient, (2) to involved third parties, or (3) to an important hospital program. Since none of these was proved, the court ordered disclosure to the persons authorized by the patient.

In a 1965 case, a federal appellate court stated that records containing information that would be adverse to the patient's health could be withheld from insurance companies.[70] It is doubtful whether this rule would be applied today since there is widespread recognition of the need for third party payers to have access to records.

Suggested Policies

Health care providers should give patients and their representatives access to medical records when authorized by the patient. When the patient is unable to authorize access, approval of the representative usually should be accepted, as discussed in the next section of this chapter. Since records contain technical information and many abbreviations and specialized terms, the protocol may offer the patient and the representative an opportunity to review the record with someone who can explain it.

Some hospitals notify the attending physician before medical records are released. The medical staff should be told the approach followed. However, physicians should not be given a veto over release of medical records.

Medical record access is recommended because in many situations the curiosity and concerns of the patient will be satisfied, avoiding any appearance of a coverup and avoiding the need for the patient to hire an attorney or file suit to obtain the records. A study that analyzed patient reactions found the following:

1. Approximately one-third of the patients who read their charts had self-induced or factitious illness and were angry to have been uncovered.
2. One-third believed their physicians to be unsympathetic to their symptoms, and some found their suspicions confirmed, while others gained renewed confidence.
3. One-third were worried about their prognosis, fearing the physician was not telling them the true severity of their illness, and all these patients were reassured.[71]

Another good reason to provide prompt access to the medical record is that some courts have ruled that any unreasonably long period from the request until the release does not count toward exhausting the statute of limitations period in which suits must be brought.[72] Thus, resistance to disclosure can reduce the protection of the statute of limitations.

ACCESS BY AUTHORIZATION OF THE PATIENT'S REPRESENTATIVE

Someone other than the patient must authorize access by persons outside the health care organization whenever the patient is unable to authorize access because of incapacity, minority, or death.

Mentally Incapacitated Patients

Guardians of mentally incompetent patients are entitled to access in circumstances when competent patients can obtain access. However, some courts have suppressed family confidences and information that may upset the patient severely.[73]

When a mentally incapacitated patient does not have a guardian, the health care organization generally may rely on authorization by the next of kin or other responsible person who is authorizing medical treatment, especially for access by the responsible person or by others for continuity of patient care or payment of charges. When the mental incapacity is temporary and the release of the information can reasonably wait, it usually is appropriate to wait for the patient's authorization.

Minors

For most minors, the decision whether to release records is made by a custodial parent. State law needs to be consulted to determine the access rights of noncustodial parents.[74]

The scope of parent and guardian access to records of adolescent and older minors is less clear.[75] Some state statutes specify that information regarding certain types of treatment, such as treatment for venereal disease and substance abuse, may not be disclosed without the minor's consent. Some statutes specify that parents must be informed before minors may obtain certain kinds of services.[76]

When minors legally consent to their own care, it is likely that parents do not have a right to information concerning the care. If the minor fails to make other arrangements to pay for the care and relies on the parents to pay, the parents may be entitled to more information. However, providers can release information concerning immature minors to their parents without substantial risk of liability unless state statutes expressly prohibit release. When a mature minor wishes information withheld from parents, the provider must make a professional judgment concerning information release to the parents except in the few circumstances where the law is settled, such as when a constitutional statute requires or forbids notification. Disclosure is generally permitted when there is likelihood of harm, such as contagious disease, to the minor or others and avoidance of that harm requires parental involvement.

State statutes should be followed. A Georgia court ruled that a father could sue a psychiatrist for releasing his minor daughter's mental health records to his former wife's attorney for use in custody litigation.[77] The daughter had requested the release and had ratified it after becoming an adult, but the release did not comply with the state statute.

Deceased Patients

After the patient's death, the responsibility to maintain confidentiality generally continues. If there is an executor of the estate, the executor's authorization should usually be sought before releasing information.[78] If there is no executor, in most states authorization should be obtained from the next of kin, such as a surviving spouse[79] or a child.[80]

In a few states the legal responsibility to maintain confidentiality ends with the patient's death. It is still prudent to insist on appropriate authorization.

ACCESS BY LAW

Even if the patient or representative opposes information release, health care providers are required by law to permit access to medical information in many circumstances. In lawsuits, parties may gain access to relevant information through subpoenas and other mechanisms to discover evidence. Providers are required (1) to report many patient conditions to law enforcement or public health authorities and (2) to provide certain persons access to information when requested.

Subpoenas and Other Discovery Mechanisms

In lawsuits and administrative proceedings, the parties are authorized by law to demand relevant unprivileged information in the control of others. Lawyers call this the "discovery" process. The most frequent discovery demand is called a *subpoena.* A subpoena is a demand for a person to appear at a certain place at a certain time, and it frequently requires the person to bring certain documents. In federal courts and in most states, demands to parties are generally called *notices of deposition* or *notices to produce*, while actual subpoenas are used only for persons who are not parties to the suit. Notices and subpoenas have essentially the same effect, so what is said about subpoenas in the rest of this chapter also applies to notices. When the demands are ignored, a court can order compliance, and further noncompliance can be punished as contempt of court. Other discovery orders can require a person to submit to a physical or mental examination or to permit inspection of land, buildings, or other property.

Medical Records

A subpoena may require that medical records (or copies) be provided to the court or to the other side in the suit. A subpoena may require a person to submit to formal questioning under oath prior to the trial. This question-and-answer session is called a *deposition* and often is used as testimony in the trial if the person questioned cannot be at the trial. If the person questioned is at the trial and gives different testimony, the deposition can be used for impeachment, which means to cast doubt on what is said at the trial.

Under the current liberal discovery practices, medical records of parties can nearly always be subpoenaed if the mental or physical condition of the party is relevant. When records can be subpoenaed, those who provided the health care usually can be ordered also to give depositions.

Sometimes the medical records custodian has a duty to refuse to provide records in response to subpoenas. For example, federal rules require a court order before substance abuse records may be released. Some states require a court order for production of medical records containing information about HIV status. Some subpoenas of mental health records may have to be resisted. In 1995, a Pennsylvania court upheld a reprimand from the state licensing board to a psychologist for disclosing patient medical records pursuant to a subpoena. The records were privileged so the subpoena did not authorize release.[81]

In most circumstances courts will not permit discovery of information concerning health care of persons who are not parties.[82] Some attorneys have sought such information to establish what happened when similar treatment was given to other patients. Providers have resisted these attempts on the basis that they invade patient privacy, violate the physician-patient privilege discussed later in this chapter, and are not relevant because of the uniqueness of the condition and reaction of each patient.

The only widely accepted exceptions in which discovery of nonparty records has been permitted have been cases of billing fraud or professional discipline.[83] Some courts have permitted access to medical records of nonparties in malpractice suits, but have required all "identifiers" to be deleted.[84] However, other courts have reaffirmed the traditional rule and declined to order access even with identifiers deleted.[85]

In 1992, the Connecticut Supreme Court ruled that the four-digit zip code suffix was an identifier.[86]

Patient Names

Some attorneys have attempted to bypass the rule against disclosure of nonparty medical records by seeking nonparty patients' names and obtaining their permission to get the records. Providers have resisted these attempts for reasons similar to those for resisting discovery of records. Most courts have not permitted discovery of nonparty patient names. For example, the Michigan Supreme Court ruled that patients' names are protected by the physician-patient privilege.[87] Similarly, in 1987, the Florida Supreme Court denied discovery of blood donor names in an AIDS case.[88] In 1976, the Arizona Supreme Court ruled that the physician-patient privilege does not protect patient names in Arizona, but still refused to order release of other names because it did not consider them relevant.[89]

In 1987, a Texas court allowed discovery of donor names in an AIDS case, but prohibited contact with the donors.[90] In 1988, the Colorado Supreme Court ordered disclosure to the court clerk of the name of a donor with AIDS so that the plaintiff could submit written questions to the donor through the clerk.[91] In 1995, a federal court allowed the deposition of a donor with AIDS under a protective order to protect the donor's identity.[92] One attorney violated a court order restricting use of donor-specific information. In 1994, a federal court ruled that, while the attorney could be punished, the case could not be dismissed as punishment.[93] There is a risk that records obtained without identifiers could be linked later to patient names through another exception.

Committee Reports

Many states have enacted statutes protecting quality improvement and peer review activities and committee reports from discovery or admission into evidence. These laws are designed to permit the candor necessary for effective peer review to improve quality and reduce morbidity and mortality. Courts have found these laws constitutional.[94]

Some courts have strictly interpreted statutory protections, reducing their effectiveness. For example, a New Jersey court refused to apply the statutory protection for "utilization review committees" to related committees, such as the medical records and audit, tissue, and infection control committees.[95] The Louisiana Supreme Court ruled that its statute did not protect nosocomial infection studies.[96] The hostility of some courts to such privileges is illustrated by a West Virginia case which ruled that courts should not rely on a hospital's assertion of the privilege, but instead should inspect all documents for which a privilege was claimed and require the hospital to prove that each document was protected by the privilege.[97]

Some courts have interpreted statutory protections broadly. For example, the Minnesota Supreme Court found that a complications conference report was protected under a statute that protected "the proceedings and records of a review organization."[98] Under some states' laws the identities of persons involved in peer review are also protected.[99]

Some state laws protect peer review records from discovery only, so if they are obtained through other channels they can be used in court.[100] Other laws protect the records from being introduced in lawsuits even if they are obtained outside discovery channels.[101]

Even when the privilege does apply, many state laws permit state licensing agencies to gain access.[102]

State law protections for peer review records do not apply in federal law suits involving federal law.[103] A few federal courts have recognized a common law qualified privilege based on the public interest in peer review activities. A District of Columbia court refused to order release of information concerning a peer review committee's activities.[104] However, other courts have refused to recognize a common law privilege for peer review.[105]

Because the status of committee reports is still an open question in many states, these reports should be carefully written so that, if they must be released, they will not inappropriately increase liability exposure.

Responses to Subpoenas and Other Discovery Orders

In most situations the proper response to a valid subpoena or discovery order is compliance. However, prompt legal assistance should be sought since some subpoenas or orders are not valid and others should be resisted.[106] A discovery order should never be ignored.

Subpoenas from state courts in other states are usually not valid unless they are given to the person being subpoenaed while that person is in the state of the issuing court. However, subpoenas from federal courts in other states are usually valid. Courts in some states have authority to issue subpoenas to persons only in a limited area. Most states have a procedure for obtaining a valid subpoena from a local court to require the release of information for a trial in a distant court that does not have the authority to issue a valid subpoena. Some state courts will order a party to sign a document requesting and authorizing release of records, especially out-of-state records, instead of going through the process of obtaining an order where the records are located.[107]

Sometimes challenges to subpoenas are successful. A New Jersey court refused to order a woman or her psychiatrist to answer questions concerning nonfinancial matters in a marriage separation case because the husband had failed to demonstrate relevance or good cause for the order.[108] When judges are not certain whether to order a release, they sometimes will order that the information be presented for court review before ruling. An Illinois court ruled that this review should be by a judge, not an administrative hearing officer.[109]

In some situations, the only way to obtain prompt appellate review of an apparently inappropriate discovery order is to risk being found in contempt of court. In one case a physician challenged a grand jury subpoena of records of 63 patients.[110] The trial court found him to be in contempt for failing to comply. The Illinois Supreme Court held that he must release the records of the one patient who had waived her physician-patient privilege, but reversed the contempt finding on the other 62 records. They were protected by the physician-patient privilege in Illinois until a showing of a criminal action relating to the treatment documented in the records was made. In another Illinois case the appellate court ruled that the trial court had erred in jailing a physician and his attorney for contempt of court concerning a deposition. The applicable statute did not permit more discovery than had been given and the trial court failed to show any accommodation for the patients scheduled for the physician's care.[111]

Valid subpoenas should never be ignored and should never be challenged except on advice of an attorney. In 1978, an Illinois court affirmed a $1,000 fine assessed against an orthopedic surgeon for ignoring a subpoena and refusing to appear at a trial involving his patient.[112] In a Kansas case, a treating physician was jailed for refusing to testify until he was paid an expert witness fee.[113] However, in 1983 the Iowa Supreme Court ruled that an expert witness who is a stranger to the litigation may not be compelled to give opinion testimony absent a demonstration of compelling necessity.[114]

Attorneys need to be cautious in giving such advice. A federal court found an attorney to be in contempt and fined the attorney for advising the client to resist a subpoena in a Medicare investigation.[115]

Statutory Duty To Disclose

Reporting Laws

The law compels disclosure of medical information in many contexts other than discovery or testimony. Reporting laws have been enacted that require medical information to be reported to governmental agencies. The most common examples are vital statistics, communicable disease, child abuse, and wound reporting laws. Familiarity with these and other reporting laws is important to assure compliance and to avoid reporting to the wrong agency. Reports to the wrong agency may not be legally protected, resulting in potential liability for breach of confidentiality.[116]

Vital Statistics. All states require the reporting of births and deaths.[117] These laws are a valid exercise of the state police power.[118]

Public Health. Most states require reports of venereal disease and other communicable diseases.[119] A California court observed that in addition to criminal penalties for not reporting, civil liability is possible in a suit by persons who contract diseases that might have been avoided by proper reports.[120] Some states require reports of cancer and other selected noncontagious diseases. A few states require reports be submitted to state driver licensing agencies of conditions such as seizures that could lead to loss of license.

In 1994, a Missouri appellate court barred enforcement of a local court rule requiring correction facilities to disclose the infectious disease reports of inmates before court appearances.[121]

Child Abuse. Most states require reports of suspected cases of child abuse or neglect.[122] Some professionals, such as physicians and nurses, are mandatory reporters and thus are required to make reports. Anyone who is not a mandatory reporter may make a report as a permissive reporter. In some states any report arising out of diagnosis or treatment in an institution must be made through the institutional administration. Most child abuse reporting laws extend some degree of immunity from liability for reports made through proper channels.[123] A mandatory reporter who fails to report child abuse is subject to both criminal penalties[124] and civil liability for future injuries to the child that could have been avoided if a report had been made.[125] There have been disputes in some states over when some activities, such as sexual activity of younger minors, must be reported as child abuse.[126]

Adult Abuse/Domestic Violence. Some states have enacted laws that require reports of abuse of certain adults, especially the older person and the disabled, and reports of domestic violence.[127]

Wounds. Many states require the reporting of certain wounds. Some states specify that all wounds of certain types must be reported. For example, New York requires the reporting of wounds inflicted by sharp instruments that may result in death and all gunshot wounds.[128] Other states limit the reporting requirement to wounds caused under certain circumstances. For example, Iowa requires the reporting of wounds that apparently resulted from criminal acts.[129] Thus, wounds that are clearly accidental or self-inflicted do not have to be reported in Iowa.

Other Reporting Laws. Some states require reports of other information, such as industrial accidents and radiation incidents.[130] National reporting laws apply to hospitals that are involved in manufacturing, testing, or using certain substances and devices. For example, fatalities due to blood transfusions must be reported to the Food and Drug Administration (FDA).[131] A sponsor of an investigational medical device must report to the FDA any unanticipated adverse effects from use of the device.[132] Device manufacturers have a duty to report to the FDA when a death or serious injury has occurred in connection with the device.[133]

Some states require that major adverse incidents be reported to a state agency.[134] A director of nursing of a nursing home was personally fined in New York for failing to make such a report.[135]

In 1977, the U.S. Supreme Court upheld a state law that required reports to a central state registry of all prescriptions of Schedule II controlled substances.[136]

At least one state requires reports to private individuals. Florida requires hospitals to notify emergency transport personnel and other individuals who bring emergency patients to the hospital if the patient is diagnosed as having a contagious disease.[137]

Access Laws

Some statutes do not mandate reporting, but authorize access to medical records, without the patient's permission, on request of certain individuals or organizations or the general public.

Workers' Compensation. Some state statutes grant all parties to a workers' compensation claim access to all relevant medical information after a claim has been made.[138] In some states, courts have ruled that filing a worker's compensation claim is a waiver of confidentiality of relevant medical information.[139] However, in 1994, the West Virginia Supreme Court ruled that the physician-patient privilege applies in workers' compensation cases.[140]

Federal Freedom of Information Act. The federal Freedom of Information Act (FOIA) applies only to federal agencies.[141] A hospital does not become a federal agency by receiving federal funds, so the FOIA applies to few hospitals outside of the VA and Defense Department hospital systems. When the FOIA applies, medical information is exempted from disclosure only when the disclosure would "constitute a clearly unwarranted invasion of personal privacy." Thus, the Act provides only limited protection of confidentiality of medical information in the possession of federal agencies. However, the federal Privacy Act may provide some additional protection to such information.[142]

State Public Records Laws. Many states have public records laws that apply to public hospitals. Some state statutes explicitly exempt hospital and medical records from disclosure.[143] In a 1974 case, Colorado's law was interpreted not to permit a publisher to obtain all birth and death reports routinely.[144] In 1983, the

Iowa Supreme Court addressed the effort of a leukemia patient to force the disclosure of an unrelated potential bone marrow donor whose name was in the records of a public hospital.[145] The court ruled that names of patients could be withheld from disclosure and that although the potential donor had never sought treatment at the hospital, the potential donor was a patient for purposes of the exemption because the medical procedure of tissue typing had been performed. However, in a 1978 Ohio case, the state law was interpreted to require access to the names and the dates of admission and discharge of all persons admitted to a public hospital.[146] In states that follow the Ohio rule it is especially important to resist discovery of nonparty records because removal of "identifiers" does not offer much protection when dates in the records may make it possible to identify the patient from the admission list.

Other Access Laws. Some federal and state statutes give governmental agencies access to medical records on request or through administrative subpoena. For example, PROs have access to all medical records pertinent to their federal review functions on request. A federal district court has ruled that Medicare surveyors have a right of access to records of non-Medicare patients, as well as to those of Medicare patients.[147] Hospital licensing laws often grant inspectors access without subpoena for audit and inspection purposes.

Common Law Duty To Disclose

In addition to these statutory requirements, the common law has recognized a duty to disclose medical information in several circumstances. Persons who could have avoided injury if information had been disclosed have won civil suits against providers who failed to disclose such information.

Contagious Diseases

When a contagious disease is diagnosed, there is a duty to warn some persons at risk of exposure unless forbidden by statute.[148] Hospital staff, family members, and others caring for the patient should be warned. In a 1928 case, an Ohio court ruled that a physician could be liable for the death of a neighbor who contracted smallpox while assisting in the care of the physician's patient with smallpox because the physician failed to warn the neighbor of the contagious nature of the disease.[149] However, in most states there is no duty to warn all members of the public individually. In a California case, the court observed that liability to the general public might result from failure to make a required report to public health authorities.[150] In at least one state there may be a duty to warn a broader range of individuals. In 1986, the South Carolina Supreme Court ruled that a hospital could be sued by the parents of a girl who had died of meningitis. Her friend had been diagnosed and treated at the hospital for meningitis, and the hospital had not notified persons who had had prior contact with its patient during the likely period of contagiousness.[151] In 1992, a Kentucky appellate court ruled that a child care center was liable for the death of a child from meningitis because it had failed to warn of other children at the center who had the disease.[152]

In 1991, the West Virginia Supreme Court ruled that a hospital security guard should have been warned that a patient had AIDS before being asked to help restrain the patient.[153] In 1994, a federal appellate court ruled that a man who got HIV infection from his brother while transporting him between hospitals could sue the first hospital for failure to disclose the brother's condition.[154] When a statute forbids disclosure of certain diseases, such as AIDS, there can be no duty to disclose.[155]

Threats to an Identified Person

Some courts have ruled that there is a duty to warn identified persons that a patient has made a credible threat to kill them. The first decision to impose this duty was *Tarasoff v. Regents of University of California.*[156] When the Tarasoffs sued for the death of their daughter, the California Supreme Court found the employer of a psychiatrist liable for the psychiatrist's failure to warn the daughter that one of his patients had threatened to kill her. The court ruled that he should have either warned the victim or advised others likely to apprise the victim of the danger. In a 1980 case, the same court clarified the scope of this duty by ruling that only threats to readily identified individuals create a duty to warn, so there is no duty to warn a threatened group.[157] In 1989, the Arizona Supreme Court ruled that foreseeable victims had to be warned even without specific threats.[158] In 1983, the Washington Supreme Court ruled that the duty to warn extended to unidentifiable victims.[159] In 1985, the Vermont Supreme Court extended the duty to warn to include property damage, imposing liability on a counseling service when a patient burned his parents' barn.[160] Some courts have declined to establish a duty to warn even readily identified individuals.[161] In states that have not addressed the issue it is prudent to follow the California rule and warn identified individuals of credible threats when the patient is not detained.

Other Duties

Courts have recognized other situations in which there is a duty to disclose. One example is the duty of referral specialists to communicate their findings to the referring physician.[162] A competent patient can waive this duty by directing the referral specialist not to communicate with the referring physician.[163]

In 1988, the Oklahoma Supreme Court held that a physician could not be sued by a patient who was convicted of rape after the physician informed police that he suspected the patient was the rapist the police were seeking. The disclosure was protected by public policy.[164]

LIMITATIONS ON DISCLOSURE

Several statutory and common law limitations on disclosure have evolved that assist in preserving confidentiality and impose sanctions for some violations of confidentiality.

It is possible that the constitutional right of privacy may preclude some disclosures.[165]

Physician-Patient Privilege

The physician-patient privilege is the rule that a physician is not permitted to testify as a witness concerning certain information gained in the physician-patient relationship. There was no physician-patient privilege from testimonial disclosure under the English common law. Nearly all American courts also have adopted this position, so with few exceptions the privilege exists only in states that have enacted privilege statutes. One exception is Alaska, which established a common law psychotherapist-patient privilege for criminal cases.[166] State privileges do not apply in most federal suits concerning federal law.[167]

Approximately two-thirds of the states have enacted a statutory physician-patient privilege. Privilege statutes address only situations in which the physician is being compelled to testify, such as in a deposition, an administrative hearing, or a trial or to release subpoenaed records. There is a widespread misconception that privilege statutes apply to other disclosures, but in most states this is not true.[168] The duty to maintain confidentiality outside of testimonial contexts is grounded on other legal principles discussed later in this chapter. Thus, privilege statutes are usually of concern only when hospitals are responding to legal compulsion.

The privilege applies only when a bona fide physician-patient relationship exists. The privilege usually does not apply to court-ordered examinations or other examinations solely for the benefit of third parties, such as insurance companies.

The scope of the privilege varies. Pennsylvania limits the privilege to communications that tend to blacken the character of the patient,[169] while Kansas extends the privilege to all communications and observations.[170] Michigan limits the privilege to physicians,[171] while New York extends the privilege to dentists and nurses.[172] When a nurse is present during a confidential communication between physician and patient, some states extend the privilege to the nurse, while other states rule that the communication is no longer privileged for the physician.

Generally the privilege extends to otherwise privileged information recorded in the hospital record.[173] However, information that is required to be reported to public authorities has generally been held not to be privileged unless the public authorities are also privileged not to disclose it.

Psychotherapist-Patient Privilege

In many states a separate statute establishes a psychotherapist-patient privilege. The definition of a psychotherapist varies. The Georgia Supreme Court ruled that the state psychiatrist-patient privilege applied to nonpsychiatrists who devoted a substantial part of their time to mental diseases.[174]

Some federal courts have recognized a federal psychotherapist-patient privilege.[175] Those that have recognized the privilege generally rule that it does not apply to criminal child abuse cases.[176]

Waiver

The patient may waive the privilege, permitting the physician to testify. The privilege can be waived by contract. Insurance applications and policies often include waivers. Other actions can constitute implied waiver. Introducing evidence of medical details or failing to object to physician testimony generally waives the privilege.[177] Authorization of disclosure outside the testimonial context usually does not waive the privilege.[178] Thus, the patient generally may authorize other persons to have access to medical records outside of court and still successfully object to having them introduced into evidence unless other actions have waived the privilege. In a few states, authorization of any disclosure to opposing parties waives the privilege.[179]

Making a claim based on emotional distress or other mental condition usually waives the psychotherapist-patient privilege.[180] In some states, if the mental claim is dropped from the suit, the privilege is restored.[181]

Waiver of the privilege usually permits only formal discovery and testimony, not informal interviews. Express patient consent is generally required before informal interviews are permitted.[182] Other courts have permitted informal interviews based on waiver of the privilege.[183] However, in some states, it may be breach of the physician's duty to the patient to engage in informal interviews.[184] Most providers limit disclosures to formal channels unless express patient consent is obtained.

Other Statutory Limitations on Disclosure

Access to medical information is limited by some federal and state statutes, such as federal substance abuse confidentiality laws and state licensing and confidentiality laws.

Substance Abuse Confidentiality

Special federal rules deal with confidentiality of information concerning patients treated or referred for treatment for alcoholism or drug abuse.[185] The rules apply to any facility receiving federal funds for any purpose, including Medicare or Medicaid reimbursement. The regulations preempt any state law that purports to authorize disclosures contrary to the regulations, but states are permitted to impose tighter confidentiality requirements. The rules apply to any disclosure, even acknowledgment of the patient's presence in the facility. Information may be released with the patient's consent if the consent is in writing and contains all the elements required by the federal rules. Many standard forms for releasing records are not sufficient to authorize release of these records.

A court order, including a subpoena, does not permit release of information unless the requirements of the regulations have all been met. The regulations require a court hearing and a court finding that the purpose for which the order is sought is more important than the purpose for which Congress mandated confidentiality. The regulations have been interpreted to permit hospitals to tell the court why they cannot comply with the order until after a hearing. After a hearing, courts have ordered disclosures to assist probation revocation and child abuse proceedings.[186] In 1981, a federal district court ordered disclosure to assist an Internal Revenue Service investigation of a surgeon.[187] Release has been ordered in other situations.[188] Courts have declined to order disclosure when the information was sought to challenge the credibility of witnesses or to assist in determining the rehabilitation potential of a convicted person for purposes of sentencing.[189]

Child abuse reports may be made under state law without patient consent or a court order, but release of records to child abuse agencies requires consent or an order.

Staff members should be oriented to these rules. In one case a nurse successfully challenged her discharge for failure to report a fellow employee's theft of patient files by establishing the reasonableness of her belief (which was actually erroneous) that these federal regulations prohibited the report.[190]

HIV/AIDS

Many states have statutes that specify when an HIV test result or a diagnosis of AIDS may be disclosed.[191] These statutes are often strictly interpreted.

A California physician was sued for writing a patient's HIV status in a medical record without the written consent required by state law even though the patient had given oral consent. The physician settled the suit.[192] A New York physician was found to have violated the law by disclosing a positive HIV test to an out-of-state workers' compensation board, where the authorization from the patient did not satisfy the statutory requirements.[193] Placing a red sticker on the possessions of an HIV-positive inmate and segregating her improperly disclosed her HIV status to persons who were not authorized to know.[194]

A Pennsylvania court permitted a hospital to make limited disclosure of a resident physician's HIV-positive status, including disclosure to patients without naming the resident.[195]

A North Carolina court upheld revocation of the clinical privileges of a physician for not complying with a hospital policy that required disclosure to the hospital of any inpatient who was HIV-positive.[196]

A federal court in Pennsylvania found that a plaintiff had waived the confidential status of his HIV status by seeking damages that required a determination of life expectancy.[197]

Professional and Hospital Licensing Laws

Professional licensing laws or regulations frequently specify that breach of confidentiality is unprofessional conduct and grounds for discipline by the licensing board. Examples are the Iowa rules pertaining to physicians and nurses.[198] Hospital licensing laws and regulations also frequently require that confidentiality of records be maintained.[199]

Other State Confidentiality Laws

Some states have statutes that establish a general responsibility to maintain confidentiality of medical records.[200] Some states have statutes that address only records regarding treatment for certain conditions, such as venereal disease.[201] Most states provide some confidentiality for the identities of biological parents of children who are adopted,[202] but this statutory protection does not usually extend to children who were not legally adopted.[203]

Accreditation Standards

The Joint Commission medical records standards specify that hospitals have the responsibility of protecting the medical record and the information in the medical record "against loss, destruction, tampering, and unauthorized access or use."[204] If a hospital accepts this responsibility to become accredited, many courts will require the hospital to follow its own rules and impose liability for injuries that result from violations.

Common Law Limitations

As discussed in the section on the physician-patient privilege, the common law usually does not provide for any protection from disclosure in testimonial contexts. Courts refuse to impose liability for testimonial disclosures.[205] Physicians and hospitals are not obligated to risk contempt of court to protect confidences (except for substance abuse records), although they may choose to do so.

In nontestimonial contexts, courts have found limitations on permissible disclosure based on the implied promise of confidentiality in the physician-patient relationship, violation of the right of privacy, and violation of professional licensing standards.[206] For example, a New York court permanently enjoined a psychoanalyst from circulating a book that included detailed information concerning a patient.[207] The patient was identifiable to close friends despite the psychoanalyst's efforts to disguise her identity. The court ruled that the book violated the implied covenant of confidentiality and the right of privacy. The plaintiff was awarded $20,000 for the 220 copies that were sold before the injunction. In 1985, the Oregon Supreme Court held that a physician could be liable for revealing his patient's identity to the patient's natural child, who had been adopted.[208] The court ruled that while it was not a violation of the patient's right of privacy, it was a breach of the professional duty to maintain secrets.

Courts have ruled in favor of health care providers in cases where disclosure was intended to prevent the spread of contagious disease.[209] As discussed in the section on the common law duty to disclose information, there could be liability in some circumstances for failing to disclose a contagious disease.

Disclosures to the patient's employer or insurance company have resulted in several suits.[210] The Alabama Supreme Court ruled that disclosures to an employer without authorization violated the implied promise of confidentiality and could result in liability.[211] The employer who induces the disclosure can also be liable.[212] However, a New York court ruled that when a patient authorized incomplete disclosure to his employer, the physician was not liable for giving a complete disclosure.[213] It is questionable whether other courts would rule this way, so the prudent practice is to refuse to release any information when only a misleading partial release is authorized. In 1992, a Missouri court found that a psychologist was not liable for sending a letter to a patient's supervisor urging the patient's transfer to a less stressful job, where the patient had authorized release on three prior occasions.[214]

Some courts have found implied authorization to release information to an insurance company based on patient actions. In a Colorado case, submission to a medical examination at the insurance company's request was considered implied authorization.[215] However, the prudent practice is to obtain the patient's written authorization. Most insurance companies do so as part of the initial application and on claim forms. In some cases, courts have ruled that insurance companies may be sued for inducing a physician to divulge confidential information.[216]

Suits for disclosures of confidential information have also been based on defamation. In most cases involving physicians, courts have found a qualified privilege to make the specific disclosures.[217] The few cases of liability have involved disclosure of a misdiagnosed embarrassing condition (such as venereal disease) that the patient did not actually have in a manner that demonstrated malice, defeating the qualified privilege.[218]

Misuse of confidential information without disclosure can also lead to sanctions. In 1991, a New York psychiatrist pled guilty to securities fraud for trading in stocks based on inside information received from a patient.[219] He was sentenced to probation and community service.

A provider can be liable for disclosure by staff members.[220]

PHOTOGRAPHY

Physicians usually may take and use photographs of patients for the medical record or for professional educational purposes unless the patient expressly forbids photographs. The highest court of Massachusetts enjoined public showing of a film of inmates of an institution for insane persons charged with crimes or delinquency, but permitted continued showings to audiences of a specialized or professional character with a serious interest in rehabilitation.[221] The court observed that the public interest in having these people informed outweighs the rights of the inmates to privacy. The Maine Supreme Court ruled that when a patient had expressly objected to being photographed, there could be liability for photographing the patient even if the photograph was solely for the medical records.[222] It is best to obtain express consent for taking and using photographs,[223] but liability for photographs taken without express consent is not likely if the patient does not object and uses are appropriately restricted. A New York appellate court ruled that a physician and nurse could not be sued for allowing a newspaper photographer to photograph a patient in the waiting areas of an infectious disease unit because the individual's presence did not indicate the individual was a patient and the individual was never identified as a patient.[224] Of course, public or commercial showing without consent can lead to liability.[225]

In 1985, a New York appellate court ruled that representatives of an incompetent patient do not have a right to photograph the patient in the hospital.[226] The petitioners failed to show a sufficient need to justify a court order that they be permitted to film an eight-hour videotape of their comatose daughter in an intensive care unit for use in a suit.

In 1986, a New York court ruled that a patient had no right, before filing a malpractice suit, to a videotape of the patient's operation. It was found not to be a part of the medical record because the physician had taken it for his personal use.[227]

DISCIPLINE OF STAFF MEMBERS

Staff members have been discharged for unauthorized disclosure of medical records. However, courts and arbitration panels tend to reinstate them unless there has been a consistent pattern of enforcement. For example, a Royal Commission that investigated the confidentiality of medical records in Ontario found many unauthorized disclosures. One of the persons responsible was a nurse who had given records to her husband, an attorney representing patients' opponents in legal proceedings. She was fired, but the arbitration board ordered her reinstated with the sanction of suspension without pay up to the time of the ruling.[228] The board accepted her position that since no one else had been disciplined, she was the scapegoat for the hospital's embarrassment concerning the Royal Commission's findings. In 1983, a Minnesota court addressed a nurse who had been dismissed for a breach of confidentiality.[229] The court found that she was not guilty of misconduct and, thus, should receive unemployment compensation because the hospital's policy had not been adequately enunciated to the staff. This misconduct disqualified the person from receiving unemployment compensation. A Texas court upheld the termination of a nurse for having revealed the identities and medical condition of patients.[230]

A consistent pattern of enforcing a well-communicated policy is important both to emphasize the importance of confidentiality to the staff and to increase the likelihood that disciplinary actions will be sustained if challenged.

Some courts have supported dismissal of employees for confidentiality violations. The Iowa Supreme Court addressed a case in which a medication aide had been fired for disclosing confidential patient information while complaining to a member of the county board of supervisors about patient care. The court ruled that the disclosure was misconduct that disqualified the aide from unemployment compensation.[231]

In 1995, the 13-year-old daughter of a Florida hospital clerk allegedly called six former emergency room patients and, as a "prank," told them falsely that they had tested positively for AIDS. Allegedly she had obtained the names and telephone numbers using a computer while visiting her mother. The girl was charged with six felony and eight misdemeanor counts for taking confidential information from a computer, making harassing phone calls, and disseminating false information about sexually transmitted diseases. She was placed in state custody. The mother was suspended from her job while an internal investigation was conducted.[232]

NOTES

1. *See* Legal Economic Evaluations v. Metropolitan Life Ins. Co., 39 F.3d 951 (9th Cir. 1994), *cert. denied*, 115 S. Ct. 1420 (U.S. 1995) [summary judgment for defendants in suit by consultants who provided services to tort claimants on costs of structured settlements and claimed antitrust violation against life insurance companies that refused to provide information to anyone other than for defense].
2. Joint Commission on Accreditation of Healthcare Organizations, 1995 COMPREHENSIVE ACCREDITATION MANUAL FOR HOSPITALS, 377–435 [hereinafter 1995 Joint Commission CAMH].
3. 42 C.F.R. § 482.24(c).

4. 1995 Joint Commission CAMH, at 397–416.

5. *E.g.*, Valendon Martinez v. Hospital Presbiteriano de la Communidad, Inc., 806 F.2d 1128 (1st Cir. 1986).

6. Lama v. Borras, 16 F.3d 473 (1st Cir. 1994).

7. Repp v. Anadarko Mun. Hosp., 43 F.3d 519 (10th Cir. 1994).

8. 1995 Joint Commission CAMH, at, *e.g.*, 408–10 (completion within 30 days of discharge), 96–97 (history, physical within 24 hours of inpatient admission), 401–05 (operative report dictated immediately after surgery, authenticated as soon as possible after surgery).

9. Hiatt v. Groce, 215 Kan. 14, 523 P.2d 320 (1974).

10. Collins v. Westlake Comm. Hosp., 57 Ill. 2d 388, 312 N.E.2d 614 (1974).

11. Engle v. Clarke, 346 S.W.2d 13 (Ky. 1961); *contra* Thome v. Palmer, 141 Ill. App. 3d 92, 489 N.E.2d 1163, 95 Ill. Dec. 435 (3d Dist. 1986); Hurlock v. Park Lane Med. Ctr., 709 S.W.2d 872 (Mo. Ct. App. 1985).

12. 42 C.F.R. § 482.24(c)(2)(viii).

13. 1995 Joint Commission CAMH, *supra* note 2, at 408.

14. *E.g.*, Board of Trustees. v. Pratt, 72 Wyo. 120, 262 P.2d 682 (1953). Some hospitals use financial incentives, *e.g.*, *Incentives spur physicians to complete record keeping*, 15 MOD. HEALTH-CARE, Dec. 6, 1985, at 64; Perry, *Emphasis on coordination hastens submission of bills*, 19 MOD. HEALTHCARE, July 14, 1989, at 39.

15. Birthisel v. Tri-Cities Health Servs. Corp., 188 W.Va. 371, 424 S.E.2d 606 (1992).

16. Kaplan v. Central Med. Group, 71 A.D.2d 912, 419 N.Y.S.2d 750 (2d Dep't 1979).

17. Mirkin v. Medical Mut. Liability Ins. Soc'y, 82 Md. App. 540, 572 A.2d 1126 (1990).

18. *E.g.*, United States ex rel. Brooks v. Pineville Comm. Hosp., No. 92-286 (E.D. Ky. Apr. 19, 1995), *as discussed in* 23 HEALTH L. DIG. (May 1995), at 31 [hospital, physicians paid $2.5 million to settle claims they submitted false claims by allowing medical records clerks to create history, physical, discharge summary documentation in medical record and authenticate it with signature stamp; prearranged, approved wording used; also settled privately with physician who brought suit, paying him $300,000 for retaliation by medical staff for suit].

19. *E.g.*, Jimenez v. Department of Professional Regulation, 556 So.2d 1219 (Fla. 4th DCA 1990) [one-year suspension of physician's license, $5,000 fine, two years' probation after suspension for adding false information to records after death of patient].

20. *E.g.*, In re Morris, 482 A.2d 369 (D.C. 1984); *see also* Caraballo v. Secretary of HHS, 670 F. Supp. 1106 (D. P.R. 1987) [judicially altered birth certificate not conclusive evidence of age].

21. Strauss v. Thorne, 490 N.W.2d 908 (Minn. Ct. App. 1992).

22. 42 C.F.R. § 482.24(b)(1); MEDICARE & MEDICAID GUIDE (CCH) ¶ 6420.85.

23. 42 U.S.C.A. § 1395x(v)(1)(I).

24. Bondu v. Gurvich, 473 So.2d 1307 (Fla. 3d DCA 1984), *rev. denied*, 484 So.2d 7 (Fla. 1986); *see also* D.R. Goodnight and D.R. Davis, *Spoliation of evidence: The unnecessary tort*, 25 J. HEALTH & HOSP. L. 232 (1992); DeLaughter v. Lawrence County Hosp., 601 So.2d 818 (Miss. 1992) [missing records create rebuttable adverse presumption]; Rodgers v. St. Mary's Hosp., 198 Ill. App. 3d 871, 556 N.E.2d 913 (4th Dist. 1990), *aff'd*, 149 Ill. 2d 302, 597 N.E.2d 616 (1992) [claim stated against hospital for loss of X-rays crucial to patient's malpractice claim]; Annotation, *Medical malpractice: presumption or inference from failure of hospital or doctor to produce relevant medical records*, 69 A.L.R. 4TH 906.

25. Elmer v. Tenneco Resins, Inc., 698 F. Supp. 535 (D. Del. 1988).

26. *E.g.*, TENN. CODE ANN. § 68-11-305(c).

27. Palmer v. New York State Dep't of Mental Hygiene, 44 N.Y.2d 958, 408 N.Y.S.2d 322, 380 N.E.2d 154 (1978).

28. Wolfe v. Beal, 477 Pa. 477, 384 A.2d 1187 (1978).

29. *Shredding documents to shield victims of sexual assault,* N.Y. TIMES, Mar. 17, 1995, at B12.

30. *E.g.,* Pyramid Life Ins. Co. v. Masonic Hosp. Ass'n, 191 F. Supp. 51 (W.D. Okla. 1961).

31. *But see* University of Tex. Med. Branch v. York, 871 S.W.2d 175 (Tex. 1994) [medical record not tangible personal property; information intangible, fact that recorded does not render information tangible].

32. *E.g.,* Cannell v. Medical & Surgical Clinic, S.C., 21 Ill. App. 3d 383, 315 N.E.2d 278 (3d Dist. 1974).

33. *E.g.,* McGarry v. J. A. Mercier Co., 272 Mich. 501, 262 N.W. 296 (1935).

34. *See* McDonald and Tierney, *Computer-stored medical records,* 259 J.A.M.A. 3433 (1988); Gardner, *Automated medical chart becoming a priority,* 18 MOD. HEALTHCARE, Sept. 2, 1988, at 29 [use of optical disk storage]; Gardner, *Computerization of records pondered,* 19 MOD. HEALTHCARE, Sept. 8, 1989, at 10 [Institute of Medicine study committee appointed]; Gardner, *Computer dilemma: Clinical access vs. confidentiality,* 19 MOD. HEALTHCARE, Nov. 3, 1989, at 32.

35. *E.g.,* ILL. ADMIN. CODE, tit. 77, pt. 250, § 250.1510.

36. *HCFA issues rules on electronic signatures,* 19 MOD. HEALTHCARE, Sept. 1, 1989, at 39 [new guidelines in Medicare hospital manual]; *Regs out for MD computer attestations,* 63 HOSPS., Oct. 20, 1989, at 72.

37. *HCFA considers changing policy prohibiting auto-authentication,* 2 HEALTH L. RPTR. [BNA] 1129 (1993) [HCFA region IX cites as deficiency, while Region X says it is desirable] [hereinafter HEALTH L. RPTR. will be cited as H.L.R.]; *Vladeck warns auto-authentication will violate Medicare conditions,* 2 H.L.R. 1423 (1993).

38. *See* A.A. Waller and D.K. Fulton, *The electronic chart: Keeping it confidential and secure,* 26 J. HEALTH & HOSP. L. 104 (1993).

39. *Medical records sold with computer,* AM. MED. NEWS, Feb. 27, 1995, at 19.

40. *E.g.,* L. Oberman, *Big boost or big brother?* AM. MED. NEWS, Jan. 9, 1995, at 4 [software offers help with diagnosis].

41. *E.g., Hospital's firing of therapist turned photographer is upheld,* WALL ST. J., May 10, 1990, at B4 [Texas state judge dismissed suit challenging firing after therapist photographed patient being brought into hospital, sold photos to newspaper].

42. S. Reiser et al., ETHICS IN MEDICINE 5 (1977).

43. American Medical Association, PRINCIPLES OF MEDICAL ETHICS (Aug. 1980).

44. *E.g.,* Board of Trustees v. Pratt, 72 Wyo. 120, 262 P.2d 682 (1953).

45. MacDonald v. United States, 767 F. Supp. 1295 (M.D. Pa. 1991), *aff'd without op.,* 983 F.2d 1051 (3d cir. 1992).

46. Hyman v. Jewish Chronic Disease Hosp., 15 N.Y.2d 317, 258 N.Y.S.2d 397, 399, 206 N.E.2d 338 (1965).

47. Klinge v. Lutheran Med. Ctr., 518 S.W.2d 157 (Mo. Ct. App. 1974).

48. In re General Accident Assurance Co. of Canada & Sunnybrook Hosp., 23 O.R.(2d) 513 (Ont. High Ct. of Justice 1979); *accord* Rea v. Pardo, 132 A.D.2d 442, 522 N.Y.S.2d 393 (4th Dep't 1987) [patient request that copy of record be sent to attorney justified physician also sending copy to his insurer].

49. *E.g.,* Lancaster v. Loyola Univ. Med. Ctr., 1992 U.S. Dist. LEXIS 15207 (N.D. Ill. Oct. 8, 1992) [hospital employees]; Morgan v. Cook County, 1993 Ill. App. LEXIS 1289 (Ill. Ct. App. Aug.

23, 1993) [treating physician, when suit seeks to make hospital vicariously liable]; Alachua Gen. Hosp. v. Stewart, 649 So.2d 357 (Fla. 1st DCA 1995) [physician, when suit seeks to make hospital vicariously liable]; *but see* Ritter v. Rush-Presbyterian-St. Luke's Med. Ctr., 177 Ill. App. 3d 313, 532 N.E.2d 327 (1st Dist. 1988) [hospital not even permitted to interview its codefendant employee treating physicians].

50. Carter v. Broadlawns Med. Ctr., 857 F.2d 448 (8th Cir. 1988), *cert. denied*, 489 U.S. 1096 (1989).

51. *See Scientists use medical-record data bases to detect adverse side effects of drugs*, WALL ST. J., Mar. 24, 1988, at 33; Gordis and Gold, *Privacy, confidentiality, and the use of medical records in research*, 207 SCIENCE 153 (1980).

52. 45 C.F.R. § 46.101(b)(5); 46 FED. REG. 8,392 (1981); *see also* 56 FED. REG. 67078 (1991) [HCFA allowed release of patient identifiable information from Uniform Clinical Data Set for research purposes].

53. *E.g.*, FLA STAT. § 395.017 [hospitals]; § 455.241 [individual professionals]; ILL. REV. STAT. ch. 110 §§ 8-2001–8-2004; Annotation, *Patient's right to disclosure of his or her own medical records under state freedom of information act*, 26 A.L.R. 4TH 701.

54. *E.g.*, Wallace v. University Hosps. of Cleveland, 84 Ohio L. Abs. 224, 170 N.E.2d 261 (Ct. App. 1960), *appeal dismissed*, 171 Ohio St. 487, 172 N.E.2d 459 (1961); Hutchins v. Texas Rehabilitation Comm'n, 544 S.W.2d 802 (Tex. Civ. App. 1976).

55. Pierce v. Penman, 357 Pa. Super. 225, 515 A.2d 948 (1986).

56. Franklin Square Hosp. v. Laubach, 318 Md. 615, 569 A.2d 693 (1990).

57. *E.g.*, Rabens v. Jackson Park Hosp. Found., 40 Ill. App. 3d 113, 351 N.E.2d 276 (1st Dep't 1976).

58. *E.g.*, Hernandez v. Lutheran Med. Ctr., 104 A.D.2d 368, 478 N.Y.S.2d 697 (2d Dep't 1984) [$1 per page reasonable]; *contra* Mauer v. Mount Sinai Hosp., 193 N.Y.L.J. No. 22 (N.Y. Sup. Ct. Feb. 1, 1985), *as discussed in* 13 HEALTH L. DIG., Mar. 1985, at 38 [$1 per page not reasonable, reduced to 25 cents].

59. Lee County v. State Farm Mut. Auto. Ins. Co., 634 So.2d 250 (Fla. 2d DCA 1994).

60. Pyramid Life Ins. Co. v. Masonic Hosp. Ass'n, 191 F. Supp. 51 (W.D. Okla. 1961).

61. Robinson v. Monaghan, 864 F.2d 622 (8th Cir. 1989).

62. Pennison v. Provident Life & Accident Ins. Co., 154 So.2d 617 (La. Ct. App. 1963), *cert. denied*, 244 La. 1019, 156 So.2d 226 (1963).

63. Cassingham v. Lutheran Sunburst Health Servs., 748 S.W.2d 589 (Tex. Ct. App. 1988).

64. MacDonald v. Clinger, 84 A.D.2d 482, 446 N.Y.S.2d 801 (4th Dep't 1982).

65. *E.g.*, IOWA CODE ANN. § 229.25.

66. Thurman v. Crawford, 652 S.W.2d 240 (Mo. Ct. App. 1983).

67. Yaretsky v. Blum, 592 F.2d 65 (2d Cir. 1979), *appeal after remand*, 629 F.2d 817 (2d Cir. 1980), *rev'd*, 457 U.S. 991 (1982) [no right to hearing before transfer].

68. Salt Lake Child & Family Therapy Clinic, Inc. v. Frederick, 890 P.2d 1017 (Utah 1995).

69. Cynthia B. v. New Rochelle Hosp. Med. Ctr., 60 N.Y.2d 452, 470 N.Y.S.2d 1221, 458 N.E.2d 363 (1983).

70. Bishop Clarkson Mem. Hosp. v. Reserve Life Ins. Co., 350 F.2d 1006 (8th Cir. 1965).

71. Altman, *Patients who read their hospital charts*, 302 N. ENGL. J. MED. 169 (1980).

72. *E.g.*, Emmett v. Eastern Dispensary & Casualty Hosp., 130 U.S. App. D.C. 50, 396 F.2d 931 (1967); *contra* Major v. North Valley Hosp., 233 Mont. 25, 759 P.2d 153 (1988).

73. *E.g.*, Gaertner v. State, 385 Mich. 49, 187 N.W.2d 429 (1971).

74. *E.g.*, Leaf v. Iowa Methodist Med. Ctr., 460 N.W.2d 892 (Iowa Ct. App. 1990) [noncustodial parent has right of access to minor's medical records].

75. *See Guidelines address medical privacy rights for teens*, Am. Med. News, Mar. 17, 1989, at 28; *see also* T.L. Cheng et al., *Confidentiality in health care*, 269 J.A.M.A. 1404 (1993) [survey of adolescent attitudes indicated they would not seek health services to avoid disclosure of certain information]; Council on Scientific Affairs, American Med. Ass'n, *Confidential health services for adolescents*, 269 J.A.M.A. 1420 (1993) [encouraging increased confidentiality].

76. *E.g.*, H.L. v. Matheson, 450 U.S. 398 (1981) [Utah parental consent requirement for abortions].

77. Mrozinski v. Pogue, 205 Ga. App. 731, 423 S.E.2d 405 (1992), *cert. denied*, 1993 Ga. LEXIS 43 (Jan. 7, 1993).

78. *E.g.*, Scott v. Henry Ford Hosp., 199 Mich. App. 241, 501 N.W.2d 259 (1993) [only executor may authorize release; wife does not have authority]; In Interest of Roy, 423 Pa. Super. 183, 620 A.2d 1172 (1992), *appeal denied*, 536 Pa. 644, 639 A.2d 30 (1994) [only executor can authorize release of mental health records]; Annotation, *Who may waive privilege of confidential communication to physician by person since deceased*, 97 A.L.R. 2D 393.

79. *E.g.*, Gerkin v. Werner, 106 Misc. 2d 643, 434 N.Y.S.2d 607 (Sup. Ct. 1980).

80. *E.g.*, Emmett v. Eastern Dispensary & Casualty Hosp., 396 F.2d 931 (D.C. Cir. 1967).

81. Rost v. State Bd. of Psychology, No. 1093 C.D. 1994 (Pa. Commw. Ct. May 22, 1995), *as discussed in* Health L. Dig., July 1995, at 67.

82. *E.g.*, Parkson v. Central Du Page Hosp., 105 Ill. App. 3d 850, 435 N.E.2d 140 (1st Dist. 1982).

83. *E.g.*, St. Lukes Reg. Med. Ctr. v. United States, 717 F. Supp. 665 (N.D. Iowa 1989) [government entitled to disclosure of physician's medical records by administrative subpoena to investigate Medicaid civil violations]; Goldberg v. Davis, 151 Ill.2d 267, 602 N.E.2d 812 (1992) [professional discipline]; Dr. K v. State Bd. of Physician Quality Assurance, 98 Md. App. 103, 632 A.2d 453, *cert. denied*, 115 S. Ct. 75 (U.S. 1994) [professional discipline].

84. *E.g.*, Amente v. Newman, 653 So.2d 1030 (Fla. 1995); Todd v. South Jersey Hosp. Sys., 152 F.R.D. 676 (D.N.J. 1993); Terre Haute Reg. Hosp. v. Trueblood, 600 N.E.2d 1358 (Ind. 1992); Community Hosp. Ass'n v. District Court, 194 Colo. 98, 570 P.2d 243 (1977); State ex rel. Lester E. Cox Med. Ctr. v. Keet, 678 S.W.2d 813 (Mo. 1984) (*en banc*).

85. *E.g.*, Buford v. Howe, 10 F.3d 1184 (5th Cir. 1994); Glassman v. St. Joseph Hosp., 259 Ill. App. 3d 730, 631 N.E.2d 1186 (1st Dist. 1994); Ekstrom v. Temple, 197 Ill. App. 3d 120, 553 N.E.2d 424 (2d Dist. 1990).

86. Connecticut State Med. Soc'y v. Commission on Hosp. & Health Care, 223 Conn. 450, 612 A.2d 1217 (1992).

87. Schechet v. Kesten, 372 Mich. 346, 126 N.W.2d 718 (1964).

88. Rasmussen v. South Fla. Blood Serv., 500 So.2d 533 (Fla. 1987); *see* Annotation, *Discovery of identity of blood donor*, 56 A.L.R. 4TH 755.

89. Banta v. Superior Court, 112 Ariz. 544, 544 P.2d 653 (1976); *accord* Mason v. Regional Med. Ctr., 121 F.R.D. 300 (W.D. Ky. 1988).

90. Tarrant County Hosp. Dist. v. Hughes, 734 S.W.2d 675 (Tex. Ct. App.), *cert. denied*, 108 S. Ct. 1027 (1987).

91. Belle Bonfils Mem. Blood Ctr. v. District Court, 763 P.2d 1003 (Colo. 1988).

92. Marcella v. Brandywine Hosp., 47 F.3d 618 (3d Cir. 1995); *accord,* Watson v. Lowcountry Red Cross, 974 F.2d 482 (4th Cir. 1992).

93. Coleman v. American Red Cross, 23 F.3d 1091 (6th Cir. 1994).

94. *E.g.*, City of Edmund v. Parr, 587 P.2d 56 (Okla. 1978); Jenkins v. Wu, 102 Ill. 2d 468, 468 N.E.2d 1162 (1984); *but see* Southwest Comm. Health Servs. v. Smith, 107 N.M. 196, 755 P.2d 40 (1988) [law upheld, but court may ignore law when records sufficiently needed in litigation].

95. Young v. King, 136 N.J. Super. 127, 344 A.2d 792 (Law Div. 1975).

96. Smith v. Lincoln Gen. Hosp., 605 So.2d 1347 (La. 1992).

97. State ex rel. Shroades v. Henry, 187 W.Va. 723, 421 S.E.2d 264 (1992).

98. Warrick v. Giron, 290 N.W.2d 166 (Minn. 1980).

99. *E.g.*, Cedars-Sinai Med. Ctr. v. Superior Court, 12 Cal. App. 4th 579, 16 Cal. Rptr. 2d 253 (2d Dist. 1993).

100. *E.g.*, Ashokan v. Department of Ins., 109 Nev. 662, 856 P.2d 244 (1993).

101. *E.g.*, FLA. STAT. §§ 395.0191–395.0193, 766.101; Young v. Saldanha, 431 S.E.2d 669 (W. Va. 1993) [physician's use of peer review materials in suit against hospital concerning clinical privileges did not waive evidentiary privilege, so patient could not use materials in malpractice suit against physician].

102. *E.g.*, St. Elizabeth's Hosp. v. State Bd. of Prof. Med. Conduct, 174 A.D. 2d 225, 579 N.Y.S.2d 457 (3d Dep't 1992).

103. Fed. R. Evid. 501; Memorial Hosp. for McHenry County v. Shadur, 664 F.2d 1058 (7th Cir. 1981); United States v. Illinois, 148 F.R.D. 587 (N.D. Ill. 1993); Pagano v. Oroville Hosp., 145 F.R.D. 683 (E.D. Cal. 1993) [patient, physician identifiers deleted; HCQIA does not create privilege].

104. Bredice v. Doctors Hosp., Inc., 50 F.R.D. 249 (D. D.C. 1970), *aff'd without op.*, 156 U.S. App. D.C. 199, 479 F.2d 920 (1973); *accord*, Laws v. Georgetown Univ. Hosp., 656 F. Supp. 824 (D. D.C. 1987).

105. *E.g.*, Pagano v. Oroville Hosp., 145 F.R.D. 683 (E.D. Cal. 1993); Davison v. St. Paul Fire & Marine Ins. Co., 75 Wis. 2d 190, 248 N.W.2d 433 (1977).

106. *E.g.*, Allen v. Smith, 179 W.Va. 360, 368 S.E.2d 924 (1988) [if not protected by statute of limitations, psychiatrist could have been sued for complying with insufficient subpoena].

107. *E.g.*, Rojas v. Ryder Truck Rental, Inc., 641 So.2d 855 (Fla. 1994); Doelfel v. Trevisani, 644 So.2d 1359 (Fla. 1994).

108. Ritt v. Ritt, 52 N.J. 177, 244 A.2d 497 (1968).

109. Laurent v. Brelji, 74 Ill. App. 3d 214, 392 N.E.2d 929 (4th Dist. 1979).

110. People v. Bickham, 89 Ill. 2d 1, 431 N.E.2d 365 (1982).

111. Roth v. Saint Elizabeth's Hosp., 241 Ill. App. 3d 407, 607 N.E.2d 1356 (5th Dist.), *appeal denied*, 151 Ill. 2d 577, 616 N.E.2d 347 (1993).

112. Schmoll v. Bray, 61 Ill. App. 3d 64, 377 N.E.2d 1172, 18 Ill. Dec. 536 (4th Dist. 1978).

113. Swope v. State, 145 Kan. 928, 67 P.2d 416 (1937).

114. Mason v. Robinson, 340 N.W.2d 236 (Iowa 1983); Annotation, *Right of independent expert to refuse to testify as to expert opinion*, 50 A.L.R. 4TH 680; *see also* Bible v. Jane Phillips Episcopal Hosp., No. 86-C-461-B (N.D. Okla. Oct. 23, 1987), *as discussed in* 21 J. HEALTH & HOSP. L. 61 (1988) [nonparty nurses could be forced to be involuntary experts].

115. United States v. Fesman, 781 F. Supp. 511 (S.D. Ohio 1991).

116. *E.g.*, Hope v. Landau, 398 Mass. 738, 500 N.E.2d 809 (1986) [immunity lost if child abuse report made to wrong agency]; *see also* Searcy v. Auerbach, 980 F.2d 609 (9th Cir. 1992) [psychologist who failed to follow statutory procedure for reporting child abuse not immune from civil liability].

117. *E.g.*, FLA. STAT. §§ 382.16, 382.081.

118. *E.g.*, Robinson v. Hamilton, 60 Iowa 134, 14 N.W. 202 (1882).

119. *E.g.*, FLA. STAT. § 381.231 [communicable diseases], § 384.25 [venereal diseases].

120. Derrick v. Ontario Comm. Hosp., 47 Cal. App. 3d 145, 120 Cal. Rptr. 566 (4th Dist. 1975).

121. State ex rel. Callahan v. Kinder, 879 S.W.2d 677 (Mo. Ct. App. 1994).

122. *E.g.*, FLA. STAT. §415.504; L.S. Wissow, *Current concepts: Child abuse and neglect,* 332 N. ENGL. J. MED. 1425 (1995).

123. *E.g.*, Martinez v. Mafchir, 35 F.3d 1486 (10th Cir. 1994) [social worker protected]; Thomas v. Beth Israel Hosp., 710 F. Supp. 935 (S.D. N.Y. 1989); Krikorian v. Barry, 196 Cal. App. 3d 1211, 242 Cal. Rptr. 312 (2d Dist. 1987); Awkerman v. Tri-County Orthopedic Group, 143 Mich. App. 722, 373 N.W.2d 204 (1985); *see also* People v. Wood, 447 Mich. 80, 523 N.W.2d 477 (1994) [social worker's duty of confidentiality to child concerning parent's alleged drug use, sale did not prevent relating information to police to obtain assistance in investigating possible neglect].

124. *E.g.*, Gladson v. State, 258 Ga. 885, 376 S.E.2d 362 (1989).

125. *E.g.*, IOWA CODE ANN. § 232.75(2); Landeros v. Flood, 17 Cal. 3d 399, 131 Cal. Rptr. 69, 551 P.2d 389 (1976); Annotation, *Validity, construction, and application of state statute requiring doctor or other person to report child abuse,* 73 A.L.R. 4TH 782.

126. *E.g.*, People v. Stockton Pregnancy Control Med. Clinic, 203 Cal. App. 3d 225, 249 Cal. Rptr. 762 (3d Dist. 1988) [must report sexual conduct of minors under age 14 if with person of disparate age]; Planned Parenthood Affiliates v. Van de Camp, 181 Cal. App. 3d 245, 226 Cal. Rptr. 361 (1st Dist. 1986) [not required to report all sexual activity of minors under age 14].

127. *E.g.*, FLA STAT. § 415.103; M.S. Lachs & K. Pillemer, *Current concepts: Abuse and neglect of elderly persons,* 332 N. ENGL. J. MED. 437 (1995) [42 states required reporting in 1991]; A. Hyman et al., *Laws mandating reporting of domestic violence: Do they promote patient well-being?* 273 J.A.M.A. 1781 (1995) [questioning helpfulness where there are inadequate responses to reports].

128. N.Y. PENAL LAW § 265.25.

129. IOWA CODE ANN. § 147.111.

130. *E.g.*, FLA. ADMIN. CODE §§ 10D-91.425, 10D-91.426, 10D-91.428 [radiation incidents].

131. 21 C.F.R. § 606.170(b).

132. 21 C.F.R. § 812.150(b).

133. 49 FED. REG. 36,326–51 (1984); *Medical device hazard reports required,* 59 HOSPS., Mar. 16, 1985, at 76.

134. *E.g.*, Beth Israel Hosp. Ass'n v. Board of Registration in Med., 401 Mass. 172, 515 N.E.2d 574 (1987).

135. Choe v. Axelrod, 141 A.D.2d 235, 534 N.Y.S.2d 739 (3d Dep't 1988).

136. Whalen v. Roe, 429 U.S. 589 (1977).

137. *E.g.*, FLA. STAT. § 395.0147.

138. *E.g.*, IOWA CODE ANN. § 85.27.

139. *E.g.*, Acosta v. Cary, 365 So.2d 4 (La. Ct. App. 1978).

140. Morris v. Consolidation Coal Co., 191 W.Va. 426, 446 S.E.2d 648 (1994).

141. 5 U.S.C. § 552.

142. 5 U.S.C. § 552a; Doe v. Stephens, 271 U.S. App. D.C. 230, 851 F.2d 1457 (1988) [effect of Privacy Act on grand jury subpoena of VA medical records]; Williams v. Department of Veterans Affairs, 879 F. Supp. 578 (E.D. Va. 1995) [Privacy Act is exclusive remedy for wrongful disclosure of medical information by VA].

143. *E.g.*, IOWA CODE ANN. § 22.7; Head v. Colloton, 331 N.W.2d 870 (Iowa 1983).

144. Eugene Cervi & Co. v. Russell, 184 Colo. 282, 519 P.2d 1189 (1974).

145. Head v. Colloton, 331 N.W.2d 870 (Iowa 1983).

146. Wooster Republican Printing Co. v. City of Wooster, 56 Ohio St. 2d 126, 383 N.E.2d 124 (1978).

147. O'Hare v. Harris, MEDICARE & MEDICAID GUIDE (CCH) ¶ 31,054 (D. N.H. Mar. 12, 1981); *see also* F.E.R. v. Valdez, 58 F.3d 1530 (10th Cir. 1995) [not violation of non-Medicaid patients' rights for state investigators to seize records in investigation of psychiatrist for Medicaid fraud].

148. *See* Annotation, *Liability of doctor or other health practitioner to third party contracting contagious disease from doctor's patient*, 3 A.L.R. 5TH 370.

149. Jones v. Stanko, 118 Ohio St. 147, 160 N.E. 456 (1928); *see also* S.A.V. v. K.G.V., 708 S.W.2d 651 (Mo. 1986) (*en banc*) [wife permitted to sue husband for failing to disclose herpes].

150. Derrick v. Ontario Comm. Hosp., 47 Cal. App. 3d 154, 120 Cal. Rptr. 566 (4th Dist. 1975).

151. Phillips v. Oconee Mem. Hosp., 290 S.C. 192, 348 S.E.2d 836 (1986).

152. Maxwell Street Creative Child Care v. Hawkins, No. 91-CA-958-MR (Ky. Ct. App. Oct. 30, 1992) [ordered not to be published], *as discussed in* 21 HEALTH L. DIG., Jan. 1993, at 41.

153. Johnson v. West Va. Univ. Hosps., 186 W.Va. 648, 413 S.E.2d 889 (1991).

154. J.B. v. Sacred Heart Hosp., 27 F.3d 506 (11th Cir. 1994).

155. *See* note 191, *infra*.

156. Tarasoff v. Regents of Univ. of Cal., 17 Cal. 3d 425, 131 Cal. Rptr. 14, 551 P.2d 334 (1976).

157. Thompson v. County of Alameda, 27 Cal. 3d 741, 167 Cal. Rptr. 70, 614 P.2d 728 (1980).

158. Hamman v. County of Maricopa, 161 Ariz. 58, 775 P.2d 1122 (1989).

159. Petersen v. State, 100 Wash. 2d 421, 671 P.2d 230 (1983).

160. Peck v. Counseling Serv., 146 Vt. 61, 499 A.2d 422 (1985).

161. *E.g.*, Shaw v. Glickman, 45 Md. App. 718, 415 A.2d 625 (1980).

162. *E.g.*, Thornburg v. Long, 178 N.C. 589, 101 S.E. 99 (1919); *see also* Gross v. Allen, 22 Cal. App. 4th 354, 27 Cal. Rptr.2d 429 (2d Dist. 1994) [original psychiatrists had duty to tell subsequent attending psychiatrist of patient's prior suicide attempts; subsequent psychiatrist called to obtain history].

163. *E.g.*, Watts v. Cumberland County Hosp. Sys., 75 N.C. App. 1, 330 S.E.2d 242 (1985), *rev'd on other grounds*, 317 N.C. 321, 345 S.E.2d 201 (1986).

164. Bryson v. Tillinghast, 749 P.2d 110 (Okla. 1988); *see also* State v. Beatty, 770 S.W.2d 387 (Mo. Ct. App. 1989) [anonymous tip by physician linking patient to robbery did not violate privilege]; Porter v. Michigan Osteopathic Hosp. Ass'n, 170 Mich. App. 619, 428 N.W.2d 719 (1988) [hospital required to disclose to court information concerning patients suspects in rape]; Ohio Att'y Gen. Op. No. 88-027 (Apr. 21, 1988) [psychologists may but do not have to report felonies].

165. *E.g.*, Doe v. City of New York, 15 F.3d 264 (2d Cir. 1994) [constitutional right to privacy of HIV status]; Schaill v. Tippecanoe County School Corp., 864 F.2d 1309 (7th Cir. 1988); *contra*, Doe v. Wigginton, 21 F.3d 733 (6th Cir. 1994); Palay v. Superior Court, 18 Cal. App. 4th 919, 22 Cal. Rptr. 2d 839 (2d Dist. 1993) [when child brought suit for malpractice for prenatal care, child waived privilege for shared prenatal records of mother, child; did not violate mother's constitutional privacy rights]; Strong v. Board of Ed., 902 F.2d 208 (2d Cir.), *cert. denied*, 498 U.S. 897 (1990) [not violation of privacy to require teacher to provide medical records, be examined before return to work after extended medical absence].

166. Allred v. State, 554 P.2d 411 (Alaska 1976).

167. Fed. R. Evid. 501; United States v. Bercier, 848 F.2d 917 (8th Cir. 1988) [criminal]; United States v. Moore, 970 F.2d 48 (5th Cir. 1992) [IRS summons]; *see* Annotation, *Situations in which federal courts are governed by state law of privilege under Rule 501 of Federal Rules of Evidence*, 48 A.L.R. FED. 259.

168. *E.g.*, Roosevelt Hotel Ltd. Partnership v. Sweeney, 394 N.W.2d 353 (Iowa 1986).

169. PA. STAT. ANN. tit. 42, § 5929.

170. KAN. STAT. ANN. § 60-427.

171. MICH. COMP. LAWS § 600.2157.

172. N.Y. CIVIL PRACTICE L. & R. § 4504.

173. *E.g.*, New York City Council v. Goldwater, 284 N.Y. 296, 31 N.E.2d 31 (1940).

174. Wiles v. Wiles, 264 Ga. 594, 448 S.E.2d 681 (1994).

175. *E.g.*, Doe v. Diamond, 964 F.2d 1325 (2d Cir. 1992); In re Zuniga, 714 F.2d 632 (6th Cir.), *cert. denied*, 464 U.S. 983 (1983); *contra*, United States v. Moore, 970 F.2d 48 (5th Cir. 1992); Hancock v. Hobbs, 967 F.2d 462 (11th Cir. 1992).

176. *E.g.*, United States v. Burtrum, 17 F.3d 1299 (10th Cir. 1994).

177. *E.g.*, Inabnit v. Berkson, 199 Cal. App. 3d 1230, 245 Cal. Rptr. 525 (5th Dist. 1988) [patient's failure to challenge subpoena waived privilege].

178. *E.g.*, Cartwright v. Maccabees Mut. Life Ins. Co., 65 Mich. App. 670, 238 N.W.2d 368 (1975), *rev'd on other grounds*, 398 Mich. 238, 247 N.W.2d 298 (1976) [when misrepresentations in insurance application, life insurer entitled to verdict when widow invoked privilege].

179. *E.g.*, Willis v. Order of R.R. Telegraphers, 139 Neb. 46, 296 N.W. 443 (1941).

180. *E.g.*, Maynard v. City of San Jose, 37 F.3d 1396 (9th Cir. 1994); Premack v. J.C.J. Ogar, Inc., 148 F.R.D. 140 (E.D. Pa. 1993).

181. *E.g.*, Sykes v. Saint Andrews School, 619 So.2d 467 (Fla. 4th DCA 1993).

182. *E.g.*, State ex rel. Kitzmiller v. Henning, 190 W. Va. 142, 437 S.E.2d 452 (1993); McClelland v. Ozenberger, 841 S.W.2d 227 (Mo. Ct. App. 1992); Loudon v. Mhyre, 110 Wash. 2d 675, 756 P.2d 138 (1988); Nelson v. Lewis, 130 N.H. 106, 534 A.2d 720 (1987).

183. *E.g.*, Huzjak v. United States, 118 F.R.D. 61 (N.D. Ohio 1987) [treating physician may voluntarily engage in ex parte contacts, but cannot be compelled to do so]; Trans-World Invs. v. Drobny, 554 P.2d 1148 (Alaska 1976); Gobuty v. Kavanagh, 795 F. Supp. 281 (D. Minn. 1992) [state law permitted defending physician to informally communicate with plaintiff's treating physician with 15 day notice].

184. *E.g.*, Requena v. Franciscan Sisters Health Care Corp., 212 Ill. App. 3d 328, 570 N.E.2d 1214 (3d Dist.), *appeal denied*, 141 Ill. 2d 559, 580 N.E.2d 133 (1991).

185. 42 C.F.R. pt. 2.

186. *E.g.*, United States v. Hopper, 440 F. Supp. 1208 (N.D. Ill. 1977) [probation revocation]; In re Baby X, 97 Mich. App. 111, 293 N.W.2d 736 (1980) [child neglect]; *see also* United States v. Corona, 849 F.2d 562 (11th Cir. 1988), *cert. denied*, 489 U.S. 1084 (1989) [trial court did not err in permitting use of records of defendant when court could have found criteria for disclosure met].

187. United States v. Providence Hosp., 507 F.Supp. 519 (E.D. Mich. 1981).

188. *E.g.*, State Bd. of Medical Examiners v. Fenwick Hall, Inc., 308 S.C. 477, 419 S.E.2d 222 (1992) [disclosure to licensing board]; O'Boyle v. Jensen, 150 F.R.D. 519 (M.D. Pa. 1993) [civil rights suit for death in police custody].

189. *E.g.*, United States v. Cresta, 825 F.2d 538 (1st Cir. 1987), *cert. denied*, 486 U.S. 1042 (1988) [credibility]; United States v. Smith, 789 F.2d 196 (3d Cir. 1986) [credibility].

190. Heng v. Foster, 63 Ill. App. 3d 30, 379 N.E.2d 688 (lst Dist. 1978).

191. *E.g.*, FLA. STAT. § 381.609(2)(f) [AIDS], § 455.2416 [permitting disclosure of AIDS to sexual partner, needlesharing partner]; Doe v. Southeastern Pa. Transp. Auth., No. 93-5988 (E.D. Pa. June 2, 1995), *as discussed in* 4 H.L.R. 901 (1995) [$125,000 awarded employee for HIV status disclosure by disclosing AZT use as prescription for drug benefit]; Woods v. White, 689 F.

Supp. 874 (W.D. Wis. 1988), *aff'd without op.*, 899 F.2d 17 (7th Cir. 1990) [prisoner could sue staff for disclosing AIDS test to other prisoners]; Doe v. Prime Health, No. 88C5149 (Kan. Dist. Ct. Johnson County Oct. 18, 1988), *as discussed in* 16 HEALTH L. DIG., Dec. 1988, at 4 [injunction on informing ex-wife, who was also patient, of ex-husband's positive AIDS test]; Annotation, *Validity, construction, and effect of state statutes or regulations expressly governing disclosure of fact that person has tested positive for acquired immunodeficiency syndrome (AIDS)*, 12 A.L.R. 5TH 149; U. Collela, *Balancing confidentiality and liberal discovery: A unified approach to discovery disputes over HIV information*, 26 J. HEALTH & HOSP. L 328 (1993).

192. Hafferty, *A new MD "nightmare": HIV status disclosure can mean lawsuits for breach of confidentiality*, AM. MED. NEWS, Nov. 4, 1988, at 27.

193. Doe v. Roe, 155 Misc. 2d 392, 588 N.Y.S.2d 236 (Sup. Ct. 1992), *modified & aff'd*, 190 A.D.2d 463, 599 N.Y.S.2d 350 (4th Dept.), *appeal dismissed*, 82 N.Y.2d 846, 606 N.Y.S.2d 597, 627 N.E.2d 519 (1993).

194. Nolley v. County of Erie, 776 F. Supp. 715 (W.D. N.Y. 1991), *supplemental op.*, 802 F. Supp. 898 (1992) [compensatory and punitive damages awarded, injunction denied], *on reconsideration*, 798 F. Supp. 123 (1992) [setting aside punitive damage award against superintendent, requiring report to court on corrective steps taken].

195. In re Milton S. Hershey Med. Ctr., 535 Pa. 9, 634 A.2d 159 (1993).

196. Weston v. Carolina Medicorp, Inc., 102 N.C. App. 370, 402 S.E.2d 653, *rev. denied*, 330 N.C. 123, 409 S.E.2d 611 (1991), *aff'g denying motion to set aside judgment*, 113 N.C. App. 415, 438 S.E.2d 751 (1994).

197. Agosto v. Trusswal Sys. Corp., 142 F.R.D. 118 (E.D. Pa. 1992).

198. IOWA ADMIN. CODE § 470-135.401(10) [physicians], § 590-1.2 (d)(6) [nurses].

199. *E.g.*, KAN. ADMIN. REGS. § 28-34-9(b).

200. *E.g.*, CAL. CIVIL CODE §§ 56–56.37.

201. *E.g.*, IOWA CODE ANN. ch. 140 [venereal disease].

202. *E.g.*, In re Assalone, 512 A.2d 1383 (R.I. 1986); Coleman v. Weiner, 139 Misc. 2d 267, 528 N.Y.S.2d 480 (Sup. Ct. 1988) [discovery of birth records allowed where need shown and mother's name deleted].

203. *E.g.*, Atwell v. Sacred Heart Hosp., 520 So.2d 30 (Fla. 1988).

204. 1995 Joint Commission CAMH, at 383.

205. *E.g.*, Boyd v. Wynn, 286 Ky. 173, 150 S.W.2d 648 (1941).

206. Annotation, *Physician's tort liability for unauthorized disclosure of confidential information about patient*, 48 A.L.R. 4TH 668.

207. Doe v. Roe, 93 Misc. 2d 201, 400 N.Y.S.2d 668 (Sup. Ct. 1977).

208. Humphers v. First Interstate Bank, 298 Or. 706, 696 P.2d 527 (1985).

209. *E.g.*, Simonsen v. Swenson, 104 Neb. 224, 177 N.W. 831 (1920) [physician]; Knecht v. Vandalia Med. Ctr., Inc., 14 Ohio App. 3d 129, 470 N.E.2d 230 (1984) [receptionist].

210. *E.g.*, Crippen v. Charter Southland Hosp., 534 So.2d 286 (Ala. 1988) [disclosure to employer's psychiatrist]; Tower v. Hirschhorn, 397 Mass. 581, 492 N.E.2d 728 (1986) [disclosure to insurer's physician].

211. Horne v. Patton, 291 Ala. 701, 287 So.2d 824 (1973).

212. *E.g.*, Alberts v. Devine, 395 Mass. 59, 479 N.E.2d 113, *cert. denied*, 474 U.S. 1013 (1985).

213. Clark v. Geraci, 29 Misc. 2d 791, 208 N.Y.S.2d 564 (Sup. Ct. 1960).

214. Childs v. Williams, 825 S.W.2d 4 (Mo. Ct. App. 1992).

215. Conyers v. Massa, 512 P.2d 283 (Colo. Ct. App. 1973).

216. *E.g.*, Hammonds v. Aetna Casualty & Sur. Co., 243 F. Supp. 793 (N.D. Ohio 1965).

217. *E.g.*, Thomas v. Hillson, 184 Ga. App. 302, 361 S.E.2d 278 (1987); *see* Annotation, *Libel and slander: privilege of statements by physician, surgeon, or nurse concerning patient*, 73 A.L.R. 2D 325.

218. *E.g.*, Beatty v. Baston, 130 Ohio L. Abs. 481 (Ct. App. 1932).

219. United States v. Willis, 778 F. Supp. 205 (S.D. N.Y. 1991), 737 F. Supp. 269 (1990); Cohen, *Doctor is accused of inside trading on patient's data*, WALL ST. J., July 28, 1989, at B8; *Psychiatrist loses bid to have securities fraud charges dropped*, WALL ST. J., Dec. 3. 1991, at B10; *Psychiatrist accused of securities fraud is sued by patient for malpractice*, WALL ST. J., Dec. 10. 1991, at B8; *Psychiatrist flip-flops and again pleads guilty to securities fraud*, WALL ST. J., Dec. 23. 1991, at B6; *Psychiatrist is sentenced*, N.Y. TIMES, Jan. 8, 1992, at C12 [5-year sentence of probation and community service]; WALL ST. J., Jan. 8, 1992, at B3 [plus fine of $150,000, plus payment of $136,580 to settle suit by SEC].

220. *E.g.*, Martin v. Baehler, 1993 Del. Super. LEXIS 199 (July 7, 1993) [award against physician for his staff's disclosure to grandmother of daughter's pregnancy], *as discussed in* 26 J. HEALTH & HOSP. L. 336 (1993).

221. Commonwealth v. Wiseman, 356 Mass. 251, 249 N.E.2d 610 (1969), *cert. denied*, 398 U.S. 960 (1970); *Film on hospital provocative after 20 years*, N.Y. TIMES, May 17, 1987, at 14; *see also* Adams v. St. Elizabeth Hosp., 1989 Ohio App. LEXIS 913 (Mar. 16, 1989) [written consent not required to show patient to teaching conference in teaching hospital], *as discussed in* 22 J. HEALTH & HOSP. L. 291 (1989).

222. Estate of Berthiaume v. Pratt, 365 A.2d 792 (Me. 1976); *see* Annotation, *Taking unauthorized photographs as invasion of privacy*, 86 A.L.R. 3D 374.

223. *E.g.*, In re Karlin, 112 Bankr. 319 (Bankr. 9th cir. 1989), *aff'd without op.*, 940 F.2d 1534 (9th Cir. 1991) [plastic surgeon's use of pictures in article was for instructional or educational purpose within meaning of authorization].

224. Anderson v. Strong Mem. Hosp., 140 Misc. 2d 770, 531 N.Y.S.2d 735 (Sup. Ct. 1988), *aff'd*, 151 A.D.2d 1033, 542 N.Y.S.2d 96 (4th Dep't 1989).

225. *E.g.*, Stubbs v. North Mem. Med. Ctr., 448 N.W.2d 78 (Minn. Ct. App. 1989) [publication in promotional, educational materials of before, after photographs of facial cosmetic surgery without patient consent may constitute breach of express warranty of silence arising from physician-patient relationship]; Feeney v. Young, 191 A.D. 501, 181 N.Y.S. 481 (1920) [public showing of film of caesarean section delivery]; Vassiliades v. Garfinckels, 492 A.2d 580 (D.C. 1985) [public use of before, after photos of cosmetic surgery in department store, on television]; *see* Annotation, *Invasion of privacy by use of plaintiff's name or likeness in advertising*, 23 A.L.R. 3D 865.

226. In re Simmons, 112 A.D.2d 806, 492 N.Y.S.2d 308 (4th Dep't 1985); *but see* North Broward Hosp. Dist. v. ABC, No. 86-026514 (Fla. Cir. Ct. Broward County Oct. 20, 1986) [hospital cannot prohibit media access to comatose patient when guardian consents].

227. Hill v. Springer, 132 Misc. 2d 1012, 506 N.Y.S.2d 255 (1986).

228. Metropolitan Gen. Hosp. v. Ontario Nurses' Ass'n, 22 L.A.C.(2d) 243 (Ont. Lab. Arb. 1979).

229. Group Health Plan, Inc. v. Lopez, 341 N.W.2d 294 (Minn. Ct. App. 1983).

230. Garay v. County of Bexar, 810 S.W.2d 760 (Tex. Ct. App. 1991).

231. Hill v. Iowa Dep't of Employment Servs., 442 N.W.2d 128 (Iowa 1989).

232. *Girl, 13, held for fake HIV calls to patients*, THE HERALD [Miami, FL], Mar. 1, 1995, at 1B; *Girl charged in prank calls taken from her mom*, THE HERALD [Miami, FL], Mar. 2, 1995, at 2B; *Felonies filed against accused HIV caller*, THE HERALD [Miami, FL], Mar. 16, 1995, at 1B.

15

Reproductive Issues

This chapter discusses the reproductive issues of contraception, conception, and abortion and the related issues of prenatal testing, genetic screening, and liability for the birth of children after negligent sterilizations or failure to inform of genetic risks.

CONTRACEPTION

Numerous contraceptive drugs, devices, and procedures are available to reduce the probability of pregnancy.[1]

Adults

Some states have attempted to restrict the sale or use of contraceptive drugs and devices. In 1965, the U.S. Supreme Court declared a Connecticut law forbidding the use of contraceptives by married persons to be an unconstitutional violation of the right of privacy.[2] In 1972, the Court declared a Massachusetts law forbidding unmarried persons to buy or use contraceptives to be unconstitutional.[3] The Court ruled that married and unmarried adults have the same right to access to contraceptives.

These two cases establish that a state may not prohibit the use of contraceptives by adults. States may regulate sales of contraceptives, but in 1977 the Supreme Court limited the permissible scope of such regulation. The Court invalidated a New York statute prohibiting the distribution of nonprescription contraceptives to persons over 16 years of age by anyone other than licensed pharmacists, finding it an undue burden on an individual's right to decide whether to bear a child.[4] The Court also invalidated a prohibition on advertising and display of both prescription and nonprescription contraceptives by persons licensed to sell such products.

Few legal barriers confront an adult who seeks to obtain contraceptives. For safety reasons, prescription contraceptives or those requiring fitted insertion often must be obtained through an authorized individual. Other contraceptives may be purchased without medical involvement.

Minors

In some states, minors still face obstacles to obtaining contraceptives. The U.S. Supreme Court's first comment on a minor's right of access to birth control came in the 1977 case discussed above.[5] The Court struck down a portion of a New York law that prohibited the sale or distribution of nonprescription contraceptives to minors under 16. In 1980, a federal appellate court ruled that minors have a right to obtain contraceptive devices from a county-run family planning center without parental notification or consent.[6] In 1988, a federal district court ruled that a Roman Catholic foster child care agency engaged in unconstitutional state action when it confiscated contraceptive devices and prescriptions of minors placed by the state in its care.[7]

A 1981 federal law required that federally funded family planning projects "encourage family participation" in counseling and decisions about services.[8] HHS proposed rules interpreting this to require parental notification after services were initially provided to any minor under age 18 unless (1) the minor was emancipated under state law or (2) the project director determined that notification would result in physical harm to the minor by a parent or guardian. The proposed rules also required compliance with all state laws concerning notification or consent.[9] The rules never took effect because they were blocked by a federal court order.[10] The court ruled that Congress intended to encourage, not require, parental involvement, so the rules exceeded statutory authority. In 1983, a federal district court declared unconstitutional a Utah law requiring parental notification before furnishing contraceptives to minors.[11] However, states may still be able to regulate a minor's access to contraceptives more strictly than would be allowed for adult access to the same materials.

While it is prudent to encourage minors to involve their parents, many minors cannot or will not accept parental involvement. Physicians must then decide whether to prescribe contraceptives in the absence of parental involvement. Physicians who choose to prescribe contraceptives to unemancipated minors face a theoretical possibility of civil liability for battery or malpractice in some states. Several states explicitly authorize minors to consent to these services. Even in states without a minor consent statute, the legal risk is small, especially when the minor is mature.

Liability

Both oral contraceptives and intrauterine devices are known to have harmful side effects in some instances. Litigation has resulted from the most serious of these situations. Much of this litigation has been against manufacturers and has been based on product liability or inadequate warnings of risks. Physicians probably will not be held liable in the absence of negligence or intentional misconduct. They will be held liable for injuries to their patients if they (1) negligently prescribe a contraceptive, (2) negligently insert a contraceptive device, (3) fail to give adequate information concerning potential side effects, or (4) fail to monitor a patient who is at risk or develops adverse reactions.

In 1989, a California appellate court ruled that a Catholic hospital could be sued for failing to provide a rape victim with access to a "morning after" pill.[12] The hospital took the position that the pill was an abortion, so it could refuse to participate. The court ruled that it was birth control, not abortion, so the hospital could be liable if the standard of care in other hospitals was to offer the pill.

VOLUNTARY STERILIZATION

Sterilization involves the termination of the ability to produce children. Sterilization may be the desired result of a surgical operation or the incidental consequence of an operation to remove a diseased reproductive organ or to cure a malfunction of such an organ. When the reproductive organs are not diseased, most sterilizations are effected by vasectomy for males and tubal ligation for females.

Adults

In the past there were concerns about the legality of voluntary sterilizations of competent adults. However, no state currently prohibits voluntary consensual sterilization of a competent adult regardless of the purpose.[13] Federal regulations require the signing of a special consent form at least 30 days prior to sterilizations funded by Medicaid.[14] Exceptions are made for some therapeutic cases. Some states, such as California, impose special requirements on all sterilizations performed in the state.[15]

The federal requirements do not apply to other patients unless required by state law. However, before an operation that may result in sterilization is performed, consent should be obtained. Absent consent, sterilization almost always constitutes a battery even if the operation is medically necessary. Courts are much less likely to find implied consent to sterilization than to other extensions of surgical procedures. When it may be predicted that an operation will sterilize, this consequence should be clearly brought to the patient's attention. It is prudent to use a consent form that indicates both the likely loss of reproductive capacity and the risk the sterilization will not be successful. Failure to inform of the risk of future reproductive ability can expose providers to liability for wrongful conception or wrongful birth as discussed later in this chapter.

Spousal Consent

The patient's consent alone is sufficient authorization for any legal operation. Some hospitals and physicians have a policy of also requiring spousal consent for sterilization of married patients. Public hospitals may not be permitted to enforce such policies. Courts have found such public hospital policies to be an unconstitutional violation of the right of privacy.[16] One federal appellate court ruled that a governmental hospital may not impose greater restrictions on sterilization procedures than on other procedures that are medically indistinguishable in the risk to the patient or the demand on staff or facilities.[17] Federal courts have declared state laws requiring spousal consent to sterilizations to be unconstitutional.[18] However, private hospitals can forbid contraceptive sterilizations or require spousal consent.[19]

Spousal involvement in the sterilization decision should be encouraged if the spouses are not estranged. Individual physicians have broader latitude to implement personal practices of not performing sterilizations without spousal consent. In 1977, a federal appellate court found no constitutional violation in a physician's personal policy to condition treatment of pregnant indigent patients on their voluntary submission to sterilization following the delivery of their third living child.[20] Serving Medicaid patients did not make his actions "state action." He applied his policy to all his patients and notified them of his practice in time for them to go elsewhere for care.

Performing a sterilization procedure without spousal consent presents little legal risk. For example, when a husband sued an Oklahoma physician for such a sterilization, the court dismissed the suit because his marital rights did not include a child-bearing wife, so he had not been legally harmed.[21]

Minors

Voluntary contraceptive sterilization of unmarried minor patients presents special problems, so local laws concerning minor consent should be carefully reviewed. Some state statutes authorize such sterilizations if the parent or guardian also consents.[22] Other state statutes forbid sterilization of an unmarried minor.[23] As discussed in the following section of this chapter, parents or guardians alone cannot authorize sterilizations. Patient consent is essential unless court authorization is obtained. Unless there is a medical reason for sterilization and the consents of the minor and the parent are clearly voluntary, informed, and unequivocal, prudent providers should be reluctant to sterilize a minor without a court order. Federal funds can be used to pay for sterilizations only if the person is competent and at least 21 years old.[24]

Conscience Clauses

Some states have enacted legislation stating that hospitals are not required to permit sterilization procedures and that physicians and hospital personnel may not be required to participate in such procedures or be discriminated against for refusal to participate.[25] In 1979, a nurse anesthetist was awarded payment from a hospital that violated the Montana conscience clause by dismissing her for refusing to participate in a tubal ligation.[26]

INVOLUNTARY STERILIZATION

Statutes and courts in some states have authorized involuntary sterilization of two groups of people. The first group to be addressed included those believed to transmit hereditary defects. In the first half of this century many states enacted eugenic sterilization laws, authorizing involuntary sterilization of these people. The U.S. Supreme Court upheld such laws in 1927.[27] Most states have repealed their eugenic sterilization laws. The second group consists of those who are severely retarded, sexually active, unable to use other forms of contraception, and unable to care properly for their offspring. Several state laws authorize sterilization of individuals a court determines to meet all of these criteria. The primary focus of these laws is the best interests of the individual and potential future offspring, rather than genetics.

These modern laws have been upheld by courts. For example, North Carolina's statute[28] was upheld by the North Carolina Supreme Court and by a federal district court.[29] The key elements of a constitutional statute appear to be (1) identification of an appropriate class of persons subject to the statute without discrimination or arbitrary bias and (2) guarantees of procedural due process, including notice, hearing, right to appeal, and assurance that decisions will be supported by qualified medical opinion.

Parents or guardians do not have the authority to consent to sterilization of retarded children or wards without a valid court authorization.[30]

Several courts have considered applications for orders authorizing involuntary sterilizations in states that do not have statutes specifically giving the court authority to issue such orders. Prior to 1978, most courts ruled that they did not have the authority and refused to issue orders authorizing sterilization. This position was largely due to two federal court decisions that judicial immunity did not protect judges who issued sterilization orders without specific statutory authority because they were not acting within their jurisdiction.[31] These decisions permitted civil rights suits against the judge and the involved health care providers. However, the U.S. Supreme Court reversed the decision in the second case in 1978, ruling that a court of broad general jurisdiction has the jurisdiction to consider a petition for sterilization of a minor unless statutes or case law in the state circumscribe the jurisdiction to foreclose consideration of such petitions.[32] Thus, the judge was protected by judicial immunity. The Court directed a lower federal court to decide the liability of the private individuals who had sought the petition and carried out the order. The lower court ruled these individuals could not be sued for federal civil rights violations because there was no showing of a conspiracy between the private individuals and the state officials.[33]

Since 1978, several state courts have ruled that they have authority to authorize involuntary sterilization of incompetents.[34] The decisions have set forth procedures and criteria that are generally similar to those specified in modern statutes.[35] However, the Alabama Supreme Court ruled that its state's courts do not have such authority.[36] In 1981, the Wisconsin Supreme Court adopted the unusual position that it had the authority, but would not exercise it.[37] Under its power to regulate lower state courts, the court ordered them not to issue authorizations. The court called on the legislature to pass appropriate legislation and said that if the legislature did not do so, the court might permit lower courts to issue authorizations.

In 1985, the California Supreme Court declared that a law that prohibited sterilizations of incompetents violated the federal and state constitutions.[38] The court found that the developmentally disabled have a constitutional right to procreative choice and that the state had not demonstrated a compelling state interest to overcome that right. However, the court declined to authorize sterilization in the particular case because there was no evidence of contraceptive necessity or of the lack of less intrusive means.

Hospitals and physicians should participate in involuntary sterilizations only when court authorization has been obtained following procedures and criteria established by statute or by the highest state court. The procedures should include notice, a hearing, and an opportunity to appeal.

ASSISTED CONCEPTION

When couples who desire children cannot achieve pregnancy, they often seek medical assistance. Techniques such as artificial insemination, surrogate mothers, and in vitro fertilization have been attempted when other approaches fail.[39]

Artificial Insemination

When the woman can conceive, but the man either cannot deliver semen or cannot produce effective semen, artificial insemination may be attempted. In the former situation the husband's semen may be injected, while in the latter situation donor semen is used. It has been estimated that 172,000 artificial inseminations occurred in 1987, resulting in 65,000 children.[40] There are few legal problems when the husband's semen is used before the husband's death. When the semen is used after the husband's death, there can be difficult questions concerning rights of the child related to the father. In 1995, a federal administrative law judge ruled that a child conceived from frozen sperm and born over 11 months after her father's death could receive his Social Security benefits.[41]

Artificial insemination with donor semen (A.I.D.) presents several legal issues, including whether the resulting child is legitimate and who is responsible for child support.[42] Several states have passed statutes concerning artificial insemination. Typical statutes specify that (1) the child is legitimate when the husband consents to A.I.D. and (2) the donor is not responsible for child support.[43] In states without statutes, some courts have ruled that the child is legitimate and the consenting husband is responsible for child support.[44] However, some courts have ruled that the child may not be legitimate under the common law.[45] At least one court has permitted a sperm donor to obtain an order of filiation.[46] Since it is unclear in most states whether the woman can waive the child's support claims, hospitals generally should limit A.I.D. procedures to married women and only with the written consent of the woman and her husband, including an acknowledgment of paternity and an acceptance of child support responsibilities.[47] If a statute or a decision of the highest state court protects the donor, the hospital, and its staff from child support responsibilities, then consideration can prudently be given to performing A.I.D. procedures in the protected situations.

Most state statutes require the procedure to be performed by a licensed physician.[48] Although the procedure can be performed by untrained persons,[49] the most prudent practice is to permit only physicians to perform it.

A fertility doctor was convicted of fraud and perjury for using his own sperm.[50]

One court has ruled that there is no policy against posthumous artificial insemination, so that the deceased's girlfriend was entitled to the frozen sperm willed to her.[51]

Surrogate Mothers

When a man has viable semen, but the woman cannot conceive, some couples seek a surrogate mother to bear a child after artificial insemination with the man's semen. The artificial insemination is legal in most states, but the agreement by the surrogate mother to give the child to the couple is probably not enforceable in many states and may be illegal. The New Jersey Supreme Court ruled against enforceability in 1988.[52] The most conservative hospital policy is not to permit artificial insemination of surrogate mothers on hospital premises. If the hospital decides to permit the practice, it is advisable to avoid involvement in the agreement to give the child to the couple. The hospital generally should release the child to persons other than the mother only with written consent signed by the mother after the birth. These arrangements lead to complex disputes.[53]

In Vitro Fertilization

Some couples produce viable reproductive cells, but conception is not possible naturally or through artificial insemination. In vitro fertilization (IVF) is available for some of these couples.[54] The reproductive cells of the couple are combined outside the woman's body, are allowed to begin growing there, and are later implanted in the woman's womb.

In one lawsuit arising from IVF, a university, a hospital, and a physician were found liable by a federal jury in New York in 1978 for the emotional distress of a couple following intentional destruction of a cell culture containing their reproductive cells.[55] This case illustrates the need for procedures that are understood by all involved, including the parents.[56]

Frozen embryos can be stored for later implantation.[57] In 1983, a California couple died in a plane crash in Chile after leaving two frozen embryos in Australia. A scholarly committee in Australia recommended that the embryos be destroyed, but in 1984 the Victoria legislature passed a law requiring that an attempt be made to implant the embryos in a surrogate mother and then place them for adoption if they were born. A California court ruled that if they were born, they could not inherit from their parents.[58] In 1989, a couple in Tennessee disputed ownership of frozen embryos in their divorce proceedings. The trial judge ruled that the embryos were children and awarded custody to the mother.[59] The intermediate appellate court granted joint custody.[60] The Tennessee Supreme Court ruled that if the parties did not agree otherwise, the embryos should be destroyed. The embryos were ultimately destroyed.[61]

A few states have passed laws that affect the use of IVF. A physician who wished to start using IVF in Illinois was concerned that the state abortion law could be interpreted to hold him liable for the care and custody of any child that resulted from IVF, so he challenged the law.[62] In 1983, the court dismissed the suit because the state attorney general informed the court that he did not intend to prosecute under the law for the use of IVF.

In 1992, a federal law was passed to develop a model program for states to certify embryo laboratories.[63]

Some courts have found that IVF is no longer experimental, so medical insurers must pay for it.[64] Some states have required coverage by statute.[65]

ABORTION

Medically, an abortion may be defined as the premature expulsion of the products of conception from the uterus. An abortion may be classified as spontaneous or induced.[66] An induced abortion can be induced to save the life of the unborn child, save the life or health of the mother, or terminate the pregnancy to preclude birth. The attention of the law has focused on induced abortions that are not intended to result in a live birth.

Historically, the common law did not prohibit induced abortions prior to the first fetal movements. By statute many states made induced abortions a crime, whether before or after fetal movements began, unless performed to preserve the life of the mother. The laws were amended in the 1960s and early 1970s to permit induced abortions when there were threats to the physical or mental health of the mother, when the child was at risk of severe congenital defects, or when the pregnancy resulted from rape or incest. A few states, such as New York, permitted induced abortions on request up to a designated stage of pregnancy if performed by a licensed physician in a licensed hospital.

In 1973, in *Roe v. Wade,* the U.S. Supreme Court declared a Texas criminal abortion law, which prohibited all abortions not necessary to save the life of the mother to be a violation of the due process clause of the Fourteenth Amendment.[67] In *Roe*, the Court adopted a three-stage analysis: (1) during the first trimester of pregnancy, the right of privacy of the woman and her physician precluded most state regulation of abortions performed by licensed physicians; (2) from the end of the first trimester until viability, states could regulate to protect maternal health; and (3) after viability, states had a compelling interest in the life of the unborn child, so that abortions could be prohibited except when necessary to preserve the life or health of the mother. After *Roe*, many laws were enacted to regulate and limit abortions. Until 1989, the U.S. Supreme Court consistently limited the scope of permitted regulation by striking down requirements that

1. first trimester abortions be performed in hospitals,[68] while allowing later abortions to be restricted to hospitals or licensed clinics;[69]
2. other physicians approve the abortion;[70]
3. restrictively defined viability;[71]
4. the woman have resided in the state for a certain period;[72]
5. the woman wait for a certain period after consenting;[73]
6. certain procedures not be used;[74] and
7. the father's consent be obtained.[75]

The Court permitted (1) restrictions on the use of public funds for abortions[76]; (2) informed consent requirements, but not requirements of specific statements designed to influence the choice[77]; (3) requirements of parental consent for minors if a timely alternative procedure was available for mature minors and other minors whose best interests indicated that their parents should not be involved[78]; and (4) record keeping and reporting requirements if confidentiality was maintained.[79]

In 1989, in *Webster v. Reproductive Health Services,* the U.S. Supreme Court upheld a state law that (1) prohibited use of public employees and facilities to perform abortions and (2) created a presumption of viability at 20 weeks' gestation which the physician could overcome by medical tests.[80] A majority of the members of the Court indicated that they questioned the three-stage analysis of *Roe*. The analysis by the majority invited greater state regulation, so it became unclear what limits, if any, on state regulation the Court would continue to recognize.

In 1991, the U.S. Supreme Court upheld a rule that prohibited federally funded family planning clinics from giving abortion advice.[81]

In 1992, the U.S. Supreme Court reaffirmed its recognition of the woman's right to choose an abortion before fetal viability, but abandoned the trimester framework, adopting in its place an undue burden test to evaluate abortion restrictions before viability and giving broader recognition to the state's interest in potential life.[82] The Court upheld several state regulations as not being undue burdens, but struck down the requirement of husband notification as an undue burden. The Court reversed its prior position on some other requirements, permitting (1) a 24-hour waiting period after consent and (2) a requirement that a physician provide certain information.

In 1993, the Court ruled that private blockades of abortion clinics do not violate the civil rights law.[83] In 1994, the Court ruled that the federal racketeering law could be used to sue antiabortion activists.[84] Also in 1994, the Court addressed the scope of permissible injunctions of abortion protestor activities.[85]

While there may continue to be some federal constitutional limits to permissible state regulation, it is likely that there will be growing attention to state legislation and to state constitutional provisions. In 1989, the Florida Supreme Court ruled that the state constitutional right of privacy protected the abortion decision prior to viability and struck down the state requirement of parental consent for abortions for unmarried minors.[86] Several state courts have ruled that the state constitution prohibits some limits on state funding of abortions.[87] At least one state has ruled that some hospitals must permit their facilities to be available for abortions.[88]

Parental approval or notification is not required for abortions for minors unless the state has enacted a requirement. However, it is prudent to encourage minors to involve their parents or other adult relatives in these decisions. Most states that require parental involvement have a procedure for mature minors to obtain judicial approval without parental involvement.

In 1984, a Massachusetts court ruled that when a court finds a minor sufficiently mature to consent to an abortion, the court's role is completed, and it cannot go further and require that a certain type of procedure be used.[89] In 1972, a Maryland court ruled that parents do not have authority to give consent for an abortion unless the minor also consents.[90] However, in 1984, a New York court ruled that a father could consent for an incompetent adult child; in 1989, another New York court permitted a husband to consent for his comatose wife; and in 1994, a Massachusetts court ruled that a guardian could consent for an incompetent adult.[91] Prudent providers will insist that a court order be obtained in each case where the woman is unable or unwilling to consent.

Several states have enacted conscience clauses that prohibit discrimination against physicians and hospital personnel who refuse to participate in abortions. These clauses were found to be constitutional.[92] In 1980, a New Jersey court ruled that it was not discrimination to transfer a refusing nurse from the maternity to the medical-surgical nursing staff with no change in seniority, pay, or shift.[93] Thus, in some jurisdictions, staff may be transferred to areas where they are not involved with the procedure without violating their right to refuse.

PRENATAL TESTING AND GENETIC SCREENING

It is possible through certain tests during pregnancy and soon after birth to detect numerous disorders.

One of the most common genetic tests during pregnancy is amniocentesis. It involves withdrawing through a long needle a small amount of amniotic fluid that surrounds the fetus. The fetal cells are studied for genetic defects. The major legal issues concerning amniocentesis involve consent and disclosure. In 1982, the Utah Supreme Court ruled that maternal consent to amniocentesis was sufficient.[94] Paternal consent need not be obtained. There are risks associated with the procedure,[95] which should be disclosed when obtaining consent.

A second type of genetic screening is a blood test within a few days after birth to detect metabolic disorders, such as phenylketonuria (PKU).[96] Some states have encouraged or required these tests to be performed on all newborns. If these conditions are detected early, special diets and other treatment can be given that preclude the severe mental retardation that is caused if the condition is not treated. Other genetic tests can now be used.[97]

WRONGFUL CONCEPTION, WRONGFUL BIRTH, AND WRONGFUL LIFE SUITS

Parents have sued physicians and hospitals for wrongful conception or wrongful birth of children they did not want or of deformed children they would have aborted had they known of the deformity. Deformed children have sued for their alleged wrongful life, claiming they were injured by being born. Courts have struggled with these suits to determine when there should be liability and what the basis for calculating the payment by the defendants should be.

Wrongful Conception and Wrongful Birth

The term *wrongful conception* is used, whether or not birth results, when (1) an unwanted pregnancy results from medical negligence or (2) a fetus with a genetic defect is conceived after the parents were not informed or were misinformed of the risk of the genetic condition. The term *wrongful birth* is used when (1) a birth results from a wrongful conception or (2) a birth follows medical negligence after conception that denies the mother the opportunity to make a timely informed decision whether to have an abortion.[98] Parents have made six basic types of wrongful conception or wrongful birth claims. Three types concern unsuccessful sterilization and abortion procedures, and the other three types concern genetic counseling and testing.

The three types that arise from unsuccessful sterilization and abortion procedures include parental claims that (1) they were not informed of risks that the procedure might be unsuccessful, (2) they were promised a successful procedure, or (3) the procedure was performed negligently. The first type is based on lack of informed consent, the second on breach of contract, and the third on malpractice.

Since pregnancy is a known risk of properly performed procedures, the occurrence of pregnancy does not establish negligent performance. Because it is usually difficult to establish negligent performance, claims tend to be of the first two types. A well-written consent form can make the first two types of claims difficult to pursue. In 1975, a Colorado court affirmed the dismissal of a parental suit because the consent form included a statement that no guarantee had been made concerning treatment results.[99]

The other three types of claims arise when an abnormal child is born who would have been aborted if the parents had known of the abnormality. The parental claims parallel the claims that arise from negligent sterilizations. The parents claim that (1) they were not advised of the possibility of the condition and the availability of tests; (2) they were told there was no risk of the particular abnormality; or (3) the tests were performed negligently, and the abnormality was not discovered. Thus, when there is reason to suspect that an abnormality is likely, parents should be advised and offered available tests. In 1987, the Minnesota Supreme Court ruled that a genetic counselor could not be liable for nondisclosure of risks that proper procedures did not reveal.[100]

Courts have generally awarded parents some payment when they are able to prove one or more of the six claims. There is some disagreement on the calculation of the payment, especially whether defendants must pay the cost of raising the child to adulthood. A few courts have permitted parents to collect the entire cost of child rearing.[101] Several courts have permitted parents to collect the cost of child rearing, reduced by the amount the jury believes the parents benefit from the joy and other advantages of parenthood.[102] Most courts have refused to permit parents to collect the cost of child rearing, especially for healthy children.[103] Courts have based their refusal on public policy considerations. They have been reluctant to label as an injury the presence of an additional child in a family. They have been concerned about the implications of the general rule that those who are injured must take steps to reduce their injuries, which could mean the parents would be required to seek an abortion or put the child up for adoption to reduce their injuries. Several courts that generally do not award the costs of child rearing do allow the special additional expenses of raising a handicapped child to adulthood.[104]

Some states have barred wrongful birth claims by statute or by court decision. These statutes have consistently been upheld.[105]

Wrongful Life

Some children with genetic defects have sued physicians and hospitals, claiming they were injured by being born. They have based their suits on the same claims that their parents have made. Most courts have refused to allow suits by these children. In one of the earliest cases addressing this issue, the New Jersey Supreme Court observed that compensation is ordinarily computed by "comparing the condition plaintiff would have been in, had the defendants not been negligent, with plaintiff's impaired condition as a result of the negligence."[106] The condition of the child, had the defendants not been negligent, would have been the "utter void of nonexistence." The court said that courts could not affix a price tag on non-life, so it would be impossible to compute the amount to award.

In 1982, the California Supreme Court adopted the unusual position of permitting a child to collect for the extraordinary expenses of living with deafness due to a genetic defect even though there was no way the child could have been born without the deafness.[107] From the perspective of the defendant's actual liability, the decision does not appear unusual. The court permitted the child to collect the same amount the parents could have collected in several other states if the suit had been in their names. A few other states have adopted this position.[108]

NOTES

1. *See* Mishell, *Contraception*, 320 N. ENGL. J. MED. 777 (1989); *but see* Djerassi, *The bitter pill*, 245 SCIENCE 356 (1989) [product liability, funding constraints on development of new contraceptives].

2. Griswold v. Connecticut, 381 U.S. 479 (1965).

3. Eisenstadt v. Baird, 405 U.S. 438 (1972).

4. Carey v. Population Servs. Int'l, 431 U.S. 678 (1977).

5. *Id.*

6. Doe v. Irwin, 615 F.2d 1162 (6th Cir.), *cert. denied*, 449 U.S. 829 (1980); *see also* Jane Does v. Utah Dep't of Health, 776 F.2d 253 (10th Cir. 1985).

7. Arneth v. Gross, 699 F. Supp. 450 (S.D. N.Y. 1988).

8. 42 U.S.C. § 300(a).

9. 48 FED. REG. 3600-14 (1983).

10. Planned Parenthood Fed'n v. Schweiker, 559 F. Supp. 658 (D. D.C.), *aff'd*, 229 U.S. App. D.C. 336, 712 F.2d 650 (1983); New York v. Heckler, 719 F.2d 1191 (2d Cir. 1983).

11. Planned Parenthood Ass'n v. Matheson, 582 F. Supp. 1001 (D. Utah 1983).

12. Brownfield v. Daniel Freeman Marina Hosp., 208 Cal. App. 3d 405, 256 Cal. Rptr. 240 (2d Dist. 1989); *see also* Ark. Att'y Gen. Op. No. 88-380 (Dec. 22, 1988) ["morning after" pill not an abortion]; *Scant use of morning-after pill is analyzed*, N.Y. TIMES, Mar. 29, 1995, at A13.

13. *E.g.*, Avila v. New York City Health & Hosps. Corp., 136 Misc. 2d 76, 518 N.Y.S.2d 574 (Sup. Ct. 1987) [mildly retarded woman could consent].

14. 42 C.F.R. §§ 441.250–441.259.

15. CAL. ADMIN. CODE tit. 22, §§ 70707.1–70707.8; California Med. Ass'n v. Lackner, 124 Cal. App. 3d 28, 177 Cal. Rptr. 188 (3d Dist. 1981) [requirement of written consent constitutional]; Kaplan v. Blank, 204 Ga. App. 378, 419 S.E.2d 127 (1992) [oral consent was no consent to tubal ligation under Voluntary Sterilization Act, so battery]; Chasse v. Mazerolle, 622 A.2d 1180 (Me. 1993) [19-year-old sterilized in 1973, claimed she was not competent to consent; failure to follow statutory consultation process can be basis for liability].

16. *E.g.*, Sims v. University of Ark. Med. Ctr., No. 1R76-C67 (E.D. Ark. Mar. 4, 1977).

17. Hathaway v. Worcester City Hosp., 475 F.2d 701 (1st Cir. 1973).

18. *E.g.*, Coe v. Bolton, No. C-87-785A (N.D. Ga. Sept. 30, 1976).

19. *E.g.*, Taylor v. St. Vincent's Hosp., 523 F.2d 75 (9th Cir. 1975), *cert. denied*, 424 U.S. 948 (1976).

20. Walker v. Pierce, 560 F.2d 609 (4th Cir. 1977), *cert. denied*, 434 U.S. 1075 (1978).

21. Murray v. Vandevander, 522 P.2d 302 (Okla. Ct. App. 1974).

22. *E.g.*, COLO. REV. STAT. ANN. § 25-6-102.

23. *E.g.*, GA. CODE ANN. § 31-20-2.

24. 42 C.F.R. §§ 50.203, 441.253.

25. *E.g.*, KAN. STAT. ANN. §§ 65-446, 65-447.

26. Swanson v. St. John's Lutheran Hosp., 182 Mont. 414, 597 P.2d 702 (1979), *judgment after remand aff'd*, 189 Mont. 259, 615 P.2d 883 (1980).

27. Buck v. Bell, 274 U.S. 200 (1927); *see also* Poe v. Lynchburg Training School, 518 F. Supp. 789 (W.D. Va. 1981) [involuntary sterilizations did not violate civil rights when under statute held constitutional].

28. N.C. GEN. STAT. §§ 35-36–35-50.

29. In re Sterilization of Moore, 289 N.C. 95, 221 S.E.2d 307 (1976); North Carolina Ass'n for Retarded Children v. North Carolina, 420 F. Supp. 451 (M.D. N.C. 1976).

30. *E.g.*, In re Grady, 85 N.J. 235, 426 A.2d 467 (1981); In re Moe, 385 Mass. 555, 432 N.E.2d 712 (1982); Annotation, *Power of parent to have mentally defective child sterilized*, 74 A.L.R. 3D 1224.

31. Wade v. Bethesda Hosp., 337 F. Supp. 671 (S.D. Ohio 1971); Wade v. Bethesda Hosp., 356 F. Supp. 380 (S.D. Ohio 1973); Sparkman v. McFarlin, 552 F.2d 172 (7th Cir. 1977).

32. Stump v. Sparkman, 435 U.S. 349 (1978).

33. Sparkman v. McFarlin, 601 F.2d 261 (7th Cir. 1979).

34. Annotation, *Jurisdiction of court to permit sterilization of mentally defective person in absence of specific statutory authority*, 74 A.L.R. 3D 1210.

35. *E.g.*, Lulos v. State, 548 N.E.2d 173 (Ind. Ct. App. 1990); In re Guardianship of Hayes, 93 Wash. 2d 228, 608 P.2d 635 (1980).

36. Hudson v. Hudson, 373 So.2d 310 (Ala. 1979).

37. In re Guardianship of Eberhardy, 102 Wis. 2d 539, 307 N.W.2d 881 (1981).

38. Conservatorship of Valerie N., 40 Cal. 3d 143, 219 Cal. Rptr. 387, 707 P.2d 760 (1985).

39. H.W. Jones and J.P. Toner, *The infertile couple*, 329 N. ENGL. J. MED. 1710 (1993).

40. *Screening for artificial insemination found lacking*, AM. MED. NEWS, Sept. 9, 1988, at 21.

41. *Tot conceived after dad died can get his benefits*, PALM BEACH [FL] POST, May 31, 1995, at 2A [decision by ALJ Elving Torres which may be appealed by government].

42. For other legal issues, see *Artificial insemination. A new frontier for medical malpractice and medical products liability*, 32 LOY. L. REV. 411 (1986); Annotation, *Rights and obligations resulting from human artificial insemination*, 83 A.L.R. 4TH 295.

43. *E.g.*, OKLA. STAT. tit. 10, §§ 551–553; FLA. STAT. § 742.11; *see also* Michael H. v. Gerald D., 491 U.S. 110 (1989) [general statutory presumption of husband's paternity does not violate due process rights of man alleging paternity].

44. *E.g.*, People v. Sorensen, 68 Cal. 2d 280, 66 Cal. Rptr. 7, 437 P.2d 495 (1968); Estate of Gordon, 131 Misc. 2d 823, 501 N.Y.S.2d 969 (Sur. Ct. 1986).

45. *E.g.*, Gursky v. Gursky, 39 Misc. 2d 1083, 242 N.Y.S.2d 406 (Sup. Ct. 1963).

46. Thomas S. v. Robin Y., 209 A.D. 2d 298, 618 N.Y.S.2d 356 (1st Dept. 1994), *recons. granted*, 85 N.Y.2d 925, 627 N.Y.S.2d 1328, 650 N.E.2d 1328 (1995).

47. *But see* Perkoff, *Artificial insemination in a lesbian*, 145 ARCH. INTERN. MED. 527 (1985); Karen T. v. Michael T., 127 Misc. 2d 14, 484 N.Y.S.2d 780 (Fam. Ct. 1985) [female declared to have paternal support responsibility because, while living as husband, consented to artificial insemination of "wife"]; *but see* V.L. Henry, *A tale of three women: A survey of rights and responsibilities of unmarried women who conceive by alternative insemination and a model for legislative reform*, 19 AM. J. L. & MED. 285 (1993).

48. *E.g.*, OR. REV. STAT. §§109.239–109.247.

49. *E.g.*, C.M. v. C.C., 152 N.J. Super. 160, 377 A.2d 821 (Juv. & Dom. Rel. Ct. 1977).

50. United States v. Jacobson, 4 F.3d 987 (*without op.*), 1993 U.S. App. LEXIS 22,534 (full report) (4th Cir. 1993), *cert. denied*, 114 S. Ct. 1643 (U.S. 1994)*; Fertility doctor starts 5-year sentence*, AM. MED. NEWS, Mar. 21, 1994, at 5; *see also* St. Paul Fire & Marine Ins. Co. v. Jacobson, 826 F. Supp. 155 (E.D. Va. 1993), *aff'd*, 48 F.3d 778 (4th Cir. 1995) [insurer must defend fertility doctor accused of using own sperm]; James v. Jacobson, 6 F.3d 233 (4th Cir. 1993) [civil suit should proceed anonymously].

51. Hecht v. Superior Court, 16 Cal. App. 4th 836, 20 Cal. Rptr. 2d 275 (2d Dist. 1993), *rev. denied*, 1993 Cal. LEXIS 4768 (Sept. 2, 1993); *Ruling left intact in sperm bequest*, N.Y. TIMES, Sept. 5, 1993, at 13.

52. In re Baby M, 109 N.J. 396, 537 A.2d 1227 (1988); *accord* Doe v. Kelly, 6 FAM. L. RPTR. 3011 (Mich. Cir. Ct. Jan. 28, 1980), *aff'd sub nom.* Doe v. Attorney Gen., 106 Mich. App. 169, 307 N.W.2d 438 (1981), *leave to appeal denied*, 414 Mich. 875 (1982), *cert. denied*, 459 U.S. 1183 (1983); *but see* Syrkowski v. Appleyard, 420 Mich. 367, 362 N.W.2d 211 (1985) [court has

jurisdiction over biological father's request for order declaring him father of child born pursuant to surrogate parenting agreement]. An English court took custody of baby born to surrogate mother, N.Y. TIMES, Jan. 10, 1985, at 7; Annotation, *Validity and construction of surrogate parenting agreement*, 77 A.L.R. 4TH 70.

53. *E.g.*, Stiver v. Parker, 975 F.2d 261 (11th Cir. 1992) [surrogate mother impregnated by husband rather than donor; her child contracted cytomegalovirus from untested donor semen]; Adoption of Matthew B., 232 Cal. App. 3d 1239, 284 Cal. Rptr. 18 (1st Dist. 1991), *reh'g denied*, 1991 Cal. App. LEXIS 995 (Aug. 28, 1991), *rev. denied*, 191 Cal. LEXIS 5522 (Nov. 21, 1991), *cert. denied*, 503 U.S. 991 (1992) [surrogate mother denied custody rights without ruling on validity of surrogate contract]; Soos v. Superior Ct., 897 P.2d 1356 (Ariz. Ct. App. 1994) [statute which allows biological father to prove paternity and grants surrogate mother status of legal mother violates equal protection by failing to give egg donor means to prove paternity]; Belsito v. Clark, 67 Ohio Misc. 54, 644 N.E.2d 760 (Cm. Pl. 1994) [when child delivered by gestational surrogate impregnated by IVF, natural parents shall be identified as persons who provided genetic imprint, genetic parents have legal status of natural parents unless relinquished or waived, so adoption required; hospital delivering child improperly told genetic mother that surrogate would be listed as mother on birth certificate].

54. *See* Lutz, *Test-tube births get scrutiny*, 19 MOD. HEALTHCARE, July 21, 1989, at 60; Raymond, *In vitro fertilization faces "R & R": (More) research and regulation*, 260 J.A.M.A. 1191 (1988).

55. Del Zio v. Presbyterian Hosp., 74 Civ. 3588 (S.D. N.Y. Apr. 12, 1978).

56. *See also* York v. Jones, 717 F. Supp. 421 (E.D. Va. 1989) [suit seeking transfer of cryopreserved human pre-zygote]; *Fertility clinic to close amid complaints*, N.Y. TIMES, May 29, 1995, at 7 [closure of U.C.L.A. clinic].

57. *See Frozen embryos: Moral, social, and legal implications*, 59 S. CAL. L. REV. 1079 (1986).

58. N.Y. TIMES, June 23, 1984, at 9; Oct. 24, 1984, at 9; Dec. 5, 1987, at 11.

59. Davis v. Davis, No. E-14496 (Tenn. Cir. Ct. Blount County Sept. 21, 1989); N.Y. TIMES, Sept. 22, 1989, at 13; Gianelli, *Judge: Embryos are "children", not "property"*, AM. MED. NEWS, Oct. 6, 1989, at 1; PALM BEACH [FL] POST, June 16, 1993, at 6A [destruction announced].

60. Davis v. Davis, 1990 Tenn. App. LEXIS 642 (Sept. 13, 1990).

61. Davis v. Davis, 842 S.W.2d 588 (Tenn. 1992), *cert. denied*, 113 S. Ct. 1259 (U.S. 1993).

62. Smith v. Hartigan, 556 F. Supp. 157 (N.D. Ill. 1983).

63. Fertility Clinic Success Rate and Certification Act of 1992, Pub. L. No. 102-493, 106 Stat. 3146 (1992) [*codified in* 42 U.S.C.A. §§ 263a-1–263a-7]; 42 C.F.R. pt. 493.

64. *E.g.*, Reilly v. Blue Cross & Blue Shield, 846 F.2d 416 (7th Cir.), *cert. denied*, 488 U.S. 856 (1988); *but see* Northwest Farm Bureau Ins. Co. v. Althauser, 90 Or. App. 13, 750 P.2d 1166, *rev. denied*, 305 Or. 672, 757 P.2d 422 (1988) [IVF not covered because not medically necessary].

65. *See Big HMO settles suit on policy concerning in-vitro fertilization*, WALL ST. J., Oct. 2, 1987, at 24.

66. For a discussion of early spontaneous abortion, *see* Wilcox et al., *Incidence of early loss of pregnancy*, 319 N. ENGL. J. MED. 189 (1988).

67. Roe v. Wade, 410 U.S. 113 (1973).

68. *E.g.*, City of Akron v. Akron Ctr. for Reproductive Health, 462 U.S. 416 (1983); Arnold v. Sendak, 416 F. Supp. 22 (S.D. Ind.), *aff'd*, 429 U.S. 968 (1976); Doe v. Bolton, 410 U.S. 179 (1973).

69. *E.g.*, Simopoulos v. Virginia, 462 U.S. 506 (1983).

70. *E.g.*, Doe v. Bolton, 410 U.S. 179 (1973).

71. *E.g.*, Colautti v. Franklin, 439 U.S. 379 (1979) ["may be" viable is too vague]; Hodgson v. Anderson, 378 F. Supp. 1008 (D. Minn. 1974), *appeal dismissed*, 420 U.S. 903 (1975), *aff'd in pertinent part*, 542 F.2d 1350 (8th Cir. 1976); Planned Parenthood v. Danforth, 428 U.S. 52 (1976).

72. *E.g.*, Doe v. Bolton, 410 U.S. 179 (1973).

73. *E.g.*, City of Akron v. Akron Ctr. for Reproductive Health, 462 U.S. 416 (1983).

74. *E.g.*, Planned Parenthood v. Danforth, 428 U.S. 52 (1976).

75. *E.g.*, *id.*; *see also* Doe v. Smith, 486 U S. 1308 (1988) [natural father of unborn child denied injunction of abortion]; Annotation, *Woman's right to have abortion without consent of, or against objections of, child's father*, 62 A.L.R. 3D 1097.

76. *E.g.*, Harris v. McRae, 448 U.S. 297 (1980); Williams v. Zbaraz, 448 U.S. 358 (1980).

77. City of Akron v. Akron Ctr. for Reproductive Health, 462 U.S. 416 (1983); Planned Parenthood Ass'n v. Fitzpatrick, 401 F. Supp. 554 (E.D. Pa 1975), *aff'd without opinion sub nom*. Franklin v. Fitzpatrick, 428 U.S. 901 (1976).

78. *E.g.*, Hartigan v. Zbaraz, 484 U.S. 171 (1987), *aff'g per curiam by equally divided court*, 763 F.2d 1532 (7th Cir. 1985); H.L. v. Matheson, 450 U.S. 398 (1981); Bellotti v. Baird, 443 U.S. 622 (1979).

79. *E.g.*, Planned Parenthood Ass'n v. Ashcroft, 462 U.S. 476 (1983); Planned Parenthood v. Danforth, 428 U.S. 52 (1976).

80. Webster v. Reproductive Health Servs., 492 U.S. 490 (1989).

81. Rust v. Sullivan, 500 U.S. 173 (1991).

82. Planned Parenthood v. Casey, 112 S. Ct. 2791 (U.S. 1992).

83. Bray v. Alexandria Women's Health Clinic, 113 S. Ct. 753 (U.S. 1993).

84. National Organization for Women v. Scheidler, 114 S. Ct. 798 (U.S. 1994).

85. Madsen v. Women's Health Care Ctr., 114 S. Ct. 2516 (U.S. 1994).

86. In re T.W., 551 So.2d 1186 (Fla. 1989).

87. *E.g.*, Moe v. Secretary of Admin. & Fin., 382 Mass. 629, 417 N.E.2d 387 (1981).

88. Doe v. Bridgeton Hosp. Ass'n, 71 N.J. 478, 366 A.2d 641 (1976), *cert. denied*, 433 U.S. 914 (1977).

89. In re Moe, 18 Mass. App. Ct. 727, 469 N.E.2d 1312 (1984); *see also* Ex parte Anonymous, 531 So.2d 901 (Ala. 1988) [abortion authorized for immature minor where best interests shown]; Annotation, *Right of minor to have abortion performed without parental consent*, 42 A.L.R. 3D 1406; Annotation, *Requisites and conditions of judicial consent to minor's abortion*, 23 A.L.R. 4TH 1061.

90. In re Smith, 16 Md. App. 209, 295 A.2d 238 (1972).

91. In re Barbara C., 101 A.D.2d 137, 474 N.Y.S.2d 799 (2d Dep't 1984), *appeal dismissed*, 64 N.Y.2d 866, 487 N.Y.S.2d 549, 476 N.E.2d 994 (1985); In re Klein, 145 A.D.2d 145, 538 N.Y.S.2d 274 (2d Dep't), *appeal denied*, 73 N.Y.2d 705, 539 N.Y.S.2d 298, 536 N.E.2d 627, *stay denied*, 489 U.S. 1003 (1989); In the Matter of Jane A., 36 Mass. App. Ct. 236, 629 N.E.2d 1337 (1994); *see also* In re Doe, 533 A.2d 523 (R.I. 1987) [state agency authorized to consent to abortion despite opposition of patient's mother who had lost custody].

92. Doe v. Bolton, 410 U.S. 179 (1973).

93. Jeczalik v. Valley Hosp., 87 N.J. 344, 434 A.2d 90 (1981).

94. Reiser v. Lohner, 641 P.2d 93 (Utah 1982).

95. *E.g.*, Bush v. Blanchard, 310 S.C. 375, 426 S.E.2d 802 (1993).

96. *E.g.*, Horvath v. Baylor Univ. Med. Ctr., 704 S.W.2d 866 (Tex. Ct. App. 1985) [PKU test not performed].

97. See M.E. D'Alton and A.H. DeCherney, *Prenatal diagnosis*, 328 N. ENGL. J. MED. 114 (1993).

98. J.R. Botkin and M.J. Mehlman, *Wrongful birth: Medical, legal, and philosophical issues*, 22 J. LAW, MED. & ETHICS 21 (1994) [as of 1993, 23 state courts, 3 federal courts, 1 state statute adopted wrongful birth, while 5 state courts and 6 state statutes rejected it].

99. Herrera v. Roessing, 533 P.2d 60 (Colo. Ct. App. 1975).

100. Pratt v. University of Minn. Affiliated Hosps., 414 N.W.2d 399 (Minn. 1987).

101. *E.g.*, Gallagher v. Duke Univ., 852 F.2d 773 (4th Cir. 1988); Ochs v. Borrelli, 187 Conn. 253, 445 A.2d 883 (1982); *see* Annotation, *Recoverability of cost of raising normal, healthy child born as result of physician's negligence or breach of contract or warranty*, 89 A.L.R. 4TH 632.

102. *E.g.*, Sherlock v. Stillwater Clinic, 260 N.W.2d 169 (Minn. 1977); Jones v. Malinowski, 299 Md. 257, 473 A.2d 429 (1984).

103. *E.g.*, C.S. v. Nielson, 767 P.2d 504 (Utah 1988); Miller v. Johnson, 231 Va. 177, 343 S.E.2d 301 (1986); Kingsbury v. Smith, 122 N.H. 237, 442 A.2d 1003 (1982).

104. *E.g.*, Haymon v. Wilkerson, 535 A.2d 880 (D.C. 1987); Smith v. Cote, 128 N.H. 231, 513 A.2d 341 (1986); Fassoulas v. Ramey, 450 So.2d 822 (Fla. 1984); *see* Annotation, *Recoverability of compensatory damages for mental anguish or emotional distress for tortiously causing another's birth*, 74 A.L.R. 4TH 798.

105. *E.g.*, Campbell v. United States, 962 F.2d 1579 (11th Cir. 1992), *cert. denied*, 113 S. Ct. 1254 (U.S. 1993) [Georgia's nonrecognition of wrongful birth such claims not violation of due process]; Bianchini v. N.K.D.S. Assocs., Ltd., 420 Pa. Super. 294, 616 A.2d 700 (1992), *appeal denied*, 534 Pa. 634, 626 A.2d 1154 (1993) [wrongful birth claim precluded by 42 PA. C.S.A. § 8305].

106. Gleitman v. Cosgrove, 49 N.J. 22, 227 A.2d 689, 692 (1967); *accord* Lininger v. Eisenbaum, 764 P.2d 1202 (Colo. 1988); Goldberg v. Ruskin, 113 Ill. 2d 482, 499 N.E.2d 406 (1986); Nelson v. Krusen, 678 S.W.2d 918 (Tex. 1984); *see also* Cowe by Cowe v. Forum Group, Inc., 575 N.E.2d 630 (Ind. 1991).

107. Turpin v. Sortini, 31 Cal. 3d 220, 643 P.2d 954 (1982); Gami v. Mullikin Med. Ctr., 18 Cal. App. 4th 870, 22 Cal. Rptr. 2d 819 (2d Dist. 1993), *rev. denied*, 1993 Cal. LEXIS 6480 (Dec. 16, 1993).

108. *E.g.*, Walker v. Rinck, 604 N.E.2d 591 (Ind. 1992); Procanik v. Cillo, 97 N.J. 339, 478 A.2d 755 (1984).

16

Death and Dead Bodies

Since many deaths in the United States occur in hospitals, hospital staffs must determine death and handle dead bodies. Death may be determined by traditional standards or by the absence of brain functions. There is well-established law concerning the handling of dead bodies which should be followed strictly because of the important societal and individual interests affected.

DEFINITION OF DEATH

The question of the definition of death is distinct from the questions concerning treatment of the living. Once the patient is legally dead, there is no longer a patient. Patient care should be discontinued. The hospital becomes the custodian of a dead body with the responsibilities discussed later in this chapter.

Irreversible cessation of brain function has been accepted as the definition of death when vital signs are being maintained artificially. The traditional definition is still applicable in all other situations.

Medical Definition of Death

For over a century the traditional definition of death has been the cessation of respiration, heartbeat, and certain indications of central nervous system activity— namely, response to pain and reaction of pupils to light. Cardiac pumps, respirators, and other procedures can maintain the first two traditional indicators of life for extended periods beyond the cessation of brain activity.[1] When these indicators of life are being artificially maintained, the medical definition of death is the irreversible cessation of all brain functions. The House of Delegates of the American Medical Association (AMA) recognized the use of this criterion in 1974.

This brain-based definition of death requires irreversible cessation of all brain functions, including the brain stem. While it may be appropriate to discontinue certain treatments for patients with only brain stem functions, this should be done pursuant to the procedures for refusing treatment discussed in Chapter 13, not by declaring the patient dead before the cessation of brain stem functions. Some writers have discussed changing the brain-based definition of death, so that death occurs upon irreversible cessation of higher brain functions without cessation of brain stem functions.[2] While conceptually there are some advantages to the higher brain standard, it is not yet an accepted medical or legal definition. In 1992, the Florida Supreme Court refused to adopt the higher brain standard in a suit seeking to have an anencephalic newborn declared dead to permit organ donation.[3] An anencephalic newborn is born with a brain stem and no higher brain and generally dies within a few days of birth. In 1994, the AMA issued a controversial opinion that it was ethically permissible to use anencephalic infants as organ donors while still alive.[4]

The irreversible cessation of the functioning of the whole brain is a well-defined clinical entity for which there are reliable diagnostic tests. The most widely accepted diagnostic criteria are the guidelines developed by medical consultants in 1981 for the President's Commission for the Study of Ethical Problems in Medicine and Biomedical and Behavioral Research.[5] Cerebral unreceptivity and unresponsiveness must be observed. Adequate stimuli of several listed types must be applied to determine lack of brain stem reflexes. Apnea testing to determine the lack of spontaneous breathing efforts is necessary. The cause of the condition should be determined. Reversible conditions, such as sedation, drug intoxication, hypothermia, neuromuscular blockade, and shock, should be ruled out. Possible confirmatory tests are listed and recommended in some cases. When cause cannot be established, direct tests of absence of blood flow to the brain may be necessary. The duration of observation depends on the condition, the cause, and what confirmatory tests have been used.

Earlier guidelines[6] placed emphasis on two flat (isoelectric) electroencephalograms (EEGs) at least 24 hours apart. Although this graphic demonstration has been emphasized in nonmedical portrayals of determinations of death based on brain criteria and may still be a useful confirmatory test in some cases, neither a flat EEG nor repeat tests are necessary for a reliable diagnosis in all cases.

The 1981 guidelines recognized that the diagnosis of death using brain criteria is more difficult for infants and younger children. Even greater caution is necessary for these patients, but it is possible to make reliable diagnoses.[7]

Legal Definition of Death

The common law definition of death includes death determined by brain criteria in accordance with usual medical standards. In the first years that followed the medical recognition of this definition, some lower courts had difficulty accepting the definition in suits involving organ donations for heart transplants. One California trial court refused to accept brain criteria, acquitting the person who had been charged with manslaughter in the death of the donor. Such trial court cases are now historical anomalies.

The statutory recognition of the use of brain criteria has superseded these decisions and resolved the question in 44 states and the District of Columbia.[8] The highest courts of the other six states have recognized death determined by brain criteria as legal death.[9] Brain criteria have been officially recognized in all states.

The details in these statutes still vary somewhat from state to state, especially in terms of consultation and documentation requirements. New Jersey requires that physicians consider the patient's religious beliefs before declaring brain death. Several groups have developed model legislation in an effort to secure more uniformity. The Uniform Determination of Death Act has been adopted by at least 32 states.[10]

While some providers still seek family consent before declaring death using brain criteria, family consent is not legally required. Death legally occurs when death is declared and family denial does not negate this reality. In 1988, the Alabama Supreme Court ruled that a provider could not be liable for declaring such death and stopping treatment without family consent.[11] It is advisable to explain the situation to the family, but not to seek their consent. Seeking consent only creates the opportunity for the impasse of family refusal, which prolongs inappropriate treatment and may require otherwise unnecessary judicial involvement. However, isolated cases of treatment of dead bodies continue to occur.[12]

While some confusion exists among the media, the public, and even some health professionals concerning the conceptual foundations and terminology for death determinations using brain criteria,[13] especially when heart function is maintained after death to facilitate transplantation, the legal status of the body is clear.

When death is declared, the patient legally becomes a dead body even if heartbeat is maintained to preserve organs for transplantation. The time of death is when death is declared, not when the equipment is disconnected and the heartbeat stops. The former patient's third party payers do not pay for maintenance of the body after death is declared. Payment, if any, for this maintenance comes from those paying for the treatment of the recipients of the transplanted organs.

After death is declared, the family is entitled to possession of the dead body so the hospital may retain possession and maintain the heartbeat only with the consent of those entitled to determine the disposition of the body. In 1988, the New Jersey Supreme Court ruled that a hospital could be sued for refusing to terminate equipment and release a body after declaration of death.[14]

Declaration and Certification of Death

Generally death must be declared by a physician. A physician generally must also sign a death certificate. Some states permit nurses to declare death using traditional criteria in some circumstances, especially when death is expected, but generally a physician still must sign the death certificate.[15]

DEAD BODIES

This section discusses the duties of hospitals and health care professionals in handling dead bodies and communicating with family and legal authorities. Autopsies and anatomical donations are discussed in the following sections.

Communications with Family

The hospital in which a patient dies has a duty to take reasonable steps to identify and inform an appropriate member of the family of the death within a reasonable time.[16] This is necessary to permit appropriate arrangements to be made for disposition of the body. Information regarding death should be confirmed before being communicated. Erroneous notification of death will be upsetting to the family and may cause them to make expenditures for funeral arrangements, possibly resulting in a lawsuit. The hospital could be liable for the emotional harm and expenses.[17] However, mistaken notification will not result in liability when an error in identity is due to a good faith reliance on identification by the police at the scene of an accident.[18]

The method by which the family is informed also is important. In 1977, a New Jersey court ruled that a hospital could be sued for the method in which a mother had been informed of the death of her baby.[19] While still in the hospital where the birth occurred, the mother had been telephoned by a person from the hospital to which her baby had been transferred for specialized care. The caller, who was otherwise unidentified, told her the baby was dead, and the mother became hysterical. If it can be avoided, family should not be informed of unexpected deaths by telephone unless someone is with them to provide support. When death is anticipated, there may be less need for immediate support.

Medical Examiners' Cases

All states have laws providing for legal investigation of certain suspicious deaths by a legal officer, such as a medical examiner or coroner. Most states require a report to the medical examiner by the physician in attendance at a death known or suspected to be of the type requiring investigation. One typical example is the Iowa requirement that physicians report any "death which affects the public interest," which is defined to include

- a. Violent death, including homicidal, suicidal, or accidental death.
- b. Death caused by thermal, chemical, electrical, or radiation injury.
- c. Death caused by criminal abortion including self-induced, or by sexual abuse.
- d. Death related to disease thought to be virulent or contagious which may constitute a public hazard.
- e. Death that has occurred unexpectedly or from an unexplained cause.
- f. Death of a person confined in a prison, jail, or correctional institution.
- g. Death of a person if a physician was not in attendance within 36 hours preceding death, excluding prediagnosed terminal or bedfast cases for which the time period is extended to 30 days, and excluding a terminally ill patient who was admitted to and had received services from a hospice program, as defined in section 135.90, if a physician or registered nurse employed by the program was in attendance within thirty days preceding death.
- h. Death of a person if the body is not claimed by a relative or friend.
- i. Death of a person if the identity of the deceased is unknown.
- j. Death of a child under the age of two years if death results from an unknown cause or if the circumstances surrounding the death indicate that sudden infant death syndrome may be the cause of death.[20]

Each state's list is somewhat different, so it is important to be familiar with the applicable list and with the local medical examiner's practices concerning the cases expected to be reported. It is a crime in many states not to make the required report to the statutorily specified official. In 1995, a Florida grand jury indicted the risk management officer and a nursing supervisor for the crime of failing to report promptly the death of a hospital patient who had accidently been injected with the wrong drug. The death was not reported until the next morning approximately nine hours after the death and after the body had been moved, the room cleaned, and the vial and syringe discarded.[21]

Physicians who are not sure whether to report should report. The medical examiner can decide whether further investigation is warranted. In 1992, the Nebraska Supreme Court ruled that there was a qualified privilege to make the report, so the hospital could not be liable for the family's distress from the medical examiner's investigation.[22] When a death is clearly not a medical examiner's case, a report is inappropriate. When it is determined that the death is a medical examiner's case, all health care providers have a duty to cooperate with the investigation. The first requirement is not to move the body without permission of the medical examiner except as authorized by law. Some states authorize moving bodies, if necessary, to preserve the body from loss or destruction, to permit travel on highways or by public transportation, or to prevent immediate danger to the life, safety, or health of others. Not all states have these exceptions.

Release of the Body

Upon the death of a patient, the hospital becomes the temporary custodian of the body. The hospital is responsible for releasing the body in the proper condition to the proper recipient in accordance with state law. Thus, hospital staff should be familiar with state law applying to handling and releasing bodies.

In general, the proper recipient of the body has a right to its prompt release in the condition at death unless the deceased has directed otherwise or the body is being retained or examined in accordance with law. Thus, the major issues are (1) the scope of the deceased's authority, (2) the authority of others to act in the absence of binding directions by the decedent, (3) the timing of the release of the body, and (4) the condition of the body when it is released.

Deceased's Authority

Some state statutes give individuals broad authority to direct the disposition of their remains.[23] All states have now enacted a version of the Uniform Anatomical Gift Act,[24] so individuals can donate their bodies or certain organs for various purposes. When the situation is not covered by statute and the person entitled to dispose of the body is not willing to carry out the decedent's wishes, the common law determines whether the individual's wishes can be enforced. Most courts have recognized a right to direct disposition of the body by will,[25] but they have recognized many exceptions. While courts have taken other documents or statements into account, they have been more likely to defer to the decedent's directions when they are in a will or a document authorized by statute. The one direction that the common law generally enforces is an autopsy authorization.

Authority of Others To Control Disposition

In the absence of binding directions by the deceased, the surviving spouse is recognized as the person who controls the disposition of the remains. However, in some states, if the surviving spouse has abandoned and is living apart from the deceased, the right is waived. If there is no surviving spouse or if the surviving spouse fails to act or waives the right, then control passes to the next of kin. Unless statute or common law precedent in the jurisdiction establishes a different order of kinship, the priority is generally recognized to be adult child, parent, and adult sibling. If the person with the highest priority either fails to act or waives the right, the next priority level becomes the highest priority level and has control.

Timing of Release of the Body

The person who is entitled to control of the body for disposition is entitled to have it released promptly, as soon as the person can show entitlement to the body and has satisfied any legal requirements, including permits. The hospital can retain the body long enough to transport it from the place of death to the usual place for releasing bodies and long enough to confirm that the person claiming control has the highest priority of those able and willing to do so. Delay in delivery or refusal to release the body, even of a stillborn, can result in liability. The 1988 New Jersey Supreme Court decision described earlier in this chapter illustrates that the maintenance of the heartbeat of a dead body does not excuse delay in delivery of the body.[26]

Condition of the Body

The person who is entitled to control the body is entitled to have it in the condition it was in at the time of death. The change in the condition that most frequently has led to litigation has been due to an autopsy. An autopsy that is done without proper consent or other lawful authority can result in liability for violation of the right to the body in the condition it was in at the time of death.

Consent of the person entitled to control should be obtained before other uses are made of the body, such as maintenance of heartbeat[27] or use in experiments.[28]

Condition of the body can be an issue even when there is cremation. In 1994, a medical school agreed to settle alleged medical waste law violations arising from medical wastes found in cremated human remains.[29]

Burial or Other Disposition of Remains

The ultimate disposition of the remains is seldom the direct responsibility of the hospital, either because others assume responsibility or because arrangements are made for a mortician to handle the disposition. In a few situations some state laws permit the hospital to dispose of certain bodies directly. For example, in some states, hospitals may dispose of a stillborn when the parents elect such a disposition.

Unclaimed Dead Bodies

When there are no known relatives or friends to claim the body, the hospital must dispose of the body in accordance with applicable laws. Some states require that unclaimed bodies be buried at public expense, and a public official is assigned to make arrangements. Most states provide that such bodies may be delivered to certain types of institutions or individuals for educational or scientific purposes. The hospital should notify the appropriate public official when it has an unclaimed body so that the official can make arrangements. Before notifying the public official, the hospital should make a reasonable attempt to locate and contact relatives so that they can claim the body. Many statutes require such an inquiry; it has also been found to be a common law duty.[30]

AUTOPSIES

Autopsies are the most frequent cause of litigation involving bodies and hospitals. This section describes the legal prerequisites to autopsies and the potential sources of liability involving them.

Autopsies are performed primarily to determine the cause of death. This finding can be crucial in detecting crime or ruling out transmittable diseases that may be a threat to the public health. The cause of death can affect whether death benefits are payable under insurance policies, workers' compensation laws, and other programs. Autopsies help to advance medical science by permitting the correlation of anatomical changes with other signs and symptoms of disease.[31] They are also educational for those involved.[32] Community mores and religious beliefs have long dictated respectful handling of dead bodies. A substantial portion of the population recognizes the benefit of autopsies. Out of respect to those who continue to find autopsies unacceptable, the law requires appropriate consent before an autopsy can be performed except when an autopsy is needed to determine the cause of death for public policy purposes.

Authorization by Decedent

Many states have statutory procedures by which people may authorize an autopsy to be performed on their bodies. In states that do not explicitly address authorization before death, the anatomical gift act can be used. The person can donate the body for the purpose of autopsy, with such conditions as are desired, by following the rules for executing an anatomical gift. Even when there is valid authorization from the decedent, many hospitals and physicians decline to perform an autopsy when it is contrary to the wishes of the family.

Authorization by Family or Others

When the decedent has not given legal authorization for an autopsy, authorization must be obtained from someone else. Many states have statutes that specify who may authorize an autopsy. Some states specify a priority ordering of people[33]; the available person with the highest priority may give the authorization. Other states specify that the person assuming responsibility for disposal of the body may consent to the autopsy.[34] This second type of autopsy statute does not specify a priority, so common law principles must be followed to determine the priority. In a few states autopsy authorization statutes do not establish a priority, but rather specify the priority of the duty to assume custody for disposal.[35] The duty of disposal statutes are used to determine the priority for autopsy authorization. In the absence of either an autopsy authorization or a duty of disposal statute, the common law priority is followed.

The general common law rule is that the surviving spouse has the highest priority and duty to arrange for disposal and, thus, is the proper person to authorize an autopsy. If there is no surviving spouse or the spouse's right is waived, the next of kin has the responsibility and may authorize an autopsy. The most common order is child, parent, sibling, and then other next of kin. Most statutes disqualify any on the list who are not adults.

Under most statutes the authorization of the highest priority person who can be located with reasonable efforts is sufficient unless the objections of a person of the same or a higher priority, or of the deceased, are actually known. In these states, objections by persons of lower priority have no legal effect. Most statutes specify others who may authorize an autopsy when no spouse or next of kin is available. In most states the final priority rests with whoever assumes responsibility for disposal of the remains. A few states permit a physician to perform an autopsy without authorization when there is neither knowledge of any objection nor anyone assuming responsibility for disposal after due inquiry.[36]

In 1991, a California court ruled that malpractice defendants could not sue the surviving spouse for cremating the decedent's body before an autopsy could be performed. It was not spoilation of evidence because the defendants could not have compelled an autopsy due to the spouse's overriding legal right to control disposition of the body.[37]

Scope of Authorization

The general rule is that whoever authorizes the autopsy may limit its scope by imposing conditions.[38] If these conditions are not met, then the autopsy is not authorized. If the conditions are unacceptable, the physician who is to perform the autopsy may decline to do so. Examples of conditions include limits on the areas to be examined, restrictions on retention of parts of the body, and requirements that certain observers be present. Unless the authorization specifically includes permission to retain parts of the body, an autopsy authorization usually is interpreted not to permit retention. Liability may be imposed for retaining organs from authorized autopsies. However, the Iowa Supreme Court held that an authorization implied permission to retain slices of tissues in accordance with usual pathology practices unless expressly forbidden.[39] It is prudent to include express permission for such retention in the autopsy authorization.

Form of Authorization

A few states require that an autopsy be authorized in writing. Many states include telegrams and recorded telephone permissions as acceptable forms of authorization. Common law does not require the authorization to be documented in a particular way. A written authorization or recorded telephone authorization is obviously the easiest to prove.[40]

Authorization by Medical Examiner or Other Legal Official

In many circumstances authorization of the deceased, a family member, or a friend is not required. Determination of the cause of death is so important in some cases that statutory authority to order an autopsy has been granted to certain public officials. In addition, courts have the authority to order an autopsy.

Each state has a state or county officer, usually called a medical examiner or coroner, who is authorized to investigate certain deaths. In most states the medical examiner has the authority to perform an autopsy when it is necessary for the investigation. In some states the power also is given to other officials, such as the industrial commissioner responsible for workers' compensation cases.

An order from a medical examiner does not ensure immunity when the order is outside the authority of the medical examiner. In many states the scope of authority is broad enough that there is little risk that the medical examiner will exceed the scope of authority, but in other states the scope is so narrow that the courts have imposed liability. Thus, each hospital must be familiar with the laws of its state regarding medical examiners' autopsies before permitting them to be conducted on hospital premises.

Liability for Unauthorized Autopsies

Under general liability principles, hospitals can be liable for unauthorized autopsies by their employees and agents. Hospitals are not insurers of the safety of dead bodies, so hospitals are not generally liable for unauthorized autopsies by persons not acting on behalf of the hospital, but they must take reasonable steps to protect bodies from unauthorized autopsies.[41]

Liability for Delayed Autopsy

In 1992, the West Virginia Supreme Court ruled that a hospital could be liable for the emotional injuries of the family due to a delayed autopsy where the information from the autopsy was needed to diagnose and potentially treat genetic illnesses in relatives.[42]

DONATION OF BODIES AND CADAVER TRANSPLANTATION

Before 1969 the uncertainty surrounding the authority of persons to make binding anatomical donations prior to death and of others to make such donations after death limited the availability of organs for transplantation. The Uniform Anatomical Gift Act was developed as a model to resolve the uncertainty.[43] It was approved by the National Conference of Commissioners on Uniform State Laws and the American Bar Association in August 1968. Laws substantially equivalent to the model were enacted in all states by the end of 1971. In 1987, a modified version of the Uniform Anatomical Gift Act was developed. The 1987 version has been adopted by 35 states.[44] Every state now has statutory authority and procedures for anatomical gifts.

The Uniform Anatomical Gift Act specifies who may donate, who may receive anatomical gifts, the documentation required, the permitted uses of the anatomical gift, and how a gift may be revoked. It also provides some limitations on liability. Many states modified the Uniform Anatomical Gift Act before enactment or by subsequent amendment. For example, the age requirements for donation and the liability limitation provisions vary.

The Uniform Anatomical Gift Act has not resulted in a high rate of donation of available organs. Hospitals and physicians are reluctant to act without next of kin authorization even when a donor card was previously signed by the decedent. Many families approached at the time of death agree to donate, but many physicians are reluctant to ask them. As a result, mandatory request laws have been enacted. All hospitals that participate in Medicare or Medicaid must have written procedures for identifying potential organ donors and assuring that their families are made aware of the option to donate or decline.[45] Many states also require that families of potential donors be asked to donate in all hospitals.[46] A 1994 report of the AMA Council on Ethical and Judicial Affairs advocated mandated choice. A decision whether to authorize donation would be required whenever a driver's license was renewed or income tax form was filed. The council also advocated increased use of presumed consent to donation unless an objection has been registered.[47]

Who May Donate?

The Act specifies that persons of sound mind who are 18 years of age or more may donate all or part of their bodies. Furthermore, the Act includes a priority list of who may donate a body if the deceased has not given actual notice of contrary intentions. Persons of lower priority may donate if (1) persons of higher priority are not available and (2) persons of the same or higher priority have not given actual notice of objection. The order of priority from highest to lowest is (1) spouse; (2) an adult son or daughter; (3) either parent; (4) an adult brother or sister; (5) a guardian of the person at the time of death; and (6) any other person authorized or under obligation to dispose of the body. Several states have enacted laws that differ from the model. A few states have different age requirements. Some states authorize some minors to make donations with the consent of their parents or guardians. In some states it may be legal to remove organs from unidentified bodies without permission after proper attempts at identification.[48]

It is generally not necessary to demand identification from the person giving authorization unless there is reason for suspicion. In 1987, a New York court ruled that a hospital could not be liable for removal of a decedent's eyes in good-faith reliance on the written authorization of a woman claiming to be his wife, especially when the decedent's father, who was the legal next of kin, had been at the hospital and had not challenged her identity.[49] A similar result was obtained in a 1994 Michigan decision.[50]

Limitations on the scope of donation must be honored. In 1994, a federal court in Kansas ruled that a hospital could be liable when whole eyes and long bones were removed after the family limited the donation to corneas and bone marrow.[51]

Conflicting Wishes

Under the Act, the authorization of the highest priority person who can be located with reasonable efforts is sufficient unless there is actual knowledge of the contrary wishes of a person of the same or a higher priority, or of the deceased. In states that have enacted the Act without modification, objections by persons of lower priority have no legal effect. However, a few states permit persons of lower priority to veto an authorization.

In 1964, the New Hampshire Supreme Court decided a case in which the decedent's will donated her eyes to an eye bank and her body to one of two medical schools.[52] The eye donation was completed, but donation of the body was not. The surviving spouse and children objected, so the medical schools declined to accept the body. The court stated that the wishes of the deceased should usually be carried out. Since the medical schools had declined, the surviving spouse was permitted to determine disposition.

Medical Examiners' Cases

The Act specifies that it is subject to all laws regarding autopsies. The medical examiner's duties are given a higher public priority than anatomical donations. Some medical examiners will cooperate in coordinating the donation with the autopsy. Removal of transplantable organs does not usually compromise the autopsy.[53] When the death may result in a criminal prosecution, it is often prudent to obtain permission from the prosecuting attorney and the medical examiner. While permission from the prosecuting attorney is not legally required in most jurisdictions, it avoids accusations of interference with criminal law enforcement and may help to maintain the public acceptance of transplantation. Prosecuting attorneys usually grant permission when donation will not compromise testimony regarding the cause of death.

In some states the medical examiner has the authority to remove some organs in the course of a legal autopsy without the consent of the next of kin.[54] In 1984, a Michigan court found a hospital not to be liable when corneas were removed during a medical examiner's autopsy.[55] The court said that the removal was authorized by the medical examiner's power to retain body parts. A similar result was reached in a 1985 Georgia Supreme Court decision.[56] The medical examiner had removed corneas pursuant to state statute. The court ruled that the legislature could authorize removal of corneas without notice to the next of kin because rights concerning dead bodies are common law quasi-property rights, not constitutional rights, and the legislature has the power to modify the common law. Florida has a similar statute, but corneal tissue may not be removed when the next of kin objects. In 1988, a Florida appellate court ruled that a physician could be sued for removal contrary to next of kin's objections recorded in the medical record accompanying the body.[57]

Limitations on Liability

The Act prohibits civil liability and criminal prosecution for actions "in good faith in accord with the terms of this Act or with the anatomical gift act laws of another state or a foreign country." In 1974, the Wisconsin Supreme Court upheld the constitutionality of this section, but ruled that it did not apply to treatment of the donor prior to death.[58] In 1975, a Michigan court ruled that the section did not preclude liability for negligent failure to have a procedure to assess the potential for disease transmission from the donor.[59] The 1987 New York case involving authorization by a woman claiming to be the wife, described earlier in this chapter, is an example of the application of this protection for good-faith actions.[60] In 1994, a federal court in Minnesota ruled that a hospital and eye bank were immune when they relied on a signed form that appeared valid even though the family erroneously believed the form only authorized an autopsy.[61]

Networks

A federal Organ Procurement and Transplantation Network has been established to control allocation of organs.[62] All hospitals that participate in Medicare or Medicaid must notify an appropriate agency of all potential organ donors and, if organ transplants are performed in the hospital, be a member of and abide by the rules of the network.[63] In 1993, a federal appellate court rejected a challenge to the network by the survivors of a patient who had died while waiting for a liver transplant.[64]

Sale of Organs

Many states have made it a crime to sell human organs.[65] Hospitals and physicians procuring organs may generally recover only their costs. In 1989, two Florida residents were convicted of stealing corneas and selling them abroad.[66]

NOTES

1. *See* Darby et al., *Approach to the management of the heart beating "brain dead" organ donor*, 261 J.A.M.A. 2222 (1989).

2. *E.g.*, R.M. Veatch, *The impending collapse of the whole-brain definition of death*, 23 HASTINGS CENTER REPORT (Jul.–Aug. 1993), at 18; Wikler and Weisbard, *Appropriate confusion over "brain death*," 261 J.A.M.A. 2246 (1989).

3. In re T.A.C.P., 609 So.2d 588 (Fla. 1992); *see* Annotation, *Tests of death for organ transplant purposes*, 76 A.L.R. 3D 913.

4. D.M. Gianelli, *AMA organ donor opinion sparks ethics debate*, AM. MED. NEWS, July 25, 1994, at 1.

5. President's Commission for the Study of Ethical Problems in Medicine and Biomedical and Behavioral Research, DEFINING DEATH, 159–66 (July 1981). The guidelines were reprinted in 246 J.A.M.A. 2184 (1981). For a discussion of standards in other countries, see Levin and Whyte, *Brain death sans frontieres*, 318 N. ENGL. J. MED. 852 (1988).

6. *E.g.*, *A definition of irreversible coma*, 205 J.A.M.A. 337 (1968) [the "Harvard criteria"].

7. *See* Task Force for the Determination of Brain Death in Children, *Guidelines for the determination of brain death in children*, 21 ANN. NEUROL. 616 (1987).

8. For a state-by-state analysis, see *Death, dying, and dead bodies*, HOSPITAL LAW MANUAL.

9. *E.g.*, State v. Fierro, 124 Ariz. 182, 603 P.2d 74 (1979); Commonwealth v. Golston, 373 Mass. 249, 366 N.E.2d 744 (1977), *cert. denied*, 434 U.S. 1039 (1978); In re Quinlan, 70 N.J. 10, 355 A.2d 647 (1976), *cert. denied*, 429 U.S. 922 (1976); People v. Eulo, 63 N.Y.2d 341, 482 N.Y.S.2d 436, 472 N.E.2d 286 (1984); In re Welfare of Bowman, 94 Wash. 2d 407, 617 P.2d 731 (1980); Cranmore v. State, 85 Wis. 2d 722, 271 N.W.2d 402 (1978).

10. 12 U.L.A. 412 (1994 Supp.); *e.g.*, S.D. CODIFIED LAWS ANN. § 34-25-18.1.

11. Gallups v. Cotter, 534 So.2d 585 (Ala. 1988).

12. *E.g., Public hospital to finance home care of brain-dead teenager*, 3 HEALTH L. RPTR. [BNA] 287 (1994) [HEALTH L. RPTR. hereinafter cited as H.L.R.]; Schleich v. Archbishop Bergan Mercy Hosp., 241 Neb. 765, 491 N.W.2d 307 (1992) [after determination of brain death put in no code status].

13. *See* Younger et al., *"Brain death" and organ retrieval*, 261 J.A.M.A. 2205 (1989).

14. Strachan v. John F. Kennedy Mem. Hosp., 109 N.J. 523, 538 A.2d 346 (1988); *see* Annotation, *Liability in damages for withholding corpse from relatives*, 48 A.L.R. 3D 240.

15. *E.g.*, MASS. GEN. LAWS ANN. ch. 46, § 9.

16. Mackey v. United States, 303 U.S. App. D.C. 422, 8 F.3d 826 (1993).

17. Annotation, *Liability of hospital or similar institution for giving erroneous notification of patient's death*, 77 A.L.R. 3D 501.

18. Hoard v. Shawnee Mission Med. Ctr., 233 Kan. 267, 662 P.2d 1214 (1983); *see also* Dooley v. Richland Mem. Hosp., 283 S.C. 372, 322 S.E.2d 669 (1984) [no liability for erroneous report of serious injury]; Hart v. United States, 894 F.2d 1539 (11th Cir.), *cert. denied*, 498 U.S. 980 (1990) [government not liable for misidentification of remains as those of flyer shot down in Vietnam].

19. Muniz v. United Hosps. Med. Ctr. Presbyterian Hosp., 153 N.J. Super. 72, 379 A.2d 57 (App. Div. 1977).

20. IOWA CODE ANN. § 331.802.

21. PALM BEACH [FL] POST, June 9, 1995, at 2B.

22. Schleich v. Archbishop Bergan Mercy Hosp., 241 Neb. 765, 491 N.W.2d 307 (1992).

23. *E.g.*, CAL. HEALTH & SAFETY Code § 7100; In re Estate of Moyer, 577 P.2d 108 (Utah 1978); *see* Annotation, *Enforcement of preference expressed by decedent as to disposition of his body after death*, 54 A.L.R. 3D 1037; Annotation, *Validity and effect of testamentary direction as to disposition of testator's body*, 7 A.L.R. 3D 747.

24. 8A U.L.A. 19, 63 (1993 & 1994 Supp.) [35 states have adopted 1968 version, 15 states have adopted 1987 version].

25. *E.g.*, Dumouchelle v. Duke Univ., 69 N.C. App. 471, 317 S.E.2d 100 (1984).

26. Strachan v. John F. Kennedy Mem. Hosp., 109 N.J. 523, 538 A.2d 346 (1988).

27. *E.g., id.*

28. *See* Koenig, *Doctors use brain-dead patient to test Centocor Inc's new anti-clotting drug*, WALL ST. J., Nov. 17, 1988, at B5 [consent obtained from next of kin]; Greenhouse, *Report of experiment on patient is clouding a French trial*, N.Y. TIMES, Feb. 29, 1988, at 4 [no consent to attempt to recreate incident as part of criminal defense]; Orlowski et al., *The ethics of using newly dead patients for teaching and practicing intubation techniques*, 319 N. ENGL. J. MED. 439

(1988); *see also* Arnaud v. Odom, 870 F.2d 304 (5th Cir.), *cert. denied*, 493 U.S. 855 (1989) [no federal remedies for deputy coroner's unauthorized experiments with dead bodies, but state remedies may be pursued]; Lacy v. Cooper Hosp./Univ. Med. Ctr., 745 F. Supp. 1029 (D. N.J. 1990) [alleged pericardiocentesis procedure after death pronounced].

29. *UCLA medical school to settle waste among human ashes mishap*, 3 H.L.R. 318 (1994).

30. *E.g.*, Burke v. New York Univ., 196 A.D. 491, 188 N.Y.S. 123 (1st Dep't 1921).

31. *E.g.*, D.N. Saller et al., *The clinical utility of perinatal autopsy*, 273 J.A.M.A. 663 (1995); H.C. Kinney et al., *Neuropathological findings in the brain of Karen Ann Quinlan—The role of the thalamus in the persistent vegetative state*, 330 N. ENGL. J. MED. 1469 (1994).

32. *See* Lundberg, *Now is the time to emphasize the autopsy in quality assurance*, 260 J.A.M.A. 3488 (1988); Landefeld et al., *Diagnostic yield of the autopsy in a university hospital and a community hospital*, 318 N. ENGL. J. MED. 1249 (1988).

33. *E.g.*, IOWA CODE ANN. § 144.56.

34. *E.g.*, COLO. REV. STAT. ANN. § 12-36-133.

35. *E.g.*, ARIZ. REV. STAT. ANN. § 36-831.

36. *E.g.*, N.Y. PUB. HEALTH LAW § 4214.

37. Walsh v. Caidin, 232 Cal. App. 3d 159, 283 Cal. Rptr. 326 (2d Dist. 1991).

38. *E.g.*, Burgess v. Perdue, 239 Kan. 473, 721 P.2d 239 (1986) [brain removed contrary to instructions].

39. Winkler v. Hawkes & Ackley, 126 Iowa 474, 102 N.W. 418 (1905).

40. *E.g.*, Lashbrook v. Barnes, 437 S.W.2d 502 (Ky. 1969).

41. *E.g.*, Grawunder v. Beth Israel Hosp. Ass'n, 266 N.Y. 605, 195 N.E. 221 (1935); Annotation, *Liability for wrongful autopsy*, 18 A.L.R. 4TH 858.

42. Ricottilli v. Summersville Mem. Hosp., 188 W.Va. 674, 425 S.E.2d 629 (1992).

43. 8A U.L.A. 63 (1993 & 1994 Supp.).

44. 8A U.L.A. 19 (1993 & 1994 Supp.).

45. 42 U.S.C.A. § 1320b-8(a)(1)(A).

46. *E.g.*, FLA. STAT. § 732.922.

47. American Medical Association, Council on Ethical and Judicial Affairs, *Strategies for Cadaveric Organ Procurement*, 272 J.A.M.A. 809 (1994); for other strategies, *see* A.L. Caplan, *Current ethical issues in organ procurement and transplantation*, 272 J.A.M.A. 1708 (1994).

48. *E.g.*, *California man's heart is transplanted without permission*, N.Y. TIMES, Apr. 24, 1988, at 14.

49. Nicoletta v. Rochester Eye & Human Parts Bank, Inc., 136 Misc. 2d 1065, 519 N.Y.S.2d 928 (Sup. Ct. 1987).

50. Kelly-Nevils v. Detroit Receiving Hosp., 207 Mich. App. 410, 526 N.W.2d 15 (1994) [immunity for relying on authorization of purported brother; no obligation to verify identity].

51. Perry v. Saint Francis Hosp., 865 F. Supp. 724 (D. Kan. 1994).

52. Holland v. Metalious, 105 N.H. 290, 198 A.2d 654 (1964).

53. *Transplants often foiled by coroners, study finds*, N.Y. TIMES, Nov. 24, 1994, at C17; T. Shafer et al., *Impact of medical examiner/coroner practices on organ recovery in the United States*, 272 J.A.M.A. 1607 (1994) [many medical examiners do not cooperate with donations due to erroneous fear of loss of evidence despite lack of any cases where autopsy or prosecution was impaired by donation].

54. Annotation, *Statutes authorizing removal of body parts for transplant: validity and construction*, 54 A.L.R. 4TH 1214.

55. Tillman v. Detroit Receiving Hosp., 138 Mich. App. 683, 360 N.W.2d 275 (1984).

56. Georgia Lions Eye Bank, Inc. v. Lavant, 255 Ga. 60, 335 S.E.2d 127 (1985), *cert. denied*, 475 U.S. 1084 (1986).

57. Kirker v. Orange County, 519 So.2d 682 (Fla. 5th DCA 1988); *accord*, Brotherton v. Cleveland, 923 F.2d 477 (6th Cir. 1991) [coroner sued for policy of not reviewing medical records before removal of corneas; due process requires a predeprivation process].

58. Williams v. Hofmann, 66 Wis. 2d 145, 223 N.W.2d 844 (1974); *see* Annotation, *Tort liability of physician or hospital in connection with organ or tissue transplant procedures*, 76 A.L.R. 3D 890.

59. Ravenis v. Detroit Gen. Hosp., 63 Mich. App. 79, 234 N.W.2d 411 (1975).

60. Nicoletta v. Rochester Eye & Human Parts Bank, Inc., 136 Misc. 2d 1065, 519 N.Y.S.2d 928 (Sup. Ct. 1987).

61. Lyon v. United States, 843 F. Supp. 531 (D. Minn. 1994).

62. 42 U.S.C. § 274; *see also* McDonald, *The national organ procurement and transplantation network*, 259 J.A.M.A. 725 (1988).

63. 42 U.S.C. § 1320b-8(a)(1)(B).

64. Wheat v. Mass, 994 F.2d 273 (5th Cir. 1993).

65. *E.g.*, FLA. STAT. § 245.16.

66. MIAMI [FL] HERALD, Jan. 21, 1989, at 23A.

Glossary of Acronyms

AAPCC	Adjusted average per capita costs
ACS	American College of Surgeons
ADA	Americans with Disabilities Act
AHA	American Hospital Association
ALJ	Administrative law judge
AMA	American Medical Association
AOA	American Osteopathic Association
APGs	Ambulatory patient groups
BFOQ	Bona fide occupational qualification
CEO	Chief executive officer
CHAMPUS	Civilian Health and Medical Program for the Uniformed Services
CLIA	Clinical Laboratory Improvement Amendments of 1988
CMO	Chief medical officer
CO	Certificate of occupancy
COBRA	Consolidated Omnibus Budget Reconciliation Act
CON	Certificate of need
CPR	Cardiopulmonary resuscitation
CPT	Physician's Current Procedural Terminology
DEA	Drug Enforcement Administration
DNR	Do not resuscitate
DOJ	Department of Justice
DRGs	Diagnosis-related groups

EEG	Electroencephalogram
EEOC	Equal Employment Opportunity Commission
EMTALA	Emergency Medical Treatment and Active Labor Act
ERISA	Employee Retirement Income Security Act
ESOP	Employee Stock Ownership Plan
FDA	Food and Drug Administration
FDCPA	Fair Debt Collection Practices Act
FEHBP	Federal Employee Health Benefits Program
FHA	Federal Housing Administration
FIOA	Freedom of Information Act
FMCS	Federal Mediation and Conciliation Service
FTC	Federal Trade Commission
GAO	General Accounting Office
GAPP	Generally accepted accounting principles
HCQIA	Health Care Quality Improvement Act of 1986
HCFA	Health Care Financing Administration
HCPCS	HCFA Common Procedure Coding System
HEW	U.S. Department of Health, Education and Welfare (predecessor to HHS)
HHS	U.S. Department of Health and Human Services
HMO	Health maintenance organization
HCQIA	Health Care Quality Improvement Act of 1986
ICD-9-CM	International Classification of Diseases, Ninth Edition, Clinical Modification
IDE	Investigational device exemption
IDS	Integrated delivery system
IND	Investigational new drug
IPA	Independent practice association
IRB	Institutional review board
IRS	Internal Revenue Service
IVF	In vitro fertilization

JCAHO	Joint Commission on Accreditation of Healthcare Organizations [This acronym is not used in this book. Instead "Joint Commission" is used because that organization opposes the widely-used acronym]
LLP	Limited liability partnership
MAAC	Maximum allowable actual charge
MFN	Most favored nation clause
MRI	Magnetic resonance imaging
MSO	Medical service organization
NCQA	National Committee for Quality Assurance
NLRA	National Labor Relations Act
NLRB	National Labor Relations Board
OIG	Office of Inspector General of HHS
OSHA	Occupational Safety and Health Act of 1970
PHO	Physician-hospital organization
PICU	Pediatric intensive care unit
PLR	I.R.S. Private letter ruling
PPO	Preferred provider organization
PRO	Peer Review Organization
PPS	Prospective payment system
PRRB	Provider Reimbursement Review Board
RBRVS	Resource-based relative value scale
RICO	Racketeer Influenced and Corrupt Organizations Act
UCC	Uniform Commercial Code
UPIN	Unique physician identification number
VA	Veterans Administration

Introduction to Index of Cases

The numbers and letters after each case name tell where to find the court's decision. For example, look at *Ravenis v. Detroit Gen. Hosp.*, 63 Mich. App. 79, 234 N.W.2d 411 (1975), which is cited in footnote 59 of Chapter 16. The numbers 63 and 234 are volume numbers. They are followed by the abbreviations for the reporter systems; "Mich. App." refers to the reports of the Michigan Court of Appeals, which is the intermediate appellate court for Michigan, while "N.W.2d" refers to the *Northwestern Reporter, Second Series.* The final numbers 79 and 411 are the page numbers in the volumes. The number in parenthesis is the year of the decision. When the abbreviation of the reporter decision does not disclose the court that rendered the decision, an abbreviation of the court's name will also appear in the parenthesis. Since the "Mich. App." tells which court rendered the *Ravenis* decision, the name of the court does not appear in the parenthesis in the example. An example where the reporter abbreviation does not disclose the name of the court is *John F. Kennedy Memorial Hosp. v. Bludworth*, 452 So.2d 921 (Fla. 1984); since the *Southern Reporter, Second Series*, abbreviated "So.2d," includes decisions from several states and Florida no longer has a separate reporting system for its court decisions, it is necessary to include the abbreviation "Fla." in the parenthesis to disclose that it is a decision of the Florida Supreme Court.

When there is another set of numbers and letters after the parenthesis, they refer to another court's decision concerning the same case. If the second court is a higher court, it will be preceded by letters such as *aff'd, rev'd*, or *cert. denied*, which indicate the court affirmed, reversed, or declined to review the lower court decisions. (See Chapter 1 for a discussion of *cert. denied.*) In some situations the order of references is reversed, so that the higher court decision is listed first. In those situations the abbreviations will be *aff'g* or *rev'g*, indication whether the higher court is affirming or reversing the lower court.

Some cases are not reported in any reporter system. For those cases, the court file number, the name of the court, and the date of the ruling are given.

Index of Cases

A

Aasum v. Good Samaritan Hosp., 7:34
Abbeville Gen. Hosp. v. Ramsey, 4:118
Abbott Labs. v. Portland Retail Druggists Ass'n, Inc., 5:61
Abdelmessih v. Board of Regents, 7:53
Abrahamson v. Illinois Dep't of Prof. Reg., 8:4
Abramson v. Florida Psychological Ass'n, 8:6
Acosta v. Cary, 14:139
Ad Hoc Exec. Comm. v. Runyan, 7:224
Adams v. Children's Mercy Hosp., 10:188
Adams v. Commonwealth, Unemployment Comp. Bd. of Review, 8:13
Adams v. St. Elizabeth Hosp., 14:221
Adamski v. Tacoma Gen. Hosp., 10:146
Addington v. Texas, 13:123
Adler v. Montefiore Hosp. Ass'n, 7:286
Adoption of Matthew B., 15:53
AFSCME v. Illinois, 9:231
AFSCME v. Washington, 9:107
Agnew-Watson v. County of Alameda, 9:247
Agosto v. Trusswal Systems Corp., 14:197
Ahern v. Veterans Admin., 11:86
Aikens v. St. Helena Hosp., 12:28, 12:24, 13:82, 13:256
Akopiantz v. Board of County Comm'rs, 7:336

Alabama Tissue Ctr. v. Sullivan, 3:60
Alachua Gen. Hosp. v. Stewart, 14:49
Albany Gen. Hosp. v. Dalton, 4:147
Albert v. Board of Trustees, 7:324
Alberts v. Devine, 14:212
Albritton v. Bossier City Hosp. Comm'n, 11:87
Aldana v. Holub, 10:171
Alexander v. Choate, 4:120
Alfonso v. Fernandez, 13:276, 13:277
Allan v. Levy, 13:87
Allan v. SWF Gulf Coast, Inc., 9:28
Allegheny Gen. Hosp. v. Board of Property Assessment, 4:301
Allen v. Smith, 14:106
Allen v. State, 10:86
Allenius v. Thomas, 10:207
Alliance for Cannabis Therapeutics v. D.E.A., 3:51
Allianz Life Ins. Co. v. Riedl, 4:164
Allred v. State, 14:166
Amente v. Newman, 14:84
American Academic Suppliers, Inc. v. Beckley-Cardy, Inc., 5:115
American Academy of Ophthalmology v. Sullivan, 4:64
American Academy of Pediatrics v. Heckler, 13:307
American Bank & Trust Co. v. Community Hosp., 10:201
American Dental Ass'n v. Martin, 9:185

Index of Statutes and Regulations

**Federal Regulations
(Federal Register—FED. REG.)**

STATE

State Statutes

State Regulations

Index

Medicare conditions of participation for
  outpatient providers, 44
Physician licensure, 221–226
  required Medicare participation, 222
Physician-hospital organization (PHO), 64,
  106, 107, 191–192
Physician-hospital relationship
  See also Medical staff; Medical staff
    appointments; Review procedures for
    medical staff actions
  antitrust attacks, 127, 128, 189–190,
    194–195
  contracts, 162, 193–195
  corporate practice of medicine, 195
  exclusive contracts, 194–195
  fraud alert, hospital incentives, 68
  future of, 202–203
  history, 196–202
  practice acquisition, 192
  recruitment/retention, 69, 192–193
  tax exemption, effect on, 39, 104–106,
    192, 193
Physician offices, 20
  free rent, illegality, 69
  laboratory services, 51
  nondiscrimination laws, 357, 358
Physician-patient privilege, 463, 465, 467,
  470–471
Physician-patient relationship, 303, 352–356
  beginning of, 352–354, 409–410
  contracts
    caring for specific population, 353
    express contracts, 353–354
    implied contracts, 354
  decision to discharge from hospital, 367
  ending of, 354–356
  nondiscrimination, 354, 356–359
  state law requiring acceptance, 354
Physicians' assistants, 223, 224, 247
Physicians' employees, 229–231
Physicians' liability
  for ambiguous orders, 335
  for consent, 382–383
  for contagious disease, 468
  criminal liability, 412, 426–427
  for denial of emergency care, 362
  despite transfusion release form, 407–408
  for equipment and supplies, 329–330
  for failure to do testing, 291–292
  for failure to examine, 345

for failure to report, 466, 468
for failure to submit insurance report, 458
for hospital staff, 301, 331
for inadequate explanation to staff, 341
for inappropriate treatment, 402–403
for infections, 329–330
for misdiagnosis, 341, 343, 345–346
for mishandling specimens, 341
for peer review, 187–191
  immunity statutes, 190–191
for release of information, 473–475
for reproductive issues, 492, 493, 494,
  497–499
for unauthorized treatment, 284
when on-call, 345, 353, 357
Podiatrists
  clinical privileges, 166, 230
  licensure, 222
Poison Prevention Packaging Act, 57
Police, voluntary report to, 469–470
Police power, 7, 45, 223, 230, 466
Practice parameters, 290
Preemption, 7, 85, 252, 304
  See also ERISA, preemption
  medical device law, 299
  substance abuse confidentiality, 472
Pregnancy
  See also Conception, Reproductive issues
  access to emergency treatment, 362–363
  discrimination and, 245–246
  involuntary treatment during, 396–397
  transfers during strikes, 261
Prenatal testing, 497
Prescription Drug Marketing Act of 1988,
  57
Prescriptions, 53, 56, 406
Preservation of assets, duty of due care,
  24–25
President's Commission for the Study of
  Ethical Problems in Medicine and
  Biomedical and Behavioral Research, brain
  death criteria, 506
Primary jurisdiction, 9
Privacy. *See* Right of privacy
Privacy Act, 467
Private credentialing, 227–231
  accreditation of education programs,
    227–228
  certification of individuals, 228–229
  hospital credentialing